Human Resource Management

Tenth Edition

Lloyd L. Byars, Ph.D.
Professor Emeritus of Management
College of Management
Georgia Institute of Technology

Leslie W. Rue, Ph.D.
Professor Emeritus of Management
Robinson College of Business
Georgia State University

McGraw-Hill
Irwin

HUMAN RESOURCE MANAGEMENT, TENTH EDITION

Published by McGraw-Hill, a business unit of The McGraw-Hill Companies, Inc., 1221 Avenue of the Americas, New York, NY 10020. Copyright © 2011 by The McGraw-Hill Companies, Inc. All rights reserved. Previous editions © 2008, 2006, and 2004. No part of this publication may be reproduced or distributed in any form or by any means, or stored in a database or retrieval system, without the prior written consent of The McGraw-Hill Companies, Inc., including, but not limited to, in any network or other electronic storage or transmission, or broadcast for distance learning.

Some ancillaries, including electronic and print components, may not be available to customers outside the United States.

⊕ This book is printed on recycled, acid-free paper containing 10% postconsumer waste.

1 2 3 4 5 6 7 8 9 0 WDQ/WDQ 1 0 9 8 7 6 5 4 3 2 1 0

ISBN 978-0-07-353055-0
MHID 0-07-353055-7

Vice President & Editor-in-Chief: *Brent Gordon*
Vice President EDP/Central Publishing Services: *Kimberly Meriwether David*
Editorial Director: *Paul Ducham*
Managing Developmental Editor: *Laura Hurst Spell*
Editorial Coordinator: *Jane Beck*
Associate Marketing Manager: *Jaime Halteman*
Project Manager: *Robin A. Reed*
Design Coordinator: *Brenda A. Rolwes*
Cover Designer: *Studio Montage, St. Louis, Missouri*
Senior Photo Research Coordinator: *Jeremy Cheshareck*
Cover Image: *© Royalty-Free/CORBIS*
Buyer: *Susan K. Culbertson*
Media Project Manager: *Balaji Sundararaman*
Compositor: *MPS Limited, A Macmillan Company*
Typeface: *10/12 Times Roman*
Printer: *Quad/Graphics*

All credits appearing on page are considered to be an extension of the copyright page.

Library of Congress Cataloging-in-Publication Data

Byars, Lloyd L.
    Human resource management / Lloyd L. Byars, Leslie W. Rue. — 10th ed.
        p. cm.
    ISBN-13: 978-0-07-353055-0 (student ed.)
    ISBN-10: 0-07-353055-7 (student ed.)
    1. Personnel management. I. Rue, Leslie W. II. Title.
    HF5549.B937 2011
    658.3—dc22
                                        2010025365

To Lloyd L. Byars, Jr., Linda S. Byars,
Susan Ashley Ross, and Elizabeth Lee Means
Lloyd L. Byars

To Elizabeth R. Norris, Margaret
Massie, Leslie W. Rue, Jr., and Passie M. Rue
Leslie W. Rue

Preface

Today's most effective and successful organizations find ways to motivate, train, compensate, and challenge their employees. This is true for all organizations, whether they are manufacturing or service companies, large or small, domestic or international, profit or nonprofit, government or nongovernment.

Since the publication of the ninth edition of *Human Resource Management,* the world has continued to change. The human resource components of most organizations have become even more diverse and more sophisticated. In addition, other significant changes have occurred that affect human resource managers. The worldwide recession and accompanying downsizing, changing government and legal requirements, increased awareness for security issues, new information systems, demands for a more skilled workforce, and intensifying global competition are just a few of the factors that have contributed to the complexity of HRM issues for today's organizations.

FEATURES OF THE BOOK

As in previous editions, the tenth edition of *Human Resource Management* continues to present both the *theoretical* and *practical* aspects of HRM. The theoretical material is presented throughout the text and highlighted via a marginal glossary. Students are assisted in learning HRM terminology through these concise definitions placed in the margins. They also provide a valuable study tool for students. The practical aspects of HRM are presented through lively and pedagogically effective examples woven throughout the text and end-of-chapter materials.

- There are detailed learning objectives for each chapter.
- Multiple "HRM in Action" boxes are included in each chapter and provide current examples that illustrate how actual organizations apply concepts presented in the chapters. The overwhelming majority of these examples are new to this edition.
- A key feature entitled "On the Job" appears after several chapters and offers numerous other practical examples.
- The URLs for companies referenced in the text have been updated and expanded.
- End-of-chapter materials include these features:
  - The "Summary of Learning Objectives" is a synopsis and review of the key learning objectives within each chapter.
  - A list of key terms is provided for each chapter. These lists are new to this edition.
  - "Review Questions" provide an opportunity to review chapter concepts through questions developed to test students' memory of key issues and concepts within the chapter.
  - "Discussion Questions" give students an opportunity to apply critical thinking skills to in-depth questions.
  - Two "Incidents" per chapter act as minicases students can use to analyze and dissect chapter concepts and applications via real-life scenarios.
  - Experential "Exercises" placed at the end of each chapter can be done in class or as homework and are designed to illustrate major points emphasized in the chapter.
  - "Notes and Additional Readings" provide references and more in-depth information on covered topics.

THE TEACHING PACKAGE

Each component of the teaching package has been carefully developed to assist faculty in teaching and students in learning the important concepts and applications of HRM. The following items are included on the book website at www.mhhe.com/byars10e:

- The *Instructor's Manual* offers opportunities for classroom instruction, student participation, and assignments or research. Each chapter includes a chapter outline, presentation suggestions, and answers for the "Discussion Questions" and "Incident Solutions" that are included within the text.

- The *Test Bank* includes over 600 questions and consists of true/false, multiple choice, and short-answer questions.
- Power Point slides contain tables and figures from the text plus additional graphic material.
- The student center provides chapter review materials and self-grading quizzes. Premium content access is also available for purchase, including Test Your Knowledge, Self-Assessments, and Manager's Hot Seat videos.

In addition, the *Human Resource Management Video DVD* contains a number of short clips providing real-world illustrations of chapter concepts.

The *Manager's Hot Seat* interactive video series is also available for purchase with this textbook or online at www.mhhe.com/mhs. This popular simulation allows students to experience, as close to real-life as possible, what it's like to be in the manager's hot seat. Students watch and comment on the situation as managers in unscripted scenarios make on-the-spot decisions in confronting real-life issues, such as hiring decisions, teamwork, or the virtual workplace.

ORGANIZATION OF THE TENTH EDITION

The book's content has been rearranged into five major sections. Part 1, "Introduction and Background of Human Resources," is designed to provide the student with the foundation necessary to embark on a study of the work of human resource management. This section also explores how the legal environment and the implementation of equal employment opportunity influence all areas of human resource management. The final chapter in this section discusses job analysis and job design. Part 2, "Acquiring Human Resources," discusses the topics of human resource planning, recruitment, and selection. Part 3, "Training and Developing Employees," describes orientation and employee training, management and organizational development, career planning, and performance management systems. Part 4, "Compensating Human Resources," presents an introductory chapter on organizational reward systems and has separate chapters describing base wage and salary systems, incentive pay systems, and employee benefits. The chapter on employee benefits has been moved to this section in this edition. Part 5, "Employee Well-Being and Labor Relations" explores employee safety and health, employee relations, the legal environment and structure of labor unions, as well as union organizing campaigns, and collective bargaining.

Reviewers for this edition:

Janet A. Henquinet
Metropolitan State University

Susan L. Kendall
Arapahoe Community College

Robert D. Lewallen
Iowa Western Community College

Tom J. Sanders
University of Montevallo

Romila Singh
University of Wisconsin-Milwaukee

As with all previous editions, we solicit any ideas and inputs that readers may have concerning the book.

Lloyd L. Byars

Leslie W. Rue

Brief Contents

Table of Contents

PART THREE
TRAINING AND
DEVELOPING EMPLOYEES   147

Chapter 8
Orientation and Employee Training   149

Chapter 9
Management and Organizational
Development   167

Chapter 10
Career Development   189

Part **One**

Introduction and Background of Human Resources

Image Source/PunchStock

Chapter **One**

Human Resource Management: A Strategic Function

Chapter Learning Objectives

After studying this chapter, you should be able to:

1. Define human resource management.
2. Describe the functions of human resource management.
3. Summarize the types of assistance the human resource department provides.
4. Explain the desired relationship between human resource managers and operating managers.
5. Identify several challenges today's human resource managers currently face.
6. Outline several potential challenges and contributions that an increasingly diverse workforce presents.
7. Discuss the role of human resource managers in the future.
8. Explain how human resource managers can affect organizational performance.
9. Summarize several guidelines to follow when communicating human resource programs.

Chapter Outline

Human Resource Functions
> *Who Performs the Human Resource Functions?*
> *The Human Resource Department*

Challenges for Today's Human Resource Managers
> *Diversity in the Workforce*
> *Regulatory Changes*
> *Structural Changes to Organizations*
> *Technological and Managerial Changes within Organizations*
> *Human Resource Management in the Future*

Organizational Performance and the Human Resource Manager
> *Metrics and the HR Scorecard*

Communicating Human Resource Programs
> *Guidelines for Communicating Human Resource Programs*

Summary of Learning Objectives

Key Terms

Review Questions

Discussion Questions
> *Incident 1.1: Human Resource Management and Professionals*
> *Incident 1.2: Choosing a Major*

Exercise 1.1: Changes in Terminology

Exercise 1.2: Justifying the Human Resource Department

Exercise 1.3: Test Your Knowledge of HR History

Exercise 1.4: Are You Poised for Success?

Notes and Additional Readings

---

human resource management
Activities designed to provide for and coordinate the human resources of an organization.

Human resource management (HRM) encompasses those activities designed to provide for and coordinate the human resources of an organization. The human resources (HR) of an organization represent one of its largest investments. In fact, government reports show that approximately 64 percent of national income is used to compensate employees.[1] The value of an organization's human resources frequently becomes evident when the organization is sold. Often the purchase price is greater than the total value of the physical and financial assets. This difference, sometimes called goodwill, partially reflects the value of an organization's human resources. In addition to wages and salaries, organizations often make other sizable investments in their human resources. Recruiting, hiring, and training represent some of the more obvious examples.

Human resource management is a modern term for what was traditionally referred to as *personnel administration* or *personnel management*. However, some experts believe human resource management differs somewhat from traditional personnel management. They see personnel management as being much narrower and more clerically oriented than human resource management. For the purposes of this book, we will only use the term *human resource management*.

HUMAN RESOURCE FUNCTIONS

human resource functions
Tasks and duties human resource managers perform (e.g., determining the organization's human resource needs; recruiting, selecting, developing, counseling, and rewarding employees; acting as liaison with unions and government organizations; and handling other matters of employee well-being).

Human resource functions refer to those tasks and duties performed in both large and small organizations to provide for and coordinate human resources. Human resource functions encompass a variety of activities that significantly influence all areas of an organization. The Society for Human Resource Management (SHRM) has identified six major functions of human resource management:

1. Human resource planning, recruitment, and selection.
2. Human resource development.
3. Compensation and benefits.
4. Safety and health.
5. Employee and labor relations.
6. Human resource research.

Table 1.1 identifies many of the activities that comprise each major human resource function. Ensuring that the organization fulfills all of its equal employment opportunity and other government obligations is an activity that overlays all six of the major human resource functions.

TABLE 1.1
Activities of the Major Human Resource Functions

Human Resource Planning, Recruitment, and Selection

- Conducting job analyses to establish the specific requirements of individual jobs within the organization.
- Forecasting the human resource requirements the organization needs to achieve its objectives.
- Developing and implementing a plan to meet these requirements.
- Recruiting the human resources the organization requires to achieve its objectives.
- Selecting and hiring human resources to fill specific jobs within the organization.

Human Resource Development

- Orienting and training employees.
- Designing and implementing management and organizational development programs.
- Building effective teams within the organizational structure.
- Designing systems for appraising the performance of individual employees.
- Assisting employees in developing career plans.

Compensation and Benefits

- Designing and implementing compensation and benefit systems for all employees.
- Ensuring that compensation and benefits are fair and consistent.

Safety and Health

- Designing and implementing programs to ensure employee health and safety.
- Providing assistance to employees with personal problems that influence their work performance.

Employee and Labor Relations

- Serving as an intermediary between the organization and its union(s).
- Designing discipline and grievance handling systems.

Human Resource Research

- Providing a human resource information base.
- Designing and implementing employee communication systems.

talent management
The broad spectrum of HR activities involved in obtaining and managing the organization's human resources.

Talent management is a relatively new and all-encompassing term used in the human resources field. Talent management refers to the broad spectrum of HR activities involved in obtaining and managing the organization's human resources. This includes everything from crafting a job advertisement to tracking an employee's progress up the career ladder to separation of the employee from the organization.[2] The specific aspects of talent management are covered in the different chapters of this book.

In an attempt to cover each of the major areas of human resource management, this book contains six major sections. Part 1 serves as an introduction and presents material that applies to all major human resource functions. It contains an introductory chapter, two chapters on equal employment opportunity, and a chapter on job analysis and design. Part 2 explores those human resource functions specifically concerned with acquiring the organization's human resources: human resource planning, recruiting, and selecting. Part 3 concentrates on those functions related to the training and development of the organization's human resources. This section includes chapters on orientation and employee training, management and organization development, career planning, and performance appraisal. Part 4 covers the basic aspects of employee compensation: the organizational reward system, base wage and salary systems, and incentive pay systems, and employee benefits. Part 5 deals with employee well-being and labor relations. This part includes chapters on safety and health, employee relations, unions, and the collective bargaining process. Issues related to globalization of HR are dispersed throughout the relevant chapters of the book.

Who Performs the Human Resource Functions?

operating manager
Person who manages people directly involved with the production of an organization's products or services (e.g., production manager in a manufacturing plant, loan manager in a bank).

human resource generalist
Person who devotes a majority of working time to human resource issues, but does not specialize in any specific areas.

human resource specialist
Person specially trained in one or more areas of human resource management (e.g., labor relations specialist, wage and salary specialist).

Most managers are periodically involved to some extent in each of the major human resource functions. For example, at one time or another, almost all managers are involved in some aspect of employee recruiting, selecting, training, developing, compensation, team building, and evaluation. In small organizations, most human resource functions are performed by the owner or by **operating managers.** These managers perform the human resource functions in addition to their normal managerial activities. Many medium-size and even some large organizations use human resource generalists. A **human resource generalist** devotes a majority of his or her working time to human resource issues, but does not specialize in any specific areas of human resource management. Large organizations usually have a human resource department that is responsible for directing the human resource functions. In addition to one or more human resource generalists, such a department is normally staffed by one or more **human resource specialists.** These specialists are trained in one or more specific areas of human resource management. However, even in large organizations that have a human resource department with many human resource generalists and specialists, most operating managers must regularly perform and be involved with many of the human resource functions.

The Human Resource Department

As mentioned previously, most medium-size and some large organizations use human resource generalists and do not have a human resource department. In these situations, the functions performed by human resource generalists are essentially the same as those that would be performed by a human resource department. Therefore, the following discussion also applies to the role of human resource generalists in organizations that do not have a human resource department.

The primary function of a human resource department is to provide support to operating managers on all human resource matters. Thus, most human resource departments fulfill a traditional staff role and act primarily in an advisory capacity. In addition to advising operating managers, a human resource department customarily organizes and coordinates hiring and training; maintains personnel records; acts as a liaison between management, labor, and government; and coordinates safety programs. Therefore, accomplishing the human resource goals of an organization requires close coordination between the human resource department and the operating managers.

Precisely how all of the functions related to human resources are split between operating managers and the human resource department varies from organization to organization. For

TABLE 1.2
Examples of the Types of Assistance Provided by a Human Resource Department

Specific Services	Advice	Coordination
Maintaining employee records	Disciplinary matters	Performance appraisals
Handling initial phases of employee orientation	Equal employment opportunity matters	Compensation matters

example, the human resource department in one company may do all the hiring below a certain level. In another company, all the hiring decisions may be made by operating managers, with the human resource department acting only in an advisory capacity.

It is helpful to view the human resource department as providing three types of assistance: (1) specific services, (2) advice, and (3) coordination. Table 1.2 presents some typical examples of each of these types of assistance. Figure 1.1 illustrates the different roles a human resource department or a human resource generalist might fill.

As stated earlier, a human resource department normally acts in an advisory capacity and does not have authority over operating managers. As a result, conflict can occur when operating managers appear to ignore the suggestions and recommendations of the human resource department. If the human resource department is to be effective, it must continually cultivate good relations with operating managers. Likewise, operating managers must understand the human resource functions to effectively utilize the human resource department.

CHALLENGES FOR TODAY'S HUMAN RESOURCE MANAGERS

Human resource management has expanded and moved beyond mere administration of the traditional activities of employment, labor relations, compensation, and benefits. Today HRM is much more integrated into both the management and the strategic planning process of the organization.[3]

One reason for this expanded role is that the organizational environment has become much more diverse and complex. Compared to a workforce historically dominated by white males, today's workforce is very diverse and projected to become more so. Diversity in the workforce encompasses many different dimensions, including sex, race, national origin, religion, age, sexual orientation, and disability. Diversity in the workplace presents new and different challenges for all managers. Other challenges are the result of changes in government requirements, organizational structures, technology, and management approaches. Each of these issues is discussed below.

Diversity in the Workforce

Recent forecasts by the U.S. Bureau of Labor Statistics project that the total U.S. labor force will consist of only 33 percent white, non-Hispanic males by the year 2018.[4] Table 1.3 shows the projected numbers of entrants and leavers in the total workforce of the groups shown for

FIGURE 1.1
Three Types of Assistance Provided by a Human Resource Department

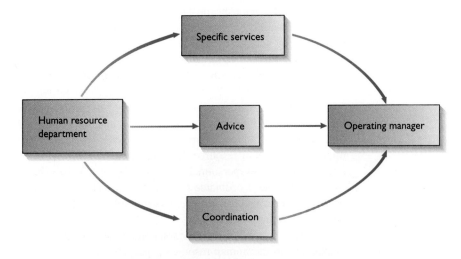

TABLE 1.3
Civilian Labor Force, 2008,
and Projected 2018;
Entrants and Leavers,
Projected 2008–18

Source: Mitra Toossi, "Labor Force
Projections to 2018: Older Workers
Staying More Active," *Monthly Labor
Review,* November 2009, p. 47.

Group*		2008–18			
	2008	**Entrants**	**Leavers**	**Stayers**	**2018**
Number, 16 years and older					
Total	154,287	37,632	25,008	129,279	166,911
Men	82,520	20,429	14,267	68,253	88,682
Women	71,767	17,203	10,741	61,026	78,229
White	125,635	27,990	21,135	104,500	132,490
Men	68,351	15,554	12,174	56,177	71,731
Women	57,284	12,436	8,961	48,323	60,759
Black	17,740	5,403	2,899	14,841	20,244
Men	8,347	2,673	1,441	6,906	9,579
Women	9,393	2,730	1,458	7,935	10,665
Asian	7,202	2,837	694	6,508	9,345
Men	3,852	1,493	450	3,402	4,895
Women	3,350	1,344	244	3,106	4,450
All other groups**	3,710	1,402	280	3,430	4,832
Men	1,970	709	202	1,768	2,477
Women	1,740	693	78	1,662	2,355
Hispanic origin	22,024	9,237	1,957	20,067	29,304
Men	13,255	5,078	1,282	11,973	17,051
Women	8,769	4,159	675	8,094	12,253
Other than Hispanic	132,263	28,395	23,051	109,212	137,607
Men	69,265	15,351	12,985	56,280	71,631
Women	62,998	13,044	10,066	52,932	65,976
White Non-Hispanic	105,209	20,847	19,222	85,987	106,834
Men	55,971	11,907	10,803	45,168	57,075
Women	49,238	8,940	8,419	40,819	49,759

*Numbers in thousands.

**The "All other groups" category includes those classed as of multiple racial origin, the race categories of American Indian and Alaska Native, or Native Hawaiian and Other Pacific Islanders.

the years 2008–2018. As the table indicates, almost half the new entrants during that time span will be women. This one dimension of diversity has many ramifications for organizations in the areas of child care, spouse relocation assistance programs, pregnancy leave programs, flexible hours, and stay-at-home jobs.

These same projections also predict that white, non-Hispanic males will comprise fewer than one-third of new labor force entrants for the years 2008–2018. In 2008, Hispanics represented approximately 14 percent of the labor force, with over 22 million workers. This figure is expected to grow by more than 7.3 million by 2018 to a total of 29.3 million. The Asian labor force, which is the smallest group in the U.S. labor force, is expected to have the second highest (behind Hispanics) annual rate of growth from 2.6 percent of the total U.S. work force in 2008 to 5.6 percent by 2018. In addition to the possibility of having differing educational backgrounds, immigrant employees are likely to have language and cultural differences. Organizations must begin now to successfully integrate these people into their workforces.

Almost everyone has heard the phrase "the graying of America." By the year 2018, the average age of employees will climb to 42.3 from 41.2 in 2008 and from 34.8 in 1978.[5] With the aging of the overall U.S. population along with the emergence of the baby boomers, the percentage of older employees in the labor force is also expected to increase. The increase in the percentage of older employees will have a mixed effect. The older workforce will likely be more experienced, reliable, and stable, but possibly less adaptable to change and retraining. One result of this trend is that the retirement age has already begun to increase.

Globalization of HR

Another dimension of diversity is related to the increasing globalization of many companies. As companies become more global, diversity must be defined in global and not just Western terms.[6] Defining diversity in global terms means looking at all people and everything that makes them different from one another, as well as the things that make them similar. Differentiating factors often go beyond race and language and may include such things as values, habits, and customs. A recent survey conducted by Jeitosa Group International and the International Association for Human Resource Information Management identified the following areas as key human resource–related challenges facing global companies:

- Cultural differences (53 percent).
- Compliance with data-privacy regulations (42 percent).
- Varying economic conditions across countries (36 percent).
- Time zone differences (32 percent).
- Legal environment (32 percent).
- International compliance (26 percent).[7]

Keeping diversity in mind, one key to a successful global HR program is to rely on local people to deal with local issues. This approach only makes sense when one considers the fact that locals almost always have a better understanding of local diversity-related issues.

Challenges and Contributions of Diversity

Organizations must successfully integrate different cultures and age groups. Photodisc/PunchStock

What challenges and contributions does the increasingly diverse workforce present? From an overall viewpoint, organizations must get away from the tradition of fitting employees into a single corporate mold.[8] Everyone will not look and act the same. Organizations must create new human resource policies to explicitly recognize and respond to the unique needs of individual employees.

Greater diversity will not only create certain specific challenges but also make some important contributions. Communication problems are certain to occur, including misunderstandings among employees and managers as well as the need to translate verbal and written materials into several languages. Solutions to these problems will necessitate additional training involving work in basic skills such as writing and problem solving. An increase in organizational factionalism will require dedicating increasing amounts of time to dealing with special interest and advocacy groups.

In addition to creating the above challenges, greater diversity presents new opportunities. Diversity contributes to creating an organizational culture that is more tolerant of different behavioral styles and wider views. This often leads to better business decisions. Another potential payoff is a greater responsiveness to diverse groups of customers.

The increasing diversification of the workplace is fact. Learning to effectively manage a diverse workforce should be viewed as an investment in the future. HRM in Action 1.1 describes how and why Scotiabank of Canada encourages diversity among its workforce.

Regulatory Changes

The deluge of government regulations and laws has placed a tremendous burden on human resource managers. Organizations face new regulations routinely issued in the areas of environment, safety and health, equal employment opportunity, pension reform, and quality of work life. Often new regulations require significant paperwork and changes in operating procedures. Implementing these changes frequently falls on human resource managers. In addition, every year thousands of cases relating to the interpretation of human resource issues are brought before the courts. Once a case has been decided, human resource managers must implement the findings. Many of the new changes to health care and health insurance will have to be implemented by human resource personnel and will have a significant impact on their activities.

Structural Changes to Organizations

In recent times, organizations have undergone many structural changes that present challenges for human resource managers—and they continue to face such changes. Some of the structural

downsizing
Laying off large numbers of managerial and other employees.

outsourcing
Subcontracting work to an outside company that specializes in that particular type of work.

changes are caused by downsizing, outsourcing, rightsizing, and reengineering. **Downsizing** is laying off large numbers of managerial and other employees. As a result of downsizing and/or attempts to reduce costs, many companies are outsourcing services that the human resource department previously provided. **Outsourcing** is subcontracting work to an outside company that specializes in that particular type of work. Some examples of human resource services being outsourced include retirement plan administration, payroll, training, and management development programs. Under the right circumstances outsourcing certain HR activities can be more efficient and less costly. A recent survey by Hewitt Associates, a global human resources services firm, of 104 organizations, approximately two-thirds of which are publicly traded companies, found that most of the responding companies have achieved their expected benefits from outsourcing. The survey also reported that one-third of the responding companies were currently more inclined to outsource than they were two years ago.[9] Organizations that human resource tasks are outsourced to are referred to as professional employer organizations (PEO's). PEO's provide integrated services to effectively manage human resource responsibilities and employer risks for clients.[10]

rightsizing
Continuous and proactive assessment of mission-critical work and its staffing requirements.

reengineering
Fundamental rethinking and radical redesign of business processes to achieve dramatic improvements in cost, quality, service, and speed.

Rightsizing is the continuous and proactive assessment of mission-critical work and its staffing requirements.[11] Rightsizing differs from downsizing in that it is an ongoing planning process to determine the optimal number of employees in every area of the organization. Other companies are implementing reengineering programs. **Reengineering** is a fundamental rethinking and radical redesign of business processes to achieve dramatic improvements in cost, quality, service, and speed.[12] In essence, reengineering usually results in sweeping changes in management and organizational structures.

Technological and Managerial Changes within Organizations

New technologies and management approaches have added to the challenges facing human resource managers. While the technological changes affecting human resource managers are widespread, none are more dramatic than those related to information systems. In addition to their uses in performing the traditional functions of accounting and payroll calculations, computerized information systems are now being used to maintain easily accessible employee data that are valuable in job placement and labor utilization. Information systems are also being used in employee training, succession planning, and compensation management, and to track and report affirmative action activity. Cyberspace and the Internet are changing the way many human resource managers operate. Today more and more human resource managers are going online to recruit personnel, conduct research using electronic databases, send e-mail, and engage in valuable networking and discussions.

Many organizations have implemented Web-based human resource systems that allow employees to complete many HR-related tasks online. These systems are sometimes referred to as electronic human resources (eHR). These self-service systems have the advantages of employee convenience, immediate response, increased accuracy, and reduced

INTRODUCING eHR AT PHILIPS ELECTRONICS AND PHILIPS NETHERLANDS

Philips Electronics Netherlands and Philips Netherlands together employ over 1,000 people in Eindhoven, Netherlands. After eHR had been implemented at both Philips facilities, a survey was conducted to determine the employees' attitudes toward the new system. The survey was conducted online and included 99 managers and 257 nommanagers.

While many factors influence employee attitudes toward eHR, two main factors were found to impact attitude towards eHR: (1) Previous experiences with Information Technology (IT) systems and (2) the employee's preferences as to the role played by HR in the organization. The first finding implies that for an eHR implementation to be successful, the broader IT environment should be taken into consideration.

If the image IT already has within an organization is positive, the eHR should be relatively easy to implement. If not, one should expect a slow process of gaining trust and credibility while implementing eHR. The second finding indicates that employees will be more positive towards an eHR implementation if they prefer a strategic role for HR as opposed to a more transactional role.

One overall conclusion from the Philips' experience is that organizations should not leave the introduction of eHR to the technical people alone.

Sources: "The Introduction of e-HRM at Philips: Some Lessons for Large Organizations: Don't Leave It All to the Technical Specialists," *Human Resource Management International Digest* 16, No. 2 (2008), p. 20; and M. Voermons and M. van Veldhoven, "Attitudes Towards e-HRM: An Empirical Study at Philips," *Personnel Review* 36, No. 6 (2007), p. 887.

costs. Some examples of self-service HR-related options include payroll systems that let employees input hours worked and requests for vacation time, payroll direct deposits that allow employees to view current and historical pay information, and various aspects of benefits administration.

Since the introduction of eHR in the 1990s, the fundamentals of eHR products haven't changed because the basic problems they address are the same.[13] However, the manner in which the eHR products are delivered and maintained has undergone a major overhaul and vast improvement. As part of this evolution, the costs have dropped and what used to take months to implement can now be done in hours. Another reason for the growth of eHR products is that today's employees are much more receptive to being sent to a Web site for information. Because of the widespread use of information systems and technology in the HR field, specific applications as related to the different HR functions are discussed throughout this book. HRM in Action 1.2 discusses some of the lessons learned from implementing eHR at two Philips facilities in the Netherlands.

telecommuting
Working at home by using an electronic linkup with a central office.

More and more frequently, companies are using **telecommuting.** Options range from allowing employees to work at home one day a week to running entire projects, or even firms, through electronic communication, with employees all over the country or even on different continents working closely together, yet never meeting face to face.

empowerment
Form of decentralization that involves giving subordinates substantial authority to make decisions.

Empowerment of employees and self-managed work teams are two specific management approaches that are having a significant impact on today's human resource managers. **Empowerment** is a form of decentralization that involves giving subordinates substantial authority to make decisions. Under empowerment, managers express confidence in the ability of employees to perform at high levels. Employees are also encouraged to accept personal responsibility for their work. In organizations using **self-managed work teams,** groups of employees do not report to a single manager; rather, groups of peers are responsible for a particular area or task.

self-managed work teams
Groups of peers are responsible for a particular area or task.

The breadth of the changes in so many areas—workforce diversity, the regulatory environment, organizational structure, new technologies, management approaches—will have a powerful impact on today's human resource managers.

Human Resource Management in the Future

To meet the challenges of the future, tomorrow's human resource departments must possess different competencies and be much more sophisticated than their predecessors.[14] Given the expanding role human resource departments must fill, it is essential that human resource managers be integrally involved in the organization's strategic and policy-making activities. Fortunately, there are signs that this is happening in many organizations. For example, in the majority of Fortune 500 companies, the head of the human resource department is an officer (usually a vice president) who answers to the chief executive officer (CEO). In many companies, the head of the human resource department sits on the board of directors, the planning committee, or both.

If tomorrow's human resource managers are to earn the respect of their colleagues and top management, they must overcome certain negative impressions and biases sometimes associated with human resource management. They can do so in several ways. First, human resource managers should become well-rounded businesspeople. In addition to having a sound background in the basic disciplines of the profession, human resource professionals need to understand business complexities and strategies.[15] The following suggestions can help human resource managers become more familiar with their businesses:

- Know the company strategy and business plan.
- Know the industry.
- Support business needs.
- Spend more time with the line people.
- Keep your hand on the pulse of the organization.
- Learn to calculate costs and solutions in hard numbers.[16]

A 2007 survey of 589 HR professionals by the Society for Human Resource Management (SHRM) found that nearly two-thirds of HR professionals viewed their department's role as equally strategic and transactional; only one-third reported their department's role as primarily transactional. HR professionals from small organizations were more likely than those from large organizations to report that they viewed their HR functions as being primarily transactional.[17] A 2008 poll also conducted by SHRM of 345 randomly selected HR professionals found that 58 percent of the respondents believed that HR's role in their organization's strategic planning had increased significantly.[18] A British survey published in 2009 of 269 HR professionals reported that 65 percent of the respondents believed that the HR profession was more strategic than when they began their careers.[19] Outsourcing many of the clerical functions, eHR, and the use of other computerized information systems (discussed further in Chapter 5) have all contributed to making today's HR managers more strategic.

HR professionals who thoroughly understand their businesses will help overcome the common idea that human resource people are unfamiliar with the operating problems and issues facing the organization. Figure 1.2 lists several pertinent questions that human resource managers should be able to answer to develop greater understanding of the organization's business strategies. HRM in Action 1.3 describes why and how Cardinal Health is expanding the strategic role of its HR functions.

Human resource managers should also become fully knowledgeable about present and future trends and issues in HR and other related fields. This will help them guard against becoming enamored with passing fads or ineffective techniques.

Finally, human resource managers should promote effective human resource utilization within the organization. Rather than taking a moralistic approach when dealing with operating managers, human resource managers should stress the importance of increasing profits through effectively using the organization's human resources. In this light, human resource managers should learn to be proactive and seize opportunities to demonstrate how they can positively affect the bottom line.

FIGURE 1.2
Questions for Understanding the Organization's Business Strategy

Source: Adapted from Daphne Woolf, "The Long Road to the Executive Boardroom," *Canadian HR Reporter,* June 17, 2002, pp. 7–8.

- What are the goals of the organization over the next year, 3 years, 5 years, and 10 years?
- How would you describe the organization's core business?
- How does your organization compare with competitors in market share and customer service?
- Will the company be growing via merger and acquisition or from internal growth?
- Will growth be local, national, or global?
- Will growth be from expansion of current businesses or from an expansion in scope?
- Instead of growth, will there be downsizing and if so, why?
- What are the organization's revenue objectives over the short and long terms?

HR TAKING A MORE STRATEGIC ROLE AT CARDINAL HEALTH

Cardinal Health, based in Dublin, Ohio, ranks 19th on the *Fortune* 500 list and is a major provider of health-care products, services, and technologies. Forty-two percent of Cardinal's 55,000 employees live outside the United States. Corporate leaders at Cardinal recently decided that the company's competitive advantage lies in its people. As a result of their decisions, the company is concentrating its human resource efforts on more strategic issues and outsourcing the more administrative functions. Cardinal is placing human resource "business partners" across the company who focus on strategic activities such as finding and developing talent while establishing new HR field operations. Cardinal has outsourced the more administrative HR functions by signing a multiyear contract with ExcellerateHRO, which is jointly owned by EDS and Towers Perrin.

Cardinal's management believes that these changes will enable the company to make HR a more strategic player and greatly increase its global HR capabilities. Cardinal's new perspective on HR comes in the aftermath of very rapid growth, zooming from $7.8 billion to $74.9 billion over the past 10 years.

Source: Mark Schoeff Jr., "Cardinal Health HR to Take More Strategic Role," *Workforce Management,* April 24, 2006, pp. 7–8.

ORGANIZATIONAL PERFORMANCE AND THE HUMAN RESOURCE MANAGER

There is no doubt that human resource managers spend considerable time working on problems and concerns related to the human side of the organization. Because of this, many people perceive human resource managers as being concerned *only* with matters that relate directly to the human side of the organization. Contrary to this view, human resource managers can have a direct impact on organizational performance in a number of specific ways:

1. Reducing unnecessary overtime expenses by increasing productivity during a normal day.
2. Staying on top of absenteeism and instituting programs designed to reduce money spent for time not worked.
3. Eliminating wasted time by employees through sound job design.
4. Minimizing employee turnover and unemployment benefit costs by practicing sound human relations and creating a work atmosphere that promotes job satisfaction.
5. Installing and monitoring effective safety and health programs to reduce lost-time accidents and keep medical and workers' compensation costs low.
6. Properly training and developing all employees so they can improve their value to the company and do a better job of producing and selling high-quality products and services at the lowest possible cost.
7. Decreasing costly material waste by eliminating bad work habits and attitudes and poor working conditions that lead to carelessness and mistakes.
8. Hiring the best people available at every level and avoiding overstaffing.
9. Maintaining competitive pay practices and benefit programs to foster a motivational climate for employees.
10. Encouraging employees, who probably know more about the nuts and bolts of their jobs than anyone else, to submit ideas for increasing productivity and reducing costs.
11. Installing human resource information systems to streamline and automate many human resource functions.[20]

Metrics and the HR Scorecard

As a direct result of increasingly available information and computer systems, the human resource department can use numerous strategies to contribute to the bottom line.[21] The basic idea behind these strategies is to translate knowledge of human resources into terms that have tangible and recognizable economic benefits, especially to operating managers.

metrics
Any set of quantitative measures used to assess workforce performance.

Metrics refers to any set of quantitative measures used to assess workforce performance. Examples of metrics that HR might use include such things as analysis of the cost per hire, average length of time to fill a position, training cost per employee, turnover cost per employee, and new-hire performance by recruiting strategy.

While the HR metrics discussed in the previous paragraph relate specifically to measures about people in the organization, there is also a need to measure the overall contribution of the HR function to the well-being of the organizations. The **HR scorecard** is one method used to do this.

HR scorecard
A measurement and control system that uses a mix of quantitative and qualititative measures to evaluate performance.

The HR scorecard is basically a modified version of the balance scorecard system applied to the human resources function. The balance scorecard system is a measurement and control system that uses a mix of quantitative and qualitative measures to evaluate performance. The HR scorecard is discussed in more depth in Chapter 11.

COMMUNICATING HUMAN RESOURCE PROGRAMS

Communicating human resource programs has been compared to marketing a new product.[22] Consider the fact that approximately 90 percent of all new consumer products fail. In some cases, the failure is due to a poor product that does not fill a current need. In other cases however, the product fails because of a breakdown in the marketing system. The product may have been inadequately researched, the salespeople may not have been properly trained, the distribution system may have been poor, or the overall marketing strategy may have been misguided. Unfortunately, many well-designed human resource programs also fail because they are not properly "marketed." In today's world of global companies, communicating with employees located throughout the world can present even greater problems. A recent survey by Watson Wyatt found that U.S. companies "are stingy when it comes to allocating human and financial resources to communicate with their workforces overseas."[23]

communication
Transfer of information that is meaningful to those involved.

Communication is much more than talking, speaking, and reading. True communication takes place when an understanding has been transferred from one party or source to another. Therefore, communication can be defined as the transfer of information that is meaningful to those involved.

In this light, each and every one of the human resource functions discussed in this book requires some degree of effective communication to succeed. For example, think of the important role communication plays in career planning, recruiting, and performance appraisal. In all too many instances, human resource managers spend tremendous amounts of time developing very good programs, only to subsequently do a poor job of communicating them. The end result is often great programs that go largely unused.

A human resource manager's first step in becoming an effective communicator is to develop an appreciation for the importance of communication. The problem is not that human resource managers tend to belittle the importance of communication; rather, they often fail to think consciously about it.

Guidelines for Communicating Human Resource Programs

As just discussed, it is helpful for human resource managers to develop a marketing approach when implementing their programs. Even when this is successfully done, numerous other communication-related guidelines remain to follow. Some of these are discussed next.[24]

Avoid communicating in peer group or "privileged-class" language. The level of communication should be determined by the receiving audience and not by the instigator of the communication. Take the common procedure for developing employee benefit information. Often a highly educated writer makes a first draft and gives it to the department head. The department head, being a specialist, then adds a few "clarifying" remarks. The company lawyer and perhaps an actuary or an insurance person then add more explanations to guard against liability and to be legally correct. Thus, the final document may be accurate and legal, but also barely understood by the employees for whom it is intended! The key is to consciously remember for whom the communication is intended.

Don't ignore the cultural and global aspects of communication. Be careful with words, symbols, and expressions. Today's workforce is much more culturally sensitive and global than it was one or two decades ago. Expressions like "They wear the black hats" or "You act like an old lady" can easily be taken out of context and offend someone in the audience.

Back up communications with management action. The old saying "People watch what you do and not what you say" is certainly true with regard to employee communications. Promises made either orally or in writing must be backed up by actions if they are to succeed.

Periodically reinforce employee communications. Most communications tend to be forgotten unless they are periodically reinforced. This is especially true with many personnel-related communications. It is a good idea, for example, to periodically remind employees of the value of the benefits they receive.

data
Raw material from which information is developed; composed of facts that describe people, places, things, or events and that have not been interpreted.

information
Data that have been interpreted and that meet a need of one or more managers.

Transmit information and not just data. **Data** can be defined as "the raw material from which information is developed; it is composed of acts that describe people, places, things, or events that have not been interpreted." Data that have been interpreted and that meet a need of one or more managers are called **information.** Employees receive piles of data from numerous sources, but until the data have been interpreted, they are of little value. Human resource managers need to guard against transmitting numbers, statistics, and other data that have little meaning without an accompanying interpretation.

Don't ignore the perceptual and behavioral aspects of communication. Try to anticipate employee reactions to communications and act accordingly. For example, it might be a good strategy to informally separate older employees from younger employees when introducing a new pension program through employee meetings. It would only be natural for these different groups to have different questions and levels of interest.

The preceding suggestions largely involve good common sense. It is not that human resource managers are not practical; rather, they often do not take the time to think through a communication. One good approach is to ask, "How could this message be misinterpreted?" The answer to this question should then be taken into account when structuring the communication.

The Web-based human resource systems (eHR) that many organizations have implemented (discussed earlier in this chapter) have greatly helped to communicate human resource programs. One survey conducted by Towers Perrin reported that 67 percent of the more than 200 respondents said that Web-based self-services for HR improved employee awareness and appreciation of company-sponsored HR programs.[25]

Summary of Learning Objectives

1. **Define *human resource management.***

   Human resource management encompasses those activities designed to provide for and coordinate the human resources of an organization. Human resource management is also a modern term for what has traditionally been referred to as personnel administration or personnel management.

2. **Describe the functions of human resource management.**

   Human resource functions are those tasks and duties performed in large and small organizations to provide for and coordinate human resources. Human resource functions include the following:
   a. Human resource planning, recruitment, and selection.
   b. Human resource development.
   c. Compensation and benefits.
   d. Safety and health.
   e. Employee and labor relations.
   f. Human resource research.

3. **Summarize the types of assistance the human resource department provides.**

   The primary function of the human resource department is to provide support to operating managers of all human resource matters. In general terms, the human resource department provides three types of assistance: (1) specific services, (2) advice, and (3) coordination.

4. Explain the desired relationship between human resource managers and operating managers.

The human resource department normally acts in an advisory capacity and does not have authority over operating managers. To be effective, human resource managers must continually cultivate good relations with operating managers. Likewise, operating managers must understand the human resource functions to effectively utilize the human resource department.

5. Identify several challenges today's human resource managers currently face.

Today's human resource managers currently face several challenges. Some of the more significant issues include an increasingly diverse workforce and changes in government regulations, organization structures, technology, and managerial approaches.

6. Outline several potential challenges and contributions that an increasingly diverse workforce presents.

An increasingly diverse workforce creates specific challenges in the areas of communication, more training, and potentially higher factionalism. On the positive side, increased diversity will contribute to an organizational culture that is more tolerant of different views, which may lead to better decisions. Another potential payoff is greater organizational responsiveness to diverse groups of customers.

7. Discuss the role of human resource managers in the future.

Human resource managers are predicted to play an increasingly important role in the management of organizations. In fulfilling this role, human resource managers should become thoroughly familiar with the business and business strategies, be knowledgeable about present and future trends, and learn to emphasize the impact human resources can have on organizational performance.

8. Explain how human resource managers can affect organizational performance.

Human resource managers can have a direct impact on organizational performance in many ways. Some of them include reducing unnecessary overtime expenses by increasing productivity, instituting programs to reduce absenteeism, eliminating wasted time through sound job design, minimizing employee turnovers and unemployment costs by practicing sound human relations and creating a work atmosphere that promotes job satisfaction, installing and monitoring effective safety and health programs, properly training and developing employees, decreasing costly material waste by eliminating bad work habits and attitudes, hiring the best people available, maintaining competitive pay practices and benefit programs, encouraging employees, and installing human resource information systems to streamline many human resource functions.

9. Summarize several guidelines to follow when communicating human resource programs.

Overall, it is helpful for human resource managers to develop a marketing approach when implementing and communicating their programs. In addition, they can follow several specific guidelines: avoid communicating in peer group or privileged-class language, remember the cultural aspects of communication, back up communications with management action, periodically reinforce employee communications, transmit information and not just data, and consider the perceptual and behavioral aspects of communication.

Key Terms

communication, *13*
data, *14*
downsizing, *9*
empowerment, *10*
HR scorecard, *13*
human resource functions, *4*
human resource generalist, *5*

human resource management, *3*
human resource specialist, *5*
information, *14*
metrics, *12*
operating manager, *5*
outsourcing, *9*

reengineering, *9*
rightsizing, *9*
self-managed work teams, *10*
talent management, *5*
telecommuting, *10*

Review Questions

1. What is human resource management? Distinguish between a human resource generalist and a human resource specialist.
2. What functions does a human resource department normally perform? Why are these functions important in today's organizations?
3. What does the term *talent management* mean?
4. List several challenges facing today's human resource managers.
5. What is meant by an "increasingly diverse workforce"?
6. Differentiate among downsizing, outsourcing, rightsizing, and reengineering.
7. What are Web-based human resource systems?
8. What are some things human resource managers should do to become more familiar with the organization's business?
9. Differentiate between the terms *HR metrics* and *HR scorecard*.
10. List several guidelines to follow when communicating human resource programs.
11. Name several specific ways human resource managers can positively affect an organization's profits.

Discussion Questions

1. Some people believe human resource management is an area reserved for those "who can't do anything else." Why do you think this belief has emerged? Is there any factual basis for it?
2. Describe some current trends that you believe will have an impact on human resource management in the next 10 years.
3. Many human resource managers claim to love their work because they like to work with people. Do you think liking people is the most important ingredient in becoming a successful human resource manager?
4. As a human resource manager, how might you go about convincing top management that you should be heavily involved in the company's strategic planning process?

Incident 1.1

Human Resource Management and Professionals

Web site: Society for Human Resource Management
www.shrm.org

You are a senior member of a national law firm in New York City. The managing partner of the firm has asked you to head up the southern branch in Raleigh, North Carolina. This branch is 1 of 10 under the main office. On the whole, the firm has been successful since its establishment in the mid-1950s, but in the last five years, many of the younger staff have elected to leave the firm. The managing partner is convinced the problem is not salary, because a recent survey indicated that the firm's salary structure is competitive with that of other major firms. However, he requests that you study this matter firsthand in your new assignment.

After getting settled in Raleigh, one of your first projects is to meet with the four senior managers to determine why the branch has had such a high attrition rate among the younger staff. Harding Smith, age 45, states that the younger staff lacks dedication and fails to appreciate the career opportunities the firm provides. Wilma Thompson, age 50, says the younger staff members are always complaining about the lack of meaningful feedback on their performance, and many have mentioned that they would like to have a sponsor in the organization to assist with their development. Thompson further explains that the firm does provide performance ratings to staff and the previous manager had always maintained an open-door policy. Brian Scott, age 40, says he has received complaints that training is not relevant and is generally dull. He explains that various persons in the firm who worked with training from time to time acted mainly on guidance from New York. Denise Rutherford, age 38, says she believes the root of the problem is the lack of a human resource department. However, she says that when the idea was mentioned to the managing partner in New York, it was totally rejected.

Questions

1. What do you think about the idea of a human resource department in a professional office?
2. How would you sell the idea of a human resource department to the managing partner?
3. What type of organizational structure would you propose?

Incident 1.2

Choosing a Major

Tom Russell is a junior in the school of business administration at a large midwestern university. Tom, who is an honor student, hasn't fully decided what his major should be. He has considered majoring in management, but just can't get excited about the field; it seems to be too general.

Tom's first course in management did appeal to him; however, this was largely because of the professor. Tom decided to talk to this professor about his dilemma. The following conversation occurred:

Tom: Professor, I would like your advice on selecting a major field of study. Right now, I just don't know what to do.

Professor: Tom, just let me say that you are making an important decision, and your concern is justified. How many courses have you taken in the School of Business Administration?

Tom: Only your introductory course in management, a basic course in marketing, and a statistics course, I do know that I don't want to major in statistics!

Professor: How about majoring in human resource management?

Tom: I don't think so. That is basically a staff job that can't really lead anywhere.

Professor: Hold on, Tom, I think I'd better tell you a little more about human resource management.

Questions

1. If you were the professor, what would you tell Tom?
2. Specifically, what future trends do you see that might help persuade Tom to major in human resource management?

EXERCISE 1.1 **Changes in** **Terminology**	Go to your college or university library or go online and search under the terms *Personnel Management* and *Human Resources Management*. Based on your findings, approximately when was the term *Personnel Management* replaced by the term *Human Resource Management?* Why do you think this change occurred? Be prepared to present your findings to the class.

EXERCISE 1.2 **Justifying the** **Human Resource** **Department**	Assume you work in the human resource department of a medium-size manufacturing company (annual sales of $300 million). The company has been unionized for many years but has never had a strike. The president of the company has just requested that all departments develop a budget for the coming fiscal year and be prepared to justify their budget requests. As part of this justification, your boss, the director of human resources, has just asked you to prepare a list of at least 10 reasons why the human resource department and its performance are important to the success of the entire company. Be prepared to present your list to the class.

EXERCISE 1.3 **Test Your Knowledge** **of HR History***	Each of these events happened in the 20th century. See if you can put them in the correct chronological order. For a greater challenge, name the year that the event occurred. Search for clues with your Web browser. Hint: Summaries of many labor laws can be found at the U.S. Department of Labor, Major Laws & Regulations Enforced by the Department of Labor, Web site.

Web site
www.dol.gov/dol/compliance/
compliance-majorlaw.htm

A. The minimum wage is raised to $7.25 an hour.

B. Executive Order 11246 is issued to provide for equal employment opportunity for those working for government contractors.

C. President Clinton signs the Family and Medical Leave Act (FMLA).

D. Congress passes the Railway Labor Act, requiring employers to bargain with unions.

E. Congress passes the Fair Labor Standards Act (FLSA), banning child labor.

F. Congress passes the Occupational Safety and Health Act.

G. President Truman seizes the steel industry when steel companies reject recommendations made by the Wage Stabilization Board.

H. The Uniformed Services Employment and Reemployment Rights Act (USERRA) is signed to protect workers who are called to active military duty.

I. Congress passes the Employment Retirement Income Security Act regulating all private pension plans.

J. The North American Free Trade Agreement is passed.

K. Congress passes the Equal Pay Act prohibiting wage differentials based on gender for workers covered by the FLSA.

L. President Reagan signs a welfare reform bill requiring single parents with children over 3 years old to get regular jobs.

M. United States enters World War II.

N. Frances Perkins becomes secretary of labor and the first woman named to a presidential cabinet.

*Source: Adapted from *Workforce,* Workforce Extra Supplement, October 1998, p. 7, and the U.S. Department of Labor, Major Laws & Regulations Enforced by the Department of Labor, Web site.

EXERCISE 1.4
Are You Poised for Success?**

As discussed in this chapter, a successful career in HR demands a broader range of skills and experiences than ever before. While designed for people currently employed in HR positions, the following exam provides good insights into what is necessary to succeed in HR today. If you are currently employed in HR, take the exam and see how well you are doing. If you are not currently in HR, go over the exam questions to learn how you might prepare yourself for a career in HR.

I. Starting Points   (10 points)

(10 points if you have a managerial, directorial, or VP title)   _____

II. Knowledge of General Business and Finance   (10 points)

During the past six months, have you initiated conversations with the CFO or other finance executive to discuss the financial implications of HR programs? If yes, add 2 points.   _____

Have you completed some general business courses at the college level? If yes, add 2 points.   _____

Do you have an MBA? If yes, add 2 points.   _____

Do you develop the first draft of the company's annual HR budget and then advocate for it during the corporate budget-setting sessions? If yes, add 2 points.   _____

Did you meet HR budget goals (+ or −5%) during the most recent fiscal year? If yes, add 2 points.   _____

III. Mastery of HR Disciplines   (10 points)

Have you initiated, developed, and implemented a specific HR program within a specific HR niche (e.g., training or compensation)? If yes, add 1 point for each program, to a maximum of 4 points.   _____

Before assuming your present position, did you hold a title of manager or director of a specific HR function, such as benefits or staffing? If yes, add 2 points for each title, to a maximum of 4 points.   _____

Have you mentored someone else in HR who was designing a program within a specific HR niche? If yes, add 2 points.   _____

IV. Knowledge of Your Organization   (10 points)

Can you state your company's earnings for the most recent fiscal year?
If yes, add 1 point.   _____

Can you state your company's profit (or loss) for the most recent fiscal year?
If yes, add 1 point.   _____

Can you identify your organization's primary product or service lines and
the relative revenue generated by each? If yes, add 1 point.   _____

Can you identify your chief competitors and state your competitive position
relative to them? If yes, add 2 points.   _____

Do you report directly to the CEO? If yes, add 2 points.   _____

During the past year, have you initiated a meeting or meetings with a line
manager or other colleague at the management level for the express
purpose of learning about their business needs or objectives? If yes, add
3 points.   _____

V. Cross-Functional Experience   (10 points)

Have you ever "shadowed" another executive or accepted a temporary
assignment to gain a better understanding of another business function?
If yes, add 2 points.   _____

Have you ever held a position in an industry outside the one in which you're
presently working? If yes, add 4 points.   _____

Have you ever held a position in a discipline outside HR (e.g., marketing,
communication, or finance)? If yes, add 4 points.   _____

VI. International/Cross-Cultural Experience   (10 points)

Have you ever participated in a cross-cultural training program? If yes,
add 1 point.   _____

Have you ever served as a member of a task force addressing a global business
issue? If yes, add 1 point.   _____

Have you ever traveled abroad? If yes, add 1 point for each country you've
visited, to a maximum of 3 points.   _____

Have you ever held an overseas assignment of six months or longer?
If yes, add 5 points.   _____

VII. Mentors   (10 points)

Have you had one or more mentors during your career? If yes, add 4 points.   _____

Have any of your mentors been

a. the opposite gender?   _____

b. another race or ethnic group?   _____

c. in a discipline other than HR?   _____

Add 2 points for each yes answer.

VIII. Career Decisions   (10 points)

Have you developed a specific career goal for yourself? If yes, add 4 points.   _____

Have you initiated activities intended to give you the skills/responsibility
needed to progress toward your career goal? If yes, add 3 points.   _____

Have you sought or accepted a lateral transfer for the purpose of expanding
your career opportunities? If yes, add 3 points.   _____

IX. Technology   (10 points)

Have you directed a project in which the application of technology (computers,
voice-response systems, etc.) improved HR's value or productivity? If yes,
add 5 points.   _____

Have you been a member of a group or task force responsible for applying
technology to solve an HR-related issue? If yes, add 3 points.   _____

Do you use a computer yourself in the course of doing your job? If yes, add
1 point.   _____

Do you consider yourself conversant in the current technological lingo
(e.g., client/server, open architecture)? If yes, add 1 point. _____

X. Continual Learning (10 points)

Do you subscribe to and read at least two business/professional publications?
If yes, add 2 points. _____

Do you keep current on general issues that have implications for HR
(e.g., health care reform)? If yes, add 2 points. _____

Do you periodically take classes or attend seminars in areas not directly
related to HR, such as creativity or statistics? If yes, add 2 points. _____

Do you participate in professional organizations or attend conferences
specifically directed to HR executives? If yes, add 2 points. _____

Do you regularly engage in right-brain activities, such as reading for pleasure,
going to museums, or attending performing-arts events? If yes, add 2 points. _____

HOW DID YOU DO?

To calculate your score, add all the numbers you entered on the spaces provided.

Enter Subtotal Here _____

Review the score sheet. For each section in which you gave yourself no points (for example, you earned no points under Career Decisions or Technology), deduct 10 points from the subtotal above.

Enter the Total Points Deducted Here _____

Subtract the deductions (if any) from the subtotal.

Enter the Grand Total Here _____

85–100	Congratulations! You're clearly a leader in HR.
70–84	The foundation you've built for your career is solid. You're on the way to the top.
55–69	You've got a good start; additional experience in one or two key areas should help you get to the top. Set specific goals.
40–54	You have valuable experience in some key areas, but to get to the top you need additional experience. Start now.
0–39	Getting to the top in HR will be very difficult.

**Source: Adapted from "Are You Poised for Success in the 90's? Take the Quiz and Find Out," *Personnel Journal,* June 1994, pp. 72–73.

Notes and Additional Readings

1. U.S. Department of Commerce, Bureau of Economic Analysis, NIPA Tables, Table 1.12, www.bea.gov/bea/dn/nipaweb/Tableview.asp. Accessed January 5, 2010.

2. "Many Actions Add Up to Successful Talent Management," *HR Focus,* July 2006, pp. 3–4.

3. Laurence O'Neil, "Executing Strategies for a New Way of Doing Business," *HR Magazine,* June 2009, p. 12; John Hobel, "The Time Is Right for Strategic HR," *Canadian HR Reporter,* October 23, 2006, p. 30; and "How Strategic Is HR Now? The Latest Research Shows Progress," *HR Focus,* December 2006, pp. 3–5.

4. Mitra Toossi, "Labor Force Projections to 2018: Older Workers Staying More Active," *Monthly Labor Review,* November 2009, pp. 44–45.

5. Ibid., p. 47.

6. Ibid., p. 46.

7. John M. Ivancevich and Jacqueline A. Gilbert, "Diversity Management: Time for a New Approach," *Public Personnel Management* 29, No. 1 (Spring 2000), pp. 75–92.

8. Much of this section is drawn from Benson Rosen and Kay Lovelace, "Piecing Together the Diversity Puzzle," *HR Magazine,* June 1991, pp. 78–84; and John D. Wheeler, "Managing Workforce Diversity," *Tax Executive,* November/December 1997, pp. 493–95.

9. "HR Outsourcing Trends and Insights 2009," www.hewitt.com. Accessed January 6, 2010.

10. "What Is a Professional Employer Organization?" www.NAPEO.org. Accessed January 6, 2010.

11. Duncan Davidson, Duane Dickson, and Jane Trice, "Rightsizing for Success," *Business Forum,* Winter–Spring 1993, pp. 10–12.

12. M. Hammer and J. Champy, *Reengineering the Corporation: A Manifesto for Business Revolution* (New York: HarperCollins, 1993).

13. Much of this paragraph is drawn from Alan Cohen, "New Electronic HR Tools Are Hitting Their Stride," *National Underwriter,* February 9, 2004, pp. 27–28.

14. Bradford S. Bell, Sae-Won Lee, and Sarah K. Yeung, "The Impact of E-HR on Professional Competencies in HRM: Implications for the Development of HR Professionals," *Human Resource Management,* Fall 2006, pp. 295–308; and Thomas W. Garvey and Brian S. Klass, "The Use and Impact of eHR: A survey of HR Professionals," *People and Strategy* 31, No. 3 (2008), pp. 50–55.

15. "Tips for Expanding Your Corporate Role," *HR Focus*, September 2000, p. 1.

16. Phil Farish, "Broader View Needed," *Personnel Administrator,* February 1987, p. 27; and Donald M. Burrows, "Increase HR's Contribution to Profits," *HR Magazine,* September 1996, pp. 103–10.

17. *HR's Evolving Role in Organizations and Its Impact on Business Strategy* (Alexandria, Va.; The Society for Human Resource Management, 2008), p. 27.

18. "Changes in the Human Resources Profession in the Last 10 Years," SHRM weekly online survey, March 18, 2008, accessed January 7, 2010.

19. Helen Williams, "HR Careering Ahead," *Personnel Today*, June 16, 2009, pp. 14–15.

20. Todd Raphael, "Think Twice: HR and an RX for the Bottom Line," *Workforce,* October 2001, p. 104; Samuel Greengard, "Increase the Value of Your Intranet," *Workforce,* March 1997, pp. 80–90.

21. Samuel Greengard, "Catch the Wave," *Personnel Journal,* July 1995, p. 59; Shari Caudron, "How HR Drives Profits," *Workforce,* December 2001, pp. 26–31, and Alan Cohen, "New Electronic HR Tools Are Hitting Their Stride," *Natural Underwriter,* February 9, 2004, pp. 27–28.

22. Joseph A. Banik, "The Marketing Approach to Communicating with Employees," *Personnel Journal,* October 1985, pp. 62–64; Joe Pasqueletto, "An HRS Marketing Strategy," *Personnel Journal,* June 1989, pp. 62–71.

23. Gina Ruiz, "Communication Often Bypasses Those Overseas," *Workforce Management,* February 13, 2006, pp. 7–8.

24. Much of this section is drawn from Banik, "The Marketing Approach," pp. 62–68.

25. "Three New Surveys Track the Growth of eHR," *HR Focus,* April 2002, pp. 4–6.

Chapter **Two**

Equal Employment Opportunity: The Legal Environment

Chapter Learning Objectives

After studying this chapter, you should be able to:

1. Define equal employment opportunity.
2. Describe the intent of the Equal Pay Act of 1963.
3. Describe the intent of Title VII of the Civil Rights Act of 1964.
4. Define disparate treatment and disparate impact.
5. Discuss the purpose of the Age Discrimination in Employment Act of 1967.
6. Discuss the purpose of the Rehabilitation Act of 1973.
7. Describe the intent of the Vietnam-Era Veterans Readjustment Assistance Act of 1974.
8. Discuss the purpose of the Pregnancy Discrimination Act of 1978.
9. Describe the intent of the Immigration Reform and Control Act of 1986.
10. Describe the purpose of the Americans with Disabilities Act of 1990.
11. Explain the purpose of the Older Workers Benefit Protection Act of 1990.
12. Discuss the intent of the Civil Rights Act of 1991.
13. Explain the intent of the Family and Medical Leave Act of 1993.
14. Discuss the purposes of Executive Orders 11246, 11375, and 11478.
15. Describe the significance of the following Supreme Court decisions: *Griggs* v. *Duke Power, McDonnell Douglas* v. *Green, Albemarle Paper* v. *Moody, University of California Regents* v. *Bakke, United Steelworkers of America* v. *Weber, Connecticut* v. *Teal, Memphis Firefighters, Local 1784* v. *Stotts, City of Richmond* v. *J. A. Crosan Company, Wards Cove* v. *Atonio, Martin* v. *Wilks, Adarand Contractors* v. *Peña, State of Texas* v. *Hopwood,* and University of Michigan's admissions procedures.
16. Name the federal agencies that have primary responsibility for enforcing equal employment opportunity.

Chapter Outline

Equal Employment Opportunity Laws
Equal Pay Act (1963)
Title VII, Civil Rights Act (1964)
Age Discrimination in Employment Act (1967)
Rehabilitation Act (1973)
Vietnam-Era Veterans Readjustment Assistance Act (1974)
Pregnancy Discrimination Act (1978)
Immigration Reform and Control Act (1986)
Americans with Disabilities Act (1990)
Older Workers Benefit Protection Act (1990)
Civil Rights Act (1991)
Family and Medical Leave Act (1993)
Executive Orders 11246, 11375, and 11478
State and Local Government Equal Employment Laws

Landmark Court Cases
Griggs v. *Duke Power Company*
McDonnell Douglas v. *Green*
Albemarle Paper v. *Moody*
University of California Regents v. *Bakke*
United Steelworkers of America v. *Weber*
Connecticut v. *Teal*
Memphis Firefighters, Local 1784 v. *Stotts*
City of Richmond v. *J. A. Crosan Company*
Wards Cove v. *Atonio*
Martin v. *Wilks*
Adarand Contractors v. *Peña*
State of Texas v. *Hopwood*
University of Michigan's Admission Procedures

Enforcement Agencies
Equal Employment Opportunity Commission
Office of Federal Contract Compliance Programs

Summary of Learning Objectives

Key Terms

Review Questions

Discussion Questions
Incident 2.1: Debate over Retirement Age
Incident 2.2: Accept Things as They Are

Exercise 2.1: Discrimination because of Sex, Religion, or National Origin

Notes and Additional Readings

Two of the most important external influences on human resource management are government legislation and regulations and court interpretations of the legislation and regulations. Numerous laws influence recruitment and selection of personnel, compensation, working conditions and hours, discharges, and labor relations. Whenever appropriate, this text describes government legislation and its court interpretations as they relate to the specific area of human resource management being discussed.

However, because equal employment opportunity is so important and covers so many areas of human resource management, two separate chapters are devoted to the topic. This chapter describes the legal framework of equal employment opportunity. Chapter 3 describes specific organizational requirements for implementing equal employment opportunity.

EQUAL EMPLOYMENT OPPORTUNITY LAWS

In 1865, the Thirteenth Amendment to the U.S. Constitution abolished slavery. In addition, Congress passed the Civil Rights Act of 1866, the Fourteenth Amendment to the U.S. Constitution in 1868, and the Civil Rights Act of 1871. Yet Americans continued to live and work in a dual society, one black and one white. Businesses often refused to hire black workers or, if they did, placed them in low-paying and low-skilled jobs.

Discrimination against women was based on the view that men should work to support their families and women should care for their families at home. Furthermore, it was a rather commonly held belief that women were not equipped to do certain jobs.

Discrimination in society and in the workplace gave impetus to the civil rights movement, which in turn pressured the U.S. Congress to pass laws designed to eliminate discrimination. As a result, Congress has passed numerous laws to ensure equal employment opportunity. Unfortunately, a common misconception is that equal employment opportunity means that an employer must give preference to women and minorities in the workplace. However, **equal employment opportunity** refers to the right of all people to work and to advance on the basis of merit, ability, and potential.

equal employment opportunity
The right of all people to work and to advance on the basis of merit, ability, and potential.

Equal Pay Act (1963)

The **Equal Pay Act of 1963** prohibits sex-based discrimination in rates of pay for men and women working on the same or similar jobs. Specifically, the act states:

Equal Pay Act
Prohibits sex-based discrimination in rates of pay for men and women working on the same or similar jobs.

No employer having employees subject to [the minimum wage provisions of the Fair Labor Standards Act] shall discriminate, within any establishment . . ., between employees on the basis of sex by paying wages to employees in such establishment at a rate less than the rate at which he pays wages to employees of the opposite sex in such establishment for equal work on jobs the performance of which requires equal skill, effort, and responsibility, and which are performed under similar working conditions.

The act permits differences in wages if the payment is based on seniority, merit, quantity and quality of production, or a differential due to any factor other than sex. The act also prohibits an employer from attaining compliance with the act by reducing the wage rate of any employee.

The Equal Pay Act is actually part of the minimum wage section of the Fair Labor Standards Act (FLSA), described in more detail in Chapter 12. Thus, coverage of the Equal Pay Act is coextensive (covers the same groups) with the coverage of the minimum wage provisions of the FLSA. Generally, the act covers employers engaged in commerce or in the production of goods for commerce, employers that have two or more employees, and labor organizations. Responsibility for enforcing the Equal Pay Act was originally assigned to the secretary of labor but was transferred to the Equal Employment Opportunity Commission (EEOC) on July 1, 1979.

Title VII, Civil Rights Act (1964)

Title VII of the Civil Rights Act of 1964 is the keystone federal legislation in equal employment opportunity. Several important provisions of Section 703 of the act state the following:

> *Sec. 703.*
> *(a) It shall be an unlawful employment practice for an employer—*
>   *(1) to fail or refuse to hire or to discharge any individual, or otherwise to discriminate against any individual with respect to his compensation, terms, conditions, or privileges of employment, because of such individual's race, color, religion, sex, or national origin; or*
>   *(2) to limit, segregate, or classify his employees or applicants for employment in any way which would deprive or tend to deprive any individual of employment opportunities or otherwise adversely affect his status as an employee, because of such individual's race, color, religion, sex, or national origin.*
> *(b) It shall be an unlawful employment practice for an employment agency to fail or refuse to refer for employment, or otherwise to discriminate against, any individual because of his race, color, religion, sex, or national origin, or to classify or refer for employment any individual on the basis of his race, color, religion, sex, or national origin.*
> *(c) It shall be an unlawful employment practice for a labor organization—*
>   *(1) to exclude or to expel from its membership, or otherwise to discriminate against any individual because of his race, color, religion, sex, or national origin;*
>   *(2) to limit, segregate, or classify its membership or applicants for membership or to classify or fail or refuse to refer for employment any individual, in any way which would deprive or tend to deprive any individual of employment opportunities, or would limit such employment opportunities or otherwise adversely affect his status as an employee or as an applicant for employment, because of such individual's race, color, religion, sex, or national origin; or*
>   *(3) to cause or attempt to cause an employer to discriminate against an individual in violation of this section.*
> *(d) It shall be an unlawful employment practice for any employer, labor organization, or joint labor–management committee controlling apprenticeship or other training or retraining, including on-the-job training programs, to discriminate against any individual because of his race, color, religion, sex, or national origin in admission to, or employment in, any program established to provide apprenticeship or other training.*

Section 703 covers two basic areas of discrimination: disparate treatment and disparate impact. **Disparate treatment,** Section 703(a)(1), refers to intentional discrimination and involves treating one class of employees differently from other employees. **Disparate impact,** Section 703(a)(2), refers to unintentional discrimination and involves employment practices that appear to be neutral but adversely affect a protected class of people.

Title VII, the name most frequently used to describe the Civil Rights Act, was amended by the Equal Employment Opportunity Act of 1972. Organizations covered by the provisions of Title VII include the following:

- All private employers of 15 or more people who are employed 20 or more weeks per year.
- All public and private educational institutions.
- State and local governments.
- Public and private employment agencies.

Title VII of the Civil Rights Act of 1964
Keystone federal legislation that covers disparate treatment and disparate impact discrimination; created the Equal Employment Opportunity Commission.

disparate treatment
Intentional discrimination; treatment of one class of employees differently from other employees.

disparate impact
Unintentional discrimination involving employment practices that appear to be neutral but adversely affect a protected class of people.

- Labor unions that maintain and operate a hiring hall or hiring office or have 15 or more members.
- Joint labor–management committees for apprenticeships and training.

Title VII also created the Equal Employment Opportunity Commission (EEOC) to administer the act and to prohibit covered organizations from engaging in any unlawful employment practices. The composition and powers of the EEOC are described later in this chapter. HRM in Action 2.1 illustrates gender discrimination.

Age Discrimination in Employment Act (1967)

Age Discrimination in Employment Act (ADEA)
Prohibits discrimination against employees over 40 years of age by all companies employing 20 or more people in the private sector.

The **Age Discrimination in Employment Act (ADEA),** passed in 1967, prohibits discrimination in employment against individuals aged 40 through 69. An amendment to the ADEA that took effect on January 1, 1987, eliminates mandatory retirement at age 70 for employees of companies with 20 or more employees. The prohibited employment practices of ADEA include failure to hire, discharge, denial of employment, and discrimination with respect to terms or conditions of employment because of an individual's age within the protected age group. Organizations covered by the ADEA include the following:

- Private employers of 20 or more employees for each working day in each of 20 or more calendar weeks in the current or preceding calendar year.
- Labor organizations.
- Employment agencies.
- State and local governments.
- Federal government agencies, with certain differences; for example, federal employees cannot be forced to retire at any age.

One exception specified in the law concerns employees in bona fide executive or high policy-making positions. The act permits mandatory retirement at age 65 for high-level executives whose pensions exceed $44,000 a year.

Section 4(f) of the ADEA sets forth several conditions under which the act does not apply. The act does not apply where age is a bona fide occupational qualification, that is, reasonably necessary to the normal operation of the particular business. For example, pilots and copilots face mandatory retirement at age 60. In addition, a bus company's refusal to consider applications of individuals between ages 40 and 65 for initial employment as intercity bus drivers was ruled legal. [1] Furthermore, it is not illegal for an employer to discipline or discharge an individual within the protected age group for good cause, such as unsatisfactory job performance.

Originally, the secretary of labor was responsible for enforcing the ADEA. On July 1, 1979, the EEOC assumed that responsibility. HRM in Action 2.2 describes growth in age-descrimination changes.

AGE DISCRIMINATION

While age-discrimination claims against employers have jumped in recent years, a U.S. Supreme Court ruling has made it more difficult for employees to win such cases. Age-discrimination allegations reached their highest point in 2008, up 29 percent from 2007 numbers. The main causes are the recession and the "graying" of the American work force.

Advocates for older workers say the June 18, 2009 Court ruling in the case of *Gross* v. *FBL Financial Services Inc.* has made it more difficult for employees to prevail in age-related discrimination cases. "The court ruled that employees who sue under a federal law that bans discrimination against those 40 or older must prove that age was the 'but-for cause'—widely interpreted as meaning the 'sole cause—of an employer's actions, rather than one of the motivating factors," says Dan Kohrman, a senior attorney with AARP. However, legislation introduced in Congress would override the Supreme Court ruling. It would require plaintiffs to show that age was only one factor behind an employment decision.

Source: Adapted from Anne Tergesen, "Age Bias Harder to Prove at Work," *Wall Street Journal*, Nov 29, 2009, pg. 2.

Rehabilitation Act (1973)

Rehabilitation Act of 1973
Prohibits discrimination against handicapped individuals.

The **Rehabilitation Act of 1973,** as amended, contains the following general provisions. It

- Prohibits discrimination against handicapped individuals by employers with federal contracts and subcontracts in excess of $2,500.
- Requires written affirmative action plans (AAPs) from employers of 50 or more employees and federal contracts of $50,000 or more.
- Prohibits discrimination against handicapped individuals by federal agencies.
- Requires affirmative action by federal agencies to provide employment opportunities for handicapped persons.
- Requires federal buildings to be accessible to handicapped persons.
- Prohibits discrimination against handicapped individuals by recipients of federal financial assistance.

handicapped individual
Person who has a physical or mental impairment that substantially limits one or more of major life activities, has a record of such impairment, or is regarded as having such an impairment.

Section 7(7)(B) of the Rehabilitation Act defines a **handicapped individual** as follows:

any person who:
(i) has a physical or mental impairment which substantially limits one or more of such person's major life activities,
(ii) has a record of such an impairment, or
(iii) is regarded as having such an impairment. . . . Such term does not include any individual who is an alcoholic or drug abuser whose current use of alcohol or drugs prevents such individual from performing the duties of the job in question or whose employment, by reason of such current alcohol or drug abuse, would constitute a direct threat to property or the safety of others.

The primary responsibility for enforcing this act lies with the Office of Federal Contract Compliance Programs (OFCCP) of the Department of Labor. OFCCP will be described in more depth later in this chapter.

Vietnam-Era Veterans Readjustment Assistance Act (1974)

Vietnam-Era Veterans Readjustment Assistance Act of 1974
Prohibits federal government contractors and subcontractors with federal government contracts of $10,000 or more from discriminating in hiring and promoting Vietnam and disabled veterans.

The **Vietnam-Era Veterans Readjustment Assistance Act of 1974** prohibits federal government contractors and subcontractors with federal government contracts of $10,000 or more from discriminating in hiring and promoting Vietnam and disabled veterans. Furthermore, the act requires employers with 50 or more employees and contracts that exceed $50,000 to have written affirmative action programs with regard to the people protected by this act. The protected class consists of disabled veterans with a 30 percent or more disability rating or veterans discharged or released for a service-connected disability and veterans on active duty for any part of the time period between August 5, 1964, and May 7, 1975. Covered contractors and subcontractors must also list job openings with the state employment service. The OFCCP enforces this act.

Pregnancy Discrimination Act (1978)

The Supreme Court decision, *General Electric Co.* v. *Gilbert,* had a significant impact on the passage of the Pregnancy Discrimination Act.[2] In that case, General Electric (GE) provided nonoccupational sickness and accident benefits to all employees under its sickness and accident insurance plan in an amount equal to 60 percent of an employee's normal straight-time weekly earnings. Several female employees at GE's Salem, Virginia, plant who were pregnant presented a claim for disability benefits under the plan to cover the period they were absent from work as a result of their pregnancies. The company denied these claims on the grounds that the plan did not provide disability benefit payments for such absences. The employees filed suit alleging a violation of Title VII, which prohibits sex discrimination. The Supreme Court ruled that the exclusion of pregnancy-related absences from the plan did not constitute sex discrimination.

Pregnancy Discrimination Act (PDA)
Requires employers to treat pregnancy just like any other medical condition with regard to fringe benefits and leave policies.

As a result of this decision, in an effort to protect the rights of pregnant workers, Congress passed the **Pregnancy Discrimination Act (PDA)** as an amendment to the Civil Rights Act in 1978. The PDA, formally referenced as Section 701(K) of Title VII, states:

> Women affected by pregnancy, childbirth, or related medical conditions shall be treated the same for all employment-related purposes, including receipt of benefits under fringe benefit programs, as other persons not so affected but similar in their ability or inability to work.

Under the PDA, employers must treat pregnancy just like any other medical condition with regard to fringe benefits and leave policies. The EEOC, which is responsible for administering the act, has taken the view that an employer may not deny its unmarried employees pregnancy benefits and that if pregnancy benefits are given to female employees, they must also be extended to the spouses of male employees.

Immigration Reform and Control Act (1986)

Recent years have seen an increasing influx of illegal aliens into the United States. When these people are unskilled or do not speak English, employment abuses may result. Thus, in 1986, the **Immigration Reform and Control Act** was passed, making it illegal for anyone to hire, recruit, or refer for employment in the United States a person known to be an unauthorized alien. To meet the requirements of the law, a company must attest, under penalty of perjury, that it has verified that the individual is not an unauthorized alien by one of the following measures:

Immigration Reform and Control Act
1986 act making it illegal to hire, recruit, or refer for U.S. employment anyone known to be an unauthorized alien.

1. Examining the individual's U.S. passport; certificate of U.S. citizenship; certificate of naturalization; unexpired foreign passport, if the passport has an appropriate, unexpired endorsement of the attorney general authorizing the individual's employment in the United States; or resident alien card.

2. Examining documents demonstrating employment authorization (Social Security card, birth certificate, or other documentation that the attorney general deems acceptable as proof).

3. Examining documentation establishing identification (e.g., state driver's license with a photograph or other documentation that the attorney general deems acceptable as proof).

Americans with Disabilities Act (1990)

Americans with Disabilities Act (ADA)
Gives disabled persons sharply increased access to services and jobs.

In May 1990, Congress approved the **Americans with Disabilities Act (ADA),** which gives people with disabilities sharply increased access to services and jobs. Under this law, employers may not:

- Discriminate, in hiring and firing, against disabled persons who are qualified for a job.
- Inquire whether an applicant has a disability, although employers may ask about his or her ability to perform a job.
- Limit advancement opportunity for disabled employees.
- Use tests or job requirements that tend to screen out disabled applicants.
- Participate in contractual arrangements that discriminate against disabled persons.

TABLE 2.1
Suggestions for Making the Workplace Accessible to Disabled Workers

- Install wheelchair ramps.
- Make curb cuts in sidewalks and entrances.
- Reposition shelves so those with disabilities can reach materials.
- Rearrange tables, chairs, vending machines, display racks, and other furniture.
- Reposition telephones and water fountains.
- Add raised markings on elevator control buttons.
- Install flashing alarm lights.
- Widen doors.
- Install offset hinges to widen doorways.
- Eliminate turnstiles or revolving doors or provide an alternative accessible path.
- Install accessible door hardware (such as levers) instead of, or in addition to, doorknobs.
- Install grab bars in toilet stalls.
- Rearrange toilet partitions to increase maneuvering space.
- Move lavatory pipes underneath sinks to prevent burns.
- Add raised toilet seats.
- Add a full-length bathroom mirror.
- Reposition paper towel dispensers.
- Create designated accessible parking spaces.
- Add a paper cup dispenser at existing accessible water fountains.
- Remove high-pile, low-density carpeting.
- Install vehicle hand controls.

Employers must accommodate the needs of disabled employees.
© Digital Vision

Older Workers Benefit Protection Act of 1990
Provides protection for employees over 40 years of age in regard to fringe benefits and gives employees time to consider an early retirement offer.

Employers must also provide reasonable accommodations for employees with disabilities, such as making existing facilities accessible, providing special equipment and training, arranging part-time or modified work schedules, and providing readers for blind employees. Employers do not have to provide accommodations that impose an undue hardship on business operations. Table 2.1 summarizes the ADA's suggestions for making the workplace accessible to disabled individuals. The bill covers all employers with 15 or more employees.

In 1997, the Equal Employment Opportunity Commission, which enforces the ADA and will be discussed in more detail later in this chapter, issued guidelines specifying that qualified individuals with psychiatric disabilities are protected from discrimination and are entitled to reasonable accommodations on the job. Mental disability is defined broadly as a mental impairment that substantially limits one or more of the major life activities of an individual, or a record of such impairment or being regarded as having such an impairment. Under this definition, the fact that an individual is regarded as having a mental disability or has a record of such disability is grounds for that person to claim that he or she has a mental disability. Obviously, these guidelines will raise many issues for human resource managers. HRM in Action 2.3 shows the complexity of issues under the ADA.

Older Workers Benefit Protection Act (1990)

The **Older Workers Benefit Protection Act of 1990** resulted from a 1989 decision of the U.S. Supreme Court. In that decision, an Ohio county agency denied disability benefits to an employee who had been laid off at age 61 because its disability plan cut off at age 60. The Court ruled that the agency had not violated the Age Discrimination in Employment Act because, it said, the law did not cover benefits, just hirings, firings, and promotions.

Under the Older Workers Benefit Protection Act, employers may integrate disability and pension pay by paying the retiree the higher of the two; integrate retiree health insurance and severance pay by deducting the former from the latter; and, in cases of plant closings or mass layoffs, integrate pension and severance pay by deducting from severance pay the amount added to the pension.

The act also gives employees time to consider a company's early retirement package—21 days for an individual or 45 days if a group is involved. Employees also have seven days to change their minds if they have signed a waiver of their right to sue. Coverage of this law is the same as that under the Age Discrimination in Employment Act.

OBESITY AND THE ADA

The case, *EEOC* v. *Watkins Motor Lines, Inc.*, 18 AD cases 641 (6th Cir. 2006), dealt with a man, Stephen Grindle, employed by the defendant company as a driver/dock worker, Grindle had been hired in August 1990. At that time, he weighed approximately 345 pounds. About 65 percent of his job involved dock work. That work included loading, unloading, and arranging freight. The job description stated that the work included "climbing, kneeling, bending, stooping, balancing, reaching, and repeated heavy lifting." Over the course of the next five years, Grindle's weight ranged from about 340 to 450 pounds. According to Grindle, he was unaware of any psychological or physiological reason that would explain his weight.

In November 1995, Grindle suffered a knee injury at work when a rung on a ladder he was climbing broke. Grindle returned to work the next day and worked 50 to 60 hours a week through December. However, in January he began a six-month leave of absence because of his knee injury. The company informed Grindle that he would be terminated if he was unable to return at the end of the six months. To return, he had to have a release from his physician and perhaps undergo a physical examination.

While on leave, Grindle's knee injury was treated by Dr. Zancan. At the end of the six months, Zancan gave Grindle a work release. However, the company would not accept it and return Grindle to work because the physician did not look at the job responsibilities before signing the release form. The company sent Zancan a list of Grindle's job responsibilities and a return to work form. However, Zancan never responded. The company ordered Grindle to see the industrial clinic physician, Dr. Lawrence. Lawrence found that Grindle had limited range of motion. Furthermore, he observed that Grindle could duck and squat but was short of breath after taking a few steps. Lawrence stated that the

most notable fact emerging from his physical examination of Grindle was that Grindle weighed 405 pounds. Lawrence concluded that, even though Grindle met Department of Transportation standards for truck drivers, he could not safely perform his job duties. The company put Grindle on safety hold. This resulted in Grindle's termination because he was unable to return to work after his six-month leave.

Grindle believed that he was terminated because of his weight and filed a claim with the EEOC in September 1998. In October 2002, the EEOC filed a federal action in which it claimed that the company violated the Americans with Disabilities Act by terminating Grindle. In February 2004, the company filed a motion for summary judgment. The district court granted the company's motion for summary judgment on the grounds that obesity not caused by a physiological reason was not an impairment under the ADA. Grindle appealed.

The EEOC acknowledged that merely being overweight did not satisfy the ADA's definition of an impairment. However, it argued that it could be an ADA impairment if an individual was overweight as a result of a physiological condition or morbid obesity no matter what the cause. Morbid obesity is defined as body weight that is more than 100 percent more than the norm. In this case, neither Grindle nor the EEOC argued that Grindle's weight resulted from a physiological condition. Rather, the argument proffered was that Grindle was morbidly obese and the cause of that condition did not matter because morbid obesity is beyond the range of what is normal. The Sixth Circuit disagreed and upheld the district court's finding that, while physiologically caused morbid obesity may be an impairment under the ADA, nonphysiological morbid obesity is not. Therefore, Grindle's morbid obesity was not an ADA impairment.

Source: Adapted from Mary Kathryn Zachary, "Obesity & the ADA—The Reason Matters," *Super Vision*, December 2006, pp. 23–27.

Civil Rights Act (1991)

Civil Rights Act (1991)
Permits women, persons with disabilities, and persons who are religious minorities to have a jury trial and sue for punitive damages if they can prove intentional hiring and workplace discrimination. Also requires companies to provide evidence that the business practice that led to the discrimination was not discriminatory but was job related for the position in question and consistent with business necessity.

The **Civil Rights Act of 1991** permits women, persons with disabilities, and persons who are religious minorities to have a jury trial and sue for punitive damages of up to $300,000 if they can prove they are victims of intentional hiring or workplace discrimination. The law covers all employers with 15 or more employees. Prior to the passage of this law, jury trials and punitive damages were not permitted except in intentional discrimination lawsuits involving racial discrimination. The law places a cap on the amount of damages a victim of nonracial, intentional discrimination can collect. The cap is based on the size of the employer: $50,000 for companies with 15 to 100 employees; $100,000 for companies with 101 to 200 employees; $200,000 for companies with 201 to 500 employees; and $300,000 for companies with more than 500 employees.

A second aspect of this act concerns the burden of proof for companies with regard to intentional discrimination lawsuits. In a series of Supreme Court decisions beginning in 1989, the Court began to ease the burden-of-proof requirements on companies. Several of these decisions are described later in this chapter. This act, however, requires that companies must provide evidence that the business practice that led to the discrimination was not discriminatory but was job related for the position in question and consistent with business necessity. Business necessity is defined in detail in Chapter 3.

ELIMINATING TRAVEL DID NOT VIOLATE FMLA

The East Baton Rouge, Louisiana, Parish School Board employed Phyllis Smith as its assistant supervisor of school accounts. Prior to her maternity leave, this position required her to travel to various schools and directly assist school principals and staff members in keeping accurate accounting records. During Smith's leave, the board restructured the school accounts department and revised her job description so that she would audit the schools' books from a central office rather than by traveling to schools.

Smith sued under the FMLA after she returned, but the 5th U.S. Circuit Court of Appeals granted summary judgment to the board, holding that Smith's position after her FMLA leave was equivalent to her former position. In discussing "equivalent," the court cited the FMLA and stated that the position must be virtually identical to the former position in pay, benefits, and working conditions; must involve substantially similar duties, skills, and authority; must have similar opportunities for promotion and pay increases; and must be viewed as equally desirable to employees.

The court concluded that "de minimis, intangible changes" to an employee's position do not violate the FMLA. The elimination of travel responsibilities when the position no longer required travel to audit the schools' accounts, combined with providing the same salary and similar job description and title, amounted to only an intangible difference in employment position that did not violate the law.

Source: Adapted from Sarah T. Zaffina, "Eliminating Travel Did Not Violate FMLA," *HRMagazine*, October 2006, p. 120.

Family and Medical Leave Act (1993)

Family and Medical Leave Act (FMLA)
Enables qualified employees to take prolonged unpaid leave for family- and health-related reasons without fear of losing their jobs.

The **Family and Medical Leave Act (FMLA)** was enacted on February 5, 1993, to enable qualified employees to take prolonged unpaid leave for family- and health-related reasons without fear of losing their jobs. Under the law, employees can use this leave if they are seriously ill, if an immediate family member is ill, or in the event of the birth, adoption, or placement for foster care of a child. To qualify for the leave, employees must have been employed for at least a year and must have worked for no less than 1,250 hours within the previous 12-month period. FMLA took effect in August 1993 for companies without collective bargaining agreements. For companies with collective bargaining agreements, the law took effect on termination of the labor contract or on February 5, 1994, whichever came first. HRM 2.4 illustrates one issue that has been decided by the courts.

Executive Orders 11246, 11375, and 11478

executive orders
Orders issued by the president of the United States for managing and operating federal government agencies.

Executive orders are issued by the president of the United States to give direction to governmental agencies. Executive Order 11246, issued in 1965, requires every nonexempt federal contractor and subcontractor not to discriminate against employees and applicants because of race, sex, color, religion, or national origin. The primary exemption from the order is for contracts and subcontracts that do not exceed $10,000. The OFCCP within the Department of Labor is responsible for administering this executive order. The equal opportunity clause specified by Executive Order 11246 requires the contractor or subcontractor to agree to do the following:

1. Comply with the provisions of the executive order.
2. Comply with those rules, regulations, and orders of the secretary of labor that are issued under the order.
3. Permit access to its books and records for purposes of investigation by the secretary of labor.
4. Include the equal employment clause in every subcontract or purchase order so that such provisions will be binding on each subcontractor or vendor.

Moreover, in the event of noncompliance with the executive order, the contract may be canceled, terminated, or suspended. After a hearing on the noncompliance, the contractor may be declared ineligible for future government contracts.

Executive Order 11246 also requires employers with 50 or more employees and contracts and subcontracts that exceed $50,000 to have a written affirmative action program (AAP). The AAP must include an identification and analysis of minority employment problem areas within the employers' workforce, and where deficiencies exist, employers must establish goals and timetables for the prompt achievement of equal employment opportunity. Part of the AAP

utilization evaluation
Part of the affirmative action plan that analyzes minority group representation in all job categories; past and present hiring practices; and upgrades, promotions, and transfers.

is called the **utilization evaluation,** which contains analyses of minority group representation in all job categories; present and past hiring practices; and upgrading, promotions, and transfers. Chapter 4 describes AAPs in more detail.

Executive Order 11246 also gave the U.S. Office of Personnel Management (OPM) authority to issue regulations dealing with discrimination within federal agencies. In 1966, the OPM (then called the Civil Service Commission) issued regulations that required agencies to correct discriminatory practices and develop affirmative action programs.

In 1967, Executive Order 11375 amended Executive Order 11246 and prohibited sex-based wage discrimination for government contractors. Finally, in 1969 the OPM issued Executive Order 11478, which in part suspended Executive Order 11246, along with revised regulations. The new regulations merely modified a number of the procedures under the previous orders and regulations.

State and Local Government Equal Employment Laws

Many state and local governments have passed equal employment laws. For example, almost all states have some form of protection against employment discrimination on the basis of disability. However, at this point it is important to note the Supremacy Clause of the U.S. Constitution,[3] which states:

> The laws of the United States dealing with matters within its jurisdiction are supreme, and the judges in every state shall be bound thereby, anything in the Constitution or Laws of any State to the contrary notwithstanding.

As a result of this clause, as would be expected, many state and local laws became invalid after the passage of the Civil Rights Act and other equal employment legislation. For example, the California Supreme Court invalidated a state statute prohibiting females from tending bar.

No federal laws prohibit states from passing laws against discrimination in areas not covered by the federal law as long as the law does not require or permit an act that is unlawful under federal legislation.

One significant development at the state level on affirmative action occurred in California. Over the years, an array of programs based on race had been adopted throughout California. One particular concern was a set of affirmative action programs that had been applied to the University of California. The California Civil Rights Initiative (CCRI), known as Proposition 209, was placed on the November 1996 election ballot and was adopted by a 54 to 46 percent margin. Proposition 209 calls for the state not to discriminate for or against any group in state employment and benefits.

As is true with most laws, however, ambiguities in language leave much room for interpretation by the federal agencies that enforce the laws. Furthermore, court decisions regarding the laws often raise additional questions of interpretation. For these reasons and others, equal employment opportunity is one of the most challenging and complex aspects of human resource management. Nevertheless, a good beginning point for understanding equal employment opportunity is to know the basic legislation covering the area. Table 2.2 provides a chronological listing of the equal employment opportunity laws and executive orders discussed in this section. It also provides a brief statement of the purpose or intent and coverage of these laws and executive orders.

LANDMARK COURT CASES

Laws passed by Congress are usually broad in nature and are refined when applied to specific situations. Furthermore, the general nature of the equal employment laws both allowed and caused enforcement agencies such as the EEOC to develop guidelines and enforce the acts as they interpreted them. Unfortunately, employers were often confused about the guidelines and enforcement of equal employment laws by the EEOC and OFCCP. The confusion and anger that resulted have led to many lawsuits concerning the interpretation of equal opportunity laws and guidelines. Again unfortunately, many court decisions have been not only confusing but, in some instances, apparently conflicting.

TABLE 2.2 **Summary of Equal Employment Opportunity Laws and Executive Orders**

Law/Executive Order	Year	Purpose or Intent	Coverage
Equal Pay Act	1963	Prohibits sex-based discrimination in rates of pay for men and women working in the same or similar jobs.	Private employers engaged in commerce or in the production of goods for commerce and with two or more employees; labor organizations.
Title VII, Civil Rights Act (as amended in 1972)	1964	Prohibits discrimination based on race, sex, color, religion, or national origin.	Private employers with 15 or more employees for 20 or more weeks per year, institutions, state and local governments, employment agencies, labor unions, and joint labor–management committees.
Executive Order 11246	1965	Prohibits discrimination on the basis of race, sex, color, religion, or national origin; requires affirmative action with regard to these factors.	Federal contractors and subcontractors with contracts in excess of $10,000; employers with 50 or more employees and contracts in excess of $50,000.
Executive Order 11375	1967	Prohibits sex-based wage discrimination.	Government contractors and subcontractors.
Executive Order 11478	1967	Supersedes Executive Order 11246 and modifies some of the procedures under the previous orders and regulations.	Same as Executive Order 11246.
Age Discrimination in Employment Act (ADEA)	1967	Prohibits discrimination against individuals who are at least 40 years of age but less than 70. An amendment eliminates mandatory retirement at age 70 for employees of companies with 20 or more employees.	Private employers with 20 or more employees for 20 or more weeks per year, labor organizations, employment agencies, state and local governments, and federal agencies, with some exceptions.
Rehabilitation Act, as amended	1973	Prohibits discrimination against handicapped persons and requires affirmative action to provide employment opportunity for handicapped persons.	Federal contractors and subcontractors with contracts in excess of $2,500, organizations receiving federal financial assistance, and federal agencies.
Vietnam-Era Veterans Readjustment Assistance Act	1974	Prohibits discrimination in hiring disabled veterans with 30 percent or more disability rating, veterans discharged or released for a service connected disability, and veterans on active duty between August 5, 1964, and May 7, 1975. Also requires written AAPs for certain employers.	Federal contractors and subcontractors with contracts in excess of $10,000; employers with 50 or more employees and contracts in excess of $50,000.
Pregnancy Discrimination Act (PDA)	1978	Requires employers to treat pregnancy just like any other medical condition with regard to fringe benefits and leave policies.	Same as Title VII, Civil Rights Act.
Immigration Reform and Control Act	1986	Prohibits hiring of illegal aliens.	Any individual or company.
Americans with Disabilities Act	1990	Increases access to services and jobs for disabled workers.	Private employers with 15 or more employees.
Older Workers Benefit Protection Act	1990	Protects employees over 40 years of age in regard to fringe benefits and gives employees time to consider an early retirement offer.	Same as ADEA.
Civil Rights Act	1991	Permits women, persons with disabilities, and persons who are religious minorities to have a jury trial and sue for punitive damages if they can prove intentional hiring and workplace discrimination. Also requires companies to provide evidence that the business practice that led to the discrimination was not discriminatory but was job-related for the position in question and consistent with business necessity.	Private employers with 15 or more employees.
Family and Medical Leave Act (FMLA)	1993	Enables qualified employees to take prolonged unpaid leave for family and health-related reasons without fear of losing their jobs.	Private employers with 15 or more employees.

Nevertheless, several Supreme Court decisions have provided guidance for interpreting equal employment opportunity laws. Some of the more important decisions are described in the following sections.

Griggs v. Duke Power Company[4]

Web site: National Employment Lawyers Association
www.nela.org

The *Griggs* case concerned the promotion and transfer policies of the Duke Power company at its Dan River Steam Station. Duke permitted incumbent employees who lacked a high school education to transfer from an "outside" job to an "inside" job by passing two tests: the Wonderlic Personnel Test, which purports to measure general verbal facility, and the Bennett Mechanical Aptitude Test. The passing scores approximated the national median for high school graduates.

In a class action suit, African American employees argued that these practices violated Title VII, since neither having a high school education nor passing the tests was necessary for successful performance on the jobs in question. The suit also argued that the practices were illegal because a much higher percentage of African Americans did not have high school educations. The company argued that the requirements were based on the company's judgment that they would generally improve the overall quality of the workforce and that the company had no discriminatory intent in instituting the requirements. The company argued that its lack of discriminatory intent was demonstrated by its efforts to help undereducated employees through financing two-thirds of the cost of tuition for high school education.

disparate impact doctrine
States that when the plaintiff shows that an employment practice disproportionately excludes groups protected by Title VII, the burden of proof shifts to the defendant to prove that the standard reasonably relates to job performance.

In 1971, the Supreme Court ruled in favor of the African American employees. The decision established several significant points concerning equal employment opportunity: (1) The consequences of employment practices, not simply the intent or motivation of the employer, are the thrust of Title VII in that practices that discriminate against one group more than another or continue past patterns of discrimination are illegal regardless of the nondiscriminatory intent of the employer; (2) the **disparate impact doctrine** provides that when the plaintiff shows that an employment practice disproportionately excludes groups protected by Title VII, the burden of proof shifts to the defendant to prove that the standard reasonably relates to job performance; and (3) the EEOC's guidelines that permitted the use of only job-related tests are appropriate.

McDonnell Douglas v. Green[5]

Percy Green, an African American man who had been employed by McDonnell Douglas, was laid off as a result of a reduction in McDonnell's workforce. After the layoff, Green participated in a protest against alleged racial discrimination by McDonnell in its employment practices. The protest included a "stall-in," whereby Green and others stopped their cars along roads leading to the plant to block access during the morning rush hour. At a later date, McDonnell advertised for mechanics. Green applied for reemployment and was rejected by the company on the grounds of his participation in the stall-in, which the company argued was unlawful conduct.

On technical grounds, the Supreme Court remanded the case back to the district court, but at the same time its ruling set forth standards for the burden of proof in discrimination cases. These standards were as follows:

1. The complainant in a Title VII case carries the initial burden of proof in establishing a *prima facie* (at first sight or before closer inspection) case of discrimination. This can be done by showing (a) that he or she belongs to a racial minority; (b) that he or she applied and was qualified for a job for which the employer was seeking applicants; (c) that, despite his or her qualifications, the applicant was rejected; and (d) that, after the rejection, the position remained open and the employer continued to seek applicants from persons of the complainant's qualifications.

2. If the complainant establishes a *prima facie* case, the burden shifts to the employer to provide some legitimate, nondiscriminatory reason for the employer's rejection.

3. The burden then shifts to the employee to prove that the employer's allegedly legitimate reason was pretextual (i.e., that the offered reason was not the true reason for the employer's action).

In its ruling, the Court stated that Green had established a *prima facie* case and that McDonnell had shown a nondiscriminatory reason for not hiring Green because of his participation in the stall-in.

Albemarle Paper v. Moody[6]

In the *Albemarle Paper* v. *Moody* case, the company required applicants for hire into various skilled lines of progression to take the Beta examination, which purportedly measures nonverbal intelligence, and the Wonderlic test, which purportedly measures general verbal facility. The company made no attempt to determine the job-relatedness of the tests and simply adopted the national norm score as a cutoff for new job applicants.

The company allowed African American workers to transfer to the skilled lines if they could pass the Beta and Wonderlic tests, but few succeeded. Incumbents in the skilled lines, some of whom had been hired before the adoption of the tests, were not required to pass them to retain their jobs or their promotion rights.

Four months before the case went to trial, Albemarle engaged an expert in industrial psychology to validate the relatedness of its testing program. He spent half a day at the plant and devised a study, which was conducted by plant officials without his supervision. This study showed the tests to be job related.

However, in June 1975, the Supreme Court found Albemarle's validation study to be materially defective. The Court's decision was based on the fact that Albemarle's study failed to comply with EEOC guidelines for validating employment tests. Thus, this decision reaffirmed that tests used in employment decisions must be job related, and it reaffirmed the use of EEOC guidelines in validating tests. The Court also held that if an employer establishes that a test is job related, it is the plaintiff's burden to demonstrate the existence of other tests that could comparably serve the employer's legitimate interests with a lesser impact on a protected group.

University of California Regents v. Bakke[7]

The medical school of the University of California at Davis opened in 1968 with an entering class of 50 students. No African American, Hispanic, or Native American students were in this class. Over the next two years, the faculty developed a special admissions program to increase the participation of minority students. In 1971, the size of the entering class doubled, and 16 of the 100 positions were to be filled by "disadvantaged" applicants chosen by a special admissions committee. In actual practice, disadvantaged meant a minority applicant.

Allan Bakke, a white male, was denied admission to the medical school in 1973 and 1974. Contending that minority students with lower grade averages and test scores were admitted under the special program, Bakke brought suit. He argued that he had been discriminated against because of his race when he was prevented from competing for the 16 reserved positions, and he alleged that the medical school's special two-track admissions system violated the Civil Rights Act of 1964. Thus, the Bakke case raised the issue of **reverse discrimination,** alleged preferential treatment of one group (minority or female) over another group rather than equal opportunity.

On June 28, 1978, the Supreme Court ruled in a five-to-four decision that Allan Bakke should be admitted to the medical school of the University of California at Davis and found the school's two-track admissions system to be illegal. However, by another five-to-four vote, the Court held that at least some forms of race-conscious admissions procedures are constitutional. The Court stated that race or ethnic background may be deemed a plus in a particular applicant's file, but it does not insulate the individual from comparison with all other candidates for the available positions. As could be expected, the somewhat nebulous decisions in the Bakke case provided an environment for further court tests of the legal status of reverse discrimination.

United Steelworkers of America v. Weber[8]

In 1974, the Kaiser Aluminum and Chemical Corporation and the United Steelworkers of America signed a collective bargaining agreement that contained an affirmative action plan designed to reduce racial imbalances in Kaiser's then almost exclusively white workforce. That plan set hiring goals and established on-the-job training programs to teach craft skills to

reverse discrimination
Condition under which there is alleged preferential treatment of one group (minority or women) over another group rather than equal opportunity.

Web site: United States National Labor Relations Board
www.nlrb.gov

unskilled workers. The plan reserved 50 percent of the openings in the training programs for African Americans.

At Kaiser's Gramercy, Louisiana, plant, Brian F. Weber, a white male, filed a class action suit against the company because African American employees were accepted into the company's in-plant craft-training program before white employees with more seniority. Lower-level courts supported Weber's suit. However, in its 1979 decision on this case, the Supreme Court ruled that the voluntarily agreed-on plan between Kaiser and the steelworkers was permissible. The Court stated that the Title VII prohibition against racial discrimination did not condemn all private, voluntary, race-conscious affirmative action programs. The Court ruled that Kaiser's affirmative action plan was permissible because it (1) was designed to break down old patterns of segregation, (2) did not involve the discharge of innocent third parties, (3) did not have any barriers to the advancement of white employees, and (4) was a temporary measure to eliminate discrimination. Thus, this decision provided important guidelines for determining the legality of an affirmative action plan.

Connecticut v. Teal[9]

A Connecticut agency promoted several African American employees to supervisory positions contingent on their passing a written examination. When they later failed the exam, the agency refused to consider them as permanent candidates for the positions. These employees alleged that Connecticut violated Title VII by requiring as an absolute condition for consideration for promotion that applicants pass a written test that disproportionately excluded African Americans and was not job related. The passing rate on the test for African Americans was only 68 percent of the passing rate for whites.

The agency gave promotions from the eligibility list generated by the written examination. As it turned out, however, the overall result was that 22.9 percent of the African American candidates and 13.5 percent of the white candidates were promoted. The district court ruled that the bottom line percentages, which were more favorable to African Americans than whites, precluded a Title VII violation. The **bottom line concept** is based on the view that the government should generally not concern itself with individual components of the selection process if the overall effect of that process is nondiscriminatory. However, the Supreme Court, on June 21, 1982, held that the nondiscriminatory bottom line results of the employer's selection process did not preclude the employees from establishing a *prima facie* case of discrimination and did not provide the employers with a defense in such a case. Thus, the conclusion reached from this case is that bottom line percentages are not determinative. Rather, the EEOC or a court will look at each test to determine whether it by itself has a disparate impact on a protected group.

bottom line concept
When the overall selection process does not have an adverse impact, the government will usually not examine the individual components of that process for adverse impact or evidence of validity.

Memphis Firefighters, Local 1784 v. Stotts[10]

The *Stotts* case concerned a conflict between a seniority system and certain affirmative action measures taken by the city of Memphis. In 1980, the Memphis Fire Department entered into a consent decree under which the department would attempt to ensure that 20 percent of the promotions in each job classification would be granted to African Americans. The decree was silent on the issues of layoffs, demotions, or seniority.

In May 1981, budget deficits made layoffs of personnel in the fire department necessary. The layoffs were to be based on seniority. The district court issued an injunction ordering the city to refrain from applying the seniority system because it would decrease the percentage of African American employees in certain jobs.

The city then used a modified plan to protect African American employees. The modified plan laid off 24 employees, 3 of whom were African American. If the traditional seniority system had been used, six African American employees would have been laid off.

The Memphis Firefighters Local 1784 filed a lawsuit objecting to this modified plan. In 1984, the Supreme Court ruled that the district court had exceeded its powers in issuing the injunction requiring white employees to be laid off when the normal seniority system would have required laying off African American employees with less seniority. This decision did not ban the use of affirmative action programs, but it does indicate that a seniority system may limit the use of certain affirmative action measures.

City of Richmond v. *J. A. Crosan Company*[11]

In 1983, the Richmond city council adopted, in an ordinance, a minority business utilization "set-aside" plan, which required nonminority-owned prime contractors awarded city construction contracts to subcontract at least 30 percent of the dollar amount of the contract to one or more minority business enterprises.

After the adoption of the ordinance, the city issued an invitation to bid on a project for the provision and installation of plumbing fixtures at the city jail. The only bidder, the J. A. Crosan Company, submitted a proposal that did not include minority subcontracting sufficient to satisfy the ordinance. The company asked for a waiver of the set-aside requirement, but the request was denied and the company was informed that the project was to be rebid. The company filed suit claiming that the ordinance was unconstitutional under the equal protection clause of the Fourteenth Amendment to the U.S. Constitution.

In January 1989, the Supreme Court ruled that the city of Richmond's plan was unconstitutional. The Court stated that state and local governments must avoid racial quotas and must take affirmative action steps only to correct well-documented examples of past discrimination. The Court went on to say that the Fourteenth Amendment to the U.S. Constitution, which guarantees equal protection of the laws, requires that government affirmative action programs that put whites at a disadvantage should be viewed with the same legal skepticism that has been applied to many state and local laws discriminating against minorities. The impact this decision will have on affirmative action plans for private companies is yet to be determined, but its implications may be wide-ranging.

Wards Cove v. *Atonio*[12]

In June 1989, the Supreme Court, in a close decision (five to four), made it easier for employers to rebut claims of racial bias based on statistical evidence. The case developed from discrimination charges against Wards Cove Packaging Company, Inc., of Seattle and Castle & Cooke, Inc., of Astoria, Oregon. The companies operate salmon canneries in remote areas of Alaska during the summer salmon run.

Minorities (in this particular case, the minorities were largely Filipinos, Alaskan natives, and Asians) alleged that while they held nearly half the jobs at the canneries, the jobs were racially stratified, with whites dominating higher-paying jobs such as machinists, carpenters, and administrators. The company argued that statistics showing that minorities held most of the lower-paying seasonal jobs and fewer better positions did not prove discrimination by the company.

The Supreme Court's decision said that when minorities allege that statistics show they are victims of discrimination, employers only have the burden of producing evidence that there is a legitimate reason for its business practices. The Court further stated that the plaintiff bears the burden of disproving an employer's assertion that the adverse employment practice is based solely on a legitimate neutral consideration. The Court also limited the statistical evidence that minorities can use to prove discrimination. It ruled that an absence of minorities in skilled jobs is not evidence of discrimination if the absence reflects a dearth of qualified minority applicants for reasons that are not the employer's fault. The Civil Rights Act of 1991 in effect reversed this Supreme Court decision.

Martin v. *Wilks*[13]

A group of white firefighters sued the city of Birmingham, Alabama, and the Jefferson County Personnel Board, alleging they were being denied promotions in favor of less qualified African American firefighters. Prior to the filing of the suit, the city had entered into two consent decrees that included goals for hiring and promoting African American firefighters. In filing their suit, the white firefighters claimed that the city was making promotion decisions on the basis of race in reliance on the consent decrees and that these decisions constituted racial discrimination in violation of the Constitution and federal statutes. The district court held that the white firefighters were precluded from challenging employment decisions taken pursuant to the decrees. However, on June 12, 1989, the Supreme Court ruled that the white firefighters could challenge the promotion decisions made pursuant to the consent decrees. Thus, the Court ruled that white firefighters could bring reverse discrimination claims against court-approved affirmative action plans.

Adarand Contractors v. *Peña*[14]

Adarand Contractors, a guardrail contracting firm, sued the U.S. government for allegedly applying race-based standards in granting public works contracts in Colorado. The lawsuit stemmed from a subcontract for guardrail work that Adarand lost in 1990 despite submitting the lowest bid. The subcontract was given to Gonzales Construction, a minority-owned business, by the main contractor, Mountain Gravel & Construction Company, because the Central Federal Lands Highway Division gave cash bonuses to prime contractors that hired minority-owned businesses. In a five-to-four decision, the Supreme Court questioned the constitutionality of government measures designed to help minorities obtain contracts, jobs, or education. The decision did not scrap outright the federal programs that for decades have given some minority-owned businesses a competitive edge over majority-owned businesses. The decision does require lower courts to apply "strict scrutiny" to those programs, meaning the government may have to prove that each program helps only those individuals who can show they were victims of past discrimination, as opposed to simply trying to help all minorities.

State of Texas v. *Hopwood*[15]

On March 18, 1996, the U.S. District Court of Appeals, 5th Circuit, rendered a decision concerning the affirmative action program at the School of Law of the University of Texas. This affirmative action program gave preferences to African Americans and Mexican Americans in the admissions program to the School of Law. This program was initiated in response to a history of discrimination against African Americans and Mexican Americans in the state of Texas. The district court decision found no compelling justification to allow the School of Law to continue to elevate some races over others, even for the purpose of correcting perceived racial imbalance in the student body. The court concluded that the law school may not use race as a factor in law school admissions. On June 25, 2001, the Supreme Court turned down an appeal by the School of Law of The University of Texas.

University of Michigan's Admission Procedures

In June 2003, the Supreme Court issued two decisions dealing with the affirmative action measures the University of Michigan used in its undergraduate and law school programs. Both cases were brought by white applicants who had been rejected for admission to the university. In the law school case (*Grutter* v. *Bollinger*)[16] the court approved the use of a holistic approach that considered race as one tool in the admission process to achieve a diverse student body. However, in the undergraduate program case (*Gratz* v. *Bollinger*)[17] the court rejected the point-based process that gave an automatic boost to African Americans, Hispanics, or Native Americans. The court said that schools cannot maintain quotas or separate admissions tracks for racial groups and that diversity cannot be defined solely on the basis of race. These two decisions are viewed as a victory for affirmative action.[18]

ENFORCEMENT AGENCIES

Two federal agencies have the primary responsibility for enforcing equal employment opportunity legislation. These agencies are the Equal Employment Opportunity Commission and the Office of Federal Contract Compliance Programs.

Equal Employment Opportunity Commission (EEOC)
Federal agency created under the Civil Rights Act of 1964 to administer Title VII of the act and to ensure equal employment opportunity; its powers were expanded in 1979.

Web site: United States Equal Employment Opportunity Commission
www.eeoc.gov

Equal Employment Opportunity Commission

The Civil Rights Act created the **Equal Employment Opportunity Commission (EEOC)** to administer Title VII of the act. The commission is composed of five members, not more than three of whom may be members of the same political party. Members of the commission are appointed by the president of the United States, by and with the advice and consent of the Senate, for a term of five years. The president designates one member to serve as chairperson of the commission and one member to serve as vice chairperson. The chairperson is responsible on behalf of the commission for its administrative operations.

In addition, a general counsel of the commission, appointed by the president with the advice of the Senate for a term of four years, is responsible for conducting litigation under the provisions of Title VII.

Originally, the EEOC was responsible for investigating discrimination based on race, color, religion, sex, or national origin. Now it is also responsible for investigating equal pay violations, age discrimination, and discrimination against disabled persons. The EEOC has the authority not only to investigate charges and complaints in these areas but also to intervene through the general counsel in a civil action on the behalf of an aggrieved party. The EEOC also develops and issues guidelines to enforce nondiscriminatory practices in all of these areas. Several of these guidelines are discussed in this and the next chapter.

Office of Federal Contract Compliance Programs

Office of Federal Contract Compliance Programs (OFCCP)
Office within the U.S. Department of Labor that is responsible for ensuring equal employment opportunity by federal contractors and subcontractors.

Unlike the EEOC, which is an independent agency within the federal government, the **Office of Federal Contract Compliance Programs (OFCCP)** is within the U.S. Department of Labor. It was established by Executive Order 11246 to ensure that federal contractors and subcontractors follow nondiscriminatory employment practices. Prior to 1978, 11 different government agencies had contract compliance sections responsible for administering and enforcing Executive Order 11246. The OFCCP generally supervised and coordinated their activities. In 1978, Executive Order 12086 consolidated the administration and enforcement functions within the OFCCP.

Summary of Learning Objectives

1. **Define *equal employment opportunity*.**

   Equal employment opportunity refers to the right of all people to work and to advance on the basis of merit, ability, and potential.

2. **Describe the intent of the Equal Pay Act of 1963.**

   This act prohibits sex-based discrimination in rates of pay for men and women working in the same or similar jobs.

3. **Describe the intent of Title VII of the Civil Rights Act of 1964.**

   Title VII of the Civil Rights Act of 1964 prohibits discrimination based on race, sex, color, religion, or national origin.

4. **Define *disparate treatment* and *disparate impact*.**

   Disparate treatment refers to intentional discrimination and involves treating one class of employees differently than other employees. *Disparate impact* refers to unintentional discrimination and involves employment practices that appear to be neutral but adversely affect a protected class of people.

5. **Discuss the purpose of the Age Discrimination in Employment Act of 1967.**

   This act prohibits discrimination against employees who are between the ages of 40 and 69.

6. **Discuss the purpose of the Rehabilitation Act of 1973.**

   This act prohibits discrimination against handicapped individuals and requires affirmative action to provide employment opportunities for such persons.

7. **Describe the intent of the Vietnam-Era Veterans Readjustment Assistance Act of 1974.**

   This act prohibits discrimination in hiring disabled veterans with a 30 percent or more disability rating, veterans discharged or released for a service-related disability, and veterans on active duty between August 5, 1964, and May 7, 1975. It also requires that employers with 50 or more employees and contracts in excess of $50,000 have a written AAP for the people protected under this act.

8. **Discuss the purpose of the Pregnancy Discrimination Act of 1978.**

   This act requires employers to treat pregnancy like any other medical condition with regard to fringe benefits and leave policies.

9. **Describe the intent of the Immigration Reform and Control Act of 1986.**

   This act prohibits the hiring of illegal aliens.

10. **Describe the purpose of the Americans with Disabilities Act of 1990.**

    This act increases access to services and jobs for disabled individuals with private employers having 15 or more employees.

11. **Explain the purpose of the Older Workers Benefit Protection Act of 1990.**

    This act protects employees over 40 years of age with respect to fringe benefits and gives employees time to consider an early retirement offer.

12. **Discuss the intent of the Civil Rights Act of 1991.**

    This act permits women, persons with disabilities, and persons who are religious minorities to have a jury trial and sue for punitive damages if they can prove intentional hiring and workplace discrimination. It also requires companies to provide evidence that the business practice that led to the discrimination was not discriminatory but was job related for the position in question and consistent with business necessity.

13. **Explain the content of the Family and Medical Leave Act of 1993.**

    The FMLA enables qualified employees to take prolonged unpaid leave for family- and health-related reasons without fear of losing their jobs.

14. **Discuss the purposes of Executive Orders 11246, 11375, and 11478.**

    Executive Order 11246 prohibits discrimination by federal contractors and subcontractors with contracts in excess of $10,000 on the basis of race, sex, color, religion, or national origin. Also, it requires contractors and subcontractors with 50 or more employees and contracts in excess of $50,000 to have a written AAP with regard to the protected classes. Executive Order 11375 prohibits sex-based wage discrimination. Executive Order 11478 supersedes Executive Order 11246 and modifies some of the procedures under the previous orders and regulations.

15. **Describe the significance of the following Supreme Court decisions:**

    Griggs v. *Duke Power*—Established that the consequences of employment practices, not simply the intent of the employer, are the thrust of Title VII.

    McDonnell Douglas v. *Green*—Set forth standards for the burden of proof in disparate treatment discrimination cases.

    Albemarle Paper v. *Moody*—Affirmed that tests used in employment decisions must be job related and affirmed the use of EEOC guidelines on validating tests.

    University of California Regents v. *Bakke*—Raised the issue of reverse discrimination. Stated that race or ethnic background may be deemed a plus in a particular applicant's file, but it does not insulate the individual from comparison with all other candidates for the available position.

    United Steelworkers of America v. *Weber*—Provided important guidelines for determining the legality of affirmative action programs.

    Connecticut v. *Teal*—Ruled that the bottom line results of an employer's selection process do not preclude employees from establishing a *prima facie* case of discrimination and do not provide the employer with a defense in such a case.

    Memphis Firefighters, Local 1784 v. *Stotts*—Provided that a seniority system may limit the use of certain affirmative action measures.

    City of Richmond v. *J. A. Crosan Company*—Stated that the Fourteenth Amendment requires government affirmative action programs that put whites at a disadvantage to be viewed with the same legal skepticism as laws that discriminate against minorities.

    Wards Cove v. *Atonio*—Changed the requirements in job discrimination suits. Now employees have to prove there was no legitimate business reason for a firm's alleged discriminatory acts.

    Martin v. *Wilks*—Ruled that whites may bring reverse discrimination claims against court-approved affirmative action plans.

    Adarand Contractors v. *Peña*—Required the lower courts to apply strict scrutiny to minority set-aside programs, meaning the government may have to prove that each program helps only those individuals who can show they were victims of past discrimination, as opposed to simply trying to help all minorities.

    Texas v. *Hopwood*—Concluded that the law school may not use race as a factor in law school admissions.

University of Michigan's Admissions Procedures—Two cases brought by white applicants who had been rejected for admission to the university upheld affirmative action provisions. In a law school case (*Grutter* v. *Bollinger*), the court approved the use of a holistic approach that considers race as one tool in the admission process to achieve a diverse student body. However, in the undergraduate program case (*Gratz* v. *Bollinger*) the court rejected the point-based process that gave an automatic boost to African Americans, Hispanics, or Native Americans. The court said that schools cannot maintain quotas or separate admissions tracts for racial groups and that diversity cannot be defined solely on the basis of race.

Key Terms

Age Discrimination in Employment Act (ADEA), *26*
Americans with Disabilities Act (ADA), *28*
bottom line concept, *36*
Civil Rights Act (1991), *30*
disparate impact, *25*
disparate impact doctrine, *34*
disparate treatment, *25*
equal employment opportunity, *24*

Equal Employment Opportunity Commission (EEOC), *38*
Equal Pay Act, *24*
executive orders, *31*
Family and Medical Leave Act (FMLA), *31*
handicapped individual, *27*
Immigration Reform and Control Act, *28*
Office of Federal Contract Compliance Programs (OFCCP), *39*

Older Workers Benefit Protection Act of 1990, *29*
Pregnancy Discrimination Act (PDA), *28*
Rehabilitation Act of 1973, *27*
reverse discrimination, *35*
Title VII of the Civil Rights Act of 1964, *25*
utilization evaluation, *32*
Vietnam-Era Veterans Readjustment Assistance Act of 1974, *27*

Review Questions

1. What is equal employment opportunity?
2. Outline the intent and coverage of each of the following laws:
   a. Equal Pay Act.
   b. Title VII, Civil Rights Act.
   c. Age Discrimination in Employment Act.
   d. Rehabilitation Act.
   e. Vietnam-Era Veterans Readjustment Assistance Act.
   f. Pregnancy Discrimination Act.
   g. Immigration Reform and Control Act.
   h. Americans with Disabilities Act.
   i. Older Workers Benefit Protection Act.
   j. Civil Rights Act of 1991.
   k. Executive Order 11246.
   l. Executive Order 11375.
   m. Executive Order 11478.
3. Define *disparate treatment* and *disparate impact*.
4. Describe the impact of the following Supreme Court decisions:
   a. *Griggs* v. *Duke Power.*
   b. *McDonnell Douglas* v. *Green.*
   c. *Albemarle Paper* v. *Moody.*
   d. *University of California Regents* v. *Bakke.*
   e. *United Steelworkers of America* v. *Weber.*
   f. *Connecticut* v. *Teal.*

     g. *Memphis Firefighters, Local 1784* v. *Stotts.*

     h. *City of Richmond* v. *J. A. Crosan Company.*

     i. *Wards Cove* v. *Atonio.*

     j. *Martin* v. *Wilks.*

     k. *Adarand Contractors* v. *Peña.*

     l. *State of Texas* v. *Hopwood.*

     m. University of Michigan's admission procedures.

5. Discuss the bottom line concept.

6. What two federal agencies have primary responsibility for enforcing equal employment opportunity legislation?

Discussion Questions

1. What area of human resource management is most affected by equal employment opportunity legislation? Discuss.

2. Do you believe most organizations meet the requirements of equal employment opportunity? Why or why not?

3. What problems do you believe have resulted from equal employment opportunity legislation?

4. Do you think misconceptions exist about equal employment opportunity? Discuss.

Incident 2.1

Debate over Retirement Age*

Hundreds of U.S. airline pilots are asking Congress to raise their mandatory retirement to 65, up from the present 60 years of age. They say the change won't threaten safety and could ease problems associated with pension cuts. Sen, James Inhofe (R-Okla.) has sponsored legislation raising the limit, which the Federal Aviation Administration (FAA) opposes. "There's just no scientific consensus that would give us a basis for changing that age-60 limit," said an FAA official. The agency has argued that the decline in a pilot's cognitive functions and the increased risk of illness over age 60 may affect safety.

Testifying before the House Aviation Subcommittee in March 2003, Paul Emens of the Air Line Pilots Against Age Discrimination (ALPAAD) said, "The world does not see this as a safety issue. Most of the world is moving to a retirement age of 65 for airline pilots. Japan and the Netherlands, to name but two, have done extensive studies which showed that raising an airline pilot's age is not a risk. Countries such as Japan, Australia, those of the Joint Aviation Authority in Europe—all have raised their pilots' retirement age. Some 45 nations now allow their airline pilots to fly past the age of 60. Some do so in United States airspace."

Testifying in March 2001 before the Senate Committee on Commerce, Science and Transportation, Nick Lacey, then the FAA's director of flight standards, said, "Proponents of raising the retirement age cite action in 1999 by the Joint Aviation Authority (JAA) in Europe which relaxed the standard, allowing a pilot in command to work until age 65, so long as the co-pilot is under age 60."

"We are not aware of any comprehensive or definitive study that was the basis for the JAA action," Lacey said.

Questions

1. Should all pilots have to retire at the age of 60?

2. How would you study this issue to raise the age to 65?

*__Source:__ "Debate over Retirement Age," *Air Safety Week*, June 13, 2005, p. 1.

Incident 2.2

Accept Things as They Are

Jane Harris came to work at the S&J department store two years ago. In Jane's initial assignment in the finance department, she proved to be a good and hard worker. It soon became obvious to both Jane and her department head, Rich Jackson, that she could handle a much more responsible job than the one she held. Jane discussed this matter with Rich. It was obvious to him that if a better position could not be found for Jane, S&J would lose a good employee. As there were no higher openings in the finance department, Rich recommended her for a job in the accounting department, which she received.

Jane joined the accounting department as payroll administrator and quickly mastered her position. She became knowledgeable in all aspects of the job and maintained a good rapport with her two employees. A short time later, Jane was promoted to assistant manager of the accounting department. In this job, Jane continued her outstanding performance.

Two months ago, Bob Thomas was hired in the accounting department. Ralph Simpson, vice president of administration for S&J, explained to Jane and Steve Smith, head of the accounting department, that Bob was a trainee. After Bob had learned all areas of the department, he would be used to take some of the load off both Jane and Steve and also undertake special projects for the department. Several days after Bob's arrival, Jane learned that Bob was the son of a politician who was a close friend of the president of S&J. Bob had worked in his father's successful election campaign until shortly before joining S&J.

Last week, Steve asked Jane to help him prepare the accounting department's budget for next year. While working on the budget, Jane got a big surprise: She found that Bob had been hired at a salary of $3,200 per month. At the time of Bob's hiring, Jane, as assistant manager of the accounting department, was making only $3,000 per month.

After considering her situation for several days, Jane went to see Ralph Simpson, the division head, about the problem. She told Ralph that she had learned of the difference in salary while assisting Steve with the budget and stated that it was not right to pay a trainee more than a manager. She reminded Ralph of what he had said several times—that Jane's position should pay $40,000 per year considering her responsibility—but S&J just could not afford to pay her that much. Jane told Ralph that things could not remain as they were at present, and she wanted to give S&J a chance to correct the situation. Ralph told Jane he would get back to her in several days.

About a week later, Ralph gave Jane a reply. He stated that while the situation was wrong and unfair, he did not feel that S&J could do anything about it. He told her that sometimes one has to accept things as they are, even if they are wrong. He further stated that he hoped this would not cause S&J to lose a good employee.

Questions

1. What options does Jane have?
2. What influence, if any, would the federal government have in this case?

EXERCISE 2.1

Discrimination because of Sex, Religion, or National Origin

The "Existing Regulations" of the Equal Employment Opportunity Commission (EEOC) are published annually in Title 29 of the *Code of Federal Regulations (CFR)*. The EEOC also publishes on a semiannual basis in the *Federal Register Notice* a regulatory agenda. The agenda lists all regulations that are scheduled for review or development during the next 12 months or that have been finalized since the publication of the last agenda.

Your professor will establish teams of three to four students. Each team will be required to use the Internet to find guidelines on discrimination because of sex, religion, or national origin. Each team will be required to make a 10–15 minute presentation of the current status of these forms of discrimination.

Notes and Additional Readings

Web site: Federal Legal Information through Electronics
www.fedworld.gov/supcourt

1. *Usery* v. *Tamiami Trail Tours, Inc.,* 531 F. 2d 224, 12FEP1233 (5th Cir. 1976).
2. *General Electric Co.* v. *Gilbert,* 429 U.S. 125 (1976).
3. Art. VI, cl. 2.
4. *Griggs* v. *Duke Power Company,* 401 U.S. 424, FEP 175.
5. *McDonnell Douglas* v. *Green,* 411 U.S. 792 (1973).
6. *Albemarle Paper* v. *Moody,* 422 U.S. 405, 95 S.CT. 2362.
7. *University of California Regents* v. *Bakke,* 483 U.S. 265.
8. *United Steelworkers of America* v. *Weber,* 99 S.CT. 2721.
9. *Connecticut* v. *Teal,* 457 U.S. 440 (1982).
10. *Memphis Firefighters, Local 1784* v. *Stotts,* 104 S.CT. 2576.
11. *City of Richmond* v. *J. A. Crosan Company,* 488 U.S. 469 (1989).
12. *Wards Cove* v. *Atonio,* 490 U.S. 642 (1989).
13. *Martin* v. *Wilks,* 490 U.S. 755 (1989).
14. *Adarand Contractors* v. *Peña,* 115 S.CT. 2097.
15. *State of Texas* v. *Hopwood,* Case H 95-1773.
16. *Grutter* v. *Bollinger,* No. 02-291, Decided June 23, 2003.
17. *Gratz* v. *Bollinger,* No. 02-516, Decided June 23, 2003.
18. See June Kronhotz, "Does a White Mom Add Diversity?—Barbara Grutter Believed She Was a Prime Candidate for Michigan's Law School," *Wall Street Journal,* June 25, 2003, p. B3.

Chapter Three

Implementing Equal Employment Opportunity

Chapter Learning Objectives

After studying this chapter, you should be able to:

1. Explain the role of the Employer Information Report, EEO–1.
2. Define employment parity, occupational parity, systemic discrimination, underutilization, and concentration.
3. Describe an affirmative action plan.
4. Define bona fide occupational qualification (BFOQ).
5. Explain what business necessity means.
6. Define sexual harassment.
7. Describe the comparable worth theory.

Chapter Outline

Web site: United States Equal Employment Opportunity Commission www.eeoc.gov

As the previous chapter indicated, the legal requirements of equal employment opportunity are quite complex. Nevertheless, each organization must develop its own approach to equal employment within the legal guidelines. Chapter 2 presents the history of equal employment opportunity. Chapter 3 presents management practice issues that HR managers confront because of EEO law. Thus, this chapter provides specific information and guidelines for implementing equal employment opportunity.[1]

MATERNITY STORE SETTLES PREGNANCY DISCRIMINATION AND RETALIATION LAWSUIT

A Philadelphia-based maternity clothes retailer will pay $375,000 to settle a pregnancy discrimination and retaliation lawsuit brought by the U.S. Equal Employment Opportunity Commission (EEOC), the agency announced today. The EEOC had charged that Mothers Work, Inc., doing business as Motherhood Maternity, refused to hire qualified female applicants because they were pregnant.

According to the EEOC's lawsuit (Case No. 3:05-CV-990-J-32TEM in U.S. District Court for the Middle District of Florida, Jacksonville Division), LaShonda Burns, a former assistant manager, complained about Motherhood's policy and practice of discrimination against pregnant applicants. The EEOC said Motherhood illegally disciplined and ultimately fired Burns because it believed she was pregnant and in retaliation for her complaints.

Such alleged conduct violates the Pregnancy Discrimination Act. The EEOC filed suit after first attempting to reach a voluntary settlement, and Burns also took part in the suit with a private attorney.

The three-year consent decree settling the suit requires Motherhood to pay Ms. Burns $135,000 in compensatory and punitive damages; $50,000 in back pay; $130,000 for Burns's private attorney's fees and costs; and $20,000 in compensatory and punitive damages to each of three women who were denied emloyment opportunities because they were pregnant—Lakevia Rollins, Aimee Tart, and Jackie Ciardiello. Motherhood must also adopt and distribute an antidiscrimination policy that specifically prohibits denying women employment opportunities because of their pregnancy; train all of its current and future Florida employees on the new policy and federal employment discrimination laws; post notice of resolution of the lawsuit; and report to EEOC twice annually regarding pregnancy discrimination complaints.

According to company information, Motherhood, which began its operations in 1982, employs over 5,000 people. It is the leading designer, manufacturer, and retailer of maternity fashion in the United States, with over 1,000 stores nationwide and Internet retailing. Motherhood owns leading brands including Mimi Maternity, A Pea in the Pod, and Maternitymail.com.

Source: Adapted from "Maternity Store Giant to Pay $375,000 to Settle EEOC Pregnancy Discrimination, Retaliation Lawsuit," *U.S. Fed News Service*, Washington, D.C., January 8, 2007.

EEOC COMPLIANCE

The Equal Employment Opportunity Commission (EEOC) and the Office of Federal Contract Compliance Programs (OFCCP), both described in the previous chapter, are the two primary enforcement agencies for equal employment opportunity. All organizations with 20 or more employees must keep records that the EEOC or OFCCP can request.

Legal Powers of the EEOC

Web site: National Employment Lawyers Association
www.nela.org

Section 713 of Title VII (Civil Rights Act of 1964), the Age Discrimination in Employment Act (ADEA), the Equal Pay Act, the Americans with Disabilities Act (ADA) of 1990, and the Civil Rights Act of 1991 authorize the EEOC to develop and publish procedural regulations regarding the enforcement of these acts. As a result, the EEOC has issued substantive regulations (or guidelines, as they are more frequently called) interpreting Title VII, the ADEA, the Equal Pay Act, the ADA, and the Civil Rights Act of 1991. The EEOC also has enforcement authority to initiate litigation and to intervene in private litigation. HRM in Action 3.1 describes a legal action undertaken by EEOC.

EEOC Posting Requirements

Web site: United States National Labor Relations Board
www.nlrb.gov

Title VII requires employers, employment agencies, and labor organizations covered by the act to post EEOC-prepared notices summarizing the requirements of Title VII, the ADEA, the Equal Pay Act, the ADA, and the Civil Rights Act of 1991. The EEOC has prepared such a poster, and a willful failure to display it is punishable by a fine of not more than $100 for each offense. Organizations subject to notice requirements by Executive Order 11246 and Title VII can display a poster meeting the requirements of both the EEOC and the OFCCP. Figure 3.1 shows a copy of this poster.

Records and Reports

Employer Information Report (Standard Form 100)
Form that all employers with 100 or more employees are required to file with the EEOC; requires a breakdown of the employer's workforce in specified job categories by race, sex, and national origin.

Employers with 100 or more employees must annually file Standard Form 100, known as the **Employer Information Report,** EEO–1. Figure 3.2 shows the form. The EEO–1 report requires a breakdown of the employer's workforce in specified job categories by race, sex, and national origin. Other, similar types of forms are required of unions, political jurisdictions,

FIGURE 3.1 EEOC Poster

Equal Employment Opportunity is

THE LAW

Employers Holding Federal Contracts or Subcontracts

Applicants to and employees of companies with a Federal government contract or subcontract are protected under the following Federal authorities:

RACE, COLOR, RELIGION, SEX, NATIONAL ORIGIN

Executive Order 11246, as amended, prohibits job discrimination on the basis of race, color, religion, sex or national origin, and requires affirmative action to ensure equality of opportunity in all aspects of employment.

INDIVIDUALS WITH DISABILITIES

Section 503 of the Rehabilitation Act of 1973, as amended, prohibits job discrimination because of disability and requires affirmative action to employ and advance in employment qualified individuals with disabilities who, with reasonable accommodation, can perform the essential functions of a job.

VIETNAM ERA, SPECIAL DISABLED, RECENTLY SEPARATED, AND OTHER PROTECTED VETERANS

38 U.S.C. 4212 of the Vietnam Era Veterans' Readjustment Assistance Act of 1974, as amended, prohibits job discrimination and requires affirmative action to employ and advance in employment qualified Vietnam era veterans, qualified special disabled veterans, recently separated veterans, and other protected veterans.

Any person who believes a contractor has violated its nondiscrimination or affirmative action obligations under the authorities above should contact immediately:

The Office of Federal Contract Compliance Programs (OFCCP), Employment Standards Administration, U.S. Department of Labor, 200 Constitution Avenue, N.W., Washington, D.C. 20210 or call (202) 693-0101, or an OFCCP regional or district office, listed in most telephone directories under U.S. Government, Department of Labor.

Private Employment, State and Local Governments, Educational Institutions

Applicants to and employees of most private employers, state and local governments, educational institutions, employment agencies and labor organizations are protected under the following Federal laws:

RACE, COLOR, RELIGION, SEX, NATIONAL ORIGIN

Title VII of the Civil Rights Act of 1964, as amended, prohibits discrimination in hiring, promotion, discharge, pay, fringe benefits, job training, classification, referral, and other aspects of employment, on the basis of race, color, religion, sex or national origin.

DISABILITY

The Americans with Disabilities Act of 1990, as amended, protects qualified applicants and employees with disabilities from discrimination in hiring, promotion, discharge, pay, job training, fringe benefits, classification, referral, and other aspects of employment on the basis of disability. The law also requires that covered entities provide qualified applicants and employees with disabilities with reasonable accommodations that do not impose undue hardship.

AGE

The Age Discrimination in Employment Act of 1967, as amended, protects applicants and employees 40 years of age or older from discrimination on the basis of age in hiring, promotion, discharge, compensation, terms, conditions or privileges of employment.

SEX (WAGES)

In addition to sex discrimination prohibited by Title VII of the Civil Rights Act of 1964, as amended (see above), the Equal Pay Act of 1963, as amended, prohibits sex discrimination in payment of wages to women and men performing substantially equal work in the same establishment.

Retaliation against a person who files a charge of discrimination, participates in an investigation, or opposes an unlawful employment practice is prohibited by all of these Federal laws.

If you believe that you have been discriminated against under any of the above laws, you should contact immediately:

The U.S. Equal Employment Opportunity Commission (EEOC), 1801 L Street, N.W., Washington, D.C. 20507 or an EEOC field office by calling toll free (800) 669-4000. For individuals with hearing impairments, EEOC's toll free TDD number is (800) 669-6820.

Programs or Activities Receiving Federal Financial Assistance

RACE, COLOR, RELIGION, NATIONAL ORIGIN, SEX

In addition to the protection of Title VII of the Civil Rights Act of 1964, as amended, Title VI of the Civil Rights Act prohibits discrimination on the basis of race, color or national origin in programs or activities receiving Federal financial assistance. Employment discrimination is covered by Title VI if the primary objective of the financial assistance is provision of employment, or where employment discrimination causes or may cause discrimination in providing services under such programs. Title IX of the Education Amendments of 1972 prohibits employment discrimination on the basis of sex in educational programs or activities which receive Federal assistance.

INDIVIDUALS WITH DISABILITIES

Sections 501, 504 and 505 of the Rehabilitation Act of 1973, as amended, prohibits employment discrimination on the basis of disability in any program or activity which receives Federal financial assistance in the federal government. Discrimination is prohibited in all aspects of employment against persons with disabilities who, with reasonable accommodation, can perform the essential functions of a job.

If you believe you have been discriminated against in a program of any institution which receives Federal assistance, you should contact immediately the Federal agency providing such assistance.

Publication OFCCP 1420
Revised 2004

FIGURE 3.2 **Standard Form 100**

Joint Reporting
Committee

- **Equal Employment
  Opportunity Com-
  mission**
- **Office of Federal
  Contract Compli-
  ance Programs (Labor)**

EQUAL EMPLOYMENT OPPORTUNITY

EMPLOYER INFORMATION REPORT EEO—1

Standard Form 100
(Rev. 3/97)

O.M.B. No. 3046-007
EXPIRES 10/31/99
100-214

Section A—TYPE OF REPORT
Refer to instructions for number and types of reports to be filed.

1. Indicate by marking in the appropriate box the type of reporting unit for which this copy of the form is submitted (MARK ONLY ONE BOX).

   (1) ☐ Single-establishment Employer Report

   Multi-establishment Employer:
   (2) ☐ Consolidated Report (Required)
   (3) ☐ Headquarters Unit Report (Required)
   (4) ☐ Individual Establishment Report (submit one for each establishment with 50 or more employees)
   (1) ☐ Special Report

2. Total number of reports being filed by this Company (Answer on Consolidated Report only) ———

Section B—COMPANY IDENTIFICATION *(to be answered by all employers)*

OFFICE USE ONLY

1. Parent Company
   a. Name of parent company (owns or controls establishment in item 2) omit if same as label

   a.

   Address (Number and street)

   b.

City or town	State	ZIP code

   c.

2. Establishment for which this report is filed. (Omit if same as label)
   a. Name of establishment

   d.

Address (Number and street)	City or Town	County	State	ZIP code

   e.

   b. Employer Identification No. (IRS 9-DIGIT TAX NUMBER)

   f.

   c. Was an EEO–1 report filed for this establishment last year? ☐ Yes ☐ No

Section C—EMPLOYERS WHO ARE REQUIRED TO FILE *(To be answered by all employers)*

☐ Yes ☐ No   1. Does the entire company have at least 100 employees in the payroll period for which you are reporting?

☐ Yes ☐ No   2. Is your company affiliated through common ownership and/or centralized management with other entitles in an enterprise with a total employment of 100 or more?

☐ Yes ☐ No   3. Does the company or any of its establishments (a) have 50 or more employees AND (b) is not exempt as provided by 41 CFR 60–1.5, AND either (1) is a prime government contractor or forst-tier subcontractor, and has a contract, subcontractor, or purchase order amounting to $50,000 or more, or (2) serves as a depository of Government funds in any amount or is a financial institution which is an issuing and paying agent for U.S. Savings Bonds and Savings Notes?

If the response to question C–3 is yes, please enter your Dun and Bradstreet identification number (if you have one): ☐☐☐☐☐☐☐☐☐☐

NOTE: If the answer is yes to questions 1, 2, or 3, complete the entire form, otherwise skip to Section G.

educational institutions, school districts, and joint labor–management committees that control apprenticeship programs. Persons willfully making false statements on EEOC reports may be punished by fine or imprisonment.

In addition to EEO–1, Title VII requires the covered organizations to make and keep certain records that may be used to determine whether unlawful employment practices have been or are being committed. Thus, it is a good practice for covered organizations to maintain records relating to job applicants, payroll records, transfers, recalls, and discharges. The length of time required for the retention of these records varies, but a good time frame for retaining such records is three years.

Since the EEOC and OFCCP are interested in the recruitment and selection of protected groups and because the collection of certain data about the protected groups is not permitted

FIGURE 3.2 **Standard Form 100 (Concluded)**

SF 100 Page 2

Section D—EMPLOYMENT DATA

Employment at this establishment—Report all permanent full-time and part-time employees including apprentices and on-the-job trainees unless specifically excluded as set forth in the instructions. Enter the appropriate figures on all lines and in all columns. Blank spaces will be considered as zeros.

JOB CATEGORIES		OVERALL TOTALS (SUM OF COL. B THRU K)	MALE					FEMALE				
			WHITE (NOT OF HISPANIC ORIGIN)	BLACK (NOT OF HISPANIC ORIGIN)	HISPANIC	ASIAN OR PACIFIC ISLANDER	AMERICAN INDIAN OR ALASKAN NATIVE	WHITE (NOT OF HISPANIC ORIGIN)	BLACK (NOT OF HISPANIC ORIGIN)	HISPANIC	ASIAN OR PACIFIC ISLANDER	AMERICAN INDIAN OR ALASKAN NATIVE
		A	B	B	D	E	F	G	H	I	J	K
Officials and Managers	1											
Professionals	2											
Technicians	3											
Sales Workers	4											
Office and Clerical	5											
Craft Workers (Skilled)	6											
Operatives (Semi-Skilled)	7											
Laborers (Unskilled)	8											
Service Workers	9											
TOTAL	10											
Total employment reported in previous EEO-1 report	11											

NOTE: Omit questions 1 and 2 on the Consolidated Report.
1. Date(s) of payroll period used: 2. Does this establishment employ apprentices?
                                                    1 ☐ Yes   2 ☐ No

Section E—ESTABLISHMENT INFORMATION *(Omit on the Consolidated Report)*

1. What is the major activity of this establishment? (Be specific, i.e., manufacturing steel castings, retail grocer, wholesale plumbing supplies, title insurance, etc. Include the specific type of product or type of service provided, as well as the principal business or industrial activity.)

OFFICE USE ONLY

g.

Section F—REMARKS

Use this item to give any identification data appearing on last report which differs from that given above, explain major changes in composition of reporting units and other pertinent information.

Section G—CERTIFICATION *(See instructions G)*

Check one
1 ☐ All reports are accurate and were prepared in accordance with the instructions (check on consolidated only)
2 ☐ This report is accurate and was prepared in accordance with the instructions.

Name of Certifying Official	Title	Signature	Date
Name of person to contact regarding this report (Type or print)	Address (Number and Street)		
Title	City and State	ZIP Code	Telephone Number (including Area Code)	Extension

All reports and information obtained from individual reports will be kept confidential as required by Section 709(e) of Title VII. WILLFULLY FALSE STATEMENTS ON THIS REPORT ARE PUNISHABLE BY LAW, U.S. CODE, TITLE 18, SECTION 1001.

on an organization's application form, the EEOC allows organizations to use a separate form, often called an *applicant diversity chart,* for collecting certain data. An example of such a form is shown in Figure 3.3. The data on this form must be maintained separately from all employment information.

Compliance Process

An individual may file a discrimination charge at any EEOC office or with any representative of the EEOC. If the charging party and respondent are in different geographic areas, the office where the charging party resides forwards the charge to the office where the respondent is located. Class action charges or charges requiring extensive investigations are processed in the EEOC's Office of Systemic Programs.

FIGURE 3.3 **Applicant Diversity Chart**

NAME OF APPLICANT	DEGREE/ EDUCATION	DATE APPLIED	POSITION APPLIED FOR	EEO JOB CATEGORY	E.I.	SEX	AGE	HANDICAP	VETERAN	DISPOSITION

Location _____   Group Code _____ 1-2

QTR. Beginning _____   QTR. Ending _____   (For EEO office use only)

CODES:

EEO JOB CATEGORY

01—Officials/Managers
02—Professionals
03—Technicians
04—Sales Workers
05—Office and Clerical
06—Craft Workers
07—Operatives
08—Laborers
09—Service Workers

ETHNIC IDENTIFICATION (E.I.)

W—White
B—Black
H—Hispanic
A—Asian or Pacific Islanders
N—American Indian or Alaskan Native

SEX

M—Male
F—Female

AGE

A—Below 40
B—40-45
C—46-50
D—51-55
F—56-60
G—61-65
H—66 & over

HANDICAP

Y—Yes
N—No

VETERAN

Y—Yes
N—No

DISPOSITION

1—Hired
2—Offer Outstanding
3—Offer Rejected
4—Applicant Rejected
5—No offer-No Opening

This Report Should Be Submitted to the Human Resource Department at the End of Every 90-Day Period

* THE NUMBERS ABOVE COLUMNS ARE FOR DATA INPUT INFORMATION ONLY.

TABLE 3.1
Steps in Processing a
Discrimination Charge

Step Number	Procedure
1.	Charge is filed with the EEOC.
2.	The EEOC evaluates charge and determines whether or not to proceed with it.
3.	If it decides to proceed with the charge, the EEOC serves respondents with a copy of the actual charge.
4.	A face-to-face, fact-finding mediation program may be offered to the charging party and the respondent.
5.	If the charge is not resolved in step 4, the EEOC conducts an investigation of the charges.
6.	In cases where the EEOC finds reasonable cause that discrimination has occurred, a proposed conciliation agreement is sent to the respondents. The proposal normally includes a suggested remedy to eliminate the unlawful practices and to take appropriate corrective and affirmative action.
7.	If the respondents do not agree to the conciliation agreement, the EEOC makes a determination on whether the charge is "litigation worthy." As a practical matter, litigation worthy means that the evidence gathered during the investigation will support a lawsuit.
8.	If the charge is deemed litigation worthy, the EEOC then files a lawsuit in the appropriate state or federal court. Decisions in these lower courts are often appealed to the Supreme Court.

employment parity
Situation in which the proportion of minorities and women employed by an organization equals the proportion in the organization's relevant labor market.

occupational parity
Situation in which the proportion of minorities and women employed in various occupations within an organization is equal to their proportion in the organization's relevant labor market.

systemic discrimination
Large differences in either occupational or employment parity.

relevant labor market
The geographical area in which a company recruits its employees.

underutilization
Practice of having fewer minorities or women in a particular job category than their corresponding numbers in the relevant labor market.

concentration
Practice of having more minorities or women in a job category than would reasonably be expected when compared to their presence in the relevant labor market.

right-to-sue letter
Statutory notice by the EEOC to the charging party if the EEOC does not decide to file a lawsuit on behalf of the charging party.

The EEOC uses two methods to determine whether discrimination against groups protected by the law has occurred: **employment parity** and occupational parity. When employment parity exists, the proportion of minorities and women employed by the organization equals the proportion in the organization's relevant labor market. **Occupational parity** exists when the proportion of minorities and women employed in various occupations within the organization is equal to their proportion in the organization's relevant labor market. Large differences in either occupational or employment parity are called **systemic discrimination.**

Relevant labor market generally refers to the geographical area in which a company recruits its employees. For example, a small company may recruit its employees only within the standard metropolitan statistical area (SMSA) within which it falls; thus, its relevant labor market would be the SMSA. On the other hand, a large company that recruits nationally may have the whole nation as its relevant labor market. Furthermore, companies can have different relevant labor markets for different occupations. For example, the relevant labor market for a company's clerical employees might be the SMSA, while the relevant labor market for its engineers might be nationwide.

The EEOC can also examine the underutilization or concentration of minorities and/or females in certain jobs. **Underutilization** refers to the practice of having fewer minorities or females in a particular job category than would reasonably be expected when compared to their presence in the relevant labor market. **Concentration** refers to the practice of having more minorities or women in a job category than would reasonably be expected when compared to their presence in the relevant labor market.

Table 3.1 summarizes the steps involved in processing a discrimination charge. These are general in nature, and many variations are possible. If the EEOC does not decide to file a lawsuit on behalf of the charging party, the individual still has the right to bring suit against the respondent. In this situation, the EEOC issues the charging party the statutory notice of a **right-to-sue letter.** The charging party must then file a civil action suit in the appropriate court within 90 days of receipt of the statutory notice of right to sue.

Preemployment Inquiry Guide

The On the Job example at the end of this chapter provides a guide to what can and cannot be asked of a job applicant in order to comply with equal employment opportunity legislation and court interpretations of that legislation. It is illustrative and attempts to answer the questions most frequently asked about equal employment opportunity law.

AFFIRMATIVE ACTION PLANS

affirmative action plan
Written document outlining specific goals and timetables for remedying past discriminatory actions.

An **affirmative action plan** is a written document outlining specific goals and timetables for remedying past discriminatory actions. All federal contractors and subcontractors with contracts over $50,000 and 50 or more employees are required to develop and implement written affirmative action plans, which are monitored by the OFCCP. In addition, all U.S. government agencies must prepare affirmative action plans. While Title VII and the EEOC do not require any specific type of written affirmative action plan, court rulings have often required affirmative action when discrimination is found.

A number of basic steps are involved in the development of an effective affirmative action plan. The EEOC has suggested the following eight steps:[2]

1. The chief executive officer of the organization should issue a written statement describing his or her personal commitment to the plan, legal obligations, and the importance of equal employment opportunity as an organizational goal.
2. A top official of the organization should be given the authority and responsibility for directing and implementing the program. In addition, all managers and supervisors within the organization should clearly understand their own responsibilities for carrying out equal employment opportunity.
3. The organization's policy and commitment to that policy should be publicized both internally and externally.
4. Present employment should be surveyed to identify areas of concentration and underutilization and determine the extent of underutilization.
5. Goals and timetables for achieving the goals should be developed to improve utilization of minorities and females in each area where underutilization has been identified.
6. The entire employment system should be reviewed to identify and eliminate barriers to equal employment. Areas for review include recruitment, selection, promotion systems, training programs, wage and salary structure, benefits and conditions of employment, layoffs, discharges, disciplinary actions, and union contract provisions affecting these areas.
7. An internal audit and reporting system should be established to monitor and evaluate progress in all aspects of the program.
8. Company and community programs supportive of equal opportunity should be developed. Programs might include training supervisors in their legal responsibilities and the organization's commitment to equal employment, and job and career counseling programs.

Several Supreme Court decisions discussed in Chapter 2 (*City of Richmond* v. *J. A. Crosan Company* and *Adarand Contractors* v. *Peña*) have removed the pressure for such plans except in cases of specific and probable acts of discrimination, *State of Texas* v. *Hopwood* and Proposition 209, which were also discussed in Chapter 2, may also have a significant impact on affirmative action programs. In addition, much discussion has been generated in both the House of Representatives and the Senate about eliminating all federal affirmative action programs.

BONA FIDE OCCUPATIONAL QUALIFICATION (BFOQ)

bona fide occupational qualification (BFOQ)
Permits employer to use religion, age, sex, or national origin as a factor in its employment practices when reasonably necessary to the normal operation of that particular business.

The **bona fide occupational qualification (BFOQ)** permits employers to use religion, age, sex, or national origin as a factor in their employment practices when it is reasonably necessary to the normal operation of that particular business. Section 703(e) of Title VII provides:

Notwithstanding any other provision of this [title], (1) it shall not be an unlawful employment practice for an employer to hire and employ employees, for an employment agency to classify or refer for employment any individual, or for an employer, labor organization, or joint labor management committee controlling apprenticeship or other training programs to admit or employ any individual in any such program, on the basis of his religion, sex, or national origin in those certain instances where religion, sex, or national origin is a bona fide occupational qualification reasonably necessary to the normal operation of that particular business or enterprise.

For example, to be able to use sex as a BFOQ in a job that requires lifting 100 pounds, the employer would be required to show that all or substantially all women cannot lift 100 pounds.

In fact, most employers most frequently raise the BFOQ exception because of sex. Section 1604.2(a) of the EEOC's *Guidelines on Discrimination Because of Sex* states:

> *The Commission believes that the bona fide occupational qualification exception as to sex should be interpreted narrowly. Labels—"men's jobs" and "women's jobs"—tend to deny employment opportunities unnecessarily to one sex or the other.*
> *(1) The Commission will find that the following situations do not warrant the application of the bona fide occupational qualification exception:*
> > *(i)   The refusal to hire a woman because of her sex based on assumptions of the comparative employment characteristics of women in general. For example, the assumption that the turnover rate among women is higher than among men.*
> > *(ii) The refusal to hire an individual based on stereotyped characterizations of the sexes. Such stereotypes include, for example, that men are less capable of assembling intricate equipment; that women are less capable of aggressive salesmanship. The principle of non-discrimination requires that individuals be considered on the basis of individual capacities and not on the basis of any characteristics generally attributed to the group.*
> > *(iii) The refusal to hire an individual because of the preferences of coworkers, the employer, clients or customers except as covered specifically in subparagraph (2) of this paragraph.*
> *(2) Where it is necessary for the purpose of authenticity or genuineness, the Commission will consider sex to be a bona fide occupational qualification, e.g., an actor or actress.*

The situations in which employers raise the BFOQ exception normally fall within three general categories:

1. Ability to perform (e.g., physical ability to perform jobs that involve strenuous manual labor).
2. Same-sex BFOQ that relates to accommodating the personal privacy of clients and customers.
3. Customer preference BFOQ where the customer states a desire to be served only by a person of a given sex.

However, the courts have very narrowly interpreted the sex discrimination defenses based on the BFOQ exception. For example, the courts permitted a same-sex BFOQ in a job that involved a potential invasion of another person's privacy in *City of Philadelphia* v. *Pennsylvania Human Relations Commission.*[3] The city, in operating youth study centers, restricted the employment of youth supervisors to persons of the same sex as those being supervised. On the other hand, in *Ludtke* v. *Kulm,*[4] the courts ruled that female reporters could not be excluded from a baseball team's postgame locker room since an interview area could be set up providing equal access for all reporters while protecting the privacy interests of the male ballplayers.

In the area of ability to perform the job, the courts have generally rejected the BFOQ defense and have usually held that each individual job applicant should be permitted an opportunity to demonstrate the ability to perform. The courts have also generally rejected customer preference as a BFOQ defense.

Age may be used as a BFOQ in certain limited situations. For example, age may be a BFOQ when public safety is involved, such as with airline pilots or interstate bus drivers.

BUSINESS NECESSITY

business necessity
Condition that comes into play when an employer has a job criterion that is neutral but excludes members of one sex at a higher rate than members of the opposite sex. The focus in business necessity is on the validity of stated job qualifications and their relationship to the work performed.

Business necessity comes into play when an employer has a job specification that is neutral but excludes members of one sex at a higher rate than members of the other. The focus in business necessity is on the validity of various stated job specifications and their relationship to the work performed. For example, in using a business necessity defense, an employer would be required to prove that the ability to lift 100 pounds is necessary in performing a warehouse job.

When a BFOQ is established, an employer can refuse to consider all persons of the protected group. When business necessity is established, an employer can exclude all persons who do not meet specifications regardless of whether the specifications have an adverse impact on a protected group.

SEXUAL HARASSMENT

sexual harassment
Unwelcome sexual conduct that has the purpose or effect of unreasonably interfering with an individual's work performance or creating an intimidating, hostile, or offensive work environment.

Sexual harassment creates a hostile work environment.
Ryan McVay/Getty Images

TABLE 3.2
EEOC's Sex Discrimination Guidelines

One of the more current issues in equal employment opportunity is **sexual harassment.** The EEOC *Guidelines on Discrimination Because of Sex* define as unlawful any unwelcome sexual conduct that "has the purpose or effect of unreasonably interfering with an individual's work performance or creating an intimidating, hostile, or offensive work environment. Section 1604.11 of the *Guidelines* is reproduced in Table 3.2.

The very nature of sexual harassment sometimes makes it difficult to prove. The fact that such conduct normally occurs secretly and outside the employer's wishes and can grow out of or be alleged to grow out of consensual relationships makes the investigation of complaints most difficult. However, when deciding to impose liability on an employer for a supervisor's sexual harassment, the courts have considered an employer's failure to investigate complaints of sexual harassment as significant.

Furthermore, the difficulty employees face in proving that an adverse decision was due to their sex and their failure to submit to sexual advances has been relaxed somewhat in favor of plaintiffs. In *Bundy* v. *Jackson,*[5] the District of Columbia Circuit Court established the allocation of the burden of proof in a sexual harassment case:

1. First, the employee must establish a *prima facie* case by proving he or she was (*a*) subjected to sexual harassment and (*b*) denied a benefit for which he or she was eligible and of which he or she had a reasonable expectation.

2. The burden then shifts to the employer to prove, by clear and convincing evidence, that its decision was based on legitimate, nondiscriminatory grounds.

3. If the employer succeeds in meeting that stringent burden, the employee may then attempt to prove that the employer's stated reasons are pretextual.

(a) Harassment on the basis of sex is a violation of Sec. 703 of Title VII. Unwelcome sexual advances, requests for sexual favors, and other verbal or physical conduct of a sexual nature constitute sexual harassment when (1) submission to such conduct is made either explicitly or implicitly a term or condition of an individual's employment, (2) submission to or rejection of such conduct by an individual is used as the basis for employment decisions affecting such individual, or (3) such conduct has the purpose or effect of unreasonably interfering with an individual's work performance or creating an intimidating, hostile, or offensive working environment.

(b) In determining whether alleged conduct constitutes sexual harassment, the Commission will look at the record as a whole and at the totality of the circumstances, such as the nature of the sexual advances and the context in which the alleged incidents occurred. The determination of the legality of a particular action will be made from the facts, on a case by case basis.

(c) Applying general Title VII principles, an employer, employment agency, joint apprenticeship committee or labor organization (hereinafter collectively referred to as "employer") is responsible for its acts and those of its agents and supervisory employees with respect to sexual harassment regardless of whether the specific acts complained of were authorized or even forbidden by the employer and regardless of whether the employer knew or should have known of their occurrence. The Commission will examine the circumstances of the particular employment relationship and the job functions performed by the individual in determining whether an individual acts in either a supervisory or agency capacity.

(d) With respect to conduct between fellow employees, an employer is responsible for acts of sexual harassment in the workplace where the employer (or its agents or supervisory employees) knows or should have known of the conduct, unless it can show that it took immediate and appropriate corrective action.

(e) An employer may also be responsible for the acts of nonemployees, with respect to sexual harassment of employees in the workplace, where the employer (or its agents or supervisory employees) knows or should have known of the conduct and fails to take immediate and appropriate corrective action. In reviewing these cases the Commission will consider the extent of the employer's control and any other legal responsibility that the employer may have with respect to the conduct of such nonemployees.

(f) Prevention is the best tool for the elimination of sexual harassment. An employer should take all steps necessary to prevent sexual harassment from occurring, such as affirmatively raising the subject, expressing strong disapproval, developing appropriate sanctions, informing employees of their right to raise and how to raise the issue of harassment under Title VII, and developing methods to sensitize all concerned.

(g) Other related practices: Where employment opportunities or benefits are granted because of an individual's submission to the employer's sexual advances or requests for sexual favors, the employer may be held liable for unlawful sex discrimination against other persons who were qualified for but denied that employment opportunity or benefit.

Many employers have implemented measures designed to avoid sexual harassment. Developing policies prohibiting sexual harassment and promptly investigating and responding to complaints of sexual harassment are essential to its prohibition. At a minimum, an organization's policy on sexual harassment should (1) define and prohibit sexual harassment and (2) encourage any employee who believes that he or she has been a victim of sexual harassment to come forward to express those complaints to management. It is important to note that acts of sexual harassment can be committed not only by men against women, but also by men against men, by women against women, and by women against men. HRM in Action 3.2 describes a case of sexual harassment.

COMPARABLE WORTH AND EQUAL PAY ISSUES

comparable worth theory
Idea that every job has a worth to the employer and society that can be measured and assigned a value.

A controversial issue in equal employment opportunity is the **comparable worth theory.** This theory holds that every job by its very nature has a worth to the employer and society that can be measured and assigned a value. Each job should be compensated on the basis of its value and paid the same as other jobs with the same value. Under this theory, market factors such as availability of qualified workers and wage rates paid by other employers would be disregarded. This theory further holds that entire classes of jobs are traditionally undervalued and underpaid because they are held by women and that this inequality amounts to sex discrimination in violation of Title VII of the Civil Rights Act.

Proponents of this theory argue that the Equal Pay Act offers little protection to female workers because the act applies only to those job classifications in which men and women are employed. Further, the most serious form of wage discrimination occurs when women arrive at the workplace with education, training, and ability equivalent to that of men and are assigned lower-paying jobs that are held primarily by women.

In the case *County of Washington* v. *Gunther,*[6] the Supreme Court considered a claim of sex-based wage discrimination between prison matrons and prison guards. Prison matrons were being paid approximately 70 percent of what the guards were being paid. In its decision, the Court ruled that sex-based wage discrimination violates Title VII of the Civil Rights Act and that the plaintiffs could file suit under the law, even if the jobs were not equal. However, the Court's decision specifically stated that it was not ruling on the comparable worth issue.

In its first policy statement on comparable worth, the EEOC stated that unequal pay for work of a similar value wasn't by itself proof of discrimination. The agency stated that it would not pursue "pure" comparable worth cases but would act in cases where it could be shown that employers intentionally paid different wages to women and men in comparable jobs. The exact meaning of this policy statement can, of course, be determined by the types of cases subsequently pursued by the EEOC.

In *AFSCME* v. *State of Washington,*[7] the employer had conducted a comparison of jobs but had not adjusted the wage rates in the female-dominated jobs to eliminate the wage differential between males and females. A district court had ordered the employer to make the adjustment partially on the basis of the comparable worth theory. However, the Ninth Circuit Court of Appeals[8] overturned this decision. The circuit court ruled that the value of a particular job to an employer is but one factor influencing the rate of compensation for that job. Other considerations may include the availability of workers willing to do the job and the effectiveness of collective bargaining in a particular industry. The court went further and said that a state could enact a comparable worth plan if it so chooses.

The parties to the *AFSCME* v. *State of Washington* suit reached an agreement that settled the dispute. Under the agreement, 35,000 employees in female-dominated jobs reached pay equity with males in 1992. The estimated cost of the settlement to the state was $482 million.

Regardless of the court and EEOC decisions, however, organizations can take certain preventive steps to guard against pay inequities:

1. Employers should attempt to avoid overconcentrations of men or women (or members of various minority groups) in particular jobs.

2. Employers should evaluate whether there is any direct evidence of bias in setting wage rates, such as discriminatory statements or admission. If so and if there are also overconcentrations of females in particular jobs, the employer should formulate a new compensation plan to correct the disparity in the future. The outline of any plan, of course, will depend on each employer's particular situation.

3. Employers should resist, as much as possible, the temptation to deviate from an internal job evaluation survey or a market survey because of difficulties encountered in hiring or retaining employees at the rates established by such surveys.

4. An employer who utilizes a certain type of job evaluation system companywide and then deviates from it obviously runs a severe risk. Job evaluation, discussed in depth in Chapter 13, is a procedure used to determine the relative worth of different jobs.

5. If an employer uses a job evaluation system or systems, it should constantly monitor the system to determine the average wages being paid to men and women for comparable jobs. Any disparities should be examined to see if they are defensible. If not, corrections should be made.

OTHER AREAS OF EMPLOYMENT DISCRIMINATION

Numerous other issues have arisen in the areas of employment discrimination. This section briefly covers some of these additional issues.

Religion

Title VII, as originally enacted, prohibited discrimination based on religion but did not define the term. The 1972 amendments to Title VII added 701(j):

> The term religion includes all aspects of religious observance and practice, as well as belief, unless an employer demonstrates that he is unable to reasonably accommodate an employee's or prospective employee's religious observance or practice without undue hardship on the conduct of the employer's business.

The most frequent accommodation issue under Title VII's religious discrimination provisions arises from the conflict between religious practices and work schedules. The conflict normally occurs for people who observe their Sabbath from sundown on Friday to sundown on Saturday. The EEOC's *Guidelines on Religious Discrimination* proposes the following:

1. Arranging for voluntary substitutes with similar qualifications; promoting an atmosphere where such swaps are regarded favorably; and providing a central file, bulletin board, or other means of facilitating the matching of voluntary substitutes.

2. Flexible scheduling of arrival and departure times; floating or optional holidays; flexible work breaks; and a plan for using lunch time and other time to make up hours lost due to the observation of religious practices.

3. Lateral transfers or changes in job assignments.

One significant case concerning religious discrimination is *TWA* v. *Hardison*.[9] Larry G. Hardison, a TWA employee whose religion required him to observe his Sabbath on Saturday, was discharged when he refused to work on Saturdays. Hardison had previously held a job with TWA that allowed him to avoid Saturday work because of his seniority. However, he voluntarily transferred to another job in which he was near the bottom of the seniority list. Due to his low seniority, he was required to work on Saturdays. TWA refused to violate the seniority provisions of the union contract and also refused to allow him to work a four-day workweek. TWA did agree, however, to permit the union to seek a change of work assignments for Hardison, but the union also refused to violate the seniority provisions of the contract.

The Supreme Court upheld the discharge on the grounds that (1) the employer had made reasonable efforts to accommodate the religious needs of the employee, (2) the employer was not required to violate the seniority provisions of the contract, and (3) the alternative plans of allowing the employee to work a four-day workweek would have constituted an undue hardship for the employer.

The Supreme Court's ruling in this case was that an employer must reasonably accommodate religious preferences unless it creates an undue hardship for the employer. Undue hardship was defined as more than a *de minimus* cost; that is, the employer can prove it has reasonably accommodated a religious preference if it can show that the employee's request would result in more than a small (i.e., *de minimus*) cost to the employer. HRM in Action 3.3 describes a case on religious discrimination.

Native Americans

Courts have found Native Americans to be protected by Title VII. In addition, Section 703(i) of Title VII benefits Native Americans by exempting them from coverage by the act, in that preferential treatment can be given to Native Americans in certain kinds of employment:

> Nothing contained in this title shall apply to any business or enterprise on or near an Indian reservation with respect to any publicly announced employment practice of such business or enterprise under which a preferential treatment is given to any individual because he is an Indian living on or near a reservation.

HIV-Positive Status

In addition, individuals who are diagnosed as HIV-positive, even if they haven't developed symptoms, are considered to be disabled and entitled to the protection of the Americans with Disabilities Act (ADA). The U.S. Supreme Court (*Bragdon* v. *Abbott*) ruled that HIV is so immediately physically devastating that it's an impairment from the moment of infection. In this case, Sidney Abbott revealed her positive status to her dentist, Randon Bragdon, and he refused to fill her tooth cavity in his office but suggested that he do the procedure at a hospital with Abbott incurring the additional expense. Abbott refused and sued Bragdon under the ADA and state law. The Supreme Court ruled in Abbott's favor and held that HIV status is a disability under the ADA.

Sexual Orientation

The EEOC and the courts have uniformly held that Title VII does not prohibit employment discrimination against effeminate males, homosexuals, or masculine-acting females. Courts have also held uniformly that adverse action against individuals who undergo or announce an intention to undergo sex-change surgery does not violate Title VII. Therefore, people who fall in those groups are protected only when a local or state statute is enacted to protect them. More court cases, however, must be decided before a clear picture can be gained concerning discrimination against people in these groups. The current controversy over gay marriages will more than likely have an impact on human resource policies and practices.

Summary of Learning Objectives

1. **Explain the role of the Employer Information Report, EEO–1.**

   This report, also known as *Standard Form 100,* must be completed by employers with 100 or more employees. It requires a breakdown of the employer's workforce in specific job categories by race, sex, and national origin.

2. **Define *employment parity, occupational parity, systemic discrimination, underutilization,* and *concentration*.**

   When employment parity exists, the proportion of minorities and women employed by an organization equals the proportion in the organization's relevant labor market. Occupational parity exists when the proportion of minorities and women employed in various occupations within an organization is equal to their proportion in the organization's relevant labor market. Large differences in either occupational or employment parity are called systemic discrimination. *Underutilization* refers to the practice of having fewer minorities or females in a particular job category than would reasonably be expected when compared to their presence in the relevant labor market. *Concentration* means having more minorities and women in a job category or department than would reasonably be expected when compared to their presence in the relevant labor market.

3. **Describe an affirmative action plan.**

   An AAP is a written document outlining specific goals and timetables for remedying past discriminatory actions.

4. **Define *bona fide occupational qualification (BFOQ)*.**

   BFOQ permits employers to use religion, age, sex, or national origin as a factor in their employment practices when doing so is reasonably necessary to the normal operation of that particular business.

5. **Explain what business necessity means.**

   Business necessity comes into play when an employer has a job requirement that is neutral but excludes members of one sex at a higher rate than members of the other.

6. **Define *sexual harassment*.**

   Sexual harassment is any unwelcome sexual conduct that has the purpose or effect of unreasonably interfering with an individual's work performance or creating an intimidating, hostile, or offensive work environment.

7. **Describe the comparable worth theory.**

   This theory holds that every job by its very nature has a worth to the employer and society and that this worth can be measured and assigned a value.

Key Terms

affirmative action plan, *52*
bona fide occupational
   qualification (BFOQ), *52*
business necessity, *53*
comparable worth
   theory, *55*

concentration, *51*
Employer Information
   Report (Standard
   Form 100), *46*
employment parity, *51*
occupational parity, *51*

relevant labor
   market, *51*
right-to-sue letter, *51*
sexual harassment, *54*
systemic discrimination, *51*
underutilization, *51*

Review Questions

Web site: Federal Legal Information through Electronics
www.fedworld.gov/supcourt

1. What legal powers does the EEOC have?
2. Explain the purpose of the Employer Information Report, EEO–1.
3. What is an applicant diversity chart?
4. Outline the steps in processing a discrimination charge.
5. What is an affirmative action plan?
6. What is BFOQ?
7. Define business necessity as it relates to equal employment opportunity.
8. Outline what actions constitute sexual harassment.
9. Explain what comparable worth means.
10. What steps can be taken to eliminate pay inequities?

Discussion Questions

1. "Comparable worth is an absurd idea." Discuss your views on this statement.
2. "We protect too many classes of people. Why can't we just let employers hire the best person for the job?" Discuss your views on these statements.
3. Identify several jobs for which you feel age or sex would be a BFOQ. Be prepared to discuss these jobs and your reasons for believing that age or sex is a BFOQ.

Incident 3.1

The Layoff

Two years ago, your organization experienced a sudden increase in its volume of work. At about the same time, it was threatened with an equal employment opportunity suit that resulted in an affirmative action plan. Under this plan, the organization has recruited and hired additional women and minority members.

Presently, the top level of management in your organization is anticipating a decrease in volume of work. You have been asked to rank the clerical employees of your section in the event that a layoff is necessary.

Following are biographical data for the seven clerical people in your section. Rank the seven people according to the order in which they should be laid off; that is, the person ranked first is to be laid off first, and so forth.

Burt Greene: White male, age 45. Married, four children, five years with the organization. Reputed to be an alcoholic; poor work record.

Nan Nushka: White female, age 26. Married, no children; husband has a steady job; six months with the organization. Hired after the affirmative action plan went into effect; average work record to date. Saving to buy a home.

Johnny Jones: Black male, age 20. Unmarried; one year with organization. High performance ratings. Reputed to be shy—a "loner"; wants to start his own business some day.

Joe Jefferson: White male, age 24. Married, no children, but wife is pregnant, three years with organization. Going to college at night; erratic performance attributed to work/study conflicts.

Livonia Long: Black female, age 49. Widow, three grown children; two years with the organization. Steady worker whose performance is average.

Ward Watt: White male, age 30. Recently divorced, one child; three years with the organization. Good worker.

Rosa Sanchez: Hispanic female, age 45. Six children, husband disabled one year ago; trying to help support her family; three months with the organization. No performance appraisal data available.

Questions

1. What criteria did you use to rank the employees?
2. What implications does your ranking have in the area of affirmative action?

Incident 3.2

Religion and Real Estate

Gloria and Robert Sapp, who run a real estate agency, are active Seventh-Day Adventists, as are most employees of the agency.

Ruth Armon, who described herself as a lapsed Lutheran at the time of her employment at the agency, states that she was emotionally upset at being unable to "tune out" statements directed to her about impending catastrophes, devil worship by Christian religions, and the asserted inadequacies of her personal religious observances.

She states that she became a target for statements critical of her beliefs and was told by Gloria Sapp that exposure to such statements was unavoidable in that workplace.

After eight months, Ruth Armon says, she had an argument with Robert Sapp growing out of her complaints about the religious talk and left the job, believing she was fired.

Questions

1. Does Ruth Armon have legitimate grounds for filing a religious discrimination case?
2. Should employees have a right to discuss their religious beliefs on the job?

EXERCISE 3.1
Affirmative Action Debate

The class divides into teams of four to five students. Each team should prepare to debate one of the following statements:

1. The federal government should not require affirmative action programs for private enterprise organizations that are federal contractors or subcontractors.
2. Affirmative action programs have been very helpful to minorities and women. Private enterprise organizations should be required to have affirmative action programs.

After the debate, the instructor should list on the board the points made by each team and discuss the issues involved.

EXERCISE 3.2
How Much Do You Know about Sexual Harassment?

A TRUE OR FALSE TEST FOR EMPLOYEES	T	F
1. If I just ignore unwanted sexual attention, it will usually stop.	☐	☐
2. If I don't mean to sexually harass another employee, there's no way my behavior can be perceived by him or her as sexually harassing.	☐	☐
3. Some employees don't complain about unwanted sexual attention from another worker because they don't want to get that person in trouble.	☐	☐
4. If I make sexual comments to someone and that person doesn't ask me to stop, then I guess my behavior is welcome.	☐	☐
5. To avoid sexually harassing a woman who comes to work in a traditionally male workplace, the men simply should not haze her.	☐	☐
6. A sexual harasser may be told by a court to pay part of a judgment to the employee he or she harassed.	☐	☐
7. A sexually harassed man does not have the same legal rights as a woman who is sexually harassed.	☐	☐
8. About 90 percent of all sexual harassment in today's workplace is done by males to females.	☐	☐
9. Sexually suggestive pictures or objects in a workplace don't create a liability unless someone complains.	☐	☐
10. Telling someone to stop his or her unwanted sexual behavior usually doesn't do any good.	☐	☐

Answers: (1) False. (2) False. (3) True. (4) False. (5) False. (6) True. (7) False. (8) True. (9) False. (10) False.

A TEST FOR MANAGEMENT PERSONNEL

		T	F
1.	An employer is not liable for the sexual harassment of one of its employees unless that employee loses specific job benefits or is fired.	☐	☐
2.	A court can require a sexual harasser to pay part of the judgment to the employee he or she has sexually harassed.	☐	☐
3.	A supervisor can be liable for sexual harassment committed by one of his or her employees against another.	☐	☐
4.	An employer can be liable for the sexually harassing behavior of management personnel even if it is unaware of that behavior and has a policy forbidding it.	☐	☐
5.	It is appropriate for a supervisor, when initially receiving a sexual-harassment complaint, to determine if the alleged recipient overreacted or misunderstood the alleged harasser.	☐	☐
6.	When a supervisor is talking with an employee about an allegation of sexual harassment against him or her, it is best to ease into the allegation instead of being direct.	☐	☐
7.	Sexually suggestive visuals or objects in a workplace don't create a liability unless an employee complains about them and management allows them to remain.	☐	☐
8.	The lack of sexual-harassment complaints is a good indication that sexual harassment is not occurring.	☐	☐
9.	It is appropriate for a supervisor to tell an employee to handle unwelcome sexual behavior if he or she thinks that the employee is misunderstanding the behavior.	☐	☐
10.	The intent behind employee A's sexual behavior is more important than the impact of that behavior on employee B when determining if sexual harassment has occurred.	☐	☐

Answers: (1) False. (2) True. (3) True. (4) True. (5) False. (6) False. (7) False. (8) False. (9) False. (10) False.

Source: Adapted from Brian S. Moskal, "Sexual Harassment: An Update," *Industry Week,* November 18, 1991, p. 40.

Notes and Additional Readings

1. For example, see *Ten-Year Check-Up: Have Federal Agencies Responded to Civil Rights Recommendations?* (Washington, D.C.: U.S. Equal Opportunity Commission, 2003).
2. See *EEOC Compliance Manual* (Washington D.C.: U.S. Equal Opportunity Commission, 1999).
3. 7 Pa. Commw. Ct. 500, 300 A. 2d 97, 5 FEP 649.
4. 461 F. Supp. 86, 18 FEP 246 (S.N.D.Y.).
5. 641 F. wd 934, 24 FEP 1155.
6. *County of Washington* v. *Gunther,* 101 Sup. Ct. 2242.
7. *AFSCME* v. *State of Washington,* 32 FEP (BNA) 1577, Western District of Washington.
8. *AFSCME* v. *State of Washington,* CA-9.
9. 432 U.S. 64.

On the Job

Preemployment Inquiry Guide

Subject	Permissible Inquiries	Inquiries That Must Be Avoided
1. Name	"Have you worked for this company under a different name?" "Is any additional information relative to change of name, use of an assumed name, or nickname necessary to enable a check on your work and educational record? If yes, explain."	Inquiries about the name that would indicate applicant's lineage, ancestry, national origin, or descent. Inquiry into previous name of applicant where it has been changed by court order or otherwise. Indicate: Miss, Mrs., Ms.

Preemployment Inquiry Guide *(continued)*

Subject	Permissible Inquiries	Inquiries That Must Be Avoided
2. Marital and Family Status	Whether applicant can meet specified work schedules or has activities, commitments, or responsibilities that may hinder the meeting of work attendance requirements. Inquiries, made to males and females alike, as to the duration of stay on job or anticipated absences.	Any inquiry indicating whether an applicant is married, single, engaged, etc.; number and age of children; information on child care arrangements; any questions concerning pregnancy; any similar question that directly or indirectly results in limitation of job opportunity in any way.
3. Age	If a minor, require proof of age in the form of a work permit or a certificate of age. Require proof of age by birth certificate after being hired. Inquiry as to whether the applicant meets the minimum age requirements as set by law and indication that, on hiring, proof of age must be submitted in the form of a birth certificate or other forms of proof of age. If age is a legal requirement: "If hired, can you furnish proof of age?" Or statement that hire is subject to verification of age. Inquiry as to whether an applicant is younger than the employer's regular retirement age.	Requirement that applicant state age or date of birth. Requirement that applicant produce proof of age in the form of a birth certificate or baptismal record. (The Age Discrimination in Employment Act of 1967 forbids discrimination against persons over the age of 40.)
4. Handicaps/ Disability *(Also see Section IV.F The Americans with Disabilities Act.)*	For employers subject to the provisions of the Rehabilitation Act of 1973, applicants may be "invited" to indicate how and to what extent they are handicapped/disabled. The employer must indicate to applicants that: (1) compliance with the invitation is voluntary; (2) the information is being sought only to remedy discrimination or provide opportunities for the handicapped/disabled; (3) the information will be kept confidential; and (4) refusing to provide the information will not result in adverse treatment. All applicants can be asked if they are able to carry out all necessary job assignments and perform them in a safe manner.	The Rehabilitation Act of 1973 forbids employers from asking job applicants general questions about whether they are handicapped or asking them about the nature and severity of their handicaps. An employer must be prepared to prove that any physical and mental requirements for a job are due to "business necessity" and the safe performance of the job. Except in cases where undue hardship can be proven, employers must make "reasonable accommodations" for the physical and mental limitations of an employee or applicant. "Reasonable accommodation" includes alteration of duties, alteration of physical setting, and provision of aids.
5. Sex	Inquiry as to sex or restriction of employment to one sex is permissible only where a bona fide occupational qualification exists. (This BFOQ exception is interpreted very narrowly by the courts and EEOC.) The burden of proof rests on the employer to prove that the BFOQ does exist and that all members of the affected class are incapable of performing the job.	Sex of applicant. Any other inquiry that would indicate sex. Sex is not a BFOQ because a job involves physical labor (such as heavy lifting) beyond the capacity of some women, nor can employment be restricted just because the job is traditionally labeled "men's work" or "women's work". Sex cannot be used as a factor for determining whether or not an applicant will be satisfied in a particular job. Avoid questions concerning applicant's height or weight unless you can prove they are necessary requirements for the job to be performed.
6. Race or Color	General distinguishing physical characteristics, such as scars.	Applicant's race. Color of applicant's skin, eyes, hair or other questions directly or indirectly indicating race or color.
7. Address or Duration of Residence	Applicant's address. Inquiry into place and length of current and previous addresses, e.g., "How long have you been a resident of this state or city?"	Specific inquiry into foreign addresses that would indicate national origin. Names or relationships of persons with whom applicant resides. Whether applicant owns or rents home.
8. Birthplace	"After employment (if employed by this institution) can you submit a birth certificate or other proof of U.S. citizenship?"	Birthplace of applicant. Birthplace of applicant's parents, spouse, or other relatives. Requirement that applicant submit a birth certificate or naturalization or baptismal record before employment. Any other inquiry into national origin.
9. Religion	An applicant may be advised concerning normal hours and days of work required by the job to avoid possible conflict with religious or other personal convictions.	Applicant's religious denomination or affiliation, church, parish, pastor or religious holidays observed. Applicants may not be told that any particular religious groups are required to work on their religious holidays. Any inquiry to indicate or identify religious denomination or customs.
10. Military record	Type of education and experience in service as it relates to a particular job.	Type of discharge.

Preemployment Inquiry Guide *(continued)*

Subject	Permissible Inquiries	Inquiries That Must Be Avoided
11. Photograph	Indicate that this may be required after hiring for identification.	Requirement that applicant affix a photograph to his or her application. Request that applicant, at his or her option, submit photograph. Requirement of photograph after interview but before hiring.
12. Citizenship	"Are you a citizen of the United States?" "If you are not a U.S. citizen, have you the legal right to remain permanently in the U.S.?" "Do you intend to remain permanently in the U.S.?" "If not a citizen, are you prevented from lawfully becoming employed because of visa or immigration status?" Statement that, if hired, applicant may be required to submit proof of citizenship or authorization to work.	"Of what country are you a citizen?" Whether applicant or his or her parents or spouse are naturalized or native born U.S. citizens. Date when applicant or parents or spouse acquired U.S. citizenship. Requirement that applicant produce his or her naturalization papers. Whether applicant's parents or spouse are citizens of the United States.
13. Ancestry or National Origin	Languages applicant reads, speaks, or writes fluently. (If another language is necessary to perform the job).	Inquiries into applicant's lineage, ancestry, national origin, descent, birthplace, or mother tongue. National origin of applicant's parents/spouse.
14. Education	Applicant's academic, vocational or professional education; school attended. Inquiry into language skills such as reading, speaking and writing foreign languages.	Any inquiry asking specifically the national, racial, or religious affiliation of a school. Inquiry as to how foreign language ability was acquired.
15. Experience	Applicant's work experience, including names and addresses of previous employers, dates of employment, reasons for leaving, salary history. Other countries visited.	
16. Conviction, Arrest, and Court Record	Inquiry into actual convictions that relate reasonably to fitness to perform a particular job. (A conviction is a court ruling where the party is found guilty as charged. An arrest is merely the apprehending or detaining of the person to answer allegations of a crime.)	Any inquiry relating to arrests. Ask or check into a person's arrest, court, or conviction record if not substantially related to functions and responsibilities of the particular job in question.
17. Relatives	Names of applicant's relatives already employed by this company. Name and addresses of parents or guardian of minor applicant.	Name or address of any relative of adult applicant, other than those employed by this company.
18. Experience *(Organizations)*	Inquiry into the organizations of which an applicant is a member, providing the name or character of the organization does not reveal the race, religion, color, or ancestry of the membership. "List all professional organizations to which you belong. What offices have you held?"	"List all organizations, clubs, societies, and lodges to which you belong." The names of organizations to which the applicant belongs if such information would indicate through character or name the race, religion, color, or ancestry of the membership.
19. References	By whom were you referred for a position here? Names of persons willing to provide professional and/or character references for applicant.	Require the submission of a religious reference. Request reference from applicant's pastor.
20. Miscellaneous	Notice to applicants that any misstatements or omissions of material facts in the application may be cause for dismissal.	

NOTE: Any inquiry should be avoided that, although not specifically listed among the above, is designed to elicit information as to race, color, ancestry, age, sex, religion, handicap, or arrest and court record unless based upon a bona fide occupational qualification.

Reprinted with permission from *Human Resource Practices for Small Colleges.* © 1992, National Association of College and University Business Officers.

Chapter **Four**

Job Analysis
and Job Design

Chapter Learning Objectives

After studying this chapter, you should be able to:

1. Define *job analysis* and *job design*.
2. Distinguish among a position, a job, and an occupation.
3. Describe several common uses of a job analysis.
4. Define *job description* and *job specification*.
5. Identify four frequently used methods of job analysis.
6. Discuss why O*NET was developed and summarize what it is.
7. Define *essential functions* and *reasonable accommodation* as interpreted under the Americans with Disabilities Act.
8. Identify several problems frequently associated with job analysis.
9. Define *job scope* and *job depth* and explain their relationship to job design.
10. Explain the sociotechnical approach to job design.
11. Distinguish among the following types of alternative work schedules: flextime, telecommuting, job sharing, and condensed workweek.
12. Define the term *contingent worker*.

Chapter Outline

Basic Terminology
Job Analysis
   Products of Job Analysis
   Job Analysis Methods
   The ADA and Job Analysis
   Potential Problems with Job Analysis
Job Design
   Job Scope and Job Depth
   Sociotechnical Approach to Job Design
   The Physical Work Environment
   Flexible Work Arrangements (FWAs)

Summary of Learning Objectives
Key Terms
Review Questions
Discussion Questions
   Incident 4.1: The Tax Assessor's Office
   Incident 4.2: Turnover Problems
Exercise 4.1: Introduction to O*NET
Exercise 4.2: Writing a Job Description
Exercise 4.3: Performing a Job Analysis
Notes and Additional Readings
On the Job: Sample Job Analysis Questionnaire

The first step in the process of acquiring the organization's human resources is to specify precisely the kind of work that needs to be done and just how that work should be done. Job analysis and job design are the processes used to determine this.

job analysis
Process of determining and reporting pertinent information relating to the nature of a specific job.

Job analysis is "the process of determining and reporting pertinent information relating to the nature of a specific job. It is the determination of the tasks that comprise the job and the skills, knowledge, abilities, and responsibilities required of the holder for successful job performance."[1] Put another way, job analysis is the process of determining, through observation and study, the pertinent information relating to the nature of a specific job.

Job analysis serves as the beginning point of many human resource functions. Jobs must be analyzed before many of the other human resource functions can be performed. For example, effective recruitment is not possible unless the recruiter knows and communicates the requirements of the job. Similarly, it is impossible to design basic wage systems without having clearly defined jobs.

Job design is the process of structuring work and designating the specific work activities of an individual or group of individuals to achieve certain organizational objectives. Job design addresses the basic question of how the job is to be performed, who is to perform it, and where it is to be performed.

Job analysis and job design are directly linked to each other. In practice, most job analyses are performed on existing jobs that have previously been designed. However, it is not unusual for a job to be redesigned as the result of a recent job analysis. For example, a job analysis might reveal that the current method of performing a job (the job design) is inefficient or contains unnecessary tasks. New technology can also cause the content of a job to change. For example, think of how computers have changed the content of thousands of jobs.

Job analysis and job design processes are usually conducted by industrial engineers and entry level human resource specialists. However, because both of these processes are basic to so many human resource functions, every human resource manager should have a thorough understanding of them.

job design
Process of structuring work and designating the specific work activities of an individual or group of individuals to achieve certain organizational objectives.

BASIC TERMINOLOGY

micromotion
Simplest unit of work; involves very elementary movements, such as reaching, grasping, positioning, or releasing an object.

element
Aggregation of two or more micromotions; usually thought of as a complete entity, such as picking up or transporting an object.

task
Consisting of one or more elements; one of the distinct activities that constitute logical and necessary steps in the performance of work by an employee. A task is performed whenever human effort, physical or mental, is exerted for a specific purpose.

Today, the word *job* has different meanings depending on how, when, or by whom it is used. It is often used interchangeably with the words *position* and *task*. This section defines terms frequently encountered in job design and job analysis and shows how these terms relate to each other.

The simplest unit of work is the micromotion. A **micromotion** involves a very elementary movement, such as reaching, grasping, positioning, or releasing an object. An aggregation of two or more micromotions forms an element. An **element** is a complete entity, such as picking up, transporting, and positioning an item. A grouping of work elements makes up a work task. Related **tasks** comprise the **duties** of a job.

Distinguishing between tasks and duties is not always easy. It is sometimes helpful to view tasks as subsets of duties. For example, suppose one duty of a receptionist is to handle all incoming correspondence. One task, as part of this duty, would be to respond to all routine inquiries. Duties, when combined with **responsibilities** (obligations to be performed), define a **position.** A group of positions that are identical with respect to their major tasks and responsibilities form a **job.** The difference between a position and a job is that a job may be held by more than one person, whereas a position cannot. For example, an organization may have two receptionists performing the same job; however, they occupy two separate positions. A group of similar jobs forms an occupation. Because the job of receptionist requires similar skills, effort, and responsibility in different organizations, being a receptionist may be viewed as an **occupation.** Figure 4.1 graphically shows the relationships among elements, tasks, duties, responsibilities, positions, jobs, and occupations.

JOB ANALYSIS

duties
One or more tasks performed in carrying out a job responsibility.

responsibilities
Obligations to perform certain tasks and assume certain duties.

position
Collection of tasks and responsibilities constituting the total work assignment of a single employee.

As defined in the introduction to this chapter, *job analysis* is the process of determining and reporting pertinent information relating to the nature of a specific job. It involves determining the tasks that comprise the job and the skills, knowledge, abilities, and responsibilities required of the holder for successful job performance. The end product of a job analysis is a job description, which is a written description of the actual requirements of the job. Job descriptions are discussed later in this section.

As mentioned in the chapter introduction, job analysis is the beginning point of many human resource functions. Specifically, data obtained from job analysis form the basis for a variety of human resource activities.[2] These activities include the following:

Job definition. A job analysis results in a description of the duties and responsibilities of the job. Such a description is useful to the current jobholders and their supervisors as well as to prospective employees.

FIGURE 4.1
Relationships among Different Job Components

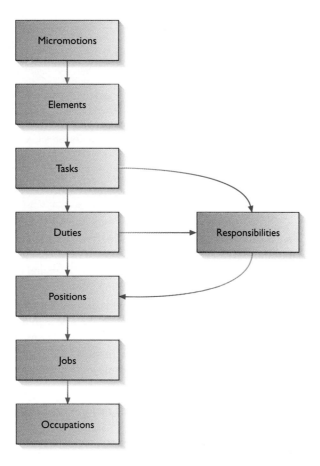

job
Group of positions that are identical with respect to their major or significant tasks and responsibilities and sufficiently alike to justify their being covered by a single analysis. One or many persons may be employed in the same job.

occupation
A grouping of similar jobs or job classes.

recruitment
Process of seeking and attracting a pool of people from which qualified candidates for job vacancies can be chosen.

selection
Process of choosing from those available the individuals who are most likely to perform successfully in a job.

orientation
Introduction of new employees to the organization, work unit, and job.

training
Learning process that involves the acquisition of skills, concepts, rules, or attitudes to increase employee performance.

Job redesign. A job analysis often indicates when a job needs to be redesigned.

Recruitment. Regardless of whether a job to be filled has been in existence or is newly created, its requirements must be defined as precisely as possible for **recruitment** to be effective. A job analysis not only identifies the job requirements but also outlines the skills needed to perform the job. This information helps identify characteristics sought in the people to be recruited.

Selection and placement. **Selection** is basically a matter of properly matching an individual with a job. For the process to be successful, the job and its requirements must be clearly and precisely known. A job analysis determines the importance of different skills and abilities. Once it has been completed, various candidates can be compared more objectively.

Orientation. Effective job **orientation** cannot be accomplished without a clear understanding of the job requirements. The duties and responsibilities of a job must be clearly defined before a new employee can be taught how to perform the job.

Training. Job analysis affects many aspects of **training.** Whether or not a current or potential jobholder needs additional training can be decided only after the specific requirements of the job have been determined through a job analysis. Similarly, establishing training objectives depends on a job analysis. Another training-related use of job analysis is to help determine whether a problem is occurring because of a training need or for some other reason.

Career counseling. Managers and human resource specialists are in a much better position to counsel employees about their careers when they have a complete understanding of the different jobs in the organization. Similarly, employees can better appreciate their career options when they understand the exact requirements of other jobs.

Employee safety. A thorough job analysis often uncovers unsafe practices and/or environmental conditions associated with a job. Focusing precisely on how a job is done usually uncovers any unsafe procedures.

TABLE 4.1
Information Provided by a Job Analysis

Area of Information	Contents
Job title and location	Name of job and where it is located.
Organizational relationship	A brief explanation of the number of persons supervised (if applicable) and the job title(s) of the position(s) supervised. A statement concerning supervision received.
Relation to other jobs	Describes and outlines the coordination required by the job.
Job summary	Condensed explanation of the content of the job.
Information concerning job requirements	The content of this area varies greatly from job to job and from organization to organization. Typically it includes information on such topics as machines, tools, and materials; mental complexity and attention required; physical demands; and working conditions.

Performance appraisal. The objective of performance appraisal is to evaluate an individual employee's performance on a job. A prerequisite is a thorough understanding of exactly what the employee is supposed to do. Then and only then can a fair evaluation be made of how an individual is performing.

Compensation. A proper job analysis helps ensure that employees receive fair compensation for their jobs. Job analysis is the first step in determining the relative worth of a job by identifying its level of difficulty, its duties and responsibilities, and the skills and abilities required to perform the job. Once the worth of a job has been established relative to other jobs, the employer can determine an equitable wage or salary schedule.

As the above list demonstrates, many of the major human resource functions depend to some extent on a sound job analysis program.

When performing a job analysis, the job and its requirements (as opposed to the characteristics of the person currently holding the job) are studied. The analyst lists the tasks that comprise the job and determines the skills, personality characteristics, educational background, and training necessary for successfully performing the job. The initial stage of a job analysis should "report the job as it exists at the time of the analysis, not as it should exist, not as it has existed in the past, and not as it exists in similar establishments."[3] Table 4.1 outlines the general information a job analysis provides.

Products of Job Analysis

Job analysis involves not only analyzing job content but also reporting the results of the analysis. These results are normally presented in the form of a job description and a job specification. A **job description** concentrates on describing the job as it is currently being performed. It explains, in written form, what the job is called, what it requires to be done, where it is to be done, and how it is to be done. While the formats for job descriptions vary somewhat, most job descriptions contain sections that include the following: the job name, a brief summary description of the job, a listing of job duties and responsibilities, and an explanation of organizational relationships pertinent to the job. A **job specification** concentrates on the knowledge, skills, abilities, and other characteristics (KSAOs) needed to perform the job. Knowledge refers to identifiable factual information necessary to perform the job. Skills are specific proficiencies necessary for performing the tasks that make up the job. Abilities refer to general and enduring capabilities for doing the job. Other characteristics include any other pertinent characteristics not covered under knowledge, skills, and abilities. A job specification may be prepared as a separate document or, as is more often the case, as the concluding section of a job description. Table 4.2 summarizes the information typically contained in a job description (including the job specification).

A potential problem with all job descriptions is that they may become outdated. Often the job description is not periodically updated to reflect changes that have occurred in the job. A good practice is to have the jobholder and his or her supervisor review the most current job description *annually* and determine whether the description needs updating. Ordinarily

job description
Written synopsis of the nature and requirements of a job.

job specification
Description of the competency, educational, and experience qualifications the incumbent must possess to perform the job.

TABLE 4.2
Contents of a Job Description

A job description should be a formal, written document, usually from one to three pages long. It should include the following:

- Date written.
- Job status (full-time or part-time; salary or wage).
- Position title.
- Job summary (a synopsis of the job responsibilities).
- Detailed list of duties and responsibilities.
- Supervision received (to whom the jobholder reports).
- Supervision exercised, if any (who reports to this employee).
- Principal contacts (in and outside the organization).
- Related meetings to be attended and reports to be filed.
- Competency or position requirements.
- Required education and experience.
- Career mobility (position[s] for which jobholder may qualify next).

this review need not take much time; however, it seldom takes place at all unless a systematic effort is made. If the job description needs updating, the jobholder should play a central role in revising it. Similarly, when a job description is being developed initially, the jobholder should be involved in the process.

Job Analysis Methods

As mentioned earlier, most job analyses are conducted by industrial engineering or entry level human resources specialists. However, it is necessary that human resources managers at all levels fully understand this process. Several methods are available for conducting a job analysis. Studies have shown that no one method is best for all situations but rather depends on the specific use of the job analysis information. Four of the most frequently used methods are discussed below, as is O*NET, an important tool that all these methods can utilize.

1. Observation

Observation is a method of analyzing jobs that is relatively simple and straightforward. It can be used independently or in conjunction with other methods of job analysis. With observation, the person making the analysis observes the individual or individuals performing the job and takes pertinent notes describing the work. This information includes such things as what was done, how it was done, how long it took, what the job environment was like, and what equipment was used.

Motion Study and Time Study   Motion study and time study are both frequently used observation methods. **Motion study** (sometimes called *methods study*) involves determining the most efficient way to do a task or job. Basically, motion study identifies the motions and movements necessary for performing a task or job and then designs the most efficient methods for putting those motions and movements together.

motion study
Job analysis method that involves determining the motions and movements necessary for performing a task or job and then designing the most efficient methods for putting those motions and movements together.

time study
Job analysis method that determines the elements of work required to perform the job, the order in which those elements occur, and the times required to perform them effectively.

Time study is the analysis of a job or task to determine the elements of work required to perform it, the order in which these elements occur, and the times required to perform them effectively. The objective of a time study is to determine how long it should take an average person to perform the job or task in question.

One drawback to using the observation method is that the observer must be carefully trained to know what to look for and what to record. It is sometimes helpful to use a form with standard categories of information to be filled in as the job is observed to ensure that certain basic information is not omitted. A second drawback of most observation methods is that the application is somewhat limited to jobs involving short and repetitive cycles. Complicated jobs and jobs that do not have repetitive cycles require such a lengthy observation period that direct observation becomes impractical. For example, it would require a tremendous amount of time to observe the work of a traveling salesperson or a lawyer. On the other hand, the job analyst can use direct observation to get a feel for a particular job and then combine this method with another method

work sampling
Job analysis method based on taking statistical samples of job actions throughout the workday and then drawing inferences about the requirements and demands of the job.

to thoroughly analyze the job. Another possibility is to use work sampling. **Work sampling** is a type of observation method based on taking statistical samples of job actions throughout the workday, as opposed to continuous observation of all actions. By taking an adequate number of samples, inferences can be drawn about the requirements and demands of the job.

2. Interviews

The *interview* method requires that the person conducting the job analysis meet with and interview the jobholder. Usually the interview is held at the job site. Interviews can be either structured or unstructured. Unstructured interviews have no definite checklist or preplanned format; the format develops as the interview unfolds. A structured interview follows a pre-designed format. Structured interviews have the advantage of ensuring that all pertinent aspects of the job are covered. Also, they make it easier to compare information obtained from different people holding the same job.

The major drawback to the interview method is that it can be extremely time-consuming because of the time required to schedule, get to, and actually conduct the interview. This problem is naturally compounded when several people are interviewed about the same job.

3. Questionnaires

Job analysis questionnaires are typically three to five pages long and contain both objective and open-ended questions. For existing jobs, the incumbent completes the questionnaire, has it checked by the immediate manager, and returns it to the job analyst. If the job analyzed is new, the questionnaire is normally sent to the manager who will supervise the employee in the new job. If the job being analyzed is vacant but is duplicated in another part of the organization, the questionnaire is completed by the incumbent in the duplicate job. The On the Job example at the end of this chapter contains a sample job analysis questionnaire.

The questionnaire method can obtain information from a large number of employees in a relatively short time period. Hence, questionnaires are used when a large input is needed and time and cost are limiting factors. A major disadvantage is the possibility that either the respondent or the job analyst will misinterpret the information. Also, questionnaires can be time-consuming and expensive to develop.

A popular variation of the questionnaire method is to have the incumbent write an actual description of the job, subject to the approval of the immediate supervisor. A primary advantage of this approach is that the incumbent is often the person most knowledgeable about the job. In addition, this method helps to identify any differences in the incumbent's and the manager's perceptions about the job.

Position Analysis Questionnaire (PAQ)   The *Position Analysis Questionnaire*[4] is a highly specialized instrument for analyzing any job in terms of employee activities. It uses six major categories of employee activities (see Table 4.3). A total of 187 descriptors, called job elements, describe the six categories in detail. Using a five-point scale, one can analyze each description for the degree to which it applies to the job. The original version now referred to as PAQc was modified in 2004 for use in research and academic settings. The original PAQc is still the version used in industry.

The primary advantage of the PAQ is that it can be used to analyze almost any type of job. Also, it is relatively easy to use. The major disadvantage is the sheer length of the questionnaire.

Management Position Description Questionnaire (MPDQ)   The *MPDQ* is a highly structured questionnaire designed specifically for analyzing managerial jobs. It contains 208 items relating to managerial responsibilities, restrictions, demands, and other miscellaneous position characteristics.[5] These 208 items are grouped under the 13 categories shown in Table 4.4. Like the PAQ, the MPDQ requires the analyst to check whether each item is appropriate to the job being analyzed.

4. Functional Job Analysis

Functional job analysis (FJA) is a job analysis method developed by the Employment and Training Administration of the Department of Labor. FJA uses standardized statements and terminology to describe the content of jobs. Functional job analysis collects detailed task

TABLE 4.3
Employee Activity Categories Used in the PAQ

Category	Description	Examples
Information	Where and how does the employee get the information used in performing the job?	Use of written materials. Near-visual differentiation.
Mental processes	What reasoning, decision-making, planning, and information-processing activities are involved in performing the job?	Level of reasoning in problem solving. Coding/decoding.
Physical activities	What physical activities does the employee perform, and what tools or devices are used?	Use of keyboard devices. Assembling/disassembling.
Relationships with other people	What relationships with other people are required in performing the job?	Instructing. Contacts with public and/or customers.
Job context	In what physical or social context is the work performed?	High temperature. Interpersonal conflict situations.
Other job characteristics	What activities, conditions, or characteristics other than those described above are relevant to the job?	Specified work pace. Amount of job structure.

statements and then rates them according to function level or function orientation. Function level describes how an employee interacts with data, people, and things. Function orientation describes the amount of time (using percentages) the employee spends on the tasks of each functional level. In addition, each task statement is analyzed and rated to determine the skills needed to perform the task it describes. Functional job analysis results in position-specific information about the work being performed and standardized information about both the work and the person performing the work.

*Occupational Information Network (O*NET)*

First compiled by the federal government in the 1930s, the Dictionary of Occupational Titles (DOT) described thousands of jobs (the last edition in 1991 described over 12,000 jobs). For over 60 years employees used the DOT to help staff jobs. However, by the early 1990s it became evident that the DOT was becoming obsolete and inefficient. The information DOT provided was very job specific and dated in many cases; the system did not provide for any type of cross-job comparisons for job similarities and differences, and the system did not directly identify what characteristics employees needed to perform the job or under what conditions the job was performed.

To overcome the problems of the DOT, the U.S. Department of Labor abandoned the DOT in 1998 and developed a new system called the **occupational information network (O*NET)**.[6] The O*NET system is the United States' primary source of occupational information. Central to the O*NET system is the O*NET database, which is a comprehensive online database of employee attributes and job characteristics. It provides definitions and

Occupational Information Network (O*NET)
The United States' primary source of occupational information. The **O*NET database** is a comprehensive online database of employee attributes and job characteristics. www.onet.center.org

TABLE 4.4
Management Position Description Questionnaire Categories

Source: Adapted from W. B. Tornov and P. R. Pinto, "The Development of a Managerial Job Taxonomy: A System for Describing, Classifying, and Evaluating Executive Positions," *Journal of Applied Psychology* 61, No. 4 (1976), p. 414.

1. Product, marketing, and financial strategy planning.
2. Coordination of other organizational units and personnel.
3. Internal business control.
4. Products and services responsibility.
5. Public and customer relations.
6. Advanced consulting.
7. Autonomy of actions.
8. Approval of financial commitments.
9. Staff service.
10. Supervision.
11. Complexity and stress.
12. Advanced financial responsibility.
13. Broad personnel responsibility.

FIGURE 4.2
The Content Model
Forming the Foundation
of O*NET

Source: O*Net Online, http://
www.onetcenter.org/content.html

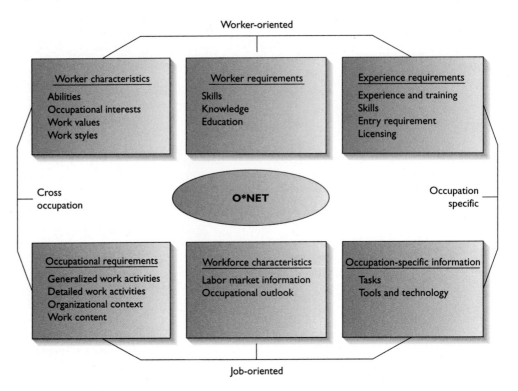

concepts for describing employee attributes and workplace requirements that can be broadly understood. By using comprehensive terms to describe knowledge, skills, abilities (KSAs), interests, and content of work, the O*NET database can accommodate rapidly changing job requirements. The O*NET database is continually updated by surveying a broad range of employees from each occupation. The goal is to replenish the entire database every five years. Figure 4.2 displays the conceptual foundation of O*NET. Called the Content Model, this model encapsulates the key features of an occupation into a standardized, measurable set of variables called "descriptors." The model starts with six domains (see Figure 4.2) that describe the day-to-day aspects of the job and the qualifications and interests of the typical worker. The model expands to 277 descriptors collected by the O*NET program, with more collected by other federal agencies such as the Bureau of Labor Statistics. As Figure 4.2 shows, the Content Model uses both job-oriented descriptors and worker-oriented descriptors. The model also allows occupational information to be applied across jobs, sectors, or industries (cross-occupation descriptors) and within occupations (occupational-specific descriptors).

While the Content Model identifies the information structure for a single occupation, the O*NET-SOC taxonomy identifies existing work occupations. The June 2009 release of the O*NET-SOC taxonomy includes 1,102 occupational titles, 965 of which have data collected from job incumbents or occupation experts. New workforce requirements brought about by changes in technology, society, law, and business practices are resulting in new and emerging (N&E) occupations. In order to reflect these changes, the O*NET system periodically incorporates the N&E occupations into the O*NET-SOC taxonomy. O*NET data can be linked to other occupational, educational, and labor market information databases. HRM in Action 4.1 describes how the American Foundation for the Blind is using O*NET.

The ADA and Job Analysis[7]

As discussed in Chapter 2, the *Americans with Disabilities Act (ADA)* and its amendments (ADAAA) prohibit discrimination against qualified individuals with disabilities in regard to all employment practices, terms, conditions, or privileges of employment. In essence, this prohibition covers the entire employment process. "Qualified individuals with disabilities" are persons who have a disability and meet the skill, education, experience, and other job-related requirements of the position held or desired and can perform the essential functions

O*NET USED TO HELP THE BLIND AND VISUALLY IMPAIRED BROADEN THEIR CAREER OPPORTUNITIES

According to studies by the American Foundation for the Blind (AFB), a majority of blind and visually impaired adults of working age are capable and want to work. However, over a million (55–60 percent) are unemployed. Dr. Karen Wolffe of AFB realized that one problem was that many blind and visually impaired people possessed a limited view of the available workplace opportunities simply because they could not see what most other employees could see. As a result of their lack of understanding about the diversity of jobs available in the labor market, many often made very poor decisions.

Aware of the O*NET system, Dr. Wolffe decided to download the database and make those items best suited to her clients accessible to them. The result was CareerConnect™, which helps the blind and visually impaired learn about the range and diversity of occupations available in the labor market. CareerConnect incorporates selected O*NET data and makes it possible for users to browse by job category, personal interest, or by title or keyword. The search results include detailed occupational descriptions, a list of related occupations, a list of available mentors as well as practical tips.

In its first year of operation, the service logged almost 3,000 visitors and 100,000 page views. Statistics suggest that visitors mostly found information of interest since the average visit was for 15 minutes.

Source: www.workforceaguirre.org. Accessed January 9, 2007.

of the position with or without reasonable accommodation. The ADA and the ADAAA also require the identification of the essential functions of each job and a reasonable accommodation to the disabilities of qualified individuals. The job analysis process is the basic method used to identify essential job functions. An *essential job function* is one that is fundamental to successful performance of the job; in contrast, *marginal job functions* may be performed at certain times but are incidental to the main purpose of the job. A particular job function is considered marginal if its performance is a matter of convenience and not a necessity. Table 4.5 presents several questions that should be asked to determine whether a particular job function is essential.

Reasonable accommodation means the employer may be required to alter the conditions of a particular job so as to enable the candidate to perform all essential functions. However, an employer cannot be required to make an accommodation that causes undue hardship for the employer. Undue hardship refers to any accommodation that would be unduly costly, substantial, or disruptive or that would fundamentally alter the nature or operation of the business.

Potential Problems with Job Analysis

In analyzing jobs, certain problems can occur. Some of these problems result from natural human behavior; others stem from the nature of the job analysis process. Some of the most frequently encountered problems associated with job analyses are the following:[8]

Top management support is missing. Top management should at least make it clear to all employees that their full and honest participation is extremely important to the process. Unfortunately, the message is often not communicated.

TABLE 4.5
Questions to Be Addressed to Determine Essential Functions

Source: Wayne E. Barlow and Edward Z. Hare, "A Practical Guide to the Americans with Disabilities Act," *Personnel Journal,* June 1992, p. 54.

1. Does the position exist to perform these functions? If the performance of a particular function is the principal purpose for hiring a person, it would be an essential function.
2. Would the removal of the function fundamentally alter the position? If the purpose of the position can be fulfilled without performing the function, it isn't essential.
3. What's the degree of expertise or skill required to perform the function? The fact that an employee is hired for his or her specialized expertise to perform a particular function is evidence that the function is essential.
4. How much of the employee's time is spent performing the function? The fact that an employee spends a substantial amount of time performing a particular function is evidence that the function is essential.
5. What are the consequences of failure to perform the function? The fact that the consequences of failure are severe is evidence that the function is essential.
6. How many other employees are available among whom the function can be distributed? The smaller the number of employees available for performing a group of functions, the greater the likelihood that any one of them will have to perform a particular function.

Only a single means and source are used for gathering data. As discussed in this chapter, there are many proven methods for gathering job data. All too often, a job analysis relies on only one of these methods when a combination of methods might provide better data.

The supervisor and the jobholder do not participate in the design of the job analysis procedure. Too many analyses are planned and implemented by one person who assumes exclusive responsibility for the project. The jobholder and his or her supervisor should be involved in the planning of the project.

No training or motivation exists for jobholders. Job incumbents are potentially a great source of information about the job. Unfortunately, they are seldom trained or prepared to generate quality data for a job analysis. Also, jobholders are rarely made aware of the importance of the data and almost never rewarded for providing good data.

Employees are not allowed sufficient time to complete the analysis. Usually a job analysis is conducted as though it were a crash program, and employees are not given sufficient time to do a thorough job analysis.

Activities may be distorted. Without proper training and preparation, employees may submit distorted data, either intentionally or not. For example, employees are likely to speed up if they know they are being watched. Employee involvement from the beginning of the project is a good way to minimize this problem.

Participants fail to critique the job. Many job analyses do not go beyond the initial phase of reporting what the jobholder currently does. These data are extremely valuable, but the analysis should not stop here. The job should be critiqued to determine whether it is being done correctly or whether improvements can be made.

JOB DESIGN

As mentioned in the introduction to this chapter, job design is the process of structuring work and designating the specific work activities of an individual or group of individuals to achieve certain organizational objectives. Designing a job involves making decisions as to who, what, where, when, why, and how the job will be performed.

The job design process can generally be divided into three phases:

1. The specification of individual tasks: What different tasks must be performed?
2. The specification of the method of performing each task: Specifically, how will each task be performed?
3. The combination of individual tasks into specific jobs to be assigned to individuals: How will the different tasks be grouped to form jobs?[9]

Phases 1 and 3 determine the content of the job, while phase 2 indicates precisely how the job is to be performed. The overall goal of job design is to develop work assignments that meet the requirements of the organization and the technology, and that satisfy the personal and individual requirements of the jobholder.[10] The key to successful job design is to balance the requirements of the organization and the jobholder. For many years, the prevailing practice in designing jobs was to focus almost entirely on simplifying the tasks to be undertaken. This usually resulted in making jobs as specialized as possible. While job specialization has many advantages, as outlined in Table 4.6, it can result in boredom and even degradation of the jobholder. A classic example of specialization is the automobile assembly line. The idea is to specialize but not overdo it. HRM in Action 4.2 discusses a very early example of specialization.

TABLE 4.6
Advantages of Job Specialization

1. Fewer skills required per person, which makes it easier to recruit and train employees.
2. Increased proficiency through repetition and practice of the same tasks.
3. More efficient use of skills by primarily utilizing each employee's best skills.
4. Low wages due to the ease with which labor can be substituted.
5. More conformity in the final product or service.
6. Different tasks performed concurrently.

Job Scope and Job Depth

job scope
Number and variety of tasks performed by the jobholder.

Job scope and job depth are two important dimensions of job design. **Job scope** refers to the number and variety of different tasks performed by the jobholder. In a job with narrow scope, the jobholder performs a few different tasks and repeats those tasks frequently. The negative effects of jobs limited in scope vary with the jobholder, but can result in more errors and lower quality. The job of a toll booth operator would be an example of a job with narrow scope.

job depth
Freedom of jobholders to plan and organize their own work, work at their own pace, and move around and communicate.

Job depth refers to the freedom of jobholders to plan and organize their own work, work at their own pace, and move around and communicate as desired. A lack of job depth can result in job dissatisfaction, which in turn can lead to tardiness, absenteeism, and even sabotage. The job of most traveling salespeople would be relatively high in job depth.

A job can be high in job scope and low in job depth, or vice versa. For example, newspaper delivery involves the same few tasks each time, but there is considerable freedom in organizing and pacing the work. Therefore, the job is low in scope but high in depth. Of course, many jobs are low (or high) in both job scope and job depth. Most assembly line jobs are narrow (or low) in job scope and low in job depth.

Sociotechnical Approach to Job Design

The *sociotechnical approach* to job design was first introduced as an alternative to viewing job design strictly as a matter of specializing the job as much as possible. The thrust of the sociotechnical approach is that both the technical system and the accompanying social system should be considered when designing jobs.[11] According to this concept, employers should design jobs by taking a holistic, or systems, view of the entire job situation, including its physical and social environment. The sociotechnical approach is situational because few jobs involve identical technical requirements and social surroundings. Specifically, the sociotechnical approach requires that the job designer carefully consider the role of the employees in the sociotechnical system, the nature of the tasks performed, and the autonomy of the work group. Ideally, the sociotechnical approach merges the technical needs of the organization with the social needs of the employees involved in decision making. The following guidelines use the sociotechnical approach to designing jobs:[12]

1. A job needs to be reasonably demanding for the individual in terms other than sheer endurance, yet provide some variety (not necessarily novelty).
2. Employees need to be able to learn on the job and to continue learning.
3. Employees need some minimum area of decision making that they can call their own.
4. Employees need some minimal degree of social support and recognition in the workplace.
5. Employees need to be able to relate what they do and what they produce to their social lives.
6. Employees need to believe that the job leads to some sort of desirable future.

The sociotechnical approach to job design has been applied in many countries, often under the heading "autonomous work groups," "Japanese-style work groups," or employee involvement

SOCIOTECHNICAL SYSTEM HUNDREDS OF YEARS AGO?

The origins of modern-day sociotechnical systems are usually attributed to the Travistock Institute in England and their work immediately following World War II. The attempt of these researchers was to "optimize" the relationship between the social and technical systems within an organization. There is evidence, however, that early forms of sociotechnical systems existed much earlier and specifically among the miners in Cornwall, England.

Mining in Cornwall can be traced back to before recorded history. Cornish miners were afforded a significant amount of political autonomy from the early 1200s, and this resulted in an economic environment conducive to successful resource development as well as technological innovation and a spirit of entrepreneurship. Individual miners organized themselves in self-selected work teams and worked under compensation arrangements that aligned the interests of the miners and the owners. The teams' immediate bosses, known as "captains," were typically elected by the miners and empowered by the owners. Miners were not considered to be laborers who, at the time, were paid straight wages. The system resulted in the miners being in a form of partnership with the mine owners. Cornish miners also made many technological advances in mining and, thus, had to integrate these changes into their jobs.

It is also interesting to note that Cornish mining expatriates were widely present in California by 1865 and that they brought their effective sociotechnical systems with them. As in Cornwall, these systems utilized the skills and abilities of the miners to effectively carry out their work roles and tasks, while meeting the goals and values of both the miners and mine management.

Source: Frederick Wolf, Bruce Finnie, and Linda Gibson, "Cornish Miners in California: 150 Years of a Unique Sociotechnical System," *Journal of Management History,* 2008, vol. 14, iss. 2, pp. 144–160.

(EI) teams.[13] Modern-day job designs based on the concepts of self-managed work teams or group productivity usually have their roots in the sociotechnical approach. HRM in Action 4.3 discusses a very early sociotechnical system.

The Physical Work Environment

The physical work environment, which includes factors such as temperature, humidity, ventilation, noise, lighting, color, and spatial density, can have an impact on the design of jobs. While studies clearly show that adverse physical conditions have a negative effect on performance and health, the degree of influence varies from individual to individual. In general, the physical work environment should allow for normal lighting, temperature, ventilation, and humidity. Baffles, acoustical wall materials, and sound absorbers should be used where necessary to reduce unpleasant noises. Soothing colors should be used whenever possible. If employees must be exposed to less-than-ideal physical conditions, it is wise to limit these exposures to short periods of time to minimize the probability that the employee will suffer any permanent physical or psychological damage.

When designing jobs, thought should also be given to the mental and psychological impacts of the physical environment. Consideration should be given to how the physical work environment of the job impacts the mental stress of the jobholder. For example, one recent study found that employees in spacially dense work areas (those with relatively little space available per person) experienced higher levels of tardiness and intentions to transfer as well as lower satisfactions with their work areas.[14] Stress in the workplace is discussed in depth in Chapter 16 (Employee Safety and Health).

The implementation of the Occupational Safety and Health Act (OSHA) in 1970 magnified the importance of safety considerations in the design process. Designed to reduce the incidence of job-related injuries and illnesses, the act outlines very specific federal safety guidelines that all organizations in the United States must follow. Chapter 16 discusses OSHA at length.

Flexible Work Arrangements (FWAs)

Other factors and arrangements that affect job design are the work schedule and alternative work arrangements. In the last several years, organizations have increasingly departed from traditional work schedules and work arrangements in an attempt to increase productivity or decrease cost. While changes in work schedules and work arrangements do not generally alter work to be done, they can affect how the work is allocated. *Flexible work arrangements*

FLEXIBILITY AT FIRST TENNESSEE BANK

First Tennessee Bank, headquartered in Memphis, has a culture that puts employees first. As explained by bank president Frank Schriner, "We learned that when our employees were delighted, they made our customers happy too." When management asked the employees what they needed to be happy at work, flexibility was a big part of their answer. The bank management took their answer seriously and subsequently implemented a wide range of practices to encourage flexible work arrangements throughout the bank.

Recruiting conversations by the bank employees emphasize flexibility from the start. The same message is interwoven into training for incoming managers. The bank's *Leadership Success Guide* and Web site also emphasize flexibility guidelines. The bank measures how it's doing with its employees through yearly surveys. The following specific examples are from the bank's Chattanooga office:

- All tellers can reschedule their hours every three weeks.
- Many employees are allowed to work from home using their laptops.
- Employees can take time to care for an ailing relative.
- Unpaid leaves of up to 16 weeks can be obtained.
- Part-time schedules can be arranged.

First Tennessee boasts one of the highest customer retention rates of any bank in the United States.

Source: *When Work Works: Making Work "Work"* (New York: Families and Work Institute, 2007), pp. 1–2.

(FWAs) is a relatively new term that refers to alternative work schedules and arrangements. FWAs allow an employee to alter the time and/or place when/where work is conducted on a regular basis, consistent and predictable with the employer's operations."[15] Some of the most commonly encountered FWAs are flextime, telecommuting, job sharing, condensed work week, and the use of contingent workers. HRM in Action 4.4 describes why and how First Tennessee Bank is utilizing flexible work arrangements.

Flextime

Flextime, or flexible working hours, allows employees to choose, within certain limits, when they start and end their workday. Usually the organization defines a core period (such as 10 A.M. to 3 P.M.) when all employees will be at work. Each employee then decides when to start and end the workday as long as the hours encompass the core period. Some flextime programs allow employees to vary the hours worked each day as long as they meet some specific weekly total, which is usually 40 hours. Flextime has the advantage of allowing employees to accommodate different lifestyles and schedules. Other potential advantages include avoiding rush hours, having less absenteeism and tardiness, and improved health.[16] From the employer's viewpoint, flextime can have the advantage of providing an edge in recruiting new employees and also in retaining hard-to-find qualified employees. Organizations with flextime schedules may also see an increase in productivity.[17] On the downside, flextime can create communication and coordination problems for supervisors and managers. The 2009 Employee Benefits Survey conducted by SHRM reported that 54 percent of the respondents offered flextime that allowed employees to select their work hours within limits established by the employer.[18]

Telecommuting

Telecommuting is the practice of working at home or while traveling and being able to interact with the office. Today's information technology (PCs, the Internet, cellular phones, etc.) has made telecommuting a reality for many companies. Higher gasoline prices have also had an impact on the popularity of telecommuting. According to a survey sponsored by the Telework Advisory Group for World at Work, approximately 17.2 million Americans worked from home or remotely at least one day per month for their employer in 2008.[19] These telecommuters are known as employee telecommuters. This same survey also reported that approximately 16.6 million Americans who work on contract, are self-employed, or are business owners work at home or remotely at least one day per month. These telecommuters are known as contract telecommuters. The sum total of employee telecommuters and contract telecommuters increased by 43 percent from 2003 to 2008. The previously referenced 2009 survey by the

Technology such as the Internet and PCs make it possible for employees to work from home, while still interacting with the office.
© image100/PunchStock

Society for Human Resource Management found that 51 percent of their respondents offered some type of telecommuting.[20] The same respondents also reported that 45 percent of their organizations offered telecommuting on an ad-hoc basis, 34 percent on a part-time basis, and 19 percent on a full-time basis.

Advantages of telecommuting include less travel time and travel expenses, avoiding rush hour, avoiding distractions at the office, and being able to work flexible hours. Potential disadvantages of telecommuting are insurance concerns relating to the health and safety of employees working at home and the lack of the professional and social environment of the workplace. Another drawback is that some state and local laws restrict just what work can be done at home. Evidence has emerged indicating that, when given a choice, employees prefer a mix of working part of the time from home and part of the time in the office.[21]

Job Sharing

Job sharing is a relatively new concept whereby two or more part-time individuals perform a job that would normally be held by one full-time person. Job sharing can be in the form of equally shared responsibilities, split duties, or a combination of both. Job sharing is especially attractive to people who want to work, but not full-time. From the organization's viewpoint, job sharing aids in the retention of valuable employees. A critical factor relating to job sharing is how benefits are handled. Often benefits are prorated between the part-time employees. Some organizations allow job-sharing employees to purchase full health insurance by paying the difference between their prorated benefit and the premium for a full-time employee. In recessionary times and when organizations are cutting back, job sharing can be used to avoid layoffs and to retain trained employees. The 2009 survey conducted by SHRM reported that 51 percent of the respondents' companies offered some type of job sharing.[22] HRM in Action 4.5 discusses how two people share the top job in one organization.

Condensed Workweek

Under the *condensed workweek*, the number of hours worked per day is increased and the number of days in the workweek is decreased. Typically, this is done by having employees work 10 hours per day for four days per week (known as 4/40). Other variations of the condensed workweek include reducing the total hours worked to 36 or 38 hours. Advantages of the condensed workweek are lower absenteeism and tardiness, less start-up time, and more time available for employees to take care of personal business. One potential disadvantage is the fatigue that often accompanies longer hours. As with telecommuting, the price of gasoline has also affected the desire of people to use a condensed workweek. A 2008 survey conducted by Chicago consultant Challenger, Gray & Christmas found that 23 percent of the responding companies offered a condensed workweek.[23] The previously referenced 2009 survey by the Society of Human Resource Management reported that 37 percent of responding companies offered some type of compressed workweek.[24]

Contingent Workers

contingent workers
Employees who are independent contractors and on-call workers or temporary short-term workers.

The U.S. Labor Department's Bureau of Labor Statistics (BLS) separates **contingent workers** into two groups: (1) independent contractors and on-call workers, who are called to work only when needed, and (2) temporary or short-term workers. Both of these groups have been growing and represented approximately 10.7 percent and 4.1 percent respectively of the U.S. workforce in 2005, which is the last year that BLS collected this data. Some people also include part-time and leased employees under the category of contingent workers.[25] In 2008, the contingent workforce was estimated to be approximately 13 percent of the entire U.S. workforce and some predicted that it could rise in the near future to as much as 30–50 percent.[26] The reasons that organizations use contingent workers include seasonal fluctuations, project-based work, the desire to acquire skill sets not available in the normal employee population, hiring freezes, and rapid growth.

Contingent workers present certain challenges for human resource people, among which are the following:

- *Management issues*. Who manages the different contingent workers and what role does HR play?
- *Tracking and reporting*. How do contingents fit into the different HR system such as payroll?
- *Compensation*. How are contingents compensated compared to other employees?
- *Retention*. Since most contingents don't receive benefits they can be hard to retain.
- *Attitude and work quality*. Most contingents do not share the same degree of commitment as other employees.
- *Orientation and training*. Orientation and training can be difficult to schedule because of scheduling conflicts with other jobs.
- *Legal issues*. Contingent workers must meet the legal definition of "independent contractor" under IRS rules.
- *Use of company resources*. This can include everything from company discounts to participation in company educational programs.
- *Physical security*. Do contingent workers have the same access to company facilities as other employees?

The above list is certainly not exhaustive but it does identify many of the major challenges that accompany contingent workers. Despite these challenges, using contingent workers can have tremendous benefits. Some of the major benefits include flexibility for dealing with fluctuating product or service demand, increasing workplace diversity, determining potential as a future full-time employee, and providing skills the organization doesn't have in-house.

Summary of Learning Objectives

1. **Define *job analysis* and *job design*.**

   Job analysis is the process of determining and reporting pertinent information relating to the nature of a specific job. It is the determination of the tasks that comprise the job and of the skills, knowledge, abilities, and responsibilities required of the holder for successful job performance. Job design is the process of structuring work and designating the specific work activities of an individual or group of individuals to achieve certain organizational objectives. Job design addresses the basic question of how the job is to be performed, who is to perform it, and where it is to be performed.

2. **Distinguish among a position, a job, and an occupation.**

   Job duties, when combined with responsibilities, define a position. A group of positions that are identical with respect to their major tasks and responsibilities form a job. A group of similar jobs forms an occupation.

3. **Describe several common uses of a job analysis.**

   Several of the most common uses of a job analysis include job definition, job redesign, recruitment, selection and placement, orientation, training, career counseling, employee safety, performance appraisal, and compensation.

4. **Define *job description* and *job specification*.**

   A job description concentrates on the job. It explains what the job is and what the duties, responsibilities, and general working conditions are. A job specification concentrates on the characteristics needed to perform the job. It describes the qualifications the incumbent must possess to perform the job.

5. **Identify four frequently used methods of job analysis.**

   Four frequently used methods of job analysis are observation, interviews, questionnaires, and functional job analysis.

6. **Discuss what O*NET is and briefly explain why it was developed.**

   O*NET stands for Occupational Information Network, which is a comprehensive online database of employee attributes and job characteristics. By using comprehensive terms to describe knowledge, skills, abilities (KSAs), interests, content, and context of work, O*NET provides a common language and form of reference for understanding what is involved in effectively performing a given job. O*NET was developed to replace the old dictionary of occupational titles (DOT) that had become obsolete and inefficient.

7. **Define *essential functions* and *reasonable accommodation* as interpreted under the Americans with Disabilities Act.**

   Under the Americans with Disabilities Act, an essential job function is one that is fundamental to successful performance of the job as compared to marginal job functions, which may be performed at certain times but are incidental to the main purpose of the job. Reasonable accommodation means the employer may be required to alter the conditions of a particular job to enable the candidate to perform all essential functions.

8. **Identify several problems frequently associated with job analyses.**

   Some of the most frequently encountered problems with job analyses include the following: top management support is missing; only a single means and source for gathering data are used; the supervisor and jobholder do not participate in the design of the job analysis procedure; no training or motivation is provided; employees are not allowed sufficient time to complete the analysis; jobholder activities may be distorted; participants fail to critique the job.

9. **Define *job scope* and *job depth* and explain their relationship to job design.**

   Job scope and job depth are both dimensions of job design. *Job scope* refers to the number and variety of tasks performed by the jobholder. *Job depth* refers to the freedom of jobholders to plan and organize their own work, work at their own pace, and move around and communicate as desired.

10. **Explain the sociotechnical approach to job design.**

    The sociotechnical approach to job design stresses that both the technical system and the accompanying social system should be considered in designing jobs.

11. **Distinguish among the following types of alternative work schedules: flextime, telecommuting, job sharing, and condensed workweek.**

    Flextime allows employees to choose, within certain limits, when they start and end their workday. Telecommuting is the practice of working at home or while traveling and being able to interact with the office. Job sharing is the practice whereby two or more part-time individuals perform a job that would normally be held by one full-time person. Under the condensed workweek, the number of hours worked per day is increased and the number of days in the workweek is decreased.

12. **Define the term *contingent worker*.**

    Contingent workers include (a) independent contractors and on-call workers, who are called to work only when needed and (b) temporary or short-term workers. Some people also consider part-time and leased employees to be contingent workers.

Key Terms

contingent workers, *79*

duties, *66*

element, *66*

job, *67*

job analysis, *65*

job depth, *75*

job description, *68*

job design, *66*

job scope, *75*

job specification, *68*

micromotion, *66*

motion study, *69*

occupation, *67*

Occupational Information
Network (O*NET), *71*

orientation, *67*

position, *66*

recruitment, *67*

responsibilities, *66*

selection, *67*

task, *66*

time study, *69*

training, *67*

work sampling, *70*

**Review
Questions**

1. Define *job analysis* and *job design*.
2. Differentiate among the terms *duties, position,* and *job.*
3. From a human resource manager's viewpoint, what are several potential uses of a job analysis?
4. Define *job descriptions* and *job specifications.* How do they relate to the job analysis process?
5. Briefly describe four of the most frequently used methods for analyzing jobs.
6. Briefly describe O*NET.
7. Define the concepts of *essential functions* and *reasonable accommodation* as interpreted under the Americans with Disabilities Act.
8. What are some potential problems associated with job analysis?
9. What is the sociotechnical approach to job design?
10. Briefly explain the following types of alternative work schedules: flextime, telecommuting, job sharing, and the condensed workweek.
11. What differentiates contingent workers from other employees?

**Discussion
Questions**

1. What method of job analysis do you think would be most applicable for jobs in a large grocery store? For jobs in a public library?
2. Comment on the following statement, which is attributed to Robert Heinlein: "A human being should be able to change a diaper, plan an invasion, butcher a hog, conn a ship, design a building, write a sonnet, balance accounts, build a wall, set a bone, comfort the dying, take orders, give orders, cooperate, act alone, solve equations, analyze new problems, pitch manure, program a computer, cook a tasty meal, fight efficiently, die gallantly. Specialization is for insects."
3. How do the requirements of the Americans with Disabilities Act affect the job analysis process?
4. Describe an actual work situation in which O*NET might be useful to you as an HR manager.

Incident 4.1

The Tax Assessor's Office

A workday begins each morning at 8 A.M. in the tax assessor's office. The staff is composed of the director, two secretaries, two computer-typists, and three file clerks. Until last year, the office operated smoothly, with even workloads and well-defined responsibilities.

Over the last year or so, the director has noticed more and more disagreements among the computer-typists and file clerks. When they approached the director to discuss their disagreements, it was determined that problems had arisen from misunderstandings concerning responsibility for particular duties. A strong undercurrent of discontent developed because the computer-typists feel the file clerks have too much free time to spend running personal errands and socializing. On the other hand, the secretaries and computer-typists frequently have to work overtime doing work they believe could easily be picked up by the file clerks. The file clerks claim they should not have to take on any additional duties because their paychecks would not reflect the extra responsibilities.

Each person in the office has a general job description that was written several years ago. However, the nature of most positions has changed considerably since then because of the implementation of the computer system. No attempt has been made to put these changes in writing. The director formerly held staff meetings to discuss problems that arose within the office; however, no meetings have been held in several months.

Questions

1. What actions would you recommend to the director?
2. Why do you think job descriptions are not updated in many organizations?

Incident 4.2

Turnover Problems

Ms. Shivers is the manager of a computer division in the federal government. Among her various responsibilities is the central data entry office, with 10 GS–4 data entry clerks and one GS–5 supervisor.

The starting salary range for a GS–4 data entry clerk with limited skills is comparable to the starting salary in private industry. However, after about six months of on-the-job experience, most data entry clerks can get a substantial pay increase by taking a job in private industry. It has become common knowledge in industry that Ms. Shivers has a very good training program for data entry clerks and that her division represents a good source of personnel. As a result of this reputation, Ms. Shivers has experienced a heavy turnover during the last several months. In fact, the problem has recently become severe enough to create a tremendous work backlog in her division. In short, she has had to oversee so many trainees that the division's overall productivity has declined.

Within the data entry section are three notable exceptions who have worked for Ms. Shivers for several years. These three have recently been responsible for most of the work turned out in the division. The GS–5 supervisor has been running the section for five years. Just recently, she informed Ms. Shivers that she had been offered a job with another company with a small pay increase and no supervisory responsibilities.

Ms. Shivers has always felt that the data entry clerks should be upgraded to the GS–5 level and the supervisor's job to GS–6. In fact, on several occasions, Ms. Shivers has mentioned this idea to her boss, John Clayton. She believes not only that these jobs should be upgraded but also that this action would go a long way toward solving her turnover problem. Unfortunately, Clayton has never shown much interest in Ms. Shivers' idea.

Questions

1. What do you suggest Ms. Shivers do to further promote the idea of upgrading the data entry clerk and supervisory positions?
2. What can Ms. Shivers do from a job design standpoint to help with the turnover problem?

EXERCISE 4.1 **Introduction to** **O*NET**	Go to the O*NET Web site at http://online.onetcenter.org and experiment with the data. Choose a job (your current job, a job you held in the past, or a job you would like to have) and see if the skills listed by O*NET match your expectations and experiences for the job.
EXERCISE 4.2 **Writing a Job** **Description**	Using Table 4.2 as a guideline, write a job description for the last job you held. Your job may have been a summer, part-time, or full-time job. If you have never had a job, choose a job of one of your parents. Your final product should normally be between one and two pages in length.

EXERCISE 4.3
Performing a Job Analysis

Your instructor may ask you to do both parts of this exercise or only part *a* or part *b*.

a. Use the job analysis questionnaire in the On the Job example at the end of this chapter (p. 84) to analyze the most recent job you have held. Your job may have been a summer, part-time, or full-time job. You need not fill in the heading information. After you have completed the questionnaire, answer the following questions:

1. Do you believe the job analysis captured the essence of your job? If not, what was left out?
2. What improvements would you recommend in the job analysis questionnaire?
3. Do you think your boss would have answered the questionnaire basically the same way you did? Why or why not?

b. Using the same job analysis questionnaire change referenced in part *a* above, go out and interview an actual jobholder of your choice. After you have completed the job analysis questionnaire, write a complete job description for the job.

Notes and Additional Readings

1. War Manpower Commission, Division of Occupational Analysis, *Training and Reference Manual for Job Analysis* (Washington, D.C.: U.S. Government Printing Office, June 1944), p. 7.
2. This list is partially adapted from J. Markowitz, "Four Methods of Job Analysis," *Training and Development Journal,* September 1981, p. 112.
3. U.S. Department of Labor, *Handbook for Analyzing Jobs* (Washington, D.C.: U.S. Government Printing Office, 1972).
4. The Position Analysis Questionnaire (PAQ) is copyrighted by the Purdue Research Foundation. The PAQ and related materials are available from PAQ Services, Inc., 11 Bellweather Way, Suite 107, Bellingham, WA 98225, phone (800) 292-2198 or (360) 733-2364 or www.paq.com.
5. W. W. Tornov and P. R. Pinto, "The Development of a Managerial Job Taxonomy: A System for Describing, Classifying, and Evaluating Executive Positions," *Journal of Applied Psychology* 61, No. 4 (1976), p. 413.
6. An updated electronic version of the abandoned DOT is available for a fee from PAQ Services, Inc., www.paq.com.
7. Much of this section is based on Wayne E. Barlow and Edward Z. Hare, "A Practical Guide to the Americans with Disabilities Act," *Personnel Journal,* June 1992, p. 53, and Eric J. Felsberg, "Conducting Job Analyses and Drafting Lawful Job Description under the Americans with Disabilities Act," *Employment Relations Today,* Fall 2004, pp. 91–93.
8. Parts of this list are adapted from Philip C. Grant, "What Use Is a Job Description?" *Personnel Journal,* February 1988, pp. 50–55; see also Brenda Paik Sunoo, "Generic or Non-Generic Job Descriptions?" *Personnel Journal,* February 1996, p. 102.
9. L. E. Davis, "Job Design and Productivity: A New Approach," *Personnel,* March 1957, p. 420; Shari Caudron, "On the Contrary: Job Stress Is in Job Design" *Workforce,* September 1998, pp. 21–23.
10. Richard B. Chase, F. Robert Jacobs, and Nicholas J. Aquilano, *Operations Management for Competitive Advantage,* 10th ed. (Burr Ridge, Ill.; McGraw-Hill/Irwin, 2004), p. 126.
11. P. B. Vaill, "Industrial Engineering and Socio-Technical Systems," *Journal of Industrial Engineering,* September 1967, p. 535.
12. Louis E. Davis, *Job Satisfaction—A Socio-Technical View,* Report 515-69 (Los Angeles: University of California, 1969), p. 14.
13. Chase, Jacobs, and Aquilano, *Operations Management,* p. 128.
14. Douglas R. May, Greg R. Oldham, and Cheryl Rathert, "Employee Affective and Behavioral Reactions to the Spatial Density of Physical Work Environments," *Human Resource Management,* Spring 2005, pp. 21–33.
15. *Workplace Flexibility in the 21st Century.* (Alexandria, Va.: The Society for Human Resource Management, 2009), p. 5.
16. "Flextime Benefits Make for Healthier Offices," *IOMA's Report on Compensation and Benefits for Law Offices* 9, No. 9 (September 2009), pp. 1–5; and "Flextime Does More Than Just Satisfy Employees," *HR Focus* 86, No. 9 (September 2009), p. 12.
17. Brian Gill, "Flextime Benefits Employees and Employers," *American Printer,* February 1998, p. 70; Sarah Fister Gale, "Expert Wisdom in Launching Flex Programs," *Workforce,* October 2001, p. 64.
18. *2009 Employee Benefits* (Alexandria, Va.: The Society for Human Resource Management, 2009), p. 32.
19. "Telework Trendlines 2009" p. 5, www.worldatwork.org. Accessed January 13, 2010.

20. *2009 Employee Benefits,* op. cit.

21. Kathy Gurchiek, "Workers Pick Office over Telecommuting," *HR Magazine,* September 2006, pp. 28–29.

22. *2009 Employee Benefits,* op. cit.

23. Pete Bach, "Workers Look to Trim Gas Costs," *McClatchy-Tribune Business News,* June 3, 2008.

24. *2009 Employee Benefits,* op. cit.

25. Much of this section is drawn from "More Contingent Workers Are a Blessing and Sometimes a Challenge for HR," *HR Focus,* January 2006, pp. 51–54. "Contingent Workforce Brings More Questions Than Answers," *HR Focus,* July 2005, pp. 6–7, and "Where Are Contract Workers Filling Talent Gaps?," *HR Focus,* March 2009, pp. 10–11.

26. Irwin Speizer, "An On-Demand Workforce," *Workforce Management,* October 19, 2009, pp. 45–49.

On the Job

SAMPLE JOB ANALYSIS QUESTIONNAIRE*

Job Analysis Information Format

Your job title _____   Code _____ Date _____
Class title _____   Department _____
Your name _____   Facility _____
Superior's title _____   Prepared by _____
Superior's name _____   Hours worked _____ AM _____ to _____ AM _____
                                                 PM   PM

1. What is the general purpose of your job?
2. What was your last job? If it was in another organization, please name it.
3. To what job would you normally expect to be promoted?
4. If you regularly supervise others, list them by name and job title.
5. If you supervise others, please check those activities that are part of your supervisory duties:

   ☐ Hiring   ☐ Coaching   ☐ Promoting
   ☐ Orienting   ☐ Counseling   ☐ Compensating
   ☐ Training   ☐ Budgeting   ☐ Disciplining
   ☐ Scheduling   ☐ Directing   ☐ Terminating
   ☐ Developing   ☐ Measuring performance ☐ Other _____

6. How would you describe the successful completion and results of your work?
7. *Job duties*—Please briefly describe WHAT you do and, if possible, HOW you do it. Indicate those duties you consider to be most important and/or most difficult.

   (a) *Daily duties:*
   (b) *Periodic duties* (Please indicate whether weekly, monthly, quarterly, etc.):
   (c) *Duties performed at irregular intervals:*

8. *Education*—Please check the blank that indicates the education requirements for the job, not your *own* educational background:

   ☐ No formal education required   ☐ 4-year college degree
   ☐ Less than high school diploma   ☐ Education beyond undergraduate
   ☐ High school diploma or equivalent   degree and/or professional license
   ☐ 2-year college certificate or equivalent

   List advanced degrees or specified professional license or certificate required.

   Please indicate the education you had when you were placed on this job.

9. *Experience*—Please check the amount needed to perform your job:

   ☐ None   ☐ More than 1 year to 3 years
   ☐ Less than 1 month   ☐ More than 3 years to 5 years
   ☐ 1 month to less than 6 months ☐ More than 5 years to 10 years
   ☐ 6 months to 1 year   ☐ Over 10 years

   Please indicate the experience you had when you were placed on this job.

*Source: Adapted from Richard I. Henderson, "Compensation Management in a Knowledge-Based World," 1st ed. © 1976, Reprinted by permission of Prentice Hall, Inc., Englewood Cliffs, NJ.

10. *Skills*—Please list any skills required in the performance of your job (e.g., amount of accuracy, alertness, precision in working with described tools, methods, systems). Please list skills you possessed when you were placed on this job.

11. *Equipment*—Does your work require the use of any equipment? Yes _____ No _____

    If yes, please list the equipment and check whether you use it rarely, occasionally, or frequently:

Equipment	Rarely	Occasionally	Frequently
(1) _____	☐	☐	☐
(2) _____	☐	☐	☐
(3) _____	☐	☐	☐
(4) _____	☐	☐	☐

12. *Physical demands*—Please check all undesirable physical demands required on your job and whether you are required to do so rarely, occasionally, or frequently:

	Rarely	Occasionally	Frequently
☐ Handling heavy material	☐	☐	☐
☐ Awkward or cramped positions	☐	☐	☐
☐ Excessive working speeds	☐	☐	☐
☐ Excessive sensory requirements (seeing, hearing, touching, smelling, speaking)	☐	☐	☐
☐ Vibrating equipment	☐	☐	☐
☐ Others _____	☐	☐	☐

13. *Emotional demands*—Please check all undesirable emotional demands placed on you by your job and whether it is rarely, occasionally, or frequently:

	Rarely	Occasionally	Frequently
☐ Contact with general public	☐	☐	☐
☐ Customer contact	☐	☐	☐
☐ Close supervision	☐	☐	☐
☐ Deadlines under pressure	☐	☐	☐
☐ Irregular activity schedules	☐	☐	☐
☐ Working alone	☐	☐	☐
☐ Excessive traveling	☐	☐	☐
☐ Other	☐	☐	☐

14. *Workplace location*—Check the type of location of your job and if you consider it to be unsatisfactory or satisfactory.

	Unsatisfactory	Satisfactory
☐ Outdoor	☐	☐
☐ Indoor	☐	☐
☐ Underground	☐	☐
☐ Pit	☐	☐
☐ Scaffold	☐	☐

15. *Physical surroundings*—Please check whether you consider the following physical conditions of your job to be poor, good, or excellent.

	Poor	Good	Excellent
☐ Lighting	☐	☐	☐
☐ Ventilation	☐	☐	☐
☐ Sudden temperature change	☐	☐	☐
☐ Vibration	☐	☐	☐
☐ Comfort of furnishings	☐	☐	☐

16. *Environmental conditions*—Please check the objectionable conditions under which you must perform your job and check whether the condition exists rarely, occasionally, or frequently:

	Rarely	Occasionally	Frequently
☐ Dust	☐	☐	☐
☐ Dirt	☐	☐	☐
☐ Heat	☐	☐	☐
☐ Cold	☐	☐	☐
☐ Fumes	☐	☐	☐
☐ Odors	☐	☐	☐
☐ Noise	☐	☐	☐
☐ Wetness	☐	☐	☐
☐ Humidity	☐	☐	☐
☐ Other _____	☐	☐	☐

17. *Health and safety*—Please check all undesirable health and safety factors under which you must perform your job and whether you are required to do so rarely, occasionally, or frequently:

	Rarely	Occasionally	Frequently
☐ Height of elevated workplace	☐	☐	☐
☐ Radiation	☐	☐	☐
☐ Mechanical hazards	☐	☐	☐
☐ Moving objects	☐	☐	☐
☐ Explosives	☐	☐	☐
☐ Electrical hazards	☐	☐	☐
☐ Fire	☐	☐	☐
☐ Other _____	☐	☐	☐

_____   _____
Signature   Date

Supervisory Review

Do the incumbent's responses to the questionnaire accurately describe the work requirements and the work performed in meeting the responsibilities of the job? Yes _____ No _____ If no, please explain and list any significant omissions or additions.

Part **Two**

Acquiring Human Resources

BananaStock/PictureQuest

Chapter **Five**

Human Resource Planning

Chapter Learning Objectives

After studying this chapter, you should be able to:

1. Define human resource planning (HRP).
2. Summarize the relationship between HRP and organizational planning.
3. Explain strategy-linked HRP.
4. Identify the steps in the HRP process.
5. Describe the different methods used for forecasting human resource needs.
6. Discuss the purpose of a skills inventory.
7. Describe succession planning.
8. Define a human resource information system (HRIS).
9. Differentiate between the Internet and an intranet.
10. Explain what Web 2.0 is.
11. Define the concept "software as a service."

Chapter Outline

human resource planning (HRP)
Process of determining the human resource needs of an organization and ensuring that the organization has the right number of qualified people in the right jobs at the right time.

Human resource planning (HRP), also referred to as *workforce planning* or *personnel planning,* has been defined as the process of "getting the right number of qualified people into the right job at the right time."[1] Put another way, HRP is "the system of matching the supply of people—internally (existing employees) and externally (those to be hired or searched for)—with the openings the organization expects to have over a given time frame."[2] The Tennessee Valley Authority (TVA) defines the HRP process as "the systematic assessment of future HR needs and the determination of the actions required to meet those needs."[3] Yet another source defines HRP as "the process of forecasting an organization's future tasks and the environment's demands on the organization and then setting HR action measures accordingly."[4] All of these definitions suggest the first challenge of HRP is to translate the organization's plans and objectives into a timed schedule of employee requirements. Once the employee requirements have been determined, HRP must devise plans for securing the necessary employees. Basically, all organizations engage in human resource planning either formally or informally. Some organizations do a good job and others a poor job.

The long-term success of any organization ultimately depends on having the right people in the right jobs at the right time. Organizational objectives and the strategies for achieving those objectives are meaningful only when people with the appropriate talents, skills, and desire are available to carry out those strategies.

Poor human resource planning can also cause substantial problems in the short term. Consider the following examples:

- The CEO of a successful company retires unexpectedly because of recent health issues. There is no obvious replacement.
- Despite an aggressive search, an important middle management position in a high-technology organization has gone unfilled for six months. Productivity in the section has plummeted.
- In another company, employees hired a few months ago have been placed on indefinite layoff because of an unforeseen lag in the workload in a specific production area.
- In still another company, thanks to the spectacular efforts of a talented marketing manager, product demand has exceeded expectations. However, because the demand was unanticipated, the company has not been able to hire enough qualified production employees.

The need for HRP is due to the significant lead time that normally exists between the recognition of the need to fill a job and securing a qualified person to fill that need. Even in recessionary times it is not always possible to go out and find an appropriate person overnight. Effective HRP can also help reduce turnover by keeping employees apprised of their career opportunities within the company.

HOW HRP RELATES TO ORGANIZATIONAL PLANNING

HRP involves applying the basic planning process to the human resource needs of the organization. To be effective, any human resource plan must be derived from the strategic and operational plans of the organization. In essence, the success of HRP depends largely on how closely the human resource department can integrate effective people planning with the organization's business planning process.[5] Unfortunately, HRP is often inadequately tied to overall corporate planning.

Strategic business planning seeks to identify various factors critical to the success of the organization. It also focuses on how the organization can become better positioned and equipped to compete in its industry. To accomplish this, the planning process should provide

- A clear statement of the organization's mission.
- A commitment from staff members to the mission.
- An explicit statement of assumptions.
- A plan of action in light of available or acquirable resources, including trained and talented people.[6]

Human resource planning contributes significantly to the strategic management process by providing the means to accomplish the outcomes desired from the planning process. In essence, the human resource demands and needs are derived from the strategic and operating planning and then compared with human resource availability. Then a variety of programs such as recruiting, training, and reallocation address the resulting gaps.

A common error occurs when human resource planners focus on the short-term replacement needs and fail to coordinate their plans with the strategic and long-term plans of the organization. Focusing on short-term replacement needs is a natural consequence of failing to integrate human resource planning with strategic planning. A nonintegrated approach almost always leads to surprises that force human resource planners to concentrate on short-term crises.

TABLE 5.1
Linking HRP to the Business Strategy

Sources: G. Christopher Wood, "Planning for People" (letters to the editor), *Harvard Business Review,* November–December 1985, p. 230; David R. Leigh, "Business Planning Is People Planning," *Personnel Journal,* May 1984, pp. 44–54.

- Be familiar with the business strategy.
- Ensure that all traditional human resource programs are satisfying the needs of senior and functional management.
- Identify the human resource implications of the organization's business strategy.
- Identify those human resource issues that may affect business objectives, and notify the appropriate functional managers.
- Convert business objectives into human resource objectives that can provide the foundation for a strategic human resource plan.
- Review the strategic planning process to identify new opportunities to involve human resource personnel.

Strategy-Linked HRP

All managers, especially line managers, should view human resource planning as one of their most important job responsibilities. Unfortunately, this is not often the case. Far too many managers view HRP as something to do only after everything else has been done. Furthermore, managers often think HRP should be handled solely by human resource personnel. But HRP is not strictly a human resource function. The role of human resource personnel is to assist operating managers in developing their individual plans and integrating those different plans into an overall scheme. The individual managers must, however, provide the basic data on which the plan is built. The process requires a joint effort by the individual managers and human resource personnel. In general, human resource personnel provide the structure, impetus, and assistance. However, individual managers must be actively involved.

One of the best ways to encourage genuine cooperation between human resource managers and line managers is to use what is called *strategy-linked HRP.* Strategy-linked HRP is based on a close working relationship between human resource staff and line managers.[7] Human resource managers serve as consultants to line managers concerning the people-management implications of business objectives and strategies. Line managers, in turn, have a responsibility to respond to the business implications of human resource objectives and strategies. Another important ingredient is the commitment of top management, which should be evident to other managers and employees.

Table 5.1 summarizes several actions human resource managers can take to link human resource planning to the organization's strategic plans.

TIME FRAME OF HRP

Because HRP is so closely tied to the organizational planning process, the time frames human resource plans cover should correspond with those covered by the organizational plans. Organizational plans are frequently classified as short-range (zero to two years), intermediate range (two to five years), or long-range (beyond five years). Ideally, an organization prepares a plan for each of these horizons. Table 5.2 summarizes the major factors affecting long-, intermediate-, and short-range human resource planning.

TABLE 5.2   Factors Affecting the Time Frame of HRP

Source: Adapted from J. Walker, "Forecasting Manpower Needs," in *Manpower Planning and Programming,* ed. E. H. Burack and J. W. Walker (Boston: Allyn & Boston, 1972), p. 94.

Forecast Factor	Short Range (0–2 Years)	Intermediate Range (2–5 Years)	Long Range (Beyond 5 Years)
Demand	Authorized employment including growth, changes, and turnover.	Operating needs from budgets and plans.	In some organizations, the same as "intermediate"; in others, an increased awareness of changes in environment and technology—essentially judgmental.
Supply	Employee census less expected losses plus expected promotions from subordinate groups.	Human resource vacancies expected from individual promotability data derived from development plans.	Management expectations of changing characteristics of employees and future available human resources.
Net needs	Numbers and kinds of employees needed.	Numbers, kinds, dates, and levels of needs.	Management expectations of future conditions affecting immediate decisions.

HRP: AN EVOLVING PROCESS

An organization's human resource planning efforts should be viewed not as an all-or-nothing process but as falling at some point along a continuum. At one end of this continuum are those organizations that do no human resource planning; at the other end are those that completely integrate long-range human resource planning into their strategic business plans.

D. Quinn Mills has identified five stages, or benchmarks, along this continuum.[8] Stage 1 companies have no long-term business plans, and they do little or no human resource planning. Companies at stage 2 have a long-term business plan, but tend to be skeptical of HRP. At the same time, such companies do realize to some degree that human resource planning is important. Stage 3 companies do engage in some aspects of human resource planning, but for the most part these efforts are not integrated into the long-range business plan. Stage 4 companies do a good deal of human resource planning, and their top managers are enthusiastic about the process. These companies have at least one human resource component integrated into the long-range plan. Stage 5 companies treat human resource planning as an important and vital part of their long-term business plan. Naturally, companies at stage 5 are highly enthusiastic about HRP.

STEPS IN THE HRP PROCESS

HRP consists of four basic steps:

1. Determining the impact of the organization's objectives on specific organizational units.
2. Defining the skills, expertise, and total number of employees (demand for human resources) required to achieve the organizational and departmental objectives.
3. Determining the additional (net) human resource requirements in light of the organization's current human resources.
4. Developing action plans to meet the anticipated human resource needs.[9]

Figure 5.1 illustrates the steps in HRP.

Determining Organizational Objectives

As emphasized earlier, human resource plans must be based on organizational strategic plans. In practice, this means the objectives of the human resource plan must be derived from organizational objectives. Specific human resource requirements in terms of numbers and characteristics of employees should be derived from the objectives of the entire organization.

organizational objectives
Statements of expected results that are designed to give the organization and its members direction and purpose.

cascade approach to setting objectives
Objective-setting process designed to involve all levels of management in the organizational planning process.

Organizational objectives, which give the organization and its members direction and purpose, should be stated in terms of expected results. The objective-setting process begins at the top of the organization with a statement of mission, which defines the organization's current and future business. Long-term objectives and strategies are formulated based on the organization's mission statement. These can then be used to establish short-term performance objectives. Short-term performance objectives generally have a time schedule and are expressed quantitatively. Divisional and departmental objectives are then derived from the organization's short-term performance objectives. Establishing organizational, divisional, and departmental objectives in this manner has been called the **cascade approach** to objective setting. Figure 5.2 illustrates this approach.

FIGURE 5.1 **Steps in the Human Resource Planning Process**

| Determine the impact of organizational objectives on specific organizational units | → | Define the skills and expertise required to meet objectives (demand for human resources) | → | Determine additional human resource requirements in light of current human resources (net human resource requirements) | → | Develop action plans to meet the anticipated human resource needs |

FIGURE 5.2   Cascade Approach to Setting Objectives

Source: Redrawn from Anthony P. Raia, *Managing by Objectives* (Glenview, IL: Scott Foresman and Company, 1974), p. 30. Reprinted by permission.

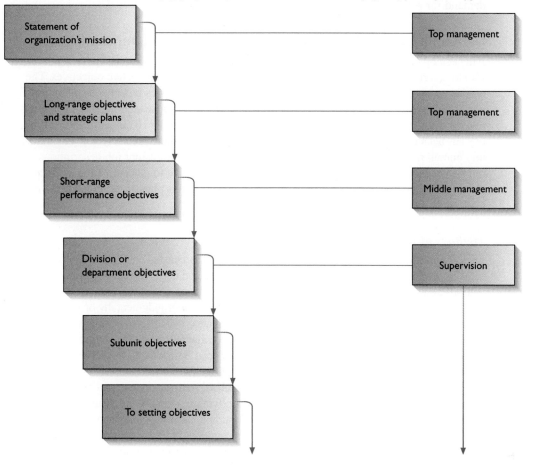

The cascade approach is not a form of top-down planning, whereby objectives are passed down to lower levels of the organization. The idea is to involve all levels of management in the planning process. Such an approach leads to an upward and downward flow of information during planning. This also ensures that the objectives are communicated and coordinated through all levels of the organization.

When properly used, the cascade approach involves both operating managers and human resource personnel in the overall planning process. During the early stages, human resource personnel can influence objective setting by providing information about the organization's human resources. For example, if human resource personnel have identified particular strengths and weaknesses in the organization's staff, this information can significantly influence the overall direction of the organization.

Environmental Factors Affecting Human Resource Needs

Many factors in the organization's external environment may have an impact on the organization's objectives and the human resources needed to realize those objectives. Some of these factors include government influences, general economic conditions, the competition, and changes in the workforce. Government influences include laws and regulations imposed by local, state, and federal governments as well as the spending patterns of the various governments. General economic conditions refer to the state of the overall economy such as recession or economic boom. Interest rates and the level of unemployment are factors that are related to general economic conditions. Competitive concerns relate primarily to the emergence or departure of direct competitors (those in the same business) as well as the emergence and departure of businesses that compete for the same labor and other resources. Changes in workforce refer not only to the workforce composition but also to its work habits. The impact of changes in technology can vary from insignificant to devastating to extremely positive. For example, consider how cell phone technology has impacted the demand for pay phone booths.

Determining the Skills and Expertise Required (Demand)

After establishing organizational, divisional, and departmental objectives, operating managers should determine the skills and expertise required to meet their respective objectives. The key here is not to look at the skills and abilities of present employees but to determine the skills and abilities required to meet the objectives. For example, suppose an objective of the production department is to increase total production of a certain item by 10 percent. Once this objective has been established, the production manager must determine precisely how this translates into human resource needs. A good starting point is to review current job descriptions. Once this has been accomplished, managers are in a better position to determine the skills and expertise necessary to meet their objectives. The final step in this phase is to translate the needed skills and abilities into types and numbers of employees.

Methods of Forecasting Human Resource Needs

The organization's future human resource needs can be forecasted using a variety of methods, some simple and some complex. Regardless of the method used, forecasts represent approximations and should not be viewed as absolutes.

managerial estimates
Judgmental method of forecasting that calls on managers to make estimates of future staffing needs.

Delphi technique
Judgmental method of forecasting that uses a panel of experts to make initially independent estimates of future demand. An intermediary then presents each expert's forecast and assumptions to the other members of the panel. Each expert is then allowed to revise his or her forecast as desired. This process continues until some consensus or composite emerges.

scenario analysis
Using workforce environmental scanning data to develop alternative workforce scenarios.

Methods for forecasting human resource needs can be either judgmentally or mathematically based. Judgmental methods include managerial estimates, the Delphi technique, and scenario analysis. Under the **managerial estimates** method, managers estimate future staffing needs based primarily on past experience. These estimates can be made by top-level managers and passed down, by lower-level managers and passed up for further revision, or by some combination of upper- and lower-level managers. With the **Delphi technique,** each member of a panel of experts independently estimates future demand, specifying any underlying assumptions. An intermediary then presents each expert's forecast and assumptions to the others and allows the experts to revise their positions if they desire. This process continues until some consensus emerges.

Scenario analysis involves using workforce environmental scanning data to develop alternative workforce scenarios.[10] These scenarios are developed in brainstorming sessions with line managers and human resource managers, who forecast what they think their workforce will look like five or more years into the future. Once these forecasts have been crystalized, the managers then work backward to identify key change points. The biggest advantage of scenario analysis is that it encourages open, out-of-the-box thinking.

Mathematically based methods for forecasting human resource needs include various statistical and modeling methods. Statistical methods use historical data in some manner to project future demand. Modeling methods usually provide a simplified abstraction of the human resource demands throughout the organization. Changing the input data allows testing the human resource ramifications of different demand scenarios. Table 5.3 summarizes four of the most frequently used statistical and/or modeling methods.

Historically, judgmental forecasts have been used more frequently than mathematically based forecasts. Judgmental methods are simpler and usually do not require sophisticated analyses. However, with the increasing proliferation of user-friendly software and computers, mathematically based methods will probably be used more frequently.

benchmarking
Thoroughly examining internal practices and procedures and measuring them against the ways other successful organizations operate.

In addition to the previously described judgmentally and mathematically based forecasting techniques, some organizations help forecast human resource needs by benchmarking what other successful organizations are doing. **Benchmarking** involves thoroughly examining internal practices and procedures and measuring them against the ways other successful organizations operate.[11] With regard to HRP, benchmarking involves learning what other successful organizations in the industry are forecasting and how they are arriving at their forecasts. Your forecasts and methods can then be compared to theirs. Consultants and professional organizations such as industry associations can be employed to help with the benchmarking process. A major advantage of benchmarking is that it forces HR professionals to look at other ways of doing things.

TABLE 5.3
Statistical Modeling Techniques Used to Forecast Human Resource Needs

Source: Kendrith M. Rowland and Gerald R. Ferris, *Personnel Management,* 1st edition, p. 59 © 1982. Reprinted by permission of Pearson Education, Inc., Upper Saddle River, NJ.

Technique	Description
1. Time-series analysis	Past staffing levels (instead of workload indicators) are used to project future human resource requirements. Past staffing levels are examined to isolate seasonal and cyclical variations, long-term trends, and random movements. Long-term trends are then extrapolated or projected using a moving average, exponential smoothing, or regression technique.
2. Personnel ratios	Past personnel data are examined to determine historical relationships among the number of employees in various jobs or job categories. Regression analysis or productivity ratios are then used to project either total or key group human resource requirements, and personnel ratios are used to allocate total requirements to various job categories or to estimate requirements for nonkey groups.
3. Productivity ratios	Historical data are used to examine past levels of a productivity index, $$P = \frac{\text{Workload}}{\text{Number of people}}$$ Where constant, or systematic, relationships are found, human resource requirements can be computed by dividing predicted workloads by P.
4. Regression analysis	Past levels of various workload indicators, such as sales, production levels, and value added, are examined for statistical relationships with staffing levels. Where sufficiently strong relationships are found, a regression (or multiple regression) model is derived. Forecasted levels of the related indicator(s) are entered into the resulting model and used to calculate the associated level of human resource requirements.

Determining Additional (Net) Human Resource Requirements

Once a manager has determined the types and numbers of employees required, he or she analyzes these estimates in light of the current and anticipated human resources of the organization. This process involves a thorough analysis of presently employed personnel and a forecast of expected changes. Sometimes this process is referred to as gap analysis, i.e., determining the gap between the organization's future human resource needs and its current human resource assets.

Skills Inventory

skills inventory
Consolidated list of biographical and other information on all employees in the organization.

A **skills inventory** consolidates information about the organization's human resources. It provides basic information on all employees, including, in its simplest form, a list of the names, certain characteristics, and skills of employees. Because the information from a skills inventory is used as input into promotion and transfer decisions, it should contain information about each employee's portfolio of skills, not just those relevant to the employee's current job. In most situations, seven broad categories of information should be included in a skills inventory:

1. Personal data: age, sex, marital status.
2. Skills: education, job experience, training.
3. Special qualifications: membership in professional groups, special achievements.
4. Salary and job history: present and past salary, dates of raises, various jobs held.
5. Company data: benefit plan data, retirement information, seniority.
6. Capacity of individual: test scores on psychological and other tests, health information.
7. Special preferences of the individual: geographic location, type of job.[12]

The popularity of skills inventories has increased rapidly since the proliferation of computers. Although traditionally most of the desired information was available from individual personnel files, compiling it was time consuming before computers became readily available. Today's intranets even have the ability to conduct comprehensive skills inventories and then place employees into training to fit the needs of the organization. Intranets are discussed later in this chapter.

The primary advantage of a skills inventory is that it furnishes a means to quickly and accurately evaluate the skills available within the organization. In addition to helping determine

MAINTAINING TALENT IN CHINA

Companies throughout China are having an increasingly difficult time retaining qualified employees. Because of China's one-child policy, not enough people are being born to supply the necessary workers. The country's outdated educational system is not producing sufficient graduates with the needed skills, and the often horrendous working conditions are resulting in employee burnout.

Those employees who do possess the desired skills are in high demand and can be extremely selective about their employer. These same employees are continually being offered higher pay, better perks, and promotions to move to another country. Throughout China, employees put in long hours, are subjected to heavy workloads and are often expected to use outdated manual processes. There is also a general lack of professional development programs and other opportunities for skill growth.

The above problems create special challenges for HR managers in China. Christopher Lynch, professional director at Manpower in Hong Kong, has summarized these challenges, "HR was previously about operational issues such as filling seats and making the payroll. Now it is a strategic one—coaching and growing an organization, retaining and nurturing talent, optimizing personnel and corporate performance to contribute to growth."

Source: Michael Taylor, "China's Talent Retention Dilemma in the New Millennium," *China Staff,* October 2008, pp. 17–19.

promotion and transfer decisions, this information is often necessary for making other decisions, such as whether to bid on a new contract or introduce a new product. A skills inventory also aids in planning future employee training and management development programs and in recruiting and selecting new employees. Figure 5.3 presents a skills inventory form that has been used by PPG Industries.

Management Inventory

management inventory
Specialized, expanded form of skills inventory for an organization's current management team; in addition to basic types of information, it usually includes a brief assessment of past performance and potential for advancement.

Because the type of information that may be required about management personnel sometimes differs from that for nonmanagerial employees, some organizations maintain a separate management inventory. In addition to biographical data, a **management inventory** often contains brief assessments of the manager's past performance, strengths, weaknesses, and potential for advancement. In essence, a management inventory is a specialized type of skills inventory just for management.

Anticipating Changes in Personnel

In addition to appraising present human resources through a skills inventory, managers must take future changes into account. Managers can accurately and easily estimate certain changes, but cannot so easily forecast other changes. However, information is almost always available to help make these forecasts.

Changes such as retirements can be forecasted with reasonable accuracy from information in the skills inventory. Other changes, such as transfers and promotions, can be estimated by taking into account such factors as the ages of individuals in specific jobs and the requirements of the organization. Individuals with potential for promotion can and should be identified. Other factors, such as deaths, resignations, and discharges, are much more difficult to predict. However, past experience and historical records often can provide useful information in these areas.

Planned training and development experiences should also be considered when evaluating anticipated changes. By combining the forecast for the human resources needed with the information from the skills inventory and from anticipated changes, managers can make a reasonable prediction of their net human resource requirements for a specified time period. HRM in Action 5.1 describes how China's shortage of talent has presented challenges for HR managers.

Developing Action Plans

Once the net human resource requirements have been determined, managers must develop action plans for achieving the desired results. The following section discusses action that can be taken to add human resources.

FIGURE 5.3   **Skills Inventory Form Used by PPG Industries**

PPG

PERSONAL HISTORY PROFILE

PRINTED FOR   DATE

PPG JOB HISTORY

DATE ASSIGNED	JOB TITLE	BUSINESS/CORPORATE DEPARTMENT	ORGANIZATIONAL UNIT

PRE-PPG JOB HISTORY   **FUNCTIONAL PREFERENCES**

COMPANY AND LOCATION	JOB TITLE	FROM	TO		
1.				1.	
2.				2.	
3.				3.	

EDUCATION   **OTHER ACHIEVEMENTS, ACTIVITIES, TRAINING**

LEVEL	YEAR	SCHOOL	STATE	SUBJECT
1.				
2.				
3.			CREDITS	
DEGREE IN PROGRESS			EARNED REQUIRED	

1.
2.
3.
4.
5.
6.
7.
8.
9.
10.

LANGUAGES   **PPG TRAINING COURSES**

	PROFICIENCY LEVEL
1.	
2.	
3.	

YEAR

1.
2.
3.
4.
5.
6.
7.
8.
9.
10.

PROFESSIONAL SOCIETIES AND ORGANIZATIONS   MEMBER STATUS   YEAR

1.		
2.		
3.		

PROFESSIONAL LICENSES AND CERTIFICATES   **RELOCATION INTEREST**

	ISSUING AUTHORITY	YR. RECD./EXP.
1.		
2.		
3.		

POTENTIAL INTEREST: YES ☐   NO ☐

GEOGRAPHIC PREFERENCE:

ANY AREA ☐   U.S. ☐   CANADA ☐

LATIN AMERICA ☐   EUROPE ☐   ASIA PACIFIC ☐

WORK EXPERIENCE AND KNOWLEDGE   ACTION

CATEGORY	DESCRIPTION	FUNCTIONAL AREA	YRS. EXP.	LAST YR.		YRS. EXP.	LAST YR.

MAILING CODE   ID   FLSA   CATG   ORIGINAL HIRE DATE   LATEST HIRE DATE   CONTINUOUS SERVICE

Adding Human Resources

Many environmental factors may impact the decision to hire permanently or temporarily or to outsource. Some of these factors include the permanency of the needs, the availability of qualified recruits, and the union contract (if applicable). If the net requirements indicate a need for additional human resources, decisions must be made whether to make permanent or temporary hires or to outsource. If the decision is to make permanent hires, plans must be made to recruit, select, orient, and train the specific numbers and types of personnel needed (Chapters 6, 7, and 8 deal with these topics).

Contingent Workers and Outsourcing Contingent workers (introduced in Chapter 4) and outsourcing (introduced in Chapter 1) have the advantage of allowing the organization to easily accommodate swings in demand for human resources. Contingent workers often do not have the same benefits as permanent employees and hence the cost of employment can be less. Other potential advantages of using contingenct workers and, specifically, temporary agencies, is that the agencies often provide both testing and training for employees before they are hired. A final potential advantage of contingent workers is that, because of their varied experiences, they can bring a new perspective to the organization.

If the decision is to outsource, then potential clients for outsourcing must be identified and evaluated. Outsourcing has become attractive in many situations because the work can often be contracted outside at a cost savings. One reason for this savings is that the company providing the service may not offer its employees benefits as attractive as those the parent company offers. Another reason to outsource is to allow the parent company to focus on its core business.

Reducing Human Resources

If a reduction in human resources is necessary, plans must be made to realize the necessary adjustments. If time is not of the essence, natural attrition can be used to reduce labor personnel. However, if the organization cannot afford the luxury of natural attrition, it can reduce human resource costs either by cutting the total number of employees or by making other adjustments that do not result in employees leaving the organization.

Downsizing As mentioned in Chapter 1, reducing the total number of employees is referred to as *downsizing.* There are four basic ways to downsize: (1) layoffs, (2) terminations, (3) early retirement inducements, and (4) voluntary resignation inducements. A layoff, as opposed to a termination, assumes it is likely that the employee will be recalled at some later date. Most early retirement and voluntary resignation plans provide some financial inducement to retire early or to resign.

Downsizing, or reducing the total number of employees, results from a number of circumstances. Steve Cole/Getty Images

Other Approaches for Reducing Human Resource Costs Approaches that do not result in employees leaving the organization include (1) reclassification, (2) transfer, (3) work sharing, and (4) job sharing. *Reclassification* involves demoting an employee, downgrading job responsibilities, or a combination of the two. Usually reclassification is accompanied by a reduction in pay. A *transfer* involves moving the employee to another part of the organization. *Work sharing* seeks to limit layoffs and terminations through the proportional reduction of hours among employees (i.e., all employees in a department could be cut back to 35 hours per week instead of 40). As discussed in Chapter 4, *job sharing* occurs when two or more part-time individuals perform a job that would normally be held by one full-time person. Job sharing can be used to downsize and still retain valuable employees.

Synthesizing the HRP Process

Figure 5.4 depicts the relationship between organizational planning and human resource planning. As the figure shows, organizational objectives are influenced by many historical and environmental factors. Environmental factors include variables such as government influences, the economy, competition, labor availability, and technology. Once the organizational objectives have been established, they are translated into divisional and departmental objectives. Individual managers then determine the human resources necessary to meet their respective objectives. Human resource personnel assimilate these different requirements and determine the total human resources demand for the organization. Similarly, HR personnel

FIGURE 5.4   Organizational and Human Resource Planning

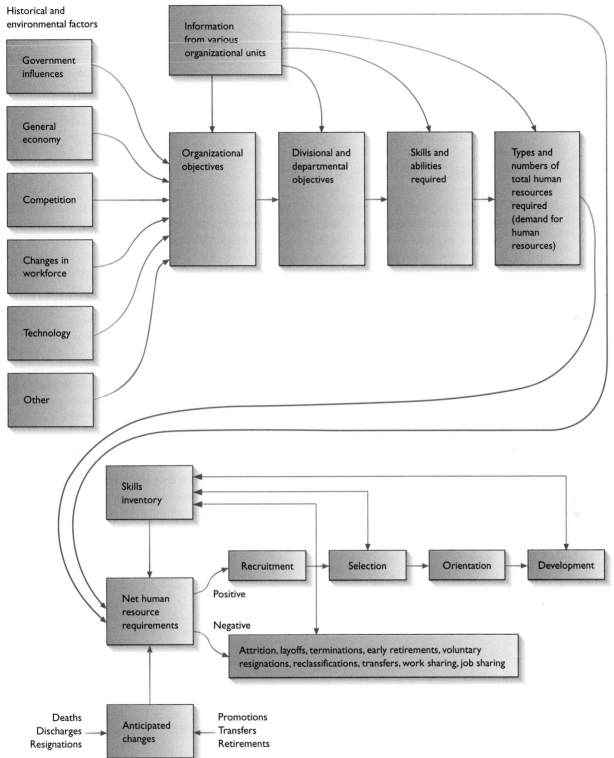

determine the additional (net) human resource requirements based on the information submitted by the various organizational units in light of available resources and anticipated changes. If the net requirements are positive, the organization implements recruitment, selection, training, and development (see Chapters 6, 7, 8, and 9). If the requirements are negative, human resource costs must be reduced through downsizing or through the use of approaches that do not result in employees actually leaving the organization. Downsizing can be realized through attrition, layoffs, terminations, early retirements, or voluntary resignations. Approaches that do not result in employees leaving the organization include reclassification, transfer, and work sharing. As these changes take place, they should be reflected in the skills inventory. Human resource planning is an ongoing process that must be continuously evaluated as conditions change.

SUCCESSION PLANNING

succession planning
Technique that identifies specific people to fill future openings in key positions throughout the organization.

Succession planning identifies a "talent pool" that can be developed in preparation for future responsibilities. Succession planning considers not only past performance but also the future potential of individuals.[13] Many organizations are engaged in a process closer to replacement planning than true succession planning. The goal of replacement planning is to identify a "backup" to fill a job when it becomes vacant. The focus is on past performance and demonstrating the skills necessary to perform the job in question. In addition to considering the future potential of individuals, succession planning anticipates changing organization needs and prepares the talent pool to meet those future needs. The emphasis of succession planning is on developing people rather than naming replacements. The idea is to build organizational bench strength so that when a vacancy occurs, there is an internal pool of qualified candidates available. True succession planning is "future focused." Under an optimal succession planning system, individuals are initially identified as candidates for the talent pool after being nominated by management. Then performance appraisal data are reviewed, potential is assessed and developmental programs are formulated. Sophisticated succession planning helps ensure that qualified internal candidates are not overlooked.

One problem with many succession plans, especially informal plans and those for large organizations, is the "crowned prince" syndrome.[14] This occurs when management considers for advancement only those who have managed to become visible to senior management. A second problem with succession planning in many organizations is that it is focused on just the senior-most levels in the organizations. Organizations should identify critical positions throughout the organization and develop talent pools for each of these positions. At the same time succession planning is not necessary for all positions; but rather the most important positions, which may not always be the most obvious.

As organizations evolve from replacement planning to succession planning, there are four important ingredients for success:

1. Define what competencies (knowledge, skills, abilities, and personal characteristics) people must possess to move the organization forward both now and in the foreseeable future.
2. Focus on critical positions, not just the very top.
3. Evaluate the current talent pools; distinguish between current performance and future potential.
4. Identify individual development needs.

Taking a proactive approach to succession planning that includes the above four ingredients will help ensure an organization's future success.

A legal notice published in October 27, 2009, by the Securities and Exchange Commission's (SEC's) Division of Corporate Finance for the first time allows shareholders to request more disclosure from companies regarding how their boards select CEOs. According to Ted Dysart, managing partner with Heidrick & Stuggles, "This change will likely mean that succession planning will now draw the same attention from shareholders that audit and compensation have been receiving."[15] There is little doubt that HR departments and managers will feel the impact of this notice and that more emphasis will be placed on succession planning. HRM in Action 5.2 discusses succession planning at McDonald's.

CEO SUCCESSION AT MCDONALD'S

The November 30, 2009 announcement that 55-year-old McDonald's Corporation president and COO Ralph Alvarez would retire at the end of the year came as a surprise to most people. Many people thought Alvarez was next in line to become the CEO of McDonald's. "After more than 30 years in the restaurant industry, the past 15 with this great brand, I've decided to retire," said Alvarez. "Seven orthopedic surgeries and years of chronic pain, culminating in two total knee replacements in the past six months, have made me realize it's time to move on."

McDonald's has faced the sudden loss of top managers before and has rarely missed a beat. McDonald's moved its current, CEO, Jim Skinner, to his position in 2004 after Charlie Bell stepped down from the post following the announcement that Bell had cancer. Bell, who died in 2005, had succeeded Jim Cantalupo earlier in 2004, after Cantalupo had died of a heart attack.

"McDonald's promotes from within, and that's a sign that they don't have to go outside," said Bruce Sherman of Chicago-based Integral Advisors. "They have enough capable internal people." "Seamless management change is a by-product of McDonald's commitment to leadership development and talent management," Skinner said. "Together with our board of directors, we have made succession planning a competitive advantage for our company."

Don Thompson, formerly president of McDonald's USA, was announced as the new president and COO on January 11, 2010.

Sources: Mark Brandau, "Alvarez Retirement Highlights Importance of Succession Plans," *Nation's Restaurant News,* December 14, 2009, pp. 1–2, and "McDonald's Corporation Elects Don Thompson as President and COO; Jan Fields and Jim Johannesen Named to Lead McDonald's USA," *PR Newswire,* January 11, 2010.

HUMAN RESOURCE INFORMATION SYSTEMS (HRIS)

human resource information system (HRIS)
A database system that contains all relevant human resource information and provides facilities for maintaining and accessing these data.

As discussed in Chapter 1, the use of information systems permeates much of the HR field. Because this is especially true in HRP, the use of information systems in HR is discussed in this section. Increased human resource requirements, government regulations, and expanded personal computer capabilities have all helped justify the need and feasibility of an information system within the human resource department. Such an information system is referred to as a **human resource information system (HRIS).** An HRIS is a database system that contains all relevant human resource information and provides facilities for maintaining and accessing these data.[16]

A major advantage of an HRIS is its potential for producing more accurate and more timely information for operating, controlling, and planning purposes than manual or payroll-based systems can produce. The speed and accuracy of an HRIS simply cannot be matched by manual systems. An HRIS also gets rid of many of the paper files human resource people and other areas of the organization maintain.

Historically the major disadvantage of an HRIS was its financial cost and the labor requirements for implementing the system. Fortunately, these problems have greatly diminished as a result of the computer hardware and software currently available. Today numerous off-the-shelf HRIS software packages and the necessary hardware are readily available at much lower prices than just a few years ago. The currently available software packages also are much more user-friendly and, thus, require less training and time to implement.

The following areas represent some specific potential applications for an HRIS:

1. *Clerical applications.* Automating certain routine clerical tasks avoids the use of additional staff, overtime, and temporary help.

2. *Applicant search expenditures.* An HRIS can easily store a summary of applicant qualifications and subsequently perform searches for candidates for certain positions. This can help the company avoid the need for an employment agency.

3. *Risk management.* Today it is critical in many industries that people in certain jobs have licenses, safety training, and even physical examinations. An HRIS can be used to monitor these requirements and report any discrepancies by jobholders.

4. *Training management.* An HRIS can compare job training requirements with the actual training experiences of individual jobholders. This system can then be used to determine both individual and organizational training needs.

5. *Training experiences.* An HRIS can provide organizationwide training development and delivery, especially for jobs using computers.

6. *Financial planning.* By using an HRIS, human resource managers can stimulate the financial impact of salary and benefit changes. It is then possible for the human resource department to recommend changes in strategy that stay within an overall budget goal.

7. *Turnover analysis.* Turnover can be closely monitored with an HRIS. Turnover characteristics can be identified and analyzed for probable causes.

8. *Succession planning.* An HRIS can identify a logical progression path and the steps required for advancement. Individual progress can then be monitored.

9. *Flexible-benefits administration.* An HRIS can be used to administer a flexible-benefits program. Without an HRIS, such programs can be expensive to implement and administer.

10. *Compliance with government regulations.* An HRIS can be used to keep up with current EEO and related government-required regulations. An HRIS can also help keep companies in compliance by more thoroughly scanning job applicants who meet specific requirements and keeping management informed of the situation.

11. *Attendance reporting and analysis.* The documentation of sick days, vacation time, personal time, and tardiness can be a significant expense if done manually. An HRIS can easily track this information.

12. *Accident reporting and prevention.* An HRIS can be used to record accident details and subsequently provide analyses that can help prevent future accidents.

13. *Strategic planning.* Today's client/server systems are transforming human resource people from simple administrators to strategic planners who can influence CEO decisions.

14. *Human resource planning.* Human resource planning can be greatly assisted by an information system that is capable of making projections based on the current workforce.[17]

A major indirect benefit of an HRIS is that it helps enable HR managers become more strategic. This is accomplished by automating much of the transaction processing and providing quality information to assist management when making strategic decisions. Thus, an HRIS provides a medium that helps HR professionals perform their jobs more effectively and it also supports strategic decision making.[18] Also, many software companies offer HRIS packages for purchase. The Web site for the International Association for Human Resource Information Management (www.ihrim.org) lists numerous sources for HRIS packages. (Go to the home page and search under "Buyers Guide.")

HR and the Internet

The Internet is an excellent source for finding many types of information related to human resource management and for keeping up with new developments in the field. Today a growing number of HR managers are using the Internet to screen and recruit personnel, conduct research, access electronic databases, send e-mail, conduct training, and network with colleagues. The real value of the Internet to HR professionals is the information that it makes available. Through the Internet, managers can access massive amounts of information. Figure 5.5 provides a list of some HR-related Web sites.

HR Intranets and Portals

An *intranet* is a private computer network that uses Internet products and technologies to provide multimedia applications within organizations. An intranet connects people to people and information and knowledge within the organization; it serves as an "information hub" for the entire organization. A Web *portal* is similar to an intranet except that portals enable other specific groups such as business partners, customers, or vendors to access an organization's intranet. The eHR systems discussed in Chapter 1 are an example of an intranet. Initially an intranet, like an internal HRIS, was seen as a luxury that could be justified only if it served thousands of employees. This is no longer true as many software companies provide a mix of intranet applications that can be purchased or leased at very reasonable rates. The Web site of the previously mentioned International Association for Human Resource Information Management (www.ihrim.org) also lists several sources for intranet packages (go to the home page and search under "Buyers Guide"). Figure 5.6 provides suggested HR-related general uses of

FIGURE 5.5
HR-Related Web Sites

Source: Adapted from "How to Enrich and Expand Your Internet Searches," *HR Focus,* June 2006, pp. 7–8, and "Progressive Business Publications PBP; Progressive Business Publications' New E-Newsletter Division Targets Advertisers Marketing to Business Executives," *Marketing Business Weekly,* July 14, 2008, p. 21.

- **SHRM (www.shrm.org).** The Society for Human Resource Management has a well-organized database for easy searching.
- **Bureau of National Affairs (www.bna.com).** Contains news and other materials on human resources and business topics.
- **IHRIM (www.ihrim.org).** IHRIM is a major organization addressing HR information systems and technology. Other useful information such as the role technology now plays in a variety of HR processes and practices is also available.
- **Human Resources Planning Society (www.hrps.org).** This group of mostly large-organization senior HR professionals addresses issues related to the developing profession and business of HR.
- **U.S. Department of Labor Bureau of Labor Statistics (www.bls.gov).** The main site for federal government information on HR topics including wages, benefits, employment, demographics, and safety.
- **National Labor Relations Board (www.nlrb.gov/nlrb/home/default.asp).** Presents federal law related to organized labor.
- **Center for Advanced HR Studies at Cornell University (www.ilr.cornell.edu/depts/cahrs/).** Research on various HR topics from a leading university.
- **HR Internet Guide (www.hrguide.com).** Links to many different HR-related Web sites, including equal employment opportunity, staffing and selection, incentive plans, job analysis, and training and development.
- **HR Software (www.hrsoftware.net).** Links to numerous vendors.
- **HR Morning (www.hrmorning.com).** Site covering general human resource management.
- **HR Tech News (www.hrtechnews.com).** Covers technology developments related to the human resources field.
- **HR Benefits Alert (www.hrbenefitsalert.com).** Information for benefits professionals.
- **HR Recruiting Alert (www.hrrecruitingalert.com).** Features recruiting and staffing information and news.
- **HR Legal News (www.hrlegalnews.com).** Information relating to workplace employment law.
- **HR Blunders (www.hrblunders.com).** Site covering HR blunders to avoid and the lighter side of HR.

FIGURE 5.6
Intranet and Portal Users

Source: Adapted from Samuel Greengard, "Ways to Make a More Powerful Portal," *Workforce,* April 2002, Crain Communications, Inc.

Basic

- Employee communication.
- Company directory.
- Company handbook, including policies and guidelines.
- Weather.
- News.
- Stock information.
- Connection for departments within the company.
- Discussion or chat rooms.

Intermediate

- Linkage to outside benefits providers.
- Employee-assistance programs.
- Web-based e-mail.
- E-learning.
- Online job postings.
- Calendar, address book, and project scheduling.
- Online travel bookings.
- Document management.
- Orientation.
- Hands-on demonstrations.

Advanced

- Benefits enrollment.
- Performance management.
- Salary and wage reviews.
- Succession planning.
- Online recruitment and hiring.
- Ability to submit electronic forms.
- Electronic paycheck information, including pay stubs and W-2s.
- Business intelligence.
- Audio and video conferencing.
- Interaction with customers.

an intranet. There is little doubt that intranets have redefined the ways that HR information is handled in many organizations.

HR and Web 2.0

Web 2.0 is the second generation of Internet use with a focus on user content control, online collaboration, and sharing between users.[19] Web 2.0 technologies use Web-based communities and hosted services such as social networking sites, blogs, and wikis. Social networking sites such as Facebook and My Space allow users the opportunity to communicate with each other in a real and personal manner. A blog, derived from the term *Web log,* is an online diary or journal that usually involves a series of short entries written in chronological order. A blog can be a personal journal or an interactive forum. A wiki is "a knowledge base developed over time by users with access to create and edit text on the site."[20] Web 2.0 technologies foster sharing and collaboration, which lend themselves to numerous HR applications.

Web 2.0 technologies can be used to perform background checks and to screen job applicants by looking them up on various social networking sites. Internal blogs and social networks can be used to keep different employees, teams and other subgroups in touch. These same technologies can also be used in many aspects of training, both formal and informal. An emerging use for HR of Web 2.0 is on the recruitment front by blogging about the organization as a great place to work. HRM in Action 5.3 describes how Capital One has used Web 2.0 to improve its internal communication and collaboration.

Software as a Service

Software as a service (SaaS) or "on-demand software" is a relatively new approach to software delivery that involves users accessing standard business applications over the Internet. Traditionally, software companies sold their software on disks and CDs, which were then installed on the client's local computers.[21] The software also had to be constantly maintained and periodically updated. With SaaS, software makers provide their products over the Internet on a pay-as-you-go basis, usually for a monthly subscription fee. Major benefits of software as a service are that no large capital expenditure is required to buy and install equipment and that there are fewer hassles related to managing the systems. Instead of waiting months and spending hundreds of thousands of dollars, with software as a service, users can be up and running within days or even hours of signing a contract. Because of these benefits, software as a service has particular appeal to HR applications. For 2009 the market research firm IDC projected SaaS growth to be 36 percent to 40 percent.[22] IDC also forecast that nearly 45 percent of U.S. companies would spend at least one-fourth of their IT budget on SaaS by the next year. Gartner, Inc., a world leading information technology research and advisory company, forecast worldwide SaaS sales to reach $7.5 billion for 2009, a healthy 17.7 percent increase from the previous year.[23] Gartner also predicts SaaS sales to almost double (14 billion) by 2013. HRM in Action 5.4 describes some HRIS software applicable to small and midsized organizations.

A LOW-COST, FLEXIBLE HRIS
www.best-software.com

HR managers in small and midsized businesses are faced with competing issues when it comes to HRIS software: controlling costs due to limited budgets and providing a fully functional system to cover all their HR needs. With the Abra Suite of HRIS software from Sage Software (formerly Best Software) of Reston, Virginia, they can choose a basic Abra HR module and add modules for other HR functions such as payroll processing, attendance tracking, attendance management, training management, online recruiting, and recruiting management. With a very affordable price for the base HR program, and additional costs for add-on modules, HR managers in smaller companies can meet budget constraints, reporting requirements, and individual organizational needs such as benefits administration and employee information storage. The system can also run on networks to provide better communication links throughout the organization.

Sage recently added Abra Workforce Connections, which can be bundled into the existing Abra offerings. Abra Workforce Connections has two main components: Abra ESS (employee self-service) and Abra Benefits Enrollment. Abra Workforce Connections offers a central online location for employees at all levels to view and manage certain personal and company information, as well as process payroll requests. Abra Workforce Connections is priced at $1,300 for a 75-employee ESS or Benefits module.

Sources: "Cream of the Crop," *Human Resource Executive,* October 16, 2005, and www.sagespecialized.com, accessed January 17, 2007.

Summary of Learning Objectives

1. Define *human resource planning* (*HRP*).

HRP is the process of getting the right number of qualified people into the right job at the right time. Put another way, HRP is the system of matching the supply of people—internally (existing employees) and externally (those to be hired or searched for)—with the openings the organization expects to have over a given time.

2. Summarize the relationship between HRP and organizational planning.

To be effective, any human resource plan must be derived from the long-range and operational plans of the organization. In essence, the success of HRP depends largely on how closely human resource personnel can integrate effective people planning with the organization's business planning process.

3. Explain strategy-linked HRP.

Strategy-linked HRP is based on a close working relationship between human resource staff and line managers. Human resource managers serve as consultants to line managers concerning the people management implications of business objectives and strategies. Line managers, in turn, have a responsibility to respond to the business implications of human resource objectives and strategies. Top management must also be committed to the HRP process.

4. Identify the steps in the HRP process.

HRP consists of four basic steps: (1) determining the impact of the organization's objectives on specific organizational units; (2) defining the skills, expertise, and total number of employees required to achieve the organizational and departmental objectives; (3) determining the additional human resource requirements; and (4) developing action plans to meet the anticipated human resource needs.

5. Identify the different methods used for forecasting human resource needs.

Methods for forecasting human resource needs can be either judgmentally or mathematically based. Judgmental methods include managerial estimates, the Delphi technique, and scenario analysis. Mathematically based methods include various statistical and modeling methods.

6. Discuss the purpose of a skills inventory.

A skills inventory consolidates information about the organization's human resources. It provides basic information on all employees, including, in its simplest form, a list of the names, certain characteristics, and skills of employees.

7. **Describe succession planning.**

    Succession planning identifies a "talent pool" that can be developed in preparation for future responsibilities and considers not only past performance but also the future potential of individuals.

8. **Define a human resource information system (HRIS).**

    Information systems developed and used exclusively for human resource applications are referred to as human resource information systems (HRIS).

9. **Differentiate between the Internet and an intranet.**

    An intranet is a private computer network that uses Internet products and technologies to provide multimedia applications *within* organizations. The Internet is a global collection of independently operating, but interconnected, computers.

10. **Explain what Web 2.0 is.**

    Web 2.0 is the second generation of internet use with a focus on user content control, online collaboration, and sharing between users.

11. **Define the concept of "software as a service."**

    Software as a service, also called on-demand software, is a relatively new approach to software delivery that involves users accessing standard business applications over the Internet.

Key Terms

benchmarking, *94*	intranet, *102*	scenario analysis, *94*
cascade approach to setting objectives, *92*	job sharing, *98*	skills inventory, *95*
	management inventory, *96*	Software as a Service
Delphi technique, *94*	managerial estimates, *94*	(SaaS), *104*
downsizing, *98*	organizational objectives, *92*	succession planning, *100*
human resource information system (HRIS), *101*	portal, *102*	Web 2.0, *104*
	reclassification, *98*	work sharing, *98*
human resource planning (HRP), *89*		

Review Questions

1. What is human resource planning (HRP)?
2. How does human resource planning relate to organizational planning?
3. What are the four basic steps in the human resource planning process?
4. Explain the cascade approach to setting objectives.
5. Identify several tools that might be used as aids in the human resource planning process.
6. What is the role of human resource personnel in the human resource planning process?
7. What is an HRIS?
8. Recount several areas or functions for which an HRIS might be used.
9. What is the difference between the Internet and an intranet?
10. Give some examples of Web 2.0 technologies.
11. What are the potential advantages of software as a service (SaaS)?

Discussion Questions

1. What role do you think HRP can play in helping organizations avoid employee layoffs?
2. Do you think most human resource planning is undertaken on the basis of organizational objectives or on an "as necessary" basis?
3. How is it possible to accomplish good organizational planning, and hence good human resource planning, in light of the many changing environmental factors over which the organization has no control?
4. Why do you think that some human resource managers might be reluctant to use information technology such as an HRIS? Do you think that the trend toward the use of Web 2.0 technologies and SaaS can have an effect on this problem?

Incident 5.1

Human Resource Planning—What Is That?

You are a human resource consultant. You have been called by the newly appointed president of a large paper manufacturing firm:

President: I have been in this job for about one month now, and all I seem to do is interview people and listen to personnel problems.

You: Why have you been interviewing people? Don't you have a human resource department?

President: Yes, we do. However, the human resource department doesn't hire top management people. As soon as I took over, I found that two of my vice presidents were retiring and we had no one to replace them.

You: Have you hired anyone?

President: Yes, I have, and that's part of the problem. I hired a guy from the outside. As soon as the announcement was made, one of my department heads came in and resigned. She said she had wanted that job as vice president for eight years. She was angry because we had hired someone from the outside. How was I supposed to know she wanted the job?

You: What have you done about the other vice president job?

President: Nothing, because I'm afraid someone else will quit because they weren't considered for the job. But that's only half my problem. I just found out that among our youngest professional employees—engineers and accountants—there has been an 80 percent turnover rate during the past three years. These are the people we promote around here. As you know, that's how I started out in this company. I was a mechanical engineer.

You: Has anyone asked them why they are leaving?

President: Yes, and they all give basically the same answer: They say they don't feel that they have a future here. Maybe I should call them all together and explain how I progressed in this company.

You: Have you ever considered implementing a human resource planning system?

President: Human resource planning? What's that?

Questions

1. How would you answer the president's question?
2. What would be required to establish a human resource planning system in this company?

Incident 5.2

New Boss

The grants management program of the Environmental Protection Agency (EPA) water division was formed several years ago. The program's main functions are to review grant applications, engineering design reports, and change orders and to perform operation and maintenance inspection of wastewater treatment facilities.

Paul Wagner, chief of the section, supervised four engineers, one technician, and one secretary. Three of the engineers were relatively new to the agency. The senior engineer, Waymon Burrell, had approximately three years' experience in the grants management program.

Because only Waymon Burrell had experience in grants management, Wagner assigned him the areas with the most complicated projects within the state. The other three engineers were given regions with less complex projects; they were assigned to work closely with Burrell and to learn all they could about the program.

At the beginning of the year, Wagner decided the new engineers had enough experience to undertake more difficult tasks; therefore, the division's territory could be allocated on a geographical basis. The territory was divided according to river basins, with each engineer assigned two or three areas.

This division according to geography worked fine as the section proceeded to meet all its objectives. However, three months ago, Wagner was offered a job with a consulting engineering company and decided to leave the EPA. He gave two months' notice to top management.

Time passed, but top management did not even advertise for a new section chief. People in the section speculated as to who might be chosen to fill the vacancy; most of them hoped it would be Waymon Burrell, since he knew the most about the workings of the section.

On the Monday of Wagner's last week, top executives met with him and the section members to announce they had decided to appoint a temporary section chief until a new one could be hired. The division chief announced that the temporary section chief would be Sam Kutzman, a senior engineer from another EPA division. This came as quite a surprise to Burrell and the others in the grants management program.

Sam Kutzman had no experience in the program. His background was in technical assistance. His previous job had required that he do research in certain treatment processes so that he could provide more technical performance information to other divisions within the EPA.

Questions

1. Do you think Sam Kutzman was a good choice for temporary section chief?
2. How well has human resource planning worked in this situation?

EXERCISE 5.1
Avoiding Layoffs?

Go to the library, Internet, or a recent publication and find a situation where an organization has recently experienced layoffs. Research the situation and determine if you think the company could have done a better job with its human resource planning and avoided or minimized the layoffs. In other words, from a human resource planning perspective, could the organization have done a better job and specifically what could have been done differently?

EXERCISE 5.2
Locating HR Software

Your instructor will assign you an HR topic or function. Your assignment is to go to the Web site of the International Association for Human Resource Information Management (www.ihrim.org) and click on the tab "Products and Services." Review the lists of possibilities and identify three to five pieces of software you think might be helpful to an organization when dealing with your HR topic. You will not be able to view the software itself but rather a brief description of what is available from different software providers.

Notes and Additional Readings

1. C. F. Russ, Jr., "Manpower Planning Systems: Part I," *Personnel Journal,* January 1982, p. 41.
2. Ibid.
3. David E. Ripley, "How to Determine Future Work-Force Needs," *Personnel Journal,* January 1995, p. 83.
4. David Liang, "Deciphering the Common Misconceptions about Human Resource Planning," *China Staff,* July/August 2009, pp. 28–31.
5. James W. Walker, "Human Resource Planning, 1990's Style," *Human Resource Planning,* December 1990, pp. 229–30; Stanley R. Case, "Ciba Creates an HR Strategy for the Next Century," *Workforce,* October 1995, pp. 109–12; and "Addressing 2003's Top Issues for HR," *HR Focus,* January 2003, pp. 1–3.
6. Ernest C. Miller, "Strategic Planning Pays Off," *Personnel Journal,* April 1989, p. 127; Patricia M. Buhler, "Workforce Development: Every Manager's Challenge," *SuperVision,* October 2001, pp. 13–15.
7. Much of this section is drawn from John A. Hooper, Ralph E. Catalanello, and Patrick L. Murray, "Showing Up the Weakest Link," *Personnel Administrator,* April 1987, pp. 49–55; Linda Davidson, "Who's Investing in HR?" *Workforce,* December 1999, pp. 66–71.

8. D. Quinn Mills, "Planning with People in Mind," *Harvard Business Review,* July–August 1985, pp. 97–105.

9. Adapted from D. L. Chicci, "Four Steps to an Organization/Human Resource Plan," *Personnel Journal,* June 1979, pp. 290–92; see also Buhler, "Workforce Development."

10. Dan Ward, "Workforce Demand Forecasting Techniques," *Human Resource Planning* 19, No. 1 (1996), pp. 54–55.

11. Samuel Greengard, "Discover Best Practices through Benchmarking," *Personnel Journal,* November 1995, pp. 62–65; Chris Mahoney, "Benchmarking HR Budgets," *Workforce,* October 2000, pp. 100–104.

12. Thomas H. Patten, *Manpower Planning and the Development of Human Resources* (New York: John Wiley & Sons, 1971), p. 243.

13. Much of this section is drawn from "Succession Planning: Four Imperatives for Success," *Workforce Management,* September 8, 2008, p. 58; and "Ten Key Steps to Effective Succession Planning," *Workforce Management,* September 8, 2008, p. 511.

14. James E. McElwain, "Succession Plans Designed to Manage Change," *HR Magazine,* February 1991, pp. 67–71; "Executive Succession: A Critical Governing Board Responsibility," *Trends On-Line,* October 2001.

15. "SEC Targets CEO Succession Plans—New Risks for Boards, Says Heidrick and Stuggles," *PR Newswire,* October 30, 2009.

16. Gerson Safran, "Human Resource Information System," *Canadian Manager,* September 1994, p. 13.

17. Adapted from William I. Travis, "Personnel Computing: How to Justify a Human Resources Information System," *Personnel Journal,* January 1994, p. 11.

18. Zahid Hussain, James Wallace, and Nelarine E. Cornelius, "The Use and Impact of Human Resource Information Systems on Human Resource Management Professionals," *Information & Management,* January 2007, pp. 74–89.

19. Much of this section is drawn from "Web 2.0 Defines Next Generation," *Knight Ridder Business News,* April 18, 2007, p. 1; and "What You Should Know about Using Web 2.0," *HR Focus,* April 2008, pp. 10–11.

20. Bill Roberts, "How to Marshal Wikis," *HR Magazine,* December 2008, pp. 54–57.

21. This section is drawn from Darren Dahl, "Service, Not Servers," *Inc.,* May 2006, pp. 41–43; and Leslie Gross Klaff, "An Ever-Changing Landscape," *Workforce Management,* December 11, 2006, pp. 4–8.

22. Patrick Thibodeau, "SaaS Still on the Rise, Despite Down Economy," *Computerworld,* February 9, 2009, pp. 12–13.

23. "Gartner Downgrade SaaS Forecast," *Informationweek-Online,* November 9, 2009.

Recruiting Employees

Chapter Learning Objectives

After studying this chapter, you should be able to:

1. Define recruitment.
2. Discuss job analysis, human resource planning, and recruitment.
3. Explain the purpose of a personnel requisition form.
4. Describe the advantages and disadvantages of using internal methods of recruitment.
5. Discuss job posting and bidding.
6. Describe the advantages and disadvantages of using external methods of recruitment.
7. Define realistic job previews.
8. Explain organizational inducements.
9. Outline some specific EEOC recommendations for job advertising.

Chapter Outline

Job Analysis, Human Resource Planning, and Recruitment

Personnel Requisition Form

Sources of Qualified Personnel

Internal Sources

External Sources

Effectiveness of Recruitment Methods

Realistic Job Previews

Who Does the Recruiting, and How?

Organizational Inducements in Recruitment

Equal Employment Opportunity and Recruitment

Summary of Learning Objectives

Key Terms

Review Questions

Discussion Questions

Exercise 6.1: Writing a Résumé

Notes and Additional Readings

recruitment
Process of seeking and attracting a pool of people from which qualified candidates for job vacancies can be chosen.

Recruitment involves seeking and attracting a pool of people from which qualified candidates for job vacancies can be chosen. Most organizations have a recruitment (or, as it is sometimes called, employment) function managed by the human resource department. In an era when the focus of most organizations has been on efficiently and effectively running the organization, recruiting the right person for the job is a top priority. HRM in Action 6.1 illustrates a creative recruiting program.

The magnitude of an organization's recruiting effort and the methods to be used in that recruiting effort are determined from the human resource planning process and the requirements of the specific jobs to be filled. As Chapter 5 explained, if the forecasted human resource

E-RECRUITMENT

Companies, while cutting traditional employee recruitment budgets in recent years, have begun to increase the amount of money and time they spend using e-recruitment techniques. This new trend has been effective in cutting costs and time spent in many cases, but as this is a new form of weeding through candidates for employment there have been some areas where improvement is needed in e-recruitment.

Depending on the open position a company may be filling, e-recruitment may be ineffective. For example, an employer may want to meet a potential sales employee in a traditional interview setting as sales is a position where personality is a huge factor in effectiveness. Yet, in the initial review an online personality assessment may allow the recruiter to weed out many potential candidates. A traditional interview process would be cost ineffective and a time drain due to the number of candidates.

A second area of weakness is cheating the system. There is a fear that potential candidates will have others fill out online applications. A way to correct that is for employers to include information that the online portion is only an initial step and further tests in person will be required. While many young potential employees are willing to go through lengthy tests, many senior-level candidates may be unwilling to spend the time for an e-recruitment process. One way to combat this is for employers to promise feedback to potential candidates on answers to their tests whether the candidate receives an offer from the company or not. This way, candidates at least can learn how to better present themselves in the e-recruitment process.

For companies, e-recruitment is a great way to be more cost-effective, and as prices for the technology continue to fall, e-recruitment will become more prevalent. As for potential candidates who may look at e-recruitment unfavorably, as the process becomes more prevalent and the problems associated with the process become fewer, the view of e-recruitment may turn more favorable as candidates recognize the ease and convenience of the process.

Source: Adapted from Nick Martindale, "The Pros and Cons of Online Assessment," *Personnel Today*, October 20, 2009, p. 12.

requirements exceed the net human resource requirements, the organization usually actively recruits new employees. Successful recruiting is difficult if the jobs to be filled are vaguely defined. Regardless of whether the job to be filled has been in existence or is newly created, its requirements must be defined as precisely as possible for recruiting to be effective.

Organizations do have options other than recruiting new employees to accomplish the work. Some of these options include using temporary workers, offering overtime to existing employees, subcontracting the work to another organization (this approach is often used on construction projects or projects that have a fixed time period for completion), and leasing employees. One final option is outsourcing the work to companies outside the United States.

JOB ANALYSIS, HUMAN RESOURCE PLANNING, AND RECRUITMENT

Figure 6.1 illustrates the relationships among job analysis, human resource planning, recruitment, and the selection process. Job analysis gives the nature and requirements of specific jobs. Human resource planning determines the specific number of jobs to be filled. Recruitment concerns providing a pool of people qualified to fill these vacancies. Questions that the recruitment process addresses include: What are the sources of qualified personnel? How are these qualified personnel to be recruited? Who is to be involved in the recruiting process? What inducements does the organization have to attract qualified personnel? The selection process, discussed in detail in the next chapter, concerns choosing from the pool of qualified candidates the individual or group of individuals most likely to succeed in a given job.

PERSONNEL REQUISITION FORM

personnel requisition form
Describes the reason for the need to hire a new person and the requirements of the job.

Most organizations use a **personnel requisition form** to officially request that the human resource manager take action to fill a particular position. The personnel requisition form describes the reason for the need to hire a new person and the requirements of the job. Figure 6.2 shows an example of a personnel requisition form. It is a good idea to attach a job description to the personnel requisition form.

FIGURE 6.1
Relationships among Job Analysis, Human Resource Planning, Recruitment, and Selection

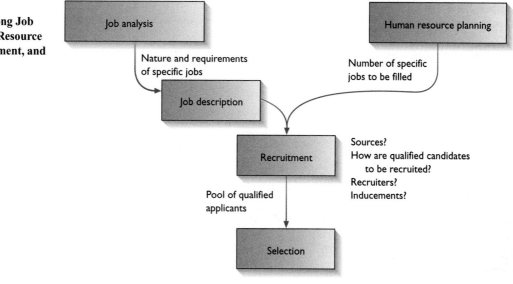

SOURCES OF QUALIFIED PERSONNEL

An organization may fill a particular job either with someone already employed by the organization or with someone from outside. Each of these sources has advantages and disadvantages.

Internal Sources

If an organization has been effective in recruiting and selecting employees in the past, one of the best sources of talent is its own employees. This has several advantages. First the organization should have a good idea of the strengths and weaknesses of its employees. If the organization maintains a skills inventory, it can use this as a starting point for recruiting from within. In addition, performance evaluations of employees are available. Present and prior managers of the employee being considered can be interviewed to obtain their evaluations of the employee's potential for promotion. In general, more accurate data are available concerning current employees, thus reducing the chance of making a wrong decision.

Not only does the organization know more about its employees, but the employees know more about the organization and how it operates. Therefore, the likelihood of the employee having inaccurate expectations and/or becoming dissatisfied with the organization is reduced when recruiting is done from within.

Another advantage is that recruitment from within can have a significant, positive effect on employee motivation and morale when it creates promotion opportunities or prevents layoffs. When employees know they will be considered for openings, they have an incentive for good performance. On the other hand, if outsiders are usually given the first opportunity to fill job openings, the effect can be the opposite.

A final advantage relates to the fact that most organizations have a sizable investment in their workforce. Full use of the abilities of the organization's employees improves the organization's return on its investment.

However, recruiting from within also has disadvantages. One danger associated with promotion from within is that infighting for promotions can become overly intense and have a negative effect on the morale and performance of people who are not promoted. Another danger involves the inbreeding of ideas. When recruiting comes only from internal sources, precautions must be taken to ensure that new ideas and innovations are not stifled by such attitudes as "We've never done it before" or "We do all right without it."

Two major issues are involved if an organization promotes from within. First, the organization needs a strong employee and management development program to ensure that its people can handle larger responsibilities. The second issue concerns the desirability of using seniority as the basis for promotions. Unions generally prefer promotions based on seniority

FIGURE 6.2
Personnel Requisition Form

Reprinted from *Human Resources: Documenting the Personnel Function* by Victor W. Eimicke, p. 23, Copyright © 1987, with permission from Elsevier.

PREPARE IN DUPLICATE, SEND ORIGINAL TO PERSONNEL

PERSONNEL REQUISITION

To Requisitioner: The Civil Rights Act of 1963 prohibits discrimination in employment because of race, color, creed, religion, sex or national origin. Federal law also prohibits other types of discrimination such as age. The laws of most States also prohibit some or all of the above types of discrimination as well as some additional types such as discrimination based upon ancestry, marital status or physical or mental handicap or disability. Any expression of limitations in these areas expressed in this requisition should be warranted by a bona fide occupational qualification or legally permissible reason.

DATE _____

FROM _____   _____
                    NAME   DEPARTMENT

I. DESCRIPTION OF NEED

DATE NEEDED	NUMBER OF EMPLOYEES	JOB TITLE	JOB CLASSIFICATION NUMBER	HIRING SALARY RANGE	JOB SALARY RANGE

PERMANENT _____   TEMPORARY _____   If temporary, for how long? _____   WHICH SHIFT? _____

PART TIME _____   FULL TIME _____   If part time, what hours or days? _____

II. REASON FOR NEED

REPLACEMENT: YES__ NO__ If yes, person(s) replaced _____   ADDITION: YES__ NO__ If yes, state reasons _____

_____   _____

_____   _____

III. REQUIREMENTS

EDUCATION: GRADE SCHOOL_____   HIGH SCHOOL_____   COLLEGE_____   COMMERCIAL_____   OTHER_____

EXPERIENCE: Please indicate, clearly, what is absolutely required as a prerequisite.

REQUIRED _____

_____

_____

DESIRABLE _____

_____

_____

ANY OTHER REQUIREMENTS: _____

_____

_____

_____

DATE _____   APPROVED BY _____

_____

DO NOT WRITE BELOW THIS LINE
_____

DATE FILLED _____   By WHOM _____

© Copyright, 1965, 1972, 1978, 1985—V.W. EIMICKE ASSOCIATES, INC., Bronxville, N.Y.   Form 116

for unionized jobs. Many organizations, on the other hand, prefer promotions based on prior performance and potential to do the new job.

Job Posting and Bidding

job posting and bidding
A method of informing employees of job vacancies by posting a notice in central locations and giving a specified period to apply for the job.

Job posting and bidding is an internal method of recruitment in which notices of available jobs are posted in central locations throughout the organization and employees are given a specified length of time to apply for the available jobs. Other methods used in publicizing jobs include memos to supervisors and listings in employee publications. Normally the job notice specifies the job title, rate of pay, and necessary qualifications. The usual procedure is for all applications to be sent to the human resource department for an initial review. The next step is an interview by the prospective manager. Then a decision is made based on qualifications, performance, length of service, and other pertinent criteria.

A successful job posting and bidding program requires the development of specific implementation policies. Some suggestions include the following:

- Both promotions and transfers should be posted.
- Openings should be posted for a specified time period before external recruitment begins.
- Eligibility rules for the job posting system need to be developed and communicated. For example, one eligibility rule might be that no employee can apply for a posted position unless the employee has been in his or her present position for six months.
- Specific standards for selection should be included in the notice.
- Job bidders should be required to list their qualifications and reasons for requesting a transfer or promotion.
- Unsuccessful bidders should be notified by the human resource department and advised as to why they were not accepted.

Naturally, the actual specifications for a job posting and bidding program must be tailored to the particular organization's needs.

In unionized organizations, job posting and bidding procedures are usually spelled out in the collective bargaining agreement. Because they are concerned about the subjective judgments of managers, unions normally insist that seniority be one of the primary determinants used in selecting people to fill available jobs.

External Sources

Organizations have at their disposal a wide range of external sources for recruiting personnel. External recruiting is needed in organizations that are growing rapidly or have a large demand for technical, skilled, or managerial employees.

One inherent advantage of recruiting from outside is that the pool of talent is much larger than that available from internal sources. Another advantage is that employees hired from outside can bring new insights and perspectives to the organization. In addition, it is often cheaper and easier to hire technical, skilled, or managerial people from the outside rather than to train and develop them internally. This is especially true when the organization has an immediate demand for this type of talent.

One disadvantage of external recruitment is that attracting, contacting, and evaluating potential employees is more difficult. A second potential disadvantage is that employees hired from the outside need a longer adjustment or orientation period. This can cause problems because even jobs that do not appear to be unique to the organization require familiarity with the people, procedures, policies, and special characteristics of the organization in which they are performed. A final problem is that recruiting from outside may cause morale problems among people within the organization who feel qualified to do the jobs.

Advertising

job advertising
The placement of help-wanted advertisements in daily newspapers, in trade and professional publications, or on radio and television.

Web site: Careers.Org
www.careers.org

**Web site:
ComputerJobs.com, Inc.**
www.computerjobs.com

**Web site: America's
Job Bank**
www.ajb.org

One of the more widely used methods of recruitment is **job advertising.** Help-wanted ads are commonly placed in daily newspapers and in trade and professional publications. Other, less frequently used media for advertising include radio, television, and billboards.

Human resource managers should ensure that their ads accurately describe the job opening and the requirements or qualifications needed to secure the position. However, it is generally true that people respond more frequently to advertisements from companies with a positive corporate image than to those companies with a lower corporate image.

The widespread use of advertising is probably more a matter of convenience than of proven effectiveness. If advertising is to be used as a primary source of recruitment, planning and evaluating the advertising program should be a primary concern of human resource personnel.

Employment Agencies

Both public and private employment agencies can be helpful in recruiting new employees. State employment agencies exist in most U.S. cities with populations of 10,000 or more. Although each state administers its respective agencies, the agencies must comply with the

headhunter
A type of private employment agency that seeks candidates for high-level, or executive, positions.

policies and guidelines of the Employment and Training Administration of the U.S. Department of Labor to receive federal funds. The Social Security Act requires all eligible individuals to register with the state employment agency before they can receive unemployment compensation. Thus, state employment agencies generally have an up-to-date list of unemployed persons. State employment agencies provide free service for individuals seeking employment and for business organizations seeking employees.

Two types of private employment agencies exist. The executive search firm (or **headhunter**) seeks candidates for high-level positions. (The term *headhunter* apparently comes from the concept of hiring a replacement head of an organization, such as chief executive officer or chief operating officer.) The second type of employment agency recruits for lower-level positions. Customers of this type of employment agency may be job applicants seeking employment or business firms seeking employees. The fees of private employment agencies are paid by the individual or the employing organization. If the fees are paid by the employing organization, the private employment agency will likely advertise the job as a "fee paid" position.

Temporary Help Agencies and Employee Leasing Companies

temporary help
People working for employment agencies who are subcontracted out to businesses at an hourly rate for a period of time specified by the businesses.

One of the fastest-growing areas of recruitment is **temporary help** hired through employment agencies. The agency pays the salary and benefits of the temporary help; the organization pays the employment agency an agreed-upon figure for the services of the temporary help. The use of temporary help is not dependent on economic conditions. When an organization is expanding, temporary employees are used to augment the current staff. When an organization is downsizing, temporary employees create a flexible staff that can be laid off easily and recalled when necessary. One obvious disadvantage of using temporary employees is their lack of commitment to the organization.

employee leasing companies
Provide permanent staffs at customer companies.

Unlike temporary agencies, which normally place people in short-term jobs at various companies, **employee leasing companies** and professional employer organizations (PEOs) provide permanent staff at customer companies, issue the workers' paychecks, take care of personnel matters, ensure compliance with workplace regulations, and provide various employee benefits.[1] In addition, they supply highly skilled technical workers such as engineers and information technology specialists for long-term projects under contract between a company and a technical services firm.

Employee Referrals and Walk-Ins/Unsolicited Applications

Many organizations involve their employees in the recruiting process. These recruiting systems may be informal and operate by word-of-mouth, or they may be structured with definite guidelines to be followed. Incentives and bonuses are sometimes given to employees who refer subsequently hired people. One drawback to the use of employee referrals is that cliques may develop within the organization because employees tend to refer only friends or relatives.

Walk-ins and unsolicited applications are also a source of qualified recruits. Corporate image has a significant impact on the number and quality of people who apply to an organization in this manner. Compensation policies, working conditions, relationships with labor, and participation in community activities are some of the many factors that can positively or negatively influence an organization's image.

campus recruiting
Recruitment activities of employers on college and university campuses.

Campus Recruiting

Recruiting on college and university campuses is a common practice of both private and public organizations. **Campus recruiting** activities are usually coordinated by the university or college placement center. Generally, organizations send one or more recruiters to the campus for initial interviews. The most promising recruits are then invited to visit the office or plant before a final employment decision is made.

Campus recruiting is one way employers can scout future employees.
BananaStock/JupiterImages

If the human resource department uses campus recruiting, it should take steps to ensure that recruiters are knowledgeable concerning the organization and the jobs to be filled and that they understand and use effective interviewing skills. Recruitment interviewing is discussed later in this chapter. College recruiters generally review an applicant's résumé before conducting the interview.

UNEMPLOYMENT FOR VETERANS

Unemployment for veterans has been running a full percentage point higher during the recession than the country's current jobless rate of 10.2 percent for the general population. The problem exists even more prominently; 185,000 veterans of the wars in Iraq and Afghanistan have gone from the front lines to the unemployment lines.

The problem has become a concern in Washington. President Barack Obama created the Council on Veterans Employment to encourage federal agencies to recruit and train veterans.

Job fairs for veterans have been running across the country ever since. Reviews from veterans of these job fairs have been mixed. Some say it has been a valuable tool in gaining steady and improved employment, while some complain that the level of job recruiting is not high.

Source: Adapted from Jeff Harrington, "Job Fair in Tampa for Veterans Draws 350," *McClatchy-Tribune Business News*, December 4, 2009.

Another method of tapping the products of colleges, universities, technical/vocational schools, and high schools is through cooperative work programs. Through these programs, students may work part-time and go to school part-time, or they may go to school and work at different times of the year. These programs attract people because they offer an opportunity for both a formal education and work experience. As an added incentive to finish their formal education and stay with the organization, employees are often promoted when their formal education is completed.

Internet Recruiting

The use of the Internet to recruit potential employees continues to grow rapidly and has become a major method of recruitment that most large firms utilize. College graduates and professionals are just as likely to send an electronic résumé as the traditional paper-based document. Examples of recruiting on the Internet include the following: IBM's CyberBlue Web site (www.cyberblue.ibm.com) offers searchable job postings, job fair information for college students, and benefits information. Other companies use Internet sources such as Job Options (www.joboptions.com), Career Builder (www.careerbuilder.com), Vault (www.vault.com), and Monster.com (www.monster.com) to list job postings on the Web. Using the Internet for recruiting may lead to having some unsuitable job candidates and some poor-quality job applications. However, the speed and time saved in recruitment seem to offset these potential problems. HRM in Action 6.2 describes job fairs for veterans.

EFFECTIVENESS OF RECRUITMENT METHODS

Organizational recruitment programs are designed to bring a pool of talent to the organization. From this pool, the organization hopes to select the person or persons most qualified for the job. An obvious and very important question human resource departments face is which method of recruitment supplies the best talent pool.

Many studies have explored this issue. One study concluded that employee referrals were the most effective recruitment source when compared to newspaper advertisements, private employment agencies, and walk-in applicants.[2] This study found that turnover rates for employees hired from employee referrals were lower than for employees hired through the other methods.

Another study examined the relationship among employee performance, absenteeism, work attitudes, and methods of recruitment.[3] This study showed that individuals recruited through a college placement office and, to a lesser extent, those recruited through newspaper advertisements were lower in performance (i.e., quality and dependability) than individuals who made contact with the company on their own initiative or through a professional journal or convention advertisement. This study concluded that campus recruiting and newspaper advertising were poorer sources of employees than were journal/convention advertisements and self-initiated contacts.

Generally, it seems safe to say that research has not identified a single best source of recruitment. Thus, each organization should take steps to identify its most effective recruitment sources. For example, a human resource department could monitor the effectiveness of recent hires in terms of turnover, absenteeism, and job performance. It might then contrast the different recruitment sources with respect to employee effectiveness and identify which of the specific recruitment sources produces the best employees.[4]

Table 6.1 summarizes the advantages and disadvantages of the internal and external methods of recruitment. HRM in Action 6.3 describes how companies monitor their recruitment.

REALISTIC JOB PREVIEWS

realistic job previews
A method of providing complete job information, both positive and negative, to the job applicant.

One method proposed for increasing the effectiveness of all recruiting methods is the use of realistic job previews. **Realistic job previews (RJPs)** provide complete job information, both positive and negative, to the job applicant.

Traditionally, organizations have attempted to sell the organization and the job to the prospective employee by making both look good. Normally this is done to obtain a favorable selection ratio, that is, a large number of applicants in relation to the number of job openings. Then, of course, the company can select the cream of the crop. Unfortunately, these attempts sometimes set the initial job expectations of the new employees too high and can produce dissatisfaction and high turnover among employees recruited in this manner. Figure 6.3 contrasts some of the outcomes that can develop from traditional and realistic job previews.

TABLE 6.1
Advantages and Disadvantages of Internal and External Recruiting

Source	Advantages	Disadvantages
Internal	• Company has a better knowledge of strengths and weaknesses of job candidate. • Job candidate has a better knowledge of company. • Morale and motivation of employees are enhanced. • The return on investment that an organization has in its present workforce is increased.	• People might be promoted to the point where they cannot successfully perform the job. • Infighting for promotions can negatively affect morale. • Inbreeding can stifle new ideas and innovation. • Attracting, contacting, and evaluating potential employees is more difficult.
External	• The pool of talent is much larger. • New insights and perspectives can be brought to the organization. • Frequently it is cheaper and easier to hire technical, skilled, or managerial employees from outside.	• Adjustment or orientation time is longer. • Morale problems can develop among those employees within the organization who feel qualified to do the job.

FIGURE 6.3
Typical Consequences of Job Preview Procedures

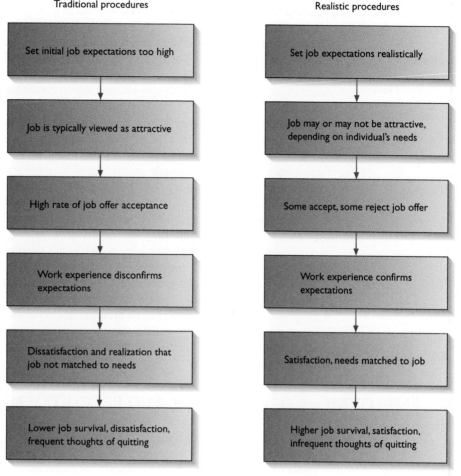

Traditional procedures

- Set initial job expectations too high
- Job is typically viewed as attractive
- High rate of job offer acceptance
- Work experience disconfirms expectations
- Dissatisfaction and realization that job not matched to needs
- Lower job survival, dissatisfaction, frequent thoughts of quitting

Realistic procedures

- Set job expectations realistically
- Job may or may not be attractive, depending on individual's needs
- Some accept, some reject job offer
- Work experience confirms expectations
- Satisfaction, needs matched to job
- Higher job survival, satisfaction, infrequent thoughts of quitting

Studies on the effectiveness of RJP indicate that it enables job candidates to self-select out of jobs that do not meet their expectations. On the other hand, if individuals are offered and accept a job, RJP can cause them to be more committed to it. Generally, it can be said that job applicants recruited using RJP who accepted the job have more job satisfaction.

WHO DOES THE RECRUITING, AND HOW?

In most large and middle-size organizations, the human resource department is responsible for recruiting. These organizations normally have an employment office within the human resource department. The employment office has recruiters, interviewers, and clerical personnel who handle the recruitment activities both at the organization's offices and elsewhere.

The role of personnel in the employment office is crucial. Walk-ins/write-ins and respondents to advertising develop an impression of the organization through their contacts with the employment office. If the applicant is treated indifferently or rudely, he or she may develop a lasting negative impression. On the other hand, if the applicant is pleasantly greeted, provided with pertinent information about job openings, and treated with dignity and respect, she or he may develop a lasting positive impression. Having employees trained in effective communication and interpersonal skills is essential in the employment office.

When recruiting is done away from the organization's offices, the role of the recruiter is equally critical. Job applicants' impressions about the organization are significantly influenced by the knowledge and expertise of the recruiter.

In small organizations, the recruitment function, in addition to many other responsibilities, is normally handled by one person, frequently the office manager. Also, it is not unusual for line managers in small organizations to recruit and interview job applicants.

ORGANIZATIONAL INDUCEMENTS IN RECRUITMENT

organizational inducements
Positive features and benefits offered by an organization to attract job applicants.

The objective of recruitment is to attract a number of qualified personnel for each particular job opening. **Organizational inducements** are all the positive features and benefits the organization offers to attract job applicants. Three of the more important organizational inducements are organizational compensation systems, career opportunities, and organizational reputation.

Starting salaries, frequency of pay raises, incentives, and the nature of the organization's fringe benefits can all influence the number of people attracted through the recruitment process. For example, organizations that pay low starting salaries have a much more difficult time finding qualified applicants than do organizations that pay higher starting salaries.

Organizations that have a reputation for providing employees with career opportunities are also more likely to attract a larger pool of qualified candidates through their recruiting activities. Employee and management development opportunities enable present employees to grow personally and professionally; they also attract good people to the organization. Assisting present employees in career planning develops feelings that the company cares. It also acts as an inducement to potential employees.

Finally, the organization's overall reputation, or image, serves as an inducement to potential employees. Factors that affect an organization's reputation include its general treatment of employees, the nature and quality of its products and services, and its participation in worthwhile social endeavors. Unfortunately, some organizations accept a poor image as "part of our industry and business." Regardless of the type of business or industry, organizations should strive for a positive image.

EQUAL EMPLOYMENT OPPORTUNITY AND RECRUITMENT

The entire subject of recruitment interviewing is made even more complex by equal employment opportunity legislation and court decisions relating to this legislation. For example, if an interviewer asks for certain information such as race, sex, age, marital status, and number of children during the interview, the company risks the chance of an employment discrimination suit. Prior to employment, interviewers should not ask for information that is potentially prejudicial unless the company is prepared to prove (in court, if necessary) that the requested information is job related.

Equal opportunity legislation has significantly influenced recruitment activities. All recruitment procedures for each job category should be analyzed and reviewed to identify and eliminate discriminatory barriers. For example, the Equal Employment Opportunity Commission (EEOC) encourages organizations to avoid recruiting primarily by employee referral and walk-ins because these practices tend to perpetuate the present composition of an organization's workforce. If minorities and females are not well represented at all levels of the organization, courts have ruled that reliance on such recruitment procedures is a discriminatory practice. HRM in Action 6.4 describes how EEOC worked with the Palm Management Corporation to ensure gender diversity.

The EEOC also suggests that the content of help-wanted ads should not indicate any race, sex, or age preference for the job unless age or sex is a bona fide occupational qualification (BFOQ). Organizations are also encouraged to advertise in media directed toward minorities and women. Advertising should indicate that the organization is an equal opportunity employer and does not discriminate.

Campus recruiting visits should be scheduled at colleges and universities with large minority and female enrollment. The EEOC also recommends that employers develop and maintain contacts with minority, female, and community organizations as sources of recruits.

Employers are encouraged to contact nontraditional recruitment sources, such as organizations that place physically and mentally handicapped persons. It is likely that hiring of both females and minority groups will continue to receive attention, and increased emphasis will be placed on hiring those groups.

EEOC AND PALM MANAGEMENT CORPORATION

The U.S. Equal Employment Opportunity Commission (EEOC) and Palm Management Corporation, which manages The Palm Restaurants, today announced the resolution of an EEOC Commissioner's Charge, ending a nationwide investigation focusing on past recruitment and hiring practices. The prelitigation agreement was voluntarily entered into by the Palm and obtained through the EEOC's conciliation process. The terms of the agreement include the Palm's already extensive diversity program with mandatory EEO training for managers and employees, and the establishment of a class fund in the amount of $500,000.

The EEOC's investigation was based on allegations that the Palm violated Title VII of the Civil Rights Act of 1964 by failing to recruit and hire women into service worker positions. However, beginning in 2000, the Palm had implemented changes in its employment practices, which included providing mandatory training to supervisors concerning the avoidance of discrimination in hiring and more effective applicant tracking and record-keeping systems.

Olophius Perry, director of EEOC's Los Angeles District Office, which led the investigation, said, "This is a prime example of how employers should work cooperatively with the EEOC as a means of effectively resolving discrimination charges to the satisfaction of all involved parties. The Palm has shown it is committed to equal employment opportunity for women. Once made aware of inconsistencies that existed in its recruitment and hiring effort, the Palm proactively created a sophisticated, centralized tracking system that should serve as a 'best practices' model for other businesses."

Palm president and chief operating officer Fred Thimm said, "I am pleased that we were able to work collaboratively with the EEOC to resolve the allegations. We have achieved an outcome which has enhanced our methods of recruitment to ensure a more diverse pool of applicants, and as a result, a more diverse workforce. As a business that experienced rapid growth, we learned that our traditional method of recruiting only through employee referrals was not the best way in terms of ensuring gender diversity. It should go without saying that the Palm does not tolerate discrimination in its workplace, and will continue rigorous enforcement of its existing EEOC policies."

Source: Adapted from "EEOC and the Palm Resolve Inquiry into Recruitment and Hiring Practices," *Women in Management Review* (2004), p. 129.

More than likely, recruiters will also have to pay more attention to the spouse, male or female, of the person being recruited. It may become necessary to assist in finding jobs for spouses of recruits. In hiring women, especially for managerial and professional jobs, it may be necessary to consider hiring the husband as well.

Summary of Learning Objectives

1. **Define *recruitment*.**

   Recruitment involves seeking and attracting a pool of people from which qualified candidates for job vacancies can be chosen.

2. **Discuss job analysis, human resource planning, and recruitment.**

   Job analysis gives the nature and requirements of specific jobs. Human resource planning determines the specific number of jobs to be filled. Recruitment provides a pool of qualified people to fill the vacancies.

3. **Explain the purpose of a personnel requisition form.**

   A personnel requisition form describes the reason for the need to hire a new person and the requirements of the job.

4. **Describe the advantages and disadvantages of using internal methods of recruitment.**

   The advantages are that the company has a better knowledge of the strengths and weaknesses of the job candidates; the job candidates have a better knowledge of the company; employee motivation and morale are enhanced; and the return on investment that an organization has in its workforce is increased. The disadvantages are that people can be promoted to the point where they cannot successfully perform the job; infighting for promotions can negatively affect morale; and inbreeding can stifle new ideas and innovation.

5. **Discuss job posting and bidding.**

   Job posting and bidding are an internal method of recruitment in which notices of available jobs are posted in central locations throughout the organization and employees are given a specified length of time to apply for the available jobs.

6. **Describe the advantages and disadvantages of using external methods of recruitment.**

   The advantages are that the pool of talent is much larger; new insights and perspectives can be brought to the organization; and it is frequently cheaper and easier to hire technical, skilled, or managerial employees from outside. The disadvantages are that attracting, contacting, and evaluating potential employees are more difficult; adjustment or orientation time is longer; and morale problems can develop among those employees within the organization who feel qualified to do the job.

7. **Define *realistic job previews*.**

   Realistic job previews provide complete job information, both positive and negative, to the job applicant.

8. **Explain organizational inducements.**

   Organizational inducements are all the positive features and benefits offered by an organization that serve to attract job applicants.

9. **Outline some specific EEOC recommendations for job advertising.**

   EEOC recommends that organizations avoid recruiting primarily by employee referral and walk-ins. Advertising should indicate that the organization is an equal opportunity employer. Campus recruiting visits should be scheduled at colleges or universities with large female and minority groups.

Key Terms

campus recruiting, *116*
employee leasing companies, *116*
headhunter, *116*
job advertising, *115*

job posting and bidding, *114*
organizational inducements, *120*

personnel requisition form, *112*
realistic job previews, *118*
recruitment, *111*
temporary help, *116*

Review Questions

1. What is recruitment?
2. Describe the relationships among job analysis, personnel planning, recruitment, and selection.
3. What is a personnel requisition form?
4. Describe several advantages of recruiting from internal sources and several advantages of recruiting from external sources.
5. Name and describe at least five methods of recruiting.
6. What are realistic job previews?
7. Define and give examples of organizational inducements.
8. Outline some specific EEOC recommendations for job advertising.

Discussion Questions

1. Discuss the following statement: "An individual who owns a business should be able to recruit and hire whomever he or she pleases."
2. Employees often have negative views on the policy of hiring outsiders rather than promoting from within. Naturally, employees believe they should always be given preference for promotion before outsiders are hired. Do you think this is in the best interest of the organization?
3. As a potential recruit who will probably be looking for a job upon completion of school, what general approach and method or methods of recruiting do you think would be most effective in attracting you?

Incident 6.1

Inside or Outside Recruiting?

Powermat, Inc., has encountered difficulty over the last few years in filling its middle management positions. The company, which manufactures and sells complex machinery, is organized into six semiautonomous manufacturing departments. Top management believes it is necessary for the managers of these departments to make many complex and technical decisions. Therefore, the company originally recruited strictly from within. However, it soon found that employees elevated to middle management often lacked the skills necessary to discharge their new duties.

A decision was then made to recruit from outside, particularly from colleges with good industrial management programs. Through the services of a professional recruiter, the company developed a pool of well-qualified industrial management graduates. Several were hired and placed in lower management positions as preparation for the middle management jobs. Within two years, all these people had left the company.

Management reverted to its former policy of promoting from within and experienced basically the same results as before. Faced with the imminent retirement of employees in several key middle management positions, the company decided to call in a consultant for solutions.

Questions

1. Is recruiting the problem in this company?
2. If you were the consultant, what would you recommend?

Incident 6.2

A Malpractice Suit against a Hospital

Hospital jumping is a term hospital personnel use to describe the movement of incompetent and potentially negligent employees from hospital to hospital. One factor contributing to hospital jumping is the reluctance of hospitals to release information to other hospitals that are checking references.

Ridgeview Hospital was sued for negligence in its screening of employees. The case involved the alleged incorrect administration to an infant of a medication that nearly caused the child's death. The party bringing suit contended that the nurse who administered the drug was negligent, as was the hospital because it had failed to make a thorough investigation of the nurse's work history and background. It was learned that the nurse had been hired by Ridgeview before it had received a letter of reference from her previous employer verifying her employment history. In support of the plaintiff's case, uncontested information was presented about a similar incident of negligence in patient care by the nurse in her previous employment.

Ridgeview Hospital's personnel director, John Reeves, took the position that reference checks were a waste of time because area hospital personnel directors would not provide what they thought might be defamatory information about former employees. He further stated that in checking reference sources, these same personnel directors would request information they themselves would not give.

Reeves's lawyer concluded that the hospital would have to choose between two potentially damaging alternatives in adopting a personnel screening policy. It could continue not to verify references, thereby risking malpractice suits such as the one discussed. Alternatively, it could implement a policy of giving out all information on past employees and risk defamation suits. The lawyers recommended the second alternative because they thought the potential cost would be significantly less if the hospital were convicted of libel or slander than if it were judged guilty of negligence.

Questions

1. Which of the two alternatives would you recommend to the hospital?
2. What questions could be asked in a recruitment interview to help eliminate the problem?

EXERCISE 6.1
Writing a Résumé

Use a résumé writer from the Internet to write your own résumé. Bring the résumé to class and have another student or your professor evaluate it.

Notes and Additional Readings

1. See Jane King, "The Web Habit Is HR's Manna from Heaven," *Personnel Today,* January 27, 2004, p. 2.
2. Michelle Neely Martinez, "The Headhunter Within," *HR Magazine,* August 2001, pp. 48–55; Carroll Lachnit, "Employee Referrals Save Time, Save Money, Deliver Quality," *Workforce,* June 2001, pp. 67–72.
3. Tina King, "Onondaga Leasing Works with People," *Business Journal,* November 3, 2000, p. 30; John M. Polson, "The PEO Phenomenon: Co-Employment at Work," *Employee Relations Law Journal,* Spring 2002, pp. 7–25.
4. James A. Breaugh and Mary Starke, "Research on Employee Recruitment: So Many Studies, So Many Remaining Questions," *Journal of Management* 26, 2000, pp. 405–34.

Chapter **Seven**

Selecting Employees

Chapter Learning Objectives

After studying this chapter, you should be able to:

1. Outline the steps in the selection process.
2. Describe aptitude, psychomotor, job knowledge, proficiency, interest, and personality tests.
3. Explain a polygraph test.
4. Describe structured and unstructured interviews.
5. Define validity.
6. Explain predictive validity.
7. Explain concurrent validity.
8. Describe content validity.
9. Discuss construct validity.
10. Define reliability.
11. Define adverse (or disparate) impact.

Chapter Outline

selection
The process of choosing from among available applicants the individuals who are most likely to successfully perform a job.

The objective of the **selection** process is to choose the individual who can successfully perform the job from the pool of qualified candidates. Job analyses, human resource planning, and recruitment are necessary prerequisites to the selection process. A breakdown in any of these processes can make even the best selection system ineffective.

THE SELECTION PROCESS

Processing an applicant for a job normally entails a series of steps. Figure 7.1 illustrates the steps in a typical selection process. The size of the organization, the types of jobs to be filled, the number of people to be hired, and outside pressures from the EEOC or union all influence the exact nature of an organization's selection process. Most organizations use a multiple

FIGURE 7.1
Steps in the Selection Process

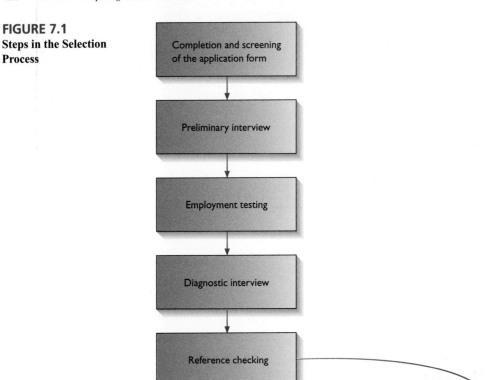

Completion and screening of the application form

↓

Preliminary interview

↓

Employment testing

↓

Diagnostic interview

↓

Reference checking

Physical examination:
Required only for individual who is offered the position. Job offer is contingent on individual passing the physical examination.

Final decision

cutoff technique in selection. With this technique, an applicant must be judged satisfactory through a series of screening devices, such as application forms, interviews, and tests. The applicant is eliminated from consideration for the job if any of these devices is unsatisfactory. All of these screening devices must be validated if they produce adverse or disparate impact.

Employment Application Form

Completing an employment application form is normally the first step in most selection procedures. The application provides basic employment information for use in later steps of the selection process and can be used to screen out unqualified applicants. For example, if the job opening requires the ability to use a word processor and the applicant indicates an inability to use a word processor, there is no need to process the application further.

EEOC Requirements

The EEOC and the courts have found that many application and interview inquiries disproportionately reject minorities and females and frequently are not job related. Many questions have therefore been explicitly prohibited. Some of the major questions that should be eliminated from preemployment inquiries (both employment application forms and interviews) because of their potential to be discriminatory include the following:

1. *Race, color, national origin, and religion.* Inquiries about race, color, national origin, or religion are not illegal per se, but asking or recording this information in employment records can invite careful scrutiny if discrimination charges are filed against the employer.

2. *Arrest and conviction records.* Courts have ruled that an individual's arrest record is an unlawful basis for refusal to hire unless the employer can show that such a policy is job related.

3. *Credit rating.* Courts have also ruled that an applicant's poor credit rating is an unlawful basis for refusal to hire unless a business necessity for such a policy can be established. Inquiries about charge accounts and home or car ownership may be unlawful unless required because of business necessity.

The On the Job example at the end of Chapter 3 provides a comprehensive listing of permissible questions and questions to be avoided, not only in preemployment interviews but also on application forms.

Processing

weighted application forms
Application forms that assign different weights or values to different questions.

Normally a member of the human resource department reviews the information on the application form to determine the applicant's qualifications in relation to the requirements of currently available jobs. Another screening procedure is the use of **weighted application forms.** These forms assign different weights to different questions. Weights are developed by determining which item responses were given more frequently by applicants who proved to be higher performers but less frequently by applicants who proved to be poorer performers. Weighted application forms are subject to the validity requirements discussed earlier in this chapter.

Accuracy of Information

The accuracy of information given on application forms is open to debate. Placing full reliance on information provided on the application form may not be prudent unless some means of verification is used. Some of the information on the application form can be verified through reference checking, which is described later in this chapter.

In an attempt to ensure that accurate information is given, many employers require the applicant to sign a statement similar to the following:

> I hereby certify that the answers given by me to the foregoing questions and statements made are true and correct, without reservations of any kind whatsoever, and that no attempt has been made by me to conceal pertinent information. Falsification of any information on this application can lead to immediate discharge at the time of disclosure.

Whether this statement actually increases the accuracy of information provided is not known. However, employers view falsification of an application form as a serious offense that, if detected, normally leads to discharge.

Applicant Flow Record

applicant flow record
A form completed voluntarily by a job applicant and used by an employer to obtain information that could be used to illegally discriminate.

At the time of completing the application form, the applicant is frequently asked to complete an applicant flow record. An **applicant flow record** is a form used by a company to obtain information from a job applicant that could be used to illegally discriminate. The applicant voluntarily completes this record. The On the Job example at the end of this chapter shows a sample combination application form and applicant flow record. Data and information from the applicant flow record can be used to provide statistical reports to the EEOC or OFCCP or in defense against charges of discrimination concerning the employer's recruitment and selection activities.

Preliminary Interview

The preliminary interview is used to determine whether the applicant's skills, abilities, and job preferences match any of the available jobs in the organization, to explain to the applicant the available jobs and their requirements, and to answer any questions the applicant has about the available jobs or the employer. A preliminary interview is usually conducted after the applicant has completed the application form. It is generally a brief, exploratory interview that is normally conducted by a specialist from the human resource department. The interview screens out unqualified or uninterested applicants. Interview questions must be job related and are subject to demonstrations of validity. The Preemployment Inquiry Guide at the end of Chapter 3 provides a summary of permissible inquiries and inquiries to

JOB APPLICANTS AND SOCIAL NETWORKS
A candidate for a job may not only have to include his or her résumé. Candidates may also be asked to turn over their information for any social or business networking Web sites such as Facebook.

In Bozeman, Montana, to be considered for a city job one must include all information regarding involvement in social networking sites. The ACLU, for one, believes this practice violates applicants' privacy. The city of Bozeman is considering changing the policy due to the media coverage it received after announcing the policy.

A more troubling aspect in the Bozeman city request is for the applicant's passwords to such sites. Applicants giving out such information could have their information stolen or misused.

Source: Adapted from Anonymous, "Apply Here, and Give Us Your Passwords," *Information Management Journal,* September/October 2009, p. 12.

be avoided during the preliminary interview. HRM in Action 7.1 describes an example of an unusual request for information made by a city.

Formal Testing

In *Albemarle* v. *Moody,* the Supreme Court ruled that any procedure used to make selection decisions is to be construed as a test. If a test is to be used in the selection process and if the selection process has adverse impact on legally protected groups, the EEOC requires the employer to establish validity and reliability using the procedures outlined in the "Uniform Guidelines on Employee Selection Procedures," which are described later in this chapter.

Many types of commercial tests are available to organizations for use in the selection process. Many of these tests have undergone validation and reliability studies. One useful source for review of these tests is the *Mental Measurements Yearbook.*[1] This handbook summarizes a wide variety of commercial tests and also provides an evaluation of the tests by several experts.

The following sections examine five categories of tests: aptitude, psychomotor, job knowledge and proficiency, interests, and personality. In addition, the use of polygraphs, graphology, and drug and AIDS testing is discussed.

Aptitude Tests

aptitude tests
Means of measuring a person's capacity or latent ability to learn and perform a job.

Aptitude tests measure a person's capacity or potential ability to learn and perform a job. Some of the more frequently used tests measure verbal ability, numerical ability, perceptual speed, spatial ability, and reasoning ability. Verbal-aptitude tests measure a person's ability to use words in thinking, planning, and communicating. Numerical tests measure ability to add, subtract, multiply, and divide. Perception speed tests measure ability to recognize similarities and differences. Spatial tests measure ability to visualize objects in space and determine their relationships. Reasoning tests measure ability to analyze oral or written facts and make correct judgments concerning these facts on the basis of logical implications.

One of the oldest and, prior to the passage of equal opportunity legislation, most frequently used aptitude tests was the general intelligence test. The EEOC views this type of test with disfavor because such tests often contain questions that are not related to successful performance on the job. Thus, employers have largely abandoned the use of intelligence tests in employee selection.

Psychomotor Tests

psychomotor tests
Tests that measure a person's strength, dexterity, and coordination.

Psychomotor tests measure a person's strength, dexterity, and coordination. Finger dexterity, manual dexterity, wrist-finger speed, and speed of arm movement are some of the psychomotor abilities that can be tested. Abilities such as these might be tested for hiring people to fill assembly-line jobs.

Job Knowledge and Proficiency Tests

job knowledge tests
Tests used to measure the job-related knowledge of an applicant.

Job knowledge tests measure the job-related knowledge possessed by a job applicant. These tests can be either written or oral. The applicant must answer questions that differentiate

proficiency tests
Tests used to measure how well a job applicant can do a sample of the work to be performed in the job.

experienced and skilled workers from less experienced and less skilled workers. **Proficiency tests** measure how well the applicant can do a sample of the work to be performed. A word processing test given to applicants for a secretarial job is an example of a proficiency test.

Interest Tests

interest tests
Tests designed to determine how a person's interests compare with the interests of successful people in a specific job.

Interest tests are designed to determine how a person's interests compare with the interests of successful people in a specific job. These tests indicate the occupations or areas of work in which the person is most interested. The basic assumption in the use of interest tests is that people are more likely to be successful in jobs they like. The primary problem with using interest tests for selection purposes is that responses to the questions are not always sincere.

Personality Tests

personality tests
Tests that attempt to measure personality traits.

Personality tests attempt to measure personality characteristics. These tests are generally characterized by questionable validity and low reliability and presently have limited use for selection purposes. Two of the better-known personality tests are the Rorschach inkblot test and the Thematic Apperception Test (TAT). In the Rorschach test, the applicant is shown a series of cards that contain inkblots of varying sizes and shapes. The applicant is asked to tell what the inkblots look like to him or her. With the TAT, the applicant is shown pictures of real-life situations for interpretation. With both of these methods, the individual is encouraged to report whatever immediately comes to mind. Interpretation of these responses requires subjective judgment and the services of a qualified psychologist. Furthermore, responses to personality tests can also be easily fabricated. For these reasons, personality tests presently have limited application in selection decisions.

The Myers-Briggs Type Indicator (MBTI) is one of the most widely used instruments. It is not a test in the sense that there are no right or wrong answers. The MBTI allows individuals to understand their personality or psychological style.

Polygraph Tests

polygraph
Device that records physical changes in a person's body as he or she answers questions (also known as a *lie detector*).

The **polygraph,** popularly known as the *lie detector,* is a device that records physical changes in the body as the test subject answers a series of questions. The polygraph records fluctuations in blood pressure, respiration, and perspiration on a moving roll of graph paper. The polygraph operator makes a judgment as to whether the subject's response was truthful or deceptive by studying the physiological measurements recorded on paper.

The use of a polygraph rests on a series of cause-and-effect assumptions: Stress causes certain physiological changes in the body; fear and guilt cause stress; lying causes fear and guilt. The theory behind the use of a polygraph test assumes a direct relationship between the subject's responses to the questions and the physiological responses recorded on the polygraph. However, the polygraph machine itself does not detect lies; it detects only physiological changes. The operator must interpret the data recorded by the machine. Thus, the operator, not the machine, is the real lie detector.

The Employee Polygraph Protection Act of 1988, with a few exceptions, prohibits employers from conducting polygraph examinations on all job applicants and most employees. It also prevents the use of voice stress analyzers and similar devices that attempt to measure honesty. Paper-and-pencil tests and chemical testing, such as for drugs or AIDS, are not prohibited.

The major exemptions to the law are as follows: (1) All local, state, and federal employees are exempt from coverage, although state laws may be passed to restrict the use of polygraphs; (2) industries with national defense or security contracts are permitted to use polygraphs; (3) businesses with nuclear power–related contracts with the Department of Energy may use polygraphs; and (4) businesses and consultants with access to highly classified information may use polygraphs.

Private businesses are also allowed to use polygraphs under certain conditions: when hiring private security personnel, when hiring persons with access to drugs, and during investigations of economic injury or loss by the employer.[2]

Graphology

graphology (handwriting analysis)
Use of a trained analyst to examine a person's handwriting to assess the person's personality, emotional problems, and honesty.

Graphology (handwriting analysis) involves using an analyst to examine the lines, loops, hooks, strokes, curves, and flourishes in a person's handwriting to assess the person's personality, performance, emotional problems, and honesty. As with the polygraph, the use of graphology is dependent on the training and expertise of the person (called *graphologist*) doing the analysis.

Graphology has had limited acceptance by organizations in the United States. However, acceptance of graphology is increasing, since the passage of the Employee Polygraph Protection Act does not prohibit its use.[3]

Drug and AIDS Testing

Many employers practice drug testing on potential employees. © liquidlibrary/ PictureQuest

Drug testing is being increasingly used by organizations. The most common practice is to test current employees when their job performance suggests substance abuse and all new potential employees. Most companies will not hire a potential employee who tests positive for drug abuse.

Urine sampling is one of the most common forms of drug testing. In addition, a more currently used technique involves measuring drug molecules from a person's hair to identify drug usage levels. Some experts believe hair testing is more accurate than urine sampling. Most experts agree that testing for drug abuse alone among current employees is a less than satisfactory solution to the problem. Testing can create an adversarial relationship in which the employee tries to escape the employer's detection. Education and employee assistance provide a much more positive relationship. This approach has led to the establishment of employee assistance programs, which are described in more detail in Chapter 16.

People with AIDS and people who test positive for HIV antibodies are protected in their jobs by the Vocational Rehabilitation Act and the Americans with Disabilities Act. However, voluntary workplace testing is not only permitted but is encouraged by some major health organizations. Furthermore, these laws permit HIV-antibody testing in certain defined circumstances. HIV testing is much more common among health-care firms because of a high potential for employee exposure to HIV-infected patients.

In some instances, AIDS in the workplace has caused fear among employers and coworkers, who often seek to be separated from those infected by the virus. If an HIV testing program is not to be considered as a violation of an employee's basic rights, the employer should be able to show that the interests to be served by testing outweigh privacy expectations. HRM in Action 7.2 describes the use of drug testing at work.

Genetic Testing

More recently, firms have considered the prospect of genetic testing for potential employees. These sophisticated medical tests use gene coding to identify individuals with gene structures that may make them susceptible to illness. Both employers and employees are concerned about the legitimate uses of genetic information and what happens to any information obtained through genetic testing. Although there is a consensus that restricting health-care benefits is not the goal of genetic testing, all parties are concerned about who will have access to the information. Another concern of employers is what liability they may have for not using genetic testing if a valid test and a reason for testing exist.[4]

Second or Follow-Up Interview

Most organizations use the second or follow-up interview as an important step in the selection process. Its purpose is to supplement information obtained in other steps in the selection process to determine the suitability of an applicant for a specific opening. All questions asked during an interview must be job-related. Equal employment opportunity legislation has placed limitations on the types of questions that can be asked during an interview (see the On the Job example at the end of Chapter 3).

Types of Interviews

structured interview
An interview conducted according to a predetermined outline.

Organizations use several types of interviews. The **structured interview** is conducted using a predetermined outline that is based on a thorough job analysis. Through the use of this outline, the interviewer maintains control of the interview so that all pertinent information on the applicant is covered systematically. Advantages of the structured interview are that it provides the same type of information on all interviewees and allows systematic coverage of all questions deemed necessary by the organization.

unstructured interview
An interview conducted without a predetermined checklist of questions.

Interviewers also conduct **unstructured interviews,** which do not have a predetermined checklist of questions. They use open-ended questions such as "Tell me about your previous job." Interviews of this type pose numerous problems, such as lack of systematic coverage of information, and are very susceptible to the personal biases of the interviewer. However, they do provide a more relaxed atmosphere.

stress interview
Interview method that puts the applicant under pressure to determine whether he or she is highly emotional.

Organizations use three other types of interviewing techniques to a limited extent. The **stress interview** is designed to place the interviewee under pressure. In the stress interview, the interviewer assumes a hostile and antagonistic attitude toward the interviewee. The purpose of this type of interview is to detect the highly emotional person. In **board or panel interviews,** two or more interviewers conduct a single interview with the applicant. **Group interviews,** in which several job applicants are questioned together in a group discussion, are also sometimes used. Panel interviews and group interviews can involve either a structured or an unstructured format.

board or panel interviews
Interview method in which two or more people conduct an interview with one applicant.

group interview
Interview method in which several applicants are questioned together.

Problems in Conducting Interviews

Although interviews have widespread use in selection procedures, they involve a host of problems. The first and certainly one of the most significant problems is that interviews are subject to the same legal requirements of validity and reliability as other steps in the selection process. However, the validity and reliability of most interviews are questionable. One primary reason seems to be that it is easy for interviewers to become either favorably or unfavorably impressed with the job applicant based on their **initial impressions.** The interviewer often draws conclusions about the applicant within the first 10 minutes of the interview. If this occurs, he or she either overlooks or ignores any additional relevant information about the applicant.

initial impressions
Interviewer draws conclusions about a job applicant within the first 10 minutes of the interview.

halo effect
Occurs when managers allow a single prominent characteristic of the employee to influence their judgment on several items of a performance appraisal.

Another problem is the **halo effect** that occurs when the interviewer allows a single prominent characteristic to dominate judgment of all other traits. For instance, it is often easy to overlook other characteristics when a person has a pleasant personality. However, merely having a pleasant personality does not necessarily ensure that the person will be a good employee.

Overgeneralizing is another common problem. An interviewee may not behave exactly the same way on the job as during the interview. For example, the interviewer must remember that the interviewee is under pressure during the interview and that some people just naturally become very nervous during an interview.

Personal preferences, prejudices, and biases can also cause problems in conducting employment interviews. Interviewers with biases or prejudices tend to look for behaviors that conform to their biases. Appearance, social status, dress, race, and gender have negatively influenced many employment interviews.

Conducting Effective Interviews

Problems associated with interviews can be partially overcome through careful planning. The following suggestions can increase the effectiveness of the interviewing process.

First, careful attention must be given to selecting and training interviewers. They should be outgoing and emotionally well-adjusted people. Interviewing skills can be learned, and the people responsible for conducting interviews should be thoroughly trained in these skills.

Second, the plan for the interview should include an outline specifying the information to be obtained and the questions to be asked. The plan should also include room arrangements. Privacy and some degree of comfort are important. If a private room is not available, the interview should be conducted in a place where other applicants are not within hearing distance.

Third, the interviewer should attempt to put the applicant at ease. The interviewer should not argue with the applicant or put the applicant on the spot. A brief conversation about a general topic of interest or offering the applicant a cup of coffee can help ease the tension. The applicant should be encouraged to talk. However, the interviewer must maintain control and remember that the primary goal of the interview is to gain information that will aid in the selection decision.

Fourth, the facts obtained in the interview should be recorded immediately. Generally, notes can and should be taken during the interview.

Finally, the effectiveness of the interviewing process should be evaluated. One way to evaluate effectiveness is to compare the performance ratings of individuals who are hired against assessments made during the interview. This cross-check can serve to evaluate the effectiveness of individual interviewers as well as that of the overall interviewing program.

Reference Checking

Reference checking can take place either before or after the second interview. Many organizations realize the importance of reference checking and provide space on the application form for listing references. Most prospective employers contact individuals from one or more of the three following categories: personal, school, or past employment references. For the most part, personal references have limited value because generally no applicant will list someone who will not give a positive recommendation. Contacting individuals who have taught the applicant in school, college, or university may be of limited value for similar reasons. Previous employers are clearly the most often used source and are in a position to supply the most objective information.

Reference checking is most frequently conducted by telephoning previous employers. However, many organizations will not answer questions about a previous employee unless the questions are put in writing. The amount and type of information a previous employer is willing to divulge varies from organization to organization. The least that normally can be accomplished is to verify the information given on the application form. However, most employers are hesitant to answer questions about previous employees because of the threat of defamation lawsuits.

Government legislation has significantly influenced the process of reference checking. The Privacy Act of 1974 prevents government agencies from making their employment records available to other organizations without the consent of the individual involved. The Fair Credit and Reporting Act (FCRA) of 1971 requires private organizations to give job applicants access to information obtained from a reporting service. It is also mandatory that an applicant be made aware that a check is being made on him or her. Because of these laws, most employment application forms now contain statements, which must be signed by the applicant, authorizing the employer to check references and conduct investigations.[5]

Physical Examination

The physical examination is normally required only for the individual who is offered the job, and the job offer is often contingent on the individual passing the physical examination. The exam is given to determine not only whether the applicant is physically capable of performing the job but also his or her eligibility for group life, health, and disability insurance. Because of the expense, physical examinations are normally one of the last steps in the selection process. The expense of physical examinations has also caused many organizations to have applicants complete a health questionnaire when they fill out their application form. If no serious medical problems are indicated on the medical questionnaire, the applicant usually is not required to have a physical examination. HRM in Action 7.3 describes the use of background checking.

The Rehabilitation Act of 1973 and the Americans with Disabilities Act of 1990 have also caused many employers to reexamine the physical requirements for many jobs. These acts do not prohibit employers from giving medical exams. However, they do encourage employers to make medical inquiries directly related to the applicant's ability to perform job-related functions and require employers to make reasonable accommodations to help handicapped

INCREASED BACKGROUND CHECKS OF POTENTIAL EMPLOYEES

As the economy rebounds, employers are stepping up background checks on potential candidates for positions. Companies have long checked employment history and education, but now the scrutiny has increased, sometimes even into a candidate's personal history.

False claims have long been reasons for employee dismissal or candidate rejection from a company. One agency specializing in candidate information verification recalls a case of a candidate rejection from a company due to the agency uncovering knowledge of the candidate's past involving an extramarital affair.

Employers have increased scrutiny due to the data they are receiving from agencies specializing in a candidate's background check. Fake résumés, dubious university records, and false claims of employment history are shown to be on the rise. Also, criminal history checks are now more comprehensive.

Source: Adapted from Anonymous, "Companies Step Up Background Checks of Prospective Employees," *McClatchy-Tribune Business News,* November 26, 2009.

people perform the job. Furthermore, the Americans with Disabilities Act requires that a physical exam cannot be conducted until after a job offer has been extended to a job candidate.

Making the Final Selection Decision

The final step in the selection process is choosing one individual for the job. The assumption made at this point is that there will be more than one qualified person. If this is true, a value judgment based on all the information gathered in the previous steps must be made to select the most qualified individual. If the previous steps have been performed properly, the chances of making a successful judgment improve dramatically.

The responsibility for making the final selection decision is assigned to different levels of management in different organizations. In many organizations, the human resource department handles the completion of application forms; conducts preliminary interviews, testing, and reference checking; and arranges for physical exams. The diagnostic interview and final selection decision are usually left to the manager of the department with the job opening. Such a system relieves the manager of the time-consuming responsibilities of screening out unqualified and uninterested applicants.

In other organizations, the human resource department handles all of the steps up to the final decision. Under this system, the human resource department gives the manager with a job opening a list of three to five qualified applicants. The manager then chooses the individual he or she believes will be the best employee based on all the information the human resource department provides. Many organizations leave the final choice to the manager with the job opening, subject to the approval of those at higher levels of management.

In some organizations, the human resource department handles all the steps in the selection process, including the final decision. In small organizations, the owner often makes the final choice.

An alternative approach is to involve peers in the final selection decision. Peer involvement has been used primarily in the selection of upper-level managers and professional employees. Peer involvement naturally facilitates the acceptance of the new employee by the work group.

In the selection of managers and supervisors, assessment centers are also sometimes used. An assessment center utilizes a formal procedure involving interviews, tests, and individual and group exercises aimed at evaluating an individual's potential as a manager/supervisor and determining his or her developmental needs. Chapter 9 describes assessment centers at length.

VALIDATION OF SELECTION PROCEDURES

The selection decision requires the decision maker to know what distinguishes successful performance from unsuccessful performance in the available job and to forecast a person's future performance in that job. Therefore, job analysis is essential in the development of a successful employee selection system. As discussed in Chapter 4, both job descriptions and job specifications are developed through job analysis. A job description facilitates determining

criteria of job success
Ways of specifying how successful performance of the job is to be measured.

criterion predictors
Factors such as education, previous work experience, and scores on tests that are used to predict successful performance of a job.

validity
Refers to how accurately a predictor actually predicts the criteria of job success.

reliability
Refers to the extent to which a criterion predictor produces consistent results if repeated measurements are made.

how successful performance of the job is to be measured. These measures are called **criteria of job success.** Possible criteria of job success include performance appraisals, production data (such as quantity of work produced), and personnel data (such as rates of absenteeism and tardiness).

A job specification facilitates identifying the factors that can be used to predict successful performance of the job. These factors are called **criterion predictors.** Possible criterion predictors include education, previous work experience, scores on tests, data from application forms, previous performance appraisals, and results of employment interviews.

Validity and reliability are extremely important concepts not only in the selection of new employees but also in promotion decisions or any other area where selection decisions are made. For example, suppose a company administers a test to all its employees in a certain unit or department. Further suppose that the employees selected for attendance in a training program are the ones who scored highest on the test. In order to use the test scores for selecting employees for attendance in a training program, the company must be able to show that the test is valid and reliable. Two landmark court cases that involved selection procedures were *Griggs* v. *Duke Power Company* and *Albemarle Paper* v. *Moody,* both of which were discussed in detail in Chapter 2.

Validity refers to how accurately a criterion predictor predicts the criterion of job success. **Reliability** refers to the extent to which a criterion predictor produces consistent results if repeated measurements are made. It is important to note that a criterion predictor such as a test score can be reliable without being valid. However, it cannot be valid if it is not reliable. Reliability is necessary but not sufficient to show the validity of a criterion predictor. Consequently, the reliability of a criterion predictor plays an important role in determining its validity. Reliability will be discussed in more detail later in this chapter.

Some criteria such as results of performance appraisals can be used as either a criterion predictor or a criterion of job success. For example, if past performance appraisals are used to forecast how successfully an employee will perform a different job, then the results of the performance appraisal system are criterion predictors. If, on the other hand, test scores are the criterion predictor, then performance appraisal results are the criterion of job success.

Figure 7.2 shows the relationship between job analysis, reliability, and validity. Three methods can be used to demonstrate the validity of a criterion predictor. These are criterion-related validity, content validity, and construct validity.

Criterion-Related Validity

Criterion-related validity is established by collecting data and using correlation analysis (a statistical method used to measure the relationship between two sets of data) to determine the relationship between a predictor and the criteria of job success. The degree of validity for a particular predictor is indicated by the magnitude of the coefficient of correlation (r), which can range from $+1$ to -1. Both $+1$ and -1 represent perfect correlation. Zero represents total lack of correlation or validity. A positive sign ($+$) on the coefficient of correlation means the two sets of data are moving in the same direction, whereas a negative ($-$) sign means the two sets of data are moving in opposite directions.

A criterion predictor never correlates perfectly with a criterion of job success. Thus, a significant issue in validity is the degree of correlation required between the criterion predictor and the criterion of job success in order to establish validity. The "Uniform Guidelines on Employee Selection Procedure" (more commonly referred to as "Uniform Guidelines"), which are described later in this chapter, take the position that no minimum correlation coefficient is applicable to all employment situations. Correlation coefficients rarely exceed 0.50; a correlation of 0.40 is ordinarily considered very good, and a correlation of 0.3 or higher is acceptable. Generally, it is safe to say that criterion predictors having a correlation coefficient of under 0.30 would not be accepted as valid.

Two primary methods for establishing criterion-related validity are predictive validity and concurrent validity.

FIGURE 7.2
Relationship between Job Analysis and Validity

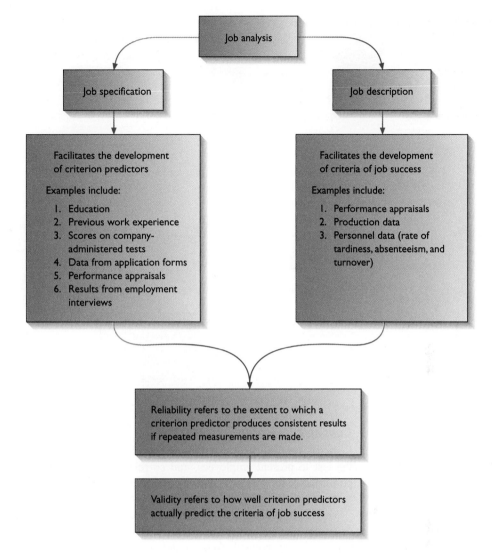

Predictive Validity

predictive validity
Validity established by identifying a predictor, administering it to applicants, hiring without regard to scores, and later correlating scores with job performance.

Predictive validity is established by identifying a predictor such as a test, administering the test to the entire pool of job applicants, and then hiring people to fill the available jobs without regard to their test scores. At a later date, the test scores are correlated with the criteria of job success to see whether those people with high test scores performed substantially better than those with low test scores.

For example, suppose the company wants to determine the validity of a test for predicting future performance of production workers. In this example, test scores would be the predictor. Further suppose the company maintains records on the quantity of output of individual workers and that quantity of output is to be used as the criterion of job success. In a predictive-validation study, the test would be administered to the entire pool of job applicants, but people would be hired without regard to their test scores. The new employees would be given the same basic orientation and training. Some time later (e.g., one year), the test scores would be correlated to quantity of output. If an acceptable correlation exists, the test is shown to be valid and can be used for selection of future employees. Figure 7.3 summarizes the steps in performing a predictive-validation study.

Predictive validation is used infrequently because it is costly and slow. To use this method, a large number of new employees must be hired at the same time without regard to their test scores. Potentially, an organization may hire both good and bad employees. Furthermore, for criteria to be predictive, all new employees must have equivalent orientation and training.

FIGURE 7.3   Predictive Validation Process

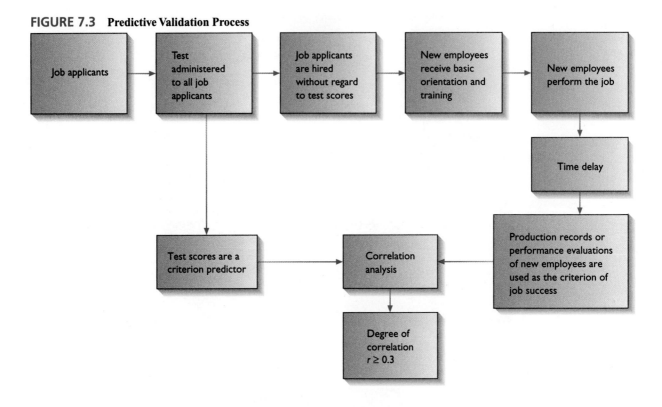

Concurrent Validity

concurrent validity
Validity established by
identifying a predictor,
administering it to current
employees, and correlating
the test data with the current
employee's job performance.

Concurrent validity is determined by identifying a predictor such as a test, administering the test to present employees, and correlating the test scores with the present employees' performance on the job. If an acceptable correlation exists, the test can be used for selection of future employees. Figure 7.4 summarizes the concurrent-validation process.

One disadvantage of concurrent validation is that in situations in which either racial or sexual discrimination has been practiced in the past, minorities and women will not be adequately represented. Another potential drawback is that among present employees in a particular job, the poorer performers are more likely to have been discharged or quit and the

FIGURE 7.4   Concurrent Validation Process

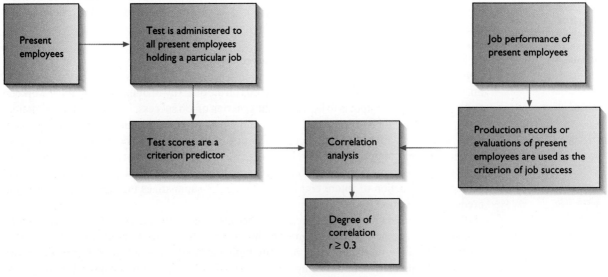

best performers have frequently been promoted. Obviously, a correlation coefficient obtained under these conditions can be misleading.

Criterion-related validation procedures (either predictive or concurrent) are preferred by the Equal Employment Opportunity Commission (EEOC) in validation studies. However, because of the cost and difficulties associated with criterion-related validation, content and construct validity are frequently used. These validation methods are also accepted by the EEOC.

Content and Construct Validity

content validity

The extent to which the content of a selection procedure or instrument is representative of important aspects of job performance.

Content validity refers to whether the content of a selection procedure or selection instrument such as a test is representative of important aspects of performance on the job. Content validity is especially useful in those situations where the number of employees is not large enough to justify the use of empirical validation methods. To use content validity, an employer must determine the exact performance requirements of a specific job and develop a selection procedure or selection instrument around an actual sample of the work that is to be performed.

construct validity

The extent to which a selection criterion measures the degree to which job candidates have identifiable characteristics determined to be important for successful job performance.

Construct validity refers to the extent to which a selection procedure or instrument measures the degree to which job candidates have identifiable characteristics that have been determined to be important for successful job performance. Examples of job-related constructs might include verbal ability, space visualization, and perceptual speed. For example, if a job requires blueprint reading, a test of space visualization might be construct valid for use in employment decisions.

Both content and construct validity are dependent on judgments. However, they may be the only available options in many validation situations.

RELIABILITY

Another important consideration for a selection system is reliability. Reliability refers to the reproducibility of results with a criterion predictor. For example, a test is reliable to the extent that the same person working under the same conditions produces approximately the same test results at different time periods. A test is not reliable if a person fails it on one day but makes an excellent grade when taking it again a week later (assuming, of course, that no learning has taken place in the meantime).

test-retest

One method of showing a test's reliability; involves testing a group and giving the same group the same test at a later time.

Three methods can be used to demonstrate the reliability of a criterion predictor. Suppose that scores on a test are to be used as the criterion predictor. One method of demonstrating the reliability of the test is called **test-retest.** This involves administering the test to a group of employees and later, usually in about two to four weeks, giving the same group the same test. Correlation analysis is used to determine the degree of correlation between the two sets of scores. The higher the correlation coefficient, the greater is the reliability of the test. Obviously, the results of the correlation can be influenced by whether members of the group studied during the time between tests.

parallel (or alternative) forms

A method of showing a test's reliability; involves giving two separate but similar forms of the test.

A second method used to determine reliability is called **parallel (or alternative) forms.** Under this method two separate but similar forms of a test would be constructed. The same group of employees would be tested at two different times using the alternative forms of the test. Again, correlation analysis is used to determine the degree of correlation between the two sets of scores. The higher the correlation coefficient, the greater is the reliability of the test.

split halves

A method of showing a test's reliability; involves dividing the test into halves.

The third method used to determine reliability is called **split-halves.** This is the simplest and easiest method of determining reliability. Under this method a test is administered to a group of employees. The results of the test are randomly split into two equal groups. The scores of the two equal groups are correlated. Again the higher the degree of correlation, the greater is the reliability.

UNIFORM GUIDELINES ON EMPLOYEE SELECTION PROCEDURES

The EEOC, the Office of Personnel Management, the Department of Justice, and the Department of Labor have adopted and published a document entitled "Uniform Guidelines on Employee Selection Procedures," more commonly referred to as "Uniform Guidelines."[6] The

Uniform Guidelines are designed to provide the framework for determining the proper use of tests and other selection procedures in any employment decision. Employment decisions include but are not limited to hiring, promotion, demotion, membership (e.g., in a labor organization), referral, retention, licensing and certification, selection for training, and transfers.

The Uniform Guidelines on Employee Selection Procedures also contain technical standards and documentation requirements for the validation of selection procedures. The guidelines broadly define selection procedures to include not only hiring but also promotion decisions, selection for training programs, and virtually every selection decision an organization makes. The guidelines are intended to be consistent with generally accepted professional standards for evaluating selection procedures. The Uniform Guidelines permit criteria-related, content, and construct validity studies. In conducting a validity study, employers are also encouraged to consider available alternatives with less adverse impact for achieving business purposes.

All validation studies must be thoroughly documented, and the Uniform Guidelines specify in detail the types of records that must be kept in any study. Since job analysis is an essential part of a validation study, specific guidelines are also provided for conducting job analyses.

Adverse (or Disparate) Impact

adverse impact
Condition that occurs when the selection rate for minorities or women is less than 80 percent of the selection rate for the majority group in hiring, promotions, transfers, demotions, or any selection decision.

4/5ths or 80 percent rule
A limit used to determine whether or not there are serious discrepancies in hiring decisions and other employment practices affecting women or minorities.

The fundamental principle underlying the Uniform Guidelines is that employment policies and practices that have an **adverse impact** on employment opportunities for any race, sex, religion, or national origin group are illegal unless justified by a demonstration of job relatedness. A selection procedure that has no adverse impact is generally considered to be legal. If adverse impact exists, however, it must be justified on the basis of job relatedness. Normally this means validation that demonstrates the relationship between the selection procedure and performance on the job.

The Uniform Guidelines adopt a rule of thumb as a practical means of determining adverse impact. This rule is known as the **4/5ths or 80 percent rule.** This rule is not a legal definition of discrimination but a practical device for determining serious discrepancies in hiring, promoting, or other employment decisions. For example, suppose an employer is doing business in an area where the labor force is 25 percent African Americans. Further, suppose that the employer has 1,000 employees and 100 (10 percent) of the employees are African Americans. Adverse impact exists because 4/5ths of 25 percent equals 20 percent and a selection rate for African Americans below 20 percent indicates adverse impact. African Americans make up only 10 percent of the employer's workforce. (See Figure 7.5.)

FIGURE 7.5
Determining Adverse Impact in an Employer's Workforce

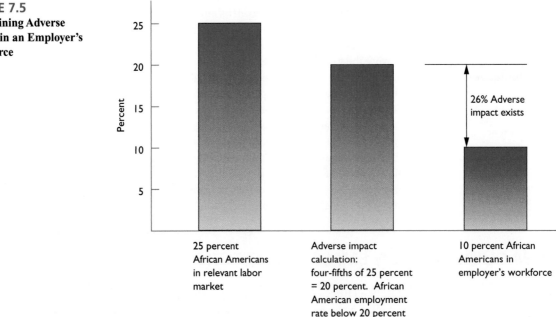

- 25 percent African Americans in relevant labor market
- Adverse impact calculation: four-fifths of 25 percent = 20 percent. African American employment rate below 20 percent indicates adverse impact
- 10 percent African Americans in employer's workforce

26% Adverse impact exists

FIGURE 7.6
Determining Adverse Impact in an Employer's Hiring Decisions

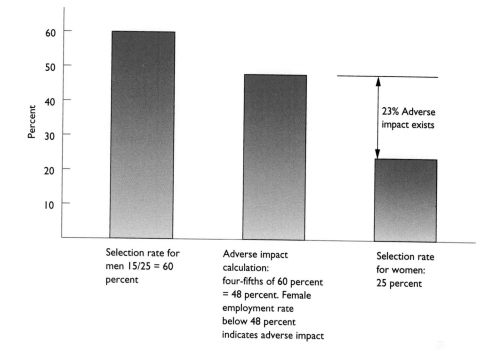

Figure 7.6 illustrates how adverse impact can be assessed in an employer's hiring decisions. Suppose 25 men have applied for a job opening and 15 of the men were hired. Suppose only 20 women applied and 5 were hired. Adverse impact exists because 4/5ths of 60 percent equals 48 percent, and a selection rate for women below 48 percent indicates adverse impact.

Where Adverse Impact Exists: The Basic Options

After it has been established that adverse impact exists, what steps do the Uniform Guidelines require? First, the employer has the option to modify or eliminate the procedure that produces the adverse impact. If the employer does not do so, it must justify the use of the procedure on the grounds of job relatedness. This normally means showing a clear relation between performance on the selection procedure and performance on the job. In the language of industrial psychology, the employer must validate the selection procedure.

Summary of Learning Objectives

1. **Outline the steps in the selection process.**

   The steps in the selection process are the application form, the preliminary interview, formal testing, the follow-up interview, reference checking, the physical examination, and making the final selection decision.

2. **Describe aptitude, psychomotor, job knowledge, proficiency, interest, and personality tests.**

   Aptitude tests measure a person's capacity or potential ability to learn and perform a job. Psychomotor tests measure a person's strength, dexterity, and coordination. Job knowledge tests measure the job-related knowledge possessed by a job applicant. Proficiency tests measure how well the applicant can do a sample of the work required in the position. Interest tests are designed to determine how a person's interests compare with the interests of successful people in a specific job. Personality tests attempt to measure personality characteristics.

3. **Explain a polygraph test.**

   The polygraph records physical changes in the body as the test subject answers a series of questions. The operator makes a judgment on whether the subject's response was truthful or deceptive by studying the physiological measurements recorded as the questions were answered.

4. **Describe structured and unstructured interviews.**

The structured interview is conducted using a predetermined outline. Unstructured interviews are conducted without a predetermined checklist of questions.

5. **Define *validity*.**

Validity refers to how well a criterion predictor actually predicts the criteria of job success.

6. **Explain predictive validity.**

Predictive validity is established by identifying a criterion predictor such as a test, administering the test to the entire pool of job applicants, and hiring people to fill the available jobs without regard to their test scores. At a later date, the test scores are correlated with the criteria of job success to see whether those people with high test scores performed substantially better than those with low test scores.

7. **Explain concurrent validity.**

Concurrent validity is established by identifying a predictor such as a test, administering the test to present employees, and correlating the test scores with the present employee's performances on the job.

8. **Describe content validity.**

Content validity refers to whether the content of a selection procedure or selection instrument, such as a test, is representative of important aspects of performance on the job.

9. **Discuss construct validity.**

Construct validity refers to the extent to which a selection procedure or instrument measures the degree to which job candidates have identifiable characteristics that have been determined to be important for successful job performance. Job-related constructs might include verbal ability, space visualization, and perceptual speed.

10. **Define *reliability*.**

Reliability refers to the extent to which a criterion predictor produces consistent results if repeated measurements are made.

11. **Define *adverse* (or *disparate*) *impact*.**

Adverse impact is a condition that occurs when the selection rate for minorities or women is less than 80 percent of the selection rate for the majority group in hiring, promotions, transfers, demotions, or other employment decisions.

Key Terms

4/5ths or 80 percent rule, *138*
adverse impact, *138*
applicant flow record, *127*
aptitude tests, *128*
board or panel interviews, *131*
concurrent validity, *136*
construct validity, *137*
content validity, *137*
criteria of job success, *134*
criterion predictors, *134*

graphology (handwriting analysis), *130*
group interview, *131*
halo effect, *131*
initial impressions, *131*
interest tests, *129*
job knowledge tests, *128*
parallel (or alternative forms), *137*
personality tests, *129*
polygraph, *129*
predictive validity, *135*

proficiency tests, *129*
psychomotor tests, *128*
reliability, *134*
selection, *125*
split halves, *137*
stress interview, *131*
structured interview, *131*
test-retest, *137*
unstructured interview, *131*
validity, *134*
weighted application forms, *127*

Review Questions

1. Outline the steps in the selection process.
2. Describe some preemployment inquiries that should be eliminated or carefully reviewed to ensure their job relatedness.
3. What is a weighted application form?

4. How is an applicant flow record used?

5. Outline and briefly describe five categories of tests.

6. What is a polygraph test?

7. What is graphology?

8. What is reference checking?

9. Briefly describe some of the procedures organizations use in making the final decision.

10. Define the following terms:

    a. Criteria of job success.

    b. Criterion predictor.

    c. Validity.

    d. Reliability.

11. Describe the following methods of validation:

    a. Predictive.

    b. Concurrent.

    c. Content.

    d. Construct.

12. What is adverse (or disparate) impact?

13. Describe the 4/5ths rule.

Discussion Questions

1. "Tests often do not reflect an individual's true ability." What are your views on this statement?

2. "Organizations should be able to hire employees without government interference." Do you agree or disagree? What do you think would happen if organizations could do this?

3. "Reference checking is a waste of time." Do you agree or disagree? Why?

4. How do you feel about establishing minimum entrance scores on national tests of acceptance to a college or university?

Incident 7.1

Promotions at OMG

Old Money Group (OMG) is a mutual fund management company based in Seattle. It operates four separate funds, each with a different goal: one each for income growth and income interest production, one for a combination or balance of growth and production, and one for dealing in short-term securities (a money market fund). OMG was formed in early 1995 as a financial management firm. By the end of 2000, OMG had almost $47 million under its management. Over this time period, the company had slightly outperformed the Standard & Poor's 500 average and done slightly better than the stock market as a whole.

The Keogh Act permits self-employed individuals to set up retirement plans. All contributions to and earnings from the plans are tax-exempt until the individual withdraws the money on retirement.

OMG recognized the great potential of using Keogh plans to help market shares in its mutual funds. It launched an aggressive marketing program aimed at persuading those with Keogh plans to buy into the fund. This was very successful. As a result, OMG found it necessary to establish a separate department to handle only Keogh plans. This new department was placed in the corporate account division under division vice president Ralph Simpson. The Keogh department grew rapidly and by the end of 2003 was managing approximately 3,000 separate Keogh plans. The department was responsible for all correspondence, personal contact, and problem solving involved with these accounts.

John Baker, who had graduated from college the previous fall with a degree in history, joined OMG in February 2004. In his interview, John had impressed the human resource department as having managerial potential. The human resource department wanted to place him in an area where he could move into such a position, but at that time none was available.

A job that could be used as a stepping-stone to more responsible positions opened up in the Keogh department. In April, John became assistant to the administrator of the department. He was told that if he handled this position well, he would be considered for a job as plan administrator when an opening occurred. This was communicated to John both by the human resource department and by the head of the Keogh department.

Over the next six months, it became apparent that John was not working out well. He seemed to show little interest in his work and did only what he had to do to get by; at times, his work was unsatisfactory. He appeared to be unhappy and not suited to the job. John let it be known that he had been looking for another position.

In October, Roy Johnson, head of the Keogh department, gave John his six-month review. Knowing that John was looking for another job, Roy decided to take the easy way out. Instead of giving John a bad review and facing the possibility of having to fire him, he gave John a satisfactory performance review. He hoped John would find another job so the problem would go away.

In early December, one of the plan administrators said she would be leaving OMG in late December. Roy faced the task of selecting someone to fill her position. Of those who had expressed an interest in the job, Fran Jenkins appeared the best suited for it. Fran was secretary to the head of the corporate division. She had become familiar with the plan administrators' work because she had helped them during their peak periods for the past three years. The only problem was Fran's lack of a college degree, which was stipulated as a requirement in the job description. Although she was currently taking night courses, she had completed only two and one-half years of college. After Roy discussed the problem with the head of the human resource department, this requirement was waived. Roy then announced that Fran would assume the position of plan administrator in December.

Two weeks later, John Baker informed the head of the human resource department that he had talked to his lawyer. He felt he had been discriminated against and believed he should have gotten the position of plan administrator.

Questions

1. Do you think John has a legitimate point?
2. What went wrong in this selection process?

Incident 7.2

The Pole Climbers

Ringing Bell Telephone Company has implemented an affirmative action plan in compliance with the Equal Employment Opportunity Commission. Under the current plan, to eliminate discrimination based on sex, women must be placed in jobs traditionally held by men. Therefore, the human resource department has emphasized recruiting and hiring women for such positions. Women who apply for craft positions are encouraged to try for outdoor craft jobs, such as those titled installer-repairer and line worker.

All employees hired as outside technicians must first pass basic installation school, which includes a week of training for pole climbing. During this week, employees are taught to climb 30-foot telephone poles. At the end of the week, they must demonstrate the strength and skills necessary to climb the pole and perform exercises while on it, such as lifting heavy tools and using a pulley to lift a bucket. Only those who pass this first week of training are allowed to advance to the segment dealing with installation.

Records have been maintained on the rates of success or failure for employees who attend the training school. For men, the failure rate has remained fairly constant at 30 percent. However, it has averaged 70 percent for women.

The human resource department has become concerned because hiring and training employees who must resign at the end of one week is a tremendous expense. In addition, the goal of placing women in outdoor craft positions is not being reached.

As a first step in solving the problem, the human resource department has started interviewing the women who have failed the first week of training. Each employee is asked her reasons for seeking the position and encouraged to discuss probable causes for failure. Interviews over the last two months disclosed that employees were motivated to accept the job because of their wishes to work outdoors, work without close supervision, obtain challenging work, meet the public, have variety in their jobs, and obtain a type of job unusual for women. Reasons for failure were physical inability to climb the pole, fear of height while on it, an accident during training such as a fall from the pole, and change of mind about the job after learning that strenuous work was involved.

In many instances, the women who mentioned physical reasons also stated they were not physically ready to undertake the training; many had no idea it would be so difficult. Even though they still wanted the job, they could not pass the physical strength test at the end of one week.

Some stated that they felt "influenced" by their interviewer from the human resource department to take the job; others said they had accepted it because it was the only job available with the company at the time.

Questions

1. What factors would you keep in mind in designing an effective selection process for the position of outdoor craft technician?

2. What would you recommend to help Ringing Bell reduce the failure rate among women trainees?

**EXERCISE 7.1
Developing
a Frequency
Distribution**

You will be given one minute to copy the letter *T* on a blank sheet of paper as many times as possible. The exercise is timed, and exactly one minute is permitted. A frequency distribution will then be developed by your instructor (or the class) to show how well the class performed. A frequency distribution is a tabular summary showing the frequency of observations in each of several nonoverlapping classes. An example of a frequency distribution would be:

I	# of People
0–10	3
10–40	6
40–60	7
60–80	5

1. What is the shape of the distribution?
2. Why is the distribution shaped in this manner?
3. Could this frequency distribution be used as a selection device for certain jobs? If so, what types of jobs?
4. How would you demonstrate the validity of this procedure?

**Notes and
Additional
Readings**

1. Barbara S. Plank, James C. Impara, and Robert A. Spies, eds. *The Fifteenth Mental Measurements Yearbook* (Lincoln, Neb.: The Buros Institute of Mental Measurement, University of Nebraska Press, 2003).

2. See Richard D. White, Jr., "Ask Me No Questions, Tell Me No Lies: Examining the Uses and Misuses of the Polygraph," *Public Personnel Management,* Winter 2001, pp. 483–93.

3. Steven L. Thomas and Steve Vaught, "The Write Stuff: What the Evidence Says about Using Handwriting Analysis in Hiring," *S. A. M. Advanced Management Journal,* Autumn 2001, pp. 31–35.

4. Gillian Flynn, "To (Genetic) Test or Not," *Workforce,* December 2000, pp. 108–109.

5. See Edward C. Andler, Dara Herbst, and David Sears, *The Complete Reference Checking Handbook,* Amazon.com, 2000.

6. For more information, enter "Uniform Guidelines on Employee Selection Procedures" through Google.

On the Job

SAMPLE ONLINE APPLICATION FOR EMPLOYMENT

This On the Job example illustrates the types of information normally asked on an application for employment and an applicant flow record. The application form in Exhibit A7.1 provides basic employment information to determine the applicant's qualifications in relation to the requirements of the available jobs and to screen out unqualified applicants. As can be seen, the applicant can also volunteer information that might be viewed as discriminatory. These data can then be used to provide statistical reports to the EEOC regarding recruitment and selection of women and minorities.

EXHIBIT A7.1

Source: Courtesy of The McGraw-Hill Companies Corporate New Media Department.

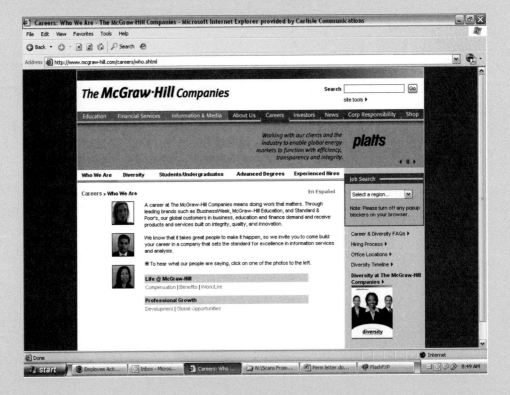

EXHIBIT A7.1
(Continued)

Part **Three**

Training and Developing Employees

Photodisc/Getty Images

Orientation and Employee Training

Chapter Learning Objectives

After studying this chapter, you should be able to:

1. Define *orientation*.
2. Describe an orientation kit.
3. Define *training*.
4. Describe needs assessment.
5. Outline three categories of training objectives.
6. Describe job rotation.
7. Explain apprenticeship training.
8. Define *virtual classroom*.
9. Outline the seven principles of learning.
10. List the four areas of training evaluation.

Chapter Outline

Web site: HR Online
www.hr2000.com

After the selection process is completed, new employees must be oriented to their job and the organization. Furthermore, all employees periodically need to update their current skills or learn new skills. Orienting new employees and training all employees are major responsibilities of the human resource function.

For orientation and training to be effective, all of the previously discussed human resource functions must be effectively accomplished. Figure 8.1 shows the relationships among human

FIGURE 8.1
Relationships among Human Resource Functions Necessary for Effective Performance

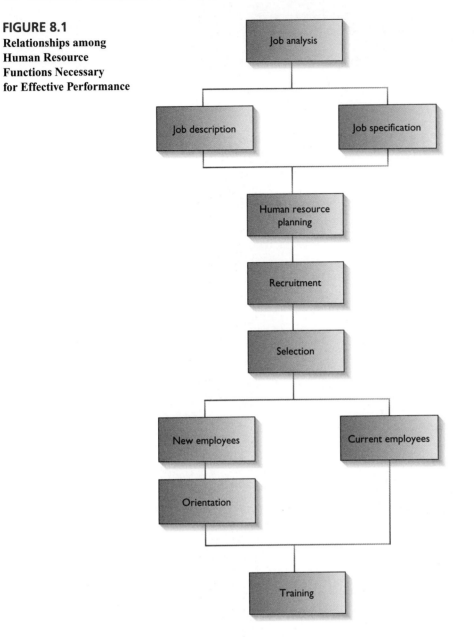

resource functions. Job analysis is the process of determining, through observation and study, the pertinent information relating to the nature of a specific job. Job analysis, as the detailed discussion in Chapter 4 showed, identifies the knowledge, skills, and abilities required to successfully perform the job. It is, therefore, necessary before other human resource functions can be performed. Job analysis leads to a job description and a job specification. A job description concentrates on describing the job as it is currently being done. It explains the name of the job, what is to be done, where it is to be done, and how it is to be done. On the other hand, a job specification concentrates on the characteristics required to successfully perform the job. Human resource planning is concerned with getting the right number of qualified people into the right job at the right time. Human resource plans must support organizational plans. For example, if an organization is laying off employees it is unlikely that human resources would be recruiting new employees. Similarly, orientation and training can only be successful if they are based on organizational needs.

ORIENTATION

orientation
The introduction of new employees to the organization, work unit, and job.

Orientation is the introduction of new employees to the organization, their work units, and their jobs. Employees receive orientation from their coworkers and from the organization. The orientation from coworkers is usually unplanned and unofficial, and it often provides the new employee with misleading and inaccurate information. This is one of the reasons the official orientation provided by the organization is so important. An effective orientation program has an immediate and lasting impact on the new employee and can make the difference between his or her success or failure.

Job applicants get some orientation to the organization even before they are hired. The organization has a reputation for the type of employer it is and the types of products or services it provides. During the selection process, the new employee usually also learns other general aspects of the organization and what the duties, working conditions, and pay will be.

After hiring the employee, the organization begins a formal orientation program. Regardless of the type of organization, orientation should usually be conducted at two distinct levels:

1. Organizational orientation—presents topics of relevance and interest to all employees.
2. Departmental and job orientation—describes topics that are unique to the new employee's specific department and job.

Shared Responsibility

Since there are two distinct levels of orientation, the human resource department and the new employee's immediate manager normally share responsibility for orientation. The human resource department is responsible for initiating and coordinating both levels of orientation, training line managers in procedures for conducting the departmental and job orientation, conducting the general company orientation, and following up the initial orientation with the new employee. The new employee's manager is usually responsible for conducting the departmental and job orientation. Some organizations have instituted a "buddy system" in which one of the new employee's coworkers conducts the job orientation. If a buddy system is to work successfully, the employee chosen for this role must be carefully selected and properly trained for such orientation responsibilities.

Organizational Orientation

organizational orientation
General orientation that presents topics of relevance and interest to all employees.

The topics presented in the **organizational orientation** should be based on the needs of both the organization and the employee. Generally, the organization is interested in making a profit, providing good service to customers and clients, satisfying employee needs and well-being, and being socially responsible. New employees, on the other hand, are generally more interested in pay, benefits, and specific terms and conditions of employment. A good balance between the company's and the new employee's needs is essential if the orientation program is to have positive results. Figure 8.2 provides a listing of suggested topics that might be covered in an organization's orientation program.

Departmental and Job Orientation

departmental and job orientation
Specific orientation that describes topics unique to the new employee's specific department and job.

The content of **departmental and job orientation** depends on the specific needs of the department and the skills and experience of the new employee. Experienced employees are likely to need less job orientation. However, even experienced employees usually need some basic orientation. Both experienced and inexperienced employees should receive a thorough orientation concerning departmental matters. Figure 8.3 presents a checklist for the development of departmental and job orientation programs.

Orientation Kit

orientation kit
A supplemental packet of written information for new employees.

Each new employee should receive an **orientation kit,** or packet of information, to supplement the verbal orientation program. This kit, which is normally prepared by the human resource department, can provide a wide variety of materials. Care should be taken in the

FIGURE 8.2   Possible Topics for Organizational Orientation Programs

Source: W. D. St. John, "The Complete Employee Orientation Program," *Personnel Journal,* May 1980, pp. 376–77. Adapted from *Personnel Journal,* Costa Mesa, California.

1. **Company overview**
   - Welcome speech
   - Founding, growth, trends, goals, priorities, and problems
   - Traditions, customs, norms, and standards
   - Current functions of the organization
   - Products/services and customers served
   - Steps in getting products/services to customers
   - Scope and diversity of activities
   - Organization, structure, and relationship of company and its branches
   - Managerial staff information
   - Community relations, expectations, and activities
2. **Policies and procedures review**
3. **Compensation**
   - Pay rates and ranges
   - Overtime
   - Holiday pay
   - Shift differential
   - How pay is received
   - Deductions: required and optional
   - Option to buy damaged products and costs thereof
   - Discounts
   - Advances on pay
   - Credit union loan information
   - Reimbursement for job expenses
4. **Benefits**
   - Insurance
   - Medical/dental
   - Life insurance
   - Disability
   - Workers' compensation
   - Holidays and vacations
   - Leave: personal illness, family illness, bereavement, maternity, military, jury duty, emergency, extended absence
   - Retirement plans and options
   - On-the-job training opportunities
   - Counseling services
   - Cafeteria
   - Recreation and social activities
   - Other company services to employees
5. **Safety and accident prevention**
   - Completion of emergency data card (if not done as part of employment process)
   - Health and first-aid clinics
   - Exercise and recreation centers
   - Safety precautions
   - Reporting of hazards
   - Fire prevention
   - Accident procedures and reporting

   - OSHA requirements (review of key sections)
   - Physical exam requirements
   - Use of alcohol, tobacco, and drugs on the job
   - Tax shelter options
6. **Employees and union relations**
   - Terms and conditions of employment review
   - Assignment, reassignment, and promotion
   - Probationary period and expected on-the-job conduct
   - Reporting of sickness and tardiness
   - Employee rights and responsibilities
   - Manager and supervisor rights
   - Relations with supervisors and shop stewards
   - Employee organizations and options
   - Union contract provisions and/or company policy
   - Supervision and evaluation of performance
   - Discipline and reprimands
   - Grievance procedures
   - Termination of employment (resignation, layoff, discharge, retirement)
   - Content of personnel record
   - Communications: channels of communication (upward and downward), suggestion system, posting materials on bulletin board, sharing new ideas
   - Sanitation and cleanliness
   - Wearing of safety equipment, badges, and uniforms
   - Bringing things to and removing things from company grounds
   - On-site political activity
   - Gambling
   - Handling of rumors
7. **Physical facilities**
   - Tour of facilities
   - Food services and cafeteria
   - Restricted areas for eating
   - Employee entrances
   - Restricted areas (e.g., from cars)
   - Parking
   - First aid
   - Rest rooms
   - Supplies and equipment
8. **Economic factors**
   - Costs of damage to select items with required sales to balance
   - Profit margins
   - Labor costs
   - Equipment costs
   - Costs of absenteeism, tardiness, and accidents

design not only to ensure that it offers essential information, but also that it does not give too much information. Some materials that might be included in an orientation kit include these:

Company organization chart.

Map of the company's facilities.

Copy of policy and procedures handbook.

FIGURE 8.3 **Possible Topics for Departmental and Job Orientation Programs**

1. **Department functions**
   - Goals and current priorities
   - Organization and structure
   - Operational activities
   - Relationship with other departments
   - Relationships of jobs within the department
2. **Job duties and responsibilities**
   - Detailed explanation of job based on current job description and expected results
   - Explanation of why the job is important and how the specific job relates to others in the department and company
   - Discussion of common problems and how to avoid and overcome them
   - Performance standards and basis of performance evaluation
   - Work hours and times
   - Overtime requirements
   - Extra duty assignments (e.g., changing duties to cover for an absent worker)
   - Required records and reports
   - Checkout of equipment to be used
   - Explanation of where and how to get tools and to have equipment maintained and repaired
   - Types of assistance available, when and how to ask for help
   - Relations with state and federal inspectors
3. **Policies and procedures**
   - Rules unique to the job and/or department
   - Handling emergencies
   - Safety precautions and accident prevention
   - Reporting of hazards and accidents
   - Cleanliness standards and sanitation (e.g., cleanup)
   - Security, theft problems, and costs
   - Relations with outside people
   - Eating, smoking, and chewing gum, etc., in department area
   - Removal of things from department
   - Damage control (e.g., smoking restrictions)
   - Time clock and time sheets
   - Breaks
   - Lunch duration and time
   - Making and receiving personal telephone calls
   - Requisitioning supplies and equipment
   - Monitoring and evaluating of employee performance
   - Job bidding and requesting reassignment
   - Going to cars during work hours
4. **Department tour**
   - Rest rooms and showers
   - Fire-alarm box and fire extinguisher stations
   - Time clocks
   - Lockers
   - Approved entrances and exits
   - Water fountains and eye-wash systems
   - Supervisors' quarters
   - Supply room and maintenance department
   - Sanitation and security offices
   - Smoking area
   - Locations of services to employees related to department
   - First-aid kit
5. **Introduction to department employees**

List of holidays and fringe benefits.

Copies of performance appraisal forms, dates, and procedures.

Copies of other required forms (e.g., expense reimbursement form).

Emergency and accident prevention procedures.

Sample copy of company newsletter or magazine.

Telephone numbers and locations of key company personnel (e.g., security personnel).

Copies of insurance plans.

Many organizations require employees to sign a form indicating they have received and read the orientation kit. This is commonly required in unionized organizations to protect the company if a grievance arises and the employee alleges he or she was not aware of certain company policies and procedures. On the other hand, it is equally important that a form be signed in nonunionized organizations, particularly in light of an increase in wrongful discharge litigation. Whether signing a document actually encourages new employees to read the orientation kit is questionable.

Orientation Length and Timing

It is virtually impossible for a new employee to absorb all the information in the company orientation program in one long session. Brief sessions, not to exceed two hours, spread over several days, increase the likelihood that the new employee will understand and retain the information presented. Too many organizations conduct a perfunctory orientation program lasting for a half day or full day. Programs of this nature can result in a negative attitude on the part of new employees.

Unfortunately, many departmental and job orientation programs produce the same results. Frequently, upon arriving in a department, new employees are given a departmental procedures manual and told to read the material and ask any questions they may have. Another frequently used departmental and job orientation method is to give new employees menial tasks to perform. Both of these methods are likely to produce poor results.

Departmental orientations should also be brief and spread over several days. Job orientations should be well planned and conducted using appropriate techniques.

Follow-Up and Evaluation

Formal and systematic follow-up to the initial orientation is essential. The new employee should not be told to drop by if any problems occur. The manager should regularly check on how well the new employee is doing and answer any questions that may have arisen after the initial orientation. The human resource department should conduct a scheduled follow-up after the employee has been on the job for a month.

The human resource department should also conduct an annual evaluation of the total orientation program. The purpose of this evaluation is to determine whether the current orientation program is meeting the company's and new employees' needs and ascertain ways to improve the present program.

Feedback from new employees is one method of evaluating the effectiveness of an organization's orientation program. Feedback can be obtained using the following methods:

Unsigned questionnaires completed by all new employees.

In-depth interviews of randomly selected new employees.

Group discussion sessions with new employees who have settled comfortably into their jobs.

Feedback of this type enables an organization to adapt its orientation program to the specific suggestions of actual participants.

Finally, organizations should realize that new employees will receive an orientation that has an impact on their performance—either from coworkers or from the company. It is certainly in the best interest of the company to have a well-planned, well-executed orientation program.

TRAINING EMPLOYEES

training
Learning process that involves the acquisition of skills, concepts, rules, or attitudes to enhance employee performance.

Training is a learning process that involves the acquisition of knowledge, skills, and abilities (KSA) necessary to successfully perform a job. Several reasons exist for an organization to conduct training for its employees. Outlined below are some of the reasons:

1. Economic, social, technological, and government changes can make the skills learned today obsolete in the future.
2. Planned organizational changes (such as the introduction of new equipment) can make it necessary for employees to update their skills or acquire new ones.
3. Performance problems within an organization such as low productivity or large scrap problems can be reduced by training.
4. Regulatory, contractual, professional, or certification issues can require an employer to provide training for its employees.

Normally, a new employee's manager has primary responsibility for her or his job training. Sometimes this training is delegated to a senior employee in the department. Regardless, the quality of this initial training can have a significant influence on the new employee's productivity and attitude toward his or her job. HRM in Action 8.1 describes orientation of students at Wake Forest University.

The steps to a successful training program include the following:

1. Perform job analysis.
2. Perform needs assessment.

ADAPTING TO UNIVERSITY LIFE FOR STUDENTS
At some universities around the country, administrators are going the extra mile to make the adjustment for incoming freshmen as painless as possible.

Staff members at Wake Forest University and Winston-Salem State have increased the level of orientation they provide for incoming students. The increased orientation includes such information as how to best enroll for their classes or going as far as how to chant at university football games.

The schools have smaller freshman classes, but the schools argue this is not due to the economic downturn.

Both institutions claim to purposefully have kept their freshman classes smaller this year. The increased orientation is due to administrators feeling overwhelmed last year by student questions regarding housing, classes, and so on. Administrators hope the increased orientation will lead to less confusion and a more productive and orderly start of the year for new students.

Source: Adapted from Lisa O'Donnell, "Starting College Life: Local Colleges Try to Make It Easier for Freshmen to Adapt to Campus Culture, Rules, and Traditions," *McClatchy-Tribune Business News*, August 21, 2009.

3. Establish training objectives.
4. Conduct training program.
5. Evaluate training outcomes.

Each of these steps is discussed in more detail in the following sections. Job analysis identifies the KSA of a job. Training programs should be designed that improve the participant's KSA. HRM in Action 8.2 describes the e-learning environment at Cathay Pacific Airways.

Needs Assessment

Training must be directed toward accomplishment of some organizational objective, such as more efficient production methods, improved quality of products or services, or reduced operating costs. This means an organization should commit its resources only to those training activities that can best help in achieving its objectives. **Needs assessment** is a systematic analysis of the specific training activities the organization requires to achieve its objectives. In general, five methods can be used to gather needs assessment information: interviews, surveys/questionnaires, observations, focus groups, and document examination.[1]

Interviews with employees can be conducted by specialists in the human resource department or by outside experts. Basic questions that should usually be asked are as follows:

1. What problems is the employee having in his or her job?
2. What additional skills and/or knowledge does the employee need to better perform the job?
3. What training does the employee believe is needed?

Of course, in conducting interviews, every organization would have several additional questions about specific issues. In addition, if interviews are to provide useful information, employees must believe their input will be valued and not be used against them.

Surveys and/or questionnaires are also frequently used in needs assessment. Normally this involves developing a list of skills required to perform particular jobs effectively and asking employees to check those skills in which they believe they need training. Figure 8.4 shows some typical areas that a needs assessment questionnaire might cover. Employee attitude surveys can also be used to uncover training needs. Usually most organizations bring in an outside party or organization to conduct and analyze employee attitude surveys. Customer surveys can also indicate problem areas that may not be obvious to employees of the organization. Responses to a customer survey may indicate areas of training for the organization as a whole or particular functional units.

To be effective, observations for determining training needs must be conducted by individuals trained in observing employee behavior and translating observed behavior into specific training needs. Specialists in the human resource department who have been trained in performing job analyses should be particularly adept at observing to identify training needs.

needs assessment
A systematic analysis of the specific training activities the organization requires to achieve its objectives.

e-LEARNING ENVIRONMENT AT CATHAY PACIFIC AIRWAYS

For Cathay Pacific Airways, the move to e-learning is part of a larger cultural shift away from passive participation toward employee initiative. A key element in this strategy is the development of an e-learning environment that the airline calls "Learner's World." Graham Higgins, manager of Cathay Pacific's learning and development team, coordinates all company training programs. He chose NetDimensions' Enterprise Knowledge Platform (EKP) as the airline's learning management system, which is the backbone of Learner's World. EKP is designed to manage the entire learning process—from enrolling students and tracking their progress, to delivering tests and reporting costs. The airline reduced its previous six-week cabin crew orientation program to five weeks, resulting in significant savings in direct and indirect costs. In the near future, NetDimensions, with direct input from Cathay Pacific, will unveil a new Web-based exam environment that features high-level security, publishing, and assessment capabilities.

"We had already learned from the introduction of our corporate intranet that we needed to offer things that would interest people. For example, we created an online travel desk where staff can enter their comments on hotels they have stayed in. This proved very popular because so many of our staff travel frequently. We also introduced online registration for some very popular lunchtime auditorium sessions. So, for example, if you wanted to attend the session on managing your personal finances, you could sign up for it via Learner's World."

In addition, some surprising areas of training have been entirely converted to e-learning. When a new reclining seat was introduced in business class, airline officials decided not to summon 300 maintenance technicians back to the classroom for training. Instead the technicians, scattered around Cathay Pacific's 49 flight destinations, were introduced to the new seat via an online self-teaching module.

Source: Adapted from Anonymous, "Airline Soars with New e-Learning Environment," *T+D*, December 2006, pp. 82–86.

Focus groups are composed of employees from various departments and various levels within the organization. A specialist in the human resource department or an outside expert can conduct the focus group sessions. Focus group topics should address issues such as the following:

1. What skills/knowledge will our employees need for our organization to stay competitive over the next five years?
2. What problems does our organization have that can be solved through training?

Document examination involves examining organizational records on the absenteeism, turnover, and accident rates to determine if problems exist and whether any identified problems can be addressed through training. Another useful source to examine is performance appraisal information gathered through the organization's performance appraisal system. Performance problems common to many employees are likely areas to address through training. Regardless of the method employed, a systematic and accurate needs assessment should be undertaken before any training is conducted.

Establishing Training Objectives

Web site: North American Training and Development Resource Center
www.trainet.com

After training needs have been determined, objectives must be established for meeting those needs. Unfortunately, many organizational training programs have no objectives. "Training for training's sake" appears to be the maxim. This philosophy makes it virtually impossible to evaluate the strengths and weaknesses of a training program.

FIGURE 8.4
Needs Assessment Questionnaire with Selected Questions

Instructions: Please read the list of training areas carefully before answering. Circle Yes if you believe you need training in that skill, either for use in your current job or for getting ready for promotion to a better position. Circle the question mark if uncertain. Circle No if you feel no need for training in that area.

1. How to more effectively manage my time	Yes	?	No
2. How to handle stress on the job	Yes	?	No
3. How to improve my written communication skills	Yes	?	No
4. How to improve my oral communication skills	Yes	?	No
5. How to improve my listening skills	Yes	?	No
6. How to improve my personal productivity	Yes	?	No

Effective training objectives should state what will result for the organization, department, or individual when the training is completed. The outcomes should be described in writing. Training objectives can be categorized as follows:

1. Instructional objectives.

   • What principles, facts, and concepts are to be learned in the training program?
   • Who is to be taught?
   • When are they to be taught?

2. Organizational and departmental objectives.

   • What impact will the training have on organizational and departmental outcomes such as absenteeism, turnover, reduced costs, and improved productivity?

3. Individual performance and growth objectives.

   • What impact will the training have on the behavioral and attitudinal outcomes of the individual trainee?
   • What impact will the training have on the personal growth of the individual trainee?

When clearly defined objectives are lacking, it is impossible to evaluate a program efficiently. Furthermore, there is no basis for selecting appropriate materials, content, or instructional methods.[2]

METHODS OF TRAINING

Several methods can be used to satisfy an organization's training needs and accomplish its objectives. Some of the more commonly used methods include on-the-job training, job rotation, apprenticeship training, and classroom training. HRM in Action 8.3 describes Cisco's Training Facilities.

on-the-job training (OJT)
Training that shows the employee how to perform the job and allows him or her to do it under the trainer's supervision.

job rotation (cross training)
Training that requires an individual to learn several different jobs in a work unit or department and perform each job for a specified time period.

On-the-Job Training and Job Rotation

On-the-job training (OJT) is normally given by a senior employee or a manager. The employee is shown how to perform the job and allowed to do it under the trainer's supervision.

One form of on-the-job training is **job rotation,** sometimes called **cross training.** In job rotation, an individual learns several different jobs within a work unit or department and performs each job for a specified time period. One main advantage of job rotation is that it makes flexibility possible in the department. For example, when one member of a work unit is absent, another can perform that job.

The advantages of on-the-job training are that no special facilities are required and the new employee does productive work during the learning process. On-the-job training has been found to be more effective than classroom training that may seldom be used when the person

TABLE 8.1
Steps Leading to Effective On-the-Job Training

A. Determining the training objectives and preparing the training area:
   1. Decide what the trainee must be taught to do the job efficiently, safely, economically, and intelligently.
   2. Provide the right tools, equipment, supplies, and material.
   3. Have the workplace properly arranged just as the trainee will be expected to keep it.
B. Presenting the instruction:
   Step 1. Preparation of the trainee for learning the job:
      a. Put the trainee at ease.
      b. Find out what the trainee already knows about the job.
      c. Get the trainee interested in and desirous of learning the job.
   Step 2. Breakdown of work into components and identification of key points:
      a. Determine the segments that make up the total job.
      b. Determine the key points, or "tricks of the trade."
   Step 3. Presentation of the operations and knowledge:
      a. Tell, show, illustrate, and question to put over the new knowledge and operations.
      b. Instruct slowly, clearly, completely, and patiently, one point at a time.
      c. Check, question, and repeat.
      d. Make sure the trainee understands.
   Step 4. Performance tryout:
      a. Test the trainee by having him or her perform the job.
      b. Ask questions beginning with *why, how, when,* or *where.*
      c. Observe performance, correct errors, and repeat instructions if necessary.
      d. Continue until the trainee is competent in the job.
   Step 5. Follow-up:
      a. Put the trainee on his or her own.
      b. Check frequently to be sure the trainee follows instructions.
      c. Taper off extra supervision and close follow-up until the trainee is qualified to work with normal supervision.

returns to the job. Its major disadvantage is that the pressures of the workplace can cause instruction of the employee to be haphazard or neglected.

In training an employee on the job, the trainer can use several steps to ensure that the training is effective. Table 8.1 summarizes the steps in the training process. Each step is explained more fully next.

Preparation of the Trainee for Learning the Job   An employee almost always desires to learn a new job. Showing an interest in the person, explaining the importance of the job, and explaining why it must be done correctly enhance the employee's desire to learn. Determining the employee's previous work experience in similar jobs enables the trainer to use that experience in explaining the present job or to eliminate unnecessary explanations.

Breakdown of Work into Components and Identification of Key Points   This breakdown consists of determining the segments that make up the total job. In each segment, something is accomplished to advance the work toward completion. Such a breakdown can be viewed as a detailed road map that guides the employee through the entire work cycle in a rational, easy-to-understand manner, without injury to the person or damage to the equipment.

A key point is any directive or information that helps the employee perform a work component correctly, easily, and safely. Key points are the "tricks of the trade" and are given to the employee to help reduce learning time. Observing and mastering the key points help the employee acquire needed skills and perform the work more effectively.

Presentation of the Operations and Knowledge   Simply telling an employee how to perform the job is usually not sufficient. An employee must not only be told but also shown how to do the job. Each component of the job must be demonstrated. While each is being demonstrated, the key points for the component should be explained. Employees should be encouraged to ask questions about each component.

Performance Tryout   An employee should perform the job under the guidance of the trainer. Generally, an employee should be required to explain what he or she is going to do at each component of the job. If the explanation is correct, the employee is then allowed to perform the component. If the explanation is incorrect, the mistake should be corrected before the employee is allowed to actually perform the component. Praise and encouragement are essential in this phase.

Follow-Up When the trainer is reasonably sure an employee can do the job without monitoring, the employee should be encouraged to work at his or her own pace while developing skills in performing the job and should be left alone. The trainer should return periodically to answer any questions and see that all is going well. Employees should not be turned loose and forgotten. They will have questions and will make better progress if the trainer is around to answer questions and help with problems.

Apprenticeship Training

apprenticeship training
Giving instruction, both on and off the job, in the practical and theoretical aspects of the work required in a highly skilled occupation.

Apprenticeship training provides beginning workers with comprehensive training in the practical and theoretical aspects of work required in a highly skilled occupation. Apprenticeship programs combine on-the-job and classroom training to prepare workers for more than 800 skilled occupations such as bricklayer, machinist worker, computer operator, and laboratory technician. About two-thirds of apprenticeable occupations are in the construction and manufacturing trades, but apprentices also work in such diverse fields as electronics, the service industries, public administration, and medical and health care. The length of an apprenticeship varies by occupation and is determined by standards adopted by the industry. Table 8.2 gives the length of some occupational apprenticeship periods.

A skilled and experienced employee conducts on-the-job training during the apprenticeship period. The purpose of this training is to learn the practical skills of the job. Apprentices learn the theoretical side of their jobs in classes they attend. Some of the subjects that might be covered in the classroom training include mathematics, blueprint reading, and technical courses required for specific occupations.

Wages paid apprentices usually begin at half those paid fully trained employees. However, the wages are generally advanced rapidly at six-month intervals.

Web site: U.S. Department of Labor Employment and Training Administration
www.doleta.gov/atels_bat/

The U.S. Department of Labor's Office of Apprenticeship Training, Employer and Labor Services (OATELS) is responsible for providing services to existing apprenticeship programs and technical assistance to organizations that wish to establish programs. The bureau has established the following minimum standards for apprenticeship programs:

1. Full and fair opportunity to apply for an apprenticeship.
2. A schedule of work processes in which an apprentice is to receive training and experience on the job.
3. Organized instruction designed to provide apprentices with knowledge in technical subjects related to their trade (e.g., a minimum of 144 hours per year is normally considered necessary).
4. A progressively increasing schedule of wages.
5. Proper supervision of on-the-job training, with adequate facilities to train apprentices.
6. Periodic evaluation of the apprentice's progress, both in job performances and related instruction, with appropriate records maintained.
7. No discrimination in any phase of selection, employment, or training.

TABLE 8.2
Length of Selected Apprenticeship Courses

Source: OATELS, U.S. Department of Labor.

Occupation	Length of Course (years)
Airplane mechanic	3–4
Automotive mechanic	3–4
Barber	2
Brewer	2–3
Butcher	2–3
Carpenter	4
Musician instrument mechanic	3–4
Photographer	3
Radio electrician	4–5
X-ray technician	4

classroom training
The most familiar training method; useful for quickly imparting information to large groups with little or no knowledge of the subject.

Classroom training is an effective way to get information to a large group of employees. BananaStock/ PictureQuest

Classroom Training

Classroom training is conducted off the job and is probably the most familiar training method. It is an effective means of imparting information quickly to large groups with limited or no knowledge of the subject being presented. It is useful for teaching factual material, concepts, principles, and theories. Portions of orientation programs, some aspects of apprenticeship training, and safety programs are usually presented utilizing some form of classroom instruction. More frequently, however, classroom instruction is used for technical, professional, and managerial employees.

Virtual Classroom

Internet technology has advanced rapidly and as a result the training of employees is changing. In some companies, employee training has moved from the classroom to the Internet. A "virtual classroom" is an online teaching and learning environment that integrates chat rooms, desktop video conferencing, Web sites, and e-mail distribution into a typical lecture-based system. Virtual classrooms offer training in either self-paced courses, real-time courses through intranets, or real-time video conferencing. In a typical virtual classroom, a professor lectures to a local class and a remote class that may be thousands of miles away. The students at the local and remote classes can ask questions of the professor. Advancing technology is likely to bring other changes in the training of employees.

EVALUATING TRAINING

When the results of a training program are evaluated, a number of benefits accrue. Less effective programs can be withdrawn to save time and effort. Weaknesses within established programs can be identified and remedied.[3]

Evaluation of training can be broken down into four areas:

1. *Reaction:* How much did the trainees like the program?
2. *Learning:* What principles, facts, and concepts were learned in the training program?
3. *Behavior:* Did the job behavior of the trainees change because of the program?
4. *Results:* What were the results of the program in terms of factors such as reduced costs or reduction in turnover?

Even when great care is taken in designing evaluation procedures, it is difficult to determine the exact effects of training on learning, behavior, and results. Because of this, evaluation of training is often limited and superficial.

Reaction

Reaction evaluation should consider a wide range of topics, including program content, program structure and format, instructional techniques, instructor abilities and style, the quality of the learning environment, the extent to which training objectives were achieved, and recommendations for improvement. Figure 8.5 illustrates a typical reaction evaluation questionnaire.

Reaction evaluation questionnaires are normally administered immediately following the training, but they can be administered several weeks later. The major flaw in using only reaction evaluation is that the enthusiasm of trainees cannot necessarily be taken as evidence of improved ability and performance.[4]

Learning

Learning evaluation concerns how well the trainees understood and absorbed the principles, facts, and skills taught. In teaching skills, classroom demonstrations by trainees are a fairly objective way to determine how much learning is occurring. Where principles and facts are being taught, paper-and-pencil tests can be used. Standardized tests can be purchased to

FIGURE 8.5
Sample Reaction Evaluation Questionnaire

Name of program _____

Instructor _____

Date _____

1. How would you rate the overall program?
   ☐ Excellent   ☐ Very Good   ☐ Good   ☐ Fair   ☐ Poor
   Comments: _____
   _____

2. How were the meeting facilities, luncheon arrangements, etc.?
   ☐ Excellent   ☐ Very Good   ☐ Good   ☐ Fair   ☐ Poor
   Comments: _____
   _____

3. Would you like to attend programs of a similar nature in the future?
   ☐ Yes   ☐ No   ☐ Not sure
   Comments: _____
   _____

4. To what extent was the program relevant to your current job?
   ☐ To a large extent   ☐ To some extent   ☐ Very little
   Comments: _____
   _____

5. How would you rate the abilities and style of the instructor?
   ☐ Excellent   ☐ Very Good   ☐ Good   ☐ Fair   ☐ Poor

6. Other comments and suggestions for future programs: _____
   _____

Signature (optional) _____

measure learning in many areas. In other areas, the trainers must develop their own tests. To obtain an accurate picture of what was learned, trainees should be tested both before and after the program.

Behavior

Behavior evaluation deals with the nature of the change in job behavior of the trainee and is much more difficult than reaction or learning evaluation. The following guidelines can help evaluate behavioral change.

1. A systematic appraisal should be made of on-the-job performance on a before-and-after basis.
2. The appraisal of performance should be made by one or more of the following groups (the more the better):

   a. The trainee.
   b. The trainee's superior or superiors.
   c. The trainee's subordinates.
   d. The trainee's peers or other people thoroughly familiar with his or her performance.

3. A statistical analysis should be made to compare performance before and after training and to relate changes to the training program.
4. The post-training appraisal should be made several months after the training so that the trainees have an opportunity to put what they have learned into practice.
5. A control group (one not receiving the training) should be used.

Results

Results evaluation attempts to measure changes in variables such as reduced turnover, reduced costs, improved efficiency, reduction in grievances, and increases in quantity and quality of production.[5] As with behavior evaluation, pretests, posttests, and control groups are required in performing an accurate results evaluation.

PRINCIPLES OF LEARNING

Previous sections of this chapter discussed not only how training needs are determined but also how they can be met. The use of sound learning principles during the development and implementation of these programs helps to ensure that the programs will succeed. The following sections discuss several principles of learning.

Motivation to Achieve Personal Goals

People strive to achieve objectives they have set for themselves. The most frequently identified objectives of employees are job security, financially and intellectually rewarding work, recognition, status, responsibility, and achievement. If a training program helps employees achieve some of these objectives, the learning process is greatly facilitated. For example, unskilled employees who are given the opportunity to learn a skilled trade may be highly motivated because they can see that more money and job security will probably result.

Knowledge of Results

Knowledge of results (feedback) influences the learning process. Keeping employees informed of their progress as measured against some standard helps in setting goals for what remains to be learned. The continuous process of analyzing progress and establishing new objectives greatly enhances learning. However, precautions should be taken to ensure that goals are not so difficult to achieve that the employee becomes discouraged.

Oral explanations and demonstrations by the trainee and written examinations are frequently used tools for providing feedback to both the trainee and the trainer. In addition, the progress of an individual or a group can be plotted on a chart to form what is commonly called a *learning curve.* The primary purpose of a learning curve is to provide feedback on the trainee's progress. It can also help in deciding when to increase or decrease training or when to change methods. Figure 8.6 illustrates two different learning curves. Although the decreasing returns curve is most frequently encountered, many other shapes of learning curves are possible.

Reinforcement

The general idea behind reinforcement is that behavior that appears to lead to a positive consequence tends to be repeated, while behavior that appears to lead to a negative consequence tends not to be repeated. A positive consequence is a reward. Praise and recognition are two typical rewards that can be used in training. For example, a trainee who is praised for good performance is likely to continue to strive to achieve additional praise.

FIGURE 8.6
Sample Learning Curves

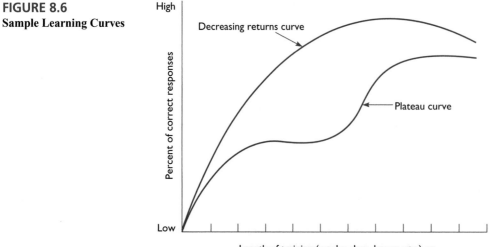

Length of training (weeks, days, hours, etc.) or number of repetitions of training program

Flow of the Training Program

Each segment of training should be organized so that the individual can see not only its purpose but also how it fits in with other parts of the program. In addition, later segments should build on those presented earlier. Gaps and inconsistencies in material are not conducive to effective learning.

Practice and Repetition

The old adage "Practice makes perfect" is applicable in learning. Having trainees perform a particular operation helps them concentrate on the subject. Repeating a task several times develops facility in performing it. Practice and repetition almost always enhance effective learning.

Spacing of Sessions

Managers frequently want to get an employee out of training and into a productive job as quickly as possible. However, trade-offs are involved in deciding whether the training should be given on consecutive days or at longer intervals. Generally, spacing out training over a period of time facilitates the learning process. However, the interval most conducive to learning depends on the type of training.

Whole or Part Training

Should training for a job be completed at once, or should the employee train separately for each job component? The decision should be based on the content of the specific job, the material being taught, and the needs of those being trained. One often successful method is to first give trainees a brief overview of the job as a whole and then divide it into portions for in-depth instruction.

Summary of Learning Objectives

1. **Define *orientation*.**

   Orientation is the introduction of new employees to the organization, work unit, and job.

2. **Describe an orientation kit.**

   An orientation kit is a packet of information given to the new employee to supplement the verbal orientation program.

3. **Define *training*.**

   Training is a learning process that involves the acquisition of skills, concepts, rules, or attitudes to enhance employee performance.

4. **Describe needs assessment.**

   Needs assessment is a systematic analysis of the specific training activities the organization requires to achieve its objectives.

5. **Outline three categories of training objectives.**

   Training objectives can be categorized as instructional objectives, organizational and departmental objectives, and individual performance and growth objectives.

6. **Describe job rotation.**

   In job rotation, an individual learns several different jobs within a work unit or department and performs each job for a specified time period.

7. **Explain apprenticeship training.**

   Apprenticeship training is a system in which an employee is given instruction and experience, both on and off the job, in all the practical and theoretical aspects of the work required in a skilled occupation, craft, or trade.

8. **Define *virtual classroom*.**

   A virtual classroom is an online teaching and learning environment that involves chat rooms, desktop video conferencing, Web sites, and e-mail distribution into a typical lecture-based system.

9. **Outline the seven principles of learning.**

The seven principles of learning are motivation to achieve personal goals, knowledge and results, reinforcement, flow of the training program, practice and repetition, spacing of sessions, and whole or part training.

10. **List the four areas of training evaluation.**

Evaluation of training consists of reaction, learning, behavior, and results evaluation.

Key Terms

apprenticeship
  training, *159*
classroom training, *160*
departmental and job
  orientation, *151*

job rotation (cross
  training), *157*
needs assessment, *155*
on-the-job training
  (OJT), *157*

organizational
  orientation, *151*
orientation, *151*
orientation kit, *151*
training, *154*

Review Questions

1. What is orientation? General company orientation? Departmental and job orientation?
2. Outline several possible topics for a general company orientation.
3. What is an orientation kit?
4. What is training?
5. Define the following:
   a. On-the-job training.
   b. Job rotation.
6. Outline five steps to follow in training a new employee to perform a job.
7. Define *apprenticeship training*.
8. List and explain the four logical areas for evaluating training.
9. What learning principles should be used in all training programs?
10. What is a virtual classroom?

Discussion Questions

1. Why are most training programs not evaluated?
2. Which principles of learning are applied in college classrooms? Which ones are most appropriate for use in college classrooms?
3. Why are training programs one of the first areas to be eliminated when an organization's budget must be cut?
4. If you were asked to develop a training program for taxicab drivers, how would you do it? How would you evaluate the program?

Incident 8.1

Starting a New Job

Jack Smythe, branch manager for a large computer manufacturer, had been told by his marketing manager, Linda Sprague, that Otis Brown had just given two weeks' notice. When Jack had interviewed Otis, he had been convinced of his tremendous potential in sales. Otis was bright and personable, an MIT honors graduate in electrical engineering who had the qualifications the company looked for in computer sales. Now he was leaving after only two months with the company. Jack called Otis into his office for an exit interview.

Jack: Come in, Otis, I really want to talk to you. I hope I can change your mind about leaving.

Otis: I don't think so.

Jack: Well, tell me why you want to go. Has some other company offered you more money?

Otis: No. In fact, I don't have another job; I'm just starting to look.

Jack: You've given us notice without having another job?

Otis: Well, I just don't think this is the place for me!

Jack: What do you mean?

Otis: Let me see if I can explain. On my first day at work, I was told that formal classroom training in computers would not begin for a month. I was given a sales manual and told to read and study it for the rest of the day.

The next day, I was told that the technical library, where all the manuals on computers are kept, was in a mess and needed to be organized. That was to be my responsibility for the next three weeks.

The day before I was to begin computer school, my boss told me that the course had been delayed for another month. He said not to worry, however, because he was going to have James Crane, the branch's leading salesperson, give me some on-the-job training. I was told to accompany James on his calls. I'm supposed to start the school in two weeks, but I've just made up my mind that this place is not for me.

Jack: Hold on a minute, Otis. That's the way it is for everyone in the first couple of months of employment in our industry. Any place you go will be the same. In fact, you had it better than I did. You should have seen what I did in my first couple of months.

Questions

1. What do you think about the philosophy of this company pertaining to a new employee's first few weeks on the job?

2. What suggestions do you have for Jack to help his company avoid similar problems of employee turnover in the future?

Incident 8.2

Implementing On-the-Job Training

The first-year training program for professional staff members of a large national accounting firm consists of classroom seminars and on-the-job training. The objectives of the training are to ensure that new staff members learn fundamental auditing concepts and procedures and develop technical, analytical, and communication skills that, with further experience and training, will help them achieve their maximum potential with the organization.

Classroom training is used to introduce concepts and theories applicable to the work environment. It consists of three two-day and two three-day seminars presented at varying intervals during the staff member's first year. Although new staff members do receive this special training, actual work experience is the principal means by which they develop the many skills necessary to become good auditors.

Teams supervised by the senior member perform most of the firm's audits. This individual is responsible for conducting the review and producing the required reports. Normally teams are assembled on the basis of member availability. For this reason, a senior auditor may be assigned one or more first-year employees for a team that must undertake a complex assignment. Because senior auditors are measured on productivity, their attention is usually focused on the work being produced. Therefore, they assign routine tasks to new staff employees, with little or no thought to furthering the career development of these employees. Most senior auditors assume the next supervisor or the individuals themselves will take care of their training and development needs.

Recently the firm has lost several capable first-year people. The reason most gave for leaving was that they were not learning or advancing in their profession.

Questions

1. What, if anything, do you think the company should do to keep its young employees?
2. Do you think on-the-job training will work in a situation such as the one described?

EXERCISE 8.1
McDonald's Training Program

Your class has recently been hired by McDonald's to make recommendations for improving the orientation and training programs of employees in the company's franchise operations. The key job activities in franchise operations are food preparation, order taking and dealing with customers, and routine cleanup operations. McDonald's wants you to make your recommendations based on your observations as customers.

Your assignment is to design a comprehensive orientation and employee training program for each of the key job activities in franchise operations. Be specific by providing an outline, methods of training, and program evaluation procedures for each activity.

1. The class divides into teams of four to five students.
2. Each group is responsible for designing the program for one of the key job activities.
3. Each team is to prepare a 10- to 15-minute presentation on its recommendations.

EXERCISE 8.2
Virtual Classroom

1. The class divides into teams of four to five students.
2. Each team is responsible for developing a virtual classroom. The teacher will specify the equipment to be used and material to be covered.
3. Each team is to prepare a 10- to 15-minute presentation on its recommendations.

Notes and Additional Readings

1. Carroll Lacnit, "Training Proves Its Worth," *Workforce,* September 2001, pp. 52–56.
2. See Joy LePree, "Target Your Training," *Industrial Maintenance & Plant Operation,* December 2000, pp. 17–18.
3. See Trevor C. Brown, et al., "What Went Wrong at University Hospital? An Exercise Assessing Training Effectiveness," *Journal of Management Education,* August 2003, p. 496.
4. See Amalia Santos and Mark Stuart, "Employee Perceptions and Their Influence on Training Effectiveness," *Human Resource Management Journal* 13, No. 1 (2003), pp. 27–46.
5. See Sandi Mann, "Assessing the Value of Your Training: The Evaluation Process from Training Needs to the Report to the Board," *Leadership & Organization Development Journal* 24, No. 5/6 (2003), p. 303.

Management and Organizational Development

Chapter Learning Objectives

After studying this chapter, you should be able to:

1. Define management development.
2. Describe a management inventory.
3. Describe a management succession plan.
4. Define the in-basket technique.
5. Describe a business simulation.
6. Describe adventure learning.
7. Define an assessment center.
8. Describe organizational development (OD).
9. Outline the four phases in organizational development.

Chapter Outline

The Management Development Process

Determining the Net Management Requirements

Organizational Objectives
Management Inventory and Succession Plan
Changes in the Management Team

Needs Assessment

Establishing Management Development Objectives

Methods Used in Management Development

Understudy Assignments
Coaching
Experience
Job Rotation
Special Projects and Committee Assignments
Classroom Training
In-Basket Technique
Web-Based Training
Business Simulations
Adventure Learning

University and Professional Association Seminars

Evaluation of Management Development Activities

Assessment Centers

Organizational Development

Diagnosis
Strategy Planning
Education
Evaluation

Summary of Learning Objectives

Key Terms

Review Questions

Discussion Questions

Incident 9.1: The 40-Year Employee
Incident 9.2: Consolidating Three Organizations

Exercise 9.1: Training Methods

Notes and Additional Readings

On the Job: Comparison of Training Methods

The previous chapter focused on the orientation and training of new employees and the training of longer-term employees. In addition, an organization must be concerned with developing the abilities of its management team, including supervisors, middle-level managers, and executives. The development and implementation of programs to improve management effectiveness are major responsibilities of the human resource department.

FIGURE 9.1
The Management
Development Process

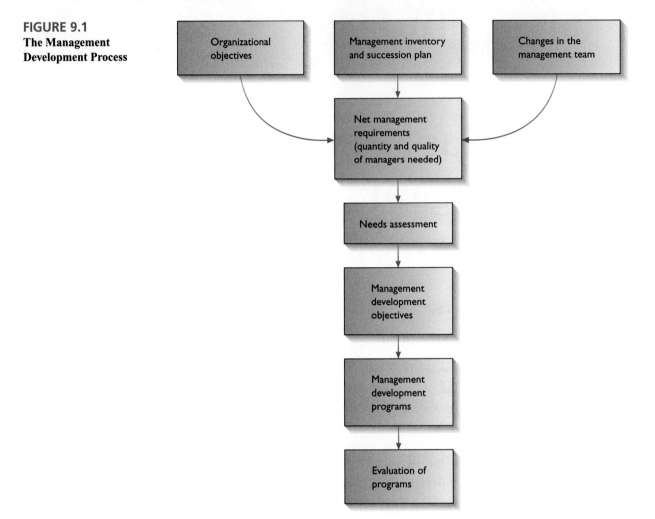

THE MANAGEMENT DEVELOPMENT PROCESS

management development
Process concerned with developing the experience, attitudes, and skills necessary to become or remain an effective manager.

Management development is concerned with developing the experience, attitudes, and skills necessary to become or remain an effective manager. To be successful, it must have the full support of the organization's top executives. Management development should be designed, conducted, and evaluated on the basis of the objectives of the organization, the needs of the individual managers who are to be developed, and anticipated changes in the organization's management team. Figure 9.1 summarizes the total management development process; the following sections discuss each of its elements in depth.

DETERMINING THE NET MANAGEMENT REQUIREMENTS

Organizational Objectives

An organization's objectives play a significant role in determining the organization's requirements for managers. For instance, if an organization is undergoing a rapid expansion program, new managers will be needed at all levels. If, on the other hand, the organization is experiencing limited growth, few new managers may be needed, but the skills of the present management team may need to be upgraded.

management inventory
Specialized, expanded form of skills inventory for an organization's current management team; in addition to basic types of information, it usually includes a brief assessment of past performance and potential for advancement.

Management Inventory and Succession Plan

A **management inventory,** which is a specialized type of skills inventory, provides certain types of information about an organization's current management team. Management inventories

TABLE 9.1 **Sample of a Simplified Management Inventory**

Name	Present Position	Length of Service	Retirement Year	Replacement Positions	Previous Training Received
James W. Burch	Industrial relations manager, Greenville plant	5 years	2007	Corporate industrial relations staff	B.B.A., University of South Carolina; middle management program, Harvard
Judy S. Chesser	Engineering trainee	9 months	2017	Plant engineering manager, corporate engineering staff	B.E.E., Georgia Tech
Thomas R. Lackey	Supervisor, receiving department, night shift	15 years	2009	Department manager, shipping and receiving	High school diploma, supervisory skills training
Brenda C. Sabo	Eastern regional marketing manager	8 years	2010	Vice president, marketing	B.B.A., UCLA; M.B.A., USC; executive development program, Stanford

often include information such as present position, length of service, retirement date, education, and past performance evaluations. Table 9.1 illustrates a simplified management inventory.

A management inventory can be used to fill vacancies that occur unexpectedly—for example, as a result of resignations or deaths. Another use is in planning the development needs of individual managers and using these plans to pinpoint development activities for the total organization.

management succession plan
Chart or schedule that shows potential successors for each management position within the organization.

A management inventory can also be used to develop a management succession plan, sometimes called a *replacement chart* or *schedule*. A **management succession plan** records potential successors for each manager within the organization. Usually presented in a format similar to an organizational chart, this plan may simply be a list of positions and potential replacements. Other information, such as length of service, retirement data, past performance evaluations, and salary, might also be shown on the replacement chart. Figure 9.2 is an example of a replacement chart for a company's administrative division.

Management inventories and succession plans are generally kept confidential and can be computerized. They are also maintained by the human resource department for the use of top executives of the organization.

Changes in the Management Team

Certain changes in the management team can be estimated fairly accurately and easily, while other changes are not so easily determined. Changes such as retirements can be predicted from information in the management inventory; changes such as transfers and promotions can be estimated from such factors as the planned retirements of individuals in specific jobs and the objectives of the organization. Deaths, resignations, and discharges are, of course, difficult to forecast. However, when these changes do occur, the management inventory and succession plan can be used to help fill these vacancies. Analyzing the organization's objectives, studying the management inventory and succession plan, and evaluating changes in the management team can give the human resource department a good picture of both the quantity and quality of managers the organization will need.

NEEDS ASSESSMENT

Every organization has physical, financial, and human resource needs. Needs relate to what the organization must have to achieve its objectives. A fundamental need of any organization is the need for an effective management team. One method of meeting this need is the use of a well-organized management development program. However, before management development activities are undertaken, the specific development needs of the managers in the

FIGURE 9.2   Replacement Plan for Administrative Division of a Typical Organization

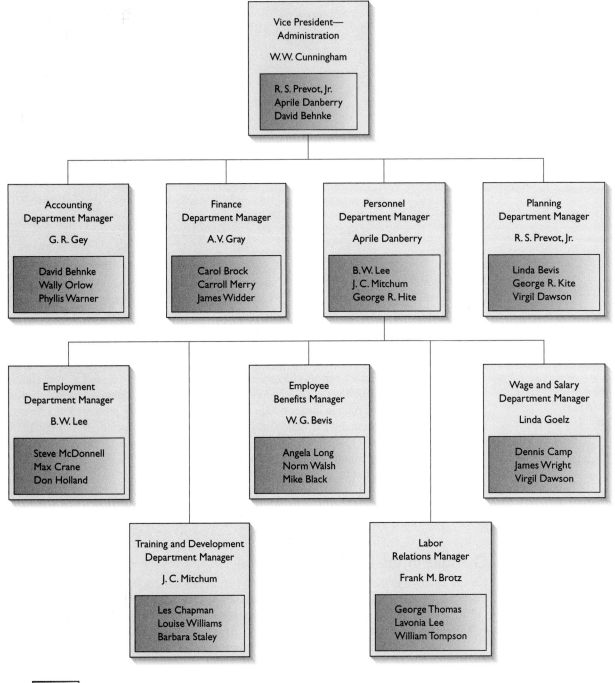

Key: Potential replacements

needs assessment
A systematic analysis of the specific management development activities required by the organization to achieve its objectives.

organization must be determined. Thus, **needs assessment** is a systematic analysis of the specific management development activities the organization requires to achieve its objectives. The management development needs of any organization result from the overall needs of the organization and the development needs of individual managers.

Basically, four methods exist to determine management development needs: a training needs survey, competency studies, task analysis, and performance analysis. A training needs survey focuses on the knowledge and skills required in performing the job. Figure 9.3 provides an example of a needs survey instrument for managerial employees. This instrument lists 18 areas of skill/knowledge managerial personnel require. Competency studies examine

FIGURE 9.3 Management Development Program Needs Assessment Questionnaire

Employee _____ Social Security No. _____

Position Title _____

Organization _____ Location _____

Supervisor (Name & Title) _____

Employee: Please review each "Supervisory/Managerial Function" to assess your need for improving related skills through appropriate developmental opportunities. Your evaluations are to be shown in the "Employee" portion of the "Developmental Requirement" section. One of the following codes should be entered in each box: O = No Need, S = Some Need, or N = Need. **Immediate Manager:** Please review the employee's assessments to indicate your findings in respective boxes ("Manager" portion of the "Developmental Requirement" section).

Supervisory/Managerial Function	Developmental Requirement	
	Employee	Manager
A. Helping Workers with Problems		
1. Help employees with job adjustment problems	☐	☐
2. Help subordinates improve performance	☐	☐
3. Help employees solve personal problems	☐	☐
4. Listening skill development	☐	☐
5. Conflict resolution	☐	☐
6. Employee assistance referral techniques	☐	☐
B. Giving Information to Employees		
1. Keeping employees informed	☐	☐
2. Conducting effective meetings	☐	☐
3. Responding to employee suggestions	☐	☐
C. Receiving Information from Employees		
1. Responding to productivity concepts	☐	☐
2. Encouraging employee participation	☐	☐
3. Consulting with employee concerning work procedures and activities to improve working conditions	☐	☐
D. Labor–Management Relations		
1. Employee rights under agreement	☐	☐
2. Handling employee grievances	☐	☐
E. Leadership		
1. Participative management concepts	☐	☐
2. Encouraging employees to assume personal responsibility for work performance	☐	☐
3. Promoting employee cooperation	☐	☐
F. Safety and Health		
1. Promoting employee understanding of health services and occupational health hazards	☐	☐
2. Promoting adherence to safety regulations	☐	☐
G. Representing Company Management		
1. Defining and defending company goals and objectives	☐	☐
2. Communicating employee views to company management	☐	☐
3. Assuming responsibility for work group's problems	☐	☐
H. Employee Development		
1. Providing detailed work instruction	☐	☐
2. Introducing change	☐	☐
3. Teaching and coaching skills	☐	☐
4. Encouraging employee skill development	☐	☐
I. Employee Utilization		
1. Assessing individual abilities to more effectively assign work	☐	☐
2. Matching individuals with jobs	☐	☐
3. Considering individual interests	☐	☐
4. Understanding employee feelings about their assignments	☐	☐
J. Planning, Scheduling, and Organizing		
1. Division of labor assignments	☐	☐
2. Planning strategies and policies	☐	☐
3. Time management	☐	☐
4. Setting priorities	☐	☐
5. Following up to ensure work completion	☐	☐

(continued)

FIGURE 9.3   (Concluded)

	Developmental Requirement	
	Employee	**Manager**
K. Controlling Work Progress		
1. Assessing daily developments and progress	☐	☐
2. Reviewing individual progress in carrying out orders	☐	☐
3. Correcting employee work problems	☐	☐
4. Early detection of productivity problems	☐	☐
5. Employee participation in setting goals and associated deadlines	☐	☐
L. Appraising Performance		
1. Establishing job performance standards	☐	☐
2. Effective employee discussion techniques; feedback on good or poor performance	☐	☐
3. Constructive criticism	☐	☐
M. Cooperation		
1. Ensuring that employees have required equipment and materials through obtaining cooperation from other company units	☐	☐
2. Effective coordination with other members of management to resolve problems	☐	☐
N. Resource Utilization		
1. Effective budgeting techniques	☐	☐
2. Financial management	☐	☐
O. Administration		
1. Properly prepare paperwork in a timely manner	☐	☐
2. Administrative policies and procedures	☐	☐
3. Preparation and maintenance of records	☐	☐
4. New employee interviewing techniques and selection criteria	☐	☐
P. Equal Employment Opportunity and Affirmative Action Plan Implementation		
1. Equal treatment of employees in work	☐	☐
2. Equal treatment of employees in advancement decisions	☐	☐
Q. Disciplinary Actions		
1. Verbal and written disciplinary actions	☐	☐
2. Resolving employee conduct problems	☐	☐
R. Personal		
1. Psychological concepts—understanding human behavior	☐	☐
2. Self-analysis for improving effectiveness	☐	☐
3. Coping with stress	☐	☐
4. Improving communications skills (oral and written)	☐	☐

Signature _____   Date _____

Manager _____   Date _____

the competencies required in performing the managerial job. Task analysis is concerned with what tasks are required in performing the managerial job. Performance analysis deals with job performance requirements in performing the managerial job. Table 9.2 summarizes the general approach, advantages, and disadvantages of each of these methods of determining management development needs.

ESTABLISHING MANAGEMENT DEVELOPMENT OBJECTIVES

After the management development needs of the organization have been determined, objectives for the overall management development program and for individual programs must be established to meet those needs. Both types of objectives should be expressed in writing and should be measurable. As discussed in the previous chapter, training objectives can be categorized within three broad areas: instructional, organizational and departmental, and individual performance and growth. This categorization scheme can also be used for management development objectives.

Instructional objectives might incorporate targets relating to the number of trainees to be taught, hours of training, cost per trainee, and time required for trainees to reach a standard

TABLE 9.2   Comparison of Four Approaches to Determining Management Development Needs

	Training Needs Survey: **What Knowledge/Skill (K/S) Is Required?**	**Competence Study:** **What Competencies Are Required?**
Approach	1. Ask key people what K/S they think/feel the trainees/performers require to do their job. 2. Prioritize the K/S recommended and summarize as a topical list, a training agenda, curriculum, etc.	1. Ask key people what competencies they think/feel the trainee/performer requires to do his or her job. 2. Determine the K/S required to attain the stated competencies. 3. Prioritize the K/S recommended and summarize as a training agenda or curriculum.
Advantages of this approach	• Fast, inexpensive. • Broad involvement. • Low risk. • Low visibility.	• Relatively fast, inexpensive. • Broad involvement. • Consensus. • In addition to training needs, articulation and agreement on a success profile for the performer. • Identify generic training needs covering a broad population (first-time supervisors, first-time managers, etc.).
Disadvantages of this approach	• Not precise or specific. • Based on opinion, albeit "expert." • Difficult to validate. • Difficult to set priorities. • Difficult to relate to output, to evaluate importance of training. • Once you ask people what training they feel is important, there is an implicit expectation that you will deliver it.	• Difficult to relate to output, to evaluate training. • Difficult to assess relative importance of competencies and therefore difficult to set priorities for K/S input. • Consensus will not necessarily identify the critical difference between exemplary and average performance. • Does not address other factors influencing performance.
	Task Analysis: What Tasks Are Required?	**Performance Analysis:** **What Job Performance Is Required?**
Approach	1. Determine what tasks are required of the trainee/performer for the job to be performed correctly/successfully. 2. Determine the K/S required to correctly perform the tasks identified. 3. Prioritize the tasks, and thereby the K/S, and summarize as a training design document, training agenda, or curriculum.	1. Determine what performance is required. 2. Determine the critical job outputs or "accomplishments." 3. Determine what tasks are required of the trainee/performer to produce the job outputs or "accomplishments." 4. Determine the K/S required to correctly perform the tasks identified. 5. Determine what other factors in addition to K/S influence job performance, such as job design, resources, consequences, and feedback. 6. Prioritize the K/S required based on impact on job performance and summarize as a training design document, training agenda, or curriculum. 7. Summarize recommendations to modify negative influences on performance, as identified in #4 above.
Advantages of this approach	• Precise identification of tasks and required K/S. • Is a form of output and can be measured. • Broad involvement. • Objective, validated by observation.	• Links K/S requirements to job performance. • Can validate, evaluate. • Addresses other factors affecting performance. • Impact of job outputs is established and therefore can prioritize K/S input.
Disadvantages of this approach	• Takes time and skill. • Difficult to assess relative importance of tasks and therefore difficult to set priorities for K/S input. • Does not address other factors affecting performance.	• Takes time and skill. • Visible.

level of knowledge. Furthermore, objectives are needed for the principles, facts, and concepts to be learned in the management development programs(s).

Organizational and departmental objectives concern the impact the programs will have on organizational and departmental outcomes, such as absenteeism, turnover, safety, and number of grievances. Individual and personal growth objectives concern the impact on the behavioral and attitudinal outcomes of the individual. They may also involve the impact on the personal growth of the individuals participating in the programs.

After the overall management development objectives have been established, individual program objectives specifying the skills, concepts, or attitudes that should result must be identified. After these objectives are developed, course content and method of instruction can be specified.

METHODS USED IN MANAGEMENT DEVELOPMENT

After the company's needs have been assessed and its objectives stated, management development programs can be implemented. This section examines some of the more frequently used methods of management development. At this point, recall the list of conditions for effective learning discussed in the previous chapter. These principles of learning also apply to management development programs.

The On the Job example at the end of this chapter defines and summarizes the strengths and weaknesses of training methods used in both management development and employee training courses. As with employee training, management development can be achieved both on and off the job. Some of the most popular methods of management development are summarized in Table 9.3 and discussed next.

Understudy Assignments

understudy assignments
Method of on-the-job training in which one individual, designated as the heir to a job, learns the job from the present jobholder.

Generally, **understudy assignments** are used to develop an individual's capabilities to fill a specific job. An individual who will eventually be given a particular job works for the incumbent. The title of the heir to the job is usually assistant manager, administrative assistant, or assistant to a particular manager.

The advantage of understudy assignments is that the heir realizes the purpose of the training and can learn in a practical and realistic situation without being directly responsible for operating results. On the negative side, the understudy learns the bad as well as the good practices of the incumbent. In addition, understudy assignments maintained over a long period can become expensive. If an understudy assignment system is used, it should generally be supplemented with one or more of the other management development methods.

Coaching

coaching
Method of management development conducted on the job that involves experienced managers advising and guiding trainees in solving managerial problems.

Coaching, which is carried out by experienced managers, emphasizes the responsibility of all managers for developing employees. Under this method of management development, experienced managers advise and guide trainees in solving managerial problems. The idea behind coaching should be to allow the trainees to develop their own approaches to management with the counsel of a more experienced manager.

One advantage to coaching is that trainees get practical experience and see the results of their decisions. However, there is a danger that the coach will neglect training responsibilities or pass on inappropriate management practices. The coach's expertise and experience are critical with this method.

TABLE 9.3
Selected Methods Used in Management Development

On the Job	Off the Job
Understudy assignments	Classroom training
Coaching	Lectures
Experience	Case studies
Job rotation	Role playing
Special projects and committee assignments	In-basket technique
	Adventure learning
	Business simulations
	University and professional association seminars
	Web-based training

Experience

Many organizations use development through experience. With this method, individuals are promoted into management jobs and allowed to learn on their own from their daily experiences. The primary advantage of this method is that the individual, in attempting to perform a specific job, may recognize the need for management development and look for a means of satisfying it. However, employees who are allowed to learn management only through experience can create serious problems by making mistakes. Also, it is frustrating to attempt to manage without the necessary background and knowledge. Serious difficulties can be avoided if the experience method is supplemented with other management development techniques.

Job Rotation

Job rotation is designed to give an individual broad experience through exposure to many different areas of the organization. In understudy assignments, coaching, and experience, the trainee generally receives training and development for one particular job. In job rotation, the trainee goes from one job to another within the organization, generally remaining in each from six months to a year. Large organizations frequently use this technique for training recent college graduates.

One advantage of job rotation is that the trainees can see how management principles can be applied in a cross section of environments. Also, the training is practical and allows the trainee to become familiar with the entire operation of the company. One serious disadvantage of this method is that the trainee is frequently given menial assignments in each job. Another disadvantage is the tendency to leave the trainee in each job longer than necessary. Both of these disadvantages can produce negative attitudes.

Special Projects and Committee Assignments

Special projects require the trainee to learn about a particular subject. For example, a trainee may be told to develop a training program on safety. This would require learning about the organization's present safety policies and problems and the safety training procedures used by other companies. The trainee must also learn to work with and relate to other employees. However, it is critical that the special assignments provide a developing and learning experience for the trainee and not just busywork.

Committee assignments, which are similar to special projects, can be used if the organization has regularly constituted or ad hoc committees. In this approach, an individual works with the committee on its regularly assigned duties and responsibilities. Thus, the person develops skills in working with others and learns through the activities of the committee.

Classroom Training

Classroom training, the most familiar type of training, can utilize several methods. Classroom training is used not only in management development programs but also in the orientating and training activities discussed in the previous chapter. Therefore, some of the material in this section also applies to those activities.

Lectures

One of the most common methods of instruction is lecturing, or teaching by the spoken word. Of course, lectures can include other media such as transparencies, slides, videotapes, or computer slides such as PowerPoint. Strengths of the lecture method of instruction include the following:

1. Lectures can communicate the intrinsic interest of the subject matter. The lecturer can communicate his or her enthusiasm for the subject, which should enhance the audience's interest in learning.
2. Lectures can cover material not otherwise available.
3. Lecturers can reach many learners at one time.

4. Lecturers can serve as effective models for their audience. An effective lecturer not only conveys information but also conveys what does and does not work in different settings.

5. The lecture method lets the instructor control what will be covered, the sequence in which it will be covered, and how much time will be devoted to each topic.

6. Lectures pose a minimal threat to the learner.

Weaknesses of the lecture method include the following:

1. Lectures often do not allow for feedback from the audience.
2. Listeners are often passive.
3. The length of lecture periods often does not match listeners' interest spans.
4. Lecturing fails to allow for individual differences in ability or experience.
5. Lectures are unsuitable for certain higher forms of learning, such as analysis and diagnosis.
6. Lectures are partially dependent on the public speaking skills and abilities of the lecturer.[1]

Case Studies

case study
Method of classroom training in which the trainee analyzes real or hypothetical situations and suggests not only what to do but also how to do it.

In the **case study** technique, popularized by the Harvard Business School, real and/or hypothetical situations are presented for the trainee to analyze. Ideally, the case study should force the trainee to think through problems, propose solutions, choose among them, and analyze the consequences of the decision.

Some major advantages of the case method are as follows:

1. Cases emphasize the analysis of a situation that is typical of the manager's world.
2. The case study method improves the learner's verbal and written communications skills.
3. Cases expose learners to a wide range of true-to-life management problems.
4. Cases inspire interest in otherwise theoretical and abstract training material.

Some possible weaknesses of the case study method include the following:

1. Cases often focus on past and static considerations.
2. Case analysis often lacks emotional involvement on the part of the student and thus is unrealistic in terms of what the trainee would actually do in the situation.
3. Case analysis can sometimes confuse students who are used to definite solutions.

incident method
Form of case study in which learners are initially given the general outline of a situation and receive additional information from the instructor only as they request it.

Furthermore, the success of the case study method depends heavily on the skills of the instructor. Asking probing questions and keeping everyone involved in the analysis of the case are critical to the success of the method.[2]

One variation of the case study is the **incident method.** The learner is initially given only the general outline of a situation. The instructor then provides additional information as the learner requests it. Theoretically, the incident method makes students probe the situations and seek additional information, much as they would be required to do in real life.[3]

Role Playing

In this method, participants are assigned different roles and required to act out those roles in a realistic situation. The idea is for the participants to learn from playing out the assigned roles. The success of this method depends on the ability of participants to assume the roles realistically. Videotaping allows for review and evaluation of the exercise to improve its effectiveness.

In-Basket Technique

in-basket technique
Method of training in which the participant is required to simulate the handling of a specific manager's mail and telephone calls and to react accordingly.

The **in-basket technique** simulates a realistic situation by requiring each participant to answer one manager's mail and telephone calls. Important duties are interspersed with routine matters. For instance, one call may come from an important customer who is angry, while a letter from a local civic club may request a donation. Participants analyze the situations and suggest alternative actions. They are evaluated on the basis of the number and quality of decisions and on the priorities assigned to each situation. The in-basket technique has been used

NEW DISTRIBUTION

Arrow Electronics Inc. is a global provider of products, services, and supply chain solutions to industrial and commercial users of electronic components and enterprise computing solutions. Arrow wanted its sales force to recognize different supply chain segments.

The solution was MAX! MAX! is a global supply chain business simulation. The simulation is set up very much like a video game with challenges and goals. It has been an effective tool for Arrow's sales force as the simulation has proved more engaging than traditional methods of training.

Source: Adapted from Jim Wexler, "Distribution: Let the Games Begin," *Industrial Distribution*, November 2009, p. 64.

not only for management development but also in assessment centers, which are discussed later in this chapter.

Web-Based Training

Many companies are turning to **Web-based training (WBT)**. Employees can gain access to online courses either via the Internet or through the company's own intranet. Participants can take the courses either independently or in real time with an instructor, through a network connection. Online courses are most often given in conjunction with instructor-led courses, so that employees still have the advantage of seeing hands-on demonstrations when necessary.[4] The flexibility of time, place and programs offered via WBT appeals to employees who often must balance school with work and home responsibilities. WBT takes advantage of the technology available in the virtual classroom. Virtual classrooms can be asynchronous or synchronous. Asynchronous classrooms allow students and instructors to engage in learning activities without being online at the same time. Synchronous classrooms allow students and instructors to be online simultaneously. It is likely that WBT will continue to grow both in large and small organizations.[5]

Web-based training allows employees to gain access to online courses. Digital Vision

Web-based training
Method of training in which material is presented on computer video screens via either the Internet or company intranet; participants are required to answer questions correctly before being allowed to proceed.

business simulation
Method of training that simulates an organization and its environment and requires a team of players to make operating decisions based on the situation.

Business Simulations

Business simulations generally provide a setting of a company and its environment and require teams of players to make decisions involving their company operations in competition with other teams. The instructor can add complexity and economic events as well as human resource challenges. This method forces individuals not only to work with other group members but also to function in an atmosphere of competition within the industry. Advantages of business simulations are that they simulate reality, decisions are made in a competitive environment, feedback is provided concerning decisions, and decisions are made using less than complete data. The main disadvantage is that many participants simply attempt to determine the key to winning.[6] When this occurs, the simulation is not used to its fullest potential as a learning device. HRM in Action 9.1 gives an interesting use of a business simulation.

Adventure Learning

adventure learning
Programs that use many kinds of challenging outdoor activities to help participants achieve their goals.

Adventure learning, or **experiential-learning programs,** use many kinds of challenging outdoor activities, often involving physical risk, to help participants achieve their objectives, which generally fall into two categories:

1. Group-focused objectives: These objectives include better communication, more creative problem solving, more effective teamwork, and improved leadership. One activity often included in adventure learning is "The Wall," a 12- to 14-foot structure that teams must get over by working together. The wall is viewed as a symbol for any business challenge.

2. Personal growth objectives: These objectives include improved self-esteem, improved risk-taking skills, increased self-awareness, and better stress management. Rope activities are favorite methods for achieving personal growth objectives. One example of a rope activity is the "electric rope" game. A team has to get every member over a rope strung high up

between two trees. Team members must try not to touch the rope, and they cannot use props. The electric rope is viewed as an analogy for a difficult business challenge the team faces at work.[7] HRM in Action 9.2 describes a firm that plans adventure learning programs.

University and Professional Association Seminars

Web site: Mind Edge
www.caso.com

Many colleges and universities offer both credit and noncredit courses intended to help meet the management development needs of various organizations. These offerings range from courses in principles of supervision to advanced executive management programs. Professional associations such as the American Management Association also offer a wide variety of management development programs. These programs use many of the previously discussed classroom techniques.

EVALUATION OF MANAGEMENT DEVELOPMENT ACTIVITIES

Four alternatives exist for evaluating management development activities. Each alternative focuses on the following questions:

Alternative I—Are the trainees happy with the course?

Alternative II—Does the training course teach the concepts?

Alternative III—Are the concepts used on the job?

Alternative IV—Does the application of the concepts positively affect the organization?

For each of the four alternatives, an organization must determine what might be measured to answer the questions posed by the alternative. Table 9.4 provides a summary of the alternatives and possible measures for evaluation.

TABLE 9.4
Evaluation Matrix

What We Want to Know	What Might Be Measured
I. Are the trainees happy with the course? If not, why?	Trainee reaction during workshop
a. Concepts not relevant	
b. Format of the presentation	Trainee reaction after workshop
II. Do the materials teach the concepts? If not, why not?	Trainee performance during workshop
a. Concepts too complex	
b. Examples not relevant	Trainee performance at end of workshop
c. Exercises not relevant	
d. Format of presentation	
III. Are the concepts used? If not, why not?	Performance improvements
a. Concepts:	
• Not relevant	
• Too complex	
b. Environment not supportive	
IV. Does application of concepts positively affect the organization? If not, why not?	Performance improvements

ASSESSMENT CENTERS

assessment center
Formal method used in training and/or selection and aimed at evaluating an individual's potential as a manager by exposing the individual to simulated problems that would be faced in a real-life managerial situation.

An **assessment center** is a method in which trained observers evaluate various personality traits of assessees based on their performance in specially chosen exercises. Assessment centers are used for making decisions on promoting, evaluating, and training managerial personnel.[8]

Developing the list of personality characteristics to be assessed is a critical element in any assessment center. The personality characteristics should be directly related to the successful performance of the particular jobs for which the assessees are being evaluated. Only when these personality characteristics have been identified can exercises be selected for use in the assessment center. Research indicates that certain exercises are more relevant for measuring some personality traits than others. Exercises used in assessment centers include in-basket exercises, business simulations, group discussions, cases, interviews, and various paper-and-pencil tests. These exercises involve the assessees in situations that require decision making, leadership, written and oral communication, planning, and organizing. Assessors observe the assessees while they are involved in the various exercises and evaluate their performance based on the personality characteristics being assessed. Assessees are generally examined in groups of approximately six persons whose personality characteristics to be assessed are similar and who occupy similar positions in the organization.

Selection of the assessment staff is another important element in an assessment center. Trained professionals such as industrial psychologists are frequently used as assessors. In addition, successful managers are often used as assessors in the belief that these people would best know the qualities required for success. Typically, several assessors are used in the evaluation process.

While the assessors observe the assessees in their performance of the various exercises, each assessor evaluates each assessee individually. The assessors then gather together and review each assessee in depth on each personality characteristic to be assessed. Each assessee is then ranked on a relative scale such as "more than acceptable," "acceptable," or "not acceptable."

The primary use of assessment centers has been as a predictor of success in some position for which the assessee is being considered. However, the method can also be used to identify special training that the assessee may require.[9] HRM in Action 9.3 illustrates one use of assessment centers.

ORGANIZATIONAL DEVELOPMENT

organizational development (OD)
Organizationwide, planned effort managed from the top to increase performance through interventions and training.

Organizational development (OD) seeks to improve the performances of groups, departments, and the overall organization. Specifically, **organizational development** is an organizationwide, planned effort managed from the top, with the goal of increasing organizational performance through planned interventions and training experiences. In particular, OD looks at the human side of organizations. It seeks to change attitudes, values, organizational structures, and managerial practices in an effort to improve organizational performance. The ultimate

Web site: Training and Development Resource Center www.tcm.com/trdev

goal of OD is to structure the organizational environment so that managers and employees can use their developed skills and abilities to the fullest.

The initial phase of an OD effort is a recognition by management that organizational performance can and should be improved. Following this initial recognition, most OD efforts include the following phases: (1) diagnosis, (2) strategy planning, (3) education, and (4) evaluation.

Diagnosis involves gathering and analyzing information about the organization to determine the areas in need of improvement. Information is usually gathered from employees through the use of questionnaires or attitude surveys. Change planning involves developing a plan for organizational improvement based on the data obtained. This planning identifies specific problem areas in the organization and outlines steps to resolve the problems. Intervention/education involves sharing diagnostic information with the people affected by it and helping them realize the need for change. The intervention/education phase often involves the use of outside consultants working with individuals or employee groups. It can also involve the use of management development programs. The evaluation phase in effect repeats the diagnostic phase. In other words, after diagnosis, strategy planning, and education, data are gathered to determine the effects of the OD effort on the total organization. This information can then lead to more planning and education.

Diagnosis

The first decision to be made in the OD process is whether the organization has the talent and available time necessary to conduct the diagnosis. If not, an alternative is to hire an outside consultant. Once the decision has been made regarding who will do the diagnosis, the next step is to gather and analyze information. Some of the most frequently used methods for doing this involve using the following.

1. *Available records.* The first step is to review any available records or documents that may be pertinent. Personnel records and financial reports are two types of generally available records that can be useful.
2. *Survey questionnaires.* The most popular method of gathering data is through questionnaires filled out by employees. Usually the questionnaires are intended to measure employee attitudes and perceptions about certain work-related factors.
3. *Personal interviews.* In this approach, employees are individually interviewed regarding their opinions and perceptions and certain work-related factors. This method takes more time than the survey questionnaire method but can result in better information.
4. *Direct observation.* In this method, the person conducting the diagnosis observes firsthand the behavior of organizational members at work. One advantage of this method is that it allows observation of what people actually do as opposed to what they say they do.

In the diagnosis stage, one should collect data for a reason. A plan for analyzing the data should be developed even before the data are collected. Too often data are collected simply because they are available and with no plan for analysis.

Strategy Planning

The data collected in the diagnosis stage must be carefully interpreted to determine the best plan for organizational improvement. If a similar diagnosis has been done in the past, it can be revealing to compare the data and look for any obvious differences. Because much of the collected data are based on personal opinions and perceptions, there will always be areas of disagreement. The key to interpreting the data is to look for trends and areas of general agreement. The end result of the strategy planning process is to identify specific problem areas and outline steps for resolving the problems.

Education

The purpose of the education phase is to share the information obtained in the diagnostic phase with the affected employees and help them realize the need for change. A thorough analysis in the change-planning phase often results in identifying the most appropriate intervention/education method to use. Some of the most frequently used intervention/education methods are discussed next.

Direct Feedback

direct feedback
Process in which the change agent communicates the information gathered through diagnosis directly to the affected people.

With the **direct feedback** method, the change agent communicates the information gathered in the diagnostic and change-planning phases to the involved parties. The change agent describes what was found and what changes are recommended. Then workshops are often conducted to initiate the desired changes.

Team Building

team building
Process by which a work group develops awareness of conditions that keep it from functioning effectively and takes action to eliminate these conditions.

The objective of **team building** is to increase the group's cohesiveness and general group spirit. Team building stresses the importance of working together. Some of the specific activities used include (1) clarifying employee roles, (2) reducing conflict, (3) improving interpersonal relations, and (4) improving problem-solving skills.

Sensitivity Training

sensitivity training
Method used in OD to make one more aware of oneself and one's impact on others.

Sensitivity training is designed to make one more aware of oneself and one's impact on others. Sensitivity training involves a group, usually called a *training group* or *T-group,* that meets with no agenda or particular focus. Normally the group has between 10 and 15 people who may or may not know one another. With no planned structure or no prior common experiences, the behavior of individuals in trying to deal with the lack of structure becomes the agenda. While engaging in group dialogue, members are encouraged to learn about themselves and others in the nonstructured environment.

Sensitivity training has been both passionately criticized and vigorously defended as to its relative value for organizations. In general, the research shows that people who have undergone sensitivity training tend to show increased sensitivity, more open communication, and increased flexibility. However, these same studies indicate that while the outcomes of sensitivity training are beneficial in general, it is difficult to predict the outcomes for any one person.

Evaluation

Probably the most difficult phase in the OD process is the evaluation phase. The basic question to be answered is: Did the OD process produce the desired results? Unfortunately, many OD efforts begin with admirable but overly vague objectives such as improving the overall health, culture, or climate of the organization. Before any OD effort can be evaluated, explicit objectives must be determined. Objectives of an OD effort should be outcome oriented and should lend themselves to the development of measurable criteria.

A second requirement for evaluating OD efforts is that the evaluation effort be methodologically sound. Ideally, an OD effort should be evaluated using hard, objective data. One approach is to compare data collected before the OD intervention against data collected after the OD intervention. An even better approach is to compare "before" and "after" data with similar data from a control group. When using this approach, two similar groups are identified, an experimental group and a control group. The OD effort is then implemented with the experimental group but not with the control group. After the OD intervention has been completed, the before and after data from the experimental group are compared with the before and after data from the control group. This approach helps rule out changes that may have resulted from factors other than the OD intervention.

From a practical standpoint, it may be desirable to use different personnel to evaluate an OD effort than those who implemented the effort. The people who implemented the effort may not be capable of objectively evaluating it.[10]

Summary of Learning Objectives

1. **Define *management development*.**

   Management development is concerned with developing the experience, attitudes, and skills necessary to become or remain an effective manager.

2. **Describe a management inventory.**

   A management inventory provides certain types of information about an organization's current management team. Information contained includes present position, length of service, retirement date, education, and past performance evaluations.

3. **Describe a management succession plan.**

   A management succession plan records potential successors for each manager within the organization.

4. **Define the in-basket technique.**

   The in-basket technique simulates a realistic situation by requiring trainees to answer one manager's mail and telephone calls.

5. **Describe a business simulation.**

   Business simulations require a team of players to make decisions involving company operations in a competitive environment.

6. **Describe adventure learning.**

   Adventure learning uses many kinds of challenging outdoor activities, often involving physical risk, to help participants reach their goals.

7. **Describe an assessment center.**

   An assessment center is a formal method aimed at evaluating an individual's potential as a manager and his or her developmental needs.

8. **Describe organizational development (OD).**

   Organizational development (OD) is an organizationwide, planned effort managed from the top, with the goal of increasing organizational performance through planned interventions and training experiences.

9. **Outline the four phases in organizational development.**

   The phases are diagnosis, strategy planning, education, and evaluation.

Key Terms

adventure learning, *177*
assessment center, *179*
business simulation, *177*
case study, *176*
coaching, *174*
direct feedback, *181*
in-basket technique, *176*

incident method, *176*
management development, *168*
management inventory, *168*
management succession plan, *169*
needs assessment, *170*

organizational development (OD), *179*
sensitivity training, *181*
team building, *181*
understudy assignments, *174*
Web-based training, *177*

Review Questions

1. Define *management development*.
2. What is a management inventory? What is a succession plan?
3. Name three classifications for overall management development objectives, and give examples of each.
4. Describe the following on-the-job methods of management development:
   a. Understudy assignments.
   b. Coaching.
   c. Experience.
   d. Job rotation.
   e. Special projects.
   f. Committee assignments.

5. Describe the following methods of training:
    a. Lectures.
    b. Case studies.
    c. Role playing.
    d. In-basket technique.
    e. Business simulations.
    f. Adventure learning.
6. What is an assessment center?
7. What is organizational development (OD)?
8. Outline the phases of organizational development.

Discussion Questions

1. Outline a system for evaluating a management development program for supervisors.
2. "It is impossible to evaluate the effectiveness of a supervisory development program." Discuss.
3. "Management games are fun, but you don't really learn anything from them." Discuss.
4. Organizational development generally takes several years to produce any positive results. Describe some of the positive results that might accrue from such a program, thus making the waiting period worthwhile.

Incident 9.1

The 40-Year Employee

John Brown, 62 years old, has been at the State Bank for 40 years. For the past 20 years, he has worked in the bank's investment department. During his first 15 years in the department, it was managed by Bill Adams. The department consisted of Bill, John, and two other employees. Bill made all decisions, while the others performed record-keeping functions.

Tom Smith took over the investment department after Bill Adams retired. Tom, 56, has worked for the State Bank for the past 28 years. Shortly after taking control of the department, Tom recognized that it needed to be modernized and staffed with people capable of giving better service to the bank's customers. As a result, he increased the department workforce to 10 people. Of the 10 employees, only John and Tom are older than 33.

When Tom took over the department, John was able to be helpful since he knew all about how the department had been run in the past. Tom considered John to be a capable employee; after about a year, he promoted John to assistant vice president.

After he had headed the department for about a year and a half, Tom purchased a new computer package to handle the bond portfolio and its accounting. When the new system was implemented, John said he did not like the new system and preferred the old system. At that time, his attitude created no real problem, since there were still many other records to be kept. John continued to handle most of the daily record keeping.

Over the next two years, further changes came about. As the other employees in the department became more experienced, they branched into new areas of investment work. The old ways of doing things were replaced by new, more sophisticated methods. John resisted these changes; he refused to accept or learn new methods and ideas. He slipped more and more into doing only simple but time-consuming busywork.

Presently a new computer system is being acquired for the investment section, and another department is being put under Tom's control. John has written Tom a letter stating he wants no part of the new computer system but would like to be the manager of the new department. In his letter, John said he was tired of being given routine tasks while the young people got all the exciting jobs. John contended that since he had been with the bank longer than anyone else, he should be given first shot at the newly created job.

Questions

1. Who has failed, John or the company?
2. Does the company owe something to a 40-year employee? If so, what?
3. What type of development program would you recommend for John?

Incident 9.2

Consolidating Three Organizations

Sitting at his desk, Ray McGreevy considered the situation he faced. His small but prosperous real estate firm had tripled in size because of two simultaneous acquisitions. He now needed to develop a management team that could coordinate the three previously independent companies into one efficient firm. He knew this would be no easy task, because the two acquired companies had each been operated as independent entities.

In the seven years since Ray had started his real estate brokerage business, he had compiled an enviable record of growth and profits. His staff, originally consisting of himself and a secretary, had grown to more than 25 employees. His organization included himself as president, 2 vice presidents, 16 sales representatives, 4 secretaries, and 2 clerical workers. These employees were distributed equally between the two branches, each supervised by a vice president. The sales representatives reported to the vice president in their particular branch. The two branches covered a large geographic area that was divided into two regions.

About a year ago, Ray had decided to add a branch in a new area. After doing considerable research, he had decided it might be more feasible to acquire one of the smaller firms already operating in the area. A bank officer whom he had contacted approved his plans and promised to help in locating a company to buy and in financing the acquisition.

Several months went by, and Ray discussed possible mergers with two firms; however, satisfactory terms could not be reached. He was becoming slightly discouraged when the banker called him to set up a meeting with the owner of another real estate firm. This firm had been in business for approximately 30 years, and the owner had only recently decided to retire. The company, which was almost equal in size to Ray's, did not sell in his firm's geographic area. Therefore, it appeared to be a natural choice, and Ray was quite excited about prospects for acquiring it. The owner had agreed to accept payment over several years. Although the price was higher than Ray had originally intended to pay, the deal was too good to refuse.

Then, when the deal seemed ready to be closed, the owners of one of the other firms Ray had been interested in buying called and said they wished to renegotiate. Ray was able to make a favorable arrangement with them. After discussing his situation with the banker, he finally decided to purchase both firms. Although this plan far exceeded his original intentions, he knew opportunities such as these did not come along every day.

Now Ray pondered his next step. He had been so busy in the negotiations that he had not had time to develop a plan for managing his enlarged company. As an entrepreneur, he knew he needed to develop a professional team to manage the new business properly. He now had three more branches and about 45 additional employees.

There were so many questions to answer. Would it be better to operate the three branches as independent divisions? Should he retain the individual identities of the two new firms, or should he rename them after his original one? He needed answers to these and all his other questions.

Questions

1. Does organizational development hold the key to Ray's questions?
2. As a personnel consultant, what recommendations would you make to him?

EXERCISE 9.1
Training Methods

The On the Job example at the end of this chapter provides a brief description of many training methods used in management development. To understand those methods better, the class breaks into teams of two students each. Each team prepares a 10-minute presentation on the uses, advantages, and disadvantages of one assigned method.

Notes and
Additional
Readings

1. See LeeAnne G. Kryder, "Large Lecture Format: Some Lessons Learned," *Business Communication Quarterly,* March 2002, pp. 88–94. Also see Tracey Sutherland, "Discussion as a Way of Teaching and How Lectures Can Build Discussion Skills," *Accounting Education News,* Winter 2003, pp. 7–11.

2. See Kevin C. Banning, "The Effect of the Case Method on Tolerance for Ambiguity," *Journal of Management Education,* October 2003, p. 556. See also W. David Rees and Christine Power, "The Use of Case Studies in Management Training and Development," *Industrial and Commercial Training,* 34, No. 1 (2002), pp. 5–9. See also Fred R. David, "Strategic Management Case Writing: Suggestions after 20 Years of Experience," *S.A.M. Advanced Management Journal,* Summer 2003, p. 36.

3. See Bruce Macfarlane, "Tales from the Front-Line: Examining the Potential of Critical Incident Vignettes," *Teaching Business Ethics,* February 2003, p. 55.

4. See Lee Chye Seng and Suliman Al-Hawamdeh, "New Mode of Course Delivery for Virtual Classroom," *Aslib Proceedings,* June 2001, pp. 238–43.

5. Mohamed Taher, "Web-Based Training," *Journal of End User Computing,* January–March 2003, pp. 57–59.

6. See A. J. Faria, "The Changing Nature of Business Simulation/Gaming Research: A Brief History," *Simulation & Gaming,* March 2001, pp. 85–97.

7. See Alvin Hwang, "Adventure Learning: Competitive (Kiasu) Attitudes and Teamwork," *Journal of Management Education* 22, No. 7/8 (2003), p. 562.

8. See Dennis A. Joiner, "Assessment Centers: What's New," *Public Personnel Management,* Summer 2002, pp. 179–86.

9. See Cam Caldwell, George C. Thornton III, and Melissa L. Gruys, "Ten Classic Assessment Center Errors: Challenges to Selection Validity," *Public Personnel Management,* Spring 2003, pp. 73–89.

10. Christopher G. Worley and Ann E. Feyerherm, "Reflections on the Future of Organization Development," *Journal of Applied Behavioral Science,* March 2003, pp. 97–116.

On the Job

Comparison of Training Methods

Method	Definition	Strengths	Weaknesses
1. Lecture	A presentation, usually spoken, by the instructor, with very limited discussions.	Clear and direct methods of presentation. Good if there are more than 20 trainees. Materials can be provided to trainees in advance to help in their preparation. Trainer has control over time. Cost effective.	Since there is no discussion, it is easy to forget. Sometimes it is not effective. Requires a high level of speaking ability. Requires a high level of quick understanding by trainees.
2. Group discussion (conference)	A lecture by the instructor, with a lot of participation (questions and comments) from the listeners. Sometimes an instructor is not necessary; however, a leader is needed.	Good if the participants are in small groups. Each participant has an opportunity to present own ideas. More ideas can be generated.	Sometimes discussions get away from the subjects. Some group leaders or instructors do not know how to guide discussions. Sometimes one strong individual can dominate others.
3. Role playing	Creating a realistic situation and having trainees assume parts of specific personalities in the situation. Their actions are based on the roles assigned to them. Emphasis is not on problem solving but on skill development.	Good if the situation is similar to the actual work situation. Trainees receive feedback that gives them confidence. Good for interpersonal skills. Teaches individuals how to act in real situations.	Trainees are not actors. Trainees sometimes are not serious. Some situations cannot be implemented in role playing. Uncontrolled role playing may not lead to any desirable results. If it is very similar to actual life, it may produce adverse reactions.

Method	Definition	Strengths	Weaknesses
4. Sensitivity training	Used for organizational development. Creating situations and examining the participants' reactions and behavior, then having feedback about behavior. Group members exchange thoughts and feelings in unstructured ways.	Helps individuals find the reasons for their behavior (self-insight). Helps individuals know the effects of their behavior on others. Creates more group interactions.	People may not like information about their behavior, especially if it is negative. May lead to conflict and anger within the group. May not be related or transferable to jobs.
5. Case study	A written narrative description of a real situation, issue, or incident that a manager faced in a particular organization. Trainees are required to propose a suitable solution or make an appropriate decision.	Cases can be very interesting. Much group discussion and interaction about many solutions, since there is no absolute solution. Develops trainees' abilities in effective communication and active participation. Develops trainees' ability to figure out various factors that influence their decision building. Develops trainees' ability to make proper decisions in real-life situations (transfer of learning).	A slow method of training. Often difficult to select the appropriate case for the specific training situation. Requires high level of skills by both trainees and trainer, as the discussion can become boring. Can create frustration on part of trainees, especially if they fail to arrive at a specific solution.
6. Business simulations	Giving the trainee information about the organization and its environment, then dividing into teams. Each team is required to make operational decisions and then evaluate them.	Develops practical experience for the trainees. Helps in transferring knowledge and applying thoughts. Helps evaluate and correct the trainees' behavior.	Often it is difficult to study the results of each team's decision. Some teams may not take it seriously. May be a slow process. Difficult to simulate a very complex system.
7. Adventure training	Several managers meet out of the workplace and live in cabins or tents for up to several days. They test their survival skills and learn about their own potentials (for creativity, cooperation, etc.).	People learn their limits and capabilities.	Very costly. May not be transferable.
8. In-basket training	Creates the same type of situations trainees face in daily work. Trainees observed on how they arrange the situations and their actions regarding them.	Effective for corrective action or reinforcement. Widely used in assessment centers for measuring management potential.	Tendency to be or become overly simplistic.
9. Incident process	Simple variation of the case study method. The basic elements are given to the trainee, who then asks the instructor for the most sufficient information that will help him or her in making a decision. The instructor will give only the requested information.	Has immediate feedback from the instructor. Develops supervisory skills in fact seeking and decision making.	Requires high degree of instruction skills in forming answers.
10. Vestibule training	Setting up a training area very similar to the work area in equipment, procedures, and environment, but separated from the actual one so trainees can learn without affecting the production schedule. Used for training typists, bank tellers, and the like.	Fast way to train employees. Trainees can get the most from this method.	Very expensive.
11. Apprenticeship training	Trainee works under guidance of skilled, licensed instructor and receives lower pay than licensed workers.	Develops special skills like mechanical, electronic, tailoring, etc. Extensive training.	Takes a long time.

Method	Definition	Strengths	Weaknesses
12. Internship training	According to agreement, individuals in these programs earn while they learn, but at a lower rate than if they worked full time.	More chance for trainees to apply what they have learned. Trainees get exposure to both the organization and the job.	Takes a long time.
13. Projects	Similar to the group discussion method. Trainees analyze data and reach conclusions together.	Helps trainees learn more about the subject.	Requires instructor's time to ensure the group is going in the right direction.
14. DVDs and movies	Recording and producing certain events or situations with clear descriptions in order to cover certain subjects. Can be shown many times, then reviewed and discussed to help trainees understand more fully.	DVDs can be played many times to ensure individual's understanding. Many events and discussions can be put on one tape. Because time length is known, presentation and follow-up can be scheduled.	Recording and producing has to be done by professionals to get good quality. Expensive.

Chapter Ten

Career Development

Chapter Learning Objectives

After studying this chapter, you should be able to:

1. Define career development and summarize its major objectives.
2. Name the three entities required to provide input for a successful career development program and briefly describe their respective responsibilities.
3. Describe the steps involved in implementing a career development program.
4. Define career pathing and career self-management.
5. List several myths employees hold related to career planning and advancement.
6. List several myths management holds related to career development.
7. Define a career plateau and a plateaued employee.
8. Describe the four principal career categories.
9. Explain the concept of a career lattice.
10. Distinguish between dual-career couples and dual-earner couples.
11. Define outplacement.
12. Explain what the glass ceiling is.
13. List some of the online career development resources that are available today.

career development
An ongoing, formalized effort by an organization that focuses on developing and enriching the organization's human resources in light of both the employees' and the organization's needs.

Not long ago, individuals joined an organization and often stayed with it for their entire working careers. Organizations frequently gave gold watches and length-of-service pins to reward loyal employees. However, the concept of organizational loyalty has faded in the decades following World War II. Starting in the mid-1960s, the average 20-year-old employee was expected to change jobs approximately six or seven times during his or her lifetime. According to mid-1990s statistics from the U.S. Department of Labor, college graduates had, on average, 8 to 10 jobs and as many as three careers in their lifetimes.[1] Recent data show that the average person born in the later years of the baby booms held slightly over 10.8 jobs from the ages of 18 to 42.[2]

Other data from different sources reveal that although most employees remain happy in their work, they sometimes grow increasingly concerned about their career prospects at their present companies.[3] Consequently, instead of thinking in terms of remaining with one organization, many employees now expect to pursue different careers. Corporate restructuring and the downsizing that often results have caused many employees to change their careers even when they did not desire a change.[4] Also, in recessioning times, employees who are unhappy with their current job and careers tend to stay where they are, but only until times get better. Thus, increased employee mobility and related environmental factors have made career development increasingly important for today's organizations. **Career development** is an ongoing, formalized effort by an organization that focuses on developing and enriching the organization's human resources in light of both the employees' and the organization's needs.

WHY IS CAREER DEVELOPMENT NECESSARY?

From the organization's viewpoint, career development can reduce costs due to employee turnover. According to a 2006 survey by the Society of Human Resource Management (SHRM), nearly three-quarters of employees were engaged in either active or passive job searches.[5] However, because of the downturn in the economy, this figure was reduced to 22 percent in 2009. Once the economy picks up, this figure will likely go back up. If a company assists employees in developing career plans, these plans are likely to be closely tied to the organization; therefore, employees are less likely to move to another organization. Taking an interest in employees' careers can also improve morale, boost productivity, and help the organization become more efficient. The fact that an organization shows interest in an employee's career development has a positive effect on that employee. Under these circumstances, employees believe the company regards them as part of an overall plan and not just as numbers. An emphasis on career development can also have a positive effect on the ways employees view their jobs and their employers. HRM in Action 10.1 discusses some of the programs IBM uses to enhance the careers of its high-performing employees.

From the organization's viewpoint, career development has three major objectives:

- To meet the immediate and future human resource needs of the organization on a timely basis.
- To better inform the organization and the individual about potential career paths within the organization.
- To utilize existing human resource programs to the fullest by integrating the activities that select, assign, develop, and manage individual careers with the organization's plans.[6]

career planning
Process by which an individual formulates career goals and develops a plan for reaching those goals.

Career planning is the process by which an individual formulates career goals and develops a plan for reaching those goals. Thus, career development and career planning should reinforce each other. Career development looks at individual careers from the viewpoint of the organization, whereas career planning looks at careers through the eyes of individual employees.

Realistic career planning forces individuals to look at the available opportunities in relation to their abilities. For example, a person might strongly desire to be a history teacher until discovering that two history teachers are available for every job.

With a career plan, a person is much more likely to experience satisfaction while making progress along the career path. A good career path identifies certain milestones along the way. When a person consciously recognizes and reaches these milestones, he or she is much more likely to experience feelings of achievement. Furthermore, these feelings increase the individual's personal satisfaction and motivation.

WHO IS RESPONSIBLE FOR CAREER DEVELOPMENT?

What are the responsibilities of both the organization and the individual with regard to career development? Which has the primary responsibility? The answer is that successful career development requires actions from three sources: the organization, the employee, and the employee's immediate manager.

Organization's Responsibilities

As defined earlier, career development is an ongoing, formalized effort by an organization that focuses on developing and enriching the organization's human resources in light of both the employee's and the organization's needs. The organization is the entity that has primary responsibility for instigating and ensuring that career development takes place. Specifically, the organization's responsibilities are to develop and communicate career options within the organization to the employee. The organization should carefully advise an employee concerning possible career paths to achieve that employee's career goals. Human resource personnel are generally responsible for ensuring that this information is kept current as new jobs are created and old ones are phased out. Working closely with both employees and their managers, human resource specialists should see that accurate information is conveyed and that interrelationships among different career paths are understood. Thus, rather than bearing the primary responsibility for preparing individual career plans, the organization should promote the conditions and create an environment that will facilitate the development of individual career plans by the employees.

Employee's Responsibilities

The primary responsibility for preparing individual career plans rests with the individual employees.[7] Career planning is not something one person can do for another; it has to come from the individual. Only the individual knows what she or he really wants out of a career, and certainly these desires vary appreciably from person to person.

Career planning requires a conscious effort on the part of the employee; it is hard work, and it does not happen automatically. Although an individual may be convinced that developing a sound career plan would be in his or her best interest, finding the time to develop such a plan is often another matter. The organization can help by providing trained specialists to encourage and guide the employee. This can best be accomplished by allotting a few hours of company time each quarter to this type of planning.

While the individual is ultimately responsible for preparing his or her individual career plan, experience has shown that when people do not receive some encouragement and direction, they make little progress.

Manager's Responsibilities

Managers have many responsibilities, including advocating on their employees' behalf.
Imageshop Punchstock

It has been said that "the critical battleground in career development is inside the mind of the person charged with supervisory responsibility."[8] Although not expected to be a professional counselor, the manager can and should play a key role in facilitating the development of a subordinate's career. First and foremost, the manager should serve as a catalyst and sounding board. The manager should show an employee how to go about the process and then help the employee evaluate the conclusions.

Table 10.1 lists several roles a manager might perform to assist subordinates in developing their careers. Unfortunately, many managers do not perceive career counseling as part of their managerial duties. They are not necessarily opposed to this role; rather, they have never considered it as part of their job. To help overcome this and related problems, many organizations have designed training programs to help their managers develop the necessary skills in this area.

Figure 10.1 illustrates how Corning, Inc., defines the roles of the different entities in the career development process. As the figure shows, successful career development results from a joint effort by the organization, the individual, and the immediate manager; the organization provides the resources and structure, the individual does the planning, and the immediate manager provides the guidance and encouragement.

IMPLEMENTING CAREER DEVELOPMENT

Successful implementation of a career development program involves four basic steps at the individual level: (1) the individual's assessment of his or her abilities, interests, and career goals; (2) the organization's assessment of the individual's abilities and potentials; (3) communication of career options and opportunities within the organization; and (4) career counseling to set realistic goals and plans for their accomplishment.[9]

Individual Assessment

Many people never stop to analyze their abilities, interests, and career goals. It isn't that most people don't want to analyze these factors; rather, they simply never take time. While this is not something an organization can do for the individual, the organization can provide the impetus and structure. A variety of self-assessment materials are available over the Internet and other commercial outlets. Some organizations have developed tailor-made forms and training programs for the use of their employees. Another option is the use of some form of psychological testing. The On-the-Job section at the end of this chapter discusses two of the most respected online self-assessment tools.

An individual's self-assessment should not necessarily be limited by current resources and abilities; career plans normally require that the individual acquire additional training and skills. However, this assessment should be based on reality. For the individual, this involves identifying personal strengths—not only the individual's developed abilities, but also the financial resources available.

vision statement
A concise statement of career goals in measurable terms.

Once an individual has a grasp of his or her interests and abilities, it is very helpful to develop a personal **vision statement.** A vision statement can help an individual stay on track and avoid events that don't positively relate to his or her career.[10] Effective vision statements are concise (not more than one or two sentences) and they are stated in measurable terms. An example of a vision statement might be, "I want to develop a career in quality by gaining the knowledge, skills, abilities, and credentials needed to become a quality manager

TABLE 10.1
Potential Career Development Roles of Managers

Source: "Training Managers for Their Role in a Career Development System," Copyright © July 1981 from *Trading and Development*, p. 74 by Zandy B. Leibowitz, and Nancy K. Schlossberg. Reprinted with permission of American Society for Training and Development; and Stuart Corger, "Fostering a Career Development Culture: Reflections on the Roles of Managers, Employees and Supervisors," *Career Development International* No. 7, 6/7 (2002), pp. 371–375.

Communicator

Holds formal and informal discussion with employees.
Listens to and understands an employee's real concerns.
Clearly and effectively interacts with an employee.
Establishes an environment for open interaction.
Structures uninterrupted time to meet with employees.

Counselor

Helps employee identify career-related skills, interests, and values.
Helps employee identify a variety of career options.
Helps employee evaluate appropriateness of various options.
Helps employee design/plan strategy to achieve an agreed-on career goal.

Appraiser

Identifies critical job elements.
Negotiates with employee a set of goals and objectives to evaluate performance.
Assesses employee performance related to goals and objectives.
Communicates performance evaluation and assessment to employee.
Designs a development plan around future job goals and objectives.
Reinforces effective job performance.
Reviews an established development plan on an ongoing basis.

Coach

Teaches specific job-related or technical skills.
Reinforces effective performance.
Suggests specific behaviors for improvement.
Clarifies and communicates goals and objectives of work group and organization.

Mentor

Arranges for employees to participate in a high-visibility activity either inside or outside the organization.
Serves as a role model in employee's career development by demonstrating successful career behaviors.
Supports employee by communicating employee's effectiveness to others in and out of organization.
Shares knowledge about how to learn and work with others.

Advisor

Communicates the informal and formal realities of progression in the organization.
Suggests appropriate training activities that could benefit employee.
Suggests appropriate strategies for career advancement.

Broker

Assists in bringing employees together who might mutually help each other in their careers.
Assists in linking employees with appropriate educational or employment opportunities.
Helps employee identify obstacles to changing present situation.
Helps employee identify resources enabling a career development change.

Referral agent

Identifies employees with problems (e.g., career, personal, health).
Identifies resources appropriate to an employee experiencing a problem.
Bridges and supports employee with referral agents.
Follows up on effectiveness of suggested referrals.

Advocate

Works with employee in designing a plan for redress of a specific issue at higher levels of management.
Works with employee in planning alternative strategies if a redress by management is not successful.
Represents employee's concern to higher-level management for redress of specific issues.

in a midsized manufacturing company in the western United States, earning an annual salary of $90,000 by the year 2013." Once a vision statement has been drafted, it is a good idea to share it with key stakeholders such as current and potential employees and family members. Depending on the feedback received, the vision statement may need to be revised. A vision statement might also be revised as one progresses throughout his or her career.

FIGURE 10.1
Career Planning Roles at Corning, Inc.

Source: Adapted from *Personnel* by Z. B. Liebowitz, B. H. Feldman, & S. H. Mosley. Copyright 1990 by American Management Association. Reproduced with permission of American Management Association in the format Textbook via Copyright Clearance Center.

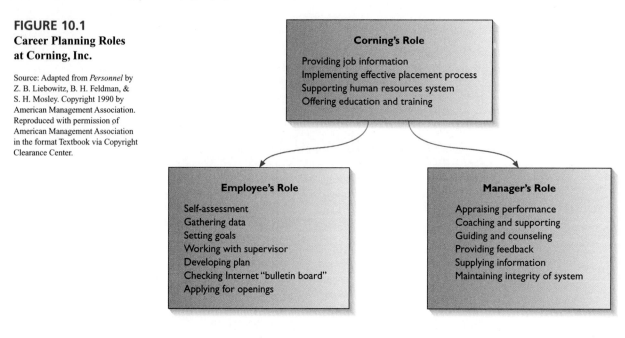

Corning's Role

Providing job information
Implementing effective placement process
Supporting human resources system
Offering education and training

Employee's Role

Self-assessment
Gathering data
Setting goals
Working with supervisor
Developing plan
Checking Internet "bulletin board"
Applying for openings

Manager's Role

Appraising performance
Coaching and supporting
Guiding and counseling
Providing feedback
Supplying information
Maintaining integrity of system

Assessment by the Organization

Organizations have several potential sources of information that can be used for assessing employees. Traditionally, the most frequently used source has been the performance appraisal process. The assessment center discussed in Chapter 9 can also be an excellent source of information. Other potential sources include personnel records reflecting information such as education and previous work experience. It is usually a good idea for an organization not to depend on any one source of information but to use as many as are readily available. Such an approach provides a natural system of checks and balances.

The organization's assessment of an individual employee should normally be conducted jointly by human resource personnel and the individual's immediate manager, who serves as a mentor.

Communicating Career Options

To set realistic career goals, an individual must know the options and opportunities that are available. The organization can do several things to facilitate such awareness. Posting on the organization's intranet and advertising job vacancies is one activity that helps employees get a feel for their options. Clearly identifying possible paths of advancement within the organization is also helpful. This can be done as part of the performance appraisal process. Another good idea is to share human resource planning forecasts with employees.

Career Pathing

career pathing
A technique that addresses the specifics of progressing from one job to another in an organization.

Career pathing is a technique that addresses the specifics of progressing from one job to another in the organization. It can be defined as a sequence of developmental activities involving informal and formal education, training, and job experiences that help make an individual capable of holding more advanced jobs.[11] Career paths exist on an informal basis in almost all organizations. However, career paths are much more useful when formally defined and documented. Such formalization results in specific descriptions of sequential work experiences, as well as how the different sequences relate to one another. Table 10.2 outlines the basic steps in career pathing. HRM in Action 10.2 describes why Molson Canada believes that career pathing is for all employees and not just those who aspire to move up several levels.

Career Self-Management

career self-management
The ability to keep up with the changes that occur within the organization and industry and to prepare for the future.

Career self-management is closely related to the concept of career pathing. **Career self-management** is "the ability to keep pace with the speed at which change occurs within the organization and the industry and to prepare for the future."[12] The basic concept of career self-management is for employees to take the responsibility for managing their own development. Under career self-management, the organization defines the necessary core competencies and

CAREER PATHING AT MOLSON

Molson Canada believes that career pathing is for all kinds of employees and not just those who aspire to move up several levels. The Montreal-based brewery started formalizing its career path program in 2007. The program, which is available online, created a guide to clearly show a career map with rules of engagement, job descriptions, and competencies for both upwards moves and cross-functional experiences. "We have a pretty large sales organization and there are some sales representatives who don't aspire to move out of sales. They love the autonomy, they value the customer interaction," says Jennifer Rigas, manager of talent acquisition and HR at Molson Canada in Toronto. "We still encourage them to build, grow, and develop within their area of specialty, whether that's a new sales technique, a systems application, or addressing the needs of the economy or customers."

The HR people at Molson believe the key is to keep all employees engaged and to not penalize employees who don't want to move or move up in the organization. Supporting this belief Molson has development plans at all levels in the organization and every employee—even those who are happy where they are.

Source: Sarah Dobson, "Unambitious Workers Still Need a Plan," *Canadian HR Reporter*, June 15, 2009, p. 16.

each employee assesses whether he or she has these competencies and, if not, how they can be developed. Career self-management emphasizes the need of individual employees to keep learning because jobs that are held today may evolve into something different tomorrow or may simply disappear entirely. Career self-management also involves identifying and obtaining new skills and competencies that allow the employee to move to a new position. The payoff of career self-management is more highly skilled and flexible employees and the retention of these employees. Career self-management requires commitment to the idea of employee self-development on the part of management and provision of self-development programs and experiences for employees. The trend today in many organizations is to emphasize career self-management.[13]

Career Counseling

Career counseling is the activity that integrates the different steps in the career-development process. Career counseling may be performed by an employee's immediate manager, a human resource specialist, or a combination of the two. In most cases, it is preferable to have the immediate manager conduct counseling with appropriate input from human resource personnel. The immediate manager generally has the advantage of practical experience, knows the company, and is in a position to make a realistic appraisal of organizational opportunities.

Some managers are reluctant to attempt counseling because they haven't been trained in the area. However, it is not necessary to be a trained psychologist to be a successful career counselor. In fact, behavioral research and actual experience suggest that the characteristics that make people likable and effective are basically the same qualities that contribute to successful counseling. Of course, the right type of training can be very beneficial to accomplished career counselors.

TABLE 10.2
Basic Steps of Career Pathing

Source: E. H. Burack and N. J. Mathys, *Career Management in Organizations: A Practical Human Resource Planning Approach* (Lake Forest, Ill.: Brace-Park Press, 1979), pp. 79–80. Used by permission.

1. *Determine or reconfirm the abilities and end behaviors of the target job.* Because jobs tend to change over time, it is important to determine or confirm requirements and review them periodically.
2. *Secure employee background data and review them for accuracy and completeness.* Because people's interests and career objectives tend to shift, these also have to be confirmed. Also, it is often necessary to update an individual's records concerning skills, experience, etc.
3. *Undertake a needs analysis comparison that jointly views the individual and the targeted job.* Determine if the individual and the targeted job tend to match. Surprisingly, many organizations neglect to query individuals when questions arise concerning their backgrounds, potential abilities, and interests.
4. *Reconcile employee career desires, developmental needs, and targeted job requirements with those of organizational career management.* Individuals formalize their career objectives or modify them as circumstances warrant.
5. *Develop individual training work and educational needs using a time-activity orientation.* Identify the individual actions (work, education, and training experiences) necessary for the individual to progress to the targeted job.
6. *Blueprint career path activities.* Create a time-oriented blueprint or chart to guide the individual.

HOW DELOITTE USES COUNSELING TO RETAIN STAFF

One of the "Big Four" accounting firms, Deloitte and Touche, has instigated a three-year-old program called Deloitte Career Connections (DCC). The program is designed to help dissatisfied staff figure out what their real interests and skills are and where they might better fit within the organization. The overriding philosophy is that it is better to retain good employees within the company than to lose them.

DCC features a Web site with a range of self-assessment tools combined with one-on-one coaching. The DCC program is based on a three-part talent management approach: (1) provide real-life development and learning experiences that people need to master a job, (2) work with individuals to identify their deep-rooted skills, interests, and knowledge and help them find their best fit within the organization, and (3) help individuals connect with the people that will help them achieve their objectives.

Confidentiality and giving staff the freedom to explore various options are key to the success of DCC. Managers are encouraged to coach employees and help them find their best fit within the organization. The company also has 14 professional coaches in the DCC program who are located throughout Deloitte's geographic regions.

Deloitte reports that over 28,600 U.S. employees have accessed the DCC Web site and more than 2,700 have received one-on-one coaching. An additional 1,260 employees have received "team" coaching. The company estimates that the firm has saved about $83.4 million, calculated with a turnover cost of twice the average annual salary of $76,000. For the tenth year Deloitte was named to *Fortune* magazine's list of "100 Best Companies to Work For."

Sources: "How Coaching Helps a 'Big Four' Accounting Firm Retain Staff," *HR Focus*, January 2006, pp. 5–6; "How Deloitte Uses Coaching to Build Staff Retention," *Partner's Report*, May 2006, pp. 1–3; and "Deloitte Marks Tenth Year on Fortune's '100 Best Companies to Work For' List," *PR Newswire*, January 23, 2009.

Generally, managers who are skilled in basic human relations are successful as career counselors. Developing a caring attitude toward employees and their careers is of prime importance. Being receptive to employee concerns and problems is another requirement. Following are some specific suggestions for helping managers become better career counselors.

1. *Recognize the limits of career counseling.* Remember that the manager and the organization serve as catalysts in the career development process. The primary responsibility for developing a career plan lies with the individual employee.

2. *Respect confidentiality.* Career counseling is very personal and has basic requirements of ethics, confidentiality, and privacy.

3. *Establish a relationship.* Be honest, open, and sincere with the subordinate. Try to be empathetic and see things from the subordinate's point of view.

4. *Listen effectively.* Learn to be a sincere listener. A natural human tendency is to want to do most of the talking. It often takes a conscious effort to be a good listener.

5. *Consider alternatives.* An important goal in career counseling is to help subordinates realize that a number of choices are usually available. Help subordinates expand their thinking and avoid being limited by past experience.

6. *Seek and share information.* Be sure the employee and the organization have completed their respective assessments of the employee's abilities, interests, and desires. Make sure the organization's assessment has been clearly communicated to the employee and that the employee is aware of potential job openings within the organization.

7. *Assist with goal definition and planning.* Remember that the employee must make the final decisions. Managers should serve as "sounding boards" and help ensure that the individual's plans are valid.[14]

HRM in Action 10.3 describes how Deloitte and Touche uses counseling to retain staff.

REVIEWING CAREER PROGRESS

Individual careers rarely go exactly according to plan. The environment changes, personal desires change, and other things happen. However, if the individual periodically reviews both the career plan and the situation, he or she can make adjustments so that career development is not impaired. On the other hand, a career plan that is not kept current rapidly becomes useless. Complacency is the greatest danger once a career plan has been developed. The plan must be updated as the circumstances and the individual change.

CAREER-RELATED MYTHS

Employees and managers hold many myths related to career development and advancement. Frequently, such myths are misleading and can inhibit career development and growth. The following sections explore these myths and provide evidence disproving them.

Myths Held by Employees[15]

Myth 1: There Is Always Room for One More Person at the Top   This myth contradicts the fact that the structures of the overwhelming majority of today's organizations have fewer positions available as one progresses up the organization. Adherence to this myth fosters unrealistic aspirations and generates self-perpetuating frustrations. There is nothing wrong with wanting to become president of the organization; however, an individual must also be aware that the odds of attaining such a position are slim. For example, Ford Motor Company has several hundred thousand employees and only one president. The major lesson to be learned from myth 1 is to pick career paths that are realistic and attainable.

Myth 2: The Key to Success Is Being in the Right Place at the Right Time   Like all the career-related myths, this one has just enough truth to make it believable. One can always find a highly successful person who attributes all of his or her success to being in the right place at the right time. People who adhere to this myth are rejecting the basic philosophy of planning: that a person, through careful design, can affect rather than merely accept the future. Adherence to myth 2 is dangerous because it can lead to complacency and a defeatist attitude.

Myth 3: Good Subordinates Make Good Superiors   This myth is based on the belief that those employees who are the best performers in their current jobs should be the ones who are promoted. This is not to imply that good performance should not be rewarded, for it should. However, when an individual is being promoted, those making the decision should look carefully at the requirements of the new job in addition to the individual's present job performance. How many times has a star engineer or salesperson been promoted into a managerial role, only to fail miserably! Similarly, outstanding athletes are frequently made head coaches, and everybody seems surprised when the former star fails in that job. Playing a sport and coaching require different talents and abilities. Because someone excels at one job does not mean she or he will excel at all jobs, or even the next-level job.

Myth 4: Career Development and Planning Are Functions of Human Resource Personnel   The ultimate responsibility for career development and planning belongs to the individual, not to human resource personnel or the individual's manager. Human resource specialists can assist the individual and answer certain questions, but they cannot develop a career plan for him or her. Only the individual can make career-related decisions.

Myth 5: All Good Things Come to Those Who Work Long, Hard Hours   People guided by this myth often spend 10 to 12 hours a day trying to impress their managers and move ahead rapidly in the organization. However, the results of these extra hours on the job often have little or no relationship to what the manager considers important, to the person's effectiveness on the job, or (most important in this context) to the individual's long-range career growth. Unfortunately, many managers reinforce this myth by designing activities "to keep everyone busy."

Myth 6: Rapid Advancement along a Career Path Is Largely a Function of the Kind of Manager One Has   A manager can affect a subordinate's rate of advancement. However, those who adhere to this myth often accept a defensive role and ignore the importance of their own actions. Belief in this myth provides a ready-made excuse for failure. It is easy and convenient to blame failures on one's manager.

Myth 7: The Way to Get Ahead Is to Determine Your Weaknesses and Then Work Hard to Correct Them   Successful salespeople do not emphasize the weak points of their products; rather, they emphasize the strong points. The same should be true in career development and planning. Individuals who achieve their career objectives do so by stressing those things they do uncommonly well. The secret is to first capitalize on one's strengths and then try to improve deficiencies in other areas.

Myth 8: Always Do Your Best, Regardless of the Task   This myth stems from the Puritan work ethic. The problem is that believers ignore the fact that different tasks have different priorities. Because there is only a limited amount of time, a person should spend that time according to priorities. Those tasks and jobs that rank high in importance in achieving one's career goals should receive the individual's best efforts. Those tasks that do not rank high should be done, but not necessarily with one's best effort. The idea is to give something less than one's best effort to unimportant tasks in order to have time to give one's best effort to the important ones.

Myth 9: It Is Wise to Keep Home Life and Work Life Separated   An individual cannot make wise career decisions without the full knowledge and support of his or her spouse or partner. Working wives and husbands should share their inner feelings concerning their jobs so that their spouses will understand the basic factors that weigh in any career decisions.

A healthy person usually has interests other than a job. Career strategy should be designed to recognize and support, not contradict, these other interests. Career objectives should be a subset of one's life objectives. Too often, however, career objectives conflict with, rather than support, life objectives.

Myth 10: The Grass Is Always Greener on the Other Side of the Fence   Regardless of the career path an individual follows, another one always seems a little more attractive. However, utopia does not exist. More than likely, the job John Doe holds involves many of the same problems every working person might face. As the individual assumes more and more personal responsibilities, the price of taking that "attractive" job becomes higher in terms of possibly having to relocate, develop a new social life, and learn new duties. This is not to say that job and related changes should not be made; however, one should avoid making such changes hastily.

Myths Held by Managers[16]

Myth 1: Career Development Will Raise Expectations   Many managers fear that an emphasis on career development will raise employee expectations to unrealistically high levels. Career development should do just the opposite: It should bring employees' aspirations into the open and match their skills, interests, and goals with opportunities that are realistically available.

Myth 2: We Will Be Overwhelmed with Requests   This myth is based on the fear that employees will deluge their managers for information about jobs in other parts of the organization and that employees will expect the organization to provide them with a multitude of career opportunities. While this fear is very realistic in the minds of many managers, it is basically unfounded.

Myth 3: Managers Will Not Be Able to Cope   Management often becomes concerned that introducing career development and planning will place managers in a counseling role for which they are ill prepared. While coaching and counseling should be an important part of any manager's job, the key to career development and planning is to place the responsibility primarily on the employee.

Myth 4: We Do Not Have the Necessary Systems in Place   This myth is based on the belief that before the organization can introduce career development, it must first put in place a whole series of other human resource planning mechanisms, such as job posting, succession planning, and certain training experiences. In reality, many organizations have implemented successful career development programs with few formal mechanisms beyond the basic requirement of providing employees with effective career-planning tools.

DEALING WITH CAREER PLATEAUS

career plateau
The point in an individual's career where the likelihood of an additional promotion is very low.

A **career plateau** has been defined as "the point in a career where the likelihood of additional hierarchical promotion is very low."[17] Career plateauing takes place when an employee reaches a position from which she or he is not likely to be promoted further.[18] Virtually all people reach a plateau in their careers; however, some individuals reach their plateaus earlier

TABLE 10.3
Classifying Managerial Careers

Source: *Academy of Management Review* by T. P. Ference, J. A. Stoner, and E. K. Warr. Copyright 1977 by Academy of Management (NY). Reproduced with permission of Academy of Management (NY) in the format Textbook via Copyright Clearance Center.

Current Performance	Likelihood of Future Promotion	
	Low	**High**
High	Solid citizens (effective plateauees)	Stars
Low	Deadwood (ineffective plateauees)	Learners (comers)

than others. Plateaued employees are those who "reach their promotional ceiling" long before they retire.[19]

Certain factors in today's work environment help explain why plateauing may become more prevalent. The fact that employers are now depending more on older employees may well cause plateauing problems. Also, today's employees are generally educated and thus enter organizations at higher positions. A third factor is that fewer promotions occur during recessionary periods. These situations ultimately mean that fewer promotion possibilities exist.

Because it is inherently true that fewer positions are available as one moves up the hierarchical ladder, plateauing does not necessarily indicate failure. However, as this section will show, the case of a plateauee may need to be handled differently in some situations than that of an employee still on the rise in the organization.

Table 10.3 presents a model for classifying careers. The four principal career categories are:

- **Learners.** Individuals with high potential for advancement who are performing below standard (e.g., a new trainee).
- **Stars.** Individuals presently doing outstanding work and having a full potential for continued advancement; these people are on fast-track career paths.
- **Solid citizens.** Individuals whose present performance is satisfactory but whose chance for future advancement is small. These people make up the bulk of the employees in most organizations.
- **Deadwood.** Individuals whose present performance has fallen to an unsatisfactory level; they have little potential for advancement.[20]

Naturally, organizations would like to have all stars and solid citizens. The challenge, however, is to transform the learners into stars or solid citizens and keep the current stars and solid citizens from slipping into the deadwood category. Furthermore, there is a tendency to overlook solid citizens. The learners, stars, and deadwood usually get most of the attention in terms of development programs and stimulating assignments. Neglect of the solid citizens may result in their slipping into the deadwood category.

Three actions can aid in managing the plateauing process: (1) Prevent plateauees from becoming ineffective (prevent a problem from occurring); (2) integrate relevant career-related information systems (improve monitoring so that merging problems can be detected and treated early); and (3) manage ineffective plateauees and frustrated employees more effectively (cure the problem once it has arisen).[21] The first action basically involves helping plateauees adjust to the solid-citizen category and realize they have not necessarily failed. There are indications that employees' attitudes toward career plateauing may have changed in the past decade or so. While plateauing has been historically viewed in a negative sense, that is not necessarily the case today. Because of the stress of continual advancement, some employees actually welcome plateauing. Others see plateauing as an opportunity to redirect their careers.[22] Available avenues for personal development and growth should also be pointed out. The second action can largely be implemented through a thorough performance appraisal system. Such a system should encourage open communication between the manager and the person being appraised (performance appraisal systems are discussed in the next chapter of this book). The following section discusses how to manage ineffective plateauees.

learners
Individuals in an organization who have a high potential for advancement but are currently performing below standard.

stars
Individuals in an organization who are presently doing outstanding work and have a high potential for continued advancement.

solid citizens
Individuals in an organization whose present performance is satisfactory but whose chance for future advancement is small.

deadwood
Individuals in an organization whose present performance has fallen to an unsatisfactory level and who have little potential for advancement.

Rehabilitating Ineffective Plateauees

Rehabilitating ineffective plateauees is difficult but certainly possible. The first question the manager might ask is "Why should we try to help ineffective plateauees; don't they often have an overall negative impact on the organization?" Certainly deadwood can have a negative impact, but there are also several good reasons to salvage these employees:

- *Job knowledge.* Plateaued employees have usually been in the job for quite some time and have amassed considerable job knowledge.
- *Organizational knowledge.* Plateaued employees not only know their jobs but also know the organization.
- *Loyalty.* Plateaued employees are usually not job-hoppers but often have demonstrated above-average loyalty to the organization.
- *Concern for the well-being of plateauees.* If the organization were to terminate all plateaued employees, this could have a disastrous impact on other employees. Also, the number of plateaued employees may be large.[23]

Given that an organization's management team wants to rehabilitate plateaued employees, what can be done? At least five possibilities exist:

1. *Provide alternate means of recognition.* If the chances for the employee to receive recognition through a future promotion are slim, look for alternative methods of recognition. Some possibilities include working on a task force or other special assignments, participating in brainstorming sessions, representing the organization to others, and training new employees.
2. *Develop new ways to make their current jobs more satisfying.* The more employees can be turned on by their current jobs, the lower the likelihood that they will remain ineffective. Some possibilities here include relating employees' performance to total organizational goals and creating competition in the job.
3. *Effect revitalization through reassignment.* The idea here is to implement systematic job switching to positions at the same level that require many similar, though not exactly the same, skills and experiences as the present job.
4. *Utilize reality-based self-development programs.* Instead of assigning plateauees to developmental programs designed to help them move into future jobs (which a majority of development programs do), assign them to development programs that can help them perform better in their present jobs.
5. *Change managerial attitudes toward plateaued employees.* It is not unusual for managers and supervisors to give up on and neglect plateaued employees. The affected employees quickly pick up on such actions, which only compounds the problem.[24]

Because plateaued employees often include a significant number of employees who are worth rehabilitating, it would pay for most organizations to address this issue seriously.

CAREER LATTICES

The idea of a career lattice first emerged in the early 1990s. Before this time careers were discussed only in terms of career ladders, going straight up or down. The idea of a career lattice is to think of employees moving at any angle, heading from side to side, supporting organizational goals while getting their career goals met at the same time.[25] Career lattices support moves in all directions, not just up or down. The lattice approach allows employees to move to different projects and locations across an organization rather than only through higher ladder-like levels. Table 10.4 presents some examples of ladder thinking compared to lattice thinking.

To facilitate the progression from a ladder to a lattice culture, Deloitte & Touche designed a framework called *mass career customization (MCC)*.[26] The goal of MCC is to align current and future career development options for the employee with current and future requirements for the organization in ways that are sustainable for both. The MCC framework outlines a definite set of options along each of four core career dimensions: (1) pace, (2) workload,

TABLE 10.4
Lattice Thinking Versus Ladder Thinking

Source: Adapted from Cliff Hakim, "Best Morale to Gain Productivity," *HR Magazine,* February 1993, pp. 46–49.

Lattice Thinking

- Movement in organization is at any angle, side to side or up and down.
- What and how employees contribute is most important.
- Be collaborative.
- Fluid long-term strategy, grow in your current position.
- Look organization-wide for expertise.
- Rewards are based on learning and performance.

Ladder Thinking

- Movement in organization is restricted to up or down.
- Promotions and titles are important.
- The boss always has the answers.
- Static short-term strategy, remembering that promotions are temporary.
- Look upward in the organization for expertise.
- Rewards are related to title.

(3) location/schedule, and (4) role. These career dimensions are interdependent, meaning that a change in one will result in adjustments to one or more of the others. Working with their managers, employees periodically select options along each dimension based on their career objectives and life circumstances within the needs of the organization. Over time each employee develops his or her own path reflecting the series of choices made in the past. A major benefit of MCC is that it allows employees to modify their activities along the four dimensions as their personal and career situations evolve.

THE IMPACT OF DUAL-EMPLOYED COUPLES AND SINGLE-PARENT EMPLOYEES

Employment by both spouses has become commonplace in the decades following World War II. Today, 71 percent of mothers with children under 18 are in the workforce.[27] As late as 1975, only 47 percent of women with children under 18 were in the labor force.

Bureau of Labor Statistics data for 2008 showed that 59 percent of married women were employed.[28] Similar data for 2008 indicated that 68 percent of mothers with children under 18 were employed.[29] Both economic and social pressures have encouraged this trend.

Dual-employed couples can usually be classified as either dual-career couples or dual-earner couples. In dual-career couples, both members are highly committed to their careers and view work as essential to their psychological sense of self and as integral to their personal identities.[30] They view their employment as part of a career path involving progressively more responsibility, power, and financial remuneration. In dual-earner couples, one or both of the members defines his or her employment as relating to rewards such as money for paying bills, an opportunity to keep busy, or an additional resource to help out. Dual-earner couples do not see their employment as an integral part of their self-definition.

Some of the biggest challenges for dual-employed couples are a lack of time followed by the difficulties in balancing personal and professional life. The biggest advantages for dual-employed couples are increased income, followed by psychological benefits as a distant second.

Dual-employed couple situations can complicate the career development process for both individuals. A career opportunity that requires a geographical move for one member creates an obvious problem for the couple and their respective organizations. Other potential problems of dual-employed couples include the need for child care, balancing time schedules, and emotional stresses. Engaging in the career-planning process can certainly help dual-employed couples address potential problems before they become real.

Single-parent employees currently make up about 5 percent of all employees in the U.S.[31] Of these single-parent working employees, there are over three times as many women as men. As with dual-employed couples, single-parent employees have needs and requirements that are different from those of families that have one parent at home. Many organizations have responded to these needs by initiating family-friendly policies and programs. Proactive corporate programs include child and elder care, flexible work scheduling, job sharing, part-time work, telecommuting, parental leave, and personal time.

OUTPLACEMENT

outplacement
Benefit provided by an employer to help an employee leave the organization and get a job someplace else.

Outplacement refers to "a benefit provided by an employer to help an employee terminate and get a job someplace else."[32] Outplacement is a way of terminating employees that can benefit both the employees and the organization. The organization gains by terminating the employees before they become deadwood; employees gain by finding new jobs and at the same time preserving their dignity. In addition, an outplacement program can have a very positive effect on employee morale.

Skill assessment, establishment of new career objectives, résumé preparation, interview training, and generation of job interviews are services generally offered through an outplacement program. Other services might include training for those who notify terminated employees, office support, spouse involvement, and individual psychological counseling.

Most company outplacement programs involve the use of outplacement consultants or an outplacement firm. The normal procedure is for the outplacement consultant to be briefed by the manager before the employee is terminated. During this session, the outplacement consultant should obtain a clear understanding from the company of why the termination was necessary. After the manager notifies the employee of his or her termination, the outplacement consultant provides immediate support to the employee. The growth of outsourcing, which was discussed in Chapters 1 and 5, has increased the need for outplacement services.

BREAKING THE GLASS CEILING

The term *glass ceiling* refers to invisible, yet real or perceived, barriers found in many organizational structures that appear to stymie the executive advancement opportunities of women and minorities.[33]

The Glass Ceiling Commission was created as part of the Civil Rights Act of 1991. The mandate of the commission was to focus greater public attention on the importance of eliminating barriers and to promote workforce diversity. The commission, which was staffed by the U.S. Department of Labor, was asked to specifically look at the compensation systems and reward structures currently used in the workplace, and at how business fills management and decision-making positions and trains and develops employees for advancement.

According to the commission's initial report, the three most common practices that contribute to the creation of a glass ceiling are (1) word-of-mouth recruiting (or using executive search firms without stating an interest in a diverse array of candidates), (2) inadequate access to developmental opportunities for women and minorities, and (3) a lack of responsibility among senior management for equal employment opportunity efforts.[34] Subsequently the commission, "which was dissolved in 1995," formulated the following suggestions for toppling job-advancement barriers:

- Demonstrate commitment. Top management should communicate its dedication to diversity and enact policies that promote it.
- Hold line managers accountable for progress by including diversity in all strategic business plans. Performance appraisals, compensation incentives, and other evaluation measures should reflect this priority.
- Use affirmative action as a tool to ensure that all qualified individuals compete based on ability and merit.
- Expand your pool of candidates. Look for prospects from noncustomary sources who may have nontraditional backgrounds and experiences.
- Educate all employees about the strengths and challenges of gender, racial, ethnic, and cultural differences.
- Initiate family-friendly programs that help men and women balance their work and family responsibilities.[35]

Because many factors that contribute to the glass ceiling stem from the common tendency "to hire in one's own image," glass ceilings will be eliminated only when all employees are evaluated, hired, and promoted on the basis of merit. If followed, the previously discussed suggestions from the Glass Ceiling Commission should go a long way toward creating such a culture. Data from the Bureau of Labor Statistics indicate that women have made gains over the last several years. For example, 2008 data show that almost 40 percent of employed women are in managerial or professional jobs, up from 36 percent in 1997 and 24 percent in 1977.[36] These same data, however, also show that women's median weekly earnings still lag behind men's by 20 percent ($638.00 per week versus $798.00 per week).[37]

Other data show that in 2008, women accounted for 15.7 percent of *Fortune* 500 corporate officer jobs (jobs with titles of at least vice president and requiring board approval).[38] These same data found that women comprised just 15.2 percent of the 5,610 director positions at these firms. *Barron's* magazine estimates that by 2020 women could hold one in five powerful posts in corporate America.[39]

CAREER DEVELOPMENT ONLINE

Today many companies are developing comprehensive, online career development centers. These online career development centers provide access to a wide variety of services to help employees manage their careers and, in some instances, even find jobs outside their present company. Online capabilities can provide many types of career-related information on demand. For example, employees can look up the competencies and skills required for jobs they aspire to have. Some of the online career planning resources being offered include these:

- Information about employment trends and job opportunities.
- Self-assessment tools, such as personality tests and interest indicators, that employees can use to determine which types of jobs they might best pursue.
- Links to online employment resources such as job listings and career development information.
- Individual online job counseling, including advice on preparing for interviews.[40]

In addition to company-sponsored online services, many resources are available on the Internet to help individuals with career development. These resources include job search guides, self-assessment tools, résumé preparation aids, job listings, career-related articles, and other similar services. There is little doubt that online career-development resources will continue to expand in the future. The On-the-Job section at the end of this chapter describes two of the most used and most respected online self assessment tools. HRM in Action 10.4 describes a recent venture of one of the leading online career development networks.

Summary of Learning Objectives

1. Define *career development* and summarize its major objectives.

Career development is an ongoing, formalized effort by an organization that focuses on developing and enriching the organization's human resources in light of both the employees' and the organization's needs. From the organization's viewpoint, career development has three major objectives: (1) to meet the immediate and future human resource needs of the organization on a timely basis, (2) to better inform the organization and the individual about potential career paths within the organization, and (3) to utilize existing human resource programs to the fullest by integrating the activities that select, assign, develop, and manage individual careers with the organization's plans.

2. Name the three entities required to provide input for a successful career development program and briefly describe their respective responsibilities.

Successful career development results from a joint effort by the organization, the employee, and the immediate manager. The organization provides the resources and structure, the employee does the planning, and the immediate manager provides the guidance and encouragement.

3. Describe the steps involved in implementing a career development program.

The implementation of a career development program involves four basic steps: (1) an assessment by the individual of his or her abilities, interests, and career goals; (2) an assessment by the organization of the individual's abilities and potential; (3) communication of career options and opportunities within the organization; and (4) career counseling to set realistic goals and plans for their accomplishment.

4. Define *career pathing* and *career self-management*.

Career pathing is a technique that addresses the specifics of progressing from one job to another in the organization. Career self-management is the ability to keep pace with the speed at which change occurs within the organization and the industry and to prepare for the future.

5. List several myths employees hold related to career planning and advancement.

Employees often hold many myths related to career planning and advancement: (1) There is always room for one more person at the top; (2) the key to success is being in the right place at the right time; (3) good subordinates make good superiors; (4) career development and planning are functions of human resource personnel; (5) all good things come to those who work long, hard hours; (6) rapid advancement along a career path is largely a function of the kind of manager one has; (7) the way to get ahead is to determine your weaknesses and then work hard to correct them; (8) always do your best, regardless of the task; (9) it is wise to keep home life and work life separated; and (10) the grass is always greener on the other side of the fence.

6. List several myths management holds related to career development.

Management personnel often hold certain myths related to career management: (1) Career development will raise expectations to unrealistically high levels; (2) management will be overwhelmed with requests; (3) managers will not be able to cope; and (4) management does not have the necessary systems in place.

7. Define a career plateau and a plateaued employee.

A career plateau is the point in a career where the likelihood of additional hierarchical promotion is very low. A plateaued employee is an employee who reaches his or her promotional ceiling long before retirement.

8. Describe the four principal career categories.

The four principal career categories are learners, stars, solid citizens, and deadwood. Learners are individuals with a high potential for advancement who are performing below standard. Stars are individuals presently doing outstanding work, with a high potential for continued advancement. Solid citizens are individuals whose present performance is satisfactory but whose chance for future advancement is small. Deadwood refers to individuals whose present performance has fallen to an unsatisfactory level and who have little potential for advancement.

9. **Explain the concept of a career lattice.**

   Career lattices support career moves in all directions within an organization, not just up or down movement.

10. **Distinguish between dual-career couples and dual-earner couples. Describe some possible ways organizations can accommodate dual-employed couples.**

    In dual-career couples, both members are highly committed to their careers and view work as essential to their psychological sense of self and as integral to their personal identities. They view their employment as part of a career path involving progressively more responsibility, power, and financial remuneration. In dual-earner couples, one or both of the members defines his or her employment as relating to rewards such as money for paying bills, an opportunity to keep busy, or an additional resource to help out. Dual-earner couples do not both see their employment as an integral part of their self-definition. Many organizations have responded to the needs of dual-employed couples by updating their human resource policies to accommodate them. Some possibilities include provision of child and elder care, flexible work scheduling, job sharing, part-time work, telecommuting, parental leave, and personal time.

11. **Define *outplacement*.**

    Outplacement refers to a benefit an employer provides to help an employee terminate employment with the organization and get a job someplace else.

12. **Explain what the glass ceiling is.**

    The term *glass ceiling* refers to invisible, yet real or projected barriers found in many organizational structures that appear to stymie the executive advancement opportunities of women and minorities.

13. **List some of the online career development resources available today.**

    Some of the online career development resources that are available today include information about employment trends and job opportunities, self-assessment tools, links to online employment services, and individual online job counseling.

Key Terms

career development, *190*	career self-management, *194*	solid citizens, *199*
career pathing, *194*	deadwood, *199*	stars, *199*
career planning, *190*	learners, *199*	vision statement, *192*
career plateau, *198*	outplacement, *202*	

Review Questions

1. Define *career development* and *career planning*.
2. What are the three major objectives of career development from the organization's viewpoint?
3. What is the role of the individual employee in career development?
4. What are the four basic steps in implementing a career development program?
5. What is a personal vision statement?
6. What are career pathing and career self-management?
7. Give some specific suggestions for helping managers become better career counselors.
8. How often should an individual review and revise his or her career plan?
9. Identify several myths employees often hold relating to career development and advancement.
10. Identify several myths managers often hold relating to career development.
11. Define the following categories: learners, stars, solid citizens, and deadwood.
12. Name and briefly describe several methods an organization might use to rehabilitate inefficient plateauees.

13. What is a career lattice?

14. Distinguish between dual-career couples and dual-earner couples and identify some of the challenges these groups face.

15. What is outplacement, and how does it usually work?

16. What is the glass ceiling and what are the three most common practices that contribute to it?

17. Name several types of online career planning resources currently available.

Discussion Questions

1. Do you think career development can adversely affect organizational performance in that the process sometimes convinces the involved parties to change jobs?

2. Is the concept of career development realistic in today's rapidly changing environment?

3. Discuss how career-related myths can inhibit career planning and growth.

4. Is it better to tell a person that he or she has reached a plateau in the organization or to allow the person to maintain hope of eventual promotion?

5. What advice would you offer today's employees regarding the problems dual-employed couples and single-parent employees face?

Incident 10.1

The Unhappy Power Line Installer

John James had been an installer-repairer for the power company for almost six years. The work kept him outdoors most of the day, and he liked the job, the pay was good, and his coworkers were congenial. John had gone to work on this job right after high school graduation and had never considered doing anything else. Through the years, others in the same job occasionally had been promoted into supervisory positions, taken advantage of company-paid educational benefits, or received recognition for outstanding service to the company.

John was close friends with Ross Bartlett, his partner on the line. Ross, who had been in his job about two years, was a good worker. About six months ago, Ross began to express dissatisfaction with the routine, monotonous work, saying there had to be some better way to make a living.

Last week, John learned the company would pay Ross's way to take college courses in business administration. That same day, John really began to feel some concern about himself and his status with the power company. He began having restless, sleepless nights as he thought back over the past years: what he had done with his life, where he was now in his career, and where he was going. His thoughts became so muddled that he realized he was going to need some help.

John had never set any personal goals for himself other than to live reasonably comfortably from day to day and month to month. He had come from a poor family and had received little encouragement or help from his parents to develop ambitions when he was young. The one thing his mother and father had insisted on was that someone in the family was going to be a high school graduate; luckily, John was that person. He never had any desire to go to college because graduation from high school had proven to be extremely difficult for him. John could not think of spending four more years in school when he needed and wanted to be out making money for himself and the family.

Now, with people around him moving on in their careers and John's career at a standstill, he felt he was at a dead end. He realized suddenly that he needed to do something, but he was not sure just what.

Questions

1. What advice might you give John?

2. Would a career plan help a person like John?

3. Is John's situation atypical of that of most employees?

Incident 10.2

Hire Me, Hire My Husband!*

Pete Gettings, director of human resources for XYZ Company's research and development laboratories, was relating a success from his State University recruiting trip to Derek Hills, XYZ's manager of computer operations.

"Derek," Gettings said excitedly, "you know how you've had me looking for engineers who could add technical strength to your operation? Well, I've found one—a senior at State University and a straight-A student, with lots of ambition, interested in computers for what they can do in applications, and anxious to work in industry. I'm bringing her in for an interview—I'm sure you'll want to hire her, and I'm positive we can.

"But," Gettings continued, "that's the good news. The bad news is that she's married and she and her husband want to work for the same company. Her husband is a marketing major and a jock. He played four years of basketball for State but is not nearly good enough to consider a pro career. I met him; he's got lots of personality and a C-grade average. I don't see any particular talent in him, and I think our marketing people will turn him down flat. But if we want her, we've got to find him a job!"

Sally Finch and her husband, Mike, were brought in for interviews with exactly the results Pete Gettings had predicted. Everybody was impressed with Sally, for she had prepared well for the interview and was able to point out some unexploited applications of computers at XYZ. Her suggestions about product performance simulation were particularly thought provoking and impressive.

Her husband, on the other hand, did very poorly in his interview. Mike could discuss his basketball prowess, but little else. His earring and ponytail hairstyle did not fit the conservative atmosphere of XYZ either.

The interviews resulted in a very attractive offer to Sally and a rejection for Mike. Sally's response was a blunt retort that she and Mike would continue to look for opportunities to work for the same company. XYZ wanted to employ Sally so badly that it made a diligent search of local employment possibilities for her husband, thinking this might be a good alternative to employing both of them at XYZ. A small telemarketing firm finally exhibited some interest in employing Mike, and because of the excellent offer that XYZ had made to Sally, the pair decided to accept both offers.

Sally subsequently proved to be a valuable asset to XYZ's R&D computer operations, and her work resulted in some excellent product development progress for the company. Derek was pleased and continued to pay for her additional training.

Sally received two promotions during her first two years at XYZ. Occasionally Derek asked about her husband, and Sally's only response was that he was doing OK and they were considering buying a home. This was good news because XYZ felt that Sally was definitely an employee they wanted to keep.

As time went on, Derek saw Mike several times at departmental social functions and noted that he had matured and become a very self-assured individual. In conversations with him, Derek observed that Mike seemed to have all the characteristics of a successful young businessman. Derek, in fact, wondered to himself if XYZ had made a mistake in not hiring him.

Derek was surprised and ill prepared one morning when Sally walked into the office and told him she was resigning.

"What's the problem?" Derek asked.

"My husband has done very well in the telemarketing business and has been offered a promotion and transfer to the West Coast. His company has asked him to open and manage a new branch operation there. I'm certain I'll be able to find employment in our new location, and we think this is the chance of a lifetime for Mike. I'm sorry to leave XYZ, but I really see no other choice. I'm willing to stay a month or so to help train a replacement if you can find one quickly. Of course, if XYZ could come up with a job for Mike equivalent to the one he's been offered on the Coast, we would stay here."

Questions

1. Should XYZ find (or "create") a job for Mike to retain Sally, a valued and well-trained employee?
2. Should XYZ management have anticipated a possible retention problem due to different career paths when it placed Sally and Mike in jobs with separate companies?
3. Do situations such as the one presented here make companies cautious about offering positions to members of dual-career families?

*Source: W. Gale Cutler, "Hire Me, Hire My Husband!" *Research-Technology Management* 38, no. 4 (July–August 1995), pp. 57–58, Copyright © 1995 Industrial Research Institute. Reprinted with permission.

EXERCISE 10.1
How Do You Rate as a Career Counselor?*

This quiz helps managers examine their knowledge of the career counseling function and discover those areas in which some skill building may be necessary. Rate your knowledge, skill, and confidence as a managerial career counselor by scoring yourself on a scale of 0 (low) to 10 (high) on each of the following statements:

_____ 1. I am aware of how career orientations and life stages can influence a person's perspective and contribute to career planning problems.

_____ 2. I understand my own career choices and changes and feel good enough about what I have done to be able to provide guidance to others.

_____ 3. I am aware of my own biases about dual-career paths and feel that I can avoid these biases in coaching others to make a decision on which way to go with their careers.

_____ 4. I am aware of how my own values influence my point of view, and I recognize the importance of helping others define their values and beliefs so they are congruent with career goals.

_____ 5. I am aware of the pitfalls of not knowing what is going on within my organization. As a result, I try to stay informed about my organization so I can help others.

_____ 6. I know the norms existing within my own department as well as those within other departments and parts of the organization, so I can help others deal with them effectively.

_____ 7. I understand the organizational reward system (nonmonetary) well enough to help others make informed decisions about career goals, paths, and plans.

_____ 8. I have access to a variety of techniques I can use to help others articulate their skills, set goals, and develop action plans to realize their career decisions.

_____ 9. I am informed on the competencies required for career success in this organization in both the managerial and technical areas, so I can advise others on the particular skills they need to build and how to go about developing that expertise.

_____ 10. I feel confident enough about my own skills as a career counselor that I can effectively help my people with their problems and plans and make midcourse corrections when necessary.

SCORING
Add up your score and rate yourself against the following scale:

0–30   It might be a good idea if you found *yourself* a career counselor.

31–60   Some of your people are receiving help from you. . . . However, do you know how many and which ones are not?

61–80   You're a counselor! You may not be ready for the big league yet, but you are providing help for your people.

81–100 Others have a lot to learn from you. You understand the importance of career counseling, and you know how to provide it.

*Source: Adapted from P. R. Jones, B. Kaye, and H. R. Taylor, "You Want Me to Do What?" *Training and Development Journal,* July 1981, p. 62. Copyright © 1981 ASTD. Reprinted with permission of American Society for Training & Development.

EXERCISE 10.2
Becoming an
Effective Career
Planner

Look over the nine potential career-planning roles of managers listed in Table 10.1. Rank-order them in terms of which roles you think would best fit you (1 being the role you would fit best, 9 being the role you would fit least). After you have completed this ranking, complete the quiz in Exercise 10.1. How does your score on this quiz correlate with how you ranked the counselor role (i.e., if you scored high on this quiz, did you rank the role of the counselor relatively high, and vice versa)? Make a list of some things you might do to become a better counselor. Be prepared to share your list with the class.

EXERCISE 10.3
Online
Self-Assessment

Take either one of the online self-assessment tests discussed in the On the Job section at the end of this chapter (pp. 210–211). The cost of either test will be $9.95. After you have finished the test and looked at your results, answer the following questions:

1. Were you surprised at which category you most closely fit?
2. Were you surprised at the occupations and work environments that most closely matched your profile?
3. Do you think that the career information you received was worth your time and money?

Notes and
Additional
Readings

1. William J. Morin, "You Are Absolutely Positively on Your Own," *Fortune,* December 9, 1996, p. 222.
2. U.S. Department of Labor, http://www.bls.gov/nls. New release June 27, 2008.
3. Anne Fisher, "Surviving the Downturn," *Fortune,* April 2, 2001.
4. Matthew Boyle, "First, You Have to Figure Out Who You Are," *Fortune,* February 18, 2002; David Firestone, "Thomaston Journal: Mill Town Mourns Its Mill, Then Reinvents Itself," *New York Times,* January 21, 2002, p. A10.
5. "The Employee Point of View: The Economic Downturn," The Society for Human Resource Management, April 1, 2009. Accessed at www.shrm.org/Research/Survey Findings, January 21, 2010.
6. B. C. Winterscheid, "A Career Development System Coordinates Training Efforts," *Personnel Administrator,* August 1980, pp. 28–32.
7. For example see H. Fred Walker, "Climbing the Career Ladder: It's Up to You," *Quality Progress,* October 2006, pp. 28–32.
8. A. B. Randolph, "Managerial Career Coaching," *Training and Development Journal,* July 1981, pp. 54–55.
9. T. H. Stone, *Understanding Personnel Management* (Hinsdale, Ill.: Dryden Press, 1981), p. 324.
10. This paragraph is drawn from H. Fred Walker, "Climbing the Career Ladder: It's Up to You," *Quality Progress,* October 2006, pp. 28–32.
11. E. H. Burack and N. J. Mathys, *Career Management in Organizations: A Practical Human Resource Planning Approach* (Lake Forest, Ill.: Brace-Park Press, 1979), p. 78; Carla Joinson, "Employee, Sculpt Thyself . . . With a Little Help," *HR Magazine,* May 2001, pp. 60–64.
12. Jeanne C. Meister, "The Quest for Lifetime Employability," *Journal of Business Strategy,* May/June 1998, pp. 25–28.
13. Mary Bambacas and Prashant Bordia, "Predicting Different Commitment Components: The Relative Effects of How Career Development HRM Practices are Perceived," *Journal of Management and Organization,* May 2009, pp. 224–240.
14. These suggestions are adapted from N. T. Meckel, "The Manager as Career Counselor," *Training and Development Journal,* July 1981, pp. 65–69.
15. Many of these myths were originally suggested by E. Staats, "Career Planning and Development: Which Way Is Up?" *Public Administration Review,* January–February 1977, pp. 73–76; and A. H. Soverwine, "Mythology of Career Growth," *Management Review,* June 1977, pp. 56–60.
16. The myths in this section were adapted from Barbara Moses, "Giving Employees a Future," *Training and Development Journal,* December 1987, pp. 25–28.
17. T. P. Ference, J. A. F. Stoner, and E. K. Warren, "Managing the Career Plateau," *Management Review,* October 1977, p. 602.

18. Steven H. Applebaum and Dvorah Firestone, "Revisiting Career Plateauing: Same Old Problems—Avant Garde Solutions," *Journal of Managerial Psychology* 9, no. 5 (1994), pp. 12–21; Suzanne Koudsi, "You're Stuck," *Fortune,* December 10, 2001.

19. Beverly Kaye, "Are Plateaued Performers Productive?" *Personnel Journal,* August 1989, p. 57; Judith M. Bardwick, *The Plateauing Trap* (New York: American Management Association, 1986), pp. 1–17.

20. Ference, Stoner, and Warren, "Managing," pp. 603–64.

21. Ibid., p. 607.

22. Patrick Chang Boon Lee, "Going Beyond Career Plateau: Using Professional Plateau to Account for Work Outcomes," *The Journal of Management Development* 22, No. 5/6 (2003), pp. 538–551; and Theresa Smith Ruig, "Exploring Career Plateau as a Multi-Faceted Phenomenon: Understanding the Types of Career Plateaux Experienced by Accounting Professionals," *British Journal of Management,* December 2009, p. 610.

23. Richard C. Payne, "Mid-Career Block," *Personnel Journal,* April 1984, p. 42.

24. Ibid., pp. 44–48.

25. Cliff Hakim, "Best Morale to Gain Productivity," *HR Magazine,* February 1993, pp. 46–49.

26. Much of this section is drawn from Cathleen Benko and Anne Weisberg, "Implementing a Corporate Career Lattice: The Mass Career Customization Model," *Strategy and Leadership* 35, No. 5 (2007), p. 29 and Cathy Benko and Anne Weisberg, "Mass Career Customization: A New Model for How Careers Are Built," *Ivey Business Journal Online,* May/June 2008, p. 1.

27. *Women in the Labor Force: A Databook 2009,* p. 1, www.bls.gov/cps/wlf-databook 2009.htm, accessed January 26, 2010.

28. Ibid., Table 4, p. 12. Accessed January 26, 2010.

29. Ibid., Table 5, p. 13. Accessed January 26, 2010.

30. Nancy Carter, "Solve the Dual-Career Challenge," *Workforce (Global Workforce Supplement),* October 1997, pp. 21–22.

31. This figure is derived from the data in Table 4 of *Employment Characteristics of Families in 2008,* www.bls.gov/news.release/pdf/famee/pdf. Accessed January 26, 2010.

32. T. M. Camden, "Using Outplacement as a Career Development Tool," *Personnel Administration,* January 1982, p. 35.

33. Cari M. Dominguez, "A Crack in the Glass Ceiling," *HR Magazine,* December 1990, pp. 65–66. It should be noted that some authors interpret the glass ceiling as applying only to women as opposed to women and minorities.

34. "The Glass Ceiling," *HR Magazine,* October 1991, pp. 91–92.

35. "Dismantling the Glass Ceiling," *HR Focus,* May 1996, p. 12.

36. *Women in the Labor Force: A Databook 2009,* Table 10, p. 26. www.bls.gov/cps/wlf-databook 2009.htm. Accessed January 27, 2010.

37. Ibid., p. 2.

38. Alexander H. Tullo, "Women in Industry," *Chemical & Engineering News,* July 20, 2009, p. 26.

39. Gene Epstein, "Breaking the Glass," *Barron's,* May 26, 2003, p. 17.

40. Jim Warner, "Creating Virtual Career Development Center," *HR Focus,* October 1997, pp. 11–12; Sarah Fister Gale, "Tapping Unused Resources in Lean Times," *Workforce,* October 2001, pp. 86–87; and Christopher J. McCarthy, Naomi Moller, and L. Michelle Beard, "Suggestions for Training Students in Using the Internet for Career Counseling," *Career Development Quarterly,* June 2003, pp. 368–78.

On the Job

ONLINE SELF-ASSESSMENT TOOLS

Many online self-assessment tools are available. Unfortunately not all of them are reliable and valid. An unreliable and/or invalid self-assessment tool can result in inaccurate information, mislead, and harm the user. The two online self-assessment tools discussed below are two of the most used and well-respected self-assessment tools available.

THE SELF-DIRECTED SEARCH (SDS)

The Self-Directed Search (SDS) has been used by over 30 million people worldwide and has been translated into 25 different languages.[1] SDS results have been supported by over 500 research studies.

SDS was developed by Dr. John L. Holland and is based on Holland's theory that most people can be loosely categorized with respect to six basic types: realistic, investigative, artistic, social, enterprising, and conventional. Under Holland's theory, occupations and work environments can also be classified by these same categories. The basic idea is that people who choose careers that match their own types are more likely to be both satisfied and successful. The SDS takes about 15 minutes and costs $9.95 to take.

THE CAREER KEY™ TEST[2]

The Career Key™ Test also measures your skills, abilities, values, and interests using the same six personality types as Holland's (described in the previous paragraph). The Career Key™ has been scientifically validated and been in use for over 23 years. The Career Key™ is currently used by over 3 million people per year. The Career Key™ takes about 10 minutes and costs $9.95 to take. The Web site for Career Key™ is www.careerkey.org.

---

[1] The information about the SDS was gathered from the SDS Web site (www.self-directed-search.com).
[2] The information about the Career Key™ was gathered from the Career Key™ Web site (www.careerkey.org).

Chapter Eleven

Performance Management Systems

Chapter Learning Objectives

After studying this chapter, you should be able to:

1. Define performance.
2. Define performance appraisal.
3. Explain management by objectives.
4. Describe multi-rater assessment.
5. Describe the graphic rating scale.
6. Explain critical-incident appraisal.
7. Describe essay appraisal.
8. Describe the checklist method of performance appraisal.
9. Explain the forced-choice method of performance appraisal.
10. Describe the work standards approach to performance appraisal.
11. Define leniency, central tendency, recency, and the halo effect.

Chapter Outline

Understanding Performance
  Determinants of Performance
  Environmental Factors as Performance Obstacles
  Responsibilities of the Human Resource Department in Performance Management
Performance Appraisal: Definition and Uses
Performance Appraisal Methods
  Management by Objectives (MBO)
  Multi-Rater Assessment (or 360-Degree Feedback)
  Graphic Rating Scale
  Behaviorally Anchored Rating Scale (BARS)
  Critical-Incident Appraisal
  Essay Appraisal
  Checklist
  Forced-Choice Rating
  Ranking Methods
  Work Standards

Potential Errors in Performance Appraisals
Overcoming Errors in Performance Appraisals
Providing Feedback through the Appraisal Interview
Developing Performance Improvement Plans
Performance Appraisal and the Law
Summary of Learning Objectives
Key Terms
Review Questions
Discussion Questions
  Incident 11.1: The College Admissions Office
  Incident 11.2: The Lackadaisical Plant Manager
Exercise 11.1: Developing a Performance Appraisal System
Notes and Additional Readings

Performance management systems that are directly tied to an organization's reward system provide a powerful incentive for employees to work diligently and creatively toward achieving organizational objectives. When properly designed and implemented, performance management systems not only let employees know how well they are presently performing but also clarify what needs to be done to improve performance.

UNDERSTANDING PERFORMANCE

performance
Degree of accomplishment of the tasks that make up an employee's job.

Performance refers to the degree of accomplishment of the tasks that make up an employee's job. It reflects how well an employee is fulfilling the requirements of a job. Often confused with *effort,* which refers to energy expended, performance is measured in terms of results. For example, a student may exert a great deal of effort in preparing for an examination and still make a poor grade. In such a case the effort expended was high, yet the performance was low.

Determinants of Performance

Job performance is the net effect of an employee's effort as modified by abilities and role (or task) perceptions. Thus, performance in a given situation can be viewed as resulting from the interrelationships among effort, abilities, and role perceptions. *Effort,* which results from being motivated, refers to the amount of energy (physical and/or mental) an individual uses in performing a task. *Abilities* are personal characteristics used in performing a job. Abilities usually do not fluctuate widely over short periods of time. *Role (task) perceptions* refer to the direction(s) in which individuals believe they should channel their effort on their jobs. The activities and behaviors people believe are necessary in the performance of their jobs define their role perceptions.

To attain an acceptable level of performance, a minimum level of proficiency must exist in each of the performance components. Similarly, the level of proficiency in any one performance component can place an upper boundary on performance. If employees put forth tremendous effort and have excellent abilities but lack a clear understanding of their roles, performance will probably not be good in the eyes of their managers. Much work will be produced, but it will be misdirected. Likewise, an employee who puts forth a high degree of effort and understands the job but lacks ability probably will rate low on performance. A final possibility is the employee who has a good ability and understanding of the role but is lazy and expends little effort. This employee's performance will likely be low. Of course, an employee can compensate up to a point for a weakness in one area by being above average in one or both of the other areas.

Environmental Factors as Performance Obstacles

Other factors beyond the control of the employee can also stifle performance. Although such obstacles are sometimes used merely as excuses, they are often very real and should be recognized. Some of the more common potential performance obstacles include the employee's lack of time or conflicting demands upon it, inadequate work facilities and equipment, restrictive policies that affect the job, lack of cooperation from others, type of supervision, temperature, lighting, noise, machine or equipment pacing, shifts, and even luck.

Environmental factors should be viewed not as direct determinants of individual performance but as modifying the effects of effort, ability, and direction. For example, poor ventilation or worn-out equipment may well affect the effort an individual expends. Unclear policies or poor supervision can also produce misdirected effort. Similarly, a lack of training can result in underutilized abilities. One of management's greatest responsibilities is to provide employees with adequate working conditions and a supportive environment to eliminate or minimize performance obstacles.

Responsibilities of the Human Resource Department in Performance Management

Performance management systems require a coordinated effort between the human resource department and the managers of the organization who are responsible for conducting performance appraisals. Generally, the responsibilities of the human resource department are to

1. Design the performance management system and select the methods and forms to be used for appraising employees.
2. Train managers in conducting performance appraisals.
3. Maintain a reporting system to ensure that appraisals are conducted on a timely basis.

EVALUATION OF DOCTORS

About five years ago, physicians and executives at three central New Jersey hospitals that encompass Meridian Health were concerned that scorecards developed by health plans and others might portray its doctors unfairly. So Jeffrey Borell, Meridian's manager of outcomes measurement, and members of Meridian's teaching hospital staff at Jersey Shore University Medical Center, created their own scorecard from scratch. The scorecards compare physician performance to members of his or her own group, members of the same specialty who work at their hospital, and to other doctors who treat similar conditions at their hospital. For readability and ease of use, Borell and his team limited color-coded scorecards to one page. Next year, Meridian plans to include patient satisfaction. One goal of the scorecards is to standardize medical practices more quickly than what has taken place in the past. While some Meridian doctors agree with the need to standardize medicine, they take issue with the methods used to grade them.

Sources: Adapted from Maureen Glabman, "Keeping Score: Scorecards, Profiles and Report Cards Rapidly Expanding to Track Physician Performance," *Physician Executive*, November/December 2005, pp. 26–32.

4. Maintain performance appraisal records for individual employees.

The responsibilities of managers in performance appraisals are to

1. Evaluate the performance of employees.
2. Complete the forms used in appraising employees and return them to the human resource department.
3. Review appraisals with employees.
4. Establish a plan for improvement with employees.

PERFORMANCE APPRAISAL: DEFINITION AND USES

performance appraisal
Process of evaluating and communicating to an employee how he or she is performing the job and establishing a plan for improvement.

Performance appraisal is the process of evaluating and communicating to an employee how he or she is performing the job and establishing a plan of improvement. When properly conducted, performance appraisals not only let employees know how well they are performing but also influence their future level of effort and task direction. Effort should be enhanced if good performance is positively reinforced. The task perception of the employee should be clarified through establishing a plan for improvement.

One of the most common uses of performance appraisals is for making administrative decisions relating to promotions, firings, layoffs, and merit pay increases.[1] For example, an employee's present job performance is often the most significant consideration for determining whether to promote the person. While successful performance in the present job does not necessarily mean an employee will be an effective performer in a higher-level job, performance appraisals do provide some predictive information.

Performance appraisal information can also provide needed input for determining both individual and organizational training and development needs. For example, this information can be used to identify an individual employee's strengths and weaknesses. These data can then be used to help determine the organization's overall training and development needs. For an individual employee, a completed performance appraisal should include a plan outlining specific training and development needs.

Another important use of performance appraisals is to encourage performance improvement. In this regard, performance appraisals are used as a means of communicating to employees how they are doing and suggesting needed changes in behavior, attitude, skills, or knowledge. This type of feedback clarifies for employees the manager's job expectations. Often this feedback must be followed by coaching and training by the manager to guide an employee's work efforts.[2] The development of a performance improvement plan is discussed in more depth later in this chapter.

Finally, two other important uses of information generated through performance appraisals are (1) input to the validation of selection procedures and (2) input to human resource planning. Both of these topics were described in detail in earlier chapters. HRM in Action 11.1 shows the use of performance appraisals in three central New Jersey hospitals.

A concern in organizations is how often to conduct performance appraisals. There seems to be no real consensus on how frequently performance appraisals should be done, but in general the answer is as often as necessary to let employees know what kind of job they are doing and, if performance is not satisfactory, the measures that must be taken for improvement. For many employees, this cannot be accomplished through one annual performance appraisal. Therefore, it is recommended that for most employees, informal performance appraisals be conducted two or three times a year in addition to an annual formal performance appraisal.

PERFORMANCE APPRAISAL METHODS

Whatever method of performance appraisal an organization uses, it must be job related. Therefore, prior to selecting a performance appraisal method, an organization must conduct job analyses and develop job descriptions. After this, one or more of the following performance appraisal methods can be used.

This section will discuss each of the following performance appraisal methods:

1. Management by objectives (MBO).
2. Multi-rater assessment (or 360-degree feedback).
3. Graphic rating scale.
4. Behaviorally anchored rating scale (BARS).
5. Critical-incident appraisal.
6. Essay appraisal.
7. Checklist.
8. Forced-choice rating.
9. Ranking methods.
10. Work standards approach.

Management by Objectives (MBO)

management by objectives (MBO)
Consists of establishing clear and precisely defined statements of objectives for the work to be done by an employee, establishing an action plan indicating how these objectives are to be achieved, allowing the employee to implement the action plan, measuring objective achievement, taking corrective action when necessary, and establishing new objectives for the future.

Management by objectives (MBO) is more commonly used with professional and managerial employees. Other names for MBO include management by results, performance management, results management, and work planning and review program.

The MBO process typically consists of the following steps:

1. Establishing clear and precisely defined statements of objectives for the work to be done by an employee.
2. Developing an action plan indicating how these objectives are to be achieved.
3. Allowing the employee to implement the action plan.
4. Measuring objective achievement.
5. Taking corrective action when necessary.
6. Establishing new objectives for the future.

For an MBO system to be successful, several requirements must be met. First, objectives should be quantifiable and measurable; objectives whose attainment cannot be measured or at least verified should be avoided where possible. Objectives should also be challenging yet achievable, and they should be expressed in writing and in clear, concise, unambiguous language.

Table 11.1 presents examples of how some poorly stated objectives might be better stated. Table 11.2 shows some typical areas in which a supervisor might set objectives.

MBO requires that employees participate in the objective-setting process. The employee's active participation is also essential in developing the action plan. Managers who set an employee's objectives without input and then ask the employee, "You agree to these, don't you?" are unlikely to get high levels of employee commitment.

A final requirement for the successful use of MBO is that the objectives and action plan must serve as a basis for regular discussions between the manager and the employee concerning the employee's performance. These regular discussions provide an opportunity for the manager and employee to discuss progress and modify objectives when necessary.[3]

TABLE 11.1
Examples of How to Improve Work Objectives

Poor:	To maximize production.
Better:	To increase production by 10 percent within the next three months.
Poor:	To reduce absenteeism.
Better:	To average no more than three absent days per employee per year.
Poor:	To waste less raw material.
Better:	To waste no more than 2 percent of raw material.
Poor:	To improve the quality of production.
Better:	To produce no more than 2 rejects per 100 units of production.

TABLE 11.2
Typical Areas of Supervisory Objectives

1. Production or output:
   Usually expressed as number of units per time period.
   Example: Our objective is to average 20 units per hour over the next year.
2. Quality:
   Usually expressed as number of rejects, number of customer complaints, amount of scrap.
   Example: Our objective is to produce fewer than 10 rejects per week for the next six months.
3. Cost:
   Usually expressed as dollars per unit produced or dollars per unit of service offered.
   Example: Our objective is that the cost of each widget produced will average less than $5 over the next three months.
4. Personnel:
   Usually expressed in terms of turnover, absenteeism, tardiness.
   Example: Our objective is to average fewer than three days of absenteeism per employee per year.
5. Safety:
   Usually expressed in terms of days lost due to injury.
   Example: Our objective is to reduce the number of days lost due to injury this year by 10 percent.

Multi-Rater Assessment (or 360-Degree Feedback)

Another method of performance appraisal is called *multi-rater assessment,* or *360-degree feedback*. With this method, managers, peers, customers, suppliers, or colleagues are asked to complete questionnaires on the employee being assessed. The person assessed also completes a questionnaire. The questionnaires are generally lengthy. Typical questions are: "Are you crisp, clear, and articulate? Abrasive? Spreading yourself too thin?" The human resources department provides the results to the employee, who in turn gets to see how his or her opinion differs from those of the group doing the assessment.[4] HRM in Action 11.2 describes the lack of use of 360-degree feedback.

Graphic Rating Scale

graphic rating scale
Method of performance appraisal that requires the rater to indicate on a scale where the employee rates on factors such as quantity of work, dependability, job knowledge, and cooperativeness.

With the **graphic rating scale** method, the rater assesses an employee on factors such as quantity of work, dependability, job knowledge, attendance, accuracy of work, and cooperativeness. Graphic rating scales include both numerical ranges and written descriptions. Table 11.3 gives an example of some items that might be included on a graphic rating scale that uses written descriptions.

The graphic rating scale method is subject to some serious weaknesses. One potential weakness is that evaluators are unlikely to interpret written descriptions in the same manner due to differences in background, experience, and personality. Another potential problem relates to the choice of rating categories. It is possible to choose categories that have little relationship to job performance or to omit categories that have a significant influence on job performance.

Behaviorally Anchored Rating Scale (BARS)

behaviorally anchored rating scale (BARS)
Method of performance appraisal that determines an employee's level of performance based on whether or not certain specifically described job behaviors are present.

The **behaviorally anchored rating scale (BARS)** method of performance appraisal is designed to assess behaviors required to successfully perform a job. The focus of BARS and, to some extent, the graphic rating scale and checklist methods is not on performance outcomes but on functional behaviors demonstrated on the job. The assumption is that these functional behaviors will result in effective job performance.

PROMOTING EMPLOYEES MISMANAGED

Some companies feel that the difficult part of finding upper management is in selecting and promoting existing employees to new higher management positions. Research, however, does not support this theory. A survey conducted by The Institute for Corporate Productivity showed only 24 percent of 324 employee respondents rated their company as good in terms of transitioning employees to managers.

Sixty percent of those employees surveyed said their companies do not utilize 360-degree feedback mechanisms or other performance metrics to gauge the transitional success of new managers. This is cause for concern because many of the promoted employees are at the point of taking their new position very seriously and want to achieve in their new position, but their company is not necessarily giving them the tools to be successful. Companies argue that these metrics are costly, but in the long run many experts feel these companies who shortchange their managers' training will pay the far more costly price of mismanagement.

Source: Adapted from Aparna Nancheria, "Mismanaged Transitions," *Training & Development,* October 29, 2009, p. 18.

Most BARSs use the term *job dimension* to mean those broad categories of duties and responsibilities that make up a job. Each job is likely to have several job dimensions, and separate scales must be developed for each. Table 11.4 illustrates a BARS written for the job dimension found in many managerial jobs of planning, organizing, and scheduling project assignments and due dates. Scale values appear on the left side of the table and define specific categories of performance. Anchors, which appear on the right side, are specific written statements of actual behaviors that, when exhibited on the job, indicate the level of performance on the scale opposite that particular anchor. As the anchor statements appear beside each scale value, they are said to "anchor" each scale value along the scale.

Rating performance using a BARS requires the rater to read the list of anchors on each scale to find the group of anchors that best describe the employee's job behavior during the period being reviewed. The scale value opposite the group of anchors is then checked. This

TABLE 11.3

Sample Items on a Graphic Rating Scale

Quantity of work—the amount of work an employee does in a workday

( )	( )	( )	( )	( )
Does not meet minimum requirements.	Does just enough to get by.	Volume of work is satisfactory.	Very industrious, does more than is required.	Has a superior work production record.

Dependability—the ability to do required jobs well with a minimum of supervision

( )	( )	( )	( )	( )
Requires close supervision; is unreliable.	Sometimes requires prompting.	Usually completes necessary tasks with reasonable promptness.	Requires little supervision; is reliable.	Requires absolute minimum of supervision.

Job knowledge—information an employee should have on work duties for satisfactory job performance

( )	( )	( )	( )	( )
Is poorly informed about work duties.	Lacks knowledge of some phases of job.	Is moderately informed; can answer most questions about the job.	Understands all phases of job.	Has complete mastery of all phases of job.

Accuracy—the correctness of work duties performed

( )	( )	( )	( )	( )
Makes frequent errors.	Careless, often makes errors.	Usually accurate, makes only average number of mistakes.	Requires little supervision; is exact and precise most of the time.	Requires absolute minimum of supervision; is almost always accurate.

TABLE 11.4

Example of a Behaviorally Anchored Rating Scale

Source: C. E. Schneier and R. W. Beatty, from *Review of Public Personnel Administration*, p. 60, copyright © 1979. Reprinted by permission of Sage Publications, Inc.

Scale Values	Anchors
7[ ] Excellent	Develops a comprehensive project plan, documents it well, obtains required approval, and distributes the plan to all concerned.
6[ ] Very good	Plans, communicates, and observes milestones; states week by week where the project stands relative to plans. Maintains up-to-date charts of project accomplishments and backlogs and uses these to optimize any schedule modifications required.
	Experiences occasional minor operational problems but communicates effectively.
5[ ] Good	Lays out all the parts of a job and schedules each part; seeks to beat schedule and will allow for slack.
	Satisfies customers' time constraints; time and cost overruns occur infrequently.
4[ ] Average	Makes a list of due dates and revises them as the project progresses, usually adding unforeseen events; instigates frequent customer complaints.
	May have a sound plan, but does not keep track of milestones; does not report slippages in schedule or other problems as they occur.
3[ ] Below average	Plans are poorly defined; unrealistic time schedules are common.
	Cannot plan more than a day or two ahead; has no concept of a realistic project due date.
2[ ] Very poor	Has no plan or schedule of work segments to be performed.
	Does little or no planning for project assignments.
1[ ] Unacceptable	Seldom, if ever, completes project because of lack of planning, and does not seem to care.
	Fails consistently due to lack of planning and does not inquire about how to improve.

process is followed for all the identified dimensions of the job. The total evaluation combines the scale values checked for all job dimensions.

BARSs are normally developed through a series of meetings that both managers and job incumbents attend. Three steps are usually followed:

1. Managers and job incumbents identify the relevant job dimensions for the job.
2. Managers and job incumbents write behavioral anchors for each job dimension. As many anchors as possible should be written for each dimension.
3. Managers and job incumbents reach a consensus concerning the scale values to be used and the grouping of anchor statements for each scale value.

The use of a BARS can result in several advantages. First, BARSs are developed through the active participation of both managers and job incumbents. This increases the likelihood that the method will be accepted. Second, the anchors are developed from the observations and experiences of employees who actually perform the job. Finally, BARSs can be used to provide specific feedback concerning an employee's job performance.

One major drawback to the use of BARSs is that they take considerable time and commitment to develop. Furthermore, separate forms must be developed for different jobs. From a technical point of view, BARS is a graphic rating scale that was developed to help overcome errors in performance appraisals that are discussed later in this chapter.

Critical-Incident Appraisal

critical-incident appraisal
Method of performance appraisal in which the rater keeps a written record of incidents that illustrate both positive and negative employee behaviors. The rater then uses these incidents as a basis for evaluating the employee's performance.

The **critical-incident appraisal** method requires the evaluator to keep a written record of incidents as they occur. The incidents recorded should involve job behaviors that illustrate both satisfactory and unsatisfactory performance of the employee being rated. As they are recorded over time, the incidents provide a basis for evaluating performance and providing feedback to the employee.

The main drawback to this approach is that the rater is required to jot down incidents regularly, which can be burdensome and time consuming. Also, the definition of a critical incident is unclear and may be interpreted differently by different people. This method may

TABLE 11.5
Sample Checklist Questions

	Yes	No
1. Does the employee lose his or her temper in public?	_____	_____
2. Does the employee play favorites?	_____	_____
3. Does the employee praise employees in public when they have done a good job?	_____	_____
4. Does the employee volunteer to do special jobs?	_____	_____

also lead to friction between the manager and employees when the employees believe the manager is keeping a "book" on them.

Essay Appraisal

essay appraisal
Method of performance appraisal in which the rater prepares a written statement describing an employee's strengths, weaknesses, and past performance.

The **essay appraisal** method requires that the evaluation describe an employee's performance in written narrative form. Instructions are often provided as to the topics to be covered. A typical essay appraisal question might be "Describe, in your own words, this employee's performance, including quantity and quality of work, job knowledge, and ability to get along with other employees. What are the employee's strengths and weaknesses?" The primary problem with essay appraisals is that their length and content can vary considerably, depending on the rater. For instance, one rater may write a lengthy statement describing an employee's potential and little about past performance; another rater may concentrate on an employee's past performance. Thus, essay appraisals are difficult to compare. The writing skill of the appraiser can also affect the appraisal. An effective writer can make an average employee look better than the actual performance warrants. It is possible to use a critical-incident method to support the essay methods, however.

Checklist

checklist
Method of performance appraisal in which the rater answers with a yes or no a series of questions about the behavior of the employee being rated.

In the **checklist** method, the rater makes yes-or-no responses to a series of questions concerning the employee's behavior. Table 11.5 lists some typical questions. The checklist can also assign varying weights to each question.

Normally the human resource department keeps the scoring key for the checklist method; the evaluator is generally not aware of the weights associated with each question. But raters can see the positive or negative connotation of each question, which introduces bias. Additional drawbacks to the checklist method are that it is time-consuming to assemble the questions for each job category, a separate listing of questions must be developed for each job category, and the checklist questions can have different meanings for different raters.

Forced-Choice Rating

forced-choice rating
Method of performance appraisal that requires the rater to rank a set of statements describing how an employee carries out the duties and responsibilities of the job.

Many variations of the **forced-choice rating** method exist. The most common practice requires the evaluator to rank a set of statements describing how an employee carries out the duties and responsibilities of the job. Table 11.6 illustrates a group of forced-choice statements. The statements are normally weighted, and the rater generally does not know the weights. After the rater ranks all the forced-choice statements, the human resource department applies the weights and computes a score.

This method attempts to eliminate evaluator bias by forcing the rater to rank statements that are seemingly indistinguishable or unrelated. However, the forced-choice method has been

TABLE 11.6
Sample Set of Forced-Choice Statements

Instructions: Rank the following statements according to how they describe the manner in which this employee carries out duties and responsibilities. Rank 1 should be given to the most descriptive, and Rank 5 to the least descriptive. No ties are allowed.

Rank	Description
_____	Is easy to get acquainted with.
_____	Places great emphasis on people.
_____	Refuses to accept criticism.
_____	Thinks generally in terms of money.
_____	Makes decisions quickly.

reported to irritate raters, who feel they are not being trusted. Furthermore, the results of the forced-choice appraisal can be difficult to communicate to employees.

Ranking Methods

ranking methods
Methods of performance appraisal in which the performance of an employee is ranked relative to the performance of others.

When it becomes necessary to compare the performance of two or more employees, ranking methods can be used. Three of the more commonly used **ranking methods** are alternation, paired comparison, and forced distribution.

Alternation Ranking

The alternation ranking method lists the names of the employees to be rated on the left side of a sheet of paper. The rater chooses the most valuable employee on the list, crosses that name off the left-hand list, and puts it at the top of the column on the right-hand side of the paper. The appraiser then selects and crosses off the name of the least valuable employee from the left-hand column and moves it to the bottom of the right-hand column. The rater repeats this process for all of the names on the left-hand side of the paper. The resulting list of names in the right-hand column gives a ranking of the employees from most to least valuable.

Paired Comparison Ranking

Paired comparison ranking is best illustrated with an example. Suppose a rater is to evaluate six employees. The names of these individuals are listed on the left side of a sheet of paper. The evaluator then compares the first employee with the second employee on a chosen performance criterion, such as quantity of work. If he or she believes the first employee has produced more work than the second employee, a check mark is placed by the first employee's name. The rater then compares the first employee to the third, fourth, fifth, and sixth employee on the same performance criterion, placing a check mark by the name of the employee who produced the most work in each paired comparison. The process is repeated until each employee has been compared to every other employee on all of the chosen performance criteria. The employee with the most check marks is considered to be the best performer. Likewise, the employee with the fewest check marks is the lowest performer. One major problem with the paired comparison method is that it becomes unwieldy when comparing more than five or six employees.

Forced Distribution

The forced-distribution method requires the rater to compare the performance of employees and place a certain percentage of employees at various performance levels. It assumes the performance level in a group of employees will be distributed according to a bell-shaped, or "normal," curve. Figure 11.1 illustrates how the forced-distribution method works. The rater is required to rate 60 percent of the employees as meeting expectations, 20 percent as exceeding expectations, and 20 percent as not meeting expectations.

FIGURE 11.1
Forced-Distribution Curve

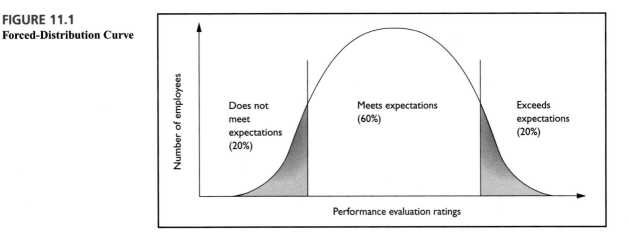

TABLE 11.7
Frequently Used Methods for Setting Work Standards

Method	Areas of Applicability
Average production of work groups	When tasks performed by all employees are the same or approximately the same.
Performance of specially selected employees	When tasks performed by all employees are basically the same and it would be cumbersome and time-consuming to use the group average.
Time study	When jobs involve repetitive tasks.
Work sampling	Noncyclical types of work where many different tasks are performed and there is no set pattern or cycle.
Expert opinion	When none of the more direct methods (described above) apply.

One problem with the forced-distribution method is that in small groups of employees, a bell-shaped distribution of performance may not be applicable. Even where the distribution may approximate a normal curve, it is probably not a perfect curve. This means some employees probably will not be rated accurately. Also, ranking methods differ dramatically from the other methods in that one employee's performance evaluation is a function of the performance of other employees in the job. Furthermore, the Civil Service Reform Act does not permit the use of ranking methods for federal employees.

Work Standards

work standards approach
Method of performance appraisal that involves setting a standard or an expected level of output and then comparing each employee's level to the standard.

The **work standards approach** to performance appraisal is most frequently used for production employees and is basically a form of goal setting for these employees. It involves setting a standard or an expected level of output and then comparing each employee's performance to the standard. Generally, work standards should reflect the average output of a typical employee. Work standards attempt to define a fair day's output. Several methods can be used to set work standards. Some of the more common ones are summarized in Table 11.7.

An advantage of the work standards approach is that the performance review is based on highly objective factors. Of course, to be effective, the affected employees must view the standards as being fair. The most serious criticism of work standards is a lack of comparability of standards for different job categories.

leniency
Occurs in performance appraisals when a manager's ratings are grouped at the positive end instead of being spread throughout the performance scale.

POTENTIAL ERRORS IN PERFORMANCE APPRAISALS

central tendency
Tendency of a manager to rate most employees' performance near the middle of the performance scale.

Several common errors have been identified in performance appraisals. **Leniency** is the grouping of ratings at the positive end instead of spreading them throughout the performance scale. The **central tendency** occurs when appraisal statistics indicate that most employees are appraised as being near the middle of the performance scale. **Recency** occurs when evaluations are based on work performed most recently—generally work performed one to two months prior to evaluation. Leniency, central tendency, and recency errors make it difficult, if not impossible, to separate the good performers from the poor performers. In addition, these errors make it difficult to compare ratings from different raters. For example, it is possible for a good performer who is evaluated by a manager committing central tendency errors to receive a lower rating than a poor performer who is rated by a manager committing leniency errors.

recency
Tendency of a manager to evaluate employees on work performed most recently—one or two months prior to evaluation.

Another common error in performance appraisals is the **halo effect.** This occurs when a rater allows a single prominent characteristic of an employee to influence his or her judgment on each separate item in the performance appraisal. This often results in the employee receiving approximately the same rating on every item.

halo effect
Occurs when a rater allows a single prominent characteristic of an employee to influence his or her judgment on each separate item in the performance appraisal.

Personal preferences, prejudices, and biases can also cause errors in performance appraisals. Managers with biases or prejudices tend to look for employee behaviors that conform to their biases. Appearance, social status, dress, race, and sex have influenced many performance appraisals. Managers have also allowed first impressions to influence later judgments of an employee. First impressions are only a sample of behavior; however, people tend to retain these impressions even when faced with contradictory evidence.[5]

OVERCOMING ERRORS IN PERFORMANCE APPRAISALS

Employers must evaluate employees based on their overall performance to avoid potential errors.
© Brand X Pictures/PunchStock

As the preceding discussion indicates, the potential for errors in performance appraisals is great. One approach to overcoming these errors is to make refinements in the design of appraisal methods. For example, one could argue that the forced-distribution method of performance appraisal attempts to overcome the errors of leniency and central tendency. In addition, behaviorally anchored rating scales are designed to reduce halo, leniency, and central tendency errors because they provide managers with specific examples of performance against which to evaluate an employee. Unfortunately, because refined instruments frequently do not overcome all the obstacles, it does not appear likely that refining appraisal instruments will totally overcome errors in performance appraisals.

A more promising approach to overcoming errors in performance appraisals is to improve the skills of raters. Suggestions on the specific training that should be given to evaluators are often vague, but they normally emphasize that evaluators should be trained to observe behavior more accurately and judge it more fairly.

More research is needed before a definitive set of topics for rater training can be established. However, at a minimum, raters should receive training in the performance appraisal method(s) used by the company, the importance of the rater's role in the total appraisal process, the use of performance appraisal information, and the communication skills necessary to provide feedback to the employee.[6]

PROVIDING FEEDBACK THROUGH THE APPRAISAL INTERVIEW

After one of the previously discussed methods for developing an employee's performance appraisal has been used, the results must be communicated to the employee. Unless this interview is properly conducted, it can and frequently does result in an unpleasant experience for both manager and employee.

To prepare for the interview, the manager should answer the following questions:

1. What results should the interview achieve?
2. What good contributions is the employee making?
3. Is the employee working up to his or her potential?
4. Is the employee clear about the manager's performance expectations?
5. What training does the employee need to improve?
6. What strengths does the employee have that can be built on or improved?

In addition, the manager should remember several basic guidelines in conducting the interview:

1. The manager must know the employee's job description.
2. The evaluation must be based on the employee's performance and not on his or her personality.
3. The manager must be positive and build on the employee's strengths.
4. The manager must be candid and specific.
5. The manager must listen to the employee as well as presenting her or his own views.
6. The manager must elicit employee feedback on how to improve performance.

Some of the more important factors influencing the success or failure of appraisal interviews are the following:

1. The more employees are allowed to participate in the appraisal process, the more satisfied they will be with the appraisal interview and with the manager and the more likely they will be to accept and meet performance improvement objectives.[7]

PERFORMANCE IMPROVEMENT PLAN

There are 10 key items to focus on when attempting to improve a performance problem and looking for ways to improve the performance of an employee. The 10 items to remember are as follows:

1. Define the problem.
2. Define the duties or behaviors where improvement is required.
3. Establish the priorities of the duties.
4. Identify the standards upon which performance will be measured for each of the duties identified.
5. Establish short-range and long-range goals and timetables for accomplishing change in performance/behavior with employee.
6. Develop an action plan.
7. Establish periodic review dates.
8. Measure actual performance against the standards to determine if expectations were met or exceeded.
9. Establish a performance improvement file for the employee.
10. Put the performance improvement plan in writing.

Source: Adapted from Indiana University Human Resources, "Performance Improvement Plan," *Indiana University Human Resource Services,* 2009.

2. The more a manager uses positive motivational techniques (e.g., recognizing and praising good performance), the more satisfied the employee is likely to be with the appraisal interview and with the manager.

3. When the manager and the employee mutually set specific performance improvement objectives more improvement in performance results than when the manager uses a general discussion or criticism.

4. Discussing and solving problems that may be hampering the employee's current job performance improve the employee's performance.

5. The more thought and preparation that both the manager and the employee devote before the appraisal interview, the greater the benefits of the interview.

6. The more the employee perceives that performance appraisal results are tied to organizational rewards, the more beneficial the interview will be.

Many of the variables that have been identified and associated with positive outcomes from performance appraisal interviews are behaviors and skills that managers responsible for conducting the interviews can learn. The human resource department should play a key role in developing and implementing these training programs. HRM in Action 11.3 describes the components of a performance improvement plan.

DEVELOPING PERFORMANCE IMPROVEMENT PLANS

Earlier in this chapter, we stated that a completed performance appraisal should include a performance improvement plan. This important step is often ignored. However, managers must recognize that an employee's development is a continuous cycle of setting performance goals, providing training necessary to achieve the goals, assessing performance related to accomplishing the goals, and then setting new, higher goals.[8] A performance improvement plan consists of the following components:

1. *Where are we now?* This question is answered in the performance appraisal process.
2. *Where do we want to be?* This requires the evaluator and the person being evaluated to mutually agree on the areas that can and should be improved.
3. *How does the employee get from where he or she is now to where he or she wants to be?* This component is critical to the performance improvement plan. The manager and employee must agree upon specific steps to be taken. The steps may include training the employee will need to improve his or her performance and how the evaluator will help the employee achieve the performance goals.

PERFORMANCE APPRAISAL AND THE LAW

Title VII of the Civil Rights Act permits the use of a bona fide performance appraisal system. Performance appraisal systems generally are not considered to be bona fide when their application results in adverse effects on minorities, women, or older employees.

A number of court cases have ruled that performance appraisal systems used by organizations were discriminatory and not job related. In one case involving layoffs, *Brito et al.* v. *Zia Company,* Spanish-surnamed workers were reinstated with back pay because the company had used a performance appraisal system of unknown validity in an uncontrolled and unstandardized manner. In *Mistretta* v. *Sandia Corporation,* performance appraisals were used as the main basis of layoff decisions, affecting a disproportionate number of older employees. The judge awarded the plaintiffs double damages plus all court costs.

In *Chamberlain* v. *Bissel, Inc.,* an evaluator expressed dissatisfaction with an employee's performance but did not inform the employee that his job was in jeopardy. On being terminated, the employee sued the company, claiming he had never been warned that he might be dismissed. The Michigan state court ruled the company had been negligent in not informing the employee that he might be fired and awarded the employee $61,354 in damages.

In *Price Waterhouse* v. *Hopkins,* the plaintiff, Ann Hopkins, charged she was denied a partnership at Price Waterhouse because of sexual stereotyping. Although Hopkins had generated more new business and logged more billable hours than any other candidate for partner, she was denied partnership consideration because the partners concluded she lacked the proper interpersonal skills. The court ruled that the interpersonal skills category was a legitimate performance evaluation measure, but it found that some of the evaluations of Hopkins were sexual stereotyping. For example, one member of the firm advised Hopkins to walk, talk, and dress in a more feminine fashion. In its decision, the Supreme Court found that Price Waterhouse had violated Title VII of the Civil Rights Act and stated that evaluating employees by assuming or insisting that they match a stereotype was illegal.

Many suggestions have been offered for making performance appraisal systems more legally acceptable. Some of these include (1) deriving the content of the appraisal system from job analyses; (2) emphasizing work behaviors rather than personal traits; (3) ensuring that the results of appraisals are communicated to employees; (4) ensuring that employees are allowed to give feedback during the appraisal interview; (5) training managers in how to conduct proper evaluations; (6) ensuring that appraisals are written, documented, and retained; and (7) ensuring that personnel decisions are consistent with the performance appraisals.[9]

Summary of Learning Objectives

1. **Define *performance.***

   Performance refers to the degree of accomplishment of the tasks that make up an employee's job.

2. **Define *performance appraisal.***

   Performance appraisal involves determining and communicating to an employee how he or she is performing the job and, ideally, establishing a plan of improvement.

3. **Explain management by objectives.**

   Management by objectives (MBO) consists of establishing clear and precisely defined statements of objectives for the work to be done by an employee, developing an action plan indicating how these objectives are to be achieved, allowing the employee to implement this action plan, measuring objective achievement, taking corrective action when necessary, and establishing new objectives for the future. MBO also requires that employees participate in the objective-setting process.

4. **Describe multi-rater assessment.**

   Multi-rater assessment is a method of assessment under which managers, customers, and colleagues evaluate performance.

5. **Describe the graphic rating scale.**

   With this method, the rater assesses an employee on factors such as quantity of work completed, dependability, job knowledge, attendance, accuracy of work, and cooperativeness.

6. **Explain critical-incident appraisal.**

   This method requires the rater to keep a written record of incidents as they occur. Incidents should involve job behaviors that illustrate both satisfactory and unsatisfactory performances of the employee being rated.

7. **Describe essay appraisal.**

   The essay appraisal method requires that the rater describe an employee's performance in narrative form.

8. **Describe the checklist method of performance appraisal.**

   In this method, the rater makes yes-or-no responses to a series of questions concerning the employee's behavior.

9. **Explain the forced-choice method of performance appraisal.**

   In this method, the rater is required to rank a set of statements describing how an employee carries out the duties and responsibilities of the job.

10. **Describe the work standards approach to performance appraisal.**

    The work standards approach involves setting a standard or expected level of output and then comparing each employee's performance to the standard.

11. **Define *leniency, central tendency, recency,* and the *halo effect*.**

    Leniency refers to grouping ratings at the positive end of a curve instead of spreading them throughout the performance scale. Central tendency occurs when appraisal statistics indicate that most employees are appraised as being near the middle of the performance scale. Recency occurs when evaluations are based only on work performed most recently. The halo effect occurs when a rater allows a single prominent characteristic of an employee to influence his or her judgment on each separate item in the performance appraisal.

Key Terms

behaviorally anchored rating scale (BARS), *217*
central tendency, *222*
checklist, *220*
critical-incident appraisal, *219*
essay appraisal, *220*

forced-choice rating, *220*
graphic rating scale, *217*
halo effect, *222*
leniency, *222*
management by objectives (MBO), *216*
performance, *214*

performance appraisal, *215*
ranking methods, *221*
recency, *222*
work standards approach, *222*

Review Questions

1. Define *performance appraisal.*
2. What is performance? What factors influence an employee's level of performance?
3. Give at least three uses of performance appraisal information.
4. Describe the following methods used in performance appraisal:
   a. Management by objectives.
   b. Multi-rater assessment.
   c. Graphic rating scale.
   d. Behaviorally anchored rating scale (BARS).
   e. Critical-incident.
   f. Essay.
   g. Checklist.
   h. Forced-choice rating.

    i. Ranking methods.

    j. Work standards.

5. Define the following types of performance appraisal errors:

    a. Leniency.

    b. Central tendency.

    c. Recency.

    d. Halo effect.

6. Outline some conditions associated with the success or failure of appraisal interviews.

7. Describe some conditions that might make a performance appraisal system illegal.

8. Outline some recommendations for ensuring a legally acceptable performance appraisal system.

Discussion Questions

1. How often do you think performance appraisals should be conducted?

2. What do you think about discussing salary raises and promotions during the performance appraisal interview?

3. What performance appraisal method do you believe would best apply to the evaluation of a college professor?

4. Was your last exam a performance appraisal? Use your last exam to discuss both the reasons for using performance appraisals and the limitations of such appraisals.

Incident 11.1

The College Admissions Office

Bob Luck was hired to replace Alice Carter as administrative assistant in the admissions office of Claymore Community College. Before leaving, Alice had given a month's notice to the director of admissions, hoping this would allow ample time to locate and train her replacement. Alice's responsibilities included preparing and mailing transcripts at the request of students, mailing information requested by people interested in attending the college, answering the telephone, assisting students or potential enrollees who came to the office, and general supervision of clerical personnel and student assistants.

After interviewing and testing many people for the position, the director hired Bob, mainly because his credentials were good and he made a favorable impression. Alice spent many hours during the next 10 days training Bob. He appeared to be quite bright and seemed to quickly pick up the procedures involved in operating a college admissions office. When Alice left, everyone thought Bob would do an outstanding job.

However, little time had elapsed before people realized that Bob had not caught on to his job responsibilities. Bob seemed to have personal problems that were severe enough to stand in the way of his work. He asked questions about subjects that Alice had covered explicitly; he should have been able to answer these himself if he had comprehended her instructions.

Bob appeared to constantly have other things on his mind. He seemed to be preoccupied with such problems as his recent divorce, which he blamed entirely on his ex-wife, and the distress of his eight-year-old daughter, who missed her father terribly. His thoughts also dwelled on his search for peace of mind and some reasons for all that had happened to him. The director of admissions was aware of Bob's preoccupation with his personal life and his failure to learn the office procedures rapidly.

Questions

1. What would you do at this point if you were the director of admissions?

2. Describe how you might effectively use a performance appraisal in this situation.

Incident 11.2

The Lackadaisical Plant Manager

Plant manager Paul Dorn wondered why his boss, Leonard Hech, had sent for him. He thought Leonard had been tough on him lately, and he was slightly uneasy at being asked to come to Leonard's office at a time when such meetings were unusual. "Close the door and sit down, Paul," invited Leonard. "I've been wanting to talk to you." After preliminary conversation, Leonard said that because Paul's latest project had been finished, he would receive the raise he had been promised on its completion.

Leonard went on to say that it was time for Paul's performance appraisal and they might as well do that now. Leonard explained that the performance appraisal was based on four criteria: (1) amount of high-quality merchandise manufactured and shipped on time, (2) quality of relationships with plant employees and peers, (3) progress in maintaining employee safety and health, and (4) reaction to demands of top management. The first criterion had a weight of 40 percent, and the rest had a weight of 20 percent each.

On the first item, Paul received an excellent rating. Shipments were at an all-time high, quality was good, and few shipments had arrived late. On the second item, Paul was also rated excellent. Leonard said plant employees and peers related well to Paul, labor relations were excellent, and there had been no major grievances since Paul had become plant manager.

However, on attention to matters of employee safety and health, the evaluation was below average. Leonard stated that no matter how much he prodded Paul about improving housekeeping in the plant, Paul never seemed to produce results. He also rated Paul below average on meeting demands from top management. He explained that Paul always answered yes to any request and then disregarded it, going about his business as if nothing had happened.

Seemingly surprised at the comments, Paul agreed that perhaps Leonard was right and that he should do a better job on these matters. Smiling as he left, he thanked Leonard for the raise and the frank appraisal.

As weeks went by, Leonard noticed little change in Paul. He reviewed the situation with an associate. "It's frustrating. In this time of rapid growth, we must make constant changes in work methods. Paul agrees but can't seem to make people break their habits and adopt more efficient ones. I find myself riding him very hard these days, but he just calmly takes it. He's well liked by everyone. But somehow he's got to care about safety and housekeeping in the plant. And when higher management makes demands he can't meet, he's got to say, 'I can't do that and do all the other things you want, too.' Now he has dozens of unfinished jobs because he refuses to say no."

As he talked, Leonard remembered something Paul had told him in confidence once. "I take Valium for a physical condition I have. When I don't take it, I get symptoms similar to a heart attack. But I only take half as much as the doctor prescribed." Now, Leonard thought, I'm really in a spot. If the Valium is what is making him so lackadaisical, I can't endanger his health by asking him to quit taking it. And I certainly can't fire him. Yet, as things stand, he really can't implement all the changes necessary to fulfill the goals we have set for the next two years.

Questions

1. What would you do if you were in Leonard's place?
2. What could have been done differently during the performance appraisal session?

EXERCISE 11.1

Developing a Performance Appraisal System

A large manufacturing company has been having difficulty with its performance evaluation system. All operating employees and clerical employees are evaluated semiannually by their supervisors. The form the organization has been using appears in Exhibit 11.A; it has been in use for 10 years. The form is scored as follows: excellent = 5, above average = 4, average = 3, below average = 2, and poor = 1. The scores for each facet are entered in the right-hand column and totaled for an overall evaluation score.

EXHIBIT 11.A
A Performance
Evaluation Form

Performance Evaluation

Supervisors: When you are asked to do so by the human resource department, please complete this form on each of your employees. The supervisor who is responsible for 75 percent or more of an employee's work should complete this form on the employee. Please evaluate each facet of the employee separately.

Facet			Rating		Score
Quality of work	Excellent	Above average	Average	Below average	Poor
Quantity of work	Poor	Below average	Average	Above average	Excellent
Dependability at work	Excellent	Above average	Average	Below average	Poor
Initiative at work	Poor	Below average	Average	Above average	Excellent
Cooperativeness	Excellent	Above average	Average	Below average	Poor
Getting along with coworkers	Poor	Below average	Average	Above average	Excellent

Total _____

Supervisor's signature _____

Employee name _____

Employee number _____

In the procedure used, each supervisor rates each employee on July 30 and January 30. The supervisor discusses the rating with the employee and then sends the rating to the human resource department. Each rating is placed in the employee's personnel file. If promotions come up, the cumulative ratings are considered at that time. The ratings are also supposed to be used as a check when raises are given.

The system was designed by Joanna Kyle, the human resource manager who retired two years ago. Her replacement was Eugene Meyer. Meyer graduated 15 years ago with a degree in business from the University of Texas. Since then, he's had a variety of work experience, mostly in manufacturing. For about five of those years, he worked in human resources.

Meyer has been reviewing the evaluation system. Employees have a mixture of indifferent and negative feelings about it. An informal survey has shown that about 60 percent of the supervisors fill the forms out, give about three minutes to each form, and send them to the human resource department without discussing them with the employees. Another 30 percent do a little better. They spend more time completing the forms but communicate about them only briefly and superficially with their employees. Only about 10 percent of the supervisors seriously try to do what was intended.

Meyer also found out that the forms were rarely used for promotion or pay raise decisions. Because of this, most supervisors may have felt the evaluation program was a useless ritual. Where he had been previously employed, Meyer had seen performance appraisal as a much more useful experience, which included giving positive feedback to employees, improving future employee performance, developing employee capabilities, and providing data for promotion and compensation.

Meyer has not had much experience with the design of a performance appraisal system. He believes he should seek advice on the topic.

Write a report summarizing your evaluation of the strengths and weaknesses of the present appraisal system. Recommend some specific improvements or data-gathering exercises to develop a better system.

Notes and Additional Readings

1. See Dayton Fandray, "The New Thinking in Performance Appraisals," *Workforce,* May 2001, pp. 36–40. See also Matthew J. Camardella, "Effective Management of the Performance-Appraisal Process," *Employment Relations Today,* Spring 2003, p. 103.
2. See David Martone, "A Guide to Developing a Competency-Based Performance-Management System," *Employment Relations Today,* Fall 2003, p. 23.
3. See Harry Levinsin, "Management by Whose Objectives?" *Harvard Business Review,* January 2003, p. 107.
4. See Ginka Toegel and Jay A. Conger, "360-Degree Assessment: Time for Reinvention," *Academy of Management Learning & Education,* September 2003, p. 297.

5. See Edwin Arnold and Marcia Pulich, "Personality Conflicts and Objectivity in Appraising Performance," *The Health Care Manager,* July–Sept., p. 227.

6. See W. David Rees and Christine Porter, "Appraisal Pitfalls and the Training Implications—Part 1," *Industrial and Commercial Training* 35 (2003), p. 280.

7. See Gary E. Roberts, "Employee Performance Appraisal System Participation: A Technique That Works," *Public Personnel Management,* Spring 2003, pp. 89–99.

8. See Terry Gillen, "Appraisal: How to Make It Achieve What You Want It To," *Training Journal,* Sept. 2003, p. 10. See also Charles N. Painter, "Ten Steps for Improved Appraisals," *SuperVision,* Oct. 2003, p. 12.

9. See Inge C. Kerssens-van Drongelen and Olaf A. M. Fisscher, "Ethical Dilemmas in Performance Measurement," *Journal of Business Ethics,* June 2003, p. 51.

Human Resources

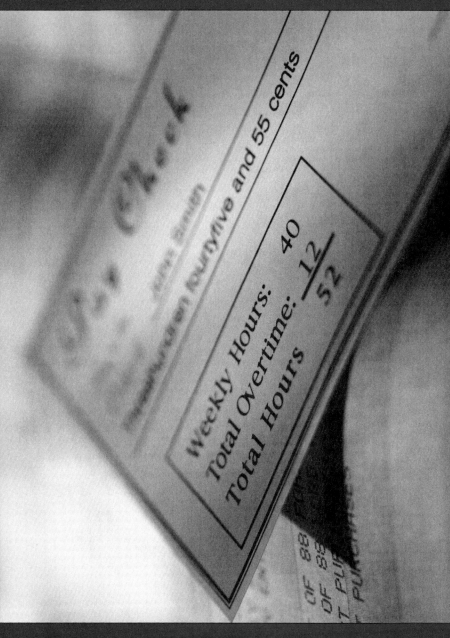

Steve Cole/Getty Images

Chapter **Twelve**

The Organizational Reward System

Chapter Learning Objectives

After studying this chapter, you should be able to:

1. Define organizational rewards.
2. Distinguish between intrinsic and extrinsic rewards.
3. List several desirable preconditions for implementing a pay-for-performance program.
4. Define job satisfaction and list its five major components.
5. Summarize the satisfaction–performance relationship.
6. Define compensation, pay, incentives, and benefits.
7. List several pieces of government legislation that have had a significant impact on organizational compensation.
8. Explain the equity theory of motivation.
9. Discuss internal, external, individual, and organizational equity.

Chapter Outline

Few things evoke as much emotion as the organization's reward system. Employees often interpret the design and use of the organizational reward system as a reflection of management attitudes, intentions, and the entire organizational climate. Because of this, the organizational reward system is one of the most effective motivation tools managers have at their disposal. The responsibility for coordinating and administering the system usually resides with the human resource manager.

TABLE 12.1
Intrinsic versus Extrinsic Rewards

Intrinsic Rewards	Extrinsic Rewards
Achievement	Formal recognition
Feelings of accomplishment	Fringe benefits
Informal recognition	Incentive payments
Job satisfaction	Pay
Personal growth	Promotion
Status	Social relationships
	Physical work environment

DEFINING THE SYSTEM

organizational reward system
Organizational system concerned with the selection of the types of rewards to be used by the organization.

organizational rewards
Rewards that result from employment with the organization; includes all types of rewards, both intrinsic and extrinsic.

The **organizational reward system** consists of the types of rewards to be offered and their distribution. **Organizational rewards** include all types of rewards, both intrinsic and extrinsic, that are received as a result of employment by the organization. **Intrinsic rewards** are internal to the individual and are normally derived from involvement in certain activities or tasks. Job satisfaction and feelings of accomplishment are examples of intrinsic rewards. Most **extrinsic rewards** are directly controlled and distributed by the organization and are more tangible than intrinsic rewards. Pay and hospitalization benefits are examples of extrinsic rewards. Table 12.1 provides examples of both types of rewards.

Though intrinsic and extrinsic rewards differ, they are also closely related. Often an extrinsic reward provides the recipient with intrinsic rewards. For example, an employee who received an extrinsic reward in the form of a pay raise may also experience feelings of accomplishment (an intrinsic reward) by interpreting the pay raise as a sign of a job well done.

SELECTION OF REWARDS

intrinsic rewards
Rewards internal to the individual and normally derived from involvement in certain activities or tasks.

extrinsic rewards
Rewards that are controlled and distributed directly by the organization and are of a tangible nature.

Selection of the rewards to be offered is critical if the reward system is to function effectively. As a first step, management must recognize what employees perceive as meaningful rewards. Pay is usually the first, and sometimes the only, reward most people think about. There is little doubt that pay is a very significant reward. However, rewards should be viewed in the larger perspective as anything employees value and may include things such as office location, the allocation of certain pieces of equipment, the assignment of preferred work tasks, and informal recognition.

If an organization is going to distribute rewards—and all do—why should it not get the maximum in return? Such a return can be realized only if the desires of employees are known. Organizations should learn what employees perceive as meaningful rewards, which is not necessarily what management perceives. Traditionally, managers have assumed they are fully capable of deciding just what rewards employees need and want. Unfortunately, this is often not true. Rewards don't necessarily have to be costly to be valued. Studies have shown that employees tend to rank lack of recognition as the most probable reason good employees quit their jobs. One survey asked employees to rank job incentives. The first choice was a personal thank-you, followed by a handwritten note of thanks from the supervisor. Money came in at a surprising sixteenth.[1]

Another closely related, and often false, assumption is exemplified by the fact that most organizations offer the same mix of rewards to all employees. Studies have shown that many variables, such as age, sex, marital status, number of dependents, and years of service, can influence employee preferences for certain rewards.[2] For example, older employees are usually much more concerned with pension and retirement benefits than are younger employees. Recent research has also shown that employees in different countries have different preferences regarding incentives.[3] This is especially relevant in today's global environment.

Another dimension to be considered when selecting the types of rewards to offer is the intrinsic benefits that might accrue as a result of the rewards. All too often, managers and employees alike consider only the tangible benefits associated with a reward.

In addition to the internal factors just mentioned are external factors that place limitations on an organization's reward system. These factors include such things as the organization's size, environmental conditions, the stage in the product life cycle, and the labor market. Since these external factors are usually beyond the control of the organization, this chapter will concentrate primarily on internal factors.

RELATING REWARDS TO PERFORMANCE

The free enterprise system is based on the premise that rewards should depend on performance. This performance–reward relationship is desirable not only at the organizational or corporate level but also at the individual level. The underlying theory is that employees will be motivated when they believe such motivation will lead to desired rewards. Unfortunately, many formal rewards provided by organizations are not related to performance. Rewards in this category, including paid vacations, insurance plans, and paid holidays, are almost always determined by organizational membership and seniority rather than by performance.

Other rewards, such as promotion, can and should be related to performance. However, opportunities for promotion may occur only rarely. When available, the higher positions may also be filled on the basis of seniority or by someone outside the organization.

The primary organizational variable used to reward employees and reinforce performance is pay. Even though many U.S. companies have some type of pay-for-performance program, most do a poor job of relating the two.[4] Surveys repeatedly show that employees do not have much confidence that a positive relationship exists between performance and pay. For example, a 2006 survey of 10,000 respondents by Hudson Talent Management, a staffing and outsourcing firm, found that only 35 percent of the respondents believed that performance was the deciding factor in determining their pay.[5] A later study by Authoria Inc. found that only 15 percent of respondents believed that compensation was used effectively for aligning individual and corporate performance.[6] There is evidence, however, that paying for performance is becoming more prevalent at the highest levels in many companies. Surveys by *The Wall Street Journal* and the Hay Group found that performance-based compensation plans overtook stock options as the most popular of long-term incentive compensation in 2007 and 2008.[7]

If relating rewards to performance is desirable, why is the practice not more widespread? One answer is that it is not easy to do; it is much easier to give everybody the same thing, as evidenced by the ever-popular across-the-board pay increase. Relating rewards to performance requires that performance be accurately measured, and this is often not easily accomplished (Chapter 11 discussed performance appraisal). It also requires discipline to actually relate rewards to performance. Another reason is that many union contracts require that certain rewards be based on totally objective variables, such as seniority. While no one successful formula for implementing a pay-for-performance program has yet been developed, a number of desirable preconditions have been identified and generally accepted:

1. *Trust in management.* If employees are skeptical of management, it is difficult to make a pay-for-performance program work.
2. *Absence of performance constraints.* Since pay-for-performance programs are usually based on an employee's ability and effort, the jobs must be structured so that an employee's performance is not hampered by factors beyond his or her control.
3. *Trained supervisors and managers.* The supervisors and managers must be trained in setting and measuring performance standards.
4. *Good measurement systems.* Performance should be based on criteria that are job specific and focus on results achieved.
5. *Ability to pay.* The merit portion of the salary increase budget must be large enough to get the attention of employees.
6. *Clear distinction among cost of living, seniority, and merit.* In the absence of strong evidence to the contrary, employees will naturally assume a pay increase is a cost-of-living or seniority increase.
7. *Well-communicated total pay policy.* Employees must have a clear understanding of how merit pay fits into the total pay picture.
8. *Flexible reward schedule.* It is easier to establish a credible pay-for-performance plan if all employees do not receive pay adjustments on the same date.[8]

**LINKING PAY TO PERFORMANCE
AT LINCOLN ELECTRIC**
www.lincolnelectric.com

Lincoln Electric Company celebrated its 115th anniversary in 2010. The Cleveland, Ohio–based manufacturer of arc welders has 9,000 employees in its global workforce. The U.S. employees do not belong to a union, have never gone out on strike, and deferred vacation when necessary to meet worldwide demand. Figures have shown that Lincoln's U.S. employees are two-and-a-half to three times more productive than employees of other, similar manufacturing companies.

The key to Lincoln's success is that the company bases pay on performance and sets virtually no limit on what employees can earn. For example, it is not unusual for top factory workers to receive sizeable bonuses and to make more than $100,000 per year. Lincoln's U.S. employees have not experienced a layoff since 1948 and have received an annual bonus every year since 1934. Once they have been with the company for three years, Lincoln's U.S. employees are also guaranteed their jobs until retirement if they agree to pay cuts or reassignment within the company when necessary. In response to demand, employees may work overtime or work fewer hours. According to John Stropki, chairman and CEO, "Most of our people get paid by the number of parts they produce. (Years ago) the Lincolns had the foresight to know that if they didn't guarantee employment, people would say (to each other), 'Make less, so we'll have a job even when things are slow.' The way we can be successful is having a high level of productivity all the time."

On December 12, 2008, Lincoln distributed profit-sharing bonuses totaling $89 million to employees. The distribution was the seventy-fifth consecutive year that Lincoln had paid a profit-sharing bonus.

Sources: Daniel Eisenberg, "When People Are Never Let Go," *Time*, June 18, 2001, p. 40; and Jennifer Gill, "How No Layoff Can Work," *BusinessWeek Online*, November 6, 2001, at http://www.businessweek.com; "Lincoln Electric Distributes 75th Consecutive Profit-Sharing Bonus—Gross Bonus Pool of $89 Million—Takes Actions to Weather Economic Uncertainty—Remains Committed to Guaranteed Employment Policy," *PR Newswire*, December 12, 2008, and www.lincolnelectric.com; accessed February 2, 2010.

HRM in Action 12.1 describes how Lincoln Electric Company has successfully related pay to performance.

JOB SATISFACTION AND REWARDS

job satisfaction
An employee's general attitude toward the job.

Organizational morale is boosted when an employee feels like part of a group.
© Brand X Pictures/PunchStock

organizational morale
An employee's feeling of being accepted by and belonging to a group of employees through adherence to common goals, confidence in the desirability of those goals, and the desire to progress toward the goals.

Job satisfaction is an employee's general attitude toward the job. The organizational reward system often has a significant impact on the level of employee job satisfaction. In addition to their direct impact, the manner in which the extrinsic rewards are dispersed can affect the intrinsic rewards (and satisfaction) of the recipients. For example, if everyone receives an across-the-board pay increase of 5 percent, it is hard to derive any feeling of accomplishment from the reward. However, if pay raises are related directly to performance, an employee who receives a healthy pay increase will more than likely also experience feelings of accomplishment and satisfaction. A 2009 study of more than 600 employees by the Society for Human Resource Management (SHRM) reported that job security was cited as the most important factor in job satisfaction by 63 percent of the respondents.[9] This same survey taken in 2008 also found job security to be the most important determinant of job satisfaction. These findings are not surprising given the economic downturn that occurred in these years: Benefits was the second most important in both 2008 and 2009. Compensation/pay came in third for both of these years. Prior to the economic downturn, compensation/pay had held or tied for the top spot for the previous two years (2006 and 2007). These figures indicate that the major determinants of job satisfaction can vary from year to year depending on both internal and external factors. Other variables that have been found to have a significant impact on job satisfaction the last several years include opportunities to use skills and abilities, feeling safe in the workplace, relationship with immediate supervisor, and flexibility to balance life and work issues.

Job satisfaction is not synonymous with **organizational morale**, which is a feeling of being accepted by and belonging to a group of employees through adherence to common goals, confidence in the desirability of those goals, and the desire to progress toward the goals. Morale is the by-product of a group, whereas job satisfaction is more an individual state of mind. Morale refers to how a person feels about the organization he or she is working for, whereas job satisfaction is about how an employee feels about his or her particular job. However, the two concepts are interrelated in that job satisfaction can contribute to morale and morale can contribute to job satisfaction. HRM in Action 12.2 discusses the status of job satisfaction in the United States.

The Satisfaction–Performance Controversy

For many years, managers generally have believed that a satisfied employee is necessarily a good employee. In other words, if management could keep all employees happy, good performance would automatically follow. Years ago Professor Charles Greene suggested that many managers subscribe to this belief because it represents "the path of least resistance."[10] Greene's thesis is that if a performance problem exists, increasing an employee's happiness is far more pleasant than discussing with the employee his or her failure to meet standards. Before discussing the satisfaction–performance controversy, we should point out that there are subtle but real differences between being satisfied and being happy. Although happiness eventually results from satisfaction, the latter goes much deeper and is far less tenuous than happiness.

The following incident illustrates two propositions concerning the satisfaction–performance relationship:

> As Ben walked by, smiling on the way to his office, Ben's boss remarked to a friend, "Ben really enjoys his job, and that's why he's the best worker I ever had. And that's reason enough for me to keep Ben happy." The friend replied, "No, you're wrong! Ben likes his job because he does it so well. If you want to make Ben happy, you ought to do whatever you can to help further improve his performance."[11]

The first proposition is the traditional view that satisfaction causes performance. The second is that satisfaction is the effect rather than the cause of performance. In this position, performance leads to rewards that result in a certain level of satisfaction. Thus, rewards constitute a necessary intervening variable in the relationship. Another position considers both satisfaction and performance to be functions of rewards. It postulates that satisfaction results from rewards, but current performance also affects subsequent performance if rewards are based on current performance.

Research evidence generally rejects the more popular view that satisfaction leads to performance. However, it does provide moderate support for the view that performance leads to satisfaction. The evidence also strongly indicates that (1) rewards constitute a more direct cause of satisfaction than does performance and (2) rewards based on current performance enhance subsequent performance.[12]

While the assumption that job satisfaction and job performance are related has much intuitive appeal, reviews of the studies in this area do not support a strong relationship. A comprehensive review of over 100 published studies involving job satisfaction and job performance found that "the best estimate of the true population correlation between satisfaction and performance is relatively low."[13] In spite of the weak correlation between job satisfaction and job performance, lay people often tend to believe strongly that satisfied employees are more productive at work.[14] One relationship that has been clearly established is that job

FIGURE 12.1
Determinants of Employee Satisfaction and Dissatisfaction

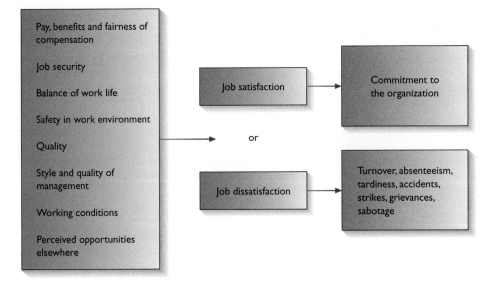

satisfaction does have a positive impact on turnover, absenteeism, tardiness, accidents, grievances, and strikes.[15] Studies have also reported that experience, gender, and performance can have a moderating effect on these relationships.[16] In addition, organizations prefer satisfied employees simply because such employees make the work environment more pleasant. Thus, even though a satisfied employee is not necessarily a high performer, there are numerous reasons for cultivating employee satisfaction.

Other Factors Affecting Job Satisfaction

As mentioned earlier, a wide range of both internal and external factors affect an employee's level of satisfaction. Throughout the 1990s employee job-satisfaction surveys generally found that base pay ranked third, fourth, or lower in factors that most influenced job satisfaction.[17] However, this has changed over the last several years. For example, the 2009 survey by SHRM (referenced earlier) found that the top drivers of employee job satisfaction were job security, benefits, pay, opportunities to use skills and abilities, and feeling safe in the work environment.[18] The left portion of Figure 12.1 summarizes these and other factors that determine an employee's level of satisfaction or dissatisfaction. The total impact of these factors causes employees to be either generally satisfied or dissatisfied with their jobs. As the right side of Figure 12.1 indicates, employees who are satisfied with their jobs tend to be committed to the organization; these employees are likely to be very loyal and dependable. Employees who are dissatisfied with their jobs tend to behave in ways that can be detrimental to the organization; these employees are likely to have higher rates of turnover, absenteeism, tardiness, accidents, strikes, and grievances.

Job satisfaction and motivation are not synonymous. Motivation is a drive to perform, whereas job satisfaction reflects the employee's attitude toward or happiness with the job situation. As Figure 12.1 suggests, a satisfied or "happy" employee is not necessarily a motivated or productive employee. The organizational reward system can influence both job satisfaction and employee motivation. The reward system affects job satisfaction by making the employee more or less comfortable as a result of the rewards received. The reward system influences motivation primarily through the perceived value of the rewards and their contingency on performance.

compensation
All the extrinsic rewards that employees receive in exchange for their work: composed of the base wage or salary, any incentives or bonuses, and any benefits.

pay
Refers only to the actual dollars employees receive in exchange for their work.

EMPLOYEE COMPENSATION

Compensation and pay are not synonymous terms. **Compensation** refers to all the extrinsic rewards employees receive in exchange for their work. **Pay** refers only to the actual dollars employees receive in exchange for their work. Usually compensation is composed of the

TABLE 12.2
Components of Employee Compensation

Base Wage or Salary	Incentives	Benefits
Hourly wage	Bonuses	Paid vacation
Weekly, monthly, or annual salary	Commissions	Health insurance
Overtime pay	Profit sharing	Life insurance
	Piece rate plans	Retirement pension

base wage or salary
Hourly, weekly, or monthly pay that employees receive for their work.

incentives
Rewards offered in addition to the base wage or salary and usually directly related to performance.

benefits
Rewards employees receive as a result of their employment and position with the organization.

base wage or salary, any incentives or bonuses, and any benefits. The base wage or salary is the hourly, weekly, or monthly pay employees receive for their work. **Incentives** are rewards offered in addition to the base wage or salary and are usually directly related to performance. **Benefits** are rewards employees receive as a result of their employment and position with the organization. Paid vacations, health insurance, and retirement plans are examples of benefits. Table 12.2 presents some examples of the different types of compensation. The next three chapters cover base wages or salaries, incentives, and benefits, respectively.

Compensation Policies

Certain policies must be formulated before a successful compensation system can be developed and implemented. Naturally, these policies are strongly influenced by the organization's objectives and its environments. Policies must deal with the following issues:

1. Minimum and maximum levels of pay (taking into consideration the worth of the job to the organization, the organization's ability to pay, government regulations, union influences, and market pressures).
2. General relationships among levels of pay (e.g., between senior management and operating management, operative employees, and supervisors).
3. The division of the total compensation dollar (i.e., what portion goes into base pay, incentive programs, and benefits).

In addition to these issues, organizations must make decisions concerning how much money will go into pay increases for the next year, who will recommend them, and how raises will generally be determined. Another important decision concerns whether pay information will be kept secret or made public.

Pay Secrecy

Many organizations have a policy of not disclosing pay-related information. This includes information about the pay system as well as individual pay received. The justification for *pay secrecy* is usually to avoid any discontent that might result from employees' knowing what everybody else is being paid. Further justification is that many employees, especially high achievers, feel very strongly that their pay is nobody else's business.[19]

On the other hand, pay secrecy makes it difficult for employees to determine whether pay is related to performance. Also, pay secrecy does not eliminate pay comparisons, and it may cause employees to overestimate the pay of their peers and underestimate the pay of their supervisors. Both situations can unnecessarily create feelings of dissatisfaction. Also, when managers refuse to disclose pay, employees naturally become suspicious and often conclude that the managers are hiding something. Prior to the National Labor Relations Board's (NLRB) ruling that it was illegal, some companies actually forbade employees to discuss and/or disclose their pay. In 1992, the NLRB ruled that forbidding employees to discuss their pay constitutes a violation of the National Labor Relations Act (the National Labor Relations Act is discussed in Chapter 18).[20] Recently, women's groups in the United States and the United Kingdom have begun to challenge pay-secrecy rules on the grounds that they perpetuate the income gap between men and women.[21]

A good compromise on the issue of pay secrecy is to disclose the pay ranges for various job levels within the organization. This approach clearly communicates the general ranges of pay for different jobs, but it does not disclose exactly what any particular employee is making.

Government and Union Influence

Government legislation and union contracts can have a significant impact on organizational compensation. Both of these factors are discussed in the following sections.

Davis-Bacon Act

Passed by Congress on March 3, 1931, the *Davis-Bacon Act* required that contractors and subcontractors on federal construction contracts in excess of $2,000 pay the prevailing wage rates for the locality of the project. This prevailing wage rate, which is determined by the secretary of labor, has normally been the same as the prevailing union rate for the area. Overtime of time-and-a-half must be paid for more than 40 hours per week.

Walsh-Healey Public Contracts Act

The *Walsh-Healey Public Contracts Act,* passed by Congress on June 30, 1936, requires that organizations manufacturing or furnishing materials, supplies, articles, or equipment in excess of $10,000 to the federal government pay at least the minimum wage for the industry as determined by the secretary of labor. Originally the Walsh-Healey Act called for overtime pay for anything over eight hours in a single day. However, the Defense Authorization Act of 1986 changed the requirement to overtime for hours worked over 40 in a week.

Fair Labor Standards Act (FLSA)

The *FLSA,* commonly called the Wage and Hour Act, was passed in 1938 and has been amended several times. Its primary requirements are that individuals employed in interstate commerce or in organizations producing goods for interstate commerce must be paid a certain minimum wage and be paid time-and-a-half for hours over 40 worked in one week. (Table 12.3 shows how the minimum wage has changed over the years.) Section 218 of the FLSA permits states, localities, and collective bargaining agreements to set a higher standard than the federal minimum. In addition, the FLSA places restrictions on the employment of individuals between ages 14 and 18. The most complex parts of the law deal with possible exemptions. Amendments to the law have reduced the number of exemptions, but careful study is necessary to determine an organization's obligations.

Discussions of compensation systems often use the terms *exempt* and *nonexempt personnel.* Nonexempt employees are covered by the FLSA; they must be paid overtime and are subject to minimum wage. Exempt employees are not covered by the FLSA and include executive, administrative, and professional employees.

Equal Pay Act

The *Equal Pay Act* was introduced and discussed in Chapter 2. Signed into law on June 10, 1963, the Equal Pay Act was an amendment to the Fair Labor Standards Act, eliminating pay differentials based solely on sex. The law makes it illegal to pay different wages to men and

TABLE 12.3
History of Minimum Wage Rates

Date	Rate per Hour	Date	Rate per Hour
October 24, 1938	$0.25	January 1, 1976	$2.30
October 24, 1939	0.30	January 1, 1978	2.65
October 24, 1945	0.40	January 1, 1979	2.90
January 25, 1950	0.75	January 1, 1980	3.10
March 1, 1956	1.00	January 1, 1981	3.35
September 3, 1961	1.15	April 1, 1990	3.80
September 3, 1963	1.25	April 1, 1991	4.25
February 1, 1967	1.40	October 1, 1996	4.75
February 1, 1968	1.60	September 1, 1997	5.15
May 1, 1974	2.00	July 24, 2007	5.85
January 1, 1975	2.10	July 24, 2008	6.55
		July 24, 2009	7.25

women for jobs that require equal skill, effort, and responsibility and are performed under similar conditions. This law does not prohibit the payment of wage differentials based on seniority systems, merit systems that measure earnings by quantity and quality of production, or systems based on any factor other than sex.

Federal Wage Garnishment Law

garnishment

A legal procedure by which an employer is empowered to withhold wages for payment of an employee's debt to a creditor.

Garnishment is a legal procedure by which an employer is empowered to withhold wages for payment of an employee's debt to a creditor. The Federal Wage Garnishment Law, which became effective on July 1, 1970, limits the amount of an employee's disposable earnings that can be garnished in any one week and protects the employee from discharge because of garnishment. However, the law did not substantially alter state laws on this subject. For instance, if the state prohibits or provides for more limited garnishment than the federal law, the state law is applied. Thus, a human resource manager must be familiar with state laws applicable to garnishment.

Lilly Ledbetter Fair Pay Act of 2009

The Lilly Ledbetter Fair Pay Act was passed in 2009 and made retroactive to May 28, 2007. Prior to the Ledbetter Act, an employee had a narrow window (180 or 300 days, depending on the state) within which to bring a lawsuit against his or her employer for unfair pay or discrimination pay practices. Under the Ledbetter Act the statute of limitations on pay discrimination claims begins running whenever a discriminatory pay decision or pay practice is adopted, when an individual becomes subject to such a decision or practice, and/or whenever the paycheck or other benefit is issued.

The Ledbetter Act is named after Lilly Ledbetter, a former supervisor at an Alabama Goodyear Tire & Rubber Company plant. Ledbetter sued Goodyear after discovering that she had been paid less than her male colleagues for almost 19 years. A jury ruled in favor of Ledbetter but that decision was overturned by the Supreme Court in 2007. The Supreme Court ruled that Ledbetter should have filed suit within 180 days of the very first time Goodyear paid her less than her peers. The Ledbetter Fair Pay Act was passed in response to that ruling and basically eliminated any time limitations.

Union Contracts

If an organization is unionized, the wage structure is usually largely determined through the collective bargaining process. Because wages are a primary concern of unions, current union contracts must be considered in formulating compensation policies. Union contracts can even affect nonunionized organizations. For example, the wage rates and increases paid to union employees often influence the wages paid to employees in nonunion organizations. Unions are discussed at length in Chapters 18 and 19.

Impact of Comparable Worth

Comparable worth theory, introduced in Chapter 3, holds that while the true worth of jobs to the employer may be similar, some jobs (especially those held by women) are often paid at a lower rate than other jobs (often held by men). A major problem associated with comparable worth theory is determining the worth of the jobs in question. How should job worth be established? U.S. courts have generally rejected cases based on comparable worth claims.[22] Although comparable worth has generally floundered in court, it has received considerable attention at the collective bargaining table and in the political arena.[23]

The Importance of Fair Pay

As discussed earlier in this chapter employee motivation is closely related to the types of rewards offered and their method of disbursement. While there is considerable debate over the motivational aspect of pay, little doubt exists that inadequate pay can have a very negative impact on an organization. Figure 12.2 presents a simple model that summarizes the reactions of employees when they are dissatisfied with their pay. According to this model, pay dissatisfaction can influence employees' feelings about their jobs in two ways: (1) It can increase the

FIGURE 12.2 **Model of the Consequences of Pay Dissatisfaction**

Source: Adapted from Edward E. Lawler III, *Pay and Organizational Effectiveness: A Psychological View* (New York: McGraw-Hill, 1971), p. 233.

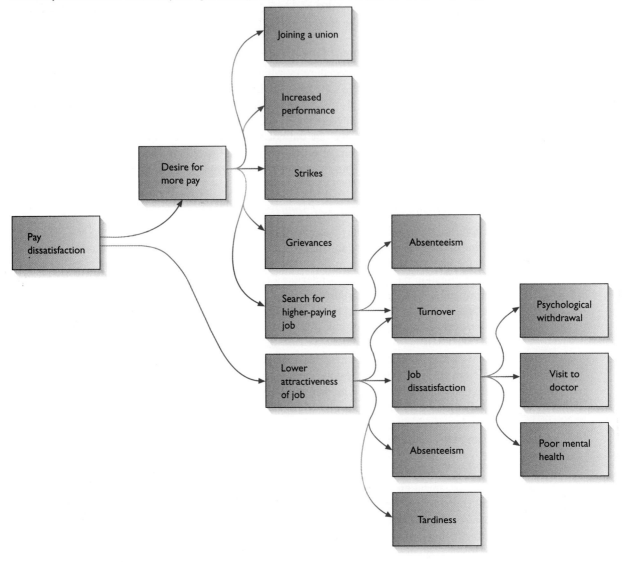

desire for more money, and (2) it can lower the attractiveness of the job. An employee who desires more money is likely to engage in actions that can increase pay. These actions might include joining a union, looking for another job, performing better, filing a grievance, or going on strike. With the exception of performing better, all of the consequences are generally classified as undesirable by management. Better performance results only in those cases where pay is perceived as being directly related to performance. On the other hand, when the job decreases in attractiveness, the employee is more likely to be absent or tardy, quit, or become dissatisfied with the job itself. Thus, while its importance may vary somewhat from situation to situation, pay satisfaction can and usually does have a significant impact on employee performance.

The fairness of executive pay has received much attention in recent years as the pay of top executives has soared to astronomical levels in some situations. This issue is discussed at length in the next chapter.

Pay Equity

The equity theory of motivation basically holds that employees have a strong need to maintain a balance between what they perceive as their inputs to their jobs and what they receive from their jobs in the form of rewards. In this theory, employees who perceive inequities will

GENDER PAY INEQUITIES

While the pay gap between women and men has narrowed over the past 30 years, it is still substantial. The good news is that while the gap closed only 1 percentage point from 1970, when women earned 59 percent as much as men, to 1980, when they earned 60 percent as much, it closed by 8 points from 1980 to 1989.

In 1992, the gap continued to close. Based on median weekly earnings, women working full-time earned 75 cents for every dollar earned by men full-time; by 1994, the figure had grown to 77 cents. Unfortunately from 1994 to 1998 the figure dropped back down to 76 cents.

In 1999 women again earned approximately 77 percent as much as men and by 2003 the figure had grown to 80 percent. The ratio was 80.3 percent in 2004 and peaked at 81 percent for 2005. The figure slipped to 80.7 percent in 2006, 80.2 percent in 2007, and 80.0 percent in 2008.

While women have made some progress regarding equal pay, the progress has been slow and still has some distance to go. The gap has not changed significantly in the last several years and remains around 20 percent.

Not surprisingly, studies have found that men tend to be more satisfied with their pay when compared to others within their organizations than do women.

Sources: Diane Crispell, "Women's Earnings Gap Is Closing—Slowly," *American Demographics,* February 1991, p. 14; Steven E. Rhoas, "Pay Equity Won't Go Away," *Across the Board,* July–August 1993, pp. 37–41; Teresa Brady, "How Equal Is Equal Pay?" *Management Review,* March 1998, pp. 59–61; "Gender Gap Narrowed in 2005," *HR Focus,* December 2006, p. 12; "Highlights of Women's Earnings in 2008," U.S. Department of Labor, July 2009, www.bls.gov.

internal equity
Addresses what an employee is being paid for doing a job compared to what other employees in the same organization are being paid to do their jobs.

external equity
Addresses what employees in an organization are being paid compared to employees in other organizations performing similar jobs.

individual equity
Addresses the rewarding of individual contributions; is very closely related to the pay-for-performance question.

organizational equity
Addresses how profits are divided up within the organizations.

take action to eliminate or reduce them. For example, if an employee believes he or she is underpaid, that employee will likely reduce expended effort by working more slowly, taking off early, or being absent. Similarly, if an employee believes she or he is being overpaid, that employee is likely to work harder or for longer hours.

Pay equity concerns whether employees believe they are being fairly paid. There are several dimensions of equity to consider in looking at pay equity. **Internal equity** concerns what an employee is being paid for doing a given job compared to what other employees in the same organization are being paid to do their jobs. **External equity** deals with what employees in other organizations are being paid for performing similar jobs. **Individual equity** addresses the issue of rewarding individual contributions and is very closely related to the pay-for-performance question. **Organizational equity** concerns how profits are divided up within the organization. In other words, do the employees believe the organization's profits are fairly distributed? It is important to recognize that employee interpretations of pay equity are based on their perceptions. Because employee feelings about pay equity are based on perceptions, organizations should do whatever they can to make these perceptions as accurate as possible. Also, it is not unusual for an employee to feel good about one or more of the equity dimensions and feel bad about the others. For example, an employee may feel good about his or her pay in comparison to what friends working in other organizations are making. She or he may also believe the company profits are fairly distributed within the company. However, this same person may be very unhappy about his or her pay relative to several other people in the same organization. HRM in Action 12.3 discusses pay inequities between women and men in today's work environment.

Pay Satisfaction Model

Figure 12.3 presents a model of the determinants of pay satisfaction. The model is based on the idea that employees will be satisfied with their pay when their perception of what their pay is and of what they think it should be agree. This happens when employees feel good about the internal and external equity of their pay.

Naturally, present pay is a primary factor influencing an employee's perception of equity. However, the person's wage history and perception of what others are getting also have an influence. For example, employees who have historically received high pay tend to lower their perception of present pay. Similarly, the higher the pay of friends and peers, the lower one's individual pay appears to be. These factors account for the fact that two people may view the same level of pay in a very different manner.

The model also shows that an employee's perception of what pay should be depends on several other factors, including job inputs, the perceived inputs and outcomes of friends and

FIGURE 12.3 **Model of the Determinants of Pay Satisfaction**

Source: Edward E. Lawler III, *Pay and Organizational Effectiveness: A Psychological View* (New York: McGraw-Hill, 1971), p. 215.

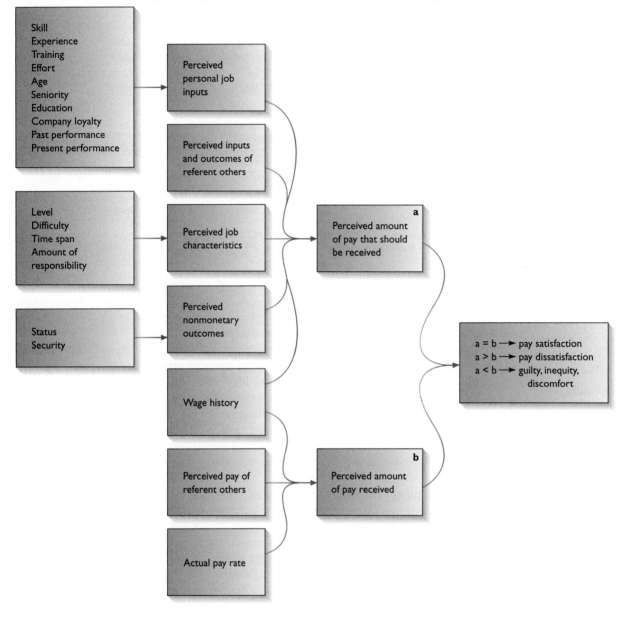

peers, and nonmonetary outcomes. Job inputs include all the experience, skills, and abilities an employee brings to the job in addition to the effort the employee puts into it. The perceived inputs and outcomes refer to the individual's perception of what friends and peers put into their jobs and what kind of pay they get in return. The nonmonetary outcomes received refer to the fact that certain nonmonetary rewards can sometimes substitute for pay, at least up to a point.

The model also makes allowances for employees who believe their pay *exceeds* what they think it should be. Research has shown that in such cases, people often experience feelings of guilt, inequity, and discomfort.[24]

THE ROLE OF THE HUMAN RESOURCE MANAGER IN THE REWARD SYSTEM

The role of the human resource manager in the overall organizational reward system is to assist in its design and to administer the system. Administering the system inherently carries the responsibility of ensuring that the system is fair to all employees and that it is clearly

COMMUNICATING THE TOTAL COMPENSATION PACKAGE

Yahoo, one of the most recognized brands in the world, has more than 10,500 employees worldwide and annual revenues of more than $5.2 billion. Because many, if not most, employees do not understand the true value of their total compensation, Yahoo believed that they were losing talent to other employers who might pay a slightly higher base salary or hourly wage. To overcome this, to "get a bigger bang for its benefits buck," Yahoo recently implemented Web-based total reward statements (TRS). Yahoo also believed that the TRS program would help pave the way for medical premium cost sharing.

Yahoo worked with Enwisen to create Yahoo's My Life: My Rewards—a secure, Web-based TRS that is available 24 hours a day from home or work, and is updated every pay period. By accessing the TRS, employees could immediately better see the true value of their total compensations including such things as the value of their stock options (the average Yahoo employee has a stock option package with one-and-a-half to two-and-a-half times their base pay), 401(k) plan value, health care value and other indirect benefits such as fitness center, subsidized cafeteria, free lattes and other drinks, and the like.

Upon launch, 96 percent of Yahoo's employees viewed the TRS and Yahoo realized the following immediate benefits:

- Voluntary turnover for the three-month period after launch went down significantly.
- There was a measurable spike in 401(k) enrollment.
- Medical premium cost sharing was implemented with little resistance from employees.

As of January 2010 Yahoo accounted for about 17 percent of the total U.S. Internet searches, a distant second to Google, who captured approximately 66 percent.

Sources: Barbara Levin, "Attracting and Retaining Employees with Total Reward Statements: The Yahoo Way," *Workspan*, October 2006, pp. 35–37, and "Yahoo Posts Profit as Revenue Lags," *Informationweek*, January 27, 2010.

communicated to all employees. Ensuring that the system is fair places the burden of minimizing reward inequities and employees' perceptions of reward inequities squarely on the human resources manager. There is little doubt that organizations need to do a better job of explaining and communicating their compensation system to employees. For example, a survey conducted by Harris International and Charlton Consulting Group found that half of the employees surveyed underestimated the value of their total compensation.[25] HRM in Action 12.4 describes a tool that Yahoo has recently implemented to better communicate the true value of its compensation package.

Many tools and techniques are available to assist human resource managers in designing and administering compensation systems. Some of them are discussed in the following three chapters.

Summary of Learning Objectives	

1. **Define *organizational rewards*.**

   Organizational rewards include all types of rewards, both intrinsic and extrinsic, that are received as a result of employment by the organization.

2. **Distinguish between intrinsic and extrinsic rewards.**

   Intrinsic rewards are rewards internal to the employee and are normally derived from involvement in certain activities or tasks. Extrinsic rewards are directly controlled and distributed by the organization and are more tangible than intrinsic rewards.

3. **List several desirable preconditions for implementing a pay-for-performance program.**

   Several preconditions have been identified for implementing a successful pay-for-performance program. These include (1) trust in management; (2) absence of performance constraints; (3) trained supervisors and managers; (4) good measurement systems; (5) ability to pay; (6) a clear distinction among cost of living, seniority, and merit; (7) a well-communicated total pay policy; and (8) a flexible reward schedule.

4. **Define *job satisfaction* and list its five major components.**

   Job satisfaction is an employee's general attitude toward the job. The five major components of job satisfaction are (1) attitude toward the work group; (2) general working conditions, (3) attitude toward the company, (4) monetary benefits, and (5) attitude toward supervision.

5. **Summarize the satisfaction–performance relationship.**

   Research evidence generally rejects the popular view that satisfaction leads to performance. The evidence does, however, provide moderate support for the view that performance leads to satisfaction. The evidence also provides strong indications that rewards constitute a more direct cause of satisfaction than does performance, and rewards based on current performance lead to subsequent performance. In general, the best estimate of the correlation between satisfaction and performance is relatively low.

6. **Define *compensation, pay, incentives,* and *benefits*.**

   Compensation refers to all the extrinsic rewards employees receive in exchange for their work. Pay includes only the actual dollars employees receive in exchange for their work. Incentives are rewards offered in addition to the base wage or salary and are directly related to performance. Benefits are rewards employees receive as a result of their employment and position with an organization.

7. **List several pieces of government legislation that have had a significant impact on organizational compensation.**

   Numerous pieces of government legislation have affected organizational compensation. Some of the most significant include the Davis-Bacon Act, the Walsh-Healey Act, the Fair Labor Standards Act (FLSA), the Equal Pay Act, the Federal Wage Garnishment Law, and the Lilly Ledbetter Fair Pay Act.

8. **Explain the equity theory of motivation.**

   The equity theory of motivation holds that employees have a strong need to maintain a balance between what they perceive as their inputs to their jobs and what they receive from their jobs in the form of rewards. In this theory, employees who perceive inequities will take action to eliminate or reduce the inequities.

9. **Discuss internal, external, individual, and organizational equity.**

   Internal equity concerns what an employee is being paid for doing a given job compared to what other employees in the same organization are being paid to do their jobs. External equity deals with what employees in other organizations are being paid for performing similar jobs. Individual equity addresses rewarding individual contributions and is very closely related to the pay-for-performance question. Organizational equity concerns how profits are divided up within the organization.

Key Terms

base wage or salary, *239*
benefits, *239*
comparable worth, *241*
compensation, *238*
Davis-Bacon Act, *240*
Equal Pay Act, *240*
external equity, *243*
extrinsic rewards, *234*
Fair Labor Standards Act
  (FLSA), *240*

garnishment, *241*
incentives, *239*
individual equity, *243*
internal equity, *243*
intrinsic rewards, *234*
job satisfaction, *236*
organizational equity, *243*
organizational morale, *236*
organizational reward
  system, *234*

organizational rewards, *234*
pay, *238*
pay secrecy, *239*
Walsh-Healey Public
  Contracts Act, *240*

Review Questions

1. What are organizational rewards?
2. Explain the differences between intrinsic and extrinsic rewards.
3. What variables have been found to influence employee preferences for certain rewards?
4. Discuss two reasons organizations do a poor job of relating rewards to performance.
5. List eight preconditions that have been found to be desirable for establishing a successful pay-for-performance program.
6. What is job satisfaction? What are its major components?
7. Discuss the satisfaction–performance controversy.

8. Define *compensation* and distinguish it from *pay*.

9. What is the primary organizational variable that can be used to reward individuals and reinforce performance?

10. Describe some of the consequences of pay dissatisfaction.

11. What are the two general factors relating to the question of fair pay?

12. Describe the pay satisfaction model. How does it determine pay satisfaction?

Discussion Questions

1. XYZ Company has just decided to take all its 200 employees to Las Vegas for an expense-paid, three-day weekend to show its appreciation for their high level of performance this past year. What is your reaction to this idea?

2. Comment on the following statement: "Employees are not capable of deciding what rewards they should receive."

3. Recently a manager was overheard making the following comment: "Most employees are never satisfied with their pay anyway, so why should we even try? I think we should pay as little as possible and just accept the fact that the employees won't like it." If you were this manager's superior, what would you say?

4. Do you think a very loyal employee is necessarily a good employee? Why or why not?

Incident 12.1

An Informative Coffee Break

On Monday morning, April 28, George Smith was given the news that effective May 1 he would receive a raise of 6 percent. This raise came two months before his scheduled performance appraisal. His manager, Loretta Weeks, informed him that the basis for the raise was his performance over the past several months and his potential worth to the company. He was told this was a very considerable increase.

On Tuesday, a group of George's coworkers were having their normal coffee break. The conversation turned to salary increases. One member of the group had received a performance review in April, but no indication of an impending salary adjustment had been given. George made a comment concerning the amount of any such increase, specifically questioning the range of increase percentages. Another coworker responded that she was surprised to have received an across-the-board 4 percent increase the previous Friday. A third individual had received a similar salary increase. Definitely astounded, George pressed for information, only to learn that several people had received increases of "around" 3 to 5 percent. George excused himself and left the group.

That evening, George wrestled with his conscience concerning the discussion that day. His first impression of his raise was that it had been given based on performance. His second impression was decidedly sour. Several questions were bothering him:

1. Why did his boss present the raise as a merit increase?
2. Was job performance really a basis for salary increases in his department?
3. Did his boss hide the truth regarding the raise?
4. Could he trust his boss in the future?
5. On what basis would further increases be issued?

Questions

1. What effect do you think this new information will have on the effort George Smith puts forth?
2. What can Loretta Weeks do to regain George Smith's confidence?
3. Has the concept of pay secrecy backfired on Loretta Weeks in this case? If so, how?

Incident 12.2

Does Money Motivate?

About four months ago, Greg Holcomb was promoted to supervisor of the claims department for a large eastern insurance company. It is now time for all supervisors to make their annual salary increase recommendations. Greg doesn't feel comfortable in making these recommendations, since he had been in his job for only a short time. To further complicate the situation, the former supervisor has left the company and is unavailable for consultation.

There are no formal company restrictions on the kinds of raises that can be given, but Greg's boss has said the total amount of money available to Greg for raises would be 8 percent of Greg's total payroll for the past year. In other words, if the sum total of the salaries for all of Greg's employees were $100,000 Greg would have $8,000 to allocate for raises. Greg is free to distribute the raises just about any way he wants, within reason.

Summarized below is the best information on his employees that Greg can find from the files of the former supervisor of the claims department. This information is supplemented by feelings Greg has developed during his short time as supervisor.

Sam Jones: Sam has been with Greg's department for only five months. In fact, he was hired just before Greg was promoted into the supervisor's job. Sam is single and seems to be a carefree bachelor. His job performance so far has been above average, but Greg has received some negative comments about Sam from his coworkers. Present salary: $44,000.

Sue Davis: Sue has been on the job for three years. Her previous performance appraisals have indicated superior performance. However, Greg does not believe the previous evaluations are accurate. He thinks Sue's performance is average at best. Sue appears to be well liked by all of her coworkers. Just last year she became widowed and is presently the sole supporter of her five-year-old child. Present salary: $46,000.

Evelyn Boyd: Evelyn has been on the job for four years. Her previous performance appraisals were all average. In addition, she has received below-average increases for the past two years. However, Evelyn recently approached Greg and told him she feels she was discriminated against in the past due to both her age and her sex. Greg believes Evelyn's work so far has been satisfactory but not superior. Most employees do not seem to sympathize with Evelyn's accusations of sex and age discrimination. Present salary: $42,000.

Jane Simond: As far as Greg can tell, Jane is one of his best employees. Her previous performance appraisals also indicate she is a superior performer. In addition, Greg knows Jane badly needs a substantial salary increase due to some personal problems. In addition, all of Greg's employees are aware of Jane's problems. She appears to be well respected by her coworkers. Present salary: $43,000.

Ralph Dubose: Ralph has been performing his present job for eight years. The job is very technical, and he could be difficult to replace. However, as far as Greg can discern, Ralph is not a good employee. He is irritable and hard to work with. In spite of this, Ralph has received above-average pay increases for the past two years. Present salary: $48,000.

Questions

1. What size raise would you give each of these employees?
2. What criteria did you use in determining the size of the raises?
3. What do you think would be the feelings of the other people in the group if they found out what raises you recommend?
4. Do you think the employees would eventually find out what raises others received? Would it matter?

EXERCISE 12.1
Relating Rewards
to Performance

Think of the most recent job you held or that you currently hold. This job could have been a summer, part-time, or full-time job. Which of the two situations described below better characterizes this job?

A. Rewards (monetary and nonmonetary) were tied directly to one's level of performance; management attempted to discriminate between the high and low performers and reward accordingly.

B. Everyone within very broad, general categories received basically the same rewards; one's level of performance did not substantially affect the rewards received.

Depending on which situation you selected, what effect do you think it had on your level of motivation? If you selected situation A, explain basically how the system worked. If you selected situation B, what specific recommendations would you make to improve the performance–reward relationship? Be prepared to discuss your answers with the class.

Notes and
Additional
Readings

1. Kevin Wallsten, "Targeted Rewards Have Greater Value—and Bigger Impact," *Workforce,* November 1998, pp. 66–71; "Do Incentive Awards Work?" *HR Focus,* October 2000, pp. 1, 14; and Greg Pallone, "Cheap—But Highly Valued—Benefits," *Canadian HR Reporter,* November 2, 2009, pp. 16–17.

2. Scott Hays, "Health Benefits: Survey This! (and That)," *Workforce,* January 1999, pp. 93–94; Morley Gunderson and Andrew Luchak, "Employee Preferences for Pension Plan Features," *Journal of Labor Research,* Fall 2001, pp. 795–808.

3. Marjaana Gunkel, Edward J. Lusk, and Birgitta Wolff, "Country-Compatible Incentive Design," *Schmalenbach Business Review: ZFBF,* July 2009, pp. 290–309.

4. Frederick S. Hills, Robert M. Madigan, K. Dow Scott, and Steven E. Markham, "Tracking the Merit of Merit Pay," *Personnel Administrator,* March 1987, p. 50; Janet Wiscombe, "Can Pay for Performance Really Work?" *Workforce,* August 2001, pp. 28–34.

5. "Employees Say Tenure Tops Performance to Determine Pay," *IOMA's Report on Salary,* August 2006, p. 8; and "Pay for Performance Increases," *The Controller's Report,* January 2009, pp. 8–9.

6. "Firms Fail to Use Compensation Strategically to Drive Business Results," *IOMA's Report on Salary Surveys,* July 2007, p. 8.

7. "*The Wall Street Journal*/Hay Group 2008 CEO Compensation Study Reveals Companies Dialed Back Pay Levels in 2008," *Business Wire,* April 3, 2009.

8. Hills, Madigan, Scott, and Markham, "Tracking the Merit," pp. 56–57, Wiscombe, "Can Pay for Performance Really Work?"

9. "2009 Employee Job Satisfaction" (Alexandria, VA: The Society for Human Resource Management, 2009), p. 6.

10. Charles N. Greene, "The Satisfaction–Performance Controversy," *Business Horizons,* October 1972, p. 31; Shari Caudron, "Job Satisfaction May Not Be Everything," *Workforce,* www.workforce.com, February 15, 2001.

11. Greene, "The Satisfaction–Performance Controversy," p. 32.

12. Ibid., p. 40; Shari Caudron, "The Myth of Job Happiness," *Workforce,* www.workforce.com, September 6, 2001.

13. Michelle T. Iaffaldano and Paul M. Muchinsky, "Job Satisfaction and Job Performance: A Meta-Analysis," *Psychological Bulletin 97,* no. 2 (1985), pp. 251–73, and Michelle D. Jones, "Which Is a Better Predictor of Job Performance: Job Satisfaction or Life Satisfaction," *Journal of Behavioral and Applied Management,* September 2006, pp. 20–42.

14. Cynthia D. Fisher, "Why Do Lay People Believe That Satisfaction and Performance Are Correlated? Possible Sources of a Commonsense Theory," *Journal of Organizational Behavioral,* September 2003, p. 753.

15. Donald P. Schwab and Larry I. Cummings, "Theories of Performance and Satisfaction: A Review," *Industrial Relations,* October 1970, pp. 408–29. For a summary of the related research, see E. A. Locke, "The Nature and Causes of Job Satisfaction," in *Handbook of Industrial and Organizational Psychology,* ed. M. D. Dunnette (Skokie, Ill.: Rand McNally, 1976), p. 1343; also see Caudron, "The Myth of Job Happiness," and T. L. Stanley, "The Joy of Working: A New Look at Job Satisfaction," *Supervision,* September 2001, pp. 3–6.

16. Frederick A. Russ and Kevin M. McNeilly, "Links among Satisfaction, Commitment, and Turnover Intentions: The Moderating Effect of Experience, Gender, and Performance," *Journal of Business Research,* September 1995, pp. 57–65; Ellen R. Auster, "Professional Women's Midcareer Satisfaction: Toward an Explanatory Framework," *Sex Roles,* June 2001, pp. 719–50.

17. Michael Hickins, "Give a Little, Get a Lot," *Management Review,* October 1998, p. 6; see also Susan J. Lambert, "Added Benefits: The Link between Work Life Benefits and Organizational Citizenship Behavior," *Academy of Management Journal,* October 2000, pp. 801–15; Peggy Simonsen, "Do Your Managers Have the Right Stuff?" *Workforce* 78, no. 2 (August 1999), pp. 47–52.

18. "2009 Employee Job Satisfaction," *op. cit.*

19. P. Thompson and J. Pronsky, "Secrecy or Disclosure in Management Compensation," *Business Horizons,* June 1975, pp. 67–74; John Case, "When Salaries Aren't Secret," *Harvard Business Review,* May 2001, pp. 37–45, and Adrienne Colella, Ramona L. Paetzold, Asghar Zardkoohi, and Michael J. Wesson, "Exposing Pay Secrecy," *Academy of Management Review,* 32, no. 1, 2007, pp. 55–71.

20. Betty Southard Murphy, Wayne E. Barlow, and D. Diane Hatch, "Rule against Discussion of Salaries Violates NLRA," *Personnel Journal,* December 1992, pp. 22; Mary Williams Walsh, "The Biggest Company Secret: Workers Challenge Employer Policies on Pay *Confidentiality,*" *New York Times,* July 28, 2000.

21. Walsh, "The Biggest Company Secret," and "Gender Pay Divide Continues to Grow," *Personnel Today,* January 27, 2004, p. 43.

22. Betty Southard Murphy, Wayne E. Barlow, and D. Diane Hatch, "Comparable Worth Claims Rejected," *Personnel Journal,* January 1990, pp. 14–18; and Linda Chavez, "Comparable Worth," *The Wall Street Journal,* August 24, 2005, p. A 10.

23. Ibid., p. 18; Laura Pincis and Bill Shaw, "Comparable Worth: An Economic and Ethical Analysis," *Journal of Business Ethics,* April 1, 1998, pp. 455–70, and Linda Chavez, "Comparable Worth."

24. E. E. Lawler III, *Pay and Organizational Effectiveness: A Psychological View* (New York: McGraw-Hill, 1971), pp. 244–47.

25. "Rewards Are Now Critical to Keep Valued Employees," *IOMA's Report on Salary Surveys,* May 2007, pp. 1–4.

Base Wage and Salary Systems

Chapter Learning Objectives

After studying this chapter, you should be able to:

1. Define base wages and salaries and state the objective of any base wage and salary system.
2. Define job evaluation.
3. Name and briefly discuss the four basic conventional methods of job evaluation.
4. Explain the concepts of key jobs and compensable factors.
5. Differentiate between subfactors and degrees.
6. Explain the purpose of wage and salary surveys.
7. Discuss wage and salary curves.
8. Define pay grades and pay ranges.
9. Explain the concepts of broadbanding, skill-based pay, competency-based pay, market-based pay, and total rewards.

Chapter Outline

Objective of the Base Wage and Salary System

Conventional Job Evaluation
   Job Ranking Method
   Job Classification Method
   Point Method
   Factor Comparison Method
   Comparison of Job Evaluation Methods

Pricing the Job
   Wage and Salary Surveys
   Wage and Salary Curves

Base Wage/Salary Structure

New Approaches to the Base Wage/Salary Structure

   Broadbanding
   Skill-Based Pay
   Competency-Based Pay
   Market-Based Pay
   Total Rewards

Summary of Learning Objectives

Key Terms

Review Questions

Discussion Questions
   Incident 13.1: Fair Pay for Pecan Workers
   Incident 13.2: A Dead-End Street?

Exercise 13.1: Ranking Jobs

Exercise 13.2: Wage/Salary Survey

Notes and Additional Readings

---

base wages and salaries
Hourly, weekly, and monthly pay that employees receive for their work.

Base wages and salaries are the hourly, weekly, or monthly pay that employees receive in exchange for their work. In most situations, base wages or salaries make up the largest portion of an employee's total compensation. In light of the facts that many organizations do not pay incentives and many employees discount or take for granted the value of benefits, base wages and salaries are often the focus of the compensation system in the eyes of employees.

Base wages and salaries form the foundation for most employees' perceptions of the fairness, or equity, of the pay system. As discussed in the previous chapter, if employees do not perceive they are being fairly paid, many possible negative effects (tardiness, absenteeism,

FIGURE 13.1
Specific Policy Issues in Developing and Implementing a Base Wage and Salary Structure

Source: Henderson, Richard I., *Compensation Management: Rewarding Performance,* 2nd ed., pp. 98–102. © 1979. Reproduced by permission of Pearson Education, Inc., Upper Saddle River, New Jersey.

1. What is the lowest rate of pay that can be offered for a job that will entice the quality of employees the organization desires to have as its members?
2. What is the rate of pay that must be offered to employees to ensure that they remain with the organization?
3. Does the organization desire to recognize seniority and meritorious performance through the base pay schedule?
4. Is it wise or necessary to offer more than one rate of pay to employees performing either identical or similar work?
5. What is considered to be a sufficient difference in base rates of pay among jobs requiring varying levels of knowledge and skills and of responsibilities and duties?
6. Does the organization wish to recognize dangerous and distressing working conditions within the base pay schedule?
7. Should there be a difference in base pay progression opportunities among jobs of varying worth?
8. Do employees have a significant opportunity to obtain higher-level jobs? If so, what should be the relationship between promotion to a higher job and changes in base pay?
9. Will policies and regulations permit employees to earn rates of pay higher than established maximums and lower than established minimums? What would be the reasons for allowing such deviations?
10. How will the pay structure accommodate across-the-board, cost-of-living, or other adjustments not related to employee tenure, performance, or responsibility and duty changes?

turnover, strikes, etc.) may result. In addition, the base wage and salary system often reflects the atmosphere of the entire organization. If the base wage and salary system is perceived as being fair and equitable, the organization is usually viewed in the same light. Of course, the reverse is also true. It is therefore critical that an organization develop and maintain a sound base wage and salary system.

OBJECTIVE OF THE BASE WAGE AND SALARY SYSTEM

Web site: Job Star Central's Salary Info
www.jobstar.org/tools/salary

The primary objective of any base wage and salary system is to establish a structure for the equitable compensation of employees, depending on their jobs and their level of performance in their jobs. While this objective is straightforward, successfully attaining it is not easy. Figure 13.1 represents some of the basic policy questions that need to be addressed as a first step in establishing a base wage and salary system.

Most base wage and salary systems establish pay ranges for certain jobs based on the relative worth of the job to the organization. An employee's performance on the job should then determine where that employee's pay falls within the job's range. The key to a sound base wage and salary system is the establishment of different pay ranges for the various jobs within the organization. A pay range for a given job establishes a range of permissible pay, with a minimum and a maximum. Establishing pay ranges involves two basic phases: (1) determining the relative worth of the different jobs to the organization (ensuring internal equity) and (2) pricing the different jobs (ensuring external equity). Job evaluation is the primary method for determining the relative worth of jobs to the organization. Wage surveys represent one of the most commonly used methods for pricing jobs. Conventional job evaluations and wage surveys, as well as some new approaches to both, are discussed in the following sections.

CONVENTIONAL JOB EVALUATION

job evaluation
Systematic determination of the value of each job in relation to other jobs in the organization.

Job evaluation is a systematic determination of the value of each job in relation to other jobs in the organization. This process is used for designing a pay structure, not for appraising the performance of employees holding the jobs. The general idea of job evaluation is to enumerate the requirements of a job and the job's contribution to the organization and then classify it according to its importance. For instance, a design engineer's job would involve more complex requirements and a potentially greater contribution to an organization than that of an assembler of the designed product. Although both jobs are important, a determination must be made concerning the relative worth of each. While the overriding purpose of job evaluation

BENEFITS OF A JOB EVALUATION IN A SMALL ORGANIZATION

The Fawcett Society is a British charity that promotes sexual equality focusing on areas such as women's representation in politics and public life, equal pay, and the treatment of women in the justice system. The society traces its roots back to the 19th century.

Prompted by high staff turnover, partially the results of erratic funding, the Fawcett Society decided to review all of its HR practices including evaluating the jobs of all 10 employees. Dorothy Telfer, an HR consultant, was called in to oversee the exercise. Telfer began by explaining the concept of job evaluation and clearly differentiated job evaluation from performance appraisal. The goal at this point was to obtain "buy-in" from the staff and to answer questions about the process. Staff members were then asked to write their own job description in an agreed-upon format. A committee composed of staff and trustees then evaluated every job. Jobs were graded according to the skills and competencies needed to perform them. Specifically five factors were assessed: knowledge and expertise; decision making; thinking; leadership; and responsibility for resources.

Telfer believes the exercise enabled each staff member to better understand what he or she needed if they were to do their jobs well and ways in which they could improve their skills. The society's director, Katherine Rake, believes the process "gave staff a clear understanding of how they could move up and it produced a transparent framework for evaluating new posts."

Source: Matthew Little, "Case Study Job Evaluation," *Third Sector,* February 8, 2006, p. 18.

is to establish the relative worth of jobs, it can serve several other purposes. Figure 13.2 lists potential uses of job evaluations.

The first step in a job evaluation program is to gather information on the jobs being evaluated. Normally, information is obtained from current job descriptions. If current job descriptions do not exist, it is usually necessary to analyze the jobs and create up-to-date descriptions.

The job evaluation process then identifies the factor or factors to be used in determining the worth of different jobs to the organization. Some frequently used factors are knowledge, responsibility, and working conditions. The job evaluation process also involves developing and implementing a plan that uses the chosen factors for evaluating the relative worth of the different jobs to the organization. Such a plan should consistently place jobs requiring more of the factors at a higher level in the job hierarchy than jobs requiring fewer of the factors. HRM in Action 13.1 describes a simple job evaluation application and the benefits derived for a small British organization.

After turning to new and different methods for valuing jobs and work (these are discussed later in this chapter), there is evidence of a renewed interest in using job-focused approaches (primarily job evaluations) to compensation.[1] Most conventional job evaluation plans are variations or combinations of four basic methods: job ranking, job classification, point, and factor comparison.

Job Ranking Method

job ranking method
Job evaluation method that ranks jobs in order of their difficulty from simplest to most complex.

Job ranking is the simplest, oldest, and least often used job evaluation technique. In the **job ranking method,** the evaluator ranks jobs from the simplest to the most difficult. Often the evaluator prepares cards with basic information about the jobs and then arranges the cards in the order of importance of the positions. The job ranking method produces only an ordering of jobs and does not indicate the relative degree of difference among them. For example, a job with a ranking of four is not necessarily twice as difficult as a job with a ranking of two.

FIGURE 13.2
Potential Uses of Job Evaluations

Source: David W. Belcher and Thomas J. Atchison, *Compensation Administration,* 2nd ed. Used by permission of Economic Research Institute.

- To provide a basis for a simpler, more rational wage structure.
- To provide an agreed-on means of classifying new or changed jobs.
- To provide a means of comparing jobs and pay rates with those of other organizations.
- To provide a base for employee performance measurements.
- To reduce pay grievances by reducing their scope and providing an agreed-on means of resolving disputes.
- To provide incentives for employees to strive for higher-level jobs.
- To provide information for wage negotiations.
- To provide data on job relationships for use in internal and external selection, human resource planning, career management, and other personnel functions.

JACKSONVILLE UPDATES JOB CLASSIFICATIONS

For years, the city code of Jacksonville, Florida generally placed employees into two categories: civil service or exempt from civil service. Different job classifications are then listed under these two major categories. For years many mid-management-level positions, including risk managers, veterinarians, and budget analysts, did not clearly fit into any existing category and classification. When one of these jobs was filled, the holder was classified as an Assistant Manager Improvement Officer (AMIO). People placed in the AMIO classification were often appointed by the mayor and many viewed this as an example of cronyism and waste.

In 2009 Councilwoman Glorious Johnson spoke out and complained that the city's roughly 200 AMIOs were being overpaid under a job classification that was too loosely defined. Johnson pointed out that since she joined the council in 2003, the number of AMIOs had nearly doubled. She also criticized the manner in which the people classified as AMIOs were hired, arguing that the job could be used to show favoritism.

Mayor John Peyton and his staff didn't agree with all the criticism about AMIOs but did agree to update the city code and its job classification system. Once the initial update has been implemented, the plan is to review the city code and job classification system every four years.

Source: "Jacksonville Mayor Making Job Class Changes: A New Bill Will Help Control about 200 Positions," *McClatchy-Tribune Business News,* November 16, 2009.

Job Classification Method

job classification method
Job evaluation method that determines the relative worth of a job by comparing it to a predetermined scale of classes or grades of jobs.

A second type of job evaluation plan is the **job classification method,** or *job grading.* Certain classes or grades of jobs are defined on the basis of differences in duties, responsibilities, skills, working conditions, and other job-related factors. The relative worth of a particular job is then determined by comparing its description with the description of each class and assigning the job to the appropriate class. This method has the advantage of simplicity, but is not always precise because it evaluates the job as a whole. The number of required classes or grades depends on the range of skills, responsibilities, duties, and other requirements among the jobs being evaluated. Normally, 5 to 15 classes will suffice. Since 1949, the U.S. government has used the job classification method to evaluate all civil service jobs. HRM in Action 13.2 discusses some of the problems the city of Jacksonville, Florida, had with its job classification system.

Point Method

point method
Job evaluation method in which a quantitative point scale is used to evaluate jobs on a factor-by-factor basis.

The **point method** has historically been the most widely used job evaluation plan in the United States.[2] It has the advantages of being relatively simple to use and reasonably objective. When the point method is used, a quantitative point scale is developed for the jobs being evaluated. One scale usually cannot be used to evaluate all types of jobs. For example, different scales are normally required for clerical and production jobs. Another scale is usually required to evaluate management and professional jobs. Usually the human resource department decides which jobs are to be included in a specific evaluation scale.

Selection of Key Jobs

After deciding which jobs are to be evaluated on each specific scale, key (benchmark) jobs are selected. Key jobs represent jobs that are common throughout the industry or in the general locale under study. The content of key jobs should be commonly understood. If there is any confusion about the description of a job or what its pay should be, it should probably not be selected as a key job. The general idea is to select a limited number (20 percent is a good guideline) of key jobs that are representative of the entire pay structure and the major kinds of work being evaluated.[3] The selection of key jobs should adequately represent the span of responsibilities, duties, and work requirements of the jobs being evaluated. Because key jobs usually represent only a small number of all jobs being evaluated, they may supply only a limited amount of data. However, the commonality and widespread acceptance of key jobs provide a basis for sound understanding and agreement. The goal here is to select enough key jobs to represent each major internal variable in the pay structure for all the jobs being evaluated. A full and detailed job description is necessary for each key job.

PRICING THE JOB

The factor comparison method of evaluation is the only conventional technique that relates the work of jobs to a monetary scale; even then, the results are derived primarily from the wage scale the organization currently uses. In general, job evaluation cannot be used to set the wage rate; however, it provides the basis for this determination. To ensure that external factors such as labor market conditions, prevailing wage rates, and living costs are recognized in the wage scale, information about these factors must be gathered.

Wage and Salary Surveys

Wage and salary surveys are used to collect comparative information on the policies, practices, and methods of wage payment from selected organizations in a given geographic location or particular type of industry. In addition to providing knowledge of the market and ensuring external equity, wage surveys can correct employee misconceptions about certain jobs. They can also have a positive impact on employee motivation.[5]

Wage or salary survey information can be obtained in two basic ways: (1) conducting your own survey or (2) purchasing or accessing a wage/salary survey undertaken by another party.

Conducting a Wage/Salary Survey

To design a wage survey, the jobs, organizations, and area to be studied must be determined, as must the method for gathering data. If the wage survey is done in conjunction with either the point or factor comparison method or job evaluation, the key jobs selected are normally the ones that are surveyed. A good rule of thumb is that a minimum of 30 percent of the jobs in an organization should be surveyed to make a fair evaluation of the organization's pay system.[6] It is also desirable to have at least 10 samples per job.[7] When using the classification or ranking method, the organization should apply the same guidelines followed for selecting jobs with the point and factor comparison methods in choosing the jobs to be surveyed.

A geographic area, an industry type, or a combination of the two may be surveyed. The size of the geographic area, the cost-of-living index for the area, and similar factors must be considered when defining the scope of the survey. The organizations to be surveyed are normally competitors or companies that employ similar types of employees. When they are willing to cooperate, it is often desirable to survey the most important and most respected organizations in the area.

The three traditional methods of surveying wage data are personal interviews, telephone interviews, and mailed questionnaires. The most reliable and most expensive method is the personal interview. Mailed questionnaires should be used only to survey jobs that have a uniform meaning throughout the industry. If there is any doubt concerning the definition of a job, the responses to a mailed questionnaire may be unreliable. Another potential problem with mailed questionnaires is that they can be answered by someone who is not thoroughly familiar with the wage structure. The telephone method, which is quick but often yields incomplete information, may be used to clarify responses to mailed questionnaires.

The Internet represents the fastest growing and latest technology for conducting wage/salary surveys. The benefits of using the Internet are that it is inexpensive and quick. The drawbacks to using the Internet for conducting salary surveys are similar to those encountered with a mailed questionnaire. Because the advantages of cost and speed are so substantial, there is little doubt that the Internet is fast becoming the method of choice for conducting salary surveys of all types. Figure 13.3 lists some topics that might be covered in a wage/salary survey.

Purchasing or Accessing Wage/Salary Surveys

Wage survey data can be purchased or accessed from a variety of sources. Since the early 1950s, consulting firms such as Mercer, Watson Wyatt, and PricewaterhouseCoopers have sold

FIGURE 13.3
Possible Topics in a Wage Survey

Length of workday	Vacation practices
Normal workweek duration	Holiday practices
Starting wage rates	Cost-of-living clauses
Base wage rates	Where paid
Pay ranges	How often paid
Incentive plans	Policy on wage garnishment
Shift differentials	Description of union contract
Overtime pay	

compensation surveys; however, these surveys are usually relatively expensive. The Bureau of Labor Statistics of the U.S. Department of Labor, state and local governments, trade associations, and chambers of commerce are all potential sources for relatively inexpensive wage/salary surveys. Also a number of wage/salary surveys and other survey information are available on the Internet. Surveys available on the Internet fall into two broad categories: (1) surveys conducted by the federal government, and (2) surveys conducted by private research organizations, professional associations, employees' associations, and consulting firms.[8] Figure 13.4 lists a sample of some different Web sites for obtaining wage/salary survey data. Most of the nongovernment sites listed in Figure 13.4 charge for accessing their information.

Pitfalls and Guidelines

Wage and salary surveys can be quite helpful if conducted and interpreted properly. If not done properly, they can yield very distorted and inaccurate information and can be the subject of much criticism. Figure 13.5 summarizes specific problems often associated with wage and salary surveys. Regardless of the type of survey used, the following guidelines should be followed to avoid problems:

1. *Assess the participating companies for comparability.* Not only should factors such as size and type of business be considered, but intangibles, such as prestige, security, growth opportunity, and location, are also important.
2. *Compare more than base wage or salary.* The total compensation package, including incentives and benefits, should be considered. For example, a company might provide few benefits but compensate for this with high base wages and salaries.
3. *Consider variations in job descriptions.* The most widely acknowledged shortcoming of wage and salary surveys is that it is difficult to find jobs that are directly comparable. Usually more information than a brief job description is needed to properly match jobs in a survey.
4. *Correlate survey data with adjustment periods.* How recently wages and salaries were adjusted before the survey affects the accuracy of the data. Some companies may have just made adjustments, whereas others may not.[9]

FIGURE 13.4
Sample of Web Sites for Wage/Salary Survey Data

The U.S. Department of Labor	http://www.dol.gov
The U.S. Department of Labor, Bureau of Labor Statistics Home Page	http://www.bls.gov
World at Work (formerly The American Compensation Association)	http://www.worldatwork.org
The AFL-CIO Executive Pay Watch	http://www.aflcio.org/paywatch/index.htm
Payscale, Inc.	http://www.payscale.com
Salary, Inc.	http://www.salary.com
Wage Web	http://www.wageweb.com
Job Search Guide offering links to more than 150 salary surveys	http://www.jobstar.org/tools/salary
Subsidiary of Career Builders.com	http://www.CBSalary.com

FIGURE 13.5
Problems Encountered When Using Salary Survey Data

Source: *Personnel* by J. C. O' Brien and R. A. Zawacki. Copyright 1985 by American Management Association. Reproduced with permission of American Management Association in the format Textbook via Copyright Clearance Center.

> Job categories too broad or imprecise.
> Industry categories too broad or imprecise.
> Unadjusted for major benefits.
> Salary categories too broad or imprecise.
> Company type/size difficult to relate to own.
> Out-of-date or undated data.
> Samples of firms unrepresentative.
> Samples of firms too small.
> Survey based on unemployed and/or job seekers.
> Survey too broad or imprecise in other ways.

Comparable worth theory, which was discussed in Chapters 3 and 12, holds that every job should be compensated on the basis of its value to the employer and society. In this theory, factors such as availability of qualified employees and wage rates paid by other employers should be disregarded. Under the comparable worth theory, wage surveys would have no value. However, as discussed in Chapter 3, the Ninth Circuit Court of Appeals has ruled that the value of a particular job to an employer is only one of many factors that should influence the rate of compensation for that job.

Wage and Salary Curves

wage and salary curves
Graphical depiction of the relationship between the relative worth of jobs and their wage rates.

Wage and salary curves graphically show the relationship between the relative worth of jobs and their wage or salary rates. In addition, these curves can be used to indicate pay classes and ranges for the jobs. Regardless of the job evaluation method used, a wage curve plots the jobs in ascending order of difficulty along the abscissa (*x*-axis) and the wage rate along the ordinate (*y*-axis). If the point method is used for evaluation, the point totals are plotted against their corresponding wage rates, as shown in Figure 13.6, to produce a general trend.

To ensure that the final wage structure is consistent with both the job evaluations and the wage survey data, it is sometimes desirable to construct one wage curve based on present wages and one based on the survey data and compare the two. Any discrepancies can be quickly detected and corrected. Points of the graph that do not follow the general trend indicate that the wage rate for that job is too low or too high or that the job has been inaccurately evaluated. Underpaid jobs are sometimes called *green-circle* jobs; when wages are overly high, the positions are known as *red-circle* jobs. These discrepancies can be remedied by granting above- or below-average pay increases for the jobs in question.

FIGURE 13.6
Wage Curve Using the Point Method

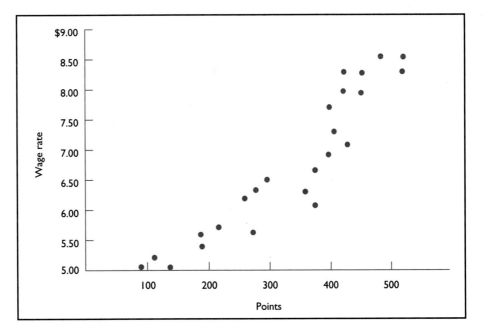

TABLE 13.8
Establishing Wage Grades

Grade	Point Range
1	0–150
2	151–250
3	251–350
4	351–450
5	451–550

Pay Grades and Ranges

pay grades

Classes or grades of jobs that for pay purposes are grouped on the basis of their worth to an organization.

pay range

Range of permissible pay, with a minimum and a maximum, that is assigned to a given pay grade.

To simplify the administration of a wage structure, jobs of similar worth are often grouped into classes, or **pay grades,** for pay purposes. If the point method is used for evaluating jobs, classes are normally defined within a certain point spread. Similarly, a money spread can be used for defining grades if the factor comparison method is used. Table 13.8 illustrates how grades might be defined for the jobs shown in Figure 13.6.

Usually, at the same time pay grades are established, **pay ranges** are determined for each grade. When this is done, each pay grade is assigned a range of permissible pay, with a minimum and a maximum. The maximum of a pay grade's range places a ceiling on the rate that can be paid to any employee whose job is classified in that grade. Similarly, the minimum of the pay grade's range places a floor on the rate that can be paid. Two general approaches for establishing pay grades and ranges are to have a relatively large number of grades with identical rates of pay for all jobs within each grade and to have a small number of grades with a relatively wide dollar range for each grade. Most pay structures fall somewhere between these extremes.

Ranges within grades are set up so that distinctions can be made among employees within grades. Ideally, the placement of employees within pay grades should be based on performance or merit. In practice, however, the distinction is often based solely on seniority. Figure 13.7 illustrates how pay ranges might be structured for the jobs in Figure 13.6.

On reaching the top of the range for a given grade, an employee can increase his or her pay only by moving to a higher grade. As shown in Figure 13.7, it is not unusual for the ranges of adjacent pay grades to overlap. Under such circumstances, it is possible for an outstanding performer in a lower grade to earn a higher salary than a below-average performer in a higher grade.

FIGURE 13.7
Establishment of Pay Grades with Ranges

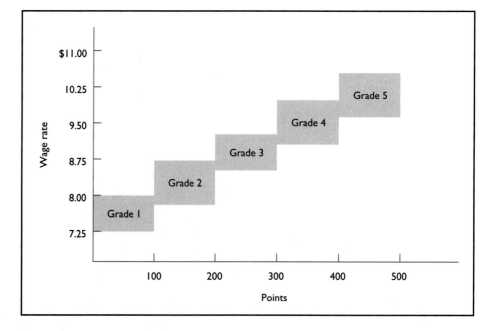

FIGURE 13.8
Developing the Base Wage
Salary Structure

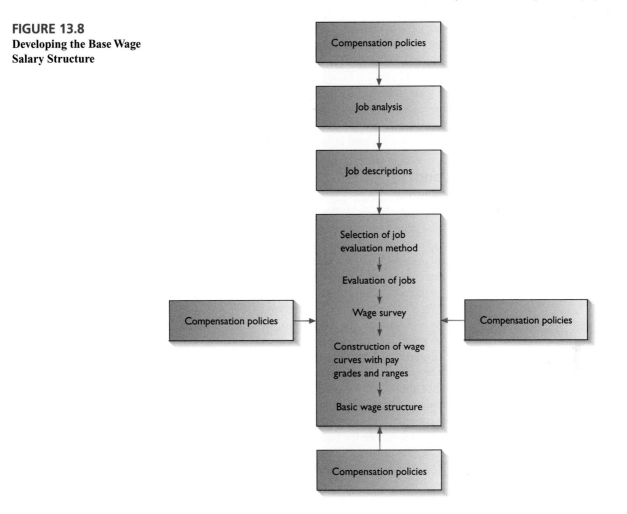

BASE WAGE/SALARY STRUCTURE

Figure 13.8 illustrates how the various segments of the compensation process fit together to establish the base wage or salary structure for an organization. Compensation policies are shown on all sides of the figure to emphasize the fact that each step in the process is influenced by the organization's current compensation policies. Ideally, an organization's compensation system should produce a base wage/salary structure that is both internally and externally equitable. The job evaluation process should ensure internal equity, while wage surveys should ensure external equity. The performance appraisal process, discussed in Chapter 11, is then used to position an individual employee within the established range.

NEW APPROACHES TO THE BASE WAGE/SALARY STRUCTURE

As described previously in this chapter, conventional base pay systems compensate employees based on the work required to do a specific job as determined by job evaluations. Mike Guthman, a partner with Hewitt Associates (a compensation/benefits consulting firm), describes conventional base pay systems in the following manner: "In the past, everything revolved around jobs. We grouped tasks, called it a job, evaluated it, put it in a salary grade and the job was unchanging. People would do that job, progress and move on to another one, but the job would stay where it was."[10] Today some people believe that even the concept of a "job" is outmoded in certain workplaces where employees frequently redirect their energies to new tasks, using different skills.[11] Following along these same lines of thought, many people today believe that narrowly defined job descriptions and pay scales that worked well in yesterday's industrial workplace do not do as well today. *Broadbanding* was created to provide additional flexibility to conventional base pay systems. Other new models of pay that have gained popularity are based on the capabilities of employees rather than on the characteristics of their job.[12] Skill-based pay and competency-based pay are specific examples of pay systems based on employee capabilities. A third type of approach to base pay is based almost exclusively on market-pricing of jobs. Each of these new approaches to the base wage/salary structure is discussed in the following sections.

Broadbanding

broadbanding
Collapsing job clusters or tiers of positions into a few wide bands to manage career growth and deliver pay.

Broadbanding is "a base-pay technique that reduces many different salary categories to several broad salary bands."[13] Put another way, broadbanding refers to collapsing job clusters or tiers of positions into a few wide bands to manage career growth and deliver pay.[14] In essence, broadbanding results in clustering jobs into wide categories or groups of jobs. The bands usually have minimum and maximum dollar amounts that overlap and an average width of 130 percent of the minimum.[15] For example, Band 1 may cover technicians earning $33,000 to $74,000 and Band 2 may cover those earning $60,000 to $140,000. Under broadbanding, a company with a conventional compensation system might have 30 salary ranges, each with a different job title. Under a banded system, these 30 ranges might be reduced to six bands with wider salary ranges and no job titles.

Major advantages of broadbanding are that managers have more autonomy in setting pay rates and it becomes easier to move employees around in the organization because broadbanding eliminates unnecessary distinctions among jobs.[16] This second advantage is especially important in today's organizations, which are flatter and have reduced promotional opportunities. Under conventional systems, employees are reluctant to take a lateral move or a downgrade even if doing so would be the best thing for their careers and for the company. Broadbanding can help overcome this reluctance. In addition, broadbanding can help improve communication teamwork by eliminating many of the frequent barriers to communication and development, namely, level, title, and status.[17] Broadbanding works especially well in organizations that are fast moving and undergoing persistent change.[18] In these situations, broadbanding provides less formal structure and allows the organizations to react quicker. A 2008 survey by Mercer Human Resource Consulting found that 21 percent of the respondents used some form of broadbanding.[19]

Skill-Based Pay

skill-based pay systems
Systems that compensate employees for the skills they bring to the job.

Skill-based pay is an effort to develop more versatile employees that are often required in today's organizations where jobs can be rapidly changing.[20] **Skill-based pay systems** (also known as knowledge-based pay systems) compensate employees for the skills they bring to the job. Specifically, these pay systems pay employees for their range of knowledge, the number of business-related skills mastered, the level of those skills or knowledge, or some combination of level and range.

Under a typical skill-based system, companies hire employees at below-market rates. As employees gain skills and knowledge, their levels of base pay increase. In general, employees are expected to learn between 5 and 10 skills over a two- to five-year period. Of course, the number of skill levels and the time required vary from organization to organization. In a conventional job-based pay system, employees must wait for a job opening before they can be promoted. Under a skill-based pay system, employees are eligible for a pay increase when they have learned a new skill and demonstrated they can progress another step. Table 13.9 lists the potential benefits of a skill-based system.

The attractive list of potential benefits listed in Table 13.9 must be weighed against several potential concerns. Increased labor costs, topped-out employees, false expectations, and union agreements are some of the more frequently mentioned potential concerns. Direct labor and training costs do often rise. However, they are usually offset by a reduced labor force and therefore lower total labor costs. Topped-out employees are those who have nowhere else to

TABLE 13.9
Potential Benefits of a Skill-Based Pay System

Source: Earl Ingram II, "The Advantages of Knowledge-Based Pay," *Personnel Journal,* April 1990, p. 138, and Brian Murray and Barry Gerhart, "An Empirical Analysis of a Skill-Based Pay Program and Plant Performance," *Academy of Management Journal,* February 1990, pp. 68–78.

Fits workforce values
Increases staffing flexibility
Builds leaner staffing requirements
Encourages flatter organizational structure
Inspires higher quality and quantity productivity levels
Broadens incentives to increase knowledge and skills
Reinforces group participation
Deepens commitment when promotions are unavailable
Decreases overall labor costs
Improves understanding of operation
Greater productivity
Favorable quality outcomes
Scrap reduction

go. The issue of topped-out employees is not new to managers and arises in most organizations regardless of the pay system used. One option is to expose topped-out employees to broader jobs in other departments. The problems of false expectations occur when there are no vacancies in the job areas for which employees have been newly trained. The key is to be realistic about the current or near-term future needs of the organization. Unrealistic expectations can even lead to increased turnover as employees become disillusioned. It is generally recognized that skill-based pay systems do not work well in unionized organizations whose pay systems are based largely on seniority.

Skill-based pay systems present formidable problems for practitioners who want to use the concept.[21] To successfully install a skill-based plan, practitioners need management information systems for identifying, valuing, certifying, and tracking employee skills. Neither these systems nor market surveys that value skills have been developed to manage plans efficiently for large groups of employees. The end result is that practitioners are often able to apply skill-based pay systems only for small groups of employees whose jobs are uncomplicated.

Because of the problems outlined above, most skill-based pay systems have focused on nonexempt employees working in manufacturing environments. This is primarily because it is relatively easy to identify and measure the skill sets needed by direct-labor employees. However, a movement has ensued to extend the skills-based pay approach to professionals and managers. The result of this movement is called *competency-based pay*.

competency-based pay system
Rewarding employees based on knowledge, skills, and behaviors that result in performance.

The concept of competency-based pay rewards employees on knowledge and special skills. RF/Corbis

Competency-Based Pay

A *competency* is defined as "a trait or a characteristic that's required by a job holder to perform that job well."[22] A similar definition is "demonstrable characteristics of the person, including knowledge, skills, and behaviors, that enable performance."[23]

An employer interested in a **competency-based pay system** in a sales organization, for example, would examine the most successful salespeople in the organization and learn what it is that those people do well.[24] The identified elements might be managing accounts, conducting competitive research, or making good technical presentations. Once the elements for predicting sales success have been identified, they are categorized as competencies. All salespeople will then be compensated based on how well they demonstrate these identified competencies.

Figure 13.9 outlines the key design choices that must be made when developing a competency-based pay system. The process involves choosing between opposing design dimensions in the eight key areas shown. Competency-based pay is intuitively compelling in that it makes sense to put money behind those things the organization values.[25] A major problem with competency-based pay is that it can be difficult to measure when a competency has been mastered and is being demonstrated.[26] Currently, competency-based pay systems are not widely used, but some prominent compensation experts continue to support the concept.[27]

FIGURE 13.9
Designing Competency-Based Pay

Source: Gerald E. Ledford, Jr., *Compensation & Benefits Review,* p. 58, Copyright 1995 by Sage Publications. Reprinted with permission of Sage Publications, Inc.

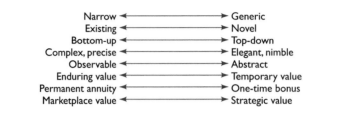

Competency-based pay plans consist of eight key dimensions. Each of these dimensions offers two basic—and polar opposite—design choices. The choices in the lefthand column are most similar to traditional pay systems, whereas those in the right are more novel.

Narrow ←——————→	Generic
Existing ←——————→	Novel
Bottom-up ←——————→	Top-down
Complex, precise ←——————→	Elegant, nimble
Observable ←——————→	Abstract
Enduring value ←——————→	Temporary value
Permanent annuity ←——————→	One-time bonus
Marketplace value ←——————→	Strategic value

Market-Based Pay

market-based pay systems
Systems that focus on external rather than internal equity and operate without traditional pay ranges.

Market-based pay systems focus on external instead of internal equity and operate without traditional pay grades and ranges.[28] Proponents of market-based pay believe that it is unnecessary to burden organizations with complex and time-consuming job evaluations when the reality of the market can fairly price jobs.[29] Market-based pay systems are meant to appeal to employees and to help attract and retain them. The basic idea is to build employee commitment by creating an atmosphere in which employees feel that their pay is logical and consistent with what the market is paying for their skills. Market-based pay systems use the same types of wage/salary surveys that were discussed earlier in this chapter. For market-based pay systems to achieve their goals of perceived fairness, great care must be taken that the surveys used be carefully selected so as to accurately represent the jobs being priced. The use of at least three or more survey sources is often recommended.[30] Some experts recommend that, because of data unreliability and underrepresented jobs, the surveys used should focus on the pricing of skill sets instead of jobs.[31] HRM in Action 13.3 discusses some of the problems incurred when the Government Accountability Office (GAO) attempted to implement a new market-based pay system.

Total Rewards

Total rewards, also referred to as *total compensation,* is a concept that emerged in the early 2000s.[32] WorldatWork defines total rewards as "all of the tools available to the employer that may be used to attract, motivate, and retain employees. Total rewards include everything the employee perceives to be of value resulting from the employment relationship."[33] The basic idea of total rewards is to consider all aspects of the work experience, not just pay and benefits, when developing a strategy to attract, motivate, and retain employees. Specifically, the total rewards concept calls for five elements to be considered: (1) compensation, (2) benefits, (3) work–life balance, (4) performance and recognition, and (5) development and career opportunities. The intent of the total rewards approach is to place more emphasis on lower-cost rewards (rewards other than compensation and benefits) and provide a flexible and broad array of rewards. The idea is to be able to effectively engage a more diverse workforce.

Since the total rewards concept emerged, much confusion and chaos has followed. The concept has gone through many revisions and been defined differently by different users. It is also difficult to quantify the adoption of the concept since many aspects of the concept have been around for a long time. The concept has made practitioners more aware of the value of the full spectrum of rewards.

All of the new approaches to the base wage/salary structure discussed in this section can be effectively used in certain situations. However, none work in all situations and all can have major execution issues if not carefully interpreted and implemented.

MARKET SURVEY CAUSES PROBLEM AT GAO

The Government Accountability Office (GAO) concluded that it was paying too much for some mid-career analysts after it commissioned Watson Wyatt Worldwide Consulting Company, which specializes in compensation and benefits, to conduct a salary market survey. As a result of the salary survey, 308 GAO employees, about 10 percent of GAO's workforce, did not receive pay increases in 2006. Even though these employees received a "meets expectation" level appraisal, they did not get a pay raise because the salary survey indicated that they were overpaid when their salaries were compared with market rates. The same study also concluded that 25 percent of the agency's employees were underpaid and they subsequently got pay raises.

One analyst, who received no pay raise as a result of the market survey, stated that he and his colleagues, who also did not receive a raise, "are losing ground without the cost-of-living adjustment. Needless to say, we're pretty ticked off about that." Subsequent additional complaints by employees forced some changes in the new pay program.

Sources: Florence Olsen, "Ticked Off about Pay at GAO," *Federal Computer Week,* May 15, 2006; Richard W. Walker, "Congress Watches Its Own Watchdog," *Federal Computer Week,* May 28, 2007; and Howard Risher and Andrew Smallwood, "Performance-Based Pay at NGA," *Public Manager,* Summer 2009, pp. 25–29.

Summary of Learning Objectives

1. Define *base wages and salaries* and state the objective of any base wage and salary system.

Base wages and salaries are the hourly, weekly, or monthly pay that employees receive in exchange for their work. The primary objective of any base wage and salary system is to establish a structure for the equitable payment of employees based on their jobs and their levels of job performance.

2. Define *job evaluation*.

Job evaluation is a systematic determination of the value of each job in relation to other jobs in the organization.

3. Name and briefly discuss the four basic conventional methods of job evaluation.

Most conventional job evaluation plans are variations or combinations of four basic methods: job classification, job ranking, point, and factor comparison. The job classification method defines certain classes or grades of jobs on the basis of differences in duties, responsibilities, skills, working conditions, and other job-related factors. In the job ranking method, the evaluator ranks whole jobs from the simplest to the most difficult. The point method develops a quantitative point scale for the jobs being evaluated. Jobs are broken down into certain recognizable factors, and the sum total value of these factors is compared against the scale to determine the job's worth. The factor comparison method is similar to the point method except that it involves a monetary scale instead of a point scale.

4. Explain the concepts of key jobs and compensable factors.

Key jobs represent jobs that are common throughout the industry or in the general locale under study. The idea is to select a limited number of jobs that will represent the spectrum of jobs being evaluated with regard to responsibilities, duties, and work requirements. Once the key jobs have been evaluated, other jobs can be compared to them. Compensable factors are those characteristics of jobs that the organization deems important to the extent that it is willing to pay for them. The degree to which a specific job possesses compensable factors determines its relative worth.

5. Differentiate between subfactors and degrees.

Subfactors are used to describe compensable factors in more detail. Degrees are profile statements used to describe the specific requirements of each subfactor.

6. Explain the purpose of wage and salary surveys.

Wage and salary surveys are used to collect comparative information on the policies, practices, and methods of wage payment from selected organizations in a given geographic location or particular type of industry.

7. Discuss wage and salary curves.

Wage and salary curves graphically show the relationship between the relative worth of jobs and their wage or salary rates. A wage curve plots the jobs in ascending levels of difficulty along the abscissa (x-axis) and the wage rate along the ordinate (y-axis).

8. **Define *pay grades* and *pay ranges*.**

A pay grade is a grouping of jobs of similar worth for pay purposes. A pay range is an assigned range of permissible pay, with a minimum and a maximum for each pay grade.

9. **Explain the concepts of broadbanding, skill-based pay, competency-based pay, market-based pay, and total rewards.**

Broadbanding reduces many different salary categories into several broad salary bands. In essence, broadbanding results in clustering jobs into wide categories or groups of jobs. Skill-based (or knowledge-based) pay systems compensate employees for the skills they bring to the job. Specifically, these pay systems pay employees for their range of knowledge, the number of business-related skills mastered, the level of those skills or knowledge, or some combination of level and range. A competency is a trait or a characteristic that a job holder needs to perform the job well. An employer interested in a competency-based pay system would examine the most successful employees in the organization and learn what those people do well. Once the elements have been identified, they are categorized as competencies, and all employees would then be compensated based on how well they demonstrated these identified competencies. Market-based pay systems focus on external instead of internal equity and operate without traditional pay grades and ranges. Market-based pay systems use wage/salary surveys, almost exclusively, to price jobs. The basic idea of total rewards is to consider all aspects of the work experience, not just pay and benefits, when developing a strategy to attract, motivate, and retain employees.

Key Terms

Review Questions

1. Define *base wages and salaries*.
2. What is the primary objective of any base wage and salary system?
3. Define *job evaluation*.
4. List the four basic conventional methods of job evaluation.
5. What are compensable factors? Subfactors? Degrees?
6. Describe wage surveys and how they might be conducted.
7. What are the two basic ways of obtaining wage or salary survey information?
8. What is the purpose of wage curves?
9. What are pay grades and ranges?
10. What are the basic arguments against the use of conventional base pay systems?
11. What is broadbanding?
12. What are the differences between skill-based pay systems and competency-based pay systems?
13. What are market-based pay systems?
14. What is total rewards?

Discussion Questions	1. Suppose your organization's recently completed wage survey showed that the pay rates of several jobs were either less or more than they should be. How might you bring these jobs into line?

2. The basic theory behind wage and salary administration is to pay people commensurately for their contributions. What should an organization do if an employee's contributions are not in line with those of others in the same type of job? For example, suppose the company accountant's contributions are deemed to be far in excess of what is usual for someone earning an accountant's pay.

3. How do you think the Internet might impact the entire area of job evaluation?

4. Discuss your views on the argument that conventional job evaluations based on narrowly defined job descriptions and pay scales do not work well in today's organizations.

Incident 13.1

Fair Pay for Pecan Workers

Cloverdale Pecan Company is one of the country's largest processors of pecans. Located in a medium-size southern town, it employs approximately 1,350 people. Although Cloverdale owns a few pecan orchards, the great majority of the nuts it processes are bought on the open market. The processing involves grading the nuts for both size and quality, and shelling, packaging, and shipping them to customers. Most buyers are candy manufacturers.

Cloverdale, which was started 19 years ago by the family of company president Jackson Massie, has been continually expanding since its inception. As do most growing companies, Cloverdale has always paid whatever was necessary to fill a vacancy without having a formal wage and salary system. Jackson Massie suspected that some wage inequities had developed over the years. His speculation was supported by complaints about such inequities from several good, long-term employees. Therefore, Massie hired a group of respected consultants to do a complete wage and salary study of all the nonexempt jobs in the company.

The study, which took five months to complete, confirmed Massie's suspicion. Wages of several jobs were found to vary from the norm. Furthermore, the situation was complicated by several factors. First, many of the employees earning too much were being paid according to union wage scales. Cloverdale is not unionized, but most of its competitors are. Second, many of those in underpaid jobs were being paid at rates equal to those for similar positions in other companies in Cloverdale's geographic area. Third, because of a tight labor market, many new employees had been hired at the top of the range for their respective grades. The study also revealed that the nature of many jobs had changed so much that they needed to be completely reclassified.

Questions

1. What should Cloverdale do to correct the existing wage inequities?

2. How could the company have prevented these problems?

3. If it is recommended that some jobs be placed in a lower pay grade, how might Cloverdale implement those adjustments?

Incident 13.2

A Dead-End Street?

Early in December, Roger Tomlin was called in for his annual salary review. Roger was a staff engineer for Zee Engineering Company, which he had been with for just over 10 years. In the past, Roger had usually received what he considered to be a fair pay raise. During this salary review his manager, Ben Jackson, informed Roger that he was recommending a 10 percent raise. Ben went on to extol the fine job Roger had done in the past year and to explain that Roger should be especially proud of the above-average pay raise he would be getting. Upon reflection, Roger was rather proud; in 10 years, he had been promoted twice and his annual salary had gone from $42,000 to $86,000.

Things were moving along just fine for Roger until he discovered a few weeks later that Zee had hired a new engineer right out of college at a starting salary of $59,000. It really upset Roger to think that a new, unproven engineer would be starting at a salary that high.

Roger's first move was to talk to several of his colleagues. Most were aware of the situation and didn't like it either. Lucy Johnson, who had been an engineer with Zee for over 12 years, asked Roger if he realized he was probably making less money, in actual dollars, than when he started at Zee. This really floored Roger. Roger realized inflation had eaten into everyone's paycheck, but he had never even considered the possibility that he had not kept up with inflation. That evening, on the way home from work, Roger stopped by the local library and looked up the consumer price index (CPI) for the past 10 years. According to Roger's figures, if his pay had kept up exactly with inflation, he would be making $85,000.

After a very restless night, the first thing Roger did upon arriving at work the next day was go straight to human resource manager Joe Dixon's office. After presenting his case about the new employee and about how inflation had eroded his pay, Roger sat back and waited for Joe's reply.

Joe started out by explaining that he understood just how Roger felt. At the same time, however, Roger had to consider the situation from the company's standpoint. The current supply and demand situation dictated that Zee had to pay $59,000 to get new engineers who were any good at all. Roger explained he could understand that, but he couldn't understand why the company couldn't pay him and other senior engineers more money. Joe again sympathized with Roger, but then went on to explain that it was a supply and demand situation. The fact was that senior engineers just didn't demand that much more pay than engineers just starting!

Questions

1. Do you think Roger is being fairly paid?
2. If you were Joe, how would you have responded to Roger?
3. Do you think a wage survey might help in this situation?
4. Should Joe establish pay grades for engineers?

EXERCISE 13.1 **Ranking Jobs**	Based on the eight job descriptions for the air transportation industry given in Exhibit 13.A, evaluate the relative worth of these jobs using the job ranking method. You may find it helpful to prepare a 3″ × 5″ card on each job and then arrange the cards accordingly to the rank you assign each job. Once you have completed your ranking, go to the library or on the Internet and find any pertinent wage survey data relating to these jobs (see Figure 13.4 on page 260 for some possible Web sites for wage/salary survey data). After you have gathered sufficient wage survey data, determine whether or not the data support your rankings. Be prepared to discuss your findings with the class.

EXERCISE 13.2 **Wage/Salary Survey**	Visit several of the Web sites listed in Figure 13.4 and look for any information you might find useful if conducting a wage/salary survey for human resource employees.

Questions

1. Did you find useful information? If so, what and where?
2. Did you find some of the Web sites to be easier to maneuver in than others? If so, which ones were easier?
3. Did any of the data surprise you as to the "going rate" for the different HR positions?

EXHIBIT 13.A
Air Transportation Industry Job Descriptions

Source: These job descriptions are taken from U.S. Department of Labor, Employment and Training Administration, O*NET® Occupational Listings, www.onetcenter.org/occupations.html.

Air Traffic Controllers Control air traffic on and within vicinity of airport and movement of air traffic between altitude sectors and control centers according to established procedures and policies. Authorize, regulate, and control commercial airline flights according to government or company regulations to expedite and ensure flight safety.

Aircraft Body and Bonded Structure Repairers Repair body or structure of aircraft according to specifications.

Aircraft Cargo Handling Supervisors Direct ground crew in the loading, unloading, securing, and staging of aircraft cargo or baggage. Determine the quantity and orientation of cargo and compute aircraft center of gravity. May accompany aircraft as member of flight crew and monitor and handle cargo in flight, and assist and brief passengers on safety and emergency procedures.

Aircraft Engine Specialists Repair and maintain the operating condition of aircraft engines. Includes helicopter engine mechanics.

Airline Pilots, Copilots, and Flight Engineers Pilot and navigate the flight of multiengine aircraft in regularly scheduled service for the transport of passengers and cargo. Requires Federal Air Transport rating and certification in specific aircraft type used.

Cargo and Freight Agents Expedite and route movement of incoming and outgoing cargo and freight shipments in airline, train, and trucking terminals, and shipping docks. Take orders from customers and arrange pickup of freight and cargo for delivery to loading platform. Prepare and examine bills of lading to determine shipping charges and tariffs.

Flight Attendants Provide personal services to ensure the safety and comfort of airline passengers during flight. Greet passengers, verify tickets, explain use of safety equipment, and serve food or beverages.

Reservation and Transportation Ticket Agents Make and confirm reservations for passengers and sell tickets for transportation agencies such as airlines, bus companies, railroads, and steamship lines. May check baggage and direct passengers to designated concourse, pier, or track.

Notes and Additional Readings

1. Jose Balderrama, "Rediscovering Job Evaluation," *Workspan*, June 2003, p. 8; Steve Watson, "Is Job Evaluation Making a Comeback—Or Did It Never Go Away?" *Benefits & Compensation International*, June 2005, p. 8; and John G. Kilgour, "Job Evaluation Revisited: The Point Factor Method," *Compensation & Benefits Review*, July/August 2008, p. 37.

2. Fred L. Eargle, "Job Evaluation and Wage Administration for Beginners," *Office Solutions*, November/December 2005, pp. 26–28; and Emin Kahya, "Revising the Metal Industry Job Evaluation System for Blue Collar Jobs," *Compensation & Benefits Review*, November/December 2006, p. 49.

3. Roger J. Plachy, "Compensation Management: Cases and Applications," *Compensation and Benefits Review*, July 1989, p. 26.

4. Richard I. Henderson, *Compensation Management: Rewarding Performance*, 4th ed. (Reston, Va.: Reston Publishing, 1985), p. 293.

5. Joan C. O'Brien and Robert A. Zawacki, "Salary Surveys: Are They Worth the Effort?" *Personnel*, October 1985, p. 72; Jill Elswick, "Online Salary Benchmark Info Mushrooms," *Employee Benefit News*, March 2001, pp. 45–46; William Dickmeyer, "How to Conduct an Effective Pay Survey," *Workforce Online*, April 2002, accessed April 9, 2004 at http://www.workforce.com.

6. Margaret Dyekman, "Take the Mystery out of Salary Survey," *Personnel Journal*, June 1990, p. 104.

7. "Essentials of Good Salary Survey," *Canadian HR Reporter*, June 4, 2007, p. S2.

8. Fay Hansen, "Guide to Salary Survey Data on the Web," *Compensation & Benefits Review*, March/April 1998, pp. 16–20; Susan J. Marks, "Can the Internet Help You Hit the Salary Mark?" *Workforce*, January 2001, pp. 86–88; Elswick, "Online Salary Benchmark Info Mushrooms"; Kathleen Carroll, "No Guessing How Much," *New York Times*, April 7, 2002, sec. 3, p. 2; and Karen Bankston, "Make Way for Web Surveys," *Association Management*, April 2003, pp. 51–55.

9. Michael A. Conway, "Salary Surveys: Avoid the Pitfalls," *Personnel Journal*, June 1985, pp. 62–65; "What Makes a Good Salary Survey?" *Workforce*, January 2001, p. 88.

10. Shari Cauldron, "Master the Compensation Maze," *Personnel Journal*, June 1993, p. 648.

11. David Barcellos, "The Reality and Promise of Market-Based Pay," *Employment Relations Today*, Spring 2005, p. 1.

12. Richard Long, "Paying for Knowledge: Does It Pay?" *Canadian HR Reporter*, March 28, 2005, pp. 12–13.

13. Bill Leonard, "New Ways to Pay Employees," *HR Magazine*, February 1994, pp. 61–62.

14. Jason C. Kovac, "Broadbanding: Creating a 'Flat' Organization," *Workspan*, November 2006, p. 67.

15. Kathryn Tyler, "Compensation Strategies Can Foster Lateral Moves and Growing in Places," *HR Magazine*, April 1998, pp. 64–71. See also Scott Hays, "Is Broadbanding Here to Stay?" *Workforce Online*, September 2, 1999, accessed September 4, 2002, at http://www.workforce.com.

16. Cauldron, "Master the Compensation Maze," p. 648; Hays, "Is Broadbanding Here to Stay?"; and Edwin W. Arnold and Clyde J. Scott, "Does Broadbanding Improve Pay System Effectiveness?" *Southern Business Review,* Spring 2002, pp. 1–8.

17. Gary L. Bergel, "Choosing the Right Pay Delivery System to Fit Banding," *Compensation,* July–August 1994, pp. 34–38; Hays, "Is Broadbanding Here to Stay?"

18. Kovac, "Broadbanding: Creating a 'Flat' Organization," p. 67.

19. Frank L. Giancola, "A Framework for Understanding New Concepts in Compensation Management," *Benefits & Compensation,* September 2009, p. 15.

20. Much of this section is based on Cauldron, "Master the Compensation Maze," p. 648; see also E. Stewart Hickman, "Pay the Person, Not the Job," *Training & Development,* October 2000, pp. 52–57; and Frank L. Giancola, "A Framework for Understanding New Concepts in Compensation Management."

21. This section is drawn from Frank L. Giancola, "A Framework for Understanding New Concepts in Compensation Management" and Frank Giancola, "Skill-Based Pay Issues for Consideration," *Benefits & Compensation,* May 2007, pp. 11–15.

22. Gerald E. Ledford, Jr., "Paying for the Skills, Knowledge, and Competencies of Knowledge Work," *Compensation & Benefits Review,* July–August 1995, pp. 55–58.

23. Ibid.; and Henry Jahja and Brian H. Kleiner, "Competency-Based Pay in Manufacturing and Service Sectors," *Industrial Management,* September/October 1997, pp. 24–27.

24. Gerald E. Ledford, Jr., "Paying for the Skills," pp. 55–58.

25. Darrell J. Cira and Ellen R. Benjamin, "Competency-Based Pay: A Concept in Evolution," *Compensation & Benefits Review,* September/October 1998, pp. 21–28; see also Howard Risher, "Compensating Today's Technical Professional," *Research Technology Management,* January/February 2000, pp. 50–56.

26. Tyler, "Compensation Strategies," pp. 64–71.

27. Frank L. Giancola, "A Framework for Understanding New Concepts in Compensation Management," p. 14.

28. Kimberly Merriman, "A Fairness Approach to Market-Based Pay," *Workspan,* March 2006, pp. 48–50.

29. David Barcellos, "The Reality and Promise of Market-Based Pay," p. 2.

30. Deb Grigson, John Delaney, and Robert Jones, "Market Pricing 101: The Science and the Art," *Workspan,* October 2004, pp. 46–52.

31. David Barcellos, "The Reality and Promise of Market-Based Pay." pp. 3–4.

32. Much of this section is drawn from Frank L. Giancola, "A Framework for Understanding New Concepts in Compensation Management"; and Frank L. Giancola, "Is Total Rewards a Passing Fad?" *Compensation and Benefits Review,* July/August 2009, pp. 29–35.

33. WorldatWork, "What Is Total Rewards?" http://www.worldatwork.org, accessed February 4, 2010.

Chapter **Fourteen**

Incentive Pay Systems

Chapter Learning Objectives

After studying this chapter, you should be able to:

1. Describe the two basic requirements of an effective incentive plan.
2. List and briefly discuss at least three types of individual incentives.
3. Distinguish between a bonus and a merit pay increase.
4. Discuss the role bonuses play in managerial compensation.
5. Differentiate between nonqualified stock options and incentive stock options (ISOs).
6. Differentiate among the following different types of stock option related plans: stock-for-stock swaps, stock appreciation rights, phantom stock plans, restricted stock plans, premium-priced options, and performance-vesting options.
7. Discuss the major issues related to the executive pay controversy.
8. Discuss the prevalence of stock options among nonmanagerial personnel.
9. Describe how group incentives work.
10. Explain what a gain-sharing plan is.
11. Discuss Scanlon-type plans.
12. Explain how an employee stock ownership plan (ESOP) works.

incentive or variable pay plans
Pay plans designed to relate pay directly to performance or productivity; often used in conjunction with a base wage and salary system.

Incentive or variable pay plans attempt to relate pay directly to the performance of the individual, group, the entire organization or some combination of these. The intent of most incentive pay is to reward above-average performance rapidly and directly. Although good performance can be rewarded through the base wage or salary structure either by raising an individual's pay within the range of the job or by promoting the individual into a higher pay grade, these rewards are often subject to delays and other restrictions. Therefore, the recipients often do not view such rewards as being directly related to performance. Incentive pay plans attempt to strengthen the performance–reward relationship and thus motivate the affected employees. The idea is to have employees think of themselves as business partners by sharing the financial risks and rewards of doing business. A major advantage to employers of incentive pay is that, unlike raises in base and salary, it is not permanent and must be earned each year. Most incentive pay programs tie pay directly to profitability, thus allowing companies to grow and shrink payroll expenses in response to the success of the business. Also, many types of incentives can be rewarded several times per year such as monthly or quarterly. This fosters a more direct link between pay and performance than if adjustments are made only annually.

Because of minimum wage laws and labor market competition, most incentive plans include a guaranteed hourly wage or salary. The guaranteed wage or salary is normally determined from the base wage or salary structure. Thus, incentive plans usually function in addition to, not in place of, the base wage/salary structure discussed in Chapter 13.

Incentive systems can be categorized on more than one basis. Probably the most popular basis is whether the plan is applied on an individual, group, or organizational level. In addition, plans are sometimes classified according to whether they apply to nonmanagerial employees or to professional and managerial employees, This chapter classifies incentives as individual, group, or organizational and, where appropriate, distinguishes between nonmanagerial and managerial employees within these categories. Some plans apply to nonmanagerial and managerial employees alike.

While base wage/salary increases hit a modern-day low in 2009, Hewitt Associates reported that incentive pay spending for 2009 was the highest on record.[1] Over the last 15 years, incentive pay as a percentage of payroll has almost doubled.

REQUIREMENTS OF INCENTIVE PLANS

There are two basic requirements for an effective incentive plan. The first concerns the procedures and methods used to appraise employee performance. If incentives are to be based on performance, employees must believe their performance and the performance of others are accurately and fairly evaluated. Naturally, performance is easier to measure in some situations than in others. For example, the performance of a commissioned salesperson is usually easy to measure, whereas the performance of a middle manager is often more difficult to evaluate. A key issue in performance measurement is the degree of trust in management. If the employees distrust management, it is almost impossible to establish a sound performance appraisal system. (Performance appraisal was discussed at length in Chapter 11).

The second requirement is that the incentives (rewards) must be based on performance. This may seem like an obvious requirement, yet it is often violated. Employees must believe there is a relationship between what they do and what they get. As discussed in Chapter 12, a 2006 survey of 10,000 respondents by Hudson Talent Management found that only 35 percent of the respondents believed that performance was the deciding factor in determining their pay.[2] A similar 2007 study by Authoria, Inc. found that only 15 percent of respondents believed that compensation was used to effectively align individual and corporate performance.[3] Individual-based incentive plans require that employees perceive a direct relationship between their own performances and their subsequent rewards. Group-based plans require employees to perceive a relationship between the group's performance and the subsequent rewards of the group's members. Furthermore, the group members must believe their individual performances have an impact on the group's overall performance. Organization-based plans have the same basic requirements group plans do. Employees must perceive a relationship between the organization's performance and their individual rewards; in addition, employees must believe their individual performances affect the performance of the organization.

INDIVIDUAL INCENTIVES

While there are many types of individual incentive plans, all are tied in some measure to the performance of the individual. At nonmanagerial levels in an organization, individual incentives are usually based on the performance of the individual as opposed to those of the group or organization. However, at managerial levels, individual incentives are often based on the performance of the manager's work unit.

The primary advantage of the individual incentive system is that the employees can readily see the relationship between what they do and what they get. With group- and organization-based plans, this relationship is often not so clear. Because of this advantage, individual incentives can also cause problems. Competition among employees can reach the point of producing negative results. For example, salespeople may not share their ideas with one another for fear that their peers will win a prize that is being offered to the top salesperson.

Piece Rate Plans

As early as 1833, many cotton mills in England used individual piece rate incentives. Piece rate plans are the simplest and most common type of incentive plan. Under such a plan, the employer pays an employee a certain amount for every unit he or she produces. In other words, an employee's wage is figured by multiplying the number of units produced by the rate of pay for each unit. The rate of pay for each unit is usually based on what a fair wage should be for an average employee. For example, if a fair wage for an average machine operator is determined to be $150 per day and it is also determined that the average machine operator should be able to produce 30 units per day, the unit rate of pay would be $5 per unit.

Several variations of the straight piece rate plan have been developed. In 1895, Frederick W. Taylor proposed his **differential piece rate plan.** Under Taylor's plan, one rate is paid for all acceptable units produced up to some standard, or predetermined amount, and then a higher rate for all units produced if the output exceeds the standard. Thus, if the standard were 30 units per day, an employee producing 30 or fewer units might receive $4.25 per unit. However, if the employee produced 31 units, he or she might receive $5 for all 31 units produced for a total of $155. Other plans pay a higher rate only for those units produced above the standard.

differential piece rate plan
Piece rate plan devised by Frederick W. Taylor that pays one rate for all acceptable units produced up to some standard and then a higher rate for all pieces produced if the output exceeds the standard.

Plans Based on Time Saved

Standard hour plans are similar to piece rate plans except that a standard time is set in terms of the time it should take to complete a particular job. Incentive plans based on time saved give an employee a bonus for reaching a given level of production or output in less than the standard time. For example, suppose a body shop repairperson is assigned to do a task for which the standard time is two hours (this is how insurance companies compute the cost of repairing damaged autos). If the repairperson completes the task in $1\frac{1}{2}$ hours, she or he is paid for two hours. If the task takes $2\frac{1}{2}$ hours, the repairperson is paid for that amount of time. Should the repairperson consistently take longer than the standard time, either the standard will need to be adjusted or the productivity of the repairperson should be examined.

commission plan
Incentive plan that rewards employees, at least in part, based on their sales volume.

Plans Based on Commissions

The previously discussed incentive plans are primarily applicable to production-type jobs. However, some incentive plans apply to other types of jobs. One of the most prevalent types is based on commission. Many salespeople work under some type of **commission plan.** Although a variety of such plans exist, they all reward employees, at least in part, based on sales volume. Some salespeople work on a straight commission basis: Their pay is entirely determined by their volume of sales. Others work on a combination of salary plus commission. Under this type of plan, a salesperson is paid a guaranteed base salary plus a

Plans based on commissions reward employees based on their sales volumes.
The McGraw-Hill Companies, Inc./Christopher Kerrigan, photographer

commission on sales. Under a third type of commission plan, salespeople are paid a monthly draw that is later subtracted from their commissions. The purpose of the draw is to provide salespeople with enough money on a monthly basis to cover their basic expenses. The difference between a draw plan and the guaranteed salary plus commission plan is that the draw is really an advance against future commissions and must be repaid. The draw plan is especially useful for salespeople whose sales tend to fluctuate dramatically from month to month or season to season.

A commission plan has the advantage of relating rewards directly to performance. Salespeople on a straight commission know that if they do not produce, they will not be paid. A major disadvantage of commission plans is that things beyond the control of an employee can adversely affect sales. For example, a product might be displaced almost overnight by a technological breakthrough. Other environmental factors, such as the national economy, the weather, and consumer preferences, can also affect an employee's sales.

Individual Bonuses

bonus
Reward that is offered on a one-time basis for high performance.

merit pay increase
Reward based on performance but also perpetuated year after year.

A **bonus** is a reward offered on a one-time basis for high performance. It should not be confused with a merit increase. A **merit pay increase** is a reward that is based on performance but is also perpetuated year after year. A bonus may be in cash or in some other form. For example, many sales organizations periodically offer prizes, such as trips, for their top salespeople. A positive aspect of bonuses is that they must be earned each year and the organization is not obligated over the long run. One potential problem with bonuses is that they can become an extension of salary. This occurs when awarding the bonus becomes practically guaranteed because the bonus is not tied to profits or some other measure of performance or because profits have been consistently high for an extended period of time. In such circumstances, the recipients begin to expect the bonus. They do not view it as resulting from their individual performances or from the profits of the organization. Serious dissatisfaction can result if the expected bonus is not granted because of a decline in profits or any other legitimate reason, such as a recession.

Suggestion Systems

Web site
http://www.eia.com

suggestion systems
Systems that usually offer cash incentives for employee suggestions that result in either increased profits or reduced costs.

Most **suggestion systems** offer cash incentives for employee suggestions that positively affect the organization. Examples include suggestions resulting in increased profits, reduced costs, or improved customer relations. In addition to the obvious organizational benefits, suggestion plans can provide a means for making employees feel more a part of the organization and for improving communications between management and employees. The key to having a successful suggestion system is to clearly communicate exactly how the system works. Employees must believe that each and every suggestion will be fairly evaluated. Modern suggestion systems generally involve specific procedures for submitting ideas and utilize committees to review and evaluate suggestions.

The Employee Involvement Association (EIA), formerly the National Association of Suggestion Systems (NASS), is a Chicago-based, not-for-profit group that represents companies regarding employee involvement programs, including suggestion programs. In 2008, the EIA estimated that its member companies saved $3,128.00 for each idea implemented.[4] For example, 291 employees at the RLI Insurance Company in Peoria, Illinois came up with 1,319 new ideas in one year.[5] One of RLI's employees came up with 49 new ideas and another employee's new ideas saved the company $145,000. Similarly, Maruti Suzuki Ltd. in India estimates that it saved a net amount of over $14 million (Rs66.5 crore) during fiscal year 2007–2008 by implementing employee suggestions to cut down on waste in its manufacturing processes.[6] HRM in Action 14.1 describes a new suggestion system at Xcel Energy.

Incentives for Managerial Personnel

Incentives for managerial personnel generally take the form of annual bonuses, long-term performance planning, or some type of stock option. These are discussed in the following sections.

NEW ONLINE SUGGESTION SYSTEM AT XCEL

Xcel Energy is a Fortune 500 company based in Minneapolis that provides electricity and natural gas to eight Midwestern and Western states. For years the company had a standard suggestion system but few employees participated and those that did rarely received any significant recognition. The standard suggestion system was overly bureaucratic, slow to respond, and resulted in very few ideas being implemented.

In order to overcome the shortcomings of the old system, Xcel devised a new online system called Xpress Ideas. Xpress Ideas directs suggestions to specific areas of need within the business by offering greater rewards for ideas that deal with those topics. Another advantage of Xpress Ideas is that employees receive a rapid response to their suggestion. Currently 74 percent of ideas are processed within 30 days, a marked contrast to the previous system. The current system rewards employees 30 points just for submitting an idea and additional points if an idea is approved. A sliding scale offers more points for ideas that relate to specific objectives. Collective points are then exchangeable for catalog points or for cash, up to $1,000.00. In 2004 alone, approximately 7,600 suggestions were submitted, resulting in a saving of $17 million. Halfway through 2007, the company had already received 4,600 suggestions. John Torres, Xcel's manager of corporate rewards and recognition, believes the new suggestion system has led to an overall culture shift at Xcel with employees taking more ownership in the company and seeking ways to make improvements.

Source: A. E. Smith, "What's the Big Idea?" *Incentive,* March 2008, pp. 30–34.

Annual Bonus

By far the most common type of incentive for managerial employees is the annual cash bonus. Although cash bonuses have always been popular among managers, they have become increasingly popular over time. Most plans provide a year-end bonus based on that year's performance, usually measured in terms of profits but sometimes measured by other means. Even though managerial bonuses are usually based on organizational or group performance, they are considered individual incentives because of the key roles managers play in the success of an organization. Typically, a bonus is paid in cash as a lump sum soon after the end of the performance year. It is not unusual for executives to defer receiving some portion of a cash bonus until a later date for income tax purposes.

One survey taken by Challenger, Gray and Christmas, a Chicago consulting company, found that 64 percent of employers planned to give an end-of-year bonus in 2009.[7] In 2008 only 54 percent planned to give a year-end bonus. Table 14.1 shows how significant bonuses are for several levels of top executives including the top human resource executive.

Long-Term Performance Plans

In recent years, some companies have adopted managerial incentive plans based on the attainment of certain long-term corporate financial performance goals as opposed to the more common annual bonus plans. Generally known as **performance share plans** or **unit plans,** these plans usually award top executives a set number of performance units at the beginning of a performance period. The actual value of the units is then determined by the company's performance over the performance period, usually from three to five years.

Stock Options for Managerial Personnel

Stock option plans are generally designed to give managers an option to buy company stock at a predetermined, fixed price. If the price of the stock goes up, the individual exercises the option to buy the stock at the fixed price and realizes a profit. If the price of the stock goes down, the stock option is said to be "underwater," and the manager does not purchase the stock. The

performance share plan (unit plan)
Incentive plan that awards top executives a set number of performance units at the beginning of the performance period; actual value of the units is then determined by the company's performance over the performance period.

TABLE 14.1
Top Executive Eligible for Bonus and/or Other Cash Compensation Payments

Source: The 2006/2007 Survey Report on Top Management Compensation, Vol. 1 (Rochelle Park, N.J.: Watson Wyatt Data Services, 2007). Reprinted with permission.

Position	Number of Executives	Eligible for Award
Chief Executive Officer	1,326	90.0%
Chief Operating Officer	628	85.3
CEO/President-Subsidiary	399	95.7
Top Division Executive	346	95.4
Executive Vice President	504	89.2
Top Human Resource Executive	482	82.6

idea behind such plans is to provide an incentive for managers to work hard and increase company profits, thus increasing the price of the stock. However, while the use of stock options was originally intended to align corporate executives' interests with those of shareholders, there is evidence that some executives have become more concerned with pumping up the short-term value of the stock to increase their personal wealth.[8] One other potentially negative effect of stock options is that it dilutes the holdings of current shareholders.

Before the passage of the Tax Reform Act of 1976, two major forms of stock options were available: qualified and nonqualified. **Qualified stock options** were those approved by the Internal Revenue Service (IRS) for favorable tax treatment. A qualified option was not taxed until the option was exercised and, in the interim, was treated as a capital asset. Income realized from the eventual sale of the stock was usually taxed as a long-term capital gain. To qualify for a tax advantage, the stock option plan and the recipient had to adhere to certain conditions prescribed by the IRS. These conditions centered primarily around the length of time the executive was required to hold the option before purchasing and selling the stock and the basis for establishing the price the executive paid for it. **Nonqualified stock options** are similar to qualified options, except that they are subject to a less favorable tax rate. They are not subject to the same restrictions.

As a result of the Tax Reform Act of 1976, no new qualified stock options were created after May 20, 1976 (with a few exceptions). In addition, the act ordered that all qualified options in existence prior to the passage of the act had to be exercised before May 21, 1981. It also affected nonqualified options by increasing the period over which one had to hold an exercised stock option to enjoy long-term capital gains tax rates. However, with the adoption of the Economic Recovery Tax Act of 1981, the qualified stock option was resurrected under the new name of **incentive stock option (ISO)**. Under an ISO, a manager does not have to pay any tax until he or she sells the stock. The major drawback to ISOs is that the company granting such options does not get tax reductions, which it does with nonqualified options. Because of tax ramifications, the recipients tend to prefer ISOs, whereas the granting organizations tend to favor nonqualified options.

In recent times, stock options have often represented the largest portion of an executive's total compensation. Table 14.2 shows the salary, bonuses, other, and stock gains for the top 10 of the country's highest-paid executives in 2008. The stock gains represent the value realized by exercising stock options. It is evident from Table 14.2 that top executives' total compensation is often many times their salary and bonuses.

Stock-for-Stock Swaps A substantial proportion of companies with stock option plans provide for **stock-for-stock swaps.** This procedure allows options to be exercised with shares of previously purchased company stock in lieu of cash. The advantage is that this arrangement postpones the taxation of any gain on stock already owned.

qualified stock options
Stock options approved by the Internal Revenue Service for favorable tax treatment.

nonqualified stock options
Similar to qualified options, except that they are subject to a less favorable tax rate and are not subject to the same restrictions.

incentive stock option (ISO)
Form of qualified stock option plan in which the manager does not have to pay any tax until the stock is sold.

stock-for-stock swap
Allows options to be exercised with shares of previously purchased company stock in lieu of cash; postpones the taxation of any gain on stock already owned.

TABLE 14.2 **Top-Paid Chief Executives**

Source: Adapted from www.forbes.com/lists/2009

	Salary (in million of dollars)	Bonus (in million of dollars)	Other*	Stock Gains**	Total
1. Lawrence J. Ellison	1.0	10.78	1.45	543.75	556.98
2. Ray R. Irani	1.3	3.63	33.32	184.39	222.64
3. John B. Hess	1.5	3.50	36.66	112.92	154.58
4. Michael D. Watford	0.60	1.75	1.10	113.48	116.93
5. Mark G. Papa	.94	1.00	18.86	69.67	90.47
6. William R. Berkley	1.00	8.50	5.42	72.56	87.48
7. Matthew K. Rose	1.18	1.68	20.70	45.06	68.62
8. Paul J. Evanson	1.12	1.23	22.28	42.63	67.62
9. Hugh Grant	1.29	3.33	9.32	50.67	64.60
10. Robert W. Lane	1.44	3.59	15.24	41.04	61.30

*Other compensation such as vested restricted stock grants and other perks
**Stock gains represent the value realized by exercising stock options

stock appreciation rights (SARs)
Type of nonqualified stock option in which an executive has the right to relinquish a stock option and receive from the company an amount equal to the appreciation in the stock price from the date the option was granted. Under an SAR, the option holder does not have to put up any money, as would be required in a normal stock option plan.

phantom stock plan
Special type of stock option plan that protects the holder if the value of the stock being held decreases; does not require the option holder to put up any money.

restricted stock plan
Plan under which a company gives shares of stock to participating managers, subject to certain restrictions; the major restriction of most plans is that shares are subject to forfeiture until "earned out" over a stipulated period of continued employment.

premium-priced options
Stock options with an exercise price significantly above stock's current market price.

performance-vesting options
Stock options priced at market price but only exercisable if stock price reaches or exceeds price goal within defined period.

Stock Appreciation Rights (SARs) **Stock appreciation rights (SARs)** are often used with stock option plans. Under an SAR, an executive has the right to relinquish a stock option and receive from the company an amount equal to the appreciation in the stock price from the date the option was granted. The gain is taxed as ordinary income at the time it is received. The advantage of SARs is that the receiver does not have to put up any money to exercise the option, as he or she would with a normal stock option plan. Holders of SARs may have as long as 10 years to exercise their rights.

Phantom Stock Plans **Phantom stock plans** can work in several ways. In one form, the company awards stock as a part of its normal bonus plan. The receiver then defers this "phantom" stock until retirement. At retirement, the holder receives the accumulated shares of stock or the equivalent value. The second form of phantom stock is very similar to SARs. The receiver is credited with phantom stock. After a stipulated period of time, usually three to five years, the receiver is paid, in cash or equivalent shares, an amount equal to the appreciation in the stock. The major advantage of phantom stock plans is that the receiver does not have to put up any money at any point in the process. Also, if the value of the stock decreases, the holder does not lose any money.

Restricted Stock Plans Under a **restricted stock plan,** a company gives shares of stock, subject to certain restrictions, to participating managers. The major restriction of most plans is that the shares are subject to forfeiture until they are "earned out" over a stipulated period of continued employment. As with SARs and phantom stock plans, the receivers do not put up or risk any of their own money. An advantage from the organization's viewpoint is that restricted stock plans provide an incentive for executives to remain with the organization.

Premium-Priced and Performance-Vesting Options **Premium-priced options** are similar to standard stock options except that the exercise price of the option is set significantly above the current market price of the stock (versus the usual practice of setting it at or near the current market price). The holder realizes a gain only when the market value exceeds the exercise price.

Performance-vesting options, also called price-vesting options, are priced at the market price but only exercisable if the stock price reaches or exceeds a price goal within a defined period. If the stock price does not reach the price goal within the stipulated time frame, the option is forfeited.

The Status of Executive Compensation

As indicated in Table 14.2, it is not uncommon for CEOs to be awarded bonuses and stock options that reach nine digits—even when the company is not doing well. In 2008, Standard & Poor's (S&P) 500 chief executive officers earned 344 times as much as their employees' average pay.[9] This is compared to a ratio of 85 to 1 in 1990 and 42 to 1 in 1980. By contrast the ratio is 22 in Britain, 20 in Canada, and 11 in Japan.[10]

The main idea behind most stock options is to link pay to performance. However, when there is a sustained bull market, tying executive reward to price may be fundamentally flawed.[11] The problem is that when most stocks are going up, stock prices often provide an inaccurate measure of a company's actual strength. The same could be said when the market is in a substantial bear market.

Because of the huge dollars often involved and because many executives have received large compensation packages when the company stock is not performing well, many employees and stockholders have become outraged with what many executives are being paid (see HRM in Action 14.2 for one example). Fuel was added to the fire in late January 2009 when the media revealed that bankers had awarded themselves nearly $18.4 billion in bonuses as the economy was further deteriorating and the federal government was spending billions to bail out financial institutions. American International Group (AIG), which has received more than $170 billion in government bailout funds, paid tens of millions in retention bonuses in 2009 and 2010. AIG chairman Edward Liddy justified the bonuses by arguing that retaining key employees was critical for the company to maintain its standing in the eyes of reinsurers and rating agencies, and furthermore it was essential if AIG was to repay taxpayers.[12] Reacting to these and other abuses, a new law was passed that prohibits cash bonuses and other incentives for the five most-senior officers and the 20 highest paid executives at companies that have received funds under the Troubled Asset Relief Program (TARP).[13] The bill further stipulates that any bonuses given out by these companies would have to be in the form of long-term incentives, such as restricted stock, and that the incentives cannot be cashed out until all the TARP money has been repaid.

Largely because of outraged employees, individuals, and institutional investors, more and more organizations and boards of directors are reexamining their entire executive compensation packages. A 2009 survey by Watson Wyatt Worldwide found that 63 percent of responding directors said U.S. companies should modify executive compensation to adapt to economic realities.[14] This same survey reported that 34 percent of the respondents said their companies had already reduced salary, bonuses, or long-term incentive awards. Surveys by Equilar (for the *New York Times*), the Hay Group, and *Forbes* magazine all showed that executive pay fell in 2008, largely because of drops in bonuses.[15] Most organizations are aware of the public furor over executive compensation and many are making changes. One common thread in many of these changes is to directly relate compensation to performance.

Say-on-Pay "Say-on-pay" proposals require an annual nonbinding shareholder vote regarding executive compensation. Most say-on-pay proposals set up advisory boards to oversee executive pay, express shareholder views, and vote on executive compensation. Some say-on-pay proposals also call for shareholder approval on golden parachutes as well as executive compensation relating to managers. The first say-on-pay victory was passed by shareholders for Blockbuster, Inc. on May 9, 2007.[16] On July 31, 2009 the U.S. House of Representatives passed the Corporate and Financial Institutions Compensation Fairness Act (CFICF). Under this bill, most publicly held companies would be required to offer shareholders a voluntary "say-on-pay" vote and the Securities and Exchange Commission (SEC) would establish conflict-of-interest standards for compensation consultants and create a requirement that only independent directors can serve on corporate board compensation committees. The bill also includes some provisions that apply only to financial companies with assets over $1 billion. As of press time, the U.S. Senate had not acted on this bill. HRM in Action 14.3 discusses preemptive actions taken by Aflac to avoid many of the executive compensation problems being experienced by many companies.

The concerns discussed above plus worries about shareholder interests being diluted by the issue of stock options and fallout from the corporate scandals of recent years have caused many companies to abandon or reduce the use of stock options. In 2004, the Financial

Accounting Standards Board (FASB) issued Statement of Financial Accounting Standard (SFAS) 123R that requires a range of equity-based compensation arrangements (such as stock options) to be treated the same as other forms of compensation. In essence, companies now have to expense stock options just like salaries. One result of this proposal is that company profits will be lowered by the value of the stock options. The International Accounting Standards Board (IASB) also ruled that international companies had to deduct the cost of stock options from corporate profits beginning in 2005.[17]

While the reaction to executive compensation has not been universal, there is a trend toward the special types of equity grants (such as premium-priced, performance-vested options, and restricted stock plans) that do relate executive rewards to actual company performance. Given the current climate, there is little doubt that executive compensation will continue to come under increasing scrutiny in the future. HRM in Action 14.3 discusses what one company has done regarding executive compensation.

Stock Options for Nonmanagerial Personnel

When stock options are mentioned, most people think only about stock options for executives and managerial personnel. Nonmanagerial personnel also widely hold stock options, however. A public opinion survey released in 2004 reported that about 13 percent of private-sector employees nationwide receive some type of stock options and that the vast majority, 94 percent, hold jobs below the top management ranks.[18] This same survey reported that at least one in every eight employees in nongovernment jobs held stock options. This number was much higher than previously thought. A 2008 Bureau of Labor Statistics survey reported that about 8 percent of all private sector employees had stock options.[19] Overall about 9 million American employees were estimated to have stock options in 2009.[20]

If companies continue to cut back on the use of stock options, as discussed in the previous section, many people believe that regular employees will be hurt more than executives.[21] Some people are even calling for legislation to encourage companies to expand stock option offerings with rank-and-file employees.

GROUP INCENTIVES

group incentives
Incentives based on group rather than individual performance.

Because jobs can be interdependent, it is sometimes difficult to isolate and evaluate individual performance. In these instances, it is often wise to establish incentives based on group or team performance. For example, an assembly-line operator must work at the speed of the line. Thus, everyone working on the line is dependent on everyone else. With **group incentives,** all group members receive incentive pay based on the performance of the entire group. Depending on the specific situation, the group may be as large as the entire organizational workforce or as small as three or four members of a work team. Many group incentive plans are based on such factors as profits or reduction in costs of operations.

Group incentive plans are designed to encourage employees to exert peer pressure on group members to perform. For instance, if a group member is not performing well and thus is lowering the production of the entire group, the group will usually pressure the individual to improve, especially if a group incentive plan is in operation. A disadvantage of group incentives is that the members of the group may not perceive a direct relationship between their individual performances and that of the group. Size and cohesiveness of the group are two factors that affect this relationship. Usually smaller groups are more cohesive because more employees are likely to perceive a relationship between their performances and that of the group. Another potential disadvantage is that different groups can become overly competitive with one another to the detriment of the entire organization.

Self-Directed Work Teams   The philosophy behind any type of work team is that teams can contribute to improved performance by identifying and solving work-related problems. The basic idea is to motivate employees by having them participate in decisions that affect them and their work. Self-directed work teams, also called self-managed work teams, are teams of employees that accomplish tasks within their area of responsibility without direct supervision. Each team makes its own job assignments, plans its own work, performs equipment maintenance, keeps records, obtains supplies, and decides on new members for the work unit.

Although self-directed work teams are well established in Europe and especially in Scandinavia, they are relatively new in the United States.[22] The past 25 years have seen a dramatic increase in the use of self-directed work teams and they are widely used in today's organizations.[23] Most companies that use self-directed work teams usually incorporate some type of group incentive pay based on the performance of the respective work teams.

organizationwide incentives
Incentives that reward all members of the organization based on the performance of the entire organization.

Organizationwide Incentives   **Organizationwide incentives** reward members based on the performance of the entire organization. With such plans, the size of the reward usually depends on the salary of the individual. Most organizationwide incentive plans are based on establishing cooperative relationships among all levels of employees. One of the first and most successful organizationwide incentive plans was the Lincoln Electric plan, developed by James F. Lincoln. (The Lincoln Electric Company was discussed in HRM in Action 12.1 on page 236). In addition to providing many other benefits, this plan calls for a year-end bonus fund for employees based on company profits. Thus, the plan encourages employees to unite with management to reduce costs and increase production so that the bonus fund will grow.

Some of the most common organizationwide incentive plans include gain-sharing plans, Scanlon-type plans, and employee stock ownership plans (ESOPs). These three types of plans are discussed in the following sections.

Gain-Sharing or Profit-Sharing Plans

gain sharing
Programs also known as *profit sharing, performance sharing,* or *productivity incentives;* generally refers to incentive plans that involve employees in a common effort to achieve the company's productivity objectives. Based on the concept that the resulting incremental economic gains are shared among employees and the company.

Different companies know **gain sharing** by different names, such as *profit sharing, performance sharing,* or *productivity incentives.* These programs generally refer to incentive plans that involve employees in a common effort to improve organizational performance and then reward employees immediately when their performance improves.[24] Gain sharing is based on the concept that employees and the company share the resulting incremental economic gains. While many variants of gain sharing exist, they are all based on the same principles. First, the company must be able to measure its output; then, when employees reduce labor costs by increasing productivity, they share in the savings. For example, if it is determined that 25 percent of net production costs should be attributable to labor costs, any improvement below this target would be put into a bonus pool to be shared with employees. The division of these gains or profits, which are given in addition to normal wages and salaries, is usually based on an employee's base salary or job level. However, many variations are possible, including plans that give all employees the same amount, plans based on seniority, and plans based on individual

COKE TIES DIRECTOR'S COMPENSATION DIRECTLY TO COMPANY PERFORMANCE

In April 2006, the Coca-Cola Company adopted a new compensation plan for its board of directors that consists entirely of equity-based renumeration payable only if the company meets certain performance targets. Directors can potentially earn $175,000 per year in Coke shares, but the stock will be granted only if the company achieves 8 percent annual earnings in growth over a three year period (8 percent is the mid-point of the company's long-term performance target). If the performance goal is met at the end of the performance period, the share units are payable. If the performance goal is not met, all share units and hypothetical dividends are forfeited.

"Shareowners understand that they are only rewarded when the company performs," said James D. Robinson, III,

chairman of the company's Committee on Directors and Corporate Governance. "The Coca Cola Company board will hold itself to the same standard. As the company performs well, directors will be appropriately compensated."

The Coca Cola Company is the world's largest beverage company, with nearly 500 sparkling and still brands. Through the world's largest distribution system, consumers in more than 200 countries enjoy the company's beverages at a rate of nearly 1.6 billion servings a day.

Sources: "The Coca Cola Company Announced New Compensation Plan for Directors; Compensation to be Entirely Based on Company's Performance over Three-Year Periods," *PR Newswire*, April 5, 2006, and "The Board of Directors of the Coca Cola Company Announces Two Officers Elections," *Business Wire*, December 10, 2009.

performance. Probably the most popular type of gain-sharing or profit-sharing plan is where employees share in a percentage of all net profits after taxes over a certain, predetermined amount.

A recent review and summation of the empirical literature concluded that the "literature to date provides support for the contention that gain-sharing plans improve organizational effectiveness. However, further empirical work is needed to prove or disprove this contention."[25] The U.S. General Accounting Office has reported that firms with gain-sharing programs experience lower turnover and absenteeism, fewer grievances, and improved labor–management relations. One potential drawback to gain-sharing/profit-sharing plans is that the average employee may not perceive a direct relationship between individual output and the performance of the entire organization. However, it is not unusual for executives and top managers to have a significant amount of their total compensation based on the profits of the company. HRM in Action 14.4 describes a new compensation plan for directors at the Coca-Cola Company. The plan ties directors' compensation directly to the performance of the entire organization.

Scanlon-Type Plans

Scanlon plan
Organizationwide incentive plan that provides employees with a bonus based on tangible savings in labor costs.

The **Scanlon plan** was developed by Joseph Scanlon in 1927 and introduced at the LaPointe Machine Tool Company in Hudson, Massachusetts.[26] The Scanlon plan provides employees with a bonus based on tangible savings in labor costs and is designed to encourage employees to suggest changes that might increase productivity. Companies establish departmental committees composed of management and employee representatives to discuss and evaluate proposed labor-saving techniques. Usually the bonus paid is determined by comparing actual productivity to a predetermined productivity norm. Companies measure actual productivity by comparing the actual payroll to the sales value of production for the time period being measured. They place any difference between actual productivity and the norm in a bonus fund. The employees and the company share the bonus fund. Most Scanlon plans pay 75 percent of the bonus fund to employees and 25 percent to the company. Under the Scanlon plan, any cost savings are paid to all employees, not just to the employees who made the suggestions. Some companies have found that it is beneficial to review and modify their Scanlon plans periodically to take into account any changes that have occurred.[27] Scanlon plans have been successfully implemented in virtually every industry utilizing a variety of bonus formulas.[28]

Employee Stock Ownership Plans (ESOPs)

employee stock ownership plan (ESOP)
Form of stock option plan in which the organization provides for employee purchase of its stock at a set price for a set time period based on the employee's length of service and salary and the profits of the organization.

An **employee stock ownership plan (ESOP)** is a plan for providing employee ownership of company stock. ESOPs are generally executed in the form of a stock bonus plan or a leveraged plan. With either plan, an ESOP is established when the company sets up a trust, called an *employee stock ownership trust (ESOT)*, to acquire a specified number of shares of its own stock for the benefit of participating employees. With a stock bonus plan, the company annually gives stock to the ESOT or gives cash to the ESOT for buying stock. With a leveraged plan, the trust borrows a sum of money to purchase a specified number of shares of the company's stock. Generally, the company guarantees the loan. Then the company annually pays into the trust an agreed-on sum necessary to amortize and pay the interest on the loan. Under either plan, as the trust receives the stock, it is credited to an account established for each employee. Allocations are usually based on relative pay, length of service, or some combination of the two. When the employee retires or leaves the company, the stock is either given to the employee or purchased by the trust under a buy-back arrangement.

Revised data indicates that ESOPs grew rather dramatically from the mid-1970s through the late 1980s.[29] For example, in 1990, over 8,000 companies had enrolled nearly 5 million employees in ESOPs. This was up from 1,600 enrolled companies covering less than 250,000 employees in 1975. Growth through the mid-1990s was steady but slow. In 2006, the National Center for Employee Ownership (NCEO) estimated that 9,225 companies had ESOPs with 10.1 million participants.[30] As of 2009, the NCEO estimated that 11,400 plans covering 13.7 million employees existed in the United States.[31]

One appealing feature of ESOPs is that they have specific tax advantages for both the organization and the employees. For example, the organization can use pretax dollars to pay back the loan used to purchase the stock. The dividends a company pays on stock held by its ESOP are treated like interest and are also deductible. An advantage that has recently emerged is using an ESOP to rebuff an unfriendly takeover. The more stock an ESOP holds, the better equipped the company is to fend off an unwanted tender offer. Employees benefit by being able to defer any capital gains until the stock is actually distributed. ESOPs can also give employees some voice in running the company. Table 14.3 summarizes the primary benefits of ESOPs for the organization, the employee, and the stockholders.

One underlying assumption of an ESOP is that having a piece of the action causes employees to take more interest in the success of the company. Several studies have shown that companies combining an ESOP with employee participation in decision making enjoy sharply higher sales and earnings growth.[32] Numerous surveys have also reported that most companies' financial figures and other performance measures improve following the implementation of an ESOP.[33] On the other hand, ESOPs can have a limited effect as incentives. This is especially true when each employee owns only a minuscule amount of stock. Also, as we have seen clearly in recent years, it is possible that the price of the stock will go down rather than up. Thus, some employees view a stock option plan warily.

Table 14.4 summarizes the most frequently used incentive plans for nonmanagerial and managerial employees.

TABLE 14.3   **Major Benefits of Employee Stock Ownership Plans**

To Organization	To Employees	To Stockholders
Allows use of pretax dollars to finance debt.	Favorable tax treatment of lump-sum distribution, deferment of tax until distribution, and gift and estate tax exemptions.	Provides ready market to sell stock.
Increases cash flow.		Establishes definite worth of shares for estate purposes.
Provides a ready buyer for stock.	Allows employees to share in the success of the company.	Maintains voting control of company.
Provides protection against unwanted tender offers.	Provides a source of capital gains income for employees.	Protects the company from having to come up with large sums of money to settle an estate.
Protects the company from estate problems.	Can allow employees some voice in running the company.	
Can result in substantial tax savings.		Can result in preferential consideration for a government-guaranteed loan.
Can motivate employees by giving them a piece of the action.		

TABLE 14.4   **Summary of Most Commonly Used Incentive Plans**

Personnel	Type of Plan		
	Individual	**Group**	**Organizational**

Nonmanagers	Piece rate plans
	Plans based on time saved
	Commission plans
	Bonuses based on individual
	  performance
	Suggestion systems
	Stock options
		Bonuses based on group
		  performance
			Lincoln Electric plan
			Gain-sharing/profit-sharing
			  plans
			Scanlon-type plans
			Employee stock ownership plans
			  (ESOPs)

Managers	Bonuses based on organizational
	  performance (annual and long-term)
	Stock option plans:
	   Stock appreciation rights (SARs)
	   Phantom stock plans
	   Restricted stock plans
	Suggestion systems
		Bonuses based on group
		  performance
			Lincoln Electric plan
			Gain-sharing/profit-sharing
			  plans
			Scanlon-type plans
			Employee stock ownership plans
			  (ESOPs)

MAKING INCENTIVE PLANS WORK

Incentive plans have existed in one form or another for a long time. New plans are periodically developed, often as a result of changes in tax laws. As several examples in this chapter demonstrated, incentive compensation can make up a significant portion of an individual's total compensation. This is especially true with executives. If an incentive plan is to function as intended and generate higher performance among employees, it must be clearly communicated to employees, must be viewed as being fair, and must be related to performance. It also follows that the more employees understand an incentive plan, the more confidence and trust they will develop in the organization.

Summary of Learning Objectives

1. **Describe the two basic requirements of an effective incentive plan.**

   For an incentive plan to be effective, employees must believe their performances and the performances of others are accurately and fairly evaluated and that the incentives (rewards) are based on performance.

2. **List and briefly discuss at least three types of individual incentives.**

   The differential piece rate plan pays employees one rate for all acceptable units produced up to some standard and then a higher rate for all pieces produced if the output exceeds the standard. Incentive plans based on time saved give an employee a bonus for reaching a given level of production or output in less than the standard time. Under the commission plan, employees are rewarded, in part for their sales volume.

3. **Distinguish between a bonus and a merit pay increase.**

   A bonus is a reward offered on a one-time basis for high performance. A merit pay increase is a reward also based on performance, but perpetuated year after year.

4. **Discuss the role bonuses play in managerial compensation.**

   Bonuses are by far the most common type of incentive pay for managers. A 2002 survey reported that bonuses made up approximately 66 percent of total salaries for CEOs and approximately 36 percent of total salaries for all top executives.

5. **Differentiate between nonqualified stock options and incentive stock options (ISOs).**

   Stock option plans generally give managers an option to buy company stock at a predetermined, fixed price within a set period of time. Nonqualified stock options do not qualify for favorable tax treatment. Incentive stock options (ISOs) have certain tax advantages. Under an ISO, a recipient does not have to pay any tax until he or she sells the stock.

6. **Differentiate among the following different types of stock option related plans: stock-for-stock swaps, stock appreciation rights, phantom stock plans, restricted stock plans, premium-priced options, and performance-vesting options.**

   Stock-for-stock swaps allow options to be exercised with shares of previously purchased company stock in lieu of cash. Stock appreciation rights (SARs) are often used with stock option plans. Under an SAR, an executive has the right to relinquish a stock option and receive from the company an amount equal to the appreciation in the stock price from the date the option was granted. In one form of phantom stock, the company awards stock as a part of its normal bonus plan. The receiver then defers this phantom stock until retirement when he or she receives the accumulated shares of stock or its equivalent value. With another form of phantom stock, the receiver is credited with phantom stock and often after a stipulated period of time (usually three to five years) he or she is paid, in cash or equivalent shares, an amount equal to the appreciation in the stock. Under a restricted stock plan, a company gives shares of stock, subject to certain restrictions. Premium priced options are similar to standard options except that the exercise price of the stock is set substantially above the current market price of the stock. Performance-vesting options are priced at market price but are only exercisable if the stock price reaches or exceeds the price goal within the defined period.

7. **Discuss the major issues related to the executive pay controversy.**

   U.S. CEOs earn many, many times as much compensation as their average employee; much more than CEOs in Britain, Canada, and Japan. The large bonuses paid by companies that received government bailout money has infuriated many people. CEOs receiving large bonuses and other forms of compensation when the company is not performing well have also angered many people.

8. **Discuss the prevalence of stock options among nonmanagerial personnel.**

   Contrary to public belief, stock options are widely held by nonmanagerial personnel. One recent survey reported that 13 percent of private-sector employees nationwide receive some type of stock options and that 94 percent of these hold jobs below the top management ranks. A second recent study reported that 14.4 percent of all employees held stock options.

9. **Describe how group incentives work.**

   Under a group incentive plan, all members of a specified group receive incentive pay based on the performance of the entire group. Many group incentive plans are based on factors such as profits or reduction in costs of operations.

10. **Explain what a gain-sharing plan is.**

    Gain sharing is also known as profit sharing, performance sharing, or productivity incentives. Gain sharing plans generally refer to incentive plans that involve employees in a common effort to achieve the company's productivity objective. Gain sharing is based on the concept that the incremental economic gains are shared among employees and the company.

11. **Discuss Scanlon-type plans.**

    Scanlon-type plans provide employees with a bonus based on tangible savings in labor costs and are designed to encourage employees to suggest changes to increase productivity. Under a Scanlon-type plan, any cost savings are paid to all employees, not just to employees who made the suggestions.

12. **Explain how an employee stock ownership plan (ESOP) works.**

    An employee stock ownership plan (ESOP) provides for employee ownership of company stock. ESOPs are generally executed in the form of a stock bonus plan or a leveraged plan. With either plan, an ESOP is established when the company sets up a trust, called an employee stock ownership trust (ESOT), to acquire a specified number of shares of its own stock for the benefit of participating employees. With a stock bonus plan, the company annually gives stock to the ESOT or gives cash to the ESOT for buying stock. With a leveraged plan, the trust borrows a sum of money to purchase a specified number of shares of the company's stock.

Key Terms

bonus, *276*
commission plan, *275*
differential piece rate
  plan, *275*
employee stock
  ownership plan
  (ESOP), *283*
gain sharing, *282*
group incentives, *281*
incentive or variable pay
  plans, *274*

incentive stock option
  (ISO), *278*
merit pay increase, *276*
nonqualified stock
  options, *278*
organizationwide
  incentives, *282*
performance share
  plan (unit plan), *277*
performance-vesting
  options, *279*

phantom stock plan, *279*
premium-priced
  options, *279*
qualified stock options, *278*
restricted stock plans, *279*
Scanlon plan, *283*
stock appreciation
  rights (SARs), *279*
stock-for-stock swap, *278*
suggestion systems, *276*

**Review
Questions**

1. What are two essential requirements of an effective incentive plan?
2. Outline the advantages and disadvantages of individual incentive plans.
3. What is a piece rate plan?
4. What is an incentive plan based on time saved?
5. Describe an incentive plan based on commission.
6. What is a suggestion plan?
7. What is a long-term performance plan?
8. Define a stock option plan.
9. Define each of the following stock option–related plans: stock-for-stock swaps, stock appreciation rights, phantom stock plans, restricted stock plans, premium-priced options, and performance-vesting options.
10. Why are many people furious about executive compensation?
11. Name the advantages and disadvantages of a group incentive plan.
12. What are self-directed work teams?
13. Describe the most common types of organizationwide incentive plans.
14. What are the benefits of an ESOP to employees? To the organization? To stockholders?

**Discussion
Questions**

1. It has been said that incentive plans work only for a relatively short time. Do you agree or disagree? Why?
2. If you were able to choose the type of incentive pay system your company offered, would you choose an individual, a group, or an organizationwide incentive plan? Why?
3. If you were president of Ford Motor Company and could design and implement any type of incentive plan, what general type would you recommend for top management? For middle management? For supervisory management? For production employees?
4. What do you think about the way executive compensation has escalated in recent years? Do you think it is usually justifiable? Why or why not?

Incident 14.1

Rewarding Good Performance at a Bank

The performance of a bank branch manager is often difficult to measure. Evaluation can include such variables as loan quality, deposit growth, employee turnover, complaint levels, or audit results. However, many other factors that influence performance, such as the rate structure, changes in the market area served by the branch, and loan policy as set by senior management, are beyond the branch manager's control. The appraisal system presently used by First Trust Bank is based on points. Points are factored in for a manager's potential productivity and for the actual quality and quantity of work. In this system, the vast majority of raises are between 4 and 10 percent of base salary.

Sales growth is a major responsibility of a branch manager. Although many salespeople are paid a salary plus bonuses and commissions, no commissions are paid on business brought in by a branch manager. Therefore, one problem for the bank has been adequately rewarding those branch managers who excel at sales.

In May 2009, First Trust Bank opened a new branch on Northside Parkway, located in a high-income area. Three competing banks had been in the neighborhood for some 15 years. Jim Bryan, who had grown up in the Northside Parkway area, was selected as branch manager. In addition to Jim, the branch was staffed with five qualified people. Senior executives of the bank had disagreed about the feasibility of opening this branch. However, it was Jim's responsibility to get the bank a share of the market, which at that time consisted of approximately $56 million in deposits.

After one year of operation, this branch had the fastest growth of any ever opened by First Trust Bank. In 12 months, deposits grew to $18 million, commercial loans to $9 million, and installment loans to $2.5 million. As measured by Federal Reserve reports, the new branch captured 50 percent of the market growth in deposits over the 12 months. The customer service provided was extremely good, and branch goals for profit were reached ahead of schedule. Aware of the success, Jim looked forward to his next raise.

The raise amounted to 10 percent of his salary. His boss said he would have liked to have given Jim more, but the system wouldn't allow it.

Questions

1. Should Jim have been satisfied with his raise since this was the maximum raise the system allowed?

2. Do you think the bank currently offers adequate sales incentives to its branch managers? If not, what would you recommend?

Incident 14.2

Part-Time Pool Personnel

Crystal Clear Pool Company builds and maintains swimming pools in a large midwestern city. Crystal Clear handles pool maintenance through a contractual arrangement with the owners of the pools. Although individualized maintenance plans are available at a premium, the basic contract calls for Crystal Clear to vacuum the pools and adjust their chemical balance once a week. For 80 percent of the maintenance customers, the standard contract covers the months of May through September. The remaining 20 percent, who have either indoor or covered pools, require service year-round.

Because of the seasonal nature of the work, Crystal Clear hires many students during the summer. The maintenance staff is divided into three-person crews, each assigned to service six pools per day. In the summer, one permanent employee and two student employees comprise a team, with the permanent employee responsible for training the students. All maintenance crews are paid on a straight hourly basis.

The present system has been in force for several years, but it has resulted in at least two problems that seem to be getting more serious each year. The first is that the students hired for the summer demand to be paid the same wage rates that apply to the permanent employees. The reason is that the college students can get other summer jobs at these rates and are simply not willing to work for less. Naturally, the permanent employees resent the idea of being paid the same wages as the students. The second major problem involves the assignment of the pools, which vary in size and geographic location. The employees claim this is unfair because of the travel time required and differences in pool size. Some pools take three to four times as long to clean as others. Thus, some teams must work harder than others to service the six assigned pools.

Questions

1. What suggestions do you have for Crystal Clear to help remedy their compensation problems?

2. Can you think of any way to implement an incentive program at Crystal Clear? (Do not ignore the scheduling problems that might be created by such a program.)

3. In general, how do you think the problem of having to pay student employees the same rate as permanent employees could be resolved?

EXERCISE 14.1
Implementing Incentives

Assume you have been hired as a consultant to a medium-size sales organization to help it structure an incentive system for its three basic categories of employees. The first category is the sales force, composed of 20 salespeople all working on a straight commission. The second category is composed of seven support employees (two secretaries and five packer/shippers). All seven work on a straight hourly wage rate. The third category is made up of the two owner/managers.

The owner/managers like the straight commission system the salespeople are on, but they suspect that many of the salespeople tend to slack off once they have attained an acceptable level of sales for any given month. The seven support employees appear to be steady workers, but management believes their performance could be enhanced with the right incentive program. The owner/managers are satisfied with their current salaries but would like to look for some tax shelter for any additional profits.

Your job is to design an incentive plan with elements that will be attractive to each of the three categories of employees. Be prepared to present your plan to the class.

EXERCISE 14.2
Proven Suggestion Systems

Go to the library and/or Internet and identify one company or organization that has implemented a successful suggestion system. Identify what you think are the reasons that this suggestion system has worked. Be prepared to report your findings to the class.

EXERCISE 14.3
The Status of the Corporate and Financial Institutions Compensation Fairness Act (CFICF)

Go to your library or on the Internet and determine the status of the current status of the CFICF legislation.

Notes and Additional Readings

1. Hewitt Associates, "Variable Pay Highest on Record," press release, August 11, 2009. http://www.hewittassociates.com, accessed February 5, 2010.

2. "Employees Say Tenure Tops Performance to Determine Pay," *IOMA's Report on Salary,* August 2006, p. 8.

3. "Firms Fail to Use Comp Strategically to Drive Business Results," *IOMA's Report on Salary Surveys,* July 2007, p. 8.

4. Paula Davis, executive director EIA, telephone conversation on February 8, 2010.

5. "What Employees in Other Companies Do, Your Employees Can Do, Also," http://www.biztrain.com/coaching/services/greatidea.htm. Accessed February 5, 2007.

6. "Maruti Saves over Rs66 cr from Employee Suggestions," *Businessline,* May 10, 2008.

7. "Despite Economy, Majority of Firms Planning Year-End Bonuses," *The Enterprise,* December 14, 2009, p. 1.

8. Kathleen Johnston Jarboe, "Future Hazy for Stock Options," *Daily Record,* April 9, 2004, p. 1.

9. Robert J. Grossman, "Executive Pay: Perception and Reality," *HR Magazine,* April 2009, pp. 26–32.

10. Ibid.

11. Gretchen Morgenson, "Pushing the Pay Envelope Too Far," *New York Times,* April 14, 2002, business section, p. 1.

12. Phil Gusman, "AIG Defends Retention Program Payments," *National Underwriter,* December 15, 2008, p. 8.

13. Jennifer Schramm, "Executive Pay: On Your Radar," *HR Magazine,* April 2009, p. 108.

14. Stephen Miller, "Directors: Executive Pay Programs Need to Change," *HR Magazine,* July 2009, p. 12.

15. George Paulin, "Changing the Economics of Executive Compensation," *Business Week,* October 14, 2009.

16. Barry B. Burr, "Proxy Season Battles Pre-empted by Peace," *Pensions & Investments,* May 14, 2007, pp. 6–7.

17. "Stock Options Update," *HR Focus,* April 2004, p. 7.

18. Mark Schwanhausser, "New Survey Shows Variety of Workers Hold Stock Options," *Knight Ridder Tribune Business News,* April 4, 2004, p. 1.

19. The National Center for Employee Ownership, "A Statistical Profile of Employee Ownership," February 2009, www.nceo.org, accessed February 9, 2010.

20. The National Center for Employee Ownership, "A Comprehensive Overview of Employee Ownership," www.nceo.org, accessed February 9, 2010.

21. Jarboe, "Future Hazy for Stock Options."

22. Renee Beckham, "Self-Directed Work Teams: The Wave of the Future?" *Hospital Material Management Quarterly,* August 1998, pp. 48–60; Thomas Capozzoli, "How to Succeed with Self-Directed Work Teams," *Supervision,* February 2002, pp. 25–26.

23. Celia Zarraga and Jaime Bonache, "The Impact of Team Atmosphere on Knowledge Outcomes in Self-Managed Teams," *Organization Studies,* 26, no. 5, 2005, pp. 661–81.

24. Kevin M. Paulsen, "Lessons Learned from Gainsharing," *HR Magazine,* April 1991, p. 70.

25. Matthew H. Roy and Sanjiv S. Dugal, "Using Employee Gainsharing Plans to Improve Organizational Effectiveness," *Benchmarking,* 12, no. 3, 2005, pp. 250–59.

26. C. W. Brennan, *Wage Administration,* rev. ed. (Homewood, Ill.: Richard D. Irwin, 1963).

27. Valerie L. Williams, "Compensation Done the 'Right' Way," *Workforce,* December 1999, pp. 75–78.

28. "Scanlon & Skill: Two Compensation Plans for These Difficult Times," *IOMA's Pay for Performance Report,* December 2002, pp. 1–5.

29. The National Center for Employee Ownership, "A Statistical Profile of Employee Ownership," December 2003, pp. 1–8 at www.nceo.org/library/eo_stat.html.

30. "A Statistical Profile of Employee Ownership," July 10, 2006, http://www.nceo.org/library/eo_stat.html. Accessed February 11, 2007.

31. The National Center for Employee Ownership," A Brief Overview of Employee Ownership in the U.S.," www.nceo.org. Accessed February 9, 2010.

32. Christopher Farrell, Tim Smart, and Keith Hammonds, "Suddenly, Blue Chips Are Red-Hot for ESOPs," *BusinessWeek,* March 20, 1989; Corey Rosen and Ed Carberry, "Ownership Matters!: A Culture of 'Doing' Is Better Than Just 'Being'," *Workspan,* October 2002, pp. 28–32; and The National Center for Employee Ownership, "A Statistical Profile of Employee Ownership."

33. Peter Weaver, "An ESOP Can Improve a Firm's Performance," *Nation's Business,* September 1996, p. 63; James C. Sesil, Maya K. Kroumova, Joseph R. Blasi, and Douglas L. Kruse, "Broad-Based Employee Stock Options in US 'New Economy' Firms," *British Journal of Industrial Relations,* June 2002, p. 273; and "A Statistical Profile of Employee Ownership," February 2009, http://www.nceo.org. Accessed February 9, 2010.

Chapter **Fifteen**

Employee Benefits

Chapter Learning Objectives

After studying this chapter, you should be able to:

1. Define employee benefits.
2. Describe how employee benefits have grown over the last several years.
3. Summarize those benefits that are legally required.
4. Differentiate between a defined-benefit pension plan and a defined-contribution pension plan.
5. Discuss the attractiveness of a cash-balance plan to employees.
6. Describe a 401(k) plan and how it differs from a 403(b) plan.
7. Explain the purposes of the Employee Retirement Income Security Act (ERISA) and the Retirement Equity Act.
8. Distinguish between an IRA and a Roth IRA.
9. Describe a health maintenance organization (HMO) and a preferred provider organization (PPO).
10. Describe a Medical Savings Account and a Health Savings Account.
11. Explain the concepts of a floating holiday and personal days.
12. Explain the concept of a flexible-benefit plan.
13. Discuss two reasons employees are often unaware of the benefits their organizations offer.

Chapter Outline

employee benefits (fringe benefits)
Rewards that employees receive for being members of the organization and for their positions in the organization; usually not related to employee performance.

Employee benefits, sometimes called fringe benefits, are those rewards that employees receive for being members of the organization and for their positions in the organization. Unlike wages, salaries, and incentives, benefits are usually not related to employee performance. Figures compiled by the U.S. Chamber of Commerce show that organizations' payments for employee benefits in 2007 averaged $14,919.[1] The single most expensive cost was medical-related payments (averaging $4,595 per employee). Payments for time not worked (vacation, holidays, and sick leave) averaged $2,851 per employee. Retirement and savings accounted for $3,551 per employee.

The term *fringe benefits* was coined over 40 years ago by the War Labor Board. Reasoning that employer-provided benefits such as paid vacations, holidays, and pensions were "on the fringe of wages," the agency exempted them from pay controls.[2] It has been argued that this action, more than any single event, led to the dramatic expansion of employee benefits that has since occurred. However, because of the significance of benefits to total compensation, many employers have dropped the word *fringe* for fear that it has a minimizing effect.

WHAT ARE EMPLOYEE BENEFITS?

Web site: HR/Benefits Job Postings
www.ifebp.org/jobs/

Table 15.1 lists potential employee benefits. In general, these can be grouped into five major categories, which are not all mutually exclusive: (1) legally required, (2) retirement related, (3) insurance related, (4) payment for time not worked, and (5) other. Table 15.2 categorizes

TABLE 15.1 **Potential Employee Benefits**

Source: D. J. Thomsen, "Introducing Cafeteria Compensation in Your Company," *Personnel Journal,* March 1977, p. 125. Adapted from *Personnel Journal,* Costa Mesa, CA.

Accidental death, dismemberment insurance	Health maintenance organization fees	Private office
Birthdays (vacation)	Holidays (extra)	Professional activities
Bonus eligibility	Home health care	Psychiatric services
Business and professional memberships	Home purchase assistance	Recreation facilities
Cash profit sharing	Hospital-surgical-medical insurance	Resort facilities
Club memberships	Incentive growth fund	Retirement gratuity
Commissions	Interest-free loans	Sabbatical leaves
Company medical assistance	Layoff pay	Salary
Company-provided automobile	Legal, estate-planning, and other professional assistance	Savings plan
Company-provided housing	Loans of company equipment	Scholarships for dependents
Company-provided or subsidized travel	Long-term disability benefit	Severance pay
Day care centers	Matching educational donations	Shorter or flexible work week
Deferred bonus	Military leave	Sickness and accident insurance
Deferred compensation plan	Nurseries	Social security
Deferred profit sharing	Nursing-home care	Social service sabbaticals
Dental and eye care insurance	Opportunity for travel	Split-dollar life insurance
Discount on company products	Outside medical services	State disability plans
Educational activities (time off)	Paid attendance at business, professional, and other outside meetings	Stock appreciation rights
Employment contract	Parking facilities	Stock bonus plan
Executive dining room	Pension/401(k) plan	Stock option plans
Fitness Center	Personal accident insurance	Stock purchase plan
Free checking account	Personal counseling	Survivors' benefits
Free or subsidized lunches	Personal credit cards	Tax assistance
Group automobile insurance	Personal expense accounts	Training programs
Group homeowners' insurance	Pet insurance	Tuition benefits
Group life insurance	Physical examinations	Vacations
	Political activities (time off)	Wages
		Weekly indemnity insurance

TABLE 15.2   Examples of Common Benefits, by Major Category

Legally Required	Retirement Related	Insurance Related	Payment for Time Not Worked	Other
Social security	Pension funds	Medical insurance	Vacation	Company discounts
Unemployment compensation	Annuity plans	Accident insurance	Holidays	Meals furnished by company
Workers' compensation	401(k) plans	Life insurance	Sick leave	Moving expenses
State disability insurance	Early retirement	Disability insurance	Military leave	Severance pay
	Disability retirement	Dental insurance	Election day	Tuition refunds
	Retirement gratuity	Survivor benefits	Birthdays	Credit union
			Funerals	Company car
			Personal time	Legal services
			Paid rest periods	Financial counseling
			Lunch periods	Recreation facilities
			Wash-up time	
			Travel time	

TABLE 15.3
Benefits Expenditures from the Payroll Dollar, by Major Categories

Source: Based on figures from U.S. Chamber of Commerce Statistics and Research Center, *The 2006 Employee Benefits Study* (Washington, D.C.: U.S. Chamber of Commerce, 2006) p. 9.

Wages	55.9¢
Medical benefits	14.5¢
Payment for time not worked	11.1¢
Legally required benefits (employer's share only)	9.3¢
Retirement and savings	8.6¢
Other benefits	0.6¢
	100.0¢

many of the most common employee benefits. Table 15.3 shows how the payroll dollar is allocated among the major categories. Most benefits apply to all employees of the organization; however, some are reserved solely for executives. Certain benefits, such as health insurance, are often extended to include spouses. An increasing number of organizations are extending benefits coverage to include unmarried heterosexual and homosexual partners of unmarried employees. Since 2006, more than half of *Fortune* 500 companies have offered health benefits for domestic partners. As of 2009, 57 percent (a total of 286) of the *Fortune* 500 companies offered domestic partner benefits.[3] HRM in Action 15.1 discusses why IBM began offering some benefits to domestic partners and changes that have been made to the program.

GROWTH IN EMPLOYEE BENEFITS

Prior to the passage of the Social Security Act in 1935, employee benefits were not widespread. Not only did the act mandate certain benefits, but its implementation greatly increased the general public's awareness of employee benefits. By this time, unions had grown in strength and had begun to demand more benefits in their contracts. Thus, the 1930s are generally viewed as the birth years for employee benefits.

As productivity continued to increase throughout and after World War II, more and more employee benefits came into existence, although the categories used differ slightly from those described earlier. The 2008 Employee Benefits study by the U.S. Chamber of Commerce of 265 companies reported that benefits averaged 29.2 percent of payroll.[4] The following sections describe many of the more popular benefits today's organizations offer.

Effective January 1, 1997, IBM extended health care coverage to the partners of gay and lesbian employees. The policy covers all of IBM's 110,000 employees throughout the United States. At the time, this made IBM the largest U.S. company to offer benefits to this group. According to company officials, the policy covers only same-sex couples because opposite-sex domestic partners have the option of getting legally married. IBM officials said they implemented the policy because a rapidly growing number of other high-tech companies had and IBM didn't want to risk losing top talent. "It was a business decision," said Jill Kanin-Lovers, IBM's vice president of human resources. "We want to be in a position to attract and retain a broad spectrum of employees." Microsoft, Apple Computer, Xerox, and Hewlett-Packard are some of the other high-tech companies to offer domestic partner benefits.

When IBM introduced same-sex partner benefits in 1997, it did so with the provision that the policy would end if a state in which employees resided recognized same-sex marriages. Brad Salavich, global program manager for workforce diversity at IBM, explained that the domestic-partner benefit "was an extension to equalize benefits for gay and lesbian employees who were not legally able to have their relationship recognized." After gay marriage became legal in Massachusetts in 2004, IBM ended domestic-partner benefits for employees in Massachusetts effective January 2006. Other well-known companies that offer benefits to domestic partners include Toyota, Ford, UPS, Lowe's, and Home Depot.

Sources: "IBM Becomes Largest Employer to Offer Domestic Partner Benefits," *Business & Health*, October 1996, p. 16; Kimberly Blanton, "Some Massachusetts Firms Dropping Benefits for Unmarried Gay Couples," *Knight Ridder Tribune Business News*, December 8, 2004, p. 1; Judy Greenwald, "Advent of Gay Marriage Alters Massachusetts Partner Benefits," *Business Insurance*, January 17, 2005, pp. 4–5; and "A Fairer System: UK Should Approve Domestic-Partner Benefits," *Knight Ridder Tribune Business News*, January 18, 2007, p. 1.

LEGALLY REQUIRED BENEFITS

As mentioned earlier, the law mandates certain benefits. This section discusses three benefits that fall in this category: social security, unemployment, and workers' compensation benefits.

Social Security

social security
Federally administered insurance system designed to provide funds upon retirement or disability or both and to provide hospital and medical reimbursement to people who have reached retirement age.

Social security is a federally administered insurance system. Under current federal laws, both employer and employee must pay into the system, and a certain percentage of the employee's salary is paid up to a maximum limit. Table 15.4 shows how social security costs have changed over the past several years.

With few exceptions, social security is mandatory for employees and employers. Self-employed persons are required to contribute to social security at a rate higher than that paid by a typical employee, but lower than the combined percentage paid by both employer and employee. The payments distributed under social security can be grouped into three major categories: retirement benefits, disability benefits, and health insurance.

Retirement Benefits under Social Security

To be eligible for periodic payments through social security, a person must have reached at least age 62, and be fully insured under the system. To be fully insured a person must have 40 credits (people born before 1929 need fewer credits, depending on their year of birth). The way a credit is determined has changed over the years but generally requires that a minimum amount of money be earned ($1,000 per credit in 2007). A maximum of four credits can be earned in a calendar year. The full periodic allotment to which the retiree is entitled begins at age 65 for persons born before 1938. The age requirement increases slightly for persons born during 1938 or later (up to a maximum of age 67 for those born during 1960 or later). Those who retire as early as age 62 may receive periodic payments of a lesser amount determined by their exact age and earnings from gainful employment. Earnings from gainful employment do not include income from investments, pensions, or other retirement programs.

The size of the retirement benefit varies according to the individual's average earnings under covered employment. However, there are maximum and minimum limits to what eligible individuals and their dependents can receive. Table 15.5 lists dependents who may be eligible for retirement benefits if an eligible employee dies.

TABLE 15.4
Changes in Social Security Costs, 1980–2010

Year	Percentage Paid by Employee	Maximum Taxable Pay	Maximum Tax
1980	6.13	25,900	1,588
1981	6.65	29,700	1,975
1982	6.70	32,400	2,171
1983	6.70	35,700	2,392
1984	7.00	37,800	2,646
1985	7.05	39,600	2,792
1986	7.15	42,000	3,003
1987	7.15	43,800	3,132
1988	7.51	45,000	3,380
1989	7.51	48,000	3,605
1990	7.65	51,300	3,924
1991	7.65	53,200	4,070
1992	7.65	55,500	4,246
1993	7.65	57,600	4,406
1994	7.65	60,600	4,636*
1995	7.65	61,200	4,682*
1996	7.65	62,700	4,797*
1997	7.65	65,400	5,003*
1998	7.65	68,400	5,233*
1999	7.65	72,600	5,554*
2000	7.65	76,200	5,829*
2001	7.65	80,400	6,151*
2002	7.65	84,900	6,495*
2003	7.65	87,000	6,656*
2004	7.65	87,900	6,724*
2005	7.65	90,000	6,885*
2006	7.65	94,200	7,206*
2007	7.65	97,500	7,459*
2008	7.65	102,000	7,803*
2009	7.65	106,800	8,170*
2010	7.65	106,800	8,170*

*As of 1994, 1.45% (of the total 7.65%) going to Medicare was not limited by a maximum taxable pay. In prior years, this portion had been limited to an amount somewhat higher than the maximum taxable pay for the remaining 6.20%. See http://ssa-custhelp.ssa.gov.

TABLE 15.5
Dependents Eligible for Retirement Benefits in the Event of Death of a Covered Employee

- A widow or widower may be able to receive full benefits at age 65 if born before 1940. (The age to receive full benefits is gradually increasing to age 67 for widows and widowers born in 1940 or later.) Reduced widow or widower benefits can be received as early as age 60. If the surviving spouse is disabled, benefits can begin as early as age 50.
- A widow or widower can receive benefits at any age if she or he takes care of the deceased worker's child who is entitled to a child's benefit and is younger than age 16 or disabled.
- A deceased worker's unmarried children who are younger than age 18 (or up to age 19 if they are attending elementary or secondary school full time) also can receive benefits. Children can get benefits at any age if they were disabled before age 22 and remain disabled. Under certain circumstances, benefits also can be paid to stepchildren, grandchildren or adopted children.
- A deceased worker's dependent parents can receive benefits if they are age 62 or older. (For parents to qualify as dependents, the deceased worker would have had to provide at least one-half of their support.)
- A deceased worker's former wife or husband who is age 60 or older (as early as age 50 if disabled) can get benefits if the marriage lasted at least 10 years. A former spouse, however, does not have to meet the age or length-of-marriage rule if he or she is caring for his/her child who is younger than age 16 or who is disabled and also entitled based on the deceased worker's work. The child must be the deceased worker's former spouse's natural or legally adopted child.

Disability Benefits

Pensions may be granted under social security to eligible employees who have a disability that is expected to last at least 12 months or to result in death. The number of credits needed to qualify for disability benefits depends on the person's age (the credits vary for people under age 31), but generally 20 credits must be earned in 10 years before becoming disabled. These benefits are calculated with basically the same methods used for calculating retirement benefits.

Health Insurance

Health insurance under social security, commonly known as Medicare, provides partial hospital and medical reimbursement for persons over 65. Hospital insurance, which is known as Part A, is financed through the regular social security funds. Most inpatient hospital expenses, skilled nursing care, hospice care, and other related expenses are covered by Part A of Medicare. The medical insurance, known as Part B, helps a participant pay for a number of different medical procedures and supplies that are completely separate from hospital care. For example, normal outpatient visits and checkups would fall under Part B. Participation in the medical insurance program (Part B) of Medicare is voluntary and requires the payment of a monthly fee by those wishing to receive coverage. This fee was $110.50 per month in 2010 for individuals earning less than $85,000 per year and married couples earning less than $170,000 per year. For those earning more, the fees are substantially higher, depending on the amount earned. Part C (Medical Advantage) plans allow the user to choose to receive all of their health care services through a provider organization. Being under Part C may help lower the costs of medical services and it may result in extra benefits for an additional monthly fee. A person must have both Parts A and B to enroll in Part C. Part D (prescription drug coverage) is voluntary and the costs are paid for by the monthly premiums of enrollees and Medicare. Unlike Part B in which a person is automatically enrolled and must opt out if he or she does not want it, with Part D, a person has to opt in by filling out a form and enrolling in an approved plan.

Problems Facing Social Security

Almost everyone is aware of the financial crisis social security faces, which stems from major demographic changes that have taken place since the system was established. The basic problem is that fewer and fewer people are and will be working to support more and more retirees as the "baby boom" generation reaches retirement age.

Because tax revenues plummeted so rapidly during the latest recession, it is projected that social security could start paying out more than it takes in by 2013 and be completely bankrupt by 2029.[5] To resolve this imbalance, Congress must cut social security benefits, increase revenue to the program, or enact some combination of these options. Many experts believe that the long-term solution to the social security program is for individuals to supplement social security by some other type of retirement plan (other types of retirement plans are discussed later in this chapter).

Unemployment Compensation

unemployment compensation
Form of insurance designed to provide funds to employees who have lost their jobs and are seeking other jobs.

Unemployment compensation is designed to provide funds to employees who have lost their jobs through no fault of their own and who are seeking other jobs. Title IX of the Social Security Act of 1935 requires employers to pay taxes for unemployment compensation. However, the law was written in such a manner as to encourage individual states to establish their own unemployment systems. If a state established its own unemployment compensation system according to prescribed federal standards, the proceeds of the unemployment taxes paid by an employer go to the state. By 1937, all states and the District of Columbia had adopted acceptable unemployment compensation plans.

To receive unemployment compensation, an individual must submit an application through the state employment office and must meet three eligibility requirements: The individual must (1) have been covered by social security for a minimum number of weeks, (2) have been laid off (in some states, discharged employees may qualify), and (3) be willing to accept any suitable employment offered through the state's unemployment compensation commission. Many disputes have arisen regarding "suitable employment." Employees fired for misconduct are not eligible.

Generally, unemployment compensation is limited to a maximum of 26 weeks. Extended benefits can continue up to an additional 13 weeks during times of high unemployment. During the recent recession some states extended coverage even further. The amount received, which varies from state to state, is calculated on the basis of the individual's wages or salary received in the previous period of employment. The upper limit paid by most states is generally quite low when compared to the employee's normal salary.

Unemployment compensation is usually funded through taxes paid by employers; however, in some states, employees also pay a portion of the tax. The Federal Unemployment Tax Act (FUTA) requires all profit-making employers to pay a tax on the first $7,000 of wages paid to each employee. The rate paid varies from employer to employer based on the number of unemployed people an organization has drawing from the state's unemployment fund. Thus, the system is designed to encourage organizations to maintain stable employment. Since the passage of the Tax Reform Act of 1986, unemployment compensation has been fully taxable.

Workers' Compensation

workers' compensation
Form of insurance that protects employees from loss of income and extra expenses associated with job-related injuries or illness.

Workers' compensation is meant to protect employees from loss of income and to cover extra expenses associated with job-related injuries or illness. Table 15.6 summarizes the types of injuries and illnesses most frequently covered by workers' compensation laws. Since 1955, several states have allowed workers' compensation payments for job-related cases of anxiety, depression, and certain mental disorders. Although some form of workers' compensation is available in all 50 states, specific requirements, payments, and procedures vary among states. However, certain features are common to virtually all programs:

1. The laws generally provide for replacement of lost income, medical expense payments, rehabilitation of some sort, death benefits to survivors, and lump-sum disability payments.

2. The employee does not have to sue the employer to get compensation; in fact, covered employers are exempt from such lawsuits.

3. The compensation is normally paid through an insurance program financed through premiums paid by employers.

4. Workers' compensation insurance premiums are based on the accident and illness record of the organization. Having a large number of paid claims results in higher premiums.

5. An element of coinsurance exists in the workers' compensation coverage. Coinsurance is insurance under which the beneficiary of the coverage absorbs part of the loss. In automobile collision coverage, for example, there is often coinsurance in the amount of a $500 deductible for each accident. In workers' compensation coverage, there is coinsurance in that the workers' loss is usually not fully covered by the insurance program. For example, most states provide for a maximum payment of only two-thirds of wages lost due to the accident or illness.

TABLE 15.6
Job-Connected Injuries Usually Covered by Workers' Compensation

Source: Reprinted with permission. Table 15.6: pp. 190–191, "Job-connected Injuries Usually Covered by Workers' Compensation," from *Personnel Administration and the Law*, Second Edition, by Greenman and Schmertz; Copyright © 1979 The Bureau of National Affairs, Inc., Washington, D.C. 20037. For BNA Books Publications call toll free 1-800-960-1220 or visit www.bnabook.com.

Accidents in which the employee does not lose time from work
Accidents in which the employee loses time from work
Temporary partial disability
Permanent partial or total disability
Death
Occupational diseases
Noncrippling physical impairments, such as deafness
Impairments suffered at employer-sanctioned events, such as social events or during travel related to organization business
Injuries or disabilities attributable to an employer's gross negligence

6. Medical expenses, on the other hand, are usually covered in full under workers' compensation laws.

7. It is a no-fault system; all job-related injuries and illnesses are covered regardless of where the fault for the disability is placed.[6]

Workers' compensation coverage is compulsory in all but a few states. In these states, it is elective for the employer. When it is elective, any employers who reject the coverage also give up certain legal protections.

Benefits paid are generally provided for four types of disability: (1) permanent partial disability, (2) permanent total disability, (3) temporary partial disability, and (4) temporary total disability. Before any workers' compensation claim is recognized, the disability must be shown to be work related. This usually involves an evaluation of the claimant by an occupational physician. One major criticism of workers' compensation involves the extent of coverage different states provide. The amounts paid, ease of collecting, and the likelihood of collecting all vary significantly from state to state.

After a decade of yearly double-digit increases in the cost of workers' compensation, in the early 1990s at least 35 states began to make changes in their workers' compensation laws.[7] These changes included tighter eligibility standards, benefit cuts, improved workplace safety, and campaigns against fraud. Data indicate that these changes paid off. The rates of increases in the cost of workers' compensation slowed considerably, and in 1993 the cost actually declined.[8] The cost of workers' compensation insurance decreased through the late 1990s.[9] However, according to Standard & Poor's, after the September 11, 2001, attack on the World Trade Center in New York, workers' compensation premiums increased from 30 to 50 percent. Companies that endured losses in the attack saw rate increases from 50 to 100 percent.[10] In 2005 workers' compensation premiums dropped almost 18 percent.[11] This drop was attributable, at least in part, to workers' compensation reforms in major states such as California and Florida. Workers' compensation premiums have continued to fall in most states over the last several years.[12]

Retirees often rely on retirement-related benefits as well as social security.
Stockbyte/PunchStock

RETIREMENT-RELATED BENEFITS

In addition to the benefits required by law under social security, many organizations provide additional retirement benefits. These benefits are in the form of private retirement and pension plans.

Company-Sponsored Retirement Plans

private plans
Employee benefit that provides a source of income to people who have retired; funded either entirely by the organization or jointly by the organization and employee during employment.

defined-benefit plan
Pension plan under which an employer pledges to provide a benefit determined by a definite formula at the employee's retirement date.

defined-contribution plan
Pension plan that calls for a fixed or known annual contribution instead of a known benefit.

Retirement and pension plans, which provide a source of income to people who have retired, represent money paid for past services. **Private plans** can be funded entirely by the organization or jointly by the organization and the employee during the time of employment. Plans requiring employment contributions are called contributory plans; those that do not are called noncontributory plans. Funded pension plans are financed by money that has been set aside previously for that specific purpose. Nonfunded plans make payments to recipients out of current contributions to the fund. One popular form of pension plan is the **defined-benefit plan.** Under a defined-benefit plan, the employer pledges to provide a benefit determined by a definite formula at the employee's retirement date. The other major type of retirement plan is the **defined-contribution plan,** which calls for a fixed or known annual contribution instead of a known benefit.

As of 2008, 59 percent of full-time, private-sector American workers were employed by companies that sponsored some type of retirement plan.[13] Approximately 51 percent of private-sector workers between the ages of 25 and 64 actually participated in retirement plans on the job.[14] The 2008 Employee Benefits Study by the U.S. Chamber of Commerce reported that 82 percent of the responding companies offered retirement plan benefits to full-time employees.[15]

Pension Rights

An inherent promise of security in some form exists in every retirement and pension plan. However, if the pension benefits are too low or the plan is seriously underfunded, this promise of security is breached, and employees who have spent most of their working lives with companies that have pension plans do not receive an adequate pension—or any, in some cases.

vesting
Right of employees to receive money paid into a pension or retirement fund on their behalf by their employer if they leave the organization prior to retirement.

Another problem involves the vested rights of employees. **Vesting** refers to the rights of employees to receive the dollars paid into a pension or retirement fund by their employer if they leave the organization prior to retirement. For example, a vested employee can receive the funds invested by the employer at some later date. If not vested, the employee cannot receive the funds paid by the employer. A frequent approach is *deferred full vesting,* in which an employee, on meeting certain age and service requirements, enjoys full vested rights. A similar approach, called *deferred graded vesting,* gradually gives the employee an increasing percentage of benefits until the age and service requirements for full vesting are met.

Vesting requirements historically have caused problems for both employees and employers. In many old plans, the employee who was terminated or quit before retirement age did not receive any pension benefits regardless of the number of years worked under the pension plan or how close he or she was to retirement age. Even under plans that did provide vesting rights, the requirements were strict in terms of length of service. Employers often make requirements for vesting stringent in an effort to keep employees from leaving the organization, at least until their rights have become fully vested. On the other hand, employers have experienced the problem of employees quitting after being vested in the pension plan to draw out the funds credited to them. To counteract this, many employers have incorporated provisions in their pension plans stating that funds other than those contributed by the employee will not be distributed until the employee reaches a certain age, even if he or she has left the organization.

Defined-Benefit Plans

Defined-benefit plans have a specified formula for calculating benefits. Although there are numerous such formulas, the most popular approach has been the *final-average-pay plan,* in which the retirement benefit is based on average earnings in the years, generally two or five, immediately preceding retirement. The actual benefit sum is then computed as a function of the person's calculated average earnings and years of service. In another common approach, the *flat-benefit plan,* all participants who meet the eligibility requirements receive a fixed benefit regardless of their earnings.

Plans affecting salaried employees usually use the final-average-pay plan. Plans limited to hourly paid employees have traditionally used the flat-benefit plan. Where hourly and salaried employers are both affected, a final-average-pay formula may be modified to provide a minimum dollar benefit for participants in the lower pay classifications. Many final-average-pay plans are now calculated with an offset, or deduction, for the employee's social security benefits. In these cases, the amount of social security a person receives is taken into account when determining how much she or he will receive from the pension plan. Because defined-benefit plans can be costly to employers they have become less and less used by employers in recent years.

Cash-Balance Plans   The *cash-balance plan* is a hybrid of the traditional defined-benefit plan. The major difference is that cash-balance plans allow employees to take their cash-balance pension money with them in the form of a lump sum when they leave the organization. Another advantage of cash-balance plans is that participants can track the growth of their retirement funds in current dollars through regular statements. Participants in traditional defined-benefit plans are apprised only of what they should get at retirement. Thus, cash-balance plans are easier for the average employee to comprehend than are traditional defined-benefit plans. One drawback to cash-balance plans is that relatively junior employees can build up sizable cash balances and, once vested, leave the organization and take the cash with them. Traditional defined-benefit plans do not offer such ease of portability and therefore

COCA-COLA MOVES TO CASH-BALANCE PLAN

In 2009, Coca-Cola announced plans to adopt a cash-balance pension plan for current and future employees. Under the cash-balance plan, employees will receive annual age-weighted credits equal to a percentage of pay. The percentage will initially be 3 percent. Employees' cash-balance accounts will also be credited with a to-be-determined interest rate formula. The plan is being offered to most U.S. salaried and hourly employees hired as of January 1, 2010. Current employees in Coke's traditional $1.5 billion final average pay plan will also begin earning future benefits in the new plan.

Coke's switch to a cash-balance plan comes at a time when many major employers are phasing out their defined benefit plans in favor of defined contribution plans. Coke's executives rejected this approach. "Offering a secure and risk-free benefit to employees is very important to us," stated Sue Fleming, director of global benefits at Coke. The main appeal of a cash-balance plan for today's mobile workplace is that retirement benefits, which are based on career average pay, accrue faster than with traditional plans, in which employees have to work many years before accruing significant retirement benefits.

Source: Jerry Geisel, "Coca-Cola Makes Move to Cash Balance Plan," *Business Insurance,* February 23, 2009, p. 3.

encourage employees not to leave. Cash-balance plans became somewhat controversial in some instances where companies reduced future benefits as they converted from a traditional defined-benefit plan to a cash-balance plan. Cash-balance plans gained popularity in the late 1990s and were initially seen as a compromise from traditional defined-benefit plans. Companies liked cash-balance plans because they were cheaper and easier to maintain than traditional pensions. Employees, and especially younger employees, liked cash-balance plans because they were portable. HRM in Action 15.2 describes Coca-Cola's recent switch to a cash-balance plan.

Defined-Contribution Plans

With defined-contribution plans, every employee has a separate pension account to which the employee and the employer contribute. If only the employer contributes, it is a *noncontributing plan.* When both the employee and the employer contribute, it is a *contributing plan.* With a defined-contribution plan, the contributed money is invested and projections are made as to expected retirement income. However, the organization is not bound by these projections and hence unfunded liability problems do not occur. The benefits paid are a function of the rules of the plan and the actual value of the plan. Because the organization does not have a potential liability problem and because they are very portable, defined-contribution plans have become increasingly popular.

401(k) Plans The most popular type of defined-contribution plan is the *401(k) plan.* These plans were named after section 401(k) of the Internal Revenue Code, which became effective in 1980. The advantage of a 401(k) plan is that contributions are tax deductible up to a limit. Usually a 401(k) plan is set up to allow employees to defer a portion of their pay into the plan. Often employers will match employee contributions to some extent. As of 2010, the maximum tax-exempt contribution was $16,500.

In August of 2006, President Bush signed the Pension Protection Act (PPA) of 2006 into law.[16] Many people think that the PPA was the most significant legislation to affect retirement plans since the passage of the Employee Retirement Income Security Act (ERISA) in 1974 (ERISA is discussed in the next major section). The PPA makes permanent the increased contribution limits for 401(k) plans that the Economic Growth and Tax Relief Reconciliation Act of 2001 (EGTRRA) initially approved. The limits are also indexed to increase in $500 increments every year. Individuals over 50 years old may contribute an extra $5,500 in 2010. A major thrust of the PPA was also to impose much stronger funding requirements on employers with traditional defined-benefit pension plans. For example, previous employers were required to fund pension plans at 90 percent of their pension liability. Under the PPA, plans will be required to be 100 percent funded (this requirement will be phased in over a period

DUPONT CHANGES ITS RETIREMENT PLAN

In August 2006 DuPont Company announced that it would close its traditional, defined-benefit pension plan to employees hired after January 1, 2007. The announcement also said that the company would sharply reduce contributions to the old-style plan for current employees. To replace the potential lost retirement income from the traditional plan, DuPont will sweeten its 401(k) defined-contribution plan. Under the new setup, all employees will receive a base contribution in a personal 401(k) account of 3 percent of their pay, including overtime and bonus. In addition, the company will also match up to 6 percent of pay that an employee contributes to his or her 401(k). Current employees will retain their accrued traditional defined-benefit plan, but company contributions will be reduced by two-thirds beginning in 2008.

The changes will affect DuPont's 30,000 U.S. employees but not its 66,000 U.S. retirees. "We have to take a look at what is taking place in the market," explained DuPont spokesperson Lori Captain, "and the trend is definitely in this direction." Working through their unions, employees in some locations have protested these changes to their pensions.

Sources: "DuPont Slashes Worker Pensions, But Boosts Savings Plan," *Financial Wire,* August 29, 2006, p. 1; and "News from USW: Richmond DuPont Workers Rally to Protest Pension and Safety Issues at Spruance Plant," *Business Wire,* May 8, 2007.

of seven years for most employers). Other requirements designed to increase the security of traditional pension plans are also included under the PPA.

Many people believe that the passage of PPA signaled a decided shift in government policy toward defined-contribution retirement plans like the 401(k) plans and away from the more traditional company-funded defined-benefit plans. Recently court rulings have also lessened companies' fear of jettisoning both traditional and cash-balance plans in favor of 401(k) plans. HRM in Action 15.3 describes how DuPont has shifted its retirement plan from a traditional defined-benefit plan to a 401(k) plan.

403(b) Plan   The *403(b),* or Tax Deferred Annuity (TDA), plans are very similar to 401(k) plans except that they may only be used in not-for-profit organizations. These organizations are usually religious, charitable, and educational but also include other entities such as social clubs organized and operated for pleasure, recreation, and other nonprofitable purposes. As of January 1, 1997, the not-for-profit organization could also use 401(k) plans for the first time. Because the differences between the two types of plans are subtle, most not-for-profit plan sponsors have chosen to stay with the familiar TDA plans rather than make changes.

Employer-Sponsored SIMPLE IRA   A relatively new retirement option that is available to employers with 100 or fewer employees receiving at least $5,000 of compensation per year is the *employer-sponsored SIMPLE IRA*. Under a SIMPLE IRA an employee can elect to have the employer make contributions to a SIMPLE IRA rather than receiving that amount in cash. An employer that establishes a SIMPLE IRA plan must make either matching contributions or nonelective contributions. Employers making matching contributions must generally match employee contributions up to 3 percent of the employee's compensation for the calendar year. In lieu of making matching contributions, the employer may make a nonelective contribution of 2 percent of compensation for each eligible employee making at least $5,000 in compensation during the calendar year.

If an employer establishes a SIMPLE IRA plan, all employees who received at least $5,000 in compensation from the employer during any two prior tax years and who are reasonably expected to receive at least $5,000 during the current year must be eligible to participate in the plan for the current year. For 2010, employee elective contributions were limited to the lesser of (1) the employee's compensation or (2) $11,500 ($14,000 if age 50 or older). The main advantage of SIMPLE IRA plans is that they do not have to meet the nondiscrimination requirements, minimum participation and minimum coverage rules, and vesting rules applicable to other types of plans.

ERISA and Related Acts

Employee Retirement Income Security Act (ERISA)
Federal law passed in 1974 designed to give employees increased security for their retirement and pension plans and to ensure the fair treatment of employees under pension plans.

In an effort to ensure the fair treatment of employees under pension plans, Congress passed the **Employee Retirement Income Security Act (ERISA)** in 1974. This law was designed to ensure the solvency of pension plans by restricting the types of investments that could be made with the plan's funds and providing general guidelines for fund management. ERISA also requires that employees have vested rights in their accrued benefits after certain minimum requirements have been met. Table 15.7 summarizes the major provisions of ERISA.

The Sarbane-Oxley Act, the accounting and financial reform legislation signed by President Bush in 2002, also contains provisions that affect ERISA. Specifically, the act substantially raises the criminal penalties for ERISA reporting and disclosure violations.

Since its inception, ERISA has been criticized as being overly costly. In fact, it has been reported that several companies dropped their pension plans rather than comply with ERISA.[17] Another major complaint has been that it causes an unwieldy amount of paperwork. The existence of ERISA is yet another reason why employers are moving toward 401(k) plans.

Retirement Equity Act
Act passed in 1984 that liberalized eligibility requirements, vesting provisions, maternity/paternity leaves, and spouse survivor benefits of retirement plans.

In 1984, Congress passed the **Retirement Equity Act.** The overall impact of this act was to liberalize the eligibility requirements, vesting provisions, maternity/paternity leaves, and spouse survivor benefits of retirement plans. Table 15.8 summarizes the major provisions of the Retirement Equity Act.

TABLE 15.7 **Major Provisions of ERISA**

Source: Reprinted by permission of *Harvard Business Review,* from "Responding to the Pension Reform Law," by D. G. Carlson, November/December 1974, p. 134. Copyright © 1974 by the Harvard Business School Publishing Corporation; all rights reserved.

Subject	Provisions
Eligibility	Prohibited plans from establishing eligibility requirements of more than one year of service, or an age greater than 25, whichever is later.

Vesting*	Established new minimum standards; employer has three choices:
	  a. 100 percent vesting after 10 years of service.
	  b. 25 percent after 5 years of service, grading up to 100 percent after 15 years.
	  c. 50 percent vesting when age and service (if the employee has at least 5 years of service) equal 45, grading up to 100 percent vesting 5 years later.

Funding	Required the employer to fund annually the full cost for current benefit accruals and amortize past-service benefit liabilities over 30 years for new plans and 40 years for existing plans.
Plan termination insurance	Established a government insurance fund to insure vested insurance pension benefits up to the lesser of $750 a month or 100 percent of the employee's average wages during highest-paid five years of employment; the employer pays an annual premium of $1 per participant and is liable for any insurance benefits paid up to 30 percent of the company's net worth.
Fiduciary responsibility	Established the "prudent man" rule as the basic standard of fiduciary responsibility; prohibits various transactions between fiduciaries and parties-in-interest; prohibits investment of more than 10 percent of pension plan assets in the employer's securities.
Portability	Permitted an employee leaving a company to make a tax-free transfer of the assets behind his vested pension benefits (if the employer agrees) or of his vested profit-sharing or savings plan funds to an individual retirement account.
Individual retirement accounts (IRAs)	Provided a vehicle for transfers as noted above and permits employees of private or public employers that do not have qualified retirement plans to deduct 15 percent of compensation, up to $1,500, each year for contributions to a personal retirement fund. Earnings on the fund are not taxable until distributed.
Reporting and disclosure	Required the employer to provide employees with a comprehensive booklet describing plan provisions and to report annually to the Secretary of Labor on various operating and financial details of the plan.
Lump-sum distributions	Changed the tax rules to provide capital gains treatment on pre-1974 amounts and to tax post-1973 amounts as ordinary income, but as the employee's only income and spread over 10 years.
Limits on contributions and benefits	Limited benefits payable from defined-benefit pension plans to the lesser of $75,000 a year or 100 percent of average annual cash compensation during the employee's three highest paid years of service. Limited annual additions to employee profit-sharing accounts to the lesser of $25,000 or 25 percent of the employees' compensation that year.

*These requirements were changed by subsequent legislation.

TABLE 15.8
Major Provisions of the Retirement Equity Act

Source: Stephen P. Kurash and Gene F. Fasoldt, "An Outline of Changes Required by the New Retirement Equity Act," *Personnel Journal,* November 1984, pp. 80–84.

- Employees must be allowed to participate in a plan that qualifies for special tax treatment no later than age 21 with one year of service (previously, it was age 25 with one year of service).
- Vesting credit must be awarded for years of service beginning at age 18 (previously, service before age 22 could be ignored in most plans).
- For both vesting and participation purposes, as many as 501 hours of service must be awarded to any employee on maternity or paternity leave.
- An election to waive spouse survivor benefits must be made in writing by both the participant and spouse and witnessed by a plan representative or notary public.

The Tax Reform Act of 1986 provided for employees to become vested sooner than under ERISA and other legislation. The provisions of the Tax Reform Act of 1986 were generally applicable for plan years beginning after December 31, 1988. For plans beginning after this date, the general vesting provisions must follow one of two schedules:

- Cliff vesting, under which no vesting is provided during the first five years of service and the participant becomes vested after five years of service.
- Graded vesting, under which the participant becomes 20 percent vested after three years of service with an additional 20 percent vesting per year until the participant is 100 percent vested after seven years of service.

Mandatory Retirement

Amended Age Discrimination in Employment Act (ADEA)
Forbids mandatory retirement at any age for all companies employing 20 or more people in the private sector and in the federal government.

An amendment to the **Age Discrimination in Employment Act (ADEA)** that took effect on January 1, 1987, forbade mandatory retirement at any age for companies employing 20 or more people in the private sector (there are certain exceptions, as covered in Chapter 2) and for federal employees.

Early Retirement

As an alternative to mandatory retirement, some organizations offer incentives to encourage early retirement. This method of reducing the workforce is often viewed as a humanitarian way to reduce the payroll and reward long-tenured employees. The types of incentives offered vary, but often include a lump-sum payment plus the extension of other benefits, such as medical insurance. Another popular incentive is to credit the employee with additional years of service that can be used under a defined-benefit plan.

Most pension plans have special allowances for voluntary early retirement. Usually an employee's pension is reduced by a stated amount for every month that he or she retires before age 65. Popular early retirement ages are 55, 60, and 62. Most plans require that an individual shall have worked a minimum number of years with the organization to be eligible for early retirement. Early retirement has grown in popularity, partly because of the pension benefits available. Presently, the earliest an employee can receive social security retirement benefits at a reduced rate is at age 62.

Employees Not Covered by Company Retirement Plans

individual retirement accounts (IRA)
Individual pension plan for employees not covered by private pension plans.

In 1981, legislation was enacted to allow employees to set up individual plans called **individual retirement accounts (IRAs).** Although the basic purpose of IRAs was to provide an option for employees not covered by private plans, anyone who has an earned income can invest in an IRA. For 2010, allowable contributions to an IRA can generally be made up to the lesser of $5,000 or the individual's compensation (wages or other earned income, plus alimony received). Also, individuals who are at least age 50 by year end may contribute an additional $1,000 to their IRA account, for a total contribution of $6,000. For married couples, this amount may be contributed for each person—if the combined compensation of both spouses is at least equal to the contributed amount (assuming a joint return is filed). While a contribution is allowable as explained above, the deductibility of an IRA contribution is dependent upon the participation of the individual—or individual's spouse—in an employer-sponsored retirement plan.

If there is no active participation in a retirement plan, the individual (and spouse) may deduct the full amount of their contribution, subject to the compensation limits described above. If one or both spouses participate in an employer plan, however, the ability to deduct the IRA contribution may be limited, based on modified adjusted gross income (AGI). (1) If an individual participates in a plan, the deduction begins to phase out with modified AGI ranging from $55,000–$65,000 for single or head-of-household filers, and $89,000–$109,000 for married couples filing jointly. (2) For married couples where only one is covered under a plan, the phase-out range begins at $166,000 with no deduction allowed after $176,000.

SEP-IRA
Retirement plan that allows small businesses and sole proprietors to make deductible contributions.

In a simplified employee pension IRA, known as a **SEP-IRA** or a SEPP-IRA, the employer contributes up to 25 percent of an employee's total salary, with a maximum of $49,000. These plans are offered by small businesses or even sole proprietors, which usually don't have any other retirement program. SEP-IRAs are subject to the same rules as regular IRAs. SEP-IRA contributions and earnings on investments are not taxable until withdrawal (presumably retirement), when they become subject to normal income tax.

Roth IRA
Retirement plan that allows individuals to make nondeductible contributions and tax-free withdrawals with certain restrictions.

The **Roth IRA,** which was also created by the Taxpayer Relief Act of 1997, allows for nondeductible contributions of up to $5,000 annually ($10,000 married filing jointly), less the total amounts contributed to any other IRAs. As with a regular IRA, a special catch-up provision has been added allowing individuals age 50 and over to contribute an additional $1,000 per year. All earnings in a Roth IRA then accumulate tax-deferred, and qualified distributions are made free of federal income tax and penalties. In order for withdrawals from a Roth IRA to be qualified as tax free, the withdrawals must have been made for at least five years, after the attainment of age 59½, or due to death or disability, or for first-time home buyer expenses up to a lifetime limit of $10,000. Contributions to Roth IRAs are phased out from $105,000 through $120,000 of income for single taxpayers and $166,000 to $176,000 for joint filers. The Roth IRA is especially attractive for young employees because of the long-term growth potential of the investment. Although it can be complicated, it is possible in many circumstances to convert a traditional IRA to a Roth IRA.

Recent broadening of retirement provisions now enable self-employed persons to have their own 401(k) plans following the same rules as other 401(k) plans.

Preretirement Planning

A recently evolved benefit is preretirement planning. The purpose of such a planning program is to help employees prepare for retirement, both financially and psychologically. At the most basic level, preretirement planning provides employees with information about the financial benefits they will receive upon retirement. The subjects include social security, pensions, employee stock ownership, and health and life insurance coverage. Other programs go beyond financial planning and cover such topics as housing, relocation, health, nutrition, sleep, exercise, part-time work, second careers, community service, recreation, and continuing education.

The rapid pace of change in today's world, accentuated by changing federal laws and uncertainty concerning social security, has enhanced the need for some type of preretirement planning. This need is not expected to diminish in the near future.

INSURANCE-RELATED BENEFITS

Insurance programs of various types represent an important part of any benefit package. For example, the 2008 Employee Benefits Survey by the U.S. Chamber of Commerce reported that 89 percent of the respondents provided some form of medical insurance to full-time employees.[18] At the same time, however, many employees of small companies are not covered by company-sponsored health insurance. Company-sponsored medical insurance programs are designed so that the employer pays either the entire premium or a portion of it, with the employee responsible for the balance. The issue of health insurance has been vigorously debated by the U.S. Congress over the last several years. The Obama administration has passed sweeping changes to the health care system and only time will reveal what ultimately evolves.

Health Insurance

In addition to normal hospitalization and outpatient doctor bills, some plans now cover prescription drugs and dental, eye, and mental health care. Many health care plans incorporate a deductible, which requires the employee to pay a certain amount of medical expenses each year (usually $50 to $300 per person) before the insurance becomes effective. The health insurance plan then pays the bulk of the remaining expenses. Some plans pay the entire cost of health insurance for both the employees and dependents, some plans require the employee to pay part of the cost for dependents only, and some plans require the employee to pay part of the cost for both.

Over the years, two distinct health insurance plans have evolved: the base plan and the major medical expense plan. *Base plans* cover expenses for specified services within certain limits established for each kind of service. *Major medical plans* define a broad range of covered expenses, including all services that may be required for successful treatment. When used alone, a major medical plan is referred to as a *comprehensive plan.* Many organizations supplement a base plan with a major medical expense plan. The reason for combining the two is usually to reduce the deductible amount for certain types of treatment. The precise coverage, size of the deductible, and other specifics vary considerably among plans.

Managed Care   Due to rapidly escalating health care costs, many organizations have turned to various forms of managed care. The idea behind *managed care* programs is for the provider of the health care, usually an insurance company, to organize and manage the program in a manner that will control costs. Managed care can be provided in a variety of forms. The health maintenance organization (HMO) and the preferred provider organization (PPO) are two of the most popular types of managed care programs.

Health Maintenance Organizations (HMOs)   The Health Maintenance Organization Act of 1973 ushered in the concept of one-stop, prepaid medical services as an alternative to traditional insurance programs. Under this arrangement, organizations contract with an approved **health maintenance organization (HMO)** to provide all the basic medical services the organization's employees need for a fixed price. HMOs can be structured in many different ways. Some HMOs own their facilities and pay doctors to work for them; others contract with a physician group to care for its patients; and still others contract either with individual doctors or with networks of independent physicians practicing in their own offices. Advantages of HMOs include emphasis on prevention of health problems and costs that are usually lower than those of traditional coverage. One major disadvantage, from the employee's viewpoint, is that employees must use physicians employed or approved by the HMO, and these may or may not be the doctors of their choice. A second disadvantage from the employee's viewpoint is that, in many instances, the HMO must preapprove certain procedures and treatments. Because of these disadvantages and the resulting general employee discontent, the picture of HMOs is not as bright as in the past. The 2008 Employee Benefits Study by the U.S. Chamber of Commerce reported that 28 percent of the respondents offered some type of HMO.[19] The 2009 Employee Benefit Study by SHRM found that 35 percent of the respondents offered some type of HMO.[20]

Preferred Provider Organizations (PPOs)   Preferred provider organizations (PPOs) are another alternative that emerged during the 1980s. A PPO is formed by contracting with a group of doctors and hospitals to provide services at a discounted or otherwise attractive price. In exchange, these providers are designated as "preferred" providers of care. The major difference between an HMO and a PPO is that under a PPO, employees have much more freedom to choose their own doctors. PPOs do not restrict the provision of care to their own providers. They do, however, offer incentives, such as higher reimbursement levels, when care is received from a PPO member. The U.S. Chamber of Commerce's 2008 Employee Benefits Study reported that 72 percent of respondents offered some type of PPO.[21] The 2009 Employee Benefits Study by SHRM found that 81 percent of the respondents offered some type of PPO.[22]

Medical Savings Accounts   Medical savings accounts, also known as medical spending accounts, allow employees to set aside pretax dollars through normal payroll deductions to pay for medical bills throughout the calendar year. The major drawback to medical savings accounts is that any money not used during the calendar year is usually forfeited. Because of this stipulation, employees using medical spending accounts must conservatively and

health maintenance organization (HMO)
Health service organization that contracts with companies to provide certain basic medical services around the clock, seven days a week, for a fixed cost.

preferred provider organizations (PPO)
Formed by contracting with a group of doctors and hospitals to provide services at a discount or otherwise attractive price. Such providers are designated as "preferred" providers of care.

**LOWERING HEALTH INSURANCE COSTS
WITH AN HSA**

Boulder, Colorado, dentist Kirk Rathburn opened his five-employee practice in 1993. From the start Rathburn believed it was a basic obligation to ensure that his employees had access to health insurance. However, Rathburn found that the cost of health insurance skyrocketed over the years to the point that he thought he might have to stop offering it.

In an attempt to lower his health insurance costs, Rathburn turned to health savings accounts (HSAs) and high deductible insurance. Rathburn found that his cost per employee dropped immediately from about $2,000 per month with traditional insurance to $1,500 monthly. Rathburn has also discovered that the premiums he and his employees pay have risen much more slowly. To say the least Rathburn was relieved.

Today, Rathburn looks at his HSA as a type of secondary retirement investment vehicle. With this view, Rathburn currently pays all of his family's routine medical expenses out-of-pocket in order to let his HSA continue to grow.

Source: Greg Avery, "Health Savings Accounts Take Center Stage," *Knight Ridder Tribune Business News,* January 27, 2007, p. 1.

accurately estimate their medical expenses. The major advantage of these plans is that these expenses are tax free.

Health Savings Accounts   In 2004, President Bush signed prescription drug legislation that made drug coverage available to Medicare's senior citizens and people with disabilities. The new law also established health savings accounts (HSAs).[23] HSAs are similar to 401(k) retirement plans in that they allow a certain amount of tax-free funds to be put aside by employers and employees. The HSA funds can then be withdrawn to pay for out-of-pocket medical expenses. In general HSAs operate as follows (the figures are for 2010):

- Employees or employers buy regular health insurance policies with high annual deductibles of at least $1,200 per year for individuals and $2,400 for families. These policies will cover the most expensive illnesses, but not routine medical costs such as doctors' visits and lab tests.

- Employees open supplemental HSAs, into which they or their employers can put up to $3,050 per year for individuals and up to $6,150 per year for families. Contributions are tax deductible. The funds will accumulate indefinitely, and can be withdrawn to pay for routine medical services, such as those now covered by traditional health plans. In addition, HSA monies can be spent on services that are not always covered by traditional plans, such as eye glasses, dental care, and some cosmetic procedures.

HSAs are expected to continue to grow in popularity. The SHRM 2009 Employee Benefits Study reported that 32 percent of the respondents offered HSAs.[24] HRM in Action 15.4 discusses why one dentist has switched his office over to an HSA.

Dental Insurance

Dental insurance has been one of the fastest-growing types of employee benefits in recent years. Surveys conducted by the Conference Board show that the number of companies providing dental plans grew from 8 percent in 1973 to 19 percent in 1975 and 41 percent in 1981. In the 2008 Employee Benefits Study of the U.S. Chamber of Commerce, 80.3 percent of the respondent companies provided dental insurance.[25] The 2009 Employee Benefits Study by SHRM reported that 96 percent of the responding companies offered some type of dental plan.[26] Some major medical expense plans include dental treatment, but most dental insurance is provided as a separate plan. The majority of dental plans specify a deductible and require the employee to pay a portion of the cost of services.

Life Insurance

Life insurance is a benefit commonly available from organizations. When provided for all employees, it is called *group life insurance.* Costs of this type of insurance, based on the characteristics of the entire group covered, are typically the same per dollar of insurance for all employees. Generally, the employer provides a minimum coverage, usually $10,000 to $20,000. Employees often have the option to purchase more insurance at their own expense. A physical examination is usually not required for coverage. Presently, employers can provide up to a maximum of $50,000 worth of life insurance for an employee without the cost of the policy being considered as income to the individual. The U.S. Chamber of Commerce's 2008

Employee Benefits Study reported that 87.3 percent of those companies surveyed provided at least some payment for life insurance for full-time employees.[27] The 2009 SHRM Employee Benefits Study found that 91 percent of the respondents provided some type of life insurance.[28]

Accident and Disability Insurance

disability insurance
Designed to protect employees who experience long-term or permanent disability.

In addition to health, dental, and life insurance, many organizations provide some form of accident or disability insurance, or both. Most accident insurance is designed to provide funds for a limited period of time, usually up to 16 weeks. The amount of benefit is often some percentage of the accident victim's weekly salary. **Disability insurance** is designed to protect the employee who experiences a long-term or permanent disability. Normally, a one- to six-month waiting period is required following the disability before the employee becomes eligible for benefits. As with accident insurance, disability insurance benefits are usually calculated as a percentage of salary.

PAYMENT FOR TIME NOT WORKED

It is now standard practice for organizations to pay employees for certain times when they do not work. Rest periods, lunch breaks, and wash-up times represent times not worked that are almost always taken for granted as part of the job. Recognized holidays, vacations, and days missed because of sickness, jury duty, and funerals represent other compensated times that are not worked. As mentioned earlier in this chapter, payments for time not worked represent over one-fourth the cost of all benefits.

Paid Holidays and Paid Vacations

floating holiday
Holiday that is observed at the discretion of the employee or the employer.

Christmas Day, New Year's Day, Thanksgiving Day, Independence Day, Labor Day, and Memorial Day are currently provided as paid holidays by most companies. One relatively new concept is the **floating holiday,** which is observed at the discretion of the employee or the employer. Another relatively new concept is referred to as personal time-off or personal days. Under this concept, organizations give employees a certain number of days with pay to attend to personal affairs. Normally these days can be taken at the employee's discretion. The number of paid holidays provided by most companies appears to have stabilized at an average of 9 to 10 per year.

Typically, an employee must meet a certain length-of-service requirement before becoming eligible for a paid vacation. Also, the time allowed for paid vacations generally depends on the employee's length of service. Unlike holiday policies that usually affect everyone in the same manner, vacation policies may differ among categories of employees. Most organizations allow employees to take vacation by the day or week but not in units of less than a day.

OTHER BENEFITS

In addition to the previously discussed major benefits, organizations may offer a wide range of additional benefits, including food services, exercise facilities, health and first-aid services, financial and legal advice, counseling services, educational and recreational programs, day care services, adoption assistance, and purchase discounts. Employee assistance programs, a type of general service related to employee well-being, are discussed in Chapter 16.

The extent and attractiveness of these benefits vary considerably among organizations. For example, purchase discounts would be especially attractive to employees of a retail store or an airline.

EMPLOYEE PREFERENCES AMONG BENEFITS

If an organization expects to get the maximum return from its benefit package in terms of such factors as retention, motivation, satisfaction, low turnover, and good relations with unions, the benefits should be those its employees most prefer. Ironically, however, organizations traditionally have done little to ensure that this is the case. Historically, they have offered uniform benefit packages selected by the human resource department and top management. Only on rare occasions or when demanded by a union contract are employees consulted concerning their benefit preferences.

Organizations that provide benefits without input from their employees assume management always knows what is best for the employees and that all employees need and desire the same benefits. Not too many years ago, a "typical" employee was a middle-aged male who worked full time, supported 2.5 children, and had a wife who stayed home. With the increasing diversity of today's workforce, there really is no such thing as a typical employee. Given that the workforce is far from homogeneous, it is not surprising that studies have shown that factors such as sex, age, marital status, number of dependents, years of service, and job title appear to influence benefit preferences.[29]

Flexible-Benefit Plans

flexible-benefit plan (cafeteria plan)
Benefit plan that allows employees to select from a wide range of options how their direct compensation and benefits will be distributed.

Because of the differences in employee preferences, some companies began to offer flexible-benefit plans in the mid-1970s. Under a **flexible-benefit plan,** individual employees have some choice as to specific benefits each will actually receive; usually employees select from among several options how they want their direct compensation and benefits to be distributed. The idea is to allow employees to select benefits most appropriate to their individual needs and lifestyles. For example, a middle-aged employee with several children in school might choose to take a set of benefits that differs from those chosen by a young, single employee.

Flexible plans are also called **cafeteria plans** because they provide a "menu," or choice of benefits, from which employees select. The selection possibilities within a flexible-benefit plan may vary considerably from plan to plan. Some plans limit the choices to only a few types of coverage, such as life insurance and health insurance. Others allow employees to choose from a wide range of options.

The number of companies offering flexible plans is not huge, but it has been growing steadily. TRW Systems and Energy Group, Education Testing Service, American Can, Northern States Power, and North American Van Lines (a subsidiary of PepsiCo) were some of the first companies to offer flexible benefits.

Why Are Flexible Plans Attractive?

Flexible plans may be of interest to organizations for several reasons:

1. Employee benefits are a very significant component of overall compensation.
2. Flexible benefits can allow employers to limit their contributions without alienating employees, since options give employees some control over the distribution of benefits.
3. Lifestyles have changed in the past several years, causing employees to reevaluate the need for certain traditional benefits. For example, in a family where both spouses work and receive family medical insurance, one coverage is sufficient.
4. Benefits can be useful in recruiting and retaining employees. However, when a mandatory benefit package is largely unresponsive to a prospective employee's needs or to the retention of present employees, the organization is wasting money.
5. The high cost of benefits is causing organizations to try to communicate effectively the real cost to the employee. By making specific benefit choices, the employee becomes highly familiar with the costs associated with each benefit.
6. There can be positive tax ramifications for employees. Also, because certain benefits are taxable and others are not, different benefit mixes can be attractive to different employees (the tax ramifications of flexible plans are discussed below).
7. A flexible plan can have a positive impact on employee attitudes and behavior.
8. It can lower overall health care costs.[30]

Problems with Flexible Plans

Flexible plans are not without their difficulties. The major problems are as follows:

1. A flexible plan requires more effort to administer.
2. Unions often oppose flexible plans because they are required to give up control over the program details or face losing some of their previously negotiated benefit improvements.
3. Employees may not choose those benefits that are in their own best interests.
4. Tax laws limit the amount of individual flexibility in certain situations.[31]

Tax Implications of Flexible Plans

Flexible plans can have certain tax advantages by allowing employees to purchase benefits on a pretax basis. Contributions made under a flexible plan are generally not subject to social security tax (FICA).

Flexible-spending plans that offer employees choices between taxable and nontaxable benefits are subject to special rules under the Internal Revenue Code's Section 125, enacted in 1978. Plans that offer choices only among nontaxable benefits are not subject to Section 125. The Deficit Reduction Act (DEFRA) of 1984 clarified many of the tax questions that had clouded flexible benefits since the inception of Section 125. The following list summarizes many of the requirements resulting from Section 125 and/or DEFRA:

- An employer cannot require an employee to complete more than three years of service before becoming eligible under the plan.
- Flexible plans must offer a choice between only taxable and statutory nontaxable benefits. Taxable benefits allowed include cash, group term life insurance in excess of $50,000, and group term life insurance for dependents. Statutory nontaxable benefits include group term life insurance, group legal services, accident and health benefits, dependent care assistance, and certain types of deferred compensation. Vacation days are also treated as nontaxable benefits.
- If more than 25 percent of the total nontaxable benefits in the plan are provided for key employees, as defined by Section 416(i)(1) of the Internal Revenue Code, the key employees will be taxed on the value of those benefits.
- Employee benefits elections must be irrevocable and made at the beginning of the period of coverage.
- No change in coverage is allowed except in the case of a change in family status.
- No cash-out or carryover of individual balances is allowed if the selected benefits are not fully used. In other words, any monies left in an account at the end of the year must be forfeited.

Although the present laws do present some restrictions, there is still considerable opportunity for establishing effective flexible plans, and the potential gains from flexible plans are large enough to merit consideration. There is evidence that flexible plans have become increasingly popular in recent years.[32]

THE BENEFIT PACKAGE

Unfortunately, many benefit packages are thrown together piecemeal and are poorly balanced. There are many reasons for this. The major problem is that companies often add or delete new benefits without examining their impact on the total package. Also, they frequently add or delete benefits for the wrong reasons, such as a whim of a top executive, union pressures, or a fad. The key to any successful benefit package is to plan the package and integrate all the different components. Such an approach ensures that any new benefit additions or deletions will fit in with the other benefits currently offered.

Many small companies have found they can lower the cost and keep benefits relatively attractive by working through their professional associations. In these cases, the professional or industry association offers different benefit options to its members. The association often can offer relatively attractive pricing because of the ability to group its members together.

COMMUNICATING THE BENEFIT PACKAGE

Although most organizations provide some form of benefits to their employees, the average employee often has little idea of what he or she is receiving. Many surveys have shown that employees often do not understand the benefit programs their respective companies provide.[33] Why are employees often unaware of their benefits? One explanation is that organizations do not make much of an effort to communicate their employee benefits.

Another possible explanation is that employees cannot easily understand descriptive material on benefits when it is available. One provision of the Employee Retirement Income Security Act of 1974 (ERISA) requires an employer to communicate at specified intervals certain types of benefit

FIGURE 15.1

Sample Employee Earnings and Benefits Letter

Source: Adapted from J. C. Claypool and J. P. Cargemi, "The Annual Employee Earnings and Benefits Letter," *Personnel Journal,* July 1980, p. 564.

```
Company Name
Address
Date

Employee's Name
Address

Dear

        Enclosed are your W-2 forms showing the amount of taxable income that
you received from _____ during the year ____.  Listed below in
Section A are your gross wages and a cost breakdown of various benefit
programs that you enjoy. In addition to the money you received as wages, the
company paid benefits for you that are not included in your W-2 statement.
These are benefits that are sometimes overlooked. In an easy-to-read form,
here's what _____ paid to you for the year ____.

    Section A—Paid to you in your W-2 earnings:

    Cost-of-living allowance       _____
    Shift premium                  _____
    Service award(s)               _____
    Vacation pay                   _____
    Holiday pay                    _____
    Funeral pay                    _____
    Jury duty pay                  _____
    Military pay                   _____
    Accident & sickness benefits _____
    Regular earnings               _____
    Overtime earnings              _____
    Allowances                     _____
        Gross wages                _____


    Section B—Paid for you and not included on your W-2 earnings:

    Company contributed to pension plan                  _____
    Company cost of your health insurance payments       _____
    Company cost of your dental insurance                _____
    Company cost of your life & accidental death insurance _____
    Company cost for social security tax on your wages   _____
    Company cost of the premium for your workers'
        compensation                                     _____
    Company cost for the tax on your wages for
        unemployment compensation                        _____
    Company cost for the tuition refund                  _____
    Company cost for safety glasses                      _____
    Company cost for exercise facilities                 _____
    Company cost for financial planning services         _____
        Total cost of benefits not included in W-2 earnings _____
        Total _____ paid for
        your services for the year ____        ========================

        You have earned the amount on the bottom line, but we want to give
you a clearer idea of the total cost of your services to the company, and the
protection and benefits that are being purchased for you and your family. Thank
you for your commitment and service to our company.

                            Sincerely,
                            Manager of Human Resources
```

information in a manner employees can understand. Several methods can be used to evaluate the readability of written documents. Generally, in these methods the number of words per sentence and the percentage of difficult polysyllabic words in the passage are counted in a readability index related to a school-grade reading level. The basic goal is to match the readability index of the benefit description to the educational level of the organization's employees.

The method used to communicate the benefit package is as important as the readability of the document. One successful method of communication is a personalized statement sent periodically to each employee. The employee earnings and benefits letter shown in Figure 15.1 is an

IMPROVING BENEFITS COMMUNICATION WITH EMPLOYEES

Dick Quinn, vice president of compensation and benefits for the Public Service Enterprise Group (PSEG) in Newark, New Jersey, had recently revamped the company's benefits package to better reflect what employees wanted. The changes included increased wellness incentives, better mental health parity, and 401(k) automatic enrollment. Once these new features were installed, Quinn wanted to be able to effectively communicate the new choices to current and prospective employees.

Quinn completely restructured the company's benefits section of its Web site. Gone are the laundry-list eyesores and computer screens filled with lengthy benefit descriptions.

In these places is a simple, easy-to-read page containing 16 colorful icons, each representing a different benefit. For example, one icon is a picture of three people riding stationary bikes, with a subheading that reads "We've Got You Covered." A brief description of PSEG's medical benefits appears when the computer cursor touches the picture. Quinn's goal for the new Web site was to present the information in a less boring and more user-friendly manner.

Quinn's ideas must be working as the new benefits Web site gets about 1,500–2,000 hits per day.

Source: Chris Silva, "Loud and Proud Approach to Benefits Marketing: Tired of the Same Old, PSEG Revamps Web Site to Better Market New Benefits," *Employee Benefit News*, February 1, 2008, p. 1.

example of such a statement. For organizations that use a computerized payroll system, some benefit information can easily be printed on each employee's check stub. The latest method for communicating benefits is to use intranet technology. Having access restricted to qualified users, the intranet, without any additional operating cost, can provide benefit information around the clock, seven days a week. With the intranet, employees can log on at work or from any location and instantly access company information regarding most employee benefits, such as medical and dental plans. With this technology, employees can even revise benefit forms and update their records. Other methods for communicating benefit information include posters and visual presentations, such as videos, slide shows, and flip charts. Meetings and conferences can also be used to explain an organization's benefits. HRM in Action 15.5 describes how one company greatly improved the way it communicates its benefits to its employees.

Summary of Learning Objectives

1. **Define *employee benefits*.**

   Employee benefits, sometimes called fringe benefits, are those rewards that organizations provide to employees for being members of the organization. In general, benefits can be grouped into five major categories: (1) legally required, (2) retirement related, (3) insurance related, (4) payment for time not worked, and (5) other.

2. **Describe how employee benefits have grown over the last several years.**

   Employee benefits have grown steadily over the past several years. Specifically, they grew from approximately 15 percent of total compensation in 1951 to approximately 39 percent of total compensation in 1994.

3. **Summarize those benefits that are legally required.**

   The three primary benefits mandated by law are social security, unemployment compensation, and workers' compensation benefits. Social security is a federally administered insurance system. Under current federal laws, both employer and employee must pay into the system, and a certain percentage of the employee's salary is paid up to a maximum limit. The payment distributed under social security can be grouped into three major categories: retirement benefits, disability benefits, and health insurance. Unemployment compensation is designed to provide funds to employees who have lost their jobs through no fault of their own and are seeking other jobs. Unemployment compensation is usually funded through taxes paid by employers; however, in some states employees also pay a portion of the tax. Workers' compensation is meant to protect employees from loss of income and extra expenses associated with job-related injuries or illnesses. Workers' compensation coverage varies significantly among different states.

4. Differentiate between a defined-benefit pension plan and a defined-contribution pension plan.

Under a defined-benefit pension plan, the employer pledges to provide a benefit determined by a definite formula at the employee's retirement date. A defined-contribution pension plan calls for a fixed or known annual contribution instead of a known benefit.

5. Discuss the attractiveness of a cash-balance plan to employees.

Cash-balance plans are attractive to employees because they allow employees to take their cash-balance pension money with them in the form of a lump sum when they leave the organization. Cash-balance plans also allow participants to track the growth of their retirement funds in current dollars through regular statements.

6. Describe a 401(k) plan and how it differs from a 403(b) plan.

A 401(k) plan is a defined-contribution pension plan named after section 401(k) of the Internal Revenue Code. A 401(k) plan allows employees to make tax deductible contributions up to certain limits ($15,000 per year in 2006). Often employers will match the employee contributions to some extent. The 403(b) or Tax Deferred Annuity (TDA) plans are very similar to 401(k) plans except that they may only be used in not-for-profit organizations.

7. Explain the purposes of the Employee Retirement Income Security Act (ERISA) and the Retirement Equity Act.

Congress passed ERISA in 1974 in an effort to ensure the fair treatment of employees under pension plans. The law was designed to ensure the solvency of pension plans by restricting the types of investments that can be made with the plan's funds and providing general guidelines for fund managers. The overall impact of the Retirement Equity Act, which was passed in 1984, was to liberalize the eligibility requirements, vesting provisions, maternity/paternity leaves, and spouse survivor benefits of retirement plans.

8. Distinguish between an IRA and a Roth IRA.

An IRA is a type of individual pension plan that can be used to make tax deductible contributions up to a limit of $4,000 per year per person. When withdrawals are subsequently made from an IRA they are taxable as ordinary income. With a Roth IRA non-tax-deductible contributions of up to $4,000 per year per person can be made. When withdrawals are subsequently made, they are tax-free.

9. Describe a health maintenance organization (HMO) and a preferred provider organization (PPO).

HMOs provide certain basic medical services for an organization's employees for a fixed price. Advantages of HMOs include an emphasis on prevention of health problems and generally lower costs. A major drawback is that employees must use physicians employed or approved by the HMO. PPOs are similar to HMOs in many ways. A PPO is formed by contracting with a group of doctors and hospitals to provide services at a discounted or otherwise attractive price. Under a PPO, employees are free to go to any doctor or facility on an approved list.

10. Describe a medical savings account and a Health Savings Account.

A medical savings account allows employees to set aside pretax dollars through payroll deduction to pay for medical bills throughout the calendar year. The major drawback to medical savings accounts is that any money not used during the calendar year is usually forfeited. Under a Health Savings Account employees or employers can put up to $2,850 for individuals or $5,650 for families in pretax dollars into an account. These funds can then be withdrawn to pay for medical services. These funds can accumulate indefinitely. In order to qualify for an HSA, employees or employers must also buy a regular health insurance policy with an annual deductible of at least $1,100 for individuals and $2,200 for families.

11. **Explain the concepts of a floating holiday and personal days.**

   A floating holiday is a holiday observed at the discretion of the employee or the employer. Personal days are paid days that employees can take, usually at their discretion, to attend to personal matters.

12. **Explain the concept of a flexible-benefit plan.**

   Under a flexible-benefit plan, individual employees have some choice as to the specific benefits they will actually receive; usually employees select from among several options how they want their direct compensation and benefits to be distributed. Flexible plans are also known as cafeteria plans or benefits.

13. **Discuss two reasons employees are often unaware of the benefits their organizations offer.**

   One reason is that organizations often make little effort to communicate their employee benefits. A second reason is that descriptive material, when provided, is often not easily understood by employees.

Key Terms

401(k) plans, *300*
403(b) plans, *301*
Amended Age Discrimination in Employment Act (ADEA), *303*
defined-benefit plan, *298*
defined-contribution plan, *298*
disability insurance, *307*
employee benefits (fringe benefits), *292*

Employee Retirement Income Security Act (ERISA), *302*
employer-sponsored SIMPLE IRAs, *301*
flexible-benefit plan (cafeteria plan), *308*
floating holiday, *307*
health maintenance organization (HMO), *305*
individual retirement accounts (IRA), *303*

preferred provider organizations (PPO), *305*
private plans, *298*
Retirement Equity Act, *302*
Roth IRA, *304*
SEP-IRA, *304*
social security, *294*
unemployment compensation, *296*
vesting, *299*
workers' compensation, *297*

Review Questions

1. What is social security? Describe the three major categories of social security.
2. Briefly explain how unemployment compensation works.
3. What types of injuries and illnesses are covered by workers' compensation?
4. Describe the differences between defined-benefit pension plans and defined-contribution pension plans.
5. What is the most popular type of defined-contribution plan? How does it work?
6. What is an employer-sponsored SIMPLE IRA?
7. What is a cash-blance plan?
8. State the overriding purpose of the Employee Retirement Income Security Act (ERISA).
9. What are three pension alternatives for individuals not covered by private pension plans?
10. Discuss some of the insurance programs offered to employees by organizations.
11. What is a health maintenance organization (HMO)? A preferred provider organization (PPO)?
12. Distinguish between medical savings accounts and Health Savings Accounts.
13. What is the flexible approach to benefits? List the advantages and disadvantages of flexible plans.
14. Why are many employees unaware of some of the benefits provided by their organization?

Discussion Questions

1. If an average production employee were given the option to have an additional $100 per month in salary or the equivalent of $200 per month in voluntary benefits, which do you think the employee would choose? Why? What are the implications of your answer for management?

2. Develop and discuss at least two arguments in support of social security. Compare and contrast your arguments.

3. If your employer offered you an option to join an HMO, would you be interested? Why or why not?

4. Many people believe employers use pension vesting requirements solely for the purpose of retaining employees. If this is completely or even partially true, do you think such behavior is ethical? Why or why not?

Incident 15.1

Who Is Eligible for Retirement Benefits?

Preston Jones, 51, had been an hourly worker in a machine shop of Armon Company for 21 years and four months. On a Christmas holiday, he suffered a severe heart attack and was hospitalized for three weeks. At his release, his doctor said he was to rest at home for a couple of months. After his recuperation period, his doctor, along with Armon Company's physicians, was to decide whether or not Preston should be retired for disability reasons. They never got the opportunity to make this decision; in February, Preston died of a second heart attack. He left a wife, four sons, two daughters, and two daughters-in-law. Mrs. Jones still had four children at home.

As a part of Preston's estate, his wife received the normal group insurance payments, the balance of his savings plan account, and the other benefits due her. However, she did not receive a pension from Armon as a survivor of an eligible employee.

When Mrs. Jones and the company representatives had discussed the settlement, she had inquired about her husband's pension and about her right to receive it. The human resource department had stated that since contributions to this fund were made only by the company, no survivor's benefits were provided.

Questions

1. What do you think Mrs. Jones should do at this point?

2. What does the Employment Retirement Income Security Act of 1974 have to say about this issue?

Incident 15.2

Benefits for Professionals

LJT, Architects, a small architectural firm organized as a sole proprietorship, serves clients in the New York metropolitan area. Anticipating a good year, Len Elmore, the principal, hopes for a gross of between $600,000 and $800,000.

In an architectural practice, revenue is produced by providing a variety of services that range from creating a design and generating the construction documents used by a contractor in executing the project to visiting the site periodically to verify that construction is progressing according to specifications. Architects are also responsible for coordinating their work with that of the engineers and other consultants associated with projects.

Many small architectural firms such as LJT, Architects, have no permanent employees. They hire workers for a particular project with the understanding that they might remain after a particular phase of the project is completed but they might also be laid off. Employees are usually needed for the functions of design, development, and production of construction documents, which include approximately 50 to 70 percent of the services provided under a standard architectural agreement.

Firms acquire the personnel needed for these projects in several ways. They hire personnel on a full-time permanent or temporary basis or on a part-time basis to moonlight (i.e., as a second job). An employee might also be borrowed from another firm whose contracted work has been completed with no new work foreseen immediately. Len believes that hiring full-time temporary or permanent employees gives him more control over the production aspect of his practice.

At this time, Len does not follow any formal personnel policies. He prefers to "work things out" as issues and problems arise. When hiring, he will agree verbally to certain broad terms of employment, compensation, and benefits common to local professional offices, such as two weeks' vacation per year. He usually insists on a two-week to one-month probationary period during which the salary paid is slightly less than normal. A spot check of some of his colleagues leads him to believe his salary rates are comparable with those of similar employers. Because the nature of the employment tends to be temporary, Len suggests a contract arrangement with his employees, in which no taxes are withheld and no government-required benefits are provided.

Len's plans for expansion include adding employees until his staff numbers 10. For him, this is the best staff size to provide high-quality professional services. However, the employment situation is easing for workers in architectural firms; more newspaper ads seek applicants, and fewer callers contact Len for jobs. Those coming for interviews ask more than "When do I start?" Many ask about vacations, sick leave, paid holidays, medical insurance, and profit-sharing plans. Others want to know about the possibilities of advancement with LJT, Architects, and about such long-range benefits as pensions and education leave.

In view of the situation, Len has decided to look into providing his employees with a benefit package. At the same time, however, he fears his practice may be too small to begin providing these benefits, which may prove to be extremely expensive. He has set aside money from his own earnings to provide these extras for himself and has difficulty understanding why his employees cannot do the same.

Questions

1. What recommendations would you make to Len?
2. How much do you think your recommendations would cost?

EXERCISE 15.1
Taking a Raise

Assume you are currently employed as a human resource specialist for a medium-size company. You have been in your job for a little over two years, and your current salary is $52,000 per year. Two months ago, your company announced it was going to implement a flexible-benefit plan in conjunction with this year's salary raises. Your annual salary review was held last week, and you were informed that your raise would be equivalent to $3,000. For your salary level, the following options are available:

1. Take the entire raise as a monthly salary increase.
2. Take as much of the $3,000 as you desire in the form of vacation at the equivalent of $200 per day.
3. Have as much as you desire of the $3,000 put into a tax-sheltered retirement plan.
4. Purchase additional term life insurance at the cost of $250 per $100,000 of face value.
5. Purchase dental insurance at the cost of $20 per month for yourself and $10 per month for each dependent.

The company currently provides full health insurance at no cost to employees. How would you elect to take your raise? Be prepared to share your answer with the class.

Notes and Additional Readings

1. U.S. Chamber of Commerce, *2008 Employee Benefits Study*, p. 8.
2. R. M. McCaffery, "Employee Benefits: Beyond the Fringe?" *Personnel Administrator*, May 1981, p. 26.
3. Christopher Cornell, "State Rep Cites Pro-Business Rationale for Bill Banning Gay Discrimination," *Northeast Pennsylvania Business Journal*, June 2009, p. 43.

4. U.S. Chamber of Commerce, *2008 Employee Benefits Study,* p. 4.

5. "Financial Fiasco," *Spartanburg Herald-Journal,* August 6, 2009.

6. S. Ledvinka, *Federal Regulations of Personnel and Human Resource Management* (Boston: Kent Publishing, 1981), p. 144.

7. *CFO,* June 1995, p. 52.

8. Ibid.

9. Bill Leonard, "Study Finds Workers' Comp Costs Have Decreased Sharply," *HR Magazine,* February 1998, p. 10; and Elaine McShulskis, "Workers' Comp Costs Drop," *HR Magazine,* March 1998, p. 28.

10. Daniel Hays, "WC Buyers Caught Between a Rock and a Hard Place," *National Underwriter/ Property & Casualty Risk & Benefits,* February 2, 2002, pp. 5–6.

11. Sally Roberts, "Market Softened in 2005: Survey," *Business Insurance,* May 29, 2006, p. 6.

12. "Workers' Compensation: Premiums Decline 10 Percent—Plus for 19 Percent of Renewals," *The Controller's Report,* May 2009, pp. 5–6.

13. Patrick Purcell, "Older Workers: Employment and Retirement Trends," *Pension Benefits,* January 2010, pp. 11–12.

14. Ibid.

15. U.S. Chamber of Commerce, *The 2008 Employee Benefits Study,* p. 7.

16. Much of this section is drawn from the following sources: Tami Luhby, "Pension Reductions Rise: Survey Shows Fewer Companies Are Offering Them to Employees as a Retirement Choice," *Knight Ridder Tribune Business News,* September 1, 2006, p. 1; Tami Luhby, "Pensions: Going, Going: Increasingly, Employers Are Giving Workers Responsibility for Their Own Retirement Plans," *Knight Ridder Tribune Business News,* August 20, 2006, p. 1; and William Neikirk, "Bill Would Boost 401(k) Plans: Measure Could Make Employers Abandon Oldstyle Pensions," *Knight Ridder Tribune Business News,* August 17, 2006, p. 1.

17. P. S. Greenlaw and W. D. Biggs, *Modern Personnel Management* (Philadelphia: W. B. Saunders, 1979), p. 513.

18. U.S. Chamber of Commerce, *The 2008 Employee Benefits Study,* p. 7.

19. U.S. Chamber of Commerce, *The 2008 Employee Benefits Study,* p. 33.

20. Society for Human Resource Management, *2009 Employee Benefits Study* (Alexandria, Va.: Society for Human Resource Management, 2009), p. 47.

21. U.S. Chamber of Commerce, *The 2008 Employee Benefits Study,* p. 33.

22. Society for Human Resource Management, *2009 Employee Benefits Study,* p. 47.

23. Much of this section is drawn from "Law Creates Health Savings Accounts," *HR Focus,* January 2004, p. 12

24. Society for Human Resource Management, *2009 Employee Benefits Study,* p. 48.

25. U.S. Chamber of Commerce, *The 2008 Employee Benefits Survey,* p. 35.

26. Society for Human Resource Management, *2009 Employee Benefits Study,* p. 47.

27. U.S. Chamber of Commerce, *The 2008 Employee Benefits Study,* p. 35.

28. Society for Human Resource Management, *2009 Employee Benefits Study,* p. 17.

29. Carolyn A. Baker, "Flex Your Benefits," *Personnel Journal,* May 1988, p. 54; and Katie Lawton and Oleksandr S. Cherniphenko, "Examining Determinants of Employee Benefit Preferences: Joint Effects of Personality, Work Values, and Demographics," *Asia Pacific Journal of Human Resources,* August 2008, p. 220.

30. Chad Daughtery, "How to Introduce Flexible Benefits," *People Management,* January 10, 2002, pp. 42–43.

31. Adapted from J. H. Shea, "Cautions about Cafeteria-Style Benefit Plans," *Personnel Journal,* January 1981, pp. 37–38.

32. "Cost Sharing Is Now the Top Way to Control Costs," *HR Focus,* February 2009, pp. 5–8; Alexandra Hain-Cole, "Increase in Popularity of Flexible Benefits: UK," *Benefits & Compensation International,* November 2009, p. 30; and Paul Stephens, "Flex Gain in Popularity," *CA Magazine,* January/February 2010, p. 10.

33. For an example, see Jennifer J. Laabs, "Use Creativity to Educate Your Benefits Audience," *Personnel Journal,* February 1992, p. 64; and Mike Berry, "Do Benefits Packages Score With Staff?" *Personnel Today,* March 2004, p. 12.

Employee Well-Being and Labor Relations

Ron Levine/Getty Images

Employee Safety and Health

Chapter Learning Objectives

After studying this chapter, you should be able to:

1. State the purpose of the Occupational Safety and Health Act (OSHA) and discuss its major provisions.
2. List the three major causes of accidents in the workplace.
3. Define *frequency rate* and *severity rate*.
4. Offer several suggestions for promoting safety in the workplace.
5. Discuss the Hazard Communication rule.
6. Differentiate between stress and burnout.
7. Name several work-related consequences of alcohol and drug abuse.
8. Offer several guidelines for implementing a drug-testing program.
9. Discuss the legal requirements for terminating an employee with acquired immunodeficiency syndrome (AIDS).
10. Explain the three basic types of employee assistance programs (EAPs).
11. Explain what work/life programs and wellness programs are.
12. List several specific things an organization can do to help reduce violence in its workplace.

Chapter Outline

Employee safety and health are important concerns in today's organizations. The National Safety Council estimates that 4,303 unintentional deaths and 3.2 million unintentional disabling injuries resulted from occupational accidents in 2008.[1] The associated total work accident cost was estimated to be $183 billion.[2]

As early as 1970, new cases of occupational diseases were estimated to exceed 300,000 each year.[3] As these figures indicate, the costs associated with workplace injuries or illnesses are high. Other indirect costs include employers' costs for health insurance and workers' compensation (both discussed in Chapter 15). Recent figures show that the average U.S. employee must produce $1,250 worth of goods and services just to offset the cost of work-related injuries.[4] These costs vividly illustrate an incentive for organizations to reduce work-related injuries and illnesses and to improve overall employee health.

While health costs have escalated dramatically in recent decades, occupational injuries and illnesses have been around for a long time. For example, 35,000 occupational deaths occurred in 1936.[5] In spite of the known injuries and associated costs, for years many organizations did very little to reduce the problem. Because of this, a bipartisan U.S. Congress passed the Occupational Safety and Health Act in 1970.

OCCUPATIONAL SAFETY AND HEALTH ACT

Occupational Safety and Health Act
Federal law enacted in 1970 to ensure safe and healthful working conditions for every working person.

general-duty clause
Clause in the Occupational Safety and Health Act covering those situations not addressed by specific standards; in essence, it requires employers to comply with the intent of the act.

Web site: Occupational Safety and Health Administration
www.osha.gov

The **Occupational Safety and Health Act** became effective on April 28, 1971. The act established federal regulations relating to employee safety and health. It applies to all businesses with one or more employees. (There are certain exceptions, such as self-employed persons.) Its original stated purpose was "to assure so far as possible every working man and woman in the nation safe and healthful working conditions and to preserve our human resources." The act contains a **general-duty clause** to cover those situations not addressed by specific standards. This clause states that each employer "shall furnish . . . a place of employment which is free from recognized hazards that are causing or likely to cause death or serious physical harm to . . . employees." In essence, the general-duty clause requires employers to comply with the intent of the act.

The Occupational Safety and Health Administration (OSHA) of the U.S. Department of Labor enforces the act and is authorized to

- Encourage employers and employees to reduce workplace hazards and to implement new safety and health management systems or improve existing programs.
- Develop mandatory job safety and health standards and enforce them through worksite inspections, employer assistance, and, sometimes, by imposing citations, penalties, or both.
- Promote safe and healthful work environments through cooperative programs, partnerships, and alliances.
- Establish responsibilities and rights for employers and employees to achieve better safety and health conditions.
- Support the development of innovative ways of dealing with workplace hazards.
- Establish requirements for employers to keep records of injury and illness and to monitor certain occupational illnesses.
- Establish training programs to increase the competence of occupational safety and health personnel.
- Provide technical and compliance assistance and training and education to help employers reduce worker accidents and injuries.
- Work in partnership with states that operate their own occupational safety and health programs.
- Support the Consultation Programs offered by all 50 states, the District of Columbia, Puerto Rico, the Virgin Islands, Guam and the Northern Mariana Islands.[6]

Since 1970 when OSHA was established, occupational fatality rates have been cut by 60 percent and at the same time, U.S. employment has doubled and now includes nearly 115 million

MARSHALL v. BARLOW'S, INC.
www.osha.gov

Barlow's, Inc., is an electrical and plumbing installation business in Pocatello, Idaho. In September 1975, an OSHA inspector asked Mr. Barlow if he could search the business for safety violations. When Mr. Barlow asked the inspector whether complaints had been filed against the business, the inspector said no, that Barlow's had turned up as part of a routine selection procedure. Mr. Barlow refused to allow the inspection.

Three months later, Secretary of Labor Ray Marshall petitioned the U.S. district court for the state of Idaho to issue an order forcing Barlow to admit the inspector. Barlow again refused and sought an injunction to prevent what he considered to be a warrantless search. On December 30, 1976, a three-judge court ruled in Barlow's favor, and Marshall appealed. On May 23, 1978, the U.S. Supreme Court ruled that OSHA's searches of work areas for safety hazards and violations were unconstitutional without a warrant.

Source: *"Marshall v. Barlow's, Inc.," Supreme Court Reporter* 98A (St. Paul, Minn.: West Publishing, 1980), pp. 1816–34.

workers at 7.2 million sites. Occupational injury and illnesses rates have declined 40 percent.[7] While OSHA cannot claim all the credit for these impressive reductions, it has certainly had a major impact.

OSHA Standards

OSHA establishes legally enforceable standards relating to employee health and safety. Usually the human resource department is responsible for being familiar with these standards and ensuring that the organization complies with them.

Currently OSHA issues standards for a wide variety of workplace hazards including toxic substances, harmful physical agents, electrical hazards, fall hazards, hazardous wastes, infectious diseases, fire and explosion hazards, dangerous atmospheres, and machine hazards. Most OSHA standards and forms can be obtained online at http://www.osha.gov. The **Federal Register,** available online (http://www.gpoaccess.gov/fr/) and in many public and college libraries, also regularly publishes all OSHA standards and amendments.

Federal Register
The official daily publication for rules, proposed rules, and notices of federal agencies and organizations. http://www.gpoaccess.gov/fr/

Establishment of Standards

OSHA can initiate standards on its own or on petitions from other parties, including the U.S. Secretary of Health and Human Services (HHS), the National Institute for Occupational Safety and Health (NIOSH), state and local governments, and nationally recognized standards-producing organizations, employers, labor organizations, or any other interested party. NIOSH, which was established by the act as an agency under HHS, conducts research on various safety and health problems. NIOSH recommends most of the standards adopted by OSHA.

Workplace Inspections

OSHA compliance officers (inspectors) are authorized under the act to conduct workplace inspections. OSHA generally conducts inspections without advance notice. However, employers do have the right to require that OSHA obtain a search warrant before being admitted. Originally employers were not given advance notice of inspections and could not refuse to admit OSHA inspectors. However, a 1978 Supreme Court decision, **Marshall v. Barlow's, Inc.,**[8] ruled that employers are not required to admit OSHA inspectors onto their premises without a search warrant. At the same time, however, the court ruled that the probable cause needed to obtain a search warrant would be much less than what would be required in a criminal matter. HRM in Action 16.1 summarizes the *Marshall v. Barlow's, Inc.,* case.

Marshall v. Barlow's, Inc.
1978 Supreme Court decision that ruled that employers are not required to admit OSHA inspectors onto their premises without a search warrant; also ruled that probable cause needed to obtain the search warrant is much less than that required in a criminal matter.

Inspection Priorities

Because OSHA does not have the resources to inspect all workplaces covered by the act, a system of inspection priorities has been established. The agency inspects under the following conditions.

> *Imminent danger,* or any condition where there is reasonable certainty that a danger exists that can be expected to cause death or serious physical harm immediately or before the danger can be eliminated through normal enforcement procedures.

Catastrophes and fatal accidents resulting in the death of any employee or the hospitalization of three or more employees.

Employee complaints involving imminent danger or an employee violation that threatens death or serious harm.

Referrals from other individuals, agencies, organizations, or the media.

Planned, or programmed, inspections in industries with a high number of hazards and associated injuries.

Follow-ups to previous inspections.

Inspection Procedures

Upon the OSHA inspector's arrival, the representatives of the employer should first ask to see the inspector's OSHA credentials. Normally the inspector then conducts a preliminary meeting with the top management of the organization. The manager of the human resource department is usually present at this meeting. At this time, the inspector explains the purpose of the visit, the scope of the inspection, and the standards that apply. The inspector then usually requests an employer representative (often someone from the human resource department), and an employee representative (usually selected directly by the employees or the union if one is present) to join in an inspection tour of the facility. Under no circumstances may the employer select the employee representative. The inspector then proceeds with the inspection tour, which may cover part or all of the facilities. Afterward the inspector meets again with the employer or the employer representatives. During this meeting, the inspector discusses what has been found and indicates all apparent violations for which a citation may be issued or recommended.

Citations

In some cases, the inspector has the authority to issue citations at the work site immediately following the closing conference. This occurs only in cases where immediate protection is necessary. Normally citations are issued by the OSHA area director and sent by certified mail. Once the citation is received, the employer is required to post a copy of the citation at or near the place where the violation occurred for three days or until the violation is corrected, whichever period is longer.

Penalties

Table 16.1 summarizes the five major types of violations that may be cited and the respective penalties that may be proposed. Under certain conditions some of the proposed penalties can be adjusted downward. Additional penalties may be imposed for such things as falsifying records and assaulting an inspector.

Reporting/Record-Keeping Requirements

All employers must report to OSHA within eight hours of learning about (1) the death of any employee from a work-related incident or (2) the in-patient hospitalization of three or more employees as a result of a work-related incident. In addition, employers must report all fatal heart attacks. Deaths from motor vehicle accidents on public streets (except those in a construction work zone) and in accidents on commercial airplanes, trains, subways, or buses do not need to be reported.

Employers of 11 or more persons must meet certain record-keeping requirements specified by OSHA. These include

- Maintaining records in each establishment of occupational injuries and illnesses as they occur and making those records accessible to employees.
- Keeping injury and illness records and posting from February 1 through April 30 an annual summary of occupational injuries and illnesses for each establishment. A company executive must certify the accuracy of the summary.
- Recording any fatality regardless of the length of time between the injury and death.
- Providing, upon request, pertinent injury and illness records for inspection and copying by any representative of the Secretaries of Labor or HHS, or the state during any investigation, research, or statistical compilation.

TABLE 16.1
Types of OSHA Violations

Source: *All about OSHA* (Washington, D.C.: U.S. Department of Labor, 2003) pp. 26–27.

Violation	Definition	Proposed Penalty
Other than serious	Violation that has a direct relationship to job safety and health but probably would not cause death or serious physical harm.	Up to $7,000 for each violation (discretionary).
Serious	Violation where there is substantial probability that death or serious physical harm could result and that the employer knew or should have known of the hazard.	Up to $7,000 for each violation (mandatory).
Willful	Violation that the employer intentionally and knowingly commits. The employer either knows that what he or she is doing constitutes a violation or is aware that a hazardous condition exists and has made no reasonable effort to eliminate it.	Up to $70,000 for each willful violation with a minimum mandatory penalty of $5,000 for each violation. A violation resulting in death of an employee is punishable by a court-imposed fine or by up to six months' imprisonment, or both; a fine of up to $250,000 for an individual or $500,000 for a corporation may be imposed for a criminal conviction.
Repeated	Violation of any standard, regulation, rule, or order where, on reinspection, another violation of the same section is found.	Up to $70,000 for each such violation.
Failure to abate prior violation	Failure to correct previous violation cited by OSHA.	Civil penalty of up to $7,000 for each day the violation continues beyond the prescribed abatement date.

OSHA Form 300 (Log of Work-Related Injuries and Illnesses) and OSHA Form 300A (Summary of Work-Related Injuries and Illnesses)
Forms for recording all occupational injuries and illnesses. Each occurrence must be recorded within six working days from the time the employer learns of the accident or illness.

OSHA Form 301 (Injury and Illness Incident Report)
Form that requires much more detail about each injury or illness. Form 301 must be completed within six working days from the time the employer learns of an occupational injury or illness.

• Complying with any additional record-keeping and reporting requirements in specific OSHA standards.

Many OSHA standards have special record-keeping and reporting requirements, but all employers covered by the act must maintain certain forms. Currently, three record-keeping forms are required. **OSHA Form 300, Log of Work-Related Injuries and Illnesses; OSHA Form 300A, Summary of Work-Related Injures and Illnesses;** and **OSHA Form 301, Injury and Illness Incident Report.** Form 300 requires employers to log each recordable occupational injury and illness within six working days from the time the employer learns of it. In general this includes all occupational illnesses, regardless of severity, and all occupational injuries resulting in death, one or more lost workdays, restriction of work or motion, loss of consciousness, transfer to another job, or medical treatment other than first-aid. Form 300A was designed to make it easier to post and calculate incident rates. Employers must post copies of the previous year's records no later than February 1 and keep them up at least through April 30. Form 301 includes more data about how the injury or illness occurred and must be completed within seven calendar days from the time the employer learns of the work-related injury or illness. These forms must be retained for five years by the organization and must be available for inspection.

THE CAUSES OF ACCIDENTS

Accidents are caused by a combination of circumstances and events, usually resulting from unsafe work acts, an unsafe work environment, or both.

Personal Acts

It has been estimated that unsafe personal acts cause as much as 80 percent of organizational accidents. Unsafe personal acts include such things as taking unnecessary risks, horseplay, failing to wear protective equipment, using improper tools and equipment, and taking unsafe shortcuts.

TABLE 16.2
Unsafe Conditions in the Work Environment

Unguarded or improperly guarded machines (such as an unguarded belt)
Poor housekeeping (such as congested aisles, dirty or wet floors, loose carpeting, and improper stacking of materials)
Defective equipment and tools
Poor lighting
Poor or improper ventilation
Improper dress (such as wearing clothes with loose and floppy sleeves when working on a machine that has rotating parts)
Sharp edges

It is difficult to determine why employees commit unsafe personal acts. Fatigue, haste, boredom, stress, poor eyesight, and daydreaming are all potential reasons. However, these reasons do not totally explain why employees intentionally neglect to wear prescribed equipment or do not follow procedures. Most employees think of accidents as always happening to someone else. Such an attitude can easily lead to carelessness or a lack of respect for what can happen. It is also true that some people get a kick out of taking chances and showing off.

Research studies have also shown that employees with positive attitudes have fewer accidents than employees with negative attitudes.[9] This is not surprising when one considers that negative attitudes are likely to be related to employee carelessness.

Physical Environment

Accidents can and do happen in all types of environments, such as offices, parking lots, and factories. Certain work conditions, however, seem to result in more accidents. Table 16.2 lists commonly encountered unsafe work conditions.

Accident Proneness

A third reason often given for accidents is that certain people are accident prone. Some employees, due to their physical and mental makeup, are more susceptible to accidents. This condition may result from inborn traits, but it often develops as a result of an individual's environment. However, this tendency should not be used to justify an accident. Given the right set of circumstances, anyone can have an accident. For example, an employee who was up all night with a sick child might very well be accident prone the next day.

HOW TO MEASURE SAFETY

frequency rate
Ratio that indicates the frequency with which disabling injuries occur.

disabling injuries
Work-related injuries that cause an employee to miss one or more days of work.

severity rate
Ratio that indicates the length of time injured employees are out of work.

Accident frequency and accident severity are the two most widely accepted methods for measuring an organization's safety record. A **frequency rate** is used to indicate how often disabling injuries occur. **Disabling injuries** cause an employee to miss one or more days of work following an accident. Disabling injuries are also known as *lost-time injuries*. A **severity rate** indicates how severe the accidents were by calculating the length of time injured employees were out of work. Only disabling injuries are used in determining frequency and severity rates. Figure 16.1 gives the formulas for calculating an organization's frequency and severity rates.

Neither the frequency rate nor the severity rate means much until they are compared with similar figures for other departments or divisions within the organization, for the previous year, or for other organizations. It is through these comparisons that an organization's safety record can be objectively evaluated.

FIGURE 16.1
Formulas for Computing Accident Frequency Rate and Severity Rate

$$\text{Frequency rate} = \frac{\text{Number of disabling injuries} \times 1 \text{ million}}{\text{Total number of labor-hours worked each year}}$$

$$\text{Severity rate} = \frac{\text{Days lost* due to injury} \times 1 \text{ million}}{\text{Total number of labor-hours worked each year}}$$

*The American National Standards Institute has developed tables for determining the number of lost days for different types of accidents. To illustrate, an accident resulting in death or permanent total disability is charged with 6,000 days (approximately 25 working years).

ORGANIZATIONAL SAFETY PROGRAMS

The heart of any organizational safety program is accident prevention. It is obviously much better to prevent accidents than to react to them. A major objective of any safety program is to get the employees to "think safety." Therefore, most programs are designed to keep safety and accident prevention on employees' minds. Many different approaches are used to make employees more aware of safety. However, four basic elements are present in most successful safety programs. First, it must have the genuine (rather than casual) support of top and middle management. If upper management takes an unenthusiastic approach to safety, employees are quick to pick up on this. Second, it must be clearly established that safety is a responsibility of operating managers. All operating managers should consider safety to be an integral part of their job. Third, a positive attitude toward safety must exist and be maintained. The employees must believe the safety program is worthwhile and produces results. Finally, one person or department should be in charge of the safety program and responsible for its operation. Often the human resource manager or a member of the human resource staff has primary responsibility for the safety program.

Promoting Safety

Many things can be done to promote safety. Suggestions include the following:

1. Make the work interesting. Uninteresting work often leads to boredom, fatigue, and stress, all of which can cause accidents. Often simple changes can be made to make the work more meaningful. Attempts to make the job more interesting are usually successful if they add responsibility, challenge, and other similar factors that increase employees' satisfaction with the job.

2. Establish a safety committee composed of operative employees and representatives of management. The safety committee provides a means of getting employees directly involved in the operation of the safety program. A rotating membership of 5 to 12 members is desirable. Normal duties for the safety committee include inspecting, observing work practices, investigating accidents, and making recommendations. Committee meetings should be held at least once a month on company time, and attendance should be mandatory.

3. Feature employee safety contests. Give prizes to the work group or employee having the best safety record for a given time period. Contests can also be held to test safety knowledge. Prizes can be awarded periodically to employees who submit good accident prevention ideas.

4. Publicize safety statistics. Monthly accident reports should be posted and put on the company intranet. Ideas as to how accidents can be avoided should be solicited.

5. Use bulletin boards and the company intranet. Pictures, sketches, and cartoons can be effective if properly presented. One thing to remember when using bulletin boards and the intranet is to change the content frequently.

6. Encourage employees, including supervisors and managers, to have high expectations for safety. Recognize positive safety actions, and acknowledge those who contribute to safety improvements.

7. Periodically hold safety training programs and meetings. Have employees attend and participate in these meetings as role players or instructors. The next section discusses how to establish a safety training program for the first time.

Establishing a Safety Training Program

Several basic steps should be followed when initially establishing a safety training program:[10]

1. Assess the training needs by examining accident and injury records and talking to department heads about their perceived needs. Regardless of severity, try to find out where problems are located, what the potential causes might be, and what has been done in the past to correct them.

2. Gauge the level of employees' safety skills. Use written tests, employee interviews, and general observations to determine the level of employee knowledge about their job.

3. Design a program to solve the program. Outside resources such as consultants, equipment vendors, and even OSHA can be helpful. For best results, use a variety of teaching methods and involve employees as much as possible.

4. Get line managers on board. Once top management has embraced a safety philosophy, inform line managers about safety problems throughout the organization. Emphasize that they can help set the proper tone through example and instruction.

5. Evaluate the program's effectiveness. Try to answer two basic questions: Did the program change employees' behavior? Did the program impact business results in a positive manner?

6. Fine-tune the safety process. Periodically review the training program and make adjustments to incorporate new safety standards and to account for business and industry changes.

HRM in Action 16.2 presents some key quotes from CEOs regarding safety.

EMPLOYEE HEALTH

Until recently, safety and accident prevention received far more attention than did employee health. However, this has changed. Statistics show that occupational diseases may cost industry as much or more than occupational accidents.[11] Furthermore, there are many diseases and health-related problems that are not necessarily job related but that may affect job performance. Many organizations now not only attempt to remove health hazards from the workplace but also have invested in programs to improve health.

Occupational Health Hazards

"A coal miner in West Virginia can't breathe. A pesticide plant worker in Texas can't walk. A hospital anesthesiologist in Chicago suffers a miscarriage."[12] These people, along with hundreds of other employees, are victims of occupational diseases. An occupational illness can be defined as any abnormal condition or disorder (other than that resulting from an occupational injury) caused by exposure to environmental factors associated with employment. Approximately 187,400 new cases of occupational illnesses were reported among U.S. employees in private industry during 2008.[13] The U.S. Department of Labor currently uses five major categories to classify occupational illnesses: (1) occupational skin diseases or disorders, (2) respiratory conditions due to toxic agents, (3) poisoning (systemic effects of toxic materials), (4) hearing loss, and (5) all other occupational illnesses. In 2008, the overall incidence rate of nonfatal occupational illnesses was 19.7 per 10,000 full-time employees in private industry.[14]

Increased awareness of occupational disease was one factor that contributed to the passage of the Occupational Safety and Health Act. In addition, the **Toxic Substance Control Act** of 1976 requires the pretesting of certain new chemicals marketed each year. A 1980 OSHA rule requires organizations to measure for safety, and record employee exposure to, certain potentially harmful substances. These medical records must be made available to employees, their designated representatives, and OSHA. Furthermore, these records must be maintained for 30 years, even if the employee leaves the job. Additional rules have been issued related to specific hazards.

Hazard Communications

Because of the threats posed by chemicals in the workplace, OSHA issued its hazard communication rule in the early 1980s. This rule is also known as the *right-to-know rule.* The basic purpose of the rule is to ensure that employers and employees know what chemical hazards exist in their workplace and how to protect themselves against those hazards. The goal of the rule is to reduce the incidence of illness and injuries caused by chemicals.

The **Hazard Communication Standard** establishes uniform requirements to ensure that the hazards of all chemicals imported into, produced in, or used in the workplace are evaluated and that the results of these evaluations are transmitted to affected employers and exposed employees. OSHA has developed a variety of materials to help employers and employees implement effective hazard communication programs. For example, a free online course at www.eduwhere.com is available to help educate employees and employers about chemical hazards in the workplace.

Stress in the Workplace

Stress is the mental and physical condition that results from a perceived threat of danger (physical or emotional) and the pressure to remove it.[15] The potential for stress exists when an environmental situation presents a demand threatening to exceed a person's capabilities and resources for meeting it.[16] Stress manifests itself among employees in several ways, including increased absenteeism, job turnover, lower productivity, and mistakes on the job. In addition, excessive stress can result in both physical and emotional problems. Some common stress-related disorders include tension and migraine headaches; coronary heart disease; high blood pressure; muscle tightness in the chest, neck, and lower back; gastritis; indigestion; ulcers; diarrhea; constipation; bronchial asthma; rheumatoid arthritis; and some menstrual and sexual dysfunctions.[17] From a psychological perspective, inordinate or prolonged stress can adversely affect personal factors such as concentration, memory, sleep, appetite, motivation, mood, and the ability to relate to others.[18] Table 16.3 lists some of the more common sources and suggested causes of job-related stress.

The National Institute for Occupational Safety and Health (NIOSH) cites the following statistics, which come from numerous studies:[19]

- 40 percent of employees reported their job was very or extremely stressful.
- 25 percent view their jobs as the number one stressor in their lives.
- 75 percent of employees believe that employees have more on-the-job stress than a generation ago.
- 29 percent of employees felt quite a bit or extremely stressed at work.
- 26 percent of employees said they were "often or very often burned out or stressed by their work."

Toxic Substance Control Act
Federal law passed in 1976 requiring pretesting of new chemicals marketed for safety.

Hazard Communication Standard
Standard issued by OSHA in the early 1980s that established uniform requirements to ensure that the hazards of all chemicals imported into, produced, or used in the workplace are evaluated and that the results of these evaluations are transmitted to affected employers and exposed employees.

stress
Mental and physical condition that results from a perceived threat of danger (physical or emotional) and the pressure to remove it.

Web site: American Institute of Stress
www.stress.org

Stress manifests itself among employees in many ways. Ryan McVay/Getty Images

TABLE 16.3
Common Sources and Suggested Causes of Job-Related Stress

Source: *Personnel.* Copyright 1983 by American Management Association. Reproduced with permission of American Management Association in the Format Textbook via Copyright Clearance Center.

Sources	Suggested Causes
Threat of job loss	Cutback due to recessionary period or other factors beyond the control of employee.
Job mismatch	Job demands skills or abilities that the employee does not possess (job incompetence).
	Job does not provide opportunity for the employee to fully utilize skills or abilities (underutilization).
Conflicting expectations	Formal organization's concept of expected behavior contradicts the employee's concept of expected behavior.
	Informal group's concept of expected behavior contradicts the employee's concept.
Role ambiguity	Employee is uncertain or unclear about how to perform on the job.
	Employee is uncertain or unclear about what is expected in the job.
	Employee is unclear or uncertain about the relationship between job performance and expected consequences (rewards, penalties, etc.).
Role overload	Employee is incompetent at job.
	Employee is asked to do more than time permits (time pressure).
Fear/responsibility	Employee is afraid of performing poorly or failing.
	Employee feels pressure for high achievement.
	Employee has responsibility for other people.
Working conditions	Job environment is unpleasant; for example, there is inadequate lighting or improper regulation of temperature and noise.
	Requirements of the job may unnecessarily produce pacing problems, social isolation, and so forth.
	Machine design and maintenance procedures create pressure.
	Job involves long or erratic work hours.
Working relationships	Individual employees have problems relating to and/or working with superiors, peers, and/or subordinates.
	Employees have problems working in groups.
Alienation	There is limited social interaction.
	Employees do not participate in decision making.

According to the American Institute of Stress (a nonprofit research organization), the cost of stress for employers is currently estimated at over $300 billion annually as assessed by accidents, absenteeism, employee turnover, diminished productivity, direct medical and insurance costs, workers' compensation, and other legal costs.[20] This same group reports that 40 percent of job turnover is due to stress and that 60 to 80 percent of accidents on the job are stress related. In an effort to combat this, many organizations conduct training programs designed to help reduce employee stress. Most of these programs attempt to teach employees self-help techniques for individually reducing their own stress.

Burnout

burnout
Occurs when work is no longer meaningful to a person; can result from stress or a variety of other work-related or personal factors.

Burnout occurs when work is no longer meaningful to a person. Burnout can result from stress or a variety of other work-related or personal factors. Figure 16.2 illustrates the sequence of events that often leads to professional burnout. As burnout has become more recognized, certain related myths have surfaced.[21]

Myth 1: Burnout is just a new-fangled notion that gives lazy people an excuse not to work. Although burnout is a relatively recent term, the behavior has been around for centuries. History is full of examples of people, such as writers, artists, and scientists, who gradually or suddenly stopped producing.

Myth 2: As long as people really enjoy their work they can work as long and hard as they want and never experience burnout. Any work that inherently includes significant and continuing frustration, conflict, and pressure can lead to burnout.

Myth 3: Individuals know when they are burning out and, when they do, all they need to do is take off for a few days or weeks and then they'll be as good as new. Unfortunately, most people do not realize that burnout is occurring until it reaches its later stages.

FIGURE 16.2   The Path to Professional Burnout

Source: Donald P. Rogers, "Helping Employees Cope with Burnout," *Business,* October–December 1984, pp. 3–7. Copyright © 1984 by the College of Business Administration, Georgia State University, Atlanta. Reprinted by permission.

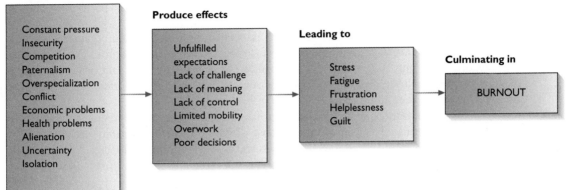

Myth 4: Individuals who are physically and psychologically strong are unlikely to experience burnout. Physically and psychologically strong individuals may indeed be able to work harder than less strong people. However, without proper stress skills, an inordinate amount of work can still cause serious damage.

Myth 5: Job burnout is always job-related. Burnout usually results from a combination of work, family, social, and personal factors.

From the organization's viewpoint, the first step in reducing burnout is to identify those jobs with the highest potential for burnout. Certain jobs, such as air traffic controller and certain computer-related jobs, are more likely to lead to burnout than others. Once those jobs have been identified, several actions are possible. Some of the possibilities include redesigning the jobs, clarifying expectations, changing work schedules, improving physical working conditions, and training the jobholders.

Alcoholism and Drug Abuse

The Substance Abuse and Mental Health Services Administration estimated for the year 2008 that nearly 20.1 million people in the United States used illicit drugs, 58.1 million people were alcohol binge drinkers, and 17.3 million people were heavy drinkers.[22] The National Council on Alcoholism and Drug Dependence estimates that alcohol and drug abuse costs the American economy $276 billion per year in lost productivity, health care expenditures, crime, motor vehicle crashes, and other conditions.[23] Compared to most employees, substance abusers

- Are late 3 times more often.
- Request time off 2.2 times more often.
- Have 2.5 times as many absences of eight days or more.
- Use 3 times the normal level of sick benefits.
- Are 5 times more likely to file a workers' compensation claim.
- Are involved in accidents 3.6 times more often.[24]

In addition, substance abuse results in reduced productivity, reduced work quality, damage to property and equipment, theft, lower morale, safety violations, and poor decision making.

Alcoholism

For years, people viewed alcoholics as people lacking self-control and morals. Today alcoholism is recognized as a disease with no single cause. Alcoholism does not strike any particular group; it can strike employees from the janitor to the chief executive officer. According to the 2008 National Survey on Drug Use & Health conducted by the U.S. Department of Health and Human Services, 79.7 percent of all adult binge and heavy drinkers are employed.[25]

The National Council on Alcoholism and Drug Dependence has estimated that the economic loss to the employer of an alcoholic employee amounts to 25 percent of the employee's wages.[26] Compared to nonalcoholic employees, alcoholics incur twice the rate of absenteeism caused by illness. Alcoholics are also two to three times more likely to be involved in a work-related accident.[27] Some people estimate that as many as 50 percent of all problem employees in industry are actually alcoholics.[28]

In spite of the well-documented costs associated with alcoholism, organizations have only recently undertaken widespread efforts to reduce employee alcoholism. A 1973 survey reported that only 400 major U.S. companies had any type of program designed to help overcome employee alcoholism.[29] Similar surveys subsequently reported that the number had grown to over 20,000 by 1998.[30]

Many organizations have established in-house alcoholic treatment programs. Most of the available information indicates that in-house alcoholic treatment programs achieve a high rate of success, based on both recovery rates and cost-effectiveness measures.[31] For example, the New York City Police Department, Du Pont, Consolidated Edison, Illinois Bell, Eastman Kodak, General Motors, and Inland Steel all report recovery rates of 60 percent or above.[32] The Comprehensive Assessment Treatment Outcomes Registry Data in Ohio have documented dramatic results from treatment, including the following:[33]

- Absenteeism decreased by 89 percent.
- Tardiness decreased by 92 percent.
- Problems with supervisors decreased by 56 percent.
- Mistakes in work decreased by 70 percent.

Programs for combating alcoholism are normally administered as part of an employee assistance program (EAP). EAPs are discussed at length later in this chapter.

Other Drugs

Widespread use of drugs other than alcohol is a relatively new phenomenon. Other than alcohol, drug usage usually falls into one of three categories: marijuana abuse, prescription drug abuse, and hard-drug abuse. According to the U.S. Department of Health and Human Services, approximately 72.7 percent of all drug users are currently employed.[34] Although most employees who use drugs are young, they are not all blue-collar employees. Employees on drugs are often much more difficult to detect than are drinking employees; alcohol can usually be smelled, whereas drugs cannot. Also, it is relatively easy to pop a pill at lunch or on a break undetected. Current estimates are that 10 percent of fulltime employees in the United States use illicit drugs.[35]

Drug Testing

As a result of the increased use of drugs in the workplace, many companies use some form of drug testing for both job applicants and existing employees. The American Management Association has reported that the percentage of employers using drug tests peaked in 1996 at 81 percent. In 1999, the percentage fell to 70 percent and to 62 percent in 2004.[36] Some people believe that workplace drug testing has increased since 2004.[37] While many, if not most, large companies do utilize drug testing, the practice is less prevalent in small businesses. Certain legal risks are involved in drug testing, and therefore extreme caution should be exercised. An employer can be exposed to substantial liability for defamation for making a false accusation of drug or alcohol use (juries have awarded amounts as high as $450,000 for such defamation). The following guidelines are suggested for implementing a drug-testing program:

- Establish a routine, uniform, organizationwide policy for substance abuse and adhere to it in a consistent and nondisciplinary manner.
- Assume employees are drug-free until proven otherwise.
- Make negative test scores a bona fide occupational qualification whenever possible.
- Include testing in uniform preemployment agreements and have them signed by new employees. For existing employees, establish drug tests as a prerequisite to recalls, promotions, and transfers.
- Train supervisors to detect and refer problem employees for testing.

- Use a high-quality type of urinalysis, not just the cheapest method.
- Use monitored laboratories that employ blind testing to ensure the integrity of the testing procedures. Blind testing requires that those performing the tests do not know the identity of those being tested.
- Use appropriate supervision and custody arrangements to ensure that the samples tested are valid.
- Require tested employees to list all legal over-the-counter drugs they are taking at the time of testing.
- Develop and maintain profiles of well-employee urinalysis results that can later be used for comparative purposes.
- Keep all results confidential.[38]

One criticism of drug-testing programs in general is that they tend to focus on off-duty conduct. Many employees view this as an invasion of privacy, which has led to morale problems and numerous lawsuits. To avoid the potential problems associated with traditional drug testing, a new form of testing, called *performance* or *impairment testing,* has emerged.[39] Instead of testing for byproducts that may or may not cause impairment, performance testing measures physical variables such as coordination and response time to certain tasks. For example, a test might consist of watching a CRT screen and manipulating a joystick or keyboard. The person's score can then be compared to a standard or to a previous score. Commercial performance tests are relatively new in most areas of the country.

AIDS

As defined by the U.S. Centers for Disease Control (CDC), AIDS is "a reliably diagnosed disease that is at least moderately indicative of an underlying cellular immunodeficiency in a person who has had no known underlying cause of cellular immunodeficiency nor any other cause of reduced resistance reported to be associated with that disease."[40] The CDC estimated that through 2007, 1,009,220 adult and adolescent cases of AIDS had been diagnosed in the United States.[41]

The Vocational Rehabilitation Act of 1973 and numerous state laws offer certain protection to employees infected with AIDS. Under these laws, AIDS-infected employees may file discrimination suits if employment opportunities are denied solely on the basis of their having AIDS. The **Vocational Rehabilitation Act** of 1973 prohibited discrimination against otherwise qualified handicapped individuals solely on the basis of their disability. It should be noted, however, that the Vocational Rehabilitation Act applies only to federal contractors who hold a contract of $2,500 or more, subcontractors to such an employer, recipients of federal financial aid, and federal agencies. Companies that do not meet the previously stated requirements of the Vocational Rehabilitation Act are subject only to applicable state and local statutes, which may vary considerably from state to state.

Vocational Rehabilitation Act
Legislation enacted in 1973 that prohibits discrimination against otherwise qualified handicapped individuals solely on the basis of their disability; applies only in certain situations involving federal contracts, recipients of federal assistance, or federal agencies.

If an individual with AIDS is covered by the Vocational Rehabilitation Act, certain other issues must be addressed. These issues include determining if the individual meets the definition of a handicapped individual, if the handicapped individual is otherwise qualified to do the job, and if the employee's contagiousness poses a threat to others. If the infected employee does not meet the provision for being handicapped, is not otherwise qualified, or does pose a threat to others, he or she is not protected by the Vocational Rehabilitation Act.

However, the Vocational Rehabilitation Act does not prevent employers from terminating an employee who can no longer perform the duties of his or her job, provided the employer made reasonable accommodations. Reasonable accommodations are defined as those that do not pose undue financial or administrative burdens on the employer.

Since no cure or vaccine for AIDS presently exists, many organizations are turning to education as the most viable means of combating both the medical and social dilemmas posed by AIDS. In addition to developing formal policies for dealing with AIDS, companies are developing in-depth training programs to educate their workforces about AIDS. One survey by the National Aids Fund reported that 65 percent of the survey respondents indicated they would like HIV/AIDS education in the workplace.[42] Only 22 percent of the respondents reported that they were currently receiving HIV/AIDS education. Table 16.4 summarizes many of the potential benefits of AIDS education in the workplace.

TABLE 16.4
Potential Benefit of AIDS Education in the Workplace

- Prevent new infections among employees by helping everyone understand how HIV is and is not transmitted.
- Alert managers and supervisors to the legal issues raised by HIV infection in the workplace. The overwhelming majority of AIDS-related lawsuits related to the workplace involve discrimination and violation of confidentiality. Good training can prevent those problems.
- Prevent discrimination against people living with HIV or AIDS.
- Prepare managers and supervisors to consider reasonable accommodation requests from people disabled by HIV infection.
- Raise morale. It is not unusual for companies to report positive effects on morale after employee HIV training.

Employee Assistance Programs (EAPs)

Many large organizations and a growing number of smaller ones are attempting to help employees with personal problems. These problems include not only alcohol and drug abuse but depression, anxiety, domestic trauma, financial problems, and other psychiatric/medical problems. This help is not purely altruistic; it is largely based on cost savings. The help is most often offered in the form of **employee assistance programs (EAPs)**.

employee assistance programs (EAPs)
Company-sponsored programs designed to help employees with personal problems such as alcohol and drug abuse, depression, anxiety, domestic trauma, financial problems, and other psychiatric/medical problems.

Cost of Personal Problems

A primary result of personal problems brought to the workplace is reduced productivity. Absenteeism and tardiness also tend to increase. Increased costs of insurance programs, including sickness and accident benefits, are a direct result of personal problems brought to the workplace. Lower morale, more friction among employees, more friction between supervisors and employees, and more grievances also result from troubled employees. Permanent loss of trained employees due to disability, retirement, and death is also associated with troubled employees. Difficult to measure, but a very real cost associated with troubled employees, is the loss of business and a damaged public image.

Organization Involvement

Until recently, organizations attempted to avoid employees' problems that were not job related. Although aware of the existence of these problems, most managers did not believe they should interfere with employees' personal lives. In the past, organizations tended to get rid of troubled employees. In recent years, however, cost considerations, unions, and government legislation altered this approach. The accepted viewpoint now is that employees' personal problems are private until they begin affecting their job performance. When and if that happens, personal problems become a matter of concern for the organization.

Studies have shown that absenteeism can be significantly reduced by employee assistance programs. It has also been found that EAPs help reduce on-the-job accidents and grievances. Workers' compensation premiums, sickness and accident benefits, and trips to the infirmary also tend to decrease with an EAP. The 2009 survey by the Society for Human Resource Management (SHRM) found that 75 percent of the responding companies offered an EAP.[43] Human resource experts estimate that 62 million Americans currently have access to EAPs.[44]

Types of EAPs

Organizations may offer employee assistance to varying degrees. For example, some organizations may offer only an education program while others may provide a complete diagnosis and treatment program. The most common type of EAP employs a coordinator who evaluates the employee's problem only sufficiently to make a referral to the proper agency or clinic for diagnosis. Sometimes the coordinator serves only as a consultant to the organization and is not a full-time employee. This type of program is especially popular with smaller employers and branch operations of large employers. In a second type of program, the organization hires a qualified person to diagnose the employee's problem; then the employee is referred to the proper agency or clinic for treatment. Under a third type of program, diagnosis and treatment are provided in-house directly by the organization. Because of the complexities of maintaining a full-service facility and hiring appropriate professional staff, most companies do not find this approach to be cost-effective.

WEGMANS' EMPLOYEE ASSISTANCE PROGRAM

Wegmans Food Markets Inc. is a Rochester, New York–based grocery chain that also operates in Dickson City and Wilkes-Barre, Pennsylvania. Wegmans has approximately 13,700 employees in Rochester and 37,400 nationally.

Wegmans began offering an employee assistance program (EAP) to its employees in 1985. At that time, Wegmans' EAP was undertaken with a contract with Park Ridge Hospital in Rochester. Since 1990, the company has maintained an internal EAP office staffed by Wegmans employees. EAP manager Vikki Wright says their on-site EAP addresses many issues from stress management, to parenting concerns, to different forms of addiction. Her office makes outside referrals when the need arises. The Wegmans' EAP does not limit how often employees or their household members can use the EAP. "We feel that as long as an employee is connected with a counselor and getting help and support that they need, and as long as they're benefiting from it, we're willing to support it as long as they need it," explains Wright.

Wegmans is known for its employee loyalty with 11 percent of its employees having been with the company for at least 15 years. In January 2010, Wegmans was named by *Fortune* magazine as the third best company in the United States to work for, up from fifth in 2009.

Sources: Shelia Livadas, "Employee Assistance Programs Evolve, Broaden Scope," *Rochester Business Journal,* May 23, 2008, p. 28, and James Haggerty, "Edward Jones, Wegmans Named Best Companies to Work for by *Fortune* Magazine," *McClatchy-Tribune Business News,* January 22, 2010.

Features of a Successful EAP

For an EAP to succeed, it must first be accepted by the employees; they must not be afraid to use it. Experience has shown that certain elements are critical to the success of an EAP. Table 16.5 summarizes several of the most important characteristics of an EAP.

A U.S. Department of Labor study found that for every dollar an employer invests in an EAP, it saves $14.[45] John Maynard, CEO of the Employee Assistance Professionals Association, believes that "EAPs can reduce absenteeism and tardiness by 10 percent and potentially boost productivity by as much as 25 percent."[46] Because of the obvious benefits to both employees and employers, EAPs are expected to continue to grow in popularity. There is evidence that EAPs are also growing in popularity in other countries and specifically in Canada, England, and China.[47] HRM in Action 16.3 describes the EAP at Wegmans Food Markets.

Work/Life Programs

A work/life program is any employer-sponsored benefit or working situation that helps employees balance work and nonwork demands. Generally these programs include such things as flexible work schedules, job sharing, telecommuting (all of which were discussed in Chapter 4), flexible benefits (discussed in Chapter 15), wellness programs, child-care and elder-care assistance, and sick-leave policies. The prevalence of both single-parent families and dual-career couples with children has had a significant impact on the need for work/life programs.

TABLE 16.5
Ten Critical Elements of an EAP

Source: Reprinted with permission of *Personnel Administrator,* published by the Society for Human Resource Management, Alexandria, VA.

Element	Significance
Management backing	Without this at the highest level, key ingredients and overall effect are seriously limited.
Labor support	The EAP cannot be meaningful if it is not backed by the employees' labor unit.
Confidentiality	Anonymity and trust are crucial if employees are to use an EAP.
Easy access	For maximum use and benefit.
Supervisor training	Crucial to employees needing understanding and support during receipt of assistance.
Union steward training	A critical variable is employees' contact with the union—the steward.
Insurance involvement	Occasionally, assistance alternatives are costly, and insurance support is a must.
Breadth of services component	Availability of assistance for a wide variety of problems (e.g., alcohol, family, personal, financial, grief, medical).
Professional leadership	A skilled professional with expertise in helping, who must have credibility in the eyes of the employee.
Follow-up and evaluation	To measure program effectiveness and overall improvement.

While many companies may not choose to relate dollar values to their work/life programs, there is substantial evidence, in both "hard" numbers and "soft" benefits, that these programs pay off.[48] Many people believe that retention, morale, and productivity can be improved from work/life programs. A 2006 survey reported that almost 50 percent of the responding companies had increased, over the past two years, the number of work/life programs they offer.[49] There is also evidence that a growing number of employers are integrating work/life and employee assistance programs.[50] Employers, consultants, and providers say that by combining these programs, companies can offer a "one-stop" option that effectively helps employees while at the same time cutting costs and eliminating administrative duplication.

Wellness Programs

As a type of work/life program, many companies have begun programs designed to prevent illness and enhance employee wellness. These programs are referred to as *wellness programs* and include such things as periodic medical exams, stop-smoking clinics, improved dietary practices, hypertension detection and control, weight control, exercise and fitness, stress management, accident-risk reduction, immunizations, and cardiopulmonary resuscitation training (CPR). Some of the documented results of wellness programs include fewer sick days, reduced coronary heart disease, and lower major medical costs. Many also believe employee productivity increases for employees participating in exercise and fitness programs. Numerous studies have reported that most types of wellness programs yield an average return on investments of $1 to almost $6 for every dollar invested.[51] Table 16.6 summarizes actual benefits obtained from wellness programs by specific companies. Experts in the wellness field report that even small companies can offer wellness programs and that they do not have to be expensive.

The 2008 Benefits Study by the Society of Human Resource Management (SHRM) found that 59 percent of respondents' organizations provided some type of wellness programs.[52] The 2008 National Compensation Survey reported that access to wellness programs for both public and private sector employees increased dramatically from 1998 to 2008.[53] In light of the continual rise in health care costs, it is predicted that company-sponsored wellness programs will continue to grow in the future. HRM in Action 16.4 describes a new approach to wellness being promoted by Premera Alaska.

TABLE 16.6
Specific Company Benefits of Wellness Programs

Source: Nancy Hatch Woodward, "Exercise Options, *HR Magazine,* June 2005, pp. 78–83.

- DuPont Corporation reported absences from illness unrelated to the job declined 14 percent at 41 individual sites where the company offered a wellness program. This compared to a 5.8 percent decline at the 19 sites where a wellness program was not offered.
- Pacific Bell found that absentee days decreased by 0.8 percent after its FitWorks program was put in place. This resulted in a $2 million savings in one year. Employees who participated in the program spent 3.3 fewer days on short-term disability, saving the company an additional $4.7 million.
- The Coca-Cola Company reported an annual reduction in health care claims for each employee who participated in its Health Works fitness program.

VIOLENCE IN THE WORKPLACE

Workplace violence includes homicides, physical attacks, rapes, aggravated and other assaults, all forms of harassment, and any other act that creates a hostile environment.[54] The FBI estimates that each year 1 million people in the United States are exposed to some form of workplace violence.[55] According to the U.S. Department of Labor, nearly 5 percent of U.S. private businesses experienced a violent incident within the 12 months prior to completing the most recent Bureau of Labor Statistics (BLS) survey on workplace violence.[56] Of those responding to the survey, 21 percent of the organizations reported that the incident affected their employees' fear level and an equal percentage said employee morale was affected by the incident.

A 2004 survey by the American Society of Safety Engineers (ASSE) found that only 1 percent of the responding companies have written policies on workplace violences.[57] Only 50 percent of these same respondents said they have procedures in place for employees to follow to discreetly report signs of impending violence. The latest Bureau of Labor Statistics survey on workplace violence reported that over 70 percent of U.S. workplaces had no formal program or policy for addressing workplace violence.[58]

Given the significance of violence in the workplace, what can organizations do to protect their employees and physical resources? It is important that companies concentrate on avoiding or heading off violence rather than simply dealing with it after it occurs.[59] Most companies can do several things to avoid falling victim to violent incidents:

- *Hire carefully, but realistically.* Screen out potential employees whose histories show a propensity to violence. A full background check can be done in many states for $50 or less.
- *Draw up a plan and involve employees in it.* Develop a plan for preventing violence and for dealing with it if it does occur. Reporting requirements for both violence and threats of violence should be an integral part of the plan. The plan should also be shaped by employee participation. Encourage employees to report any suspicions they may have and require supervisors to take action when a suspicion is reported to them.
- *As part of the plan, adopt a "zero tolerance" policy.* "Zero tolerance" does not necessarily mean dismissal; rather, it means the perpetrator of the violence will face consequences of some kind. When discipline is called for, its purpose should be to teach, not to punish.
- *Enlist the aid of professionals—with an eye on the cost.* Go to external resources when necessary to get help if a problem or a potential problem reveals itself. A few hours with a psychologist or a legal professional can defuse a simmering situation. It might even be necessary to hire a security firm temporarily in some instances.

While all of the above measures should help a company avoid violence in the workplace, the best protection may lie in developing a corporate culture that makes violence all but unthinkable. Violence is much less likely to take place in an environment where employees feel appreciated and believe they are treated with respect.

Summary
of Learning
Objectives

1. **State the purpose of the Occupational Safety and Health Act and discuss its major provisions.**

   The stated purpose of the act is "to assure so far as possible every working man and woman in the nation safe and healthful working conditions." The act established the Occupational Safety and Health Administration (OSHA) to set up standards and to conduct workplace inspections. Many OSHA standards have special record-keeping and reporting requirements that companies must adhere to.

2. **List the three major causes of accidents in the workplace.**

   The three major causes of work-related accidents are unsafe personal acts, an unsafe physical environment, and accident proneness.

3. **Define *frequency rate* and *severity rate*.**

   A frequency rate indicates how often disabling injuries occur. A severity rate indicates how severe accidents were by calculating the average length of time injured employees were unable to work.

4. **Offer several suggestions for promoting safety in the workplace.**

   Many things can be done to promote safety in the workplace. Some suggestions include these: (1) make the work interesting; (2) establish a safety committee; (3) feature employee safety contests; (4) publicize safety statistics; (5) hold periodic safety meetings; and (6) post safety-related pictures, cartoons, and sketches on bulletin boards.

5. **Discuss the Hazard Communication rule.**

   The Hazard Communication rule, also known as the right-to-know rule, is intended to ensure that employers and employees know what chemical hazards exist in the workplace and how to protect themselves against these hazards. The rule requires that certain chemicals be evaluated for danger and that the results be communicated to affected employers and exposed employees.

6. **Differentiate between stress and burnout.**

   Stress is the mental and physical condition that results from a perceived threat of danger (physical or emotional) and the pressure to remove it. Burnout occurs when work is no longer meaningful to a person. Burnout can result from stress or from a variety of other work-related or personal factors.

7. **Name several work-related consequences of alcohol and drug abuse.**

   Possible work-related consequences of alcohol and drug abuse include absenteeism, tardiness, reduced productivity, poor decision making, equipment damage, safety violations, lower morale, and even outright theft to pay for drugs.

8. **Offer several guidelines for implementing a drug-testing program.**

   Suggested guidelines for implementing a drug-testing program include these: (1) establish a routine, uniform, organizationwide policy for substance abuse and adhere to it in a consistent manner; (2) assume employees are drug-free until proven otherwise; (3) make negative drug testing scores a bona fide occupational qualification whenever possible; (4) include drug testing as a part of a preemployment agreement; (5) train supervisors to detect and refer problem employees for testing; (6) use a high-quality type of test; (7) use monitored laboratories to process and interpret the test results; (8) use appropriate supervision and custody arrangements to ensure that the samples tested are valid; (9) require tested employees to list all legal drugs they are taking; (10) develop and maintain profiles of well-employee urinalysis results that can later be used for comparative purposes; and (11) keep all results confidential.

9. **Discuss the legal requirements for terminating an employee with acquired immuno-deficiency syndrome (AIDS).**

   First, it must be determined if the employee is covered by the Vocational Rehabilitation Act of 1973. If the employee is not covered by this act, the company is subject only to applicable state and local statutes, which vary considerably from state to state. If the individual is covered by the Vocational Rehabilitation Act, it must be determined if he or she meets the provisions of a handicapped individual or is otherwise qualified, and whether his or her contagiousness poses a threat to others. If the infected employee does not meet the provisions for being handicapped, is not otherwise qualified, or poses a threat to others, she or he is not protected by the act. The act does not prevent employers from terminating employees who can no longer perform their job duties, provided the company made reasonable accommodations.

10. **Explain the three basic types of employee assistance programs (EAPs).**

    The most common type of EAP employs a coordinator who evaluates the employee's problem sufficiently to make a referral to the proper agency or clinic for diagnosis. In a second type, the organization hires a qualified person to diagnose the employee's problem and then refers the employee to a proper agency or clinic for treatment. Under a third type of EAP, diagnosis and treatment of the problem are provided directly by the organization.

11. **Explain what work/life programs and wellness programs are.**

    A work/life program is any employer-sponsored benefit or working situation that helps employees balance work and nonwork demands. A wellness program is a program designed and implemented by an employer to prevent illness and enhance employee wellness.

12. List several specific things an organization can do to help reduce violence in its workplace.

Most companies can do several things to avoid incidents. These include (1) hiring carefully, (2) drawing up a plan and involving employees in its development, (3) adopting a "zero tolerance" policy, and (4) enlisting the aid of professionals when necessary.

Key Terms

burnout, *328*
disabling injuries, *324*
employee assistance
 programs (EAPs), *332*
Federal Register, 321
frequency rate, *324*
general-duty clause,
 320
Hazard Communication
 Standard, *327*

Marshall v. *Barlow's,
 Inc., 321*
Occupational Safety
 and Health Act, *320*
OSHA Form 300 (Log of
 Work-Related Injuries
 and Illnesses) and OSHA
 Form 300A (Summary of
 Work-Related Injuries
 and Illnesses), *323*

OSHA Form 301
 (Injury and Illness
 Incident Report), *323*
severity rate, *324*
stress, *327*
Toxic Substance
 Control Act, *327*
Vocational
 Rehabilitation Act, *331*
wellness programs, *334*

Review Questions

1. What is the Occupational Safety and Health Administration (OSHA) authorized to do?
2. What is the general-duty clause as it relates to OSHA?
3. List the inspection priorities established by OSHA.
4. What is the usual inspection procedure followed by OSHA?
5. Name and discuss the three primary causes of accidents.
6. How do organizations measure their safety records?
7. What four basic elements are present in most successful safety programs?
8. What can be done to promote safety in organizations?
9. What does the Toxic Substance Control Act of 1976 require?
10. Distinguish between stress and burnout.
11. List several guidelines that should be followed when implementing a drug-testing program.
12. Define *performance testing* and describe how it differs from normal drug testing.
13. How does the Vocational Rehabilitation Act of 1973 affect the dismissal of employees with AIDS?
14. Describe the three general types of employee assistance programs (EAPs).
15. What is a work/life program?
16. List four things an organization might do to avoid violent incidents in the workplace.

Discussion Questions

1. Express your personal philosophy regarding the responsibilities of management, especially human resource managers, for the well-being of employees.
2. On July 1, 1985, the president, plant manager, and foreman of Film Recovery Systems, Inc., were sentenced to 25 years in the Illinois state prison and fined $10,000 each after being found guilty of murder in the 1983 death of an employee exposed to cyanide in a silver-recovery process.* The court found that the three executives were "totally knowledgeable of the hazards of cyanide" and failed to communicate those hazards to employees, who were mostly undocumented Polish and Mexican immigrants. What is your reaction to what were the first work-related homicide convictions in the United States?
3. Do you think an organization has any responsibility to help employees with health problems totally unrelated to their work environment?
4. Why do you think that the overwhelming majority of organizations do not have written policies relating to violence in the workplace? Additionally, why do you think that most organizations do not change or try to improve their workplace violence policies or programs following an incident?

*See Betty S. Murphy, Wayne E. Barlow, and D. Diane Hatch, "Murder in the Workplace," *Personnel Journal,* October 1985, p. 27.

Incident 16.1

Safety Problems at Blakely

Several severe accidents have recently occurred in the 12-employee assembly department of Blakely Company, which has a total workforce of 65 employees. The supervisor of this department, Joe Benson, is quite perturbed and, in response to questions by the general manager and owner of the company, claimed the employees do not listen to him. He has warned them about not taking safety precautions, he explained, but he can't police their every move. The general manager countered, "Accidents cost us money for repairs, lost time, medical expenses, human suffering, and what not. It's important that you stop it. Your department has a bad safety record—the worst in the company. You are going to have to correct it."

Joe believed he had taken the necessary precautions but was not getting satisfactory results. He also believed there were more possibilities of accidents occurring in his department than in any other department of the company. He decided to talk it over with the human resource manager, Fay Thomas. Fay suggested scheduling a 10-minute safety talk by a different employee each week. The first subject would be "using machine guards." Joe thought that "good housekeeping and safety" and "no smoking" would also be good subsequent subjects.

Fay suggested that Joe schedule part of his time to review his department periodically. Furthermore, she suggested that any unsafe act he discovered should result in an immediate two-day suspension for the offender. "You have to get tough when it comes to safety. Your people are taking safety much too lightly. Of course, you start by making an announcement of what you are going to do. Put a notice to that effect on the bulletin board. Then enforce it to the letter."

Joe believed that simply talking personally to each of his employees and urging them to work safely might get better results. However, he was convinced that some type of incentive was needed. As a result, he devised a plan in which the employee with the fewest safety violations over the next three months would be given a day off with pay. Joe's plan was approved by his boss.

Questions

1. What is Joe's problem?

2. In your opinion, how did this problem develop? What were its main causes? Discuss.

3. What actions do you recommend Joe take? Why?

Incident 16.2

To Fire or Not to Fire?*

David Butler is a former drug user who has spent time in jail. For the past three years he has been straight, as far as everyone knows. Currently David operates a forklift for Adams, Inc., a small construction company. Lately David has begun having seizures, or "flashbacks," as a result of his earlier use of the drug PCP. David has been carefully evaluated by EAP professionals and found to be clean of current drug use. The professionals say that flashbacks of this nature are quite common in ex-addicts. Mishandling of David's machine could be potentially dangerous to him and his coworkers. David has already had some flashbacks while at the controls, and in every case the seizure merely caused him to release the handle, which simply stopped the machine automatically. This is the only job David is qualified to do within the company.

Questions

1. Should David be allowed to continue on the job?

2. Are there any options other than leaving David alone or firing him?

*This case is adapted from an actual situation reported in *Management Review,* August 1991, p. 23.

**EXERCISE 16.1
Filing OSHA
Reports**

Assume you are the director of human resources for your company and that one of your responsibilities is to handle all contact with OSHA. Three days ago, on Monday, two injuries occurred in the plant. In the first case, a machine operator got careless and smashed his thumb. The operator received first aid on the floor, went home early, and was back on the job the next morning. In the second case, an office worker slipped while going down some steps and broke her arm. She is expected to report back to work at the start of the next week.

Questions

1. What OSHA forms should be filed in each of these cases? When should the forms be filed?
2. Go online (www.osha.gov) or to your library or a local OSHA office and get copies of the OSHA forms needed for each of the cases described above. Complete the forms. Make any reasonable assumptions about the accidents that you deem necessary.

**EXERCISE 16.2
Preventing Violence
in the Workplace**

Go online or to the library and identify a specific and recent incidence of violence in a workplace. As best you can, try to identify the circumstances surrounding the incident. Do you think the organization's management could have done anything to help prevent the violence from occurring?

Notes and Additional Readings

1. *Injury Facts,* 2010 ed. (Itasca, Ill.: National Safety Council, 2010), p. 52.
2. Ibid.
3. *All About OSHA* (Washington, D.C.: U.S. Department of Labor, 2003), p. 2.
4. *Injury Facts,* p. 55.
5. David S. Thelan, Donna Ledgerwood, and Charles F. Walters, "Health and Safety in the Workplace: A New Challenge for Business Schools," *Personnel Administrator,* October 1985, p. 37.
6. *All About OSHA* (Washington, D.C.: U.S. Department of Labor, 2006), pp. 5–6.
7. Ibid., p. 4.
8. *Marshall v. Barlow's, Inc.* 76-1143 (1978).
9. John D. Jordan and Rabbi D. Simons, "It's No Accident: What You Think Is What You Do," *Personnel Journal,* April 1984, pp. 16–20; and Russ Tarbell, "Gaining More Safety Success," *Professional Safety,* February 1997, p. 42.
10. "Developing a Safety Training Program," *HR Focus,* September 1996, p. 10; see also George Robotham, "Safety Training That Works," *Professional Safety,* May 2001, pp. 33–37.
11. Craig S. Weaver, "Understanding Occupational Disease," *Personnel Journal,* June 1989, pp. 86–94.
12. "Is Your Job Dangerous to Your Health?" *U.S. News & World Report,* February 5, 1979, p. 41; see also Michelle Conlin and John Carey, "Is Your Office Killing You?" *BusinessWeek,* June 5, 2000, pp. 114–22.
13. http://www.bls.gov/iif/home.htm. Accessed February 18, 2010.
14. Ibid.
15. Genevieva La Greca, "The Stress You Make," *Personnel Journal,* September 1985, p. 43.
16. J. E. McGrath, "Stress and Behavior in Organizations," in *Handbook of Industrial and Organizational Psychology,* ed. M. D. Dunnette (Skokie, Ill.: Rand McNally, 1976), pp. 1, 352.
17. Michael E. Cavanagh, "What You Don't Know About Stress," *Personnel Journal,* July 1988, p. 55; "The Warning Signs of Stress," *Restaurant Business,* March 1, 1991, p. 140.
18. Cavanagh, "What You Don't Know," p. 55.
19. National Institute for Occupational Safety and Health, "Stress at Work," http://www.cdc.gov/niosh. Accessed February 17, 2010.
20. http://www.stress.org/job.htm. Accessed February 17, 2010.
21. These myths are adapted from Cavanagh, "What You Don't Know," pp. 56–57.
22. Substance Abuse and Mental Health Services Administration (SAMHSA), "Highlights from the 2008 National Survey on Drug Use and Health," http://www.oas.samhsa.gov/nhsda.htm. Accessed February 17, 2010.

23. The National Council on Alcoholism and Drug Dependence, "Alcohol and Drug Dependence Are America's Number One Health Problem," http://www.ncadd.org/facts/numberoneprob.html. Accessed February 17, 2010.

24. Rhoda Cooke, "Hotline for Help," *Credit Union Management,* March 1997, pp. 23–24; Clyde E. Witt, "Just Say Yes: Drug Testing in the Workplace," *Material Handling Management,* May 2006, pp. 36–39; and Janet Rorholm, "Worker Put to Test," *McClatchy-Tribune Business News,* October 14, 2008.

25. *Results from the 2008 National Survey on Drug Use and Health: National Findings,* Department of Health and Human Services, Substance Abuse and Mental Health Services Administration. http://www.oas.samhsa.gov/nsduh.

26. Steven H. Appelbaum and Barbara T. Shapiro, "The ABCs of EAPs," *Personnel,* July 1989, p. 40.

27. Ibid.

28. Gopal C. Pati and John I. Adkins, Jr., "The Employer's Role in Alcoholism Assistance," *Personnel Journal,* July 1983, p. 69.

29. "Battling Employee Alcoholism," *Dun's Business Monthly,* June 1982, p. 48.

30. Ibid.; Leslie Stackel, "EAPs in the Work Place," *Employee Relations Today,* Autumn 1987, p. 289; and Roberta Reynes, "Programs That Aid Troubled Workers," *Nation's Business,* June 1998, pp. 73–74.

31. Pati and Adkins, "The Employer's Role," p. 69.

32. Ibid.

33. The National Council on Alcoholism and Drug Dependence, "Alcohol and Drug Dependence Are America's Number One Health Problem," pp. 2–3.

34. *Results from the 2008 National Survey on Drug Use and Health: National Findings.* Department of Health and Human Services, Substance Abuse and Mental Health Services Administration http://www.oas.samhsa.gov/nsduh/2k8nsduh/2k8Results.pdf., p. 27.

35. Witt, "Just Say Yes: Drug Testing in the Workplace."

36. Evelyn Beck, "Is the Time Right for Impairment Testing?" *Workforce,* February 2001, pp. 69–71; Sharon Linstedt, "More Employers Test Applicants for Drugs," *Knight Ridder Tribune Business News,* January 13, 2003, p. 1; and Dana Knight, "Employers' Use of Drug Screening Is Tapering Off," *Knight Ridder Tribune Business News,* January 31, 2005, p. 1.

37. Gene Stowe, "More Companies Are Using Drug Testing," *Tribune Business Weekly,* September 15, 2008.

38. These guidelines are adapted from Ian A. Miners, Nick Nykadyn, and Diane Traband, "Put Drug Detection to the Test," *Personnel Journal,* August 1987, p. 97.

39. Beck, "Is the Time Right for Impairment Testing?"

40. David L. Wing, "AIDS: The Legal Debate," *Personnel Journal,* August 1986, p. 114.

41. *Basic Statistics,* Department of Health and Human Services, Centers for Disease Control and Prevention, http://www.cdc.gov/hiv/topics/surveillance/basic.htm. Accessed February 17, 2010.

42. National AIDS Fund, "National AIDS Fund Survey Finds Worker Concern for HIV Positive Employees," http://www.aidsfund.org. Accessed May 6, 2004.

43. The Society for Human Resource Management, *The 2009 Employee Benefits Study* (Alexandria, VA: 2009), p. 10.

44. Sheila Liradas, "Employee Assistance Programs Evolve, Broader Scope," *Rochester Business Journal,* May 23, 2008, p. 28.

45. Fonda Phillips, "Employee Assistance Programs: A New Way to Control Health Care Costs," *Employee Benefit Plan Review,* August 2003, pp. 22–24.

46. Gina Rutz, "Expanded EAPs Lend a Hand to Employers' Bottom Line," *Workforce Management,* January 16, 2006, pp. 46–47.

47. Rick Csiernik, "EAPs in Numbers," *Canadian HR Reporter,* April 24, 2006, pp. 22–23; Cecilia Lui, "Corporate Wellness Programs Help Those Who Help Themselves," *China Staff,* September 2006, pp. 14–17, and "EAPS: Dial EAP for Help," *Employee Benefits,* July 12, 2006, p. 36.

48. Elayne Robertson Demby, "Do Your Family-Friendly Programs Make Cents?" *HR Magazine,* January 2004, p. 74.

49. "Work–Life Programs on the Rise," *Non-Profit World,* March/April 2006, p. 7.

50. Judy Greenwald, "Joint EAP, Work/Life Programs Cut Costs," *Business Insurance,* March 29, 2004, pp. T3–T6, and Karen Pallarito, "Wellness Features Fused with Work/Life Programs," *Business Insurance,* June 19, 2006, pp. 11–13.

51. "A Measurable Difference," *Best's Review,* April 2006, p. 54; "Employee Wellness Programs Demonstrate Positive Return on Investment for Business," *PR Newswire,* July 23, 2009; and Stephen Miller, "Wellness Incentives Grow in Size and Scope," *HR Magazine,* January 2010, p. 23.

52. Stephen Miller, "Firms Spend Now to Curtail Costs Later," *HR Magazine,* August 2006, p. 34.

53. Eli R. Stolzfus, "Access to Wellness and Employee Assistance Programs in the United States," April 22, 2009, www.bls.gov/opub/cwc/cm20090416ar01p1.htm.

54. "Employers Ignoring Workplace Violence," *Safety Now,* October 2006, p. 3.

55. Chuck Mannila, "How to Avoid Becoming a Workplace Violence Statistic," *T&D,* July 2008, pp. 60–66.

56. "Most Employers Don't Change Policies after Workplace Violence Occurs," HR Focus, January 2007, p. 9.

57. Paul Viollis, "Most Workplace Violence Avoidable," *Business Insurance,* April 11, 2005, p. 10.

58. "Workplace Violence: Where Are The Preventive Programs?" *ISHN,* May 2008, p. 12.

59. Much of this section is drawn from Michael Barrier, "The Enemy Within," *Nation's Business,* February 1995, pp. 18–21.

Chapter **Seventeen**

Employee Relations

Chapter Learning Objectives

After studying this chapter, you should be able to:

1. Explain employment at will.
2. Explain employment arbitration programs.
3. Explain the causes of disciplinary actions.

4. Describe progressive discipline.
5. Define grievance procedures.
6. Define just cause.
7. Explain due process.
8. Describe the duty of fair representation.
9. Define grievance arbitration.

Employee relations are concerned with the administration of discipline and grievance-handling procedures. When a manager must take action against an employee for violating an organizational work rule, the manager uses the organization's disciplinary procedure. When an employee has a complaint against the organization or its management, the employee normally uses the grievance procedure to resolve the problem. Some organizations have very formal discipline and grievance procedures, others are less formal, and some organizations have no set procedures at all.

EMPLOYMENT AT WILL

employment at will
Allows either the employer or employee to terminate his or her employment relationship at any time for virtually any reason or for no reason at all.

Until recently, management decisions on discipline or discharge in nonunionized organizations have been relatively free of judicial review. Courts intervened only in those cases violating legislation concerning equal employment opportunity. Generally, the concept of employment at will has applied. **Employment at will** allows either the employer or employee to terminate their employment relationship at any time for virtually any reason or for no reason at all.[1]

The situation has been gradually changing as the courts have begun to hear discharge cases involving allegations of capricious or unfair treatment in nonunionized organizations. In some cases, the courts have ruled in favor of the discharged employees when the employee had not been guaranteed due process under company procedures. In light of these developments, many organizations have established appeal procedures for disciplinary actions taken by management. The most common type of appeal procedure is an open-door policy that allows employees to bring appeals to successively higher levels of management. An open-door policy gives an employee the right to appeal a disciplinary action taken against him or her to the manager's superior.

employment arbitration program
A dispute resolution program for employees in nonunionized organizations that requires a signed arbitration agreement as a condition of employment.

Another appeal procedure is for the employer to establish an **employment arbitration program.** Employment arbitration is a dispute resolution program for employees in nonunionized organizations. Under this program a new employee must sign an arbitration agreement as a condition of employment. Two issues are of significant importance in these programs. First, who will administer the program? If an employment arbitration program is administered internally, there is always a question of fairness. Most programs provide for arbitration of disputes and program administration under the rules of an organization such as the American Arbitration Association (AAA). A second consideration is whether the program will be imposed only on new hires or also on current employees. The legality of imposing an arbitration program on existing employees is questionable so most employers start the program with new hires only.[2]

CAUSES OF DISCIPLINARY ACTIONS

discipline
Action taken against an employee who has violated an organizational rule or whose performance has deteriorated to the point where corrective action is needed.

Organizational **discipline** is action taken against an employee who has violated an organizational rule or whose performance has deteriorated to the point where corrective action is needed. Sixty years ago, a manager who objected to an employee's performance or behavior could simply say, "You're fired!" and that was it. Justification often played little, if any, part in the decision. At that time, managers had the final authority to administer discipline at will.

In applying organizational discipline, the primary question should be, "Why are employees disciplined?" Too many managers, when faced with a discipline problem in their organization, immediately think of what and how much: What should the penalty be? How severely should the employee be punished? The ultimate form of discipline is discharge, or organizational capital punishment as it is sometimes called. Organizations should use discharge in the case of repeated offenses or when the act committed is such that discharge is believed to be the only reasonable alternative.

Generally disciplinary actions are taken against employees for two types of conduct:

1. Poor job performance or conduct that negatively affects an employee's job performance. Absenteeism, insubordination, and negligence are examples of behaviors that can lead to discipline.
2. Actions that indicate poor citizenship. Examples include fighting on the job or theft of company property.

Table 17.1 lists the reasons that often lead to disciplinary actions against or the discharge of employees.

ADMINISTERING DISCIPLINE

The first step in the disciplinary process is the establishment of performance requirements and work rules. Performance requirements are normally established through the performance appraisal process, discussed in Chapter 11. Work rules should be relevant to successful performance of the job. Because implementation of work rules partially depends on the employee's willingness to accept them, periodic review of their applicability is essential. In addition, it is often desirable to solicit employee input either directly or indirectly when

TABLE 17.1

Reasons for Discipline or Discharge of Employees

Source: Reprinted with permission. Table 17.1: pp. 671–707, "Reasons for Discipline or Discharge of Employees," from *How Arbitration Works,* Fourth Edition, by Elkouri & Elkouri. Copyright © 1985 by The Bureau of National Affairs, Inc., Washington, D.C. 20037. For BNA Books Publications call toll free 1-800-960-1220 or visit www. bnabooks.com.

Absenteeism	Theft
Tardiness	Disloyalty to employer (includes competing with employer, conflict of interest)
Loafing	
Absence from work	Moonlighting
Leaving place of work (includes early quitting)	Negligence
	Damage to or loss of machinery or materials
Sleeping on job	Unsatisfactory performance
Assault and fighting among employees	Refusal to accept job assignment
Horseplay	Refusal to work overtime
Insubordination	Participation in prohibited strike
Sexual harassment	Misconduct during strike
Racial slur	Slowdown
Threat to or assault of management representative	Possession or use of drugs
Abusive language to supervisor	Possession or use of intoxicants
Profane or abusive language	Distribution of drugs
Falsifying company records (including time records, production records)	Obscene or immoral conduct
	Attachment or garnishment of wages
Falsifying employment application	Gambling
Dishonesty	Abusing customers

establishing work rules. Work rules are more easily enforced when employees perceive them as being fair and relevant to the job.

The second step in the process is to communicate the performance requirements and work rules to employees. This is normally handled through orientation and performance appraisal. Work rules are communicated in a variety of ways. Generally, an individual who is hired receives a manual that describes the work rules and policies of the organization. The human resource department or the new employee's supervisor explains these work rules and policies to the new employee during orientation. Furthermore, new employees may be required to sign a document indicating they have received and read the manual. In unionized organizations, work rules and the corresponding disciplinary actions for infractions are frequently part of the labor contract. Bulletin boards, company newsletters, and memos are also commonly used to communicate work rules. In any case, management bears the responsibility for clearly communicating all work rules to employees.

The final step in the disciplinary process is the application of corrective action (discipline) when necessary. Corrective action is needed when an employee's work performance is below expectations or when violations of work rules have occurred.

Prediscipline Recommendations

An employee must be advised of an infraction if it is to be considered a warning. Ryan McVay/Getty Images

Before an employee is disciplined, management can take several steps to ensure that the action will be constructive and will not likely be rescinded by higher levels of management. Adequate records are of utmost importance in discipline cases. Written records often have a significant influence on decisions to overturn or uphold a disciplinary action. Past rule infractions and overall performance should be recorded.

Another key responsibility of management is the investigation. Things that appear obvious on the surface are sometimes completely discredited after investigation. Accusations against an employee must be supported by facts. Many decisions to discipline employees have been overturned due to an improper or less than thorough investigation. Undue haste in taking disciplinary action, taking the action when the manager is angry, and improper and incomplete investigations frequently cause disciplinary actions to be rescinded. An employee's work record should also be considered a part of the investigation. Good performance and long tenure with the organization are considerations that should influence the severity of a disciplinary action. Naturally, the investigation must take place before any discipline is administered. A manager should not discipline an employee and then look for evidence to support the decision.

A typical first step in the investigation of the facts is for management to discuss the situation with the employee. Providing the employee with an opportunity to present his or her side of the situation is essential if a disciplinary system is to be viewed positively by employees.

Employees represented by a union are allowed to have a union representative present during any disciplinary interview. This right is protected by the National Labor Relations Board (NLRB).[3] The most significant NLRB policy in this area was supported by a Supreme Court decision in 1975. In ***NLRB* v. *Weingarten,*** an employee was investigated for allegedly underpaying for food purchased from the employer. The employee requested and was denied union representation at an interview held after the employee was charged with the underpayments. The union filed unfair labor practice charges against the company with the NLRB. The NLRB ruled that the employee had a right to refuse to submit to an interview without union representation but also ruled that this right was available only if the employee requested union representation and applied only when disciplinary actions might reasonably be expected as a result of the interview. However, in *Baton Rouge Water Works,* the NLRB ruled that an employee does not have the right to union representation when management meets with the employee simply to inform him or her of discipline that has been previously determined.

Thus, as the law presently stands, management must be prepared to allow the presence of a union representative in any investigatory meeting. This means management must not only deal with the employee and the problem but also must do so in the presence of a union representative, who normally acts in the role of an employee advocate.

Besides being involved in the investigation, the union should be kept informed on matters of discipline. Some organizations give unions advance notice of their intention to discipline an employee. Also, copies of warnings are sometimes sent to the union.

NLRB v. Weingarten
Supreme Court decision in 1975 holding that an employee has the right to refuse to submit to a disciplinary interview without union representation.

Guidelines for Administering Discipline

Key points in administering discipline are immediacy, advance warning, and consistency. *Immediacy* refers to the length of time between the misconduct and the discipline. For discipline to be most effective, it must be taken as soon as possible but without involving an emotional, irrational decision. Notation of rules infractions in an employee's record does not constitute *advance warning* and is not sufficient to support disciplinary action. An employee must be advised of the infraction for it to be considered a warning. Noting that the employee was warned about the infraction and having the employee sign a form acknowledging the warning are both good practices. Failure to warn an employee of the consequences of repeated violations of a rule is one reason often cited for overturning a disciplinary action.

Another element in administering discipline is *consistency.* Inconsistency lowers morale, diminishes respect for management, and leads to grievances. Striving for consistency does not mean that past infractions, length of service, work record, and other mitigating factors should not be considered when applying discipline. However, an employee should believe that any other employee under essentially the same circumstances would receive the same penalty. Similarly, management should take steps to ensure that personalities are not a factor when applying discipline. The employee should understand that the disciplinary action is a consequence of what was done and not caused by his or her personality. A manager should avoid arguing with the employee and should administer the discipline in a straightforward, calm manner. Administering discipline without anger or apology and then resuming a pleasant relationship aids in reducing the negative effects of discipline. A manager should also administer discipline in private. The only exception would be in the case of gross insubordination or flagrant and serious rule violations, where a public reprimand would help the manager regain control of the situation. Even in this type of situation, the objective should be to gain control and not to embarrass the employee.

Lower-level managers should be very reluctant to impose disciplinary suspensions and discharges. Usually discipline of this degree is reserved for higher levels of management. Even a lower-level manager who does not have the power to administer disciplinary suspensions or discharges, however, is nearly always the one who must recommend the action to higher management. Since discipline of this nature is more likely to be reviewed, more costly to the organization, and more likely to be reflected in overall morale and productivity, it is very important for lower-level managers to know when it should be recommended.

Immediacy, advance warning, and consistency are essential for administering suspensions and discharges.

corrective (progressive) discipline
The normal sequence of actions taken by management in disciplining an employee: oral warning, written warning, suspension, and finally discharge.

Management is expected to use **corrective,** or **progressive, discipline** whenever possible. Progressive, or corrective, discipline means the normal sequence of actions taken by management in disciplining an employee would be oral warning, written warning, suspension, and discharge. Some offenses, however, may justify discharge, such as stealing, striking a coworker or member of management, and gross insubordination. Management must be able to show, generally through the preponderance of evidence, that the offense was committed. Attention to the points covered regarding prediscipline recommendations is especially important in supporting a decision to discharge an employee.

As in any lesser discipline, but even more essential in suspension and discharge, the employee has the right to a careful and impartial investigation. This involves allowing the employee to state his or her side of the case, gather evidence to support that side, and, usually, question the accuser. In the case of very serious offenses, the employee may be suspended pending a full investigation.

The suggestions outlined in the preceding paragraphs are designed to assist managers in applying discipline in a positive manner and with minimal application of the harsher forms of discipline. In the disciplinary procedure, observing these suggestions should reduce the chance of a grievance or, if a grievance is filed, the chance of having the disciplinary action overruled. Table 17.2 provides a checklist of rules to observe when applying discipline.

Legal Restrictions

Alexander v. Gardner-Denver
Supreme Court decision in 1974 that ruled that using the final and binding grievance procedure in an organization does not preclude an aggrieved employee from seeking redress through court action.

The Civil Rights Act of 1964 and the Age Discrimination in Employment Act of 1967 as amended in 1978 changed an employer's authority in making decisions and taking actions involving employment conditions. Specifically, Title VII of the Civil Rights Act prohibits the use of race, color, religion, sex, or national origin as the basis of any employment condition. The Age Discrimination in Employment Act makes similar prohibitions involving persons over 40 years of age. Discipline is, of course, a condition of employment and is subject to these laws. Under these laws, employees have the right to appeal to the Equal Employment Opportunity Commission (EEOC) and to the courts any disciplinary action they consider discriminatory.

The landmark case guaranteeing employees this right was decided in 1974 by the Supreme Court in ***Alexander* v. *Gardner-Denver.*** In that case, the Supreme Court ruled that using

TABLE 17.2
Considerations in Disciplining or Discharging Employees

1. Avoid hasty decisions.
2. Document all actions and enter the evidence in the personnel file.
3. Thoroughly and fully investigate the circumstances and facts of the alleged offense.
    a. Notify the employee of the nature of the offense.
    b. Obtain the employee's version of the circumstances, reasons for the actions, and the names of any witnesses.
    c. If suspension is required until the investigation is completed, inform the employee:
        (1) To return 24 to 72 hours later to receive the decision.
        (2) That there will be reinstatement with pay if the decision is in the employee's favor.
        (3) Of the discipline to be imposed if it is not in the employee's favor.
    d. Interview all witnesses to the alleged misconduct. Obtain signed statements if necessary.
    e. Check all alternative possible causes (e.g., broken machinery).
    f. Decide whether the employee committed the alleged offense.
4. Determine the appropriate discipline. Consider:
    a. Personnel record: length of service, past performance, past disciplinary record. Has corrective discipline ever been applied?
    b. Nature of the offense.
    c. Past disciplinary action for other employees in similar situations.
    d. Existing rules and disciplinary policies.
    e. Provisions in the labor contract if one exists.
5. Advise the employee of the nature of the offense, the results of the investigation, the discipline to be imposed, and the rationale behind the discipline.

TABLE 17.3
Discipline Rules in Typical Labor Contracts

Offense	Discipline
Minor:	
Absence without notification as per existing absentee and lateness policy	First offense—written warning
	Second offense—one-day suspension
Horseplay	Third offense—two-day suspension
Major:	
Possession of, drinking, smoking, or being under the influence of, intoxicants or narcotics on company property	First offense—written warning that may result in suspension of up to three days without pay
Sleeping on the job	Second offense treated as an intolerable offense
Gambling on company property	
Intolerable:	
Stealing company or personal property	First offense—subject to discharge
Fighting on company property	

the grievance procedure in an organization did not preclude the aggrieved employee from seeking redress through court action. Basically, the Court decided that the Civil Rights Act guaranteed individuals the right to pursue remedies of illegal discrimination regardless of prior rejections in another forum.

Table 17.3 gives a sample of rules for discipline from a typical union contract.

GRIEVANCE PROCEDURES

grievance procedures
Outline of the steps to be taken by employees in appealing any management action they believe violates the union contract for corporate procedures agreed to in negotiations.

Grievance procedures outline the steps to be taken by employees in appealing any management action they believe violates the union contract and/or corporate procedures. Grievance procedures are used not only to appeal disciplinary actions but also to resolve matters concerning contract interpretation.

Generally, in unionized organizations the grievance process is initiated by an employee who has a complaint regarding some action perceived to be inconsistent with the terms of the union contract. While it is highly unlikely that the organization would initiate a grievance, it can do so. Initially, the grievant (aggrieved employee) contacts the union representative (usually called a *union steward*), and they discuss the events causing the grievance. The grievant and the union steward then meet with the grievant's supervisor. If a mutually agreeable settlement cannot be reached at this meeting, the grievance is then put into writing. Generally, in the next step, the union steward discusses the grievance with the department manager or another appropriate management representative. Management then presents a reaction, usually in writing. If the grievance is not resolved at this point, the next step usually involves the human resource or labor relations manager and higher officials of the union, such as the business agent or international representative. After fully investigating and discussing the grievance, the human resource department usually issues the final company decision. In the event the grievance is still unresolved, the party initiating the grievance can request arbitration. Grievance arbitration (discussed later in this chapter) is a process whereby the employer and union agree to settle a dispute through an independent third party. Because of the expense to both the union and management, every attempt should be made to resolve grievances in the stages before arbitration. Figure 17.1 illustrates the steps normally involved in a grievance procedure.

Just Cause

Grievance procedures for nonunionized organizations are similar to those in unionized organizations. Both types of procedures have appeals to higher levels of management leading ultimately to employment or grievance arbitration. Generally, both unionized and nonunionized employees recognize the right of management to discipline or discharge employees for just cause. In fact, in most discipline or discharge cases, the basic issue is whether or not management acted with

FIGURE 17.1
General Process Followed in a Union Grievance Procedure

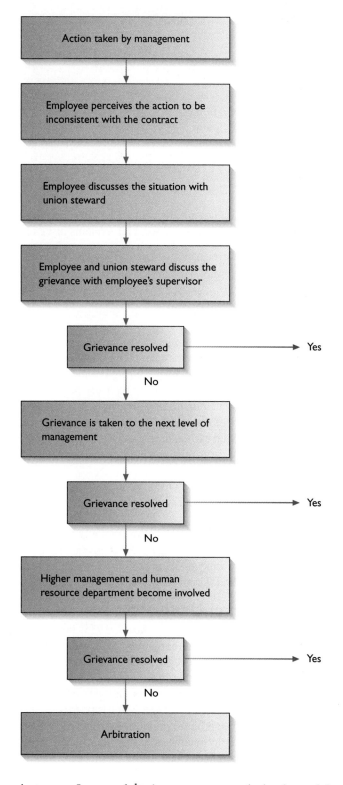

just cause
Requires that management initially bear the burden of proof of wrongdoing in discipline cases and that the severity of the punishment must coincide with the seriousness of the offense.

just cause. In general, **just cause** concerns the burden and degree of proof of wrongdoing and the severity of punishment.[4]

It is generally agreed that the burden of proof in matters of discipline and discharge lies with the company. However, once the company has established the case, the burden of proof shifts to the union to disprove or discredit the company's contention.

Once an organization proves that an employee was guilty of wrongdoing, the second area of concern in determining just cause relates to the severity of the punishment. Just cause results when the severity of the punishment coincides with the seriousness of the wrongdoing. The

JUST CAUSE

Potential liability through a summary dismissal is often a problem for employers because such dismissals are often undertaken in the heat of the moment. Liability can often be limited by proper investigations and thorough consideration of the case's strengths and weaknesses. The company should take its time and consider all options rather than responding in the heat of the moment.

Courts have stated that companies should not just use the misconduct at hand when dismissing an employee but should review the entirety of the employment relationship. The goal for the company is not to show misconduct by an employee, but also to show that said misconduct irreparably harmed the employment relationship.

Source: Adapted from Stuart Rudner, "Just Cause Can Be Justified," *Canadian HR Reporter,* June 15, 2009, p. 14.

following general guidelines are frequently used for determining just cause as it relates to the severity of punishment. HRM in Action 17.1 explains just cause in more detail.

1. Consider the past performance of the employee.
2. Consider previous disciplinary actions taken against other employees in similar situations.
3. Consider unusual circumstances surrounding the alleged offense.

Due Process

due process
Right of an employee to be dealt with fairly and justly during the investigation of an alleged offense and the administration of any subsequent disciplinary action.

Two principles that are central to just cause are due process and progressive discipline. Progressive discipline was described earlier in this chapter. **Due process** refers to the employee's right to be dealt with fairly and justly during the investigation of an alleged offense and the administration of discipline. Due process typically guarantees that the employee will receive notification and an explanation of the allegations, that an impartial investigation will be held prior to the imposition of discipline, and that the employee can present his or her version of the incident. As discussed earlier, unionized employees have the right to union representation in the disciplinary review if they request it and if disciplinary actions might reasonably be expected to result.

A breach of due process during the grievance procedure can result in either a modification or a complete reversal of a disciplinary action. Procedural requirements are often spelled out in the grievance procedures of the contract. Failure to follow such provisions may constitute a breach of due process. In general, to ensure that an employee is afforded due process, all contract terms should be followed, adequate warning should be given prior to the discipline, explicit statements should be made to the employee about possible disciplinary action if the employee's actions do not change, and a full and fair investigation should be conducted immediately after the offense.

Duty of Fair Representation

duty of fair representation
Under the National Labor Relations Act of 1935, the statutory duty of a union to fairly represent all employees in the bargaining unit, whether or not they are union members.

Vaca v. *Sipes*
Supreme Court decision that held that a union is not obligated to take all grievances to arbitration but has the authority to decide whether or not the grievance has merit. If such a decision is made fairly and nonarbitrarily, the union has not breached its duty of fair representation.

Under the National Labor Relations Act of 1935, the union has a statutory duty to fairly represent all employees in the bargaining unit, whether or not they are union members. This duty has been termed **duty of fair representation.** The rationale underlying the duty of fair representation is that the union is the exclusive representative of all employees in the bargaining unit. The extent of the union's duty to fairly represent its members and other employees was defined in a landmark case, *Vaca* v. *Sipes.* In this case, an employee who had a history of high blood pressure returned to work after six months of sick leave. Although his personal physician and another doctor had certified his fitness to resume work, the company doctor concluded that his blood pressure was too high to permit his reinstatement, and as a result he was permanently discharged. The employee filed a grievance, and the union took the grievance through the steps leading up to arbitration. The employee was then sent to a new doctor at the union's expense. When this examination did not support the employee's contention that he could safely return to work, the union decided not to take the grievance to arbitration, even though the employee demanded it. The employee sued the officers and representatives of the union for breach of their duty of fair representation. The case ultimately went to the Supreme Court, which held that (1) an individual does not have the absolute right to have a grievance taken to arbitration; (2) a union must make decisions as to the merits of particular grievances in good faith and nonarbitrarily; and (3) if a union decides in good faith and in a nonarbitrary manner that a grievance is not meritorious, a breach of fair representation does not exist, even if it is proved that the grievance was, in fact, meritorious.

An exception to this court ruling is included in a provision of the Taft–Hartley Act, which states that an individual employee may present a grievance to the employer without the aid of the union. However, this is contingent on the fact that any resulting adjustments must be consistent with the terms of the contract and must be conveyed to the union. This has been interpreted as meaning that the employer is under no obligation to consider such grievances. However, if the union presents a grievance to the employer, the employer is obligated to consider it and to resolve it through arbitration (if this is provided for in the contract) when the grievance has not been resolved in the earlier stages of the grievance process.

In addition, individuals cannot take the case into their own hands if they think it is not being effectively handled. Courts have held that the employee must thoroughly exhaust the grievance procedure before taking individual action, and such action is then contingent on proof of a breach of the duty of fair representation.

Bowen v. United States Postal Service (1983)
Supreme Court decision that established that an employee may be entitled to recover damages from both the union and the employer is cases where the employer has violated the labor agreement and the union has breached its duty of fair representation.

A Supreme Court decision, **Bowen v. United States Postal Service,** established that an employee may be entitled to recover damages from both the union and the employer in cases where the employer has violated the labor agreement and the union has breached its duty of fair representation. HRM in Action 17.2 details a case in which the court ruled that the union did not violate its duty of fair representation.

Time Delays

Perhaps the greatest criticism of the grievance procedure is that a great deal of time may be necessary to resolve a grievance that goes through the entire process. Often the internal stages of appeal may take several months to complete. If the case goes to arbitration, the parties usually request a list of potential arbitrators from an arbitration service. The parties must contact the arbitrator and must agree on an acceptable date for the hearing. Furthermore, after the hearing has taken place, the parties may desire to submit briefs, which can take several additional weeks. When the hearing is closed upon receipt of all briefs, the arbitrator normally renders a decision within 30 to 60 days. Thus, many months and sometimes a year or more may elapse before a final decision is reached. An argument could be made that this time delay in itself denies the grievant due process.

GRIEVANCE ARBITRATION

grievance arbitration
Arbitration that attempts to settle unresolved disputes arising during the term of the collective bargaining agreement that involve questions of its interpretation or application.

Grievance arbitration is the process whereby the involved parties voluntarily agree to settle a dispute through the use of an independent third party. In the United States, arbitration evolves from the voluntary agreement by two parties to submit their unresolved disputes to a privately selected neutral third party (an arbitrator). Both parties agree in advance to abide by the arbitrator's decision. The arbitrator, who functions in a quasi-judicial role, must work within the framework that the parties have negotiated in their collective bargaining agreement. Arbitrators have no legal power to subpoena witnesses or records and are not required to conform to legal rules of hearing procedures, other than that of

DISCHARGE AT AMERICAN MOTORS
www.daimlerchrysler.com

The grievant had been employed as a shipping and receiving clerk at American Motors (now a subsidiary of Daimler Chrysler) for 10 years. On November 30, the grievant asked a purchasing clerk to look up the purchasing information (part number, location, and price) on several parts, including a Jeep door. The grievant testified that his intention was to buy the door for a sheriff friend who was going to fix a DUI ticket for him. The grievant obtained the door and stored it on a shelf near his workplace until he completed his shift. At quitting time, the grievant left his workplace, carrying the door, and proceeded to the parking lot.

The grievant was seen putting the door in his van by a member of management. Later that evening, another employee contacted the grievant and informed him that a member of management had seen him carrying the door to

his van. On December 1, the grievant brought in a check to cover the price of the door. The company refused to accept the check and fired the employee for misappropriation of company property.

Union witnesses testified to many instances where employees removed parts from the company without the prior knowledge or approval of management and paid for them at a later date. Much evidence was also presented that procedures for removing and paying for parts were haphazardly observed and not in writing.

The arbitrator overruled the discharge because of management's failure to establish, communicate, and properly administer a procedure for removing parts.

Source: Labor arbitration award by Lloyd L. Byars. Case involved the American Motors Corporation and the United Automobile Workers.

Web site: Federal Mediation & Conciliation Service
www.fmcs.gov

Web site: American Arbitration Association
www.adr.org

Enterprise Wheel
Supreme Court ruling in 1960 holding that as long as an arbitrator's decision involves the interpretation of a contract, the courts should not overrule the arbitrator merely because their interpretation of the contract was different from that of the arbitrator.

giving all parties the opportunity to present evidence. HRM in Action 17.3 describes a discipline situation that an arbitrator overturned.

Grievance arbitration attempts to settle unresolved disputes arising during the term of the collective bargaining agreement that involve questions of its interpretation or application. Provision for grievance arbitration generally is not mandated by law. However, most labor contracts provide an arbitration clause as the final step in the grievance process. This is considered to be the *quid pro quo* (even exchange) for the union's agreement to a no-strike clause.

An arbitrator may serve on either a temporary (ad hoc) or permanent basis. In ad hoc arbitration, the parties select an arbitrator to hear a single case. Permanent arbitrators settle all grievance disputes arising between the parties for a period of time.

Arbitrators charge for their services. Normally arbitrators' charges are paid on a 50–50 basis by the company and the union. Both the Federal Mediation and Conciliation Service (FMCS) and the American Arbitration Association (AAA) provide lists of qualified arbitrators to the parties upon request. FMCS's services are available to both the private and public sector. AAA is a private, nonprofit organization that also provides lists of arbitrators to both the private and public sectors.

Generally, court reviews of arbitration awards have been extremely narrow in scope. The attitude of the U.S. Supreme Court was expressed in the ***Enterprise Wheel*** case: "It is the arbitrator's interpretation which was bargained for, and so far as the arbitrator's decision concerns interpretation of the contract, the courts have no business overruling him because their interpretation of the contract is different from his."[5] In spite of this opinion, courts have overturned some arbitration awards in discharge cases. However, the tendency, for the most part, has been to defer to the arbitrator's decision.

Summary of Learning Objectives

1. **Explain employment at will.**

   Employment at will allows either the employer or employee to terminate his or her employment relationship at any time for virtually any reason or for no reason at all.

2. **Explain employment arbitration programs.**

   Employment arbitration is a dispute resolution program for employees in nonunionized organizations.

3. **Explain the causes of disciplinary actions.**

   Two types of conduct that lead to discipline are poor job performance and actions that indicate poor citizenship.

4. **Describe progressive discipline.**

   Progressive discipline means that the normal sequence of actions taken by management in disciplining an employee would be oral warning, written warning, suspension, and discharge.

5. **Define grievance procedures.**

Grievance procedures are a systematic means of resolving disagreements over the collective bargaining agreement and providing assurance that the terms and conditions agreed to in negotiations are properly implemented.

6. **Define just cause.**

Just cause concerns the burden and degree of proof of wrongdoing and the severity of punishment.

7. **Explain due process.**

Due process refers to the employee's right to be dealt with fairly and justly during the investigation of an alleged offense and the administration of discipline.

8. **Describe the duty of fair representation.**

The duty of fair representation refers to the union's statutory duty to fairly represent all employees in the bargaining unit, whether or not they are union members.

9. **Define grievance arbitration.**

Under grievance arbitration, the involved parties voluntarily agree to settle a dispute through the use of an independent third party. Grievance arbitration attempts to settle unresolved disputes arising during the term of the collective bargaining agreement that involve questions of its interpretation or application.

Key Terms

Alexander v. *Gardner-Denver, 347*
Bowen v. *United States Postal Service* (1983), *351*
corrective (progressive) discipline, *347*
discipline, *344*
due process, *350*
duty of fair representation, *350*
employment arbitration program, *344*
employment at will, *343*
Enterprise Wheel, 352
grievance arbitration, *351*
grievance procedures, *348*
just cause, *349*
NLRB v. *Weingarten, 346*
Vaca v. *Sipes, 350*

Review Questions

1. What types of conduct normally result in disciplining an employee?
2. What was the significance of the decision in the *NLRB* v. *Weingarten* case?
3. List the key points in administering discipline.
4. What was the significance of the decision in the *Alexander* v. *Gardner-Denver* case?
5. What are grievance procedures?
6. Define *just cause, due process,* and *duty of fair representation.*
7. What is arbitration?

Discussion Questions

1. "Unions make it almost impossible to discipline employees." Do you agree or disagree? Discuss.
2. Two employees violate the same work rule. One is above average in performance and has been with your company for eight years. The other employee is an average performer who has been with your company for a little over a year. Should these employees receive the same discipline? Why or why not?
3. Under the doctrine of fair representation, unions are required to represent both members and nonmembers in the bargaining unit. Do you think unions should be required to represent nonmembers? Explain.
4. If you were starting your own company, what type of grievance procedure would you establish for your employees?

Incident 17.1

Tardy Tom

On September 30, 2009, a large, national automobile-leasing firm in Columbus, Ohio, hired Tom Holland as a mechanic. Tom, the only mechanic employed by the firm in Columbus, was to do routine preventive maintenance on the cars. When he first began his job, he was scheduled to punch in on the time clock at 7 A.M. On October 30, 2009, Tom's supervisor, Russ Brown, called him to his office and said, "Tom, I've noticed during October that you've been late for work seven times. What can I do to help you get here on time?"

Tom replied, "It would be awfully nice if I could start work at 8 A.M. instead of 7 A.M." Russ then stated, "Tom, I'm very pleased with your overall work performance, so it's OK with me if your workday begins at 8 A.M."

During the month of November 2009, Tom was late eight times. Another conversation occurred similar to the one at the end of October. As a result of it, Tom's starting time was changed to 9 A.M.

On January 11, 2010, Russ Brown posted the following notice on the bulletin board:

> Any employee late for work more than two times in any one particular pay period is subject to termination.

On January 20, 2010, Russ called Tom into his office and gave him a letter that read, "During this pay period, you have been late for work more than two times. If this behavior continues, you are subject to termination." Tom signed the letter to acknowledge that he had received it.

During February 2010, Tom was late eight times and between March 1 and March 11, five times. On March 11, 2010, Russ notified Tom that he had been fired for his tardiness.

On March 12, 2010, Tom came in with his union representative and demanded that he get his job back. Tom alleged that there was another employee in the company who had been late as many times as he had, or more. Tom further charged that Russ was punching the time clock for this employee because Russ was having an affair with her. The union representative stated that three other people in the company had agreed to testify, under oath, to these facts. The union representative then said, "Russ, rules are for everyone. You can't let one person break a rule and penalize someone else for breaking the same rule. Therefore, Tom should have his job back."

Questions

1. What is your position regarding this case?
2. What would you do if you were an arbitrator in this dispute?

Incident 17.2

Keys to the Drug Cabinet

John Brown, a 22-year-old African American, had been employed for only two-and-a-half weeks as a licensed practical nurse in a local hospital's alcohol and drug treatment center. John worked the 11 P.M. to 7 A.M. shift. His responsibilities included having charge of the keys to the drug cabinet.

One morning at 1 A.M., he became ill. He requested and received permission from the night supervisor, Margaret Handley, to go home. A short time later, the supervisor realized that John had failed to leave the keys when he signed out. She immediately tried to reach him by telephoning his home.

More than a dozen attempts to call John proved futile; each time Margaret got a busy signal. Finally, at 3 A.M., a man answered but refused to call John to the phone, saying John was too ill to talk. She became frantic and decided to call the police to retrieve the keys.

The police arrived at John's home at 6:30 A.M. They found him preparing to leave to return the keys to the hospital. The police took the keys and returned them.

Later that day, John reported to work on his assigned shift, apologized for not returning the keys, and questioned the necessity of calling the police.

Two days later, the unit director, Marcus Webb, informed John that he had been terminated. The reason cited for the discharge was that he had failed to leave the drug cabinet keys before leaving the hospital and that the keys had been in his possession from 1 A.M. to 7 A.M. the following day. John learned that Margaret Handley had been verbally reprimanded for her handling of the case.

John filed an appeal regarding his dismissal with the human resource director of the hospital. However, the unit director's recommendation was upheld.

Following this decision, John immediately filed charges with the EEOC that he had been discriminated against because of his race. Both the night supervisor and the unit director were white. He requested full reinstatement with back pay. He also requested that his personnel file be purged of any damaging records that alluded to the incident.

Questions

1. What would your decision be if you were asked to decide this case?
2. Should a supervisor and a lower-level employee be disciplined equally? Explain.

EXERCISE 17.1

MOCK ARBITRATION

Following is a situation in which you are to conduct a mock arbitration. The class will be divided into teams, five to six students per team. Each team will then be assigned to represent either the union or the company. Your team must decide on the witnesses you want at the hearing. Your opposing team must be given the names and job titles of your witnesses. During class time, two teams will conduct the mock arbitration.

SITUATION

Background

General Telephone Company of the Southeast (Georgia), hereinafter referred to as the company, provides local telephone service within certain areas of the state of Georgia. Its employees, as defined by Article I and Appendix A of the Agreement, are represented by the Communication Workers of America, hereinafter referred to as the union. The parties are operating under an agreement that became effective June 27, 2005.

The grievant, Cassandra Horne, was hired by the company as a service representative on June 4, 1999. On August 30, 2006, she was promoted to installer-repairer and was responsible for installing and repairing residential and single-line business for customers. The grievant's record is free of any disciplinary entries, and she is considered by her supervisor, Fred Carter, to be a satisfactory employee.

On May 19, 2007, the grievant suffered an on-the-job injury to her knee while attempting to disconnect a trailer from a company van. At some time after the injury, the grievant went on disability for approximately eight weeks. She then returned to work with a statement from the company physician, allowing her to perform her normal work. After approximately three weeks, the grievant was still experiencing pain in her knee and was diagnosed by a different physician as having a tear in the cartilage below her kneecap. She went back on disability and had surgery performed on October 19, 2007, to repair cartilage and ligament damage to her knee.

During the grievant's absence, her disability benefits expired, and she agreed to take a six-month leave of absence beginning November 10, 2007. When the grievant's leave expired on May 11, 2008, she was terminated from her employment with the company.

The company argued that the company physician had stated the grievant could not perform installer–repairer work and that no other jobs were open that the grievant could perform. The union argued that the grievant had been cleared by her personal physician and that she felt she could do the work of installer–repairer. A grievance was filed at Step 1 on May 12, 2008, and was denied by the division personnel manager, Jerry L. Leynes. The grievance was submitted to arbitration and is now properly before the arbitrator for decision and award.

The company states that the issue before the arbitrator is as follows: Did the company violate the contract by separating the grievant from her position as an installer–repairer, and if so, what should be the remedy? The union states that the issue before the arbitrator is as follows: Is the discharge of the grievant for just or proper cause; and if not, what should the remedy be?

Pertinent Provisions of the Agreement

Article 1, Recognition:

The company recognizes the union as the whole and exclusive collective bargaining agency with respect to rates of pay, hours of employment, and other conditions of employment for all employees within the exchanges coming under the operating jurisdiction of the above-named company. All supervisory and professional employees and those performing confidential labor relations duties are excluded from the bargaining unit.

Article 4, Work Jurisdiction:

1. The company recognizes the right of its employees to perform its work and will make every reasonable effort to plan its work to accomplish this end.
2. The company agrees that in its employment of contract labor to assist in the carrying out of its programs of construction, installation, removal, maintenance, and/or repair of telephone plant, it will not lay off or reduce to part-time status, nor continue on layoff or part-time status, any regular employee performing the same work as that which is being performed by contract labor.

Article 11, Absences from Duty:

1. Leave of absence, without pay, not to exceed six (6) months will be granted by the company for good and compelling reason upon receipt of written request for such leave. Each such request will be approved or disapproved dependent on the merit of the request. Such leaves may be extended for an additional period of not to exceed three (3) months.
   1.1 Working for another employer during leave shall constitute grounds for termination of employment.
   1.2 Applying for unemployment compensation during leave may constitute grounds for termination of employment, except this shall not be applicable where the employee has requested reinstatement in accordance with the provisions of this article and no work is available.
   1.3 A leave of absence shall not carry a guarantee of reemployment, but the employee concerned, desiring to return from leave, shall be given opportunity for reemployment before any new employees are hired, provided the returning employee is qualified to perform the work.

Article 12, Paid Absences:

4. In cases of physical disability resulting from compensable accidental injury while on the job, the company will pay the difference, if any, between the amount paid to the employee under workers' compensation and the employee's basic rate in accordance with the schedule set forth below. No waiting period will be required.
   4.1 Up to five (5) years' accredited service, full pay not to exceed thirteen (13) weeks.

Article 23, Discharges, Suspensions, and Demotions:

1. Requirements and limitations
   1.1 Any discharge, suspension, or demotion shall be only for proper cause and by proper action.
   1.2 Any employee who is discharged, suspended, or demoted shall, at the time of discharge, suspension, or demotion, be given a written statement setting forth the complete reasons for such action.

Notes and Additional Readings

1. Tara J. Radin, and Patricia H. Werhane, "Employment-at-Will, Employee Rights, and Future Directions for Employment," *Business Ethics Quarterly* 13, 2003, pp. 113–30.
2. Susan C., Zuckerman, "Supreme Court Decides Employment Case in Favor of Arbitration," *Dispute Resolution Journal,* May–July 2001, p. 5.
3. See Chapter 18 for a description of the NLRB.
4. See John J. McCall, "A Defense of Just Cause Dismissal Rules," *Business Ethics Quarterly* 13, 2000, pp. 151–75.
5. *United Steelworkers of America* v. *Enterprise Wheel and Car Corporation,* 46 LARM 2423 S.Ct. (1960).

Chapter **Eighteen**

The Legal Environment and Structure of Labor Unions

Chapter Learning Objectives

After studying this chapter, you should be able to:

1. Describe the conspiracy doctrine.
2. Define injunction.
3. Explain a yellow-dog contract.
4. Define the Railway Labor Act (1926).
5. Describe the Norris–La Guardia Act (1932).
6. Define the Wagner Act (1935).
7. Explain the Taft–Hartley Act (1947).
8. Describe right-to-work laws.
9. Explain the Landrum–Griffin Act (1959).
10. Describe the AFL–CIO.
11. Define amalgamation and absorption.

Chapter Outline

Prior to the Industrial Revolution in the 19th century, an individual was usually born into a level in society with a predestined standard of living. Custom and tradition kept a person's position relatively stable. After the Industrial Revolution, people were able to contract for employment by offering their skills and services for a wage. However, once people had been hired, they and their work output became the property of the employer.

Before long employees resorted to joint action to gain some influence over the terms and conditions of their employment. Initially, the public and the courts frowned on these attempts. For the most part, the relationships between employees and management were unilateral: Employees

STRIKE AT COLORADO FUEL AND IRON COMPANY (CFI)

During the early 20th century, Colorado Fuel and Iron Company (CFI) owned about 300,000 acres of mineral-rich land in southern Colorado. This geographical insulation enabled CFI to impose rather primitive conditions over its 30,000 workers. Most of the workers lived in company-owned camps located 10 to 30 miles from any big towns. Within the camps, 151 persons contracted typhoid in 1912 and 1913 because of unsanitary conditions. Wages were paid in currency valid only in company stores.

These conditions sparked union-organizing activity. The United Mine Workers (UMW) demanded an eight-hour day, enforcement of safety regulations, removal of armed guards, and abolition of company currency. The company refused to negotiate on these issues.

Thus, in September 1913, up to 10,000 workers at Colorado Fuel and Iron Company went on strike. After the strike began, tension rose quickly. CFI hired a large number of guards from outside the state, armed them, and paid their salaries.

Violence erupted almost immediately. First, a company detective and a union organizer were killed. A few days later, CFI troops broke up a strikers' mass meeting and killed three workers. Vengeful miners then killed four company men. Governor Ammons called out the National Guard to protect all property and those people who were still working.

On April 20, 1914, a major battle erupted between the strikers and the National Guardsmen. A fire that resulted led to the deaths of two women and 11 children. Several battles occurred over the next several days, and finally, on April 28, 1914, several regiments of federal troops were called in to end the war.

Source: Graham Adams, Jr., *Age of Industrial Violence, 1910–1915* (New York: Columbia University Press, 1966), pp. 146–75.

asking for higher wages approached their employers with a "take it or we'll strike" attitude, and employers usually refused or ignored their requests. Generally, the result was a test of economic strength to determine whose wage decisions would prevail. In most instances, employers prevailed. HRM in Action 18.1 illustrates some of the consequences of early strikes.

As time passed, society became more aware of the plight of employees. Legislation was enacted that was much more favorable toward employees and unions. This chapter explores how the legal environment surrounding union–management relations has evolved. It also describes the organizational structure of unions and current issues facing unions.

THE LEGAL ENVIRONMENT OF LABOR–MANAGEMENT RELATIONS

The first unions in America appeared between 1790 and 1820. These were local organizations of skilled craftspeople, such as shoemakers in Philadelphia, printers in New York, tailors in Baltimore, and other similar groups.

The demands of these unions were similar to those of unions today. Unions wanted job security, higher wages, and shorter working hours. When management did not agree to these demands, these early unions resorted to strikes, or "turn-outs," as they were then called. A *strike* is the collective refusal of employees to work.

Philadelphia Cordwainers (shoemakers) case of 1806
Case in which the jury ruled that groups of employees banded together to raise their wages constituted a conspiracy in restraint of trade.

To offset the pressure of these unions, employers formed associations and took legal action against the unions. In the *Philadelphia Cordwainers (shoemakers) case of 1806,* the jury ruled that groups of employees banded together to raise their wages constituted a conspiracy in restraint of trade. This decision established the **conspiracy doctrine,** which stated that a union could be punished if either the means used or the ends sought were deemed illegal by the courts.

conspiracy doctrine
Notion that courts can punish a union if they deem that the means used or the ends sought by the union are illegal.

Over the next 35 years, unions ran up against the conspiracy doctrine on numerous occasions. Some courts continued to rule that labor unions were illegal per se. Others ruled that the means unions used (e.g., strikes) to achieve their demands were illegal or that the ends sought (e.g., closed shops) were illegal. A *closed shop* prohibits an employer from hiring anyone other than a union member.

Commonwealth v. Hunt
Landmark court decision in 1842 that declared unions were not illegal per se.

In 1842, in the landmark Massachusetts case **Commonwealth v. Hunt,** the Supreme Court of Massachusetts rejected the doctrine that the actions of labor unions were illegal per se. The court noted that the power of a labor union could be used not only for illegal purposes but also for legal purposes. This decision, of course, left open the door for legal actions questioning the means used and ends sought by labor unions. Thus, even after 1842, the legal environment for unions remained vague and uncertain. Some courts held that a closed shop was a lawful objective; thus, strikes to obtain a closed shop were legal. Other courts reached an opposite conclusion. During this time, the legality of union activities depended to a large extent on the court jurisdiction in which the case occurred.

By the 1880s, most courts had moved away from the use of the conspiracy doctrine, and the injunction became a favorite technique used by the courts to control union activities. An **injunction** is a court order to stop an action that could result in irreparable damage to property when the situation is such that no other adequate remedy is available to protect the interests of the injunction-seeking party. During this time, the normal procedure used in seeking an injunction in a labor dispute was as follows:

1. The complainant (usually the employer) went to court, filed a complaint stating the nature of the property threat, and requested relief.
2. The judge normally issued a temporary restraining order halting the threatened action until a case could be heard.
3. Shortly thereafter, a preliminary hearing was held so the judge could decide whether to issue a temporary injunction.
4. Finally, after a trial, a decision was made as to whether a permanent injunction should be issued.

Injunctions had three effects. First, failure of the union to abide by the temporary restraining order or the temporary injunction meant risking contempt-of-court charges. Second, compliance meant a waiting period of many months before the matter came to trial. Often this waiting period was enough to destroy the effectiveness of the union. Third, the courts placed a broad interpretation on the term *property*. Historically, courts had issued injunctions to prevent damage to property where an award of money damages would be an inadequate remedy. However, during this time, the courts held that an employer's property included the right to operate the business and make a profit. Thus, the expectation of making a profit became a property right. Any strike, even a peaceful one, could be alleged to be injurious to the expectation of making a profit and could be stopped by an injunction.

Injunctions were generally granted by the courts upon request and were frequently used to control union activities until the 1930s. The attitude of the courts over this time seems to have been that management had the right to do business without the interference of unions.

Another device used by employers to control unions during this time was the **yellow-dog contract.** The name was coined by the labor unions to describe an agreement between an employee and an employer that, as a condition of employment, the employee would not join a labor union. These contracts could be oral, written, or both.

In 1917, the Supreme Court upheld the legality of yellow-dog contracts in ***Hitchman Coal & Coke Co. v. Mitchell.*** This case involved the management of Hitchman Coal & Coke Company, whose employees had been unionized in 1903, and the United Mine Workers (UMW) in West Virginia. In 1906, the union called a strike against the company. However, management defeated the union and resumed operations as a nonunionized company. To ensure that it remained nonunionized, management required all of its employees, as a condition of employment, to sign an agreement saying that they would not join a union as long as they were employed by Hitchman.

Later the United Mine Workers sent an organizer back into West Virginia. The organizer secretly contacted and signed up the employees of Hitchman Coal. When enough employees signed up, a strike was called and the mine was closed. However, Hitchman management brought a suit against the union, alleging that the organizer had deliberately induced the employees to break their agreements with the company. The Supreme Court ruled in favor of management and thus upheld the enforceability of the yellow-dog contract. Yellow-dog contracts were used until they were declared illegal by the Norris–La Guardia Act of 1932 (discussed later in this chapter).

Sherman Anti-Trust Act (1890)

The Sherman Anti-Trust Act was signed into law in 1890. The law made trusts and conspiracies that restrain interstate commerce illegal and forbade persons from monopolizing or attempting to monopolize interstate trade or commerce. Furthermore, any person who believed he or she

---

injunction
Court order to stop an action that could result in irreparable damage to property when the situation is such that no other adequate remedy is available to protect the interest of the injunction-seeking party.

yellow-dog contract
Term coined by unions to describe an agreement between an employee and an employer stipulating that, as a condition of employment, the worker would not join a labor union. Yellow-dog contracts were made illegal by the Norris–La Guardia Act of 1932.

Hitchman Coal & Coke Co. v. Mitchell
Supreme Court case of 1917 that upheld the legality of yellow-dog contracts.

had been injured by violations of the act was given the right to sue for triple the amount of damages sustained and the costs of the suit, including a reasonable attorney's fee.

Generally, it is agreed that the primary intent of Congress in passing the Sherman Anti-Trust Act was to protect the public from the abuses of corporate monopolies. However, in 1908, in the landmark ***Danbury Hatters* case,** the Supreme Court decided that the Sherman Anti-Trust Act applied to all unions. In this case, the United Hatters Union, while attempting to unionize Loewe & Company of Danbury, Connecticut, called a strike and initiated a national boycott against the company's products. The boycott was successful, and Loewe filed a suit against the union alleging violation of the Sherman Anti-Trust Act. The Court further held that the individual members of the union were jointly liable for the money damages awarded.

***Danbury Hatters* case**
Landmark case of 1908 in which the Supreme Court decided that the Sherman Anti-Trust Act applied to all unions.

Clayton Act (1914)

Labor unions rejoiced at the passage of the Clayton Act in 1914. In fact, Samuel Gompers, one of the leading spokespersons of the early labor movement, called the Clayton Act the "Industrial Magna Carta."[1] Sections 6 and 20 were of particular importance to labor:

> Section 6: The labor of a human being is not a commodity or article of commerce. Nothing contained in the antitrust law shall be construed to forbid the existence and operating of labor . . . organizations . . . or to forbid or restrain individual members of such organizations from lawfully carrying out the legitimate objects thereof; nor shall such organizations, or the members thereof be held or construed to be illegal combinations or conspiracies in restraint of trade under the antitrust laws.
>
> Section 20: No restraining order or injunction shall be granted by any court of the United States . . . in any case between an employer and employees, or between persons employed and persons seeking employment, unless necessary to prevent irreparable injury to property, or to a property right, of the party making the application, for which injury there is no adequate remedy of law.

Duplex Printing Co.* v. *Deering
Case in which the Supreme Court ruled that unions were not exempt from the control of the Sherman Anti-Trust Act.

However, the joy of the unions was short-lived. The Supreme Court, in the 1921 case ***Duplex Printing Co.* v. *Deering*,** basically gutted the intent of the Clayton Act because of the vague wording of the law. At the time, Duplex was the only nonunionized company manufacturing printing presses. The union attempted to organize the company, requesting that customers not purchase Duplex presses, that a trucking company not transport Duplex presses, and that repair shops not repair Duplex presses. The company asked for an injunction against the union but was denied by both the U.S. district and circuit owners on the basis of Section 20 of the Clayton Act. However, in a split decision, the Supreme Court overruled the lower courts. In this decision, the Court ruled that Section 6 of the Clayton Act did not exempt unions from the control of the Sherman Act. Furthermore, the Court's decision meant that the issuance of injunctions was largely unchanged by the Clayton Act.

Railway Labor Act (1926)

Legislation and its interpretations by the courts were largely antiunion prior to the passage of the **Railway Labor Act** in 1926. This act, which set up the administrative machinery for handling labor relations within the railroad industry, was the first important piece of prolabor legislation in the United States. The act was extended to airlines in 1936.[2]

Railway Labor Act
An act enacted in 1926 that set up the administrative machinery for handling labor relations within the railroad industry; the first important piece of prolabor legislation.

One provision established the National Mediation Board to administer the act. Another provision eliminated yellow-dog contracts for railroad employees. The act also established mechanisms for mediation and arbitration of disputes between employers and unions within the industry. However, the original act applied only to railroad employees and not to those employed in other industries.

Norris–La Guardia Act (1932)

The **Norris–La Guardia Act of 1932** was particularly important to labor unions because it made yellow-dog contracts unenforceable and severely restricted the use of injunctions. The law prohibited federal courts from issuing injunctions to keep unions from striking, paying strike benefits, picketing (unless the picketing involved fraud or violence), and peacefully assembling.

Norris–La Guardia Act of 1932
Prolabor act that eliminated the use of yellow-dog contracts and severely restricted the use of injunctions.

Other parts of the law further restricted the issuance of injunctions. For example, the law required the employer to show that the regular police force was either unwilling or unable to protect the employer's property before an injunction could be issued. Temporary restraining orders could not be issued for more than five days.

The Norris–La Guardia Act also gave employees the right to organize and bargain with employers on the terms and conditions of employment. However, its major weakness was that it established no administrative procedures to ensure implementation of the rights. Employees could gain bargaining rights only if their employer voluntarily agreed to recognize the union or if the employees struck and forced recognition. In other words, the law gave employees the right to organize but did not require management to bargain with their union.

National Labor Relations (Wagner) Act (1935)

National Labor Relations Act (Wagner Act)
Prolabor act of 1935 that gave workers the right to organize, obligated the management of organizations to bargain in good faith with unions, defined illegal management practices relating to unions, and created the National Labor Relations Board (NLRB) to administer the act.

The **National Labor Relations Act,** commonly known as the **Wagner Act** (named after its principal sponsor, Senator Robert Wagner Sr., of New York) was passed in 1935. The bill signaled a change in the federal government's role in labor–management relations. As a result of this law, government took a much more active role.

The Wagner Act gave employees the right to organize unions, bargain collectively with employers, and engage in other concerted actions for the purpose of mutual protection. Of course, the Norris–La Guardia Act had already granted these rights. However, the Wagner Act went further in that it required employers to recognize unions chosen by employees and to bargain with such unions in good faith. Furthermore, the act prohibited employers from engaging in uncertain unfair labor practices, including

1. Interference with, restraint of, or coercion of employees in exercising their rights under the act.
2. Domination of, interference with, or financial contributions to a union.
3. Discrimination in regard to hiring, firing, or any term or condition of employment to encourage or discourage membership in a union.
4. Discharge of or discrimination against an employee for filing charges or giving testimony under the act.
5. Refusal to bargain in good faith with the legal representative of the employees.

In addition, the act established a three-member National Labor Relations Board (NLRB) to administer the Wagner Act (the NLRB is discussed later in this chapter). The act also established procedures for use in union elections and directed the NLRB to conduct such elections and investigate unfair practices.

HRM in Action 18.2 describes the Employee Free Choice Act (EFCA), which has not presently been passed by Congress.

Labor–Management Relations (Taft–Hartley) Act (1947)

After the passage of the Wagner Act, union membership grew from approximately 6 percent of the total workforce to approximately 23 percent in 1947. Accompanying this growth was an increase in union militancy. Strikes became much more frequent and widespread. In 1946, a record 4.6 million employees participated in strikes. A nationwide steel strike, an auto strike, two coal strikes, and a railroad strike negatively influenced scores of other industries, causing shortages and layoffs.

Labor–Management Relations Act (Taft–Hartley Act)
Legislation enacted in 1947 that placed the federal government in a watchdog position to ensure that union–management relations are conducted fairly by both parties.

It was against this background of events that the **Labor–Management Relations Act** was passed in 1947. Known as the **Taft–Hartley Act,** it was an amendment and extension of the Wagner Act. The Taft–Hartley Act marked another change in the legislative posture toward union–management relations. The act basically placed government in the role of referee to ensure that both unions and management dealt fairly with each other.

Under the Taft–Hartley Act, employees have the right to organize a union, bargain collectively with an employer, and engage in other concerted activities for the purpose of collective bargaining. The act also spelled out unfair labor practices by employers and prohibited managers from forming or joining a labor union. Most provisions of the act are identical to those of the Wagner Act, but one unfair practice was changed significantly. Under the Wagner Act, employers were prohibited from discriminating in regard to hiring, firing, or any term or condition of employment to encourage or discourage membership in a union. However, the Wagner Act permitted closed and preferential shop agreements. With a closed shop, only union members can be hired, and the preferential shop requires that union members be given preference in filling job vacancies. The Taft–Hartley Act made closed and preferential shops illegal. However, the act permitted agreements in the construction industry, which required union membership within seven days of employment. The act also permitted a practice in the construction industry referred to as a *union hiring hall,* under which unions referred people to employers with existing job openings.

Unlike the Wagner Act, the Taft–Hartley Act also established a number of unfair union practices. In general, unions were forbidden to

1. Coerce employees who do not want to join.
2. Force employers to pressure employees to join a union.
3. Refuse to bargain in good faith with an employer.
4. Force an employer to pay for services not performed (featherbedding).
5. Engage in certain types of secondary boycotts (taking action against an employer that is not directly engaged in a dispute with a union).
6. Charge excessive initiation fees when union membership is required because of a union shop agreement. A *union shop agreement* requires employees to join the union and remain members as a condition of employment.

The Taft–Hartley Act also contained an important provision, the so-called free-speech clause. This clause stated that management has the right to express its opinion about unions or unionism to its employees, provided they carry no threat of reprisal or force.

secondary boycott
Issue involving other employers (secondary employers) in the relationship between a union and an employer (the primary employer).

The Taft–Hartley Act also prohibited secondary boycotts. The concept of **secondary boycott** is a complex issue, but basically concerns involving other employers (secondary employers) in the relationship between a union and an employer (the primary employer). For example, if a union attempts to persuade a large customer of a primary employer to stop doing business with the primary employer until the primary employer agrees to the union's demands, this is a secondary boycott, which is illegal. However, distinguishing between a primary and secondary employer is very complex and has been the subject of many unfair labor practice charges that the NLRB has ruled on.[3]

National Labor Relations Board (NLRB)
Five-member panel created by the National Labor Relations Act and appointed by the president of the United States with the advice and consent of the Senate and with the authority to administer the Wagner Act.

National Labor Relations Board

The Taft–Hartley Act also expanded the size of the **National Labor Relations Board (NLRB)** and created the **Office of the General Counsel.** Presently, the board is a five-member panel appointed by the president of the United States with the advice and consent of the Senate. Each member serves for a five-year term. One of the five is appointed as board chairperson by the president, with Senate confirmation. The general counsel, a separate office independent from the board, is appointed by the president and approved by the Senate for a four-year term.

Office of the General Counsel
Separate and independent office created by the Taft–Hartley Act to investigate unfair labor practice charges and present those charges with merit to the NLRB.

The relationship between the five-member board and the general counsel is similar to the relationship between the judge (or jury) and the prosecutor. In unfair labor practice cases, the board sits as the judge and the general counsel acts as the prosecutor. Anyone can file an unfair labor practice complaint with the general counsel. Frequently, people refer to filing an unfair labor practice charge with the board, but it is actually filed with the general counsel. After the charge is filed, the general counsel investigates it and decides the merit of the charge. If the general counsel decides the act has been violated, a complaint is issued. The case is then tried before the board, which decides whether a violation has occurred.

The division of authority between the board and the general counsel applies only to unfair labor practice charges. Union election procedures are handled solely by the board. The role of the board in union election campaigns is described in greater depth in Chapter 19.

Much of the work of the board and the Office of the General Counsel is carried out in regional offices established by the board. Each regional office is headed by a regional director appointed by the board. The regional director serves as the local representative of the general counsel in processing unfair labor practice charges and as the local representative of the board in administering union election procedures.

Right-to-Work Laws

Section 14(b) of the Taft–Hartley Act is one of the most controversial sections of the law. It states:

> Nothing in this act shall be construed as authorizing the execution or application of agreements requiring membership in a labor organization as a condition of employment in any state or territory in which such execution or application is prohibited by state or territory law.

right-to-work laws
Legislation enacted by individual states under the authority of Section 14(b) of the Taft–Hartley Act that can forbid various types of union security arrangements, including compulsory union membership.

Thus, section 14(b) leaves to the states and territories the right to pass laws prohibiting union shops and other arrangements for compulsory union membership. Laws passed by individual states prohibiting compulsory union membership are called **right-to-work laws,** and states that have passed such legislation are right-to-work states. Presently there are 21 right-to-work states: Alabama, Arizona, Arkansas, Florida, Georgia, Idaho, Iowa, Kansas, Louisiana, Mississippi, Nebraska, Nevada, North Carolina, North Dakota, South Carolina, South Dakota, Tennessee, Texas, Utah, Virginia, and Wyoming (see Figure 18.1). In these states, employees in unionized organizations are represented by the union but are not required to belong to the union or pay union dues. Unions argue that employees who choose not to belong or pay union dues get a free ride.[4]

The Taft–Hartley Act also created an independent agency known as the Federal Mediation and Conciliation Service within the federal government. This agency assists parties in labor disputes to settle such disputes through conciliation and mediation. Finally, the act also established procedures that the president of the United States can use for resolving labor disputes that imperil the national health and safety.

HRM in Action 18.3 describes a criminal investigation being conducted by the U.S. Department of Labor against the International Brotherhood of Electrical Workers (IBEW) Local 1505.

FIGURE 18.1
Map of Right-to-Work States

Source: National Right to Work Legal Defense Foundation.

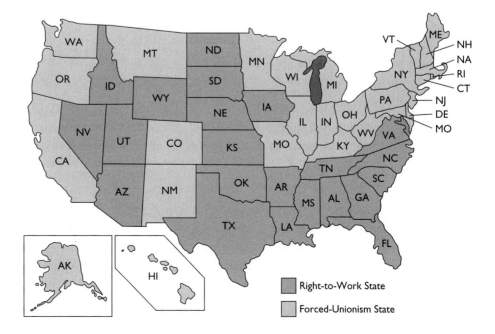

Right-to-Work State

Forced-Unionism State

IBEW LOCAL 1505

The U.S. Department of Labor notified Local 1505 of the IBEW of a criminal investigation that was being conducted concerning financial matters within the local union. Local 1505 represents approximately 2,400 of Raytheon's 11,500 employees in Massachusetts. Investigators are examining financial records of the union. They have requested all credit card statements and receipts from January 1999 to present; all bank statements, canceled checks, and bonds for the same period; and all expense vouchers. In addition, the investigators have asked for all information regarding the sale of Local 1505's building and have advised the union's leadership not to destroy any information. This investigation is likely to cause more internal strife within Local 1505.

Michael Zagami was elected business manager of Local 1505 in 1996; Stanley Lichwala was elected president of Local 1505 in 1999. These two leaders have provoked a great deal of criticism within Local 1505. Zagami and Lichwala had a fallout over finances and management styles in March 2002. Both of these men ran for business manager of the union in June 2002, but were defeated by George Noel, a longtime internal critic of the union's leadership. Lichwala admitted he had returned some funds to the local union after an investigation conducted by the IBEW national offices.

Source: Adapted from Ross Kerber, "U.S. Launches Probe of Massachusetts Union Local Representing Raytheon Workers," *Knight Ridder Tribune Business News,* Washington, D.C., August 13, 2002, p. 1.

Labor–Management Reporting and Disclosure (Landrum–Griffin) Act (1959)

Even after the passage of the Taft–Hartley Act, complaints continued concerning corruption and heavyhanded activity by certain unions. Thus, Congress created the Senate Select Committee on Improper Activities in the Labor or Management Field, better known as the McClellan Committee. Between 1957 and 1959, the McClellan Committee held hearings on union activities. As a result of these hearings, in 1959 Congress passed the **Labor–Management Reporting and Disclosure Act (LMRDA),** usually called the **Landrum–Griffin Act.** This act, which was also an amendment to and extension of the Wagner Act, was aimed primarily at regulating internal union affairs and protecting the rights of individual union members.

The main provisions of the act are as follows:

Labor–Management Reporting and Disclosure Act (LMRDA) (Landrum–Griffin Act)
Legislation enacted in 1959 regulating labor unions and requiring disclosure of certain union finance information to the government.

1. Union members are guaranteed the right to vote in union elections.
2. Union members are guaranteed the right to oppose their incumbent leadership both in union meetings and by nominating opposition candidates.
3. A majority affirmative vote of members by a secret ballot is required before union dues can be increased.
4. Reports covering most financial aspects of the union must be filed with the U.S. Department of Labor.
5. Officers and employees of unions are required to report any financial dealings with employees that might potentially influence the union members' interests.
6. Each union is required to file a constitution and bylaws with the U.S. Department of Labor.
7. Rigid formal requirements are established for conducting both national and local union elections.
8. Union members are allowed to bring suit against union officials for improper management of the union's funds and for conflict-of-interest situations.
9. Trusteeships that allow national or international unions to take over the management of a local union can be established only under provisions specified in the constitution and by-laws of the union and only to combat corruption or financial misconduct.

Civil Service Reform Act (1978)

Prior to 1978, labor–management relations within the federal government were administered through **executive orders.** These orders are issued by the president of the United States and relate to the management and operation of federal government agencies. Executive Order 10988, issued by President Kennedy, gave federal employees the right to join unions and required good-faith bargaining by both unions and federal agency management. Executive Order 11491, issued by President Nixon, defined more precisely the rights of federal employees

executive orders
Orders issued by the president of the United States for managing and operating federal government agencies.

in regard to unionization by establishing unfair labor practices for both unions and federal agency management. It also established procedures to safeguard these rights.

Civil Service Reform Act
Legislation enacted in 1978 regulating labor–management relations for federal government employees.

In 1978, the **Civil Service Reform Act** was passed. Basically, it enacted into law the measures that had previously been adopted under Executive Orders 10988 and 11491. The act gave federal employees the right to organize and establish procedures for handling labor–management relations within the federal government. The main provisions of the act are as follows:

1. Established the **Federal Labor Relations Authority (FLRA)** to administer the act. The FLRA is composed of three members, not more than two of whom may be members of the same political party. Members of the authority are appointed by the president, with approval of the Senate, for a term of five years.

Federal Labor Relations Authority (FLRA)
Three-member panel created by the Civil Service Reform Act whose purpose is to administer the act.

2. Created the Office of the General Counsel within the FLRA to investigate and prosecute unfair labor practices. The general counsel is appointed by the president, with approval of the Senate, for a term of five years.

3. Created the **Federal Services Impasses Panel (FSIP)** within the FLRA to provide assistance in resolving negotiation impasses between federal agencies and unions. The panel is composed of a chairperson and at least six other members who are appointed by the president for a term of five years.

Federal Services Impasses Panel (FSIP)
Entity within the FLRA whose function is to provide assistance in resolving negotiation impasses within the federal sector.

4. Established unfair labor practices for the management of federal agencies and unions.
5. Established the general areas that are subject to collective bargaining.
6. Required binding arbitration for all grievances that have not been resolved in earlier stages of the grievance procedure.
7. Prohibited strikes in the federal sector.

UNION STRUCTURES

Web site: AFL–CIO
www.aflcio.org

As the previously described legislation was passed and court actions taken, organizational units were developed within the union movement to deal with problems and take advantage of opportunities. Four basic types of such units exist:

- Federations of local, national, and international unions (e.g., AFL–CIO).
- National or international unions.
- City and state federations.
- Local unions.

American Federation of Labor–Congress of Industrial Organizations (AFL–CIO)
Combination of national, international, and local unions joined together to promote the interest of union and workers. The AFL–CIO was formed in 1955 by the amalgamation of the American Federation of Labor (AFL) and the Congress of Industrial Organizations (CIO).

Some important dates relating to the development of the different union organizational units are shown in Table 18.1.

AFL–CIO

Structurally speaking, the **American Federation of Labor–Congress of Industrial Organizations (AFL–CIO)** is the largest organizational unit within the union movement. Its primary goal is to promote the interests of unions and workers. The AFL–CIO resulted from the 1955 merger of the American Federation of Labor and the Congress of Industrial Organizations.

TABLE 18.1
Important Dates in the Labor Movement

Year	Event
1792	First local union: Philadelphia Shoemaker's Union
1833	First city federation: New York, Philadelphia, Baltimore
1850	First national union: International Typographical Union
1869	First attempt to form a federation of unions: Knights of Labor
1886	Formation of American Federation of Labor (AFL)
1938	Formation of Congress of Industrial Organizations (CIO)
1955	AFL–CIO merger

craft unions
Unions having only skilled
workers as members. Most
craft unions have members
from several related trades
(e.g., Bricklayers, Masons, and
Plasterers International Union).

industrial unions
Unions having as members
both skilled and unskilled
workers in a particular industry
or group of industries.

Formed in 1886, the AFL was composed primarily of **craft unions,** which had only skilled workers as members. Most such unions had members from several related trades (e.g., the Bricklayers, Masons, and Plasterers International Union). The CIO, formed in 1938, was developed to organize **industrial unions,** which have as members both skilled and unskilled workers in a particular industry or group of industries. The United Automobile Workers is an example of an industrial union.

Technically speaking, the AFL–CIO is not itself a union but is merely an organization composed of affiliated national and international unions, affiliated state and local bodies, local unions affiliated directly with the AFL–CIO, and eight trade and industrial departments. The AFL–CIO is merely a loose, voluntary federation of unions. Not all national and international unions belong to the AFL–CIO. However, a majority of unions are affiliated with the AFL–CIO.

The basic policies of the AFL–CIO are set and its executive council elected at a national convention held every two years. The executive council—composed of the president, the secretary-treasurer, the executive vice president, and 29 other members—carries out the policies established at the convention. Each affiliated national and international union sends delegates to the convention. The number of delegates a particular union sends is determined by the size of its membership.

To deal with specific concerns, the AFL–CIO president appoints and supervises standing committees that work with staff departments to provide services to the union membership. The general board meets at the call of the president or the executive council and acts on matters referred to it by the executive council.

National and International Unions

The organizational structure of most national and international unions is similar to that of the AFL–CIO. Unions are called international because they often have members in both the United States and Canada. In general, both national and international unions operate under a constitution and have a national convention with each local union represented in proportion to its membership. Usually the convention elects an executive council, which normally consists of a president, a secretary-treasurer, and several vice presidents. Normally, the president appoints and manages a staff for handling matters such as organizing activities, research, and legal problems.

The field organization of a national or an international union usually has several regional or district offices headed by a regional director. Under the regional director are field representatives who are responsible for conducting union organizing campaigns and assisting local unions in collective bargaining and handling grievances.

City and State Federations

City federations receive charters from the AFL–CIO and are composed of local unions within a specified area. Local unions send delegates to city federation meetings, which are generally held on a biweekly or monthly basis.

The primary function of city federations is to coordinate and focus the political efforts of local unions. During elections, city federations usually endorse a slate of candidates. Most city federations maintain an informal lobby at the city hall and present labor issues to legislative committees. City federations do not always focus their efforts only on labor issues. Other issues and activities that city federations frequently address include school board policies, community fund-raising drives, and public transportation problems.

State federations are also chartered by the AFL–CIO and are composed of local unions and city federations. The main goal of state federations is to influence political action favorable to unions. They try to persuade union members to vote for union-endorsed candidates. During state legislative sessions, the state federation actively lobbies for passage of bills endorsed by labor unions.

Local Unions

Most local unions operate under the constitution of their national or international union. However, a number are independent in that they operate without a national affiliation. Furthermore, a local union can be affiliated directly with the AFL–CIO without being connected with a national or international union.

As a rule, the membership of a local union elects officers, who carry out the union activities. In a typical local union, the members elect a president, vice president, and secretary-treasurer and usually form several committees. For example, a bargaining committee is usually appointed to negotiate the contract for the union, and a grievance committee is usually appointed to handle grievances for the membership. The latter committee is generally composed of a chief steward and several departmental stewards. The stewards recruit new employees into the union, listen to employee complaints, handle grievances, and observe management's administration of the union contract. Generally, most local union officials work at a regular job but have some leeway in using working time to conduct union business. In large locals, most officials are full-time, paid employees of the union. The local usually depends heavily on the field representative of its national or international union for assistance in handling contract negotiations, strikes, and arbitration hearings.

In those industries where membership is scattered among several employers, local unions often have a business agent who is a full-time, paid employee of the local union. This agent manages internal union activities, negotiates contracts, meets with company officials to resolve contract interpretation issues, handles grievances, and serves as an active participant in arbitration hearings.

CURRENT AND FUTURE DEVELOPMENTS IN THE LABOR MOVEMENT

Web site: FindLaw
www.findlaw.com

Between 1935 (the year the National Labor Relations Act was passed) and the end of World War II, union membership quadrupled (see Figure 18.2). During the post–World War II era through 1970, union membership continued to grow. Between 1970 and 1980, union membership grew by slightly more than 1 million members, but as a percentage of the total workforce it dropped significantly. In addition, union membership dropped in the 1980s by approximately 5 million workers, and it has continued to drop as a percentage of the total workforce. In contrast, union membership for government employees has grown recently. Unions also hold a much higher percentage of the government workforce.

In January 2004, the U.S. Department of Labor published a report indicating that 12.9 percent of wage and salary workers were union members, down from 13.3 percent in 2002. The 2003 data include these highlights:

- Men were more likely to be union members than women.
- African Americans were more likely to be union members than were whites, Asians, and Hispanics.
- Nearly 4 in 10 government workers were union members in 2003, compared with less than 1 in 10 workers in private-sector industries.
- Nearly two of five workers in the education, training, and library occupations were union members.
- Nearly two of five workers in the protective service occupation which includes fire fighters and police officers.
- Four states had union membership rates over 20 percent in 2003: New York (24.6 percent), Hawaii (23.8 percent), Alaska (22.3 percent), and Michigan (21.9 percent).
- North Carolina (3.1 percent) and South Carolina (4.2 percent) reported the lowest union membership rates.[5]

FIGURE 18.2
Union Membership History as a Percentage of the U.S. Workforce, 1921–2003.

Source: U.S. Department of Labor.

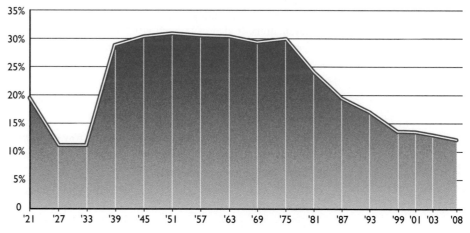

Web site: Internet Law Library
www.lectlaw.com

Historically, labor unions have gained their strength from blue-collar production workers. However, the workforce has grown and will continue to grow principally in the service sector of the economy. Less than 10 percent of the service sector is currently organized. Unions have been successful in organizing narrow segments of the service sector, such as teachers, pilots, and musicians. However, it is expected that a major emphasis of future organizing campaigns will be directed toward convincing unorganized white-collar employees that their personal and professional needs can be satisfied through union representation.

By the late 1990s, investments in private pension plans reached approximately $3 trillion. Labor unions are likely to attempt to influence how these monies are invested. Specifically, unions will probably request that the funds not be invested in stock of antiunion companies or companies that engage in antiunion practices.

The AFL–CIO has lost about 3.6 million of its nearly 13 million members and about $26 million of its $126 million budget as a result of the disaffiliation of three large unions. The 1.8-million-member Service Employees International Union, the 1.4-million-member International Brotherhood of Teamsters, and the 1.4-million-member United Food and Commercial Workers Union all disaffiliated with the federation in July, 2009.

Another likely development is the continued increase in union mergers. Union mergers take two basic forms. An **amalgamation** involves two or more unions, normally of roughly equal size, forming a new union. An **absorption** involves the merging of one union into a considerably larger one. Roughly 50 of the AFL–CIO affiliates have under 50,000 members, and another 30 have under 100,000 members. Larger unions can, of course, bring much more pressure on management, not only in negotiating collective bargaining agreements but also in union organizing campaigns.

amalgamation
Union merger that involves two or more unions, usually of approximately the same size, forming a new union.

absorption
Union merger that involves the merger of one union into a considerably larger one.

Summary of Learning Objectives

1. **Describe the conspiracy doctrine.**

   The conspiracy doctrine established that a union could be punished if either the means used or ends sought by the union were deemed illegal by the courts.

2. **Define *injunction*.**

   An injunction is a court order to stop an action that can result in irreparable damage to property when the situation is such that no adequate remedy is available to protect the interests of the injunction-seeking party.

3. **Explain a yellow-dog contract.**

   A yellow-dog contract (a term coined by labor unions) is an agreement between a worker and an employer stipulating, as a condition of employment, that the worker will not join a labor union. Yellow-dog contracts are now illegal.

4. **Define the Railway Labor Act (1926).**

   This act set up the administrative machinery for handling labor relations within the railroad and airline industries.

5. **Describe the Norris–La Guardia Act (1932).**

   This act made yellow-dog contracts unenforceable and severely limited the use of injunctions. It also gave employees the right to organize and bargain with employers on the terms and conditions of employment.

6. **Define the Wagner Act (1935).**

   This act gave employees the right to organize unions, bargain collectively with employers, and engage in other concerted actions for the purpose of mutual protection.

7. **Explain the Taft–Hartley Act (1947).**

   This act basically placed government in the role of referee to ensure that both unions and management deal fairly with each other.

8. **Describe right-to-work laws.**

   Right-to-work laws were passed by individual states and prohibit compulsory union membership.

9. **Explain the Landrum–Griffin Act (1959).**

This act aimed primarily to regulate internal union affairs and protect the rights of individual union members.

10. **Describe the AFL–CIO.**

The AFL–CIO is a voluntary federation of unions whose primary goal is to promote the interests of unions and workers.

11. **Define amalgamation and absorption.**

An amalgamation involves two or more unions, normally of roughly equal size, forming a new union. An absorption involves the merging of one union into a considerably larger one.

Key Terms

absorption, *368*
amalgamation, *368*
American Federation of Labor–Congress of Industrial Organizations (AFL–CIO), *365*
Civil Service Reform Act, *365*
Commonwealth v. *Hunt*, *358*
conspiracy doctrine, *358*
craft unions, *366*
Danbury Hatters case, *360*
Duplex Printing Co. v. *Deering*, *360*
executive orders, *364*

Federal Labor Relations Authority (FLRA), *365*
Federal Services Impasses Panel (FSIP), *365*
Hitchman Coal & Coke Co. v. *Mitchell*, *359*
industrial unions, *366*
injunction, *359*
Labor–Management Relations Act (Taft–Hartley Act), *362*
Labor–Management Reporting and Disclosure Act (LMRDA) (Landrum–Griffin Act), *364*

National Labor Relations Act (Wagner Act), *361*
National Labor Relations Board (NLRB), *362*
Norris–La Guardia Act of 1932, *360*
Office of the General Counsel, *362*
Philadelphia Cordwainers (shoemakers) case of 1806, *358*
Railway Labor Act, *360*
right-to-work laws, *363*
secondary boycott, *362*
yellow-dog contract, *359*

Review Questions

1. Explain the ruling in the *Philadelphia Cordwainers* case of 1806.
2. What was the decision in the *Commonwealth* v. *Hunt* case of 1842?
3. What is an injunction? How were injunctions used against labor unions?
4. What is a yellow-dog contract?
5. List the major benefits unions gained with the passage of the Norris–La Guardia Act of 1932.
6. What unfair employer practices were specified by the Wagner Act of 1935?
7. What unfair union practices were specified by the Taft–Hartley Act of 1947?
8. Outline the main areas covered by the Landrum–Griffin Act of 1959.
9. Outline the main areas covered by the Civil Service Reform Act of 1978.
10. Briefly describe the four basic types of union organizational units.
11. What trends have occurred in labor union membership from 1935 to the present?

Discussion Questions

1. Why did legislation take a prounion turn in the 1930s?
2. Discuss your feelings about the following statement: "Management should always fight hard to keep unions out of their organization."
3. Do you think white-collar employees should join unions? Why or why not?
4. Do you believe college professors and nurses are good candidates for unionization? Why or why not?

Incident 18.1

Unions and Management

International Association of Machinists and Aerospace Workers (IAMAW) Local 709 voted to end a strike against the Marietta plant of Lockheed-Georgia Company. The contract that was agreed on contained a wage increase of about 13 percent and improved retirement, insurance, and other benefits. The company also agreed to pay employees for the seven days over the Christmas holidays and the two days over the Thanksgiving holidays that were missed during the strike.

For the Marietta workers, the main issue was their right to "bump" workers with less seniority from projects during times when there are not enough jobs to go around. Lockheed officials claimed the bumping procedure, whereby an employee having at least one day's seniority over another could take the junior's job, would hurt production so badly that it could force the company to abandon projects. Lockheed's initial proposal had been that an employee without at least three months' seniority over the junior employee would not be allowed to bump. After the union rejected this proposal, the company proposed to change the seniority requirement to at least one month. At that point, negotiations broke down.

The last Lockheed offer, which was accepted, was that the seniority system remain the same for all current Lockheed employees. However, anyone hired after Lockheed's offer was accepted would have to have at least one month's seniority to be able to bump another worker.

Questions

1. Why do you think unions insisted on seniority as the criterion in the preceding example?
2. Do you think seniority should be used in any process within a company? Why or why not?

Incident 18.2

Voluntary Resignations during a Strike

The Supreme Court ruled in a five-to-four decision that unions cannot fine employees who resign their union membership during a strike and return to work in violation of union rules.

The case involved a seven-month strike by the Pattern Makers' League against clothing companies in Illinois and Wisconsin. The union had a rule prohibiting resignations during a strike and enforced it by fining 10 employees the approximate amount they earned after they returned to work during the strike.

The Court, upholding the view of the National Labor Relations Board, said that imposing fines and other restrictions on employees who quit the union during a strike "impairs the policy of voluntary unionism."

Source: Adapted from Stephen Wermiel, "Justices Rule Unions Can't Fine Members Who Quit, Resume Work during a Strike," *The Wall Street Journal*, June 28, 1985, p. 5.

Questions

1. Do you think unions should be able to restrict resignations during a strike? Why or why not?
2. Do you think this decision has had any effect on union membership?

EXERCISE 18.1
Need for Unions

The class breaks into teams of four to five students. Each team should prepare to debate the following statements:

1. Unions served a useful purpose in the past but have outlived their usefulness.
2. Unions are needed today as much as they have been in the past. Without unions, wages and working conditions of the average employee would deteriorate.

After the debate, the instructor will list on the board some points made by each team, and the class will discuss the issues involved.

Notes and Additional Readings

1. Samuel Gompers, "The Charter of Industrial Freedom," *American Federationist,* November 1914, pp. 971–72.

2. See Frank N. Wilner, "Should the Railway Labor Act Be Updated?" *Railway Age,* July 2001, p. 56.

3. See Joseph Bonney, "NLRB Investigating Evergreen Charges," *Journal of Commerce,* May 23, 2003, p. 1.

4. See Clay Walker, "The Myth of Right-to-Work Laws," *Area Development Site and Facility Planning,* June 2001, pp. 121–24.

5. *Union Members Summary,* U.S. Department of Labor, Bureau of Labor Statistics, January 21, 2004, pp. 1–2.

Chapter **Nineteen**

Union Organizing Campaigns and Collective Bargaining

Chapter Learning Objectives

After studying this chapter, you should be able to:

1. Define collective bargaining.
2. Explain the captive-audience doctrine.
3. Define bargaining unit.
4. Explain certification, recognition, and contract bars.
5. Describe good-faith bargaining.
6. Discuss boulwarism.
7. Explain mediation.
8. Define checkoff.
9. Explain seniority.
10. Define lockout and strike.

Chapter Outline

Union Membership Decision
  Reasons for Joining
  The Opposition View
Union Organizing Campaign
  Determining the Bargaining Unit
  Election Campaigns
  Election, Certification, and Decertification
Good-Faith Bargaining
Participants in Negotiations
  Employer's Role
  Union's Role
  Role of Third Parties
Collective Bargaining Agreements
Specific Issues in Collective Bargaining Agreements
  Management Rights

  Union Security
  Wages and Employee Benefits
  Individual Security (Seniority) Rights
  Dispute Resolution
Impasses in Collective Bargaining
Trends in Collective Bargaining
Summary of Learning Objectives
Key Terms
Review Questions
Discussion Questions
  Incident 19.1: Florida National Guard and NAGE
  Incident 19.2: Retiree Benefits
Exercise 19.1: Contract Negotiations
Notes and Additional Readings

collective bargaining
Process that involves the negotiation, drafting, administration, and interpretation of a written agreement between an employer and a union for a specific period of time.

Collective bargaining is a process that involves the negotiation, drafting, administration, and interpretation of a written agreement between an employer and a union for a specific period of time. The end result of collective bargaining is a contract that sets forth the joint understandings of the parties as to wages, hours, and other terms and conditions of employment. Contracts cover a variety of time periods, the most common being three years.

The basic components of the collective bargaining process are the following:

1. Negotiation of relevant issues in good faith by both management and the union.
2. Incorporation of the parties' understandings into a written contract.

3. Administration of the daily working relationships according to the terms and conditions of employment specified in the contract.

4. Resolution of disputes in the interpretation of the terms of the contract through established procedures.

Normally the human resource department serves as management's primary representative in all aspects of the collective bargaining process.

UNION MEMBERSHIP DECISION

Before the collective bargaining process begins, the employees of an organization must decide whether they want to be represented by a union. Thus, an important prerequisite to understanding the collective bargaining process is knowledge of what attracts employees to unions.

Reasons for Joining

A variety of factors influence an employee's desire to join a union. Employees who are dissatisfied with their wages, job security, benefits, the treatment they receive from management, and their chances for promotion are more likely to vote for union representation. Another important factor in determining employees' interest in union membership is their perception of the ability of the union to change the situation. If employees do not believe unionization will change the economic and working conditions that dissatisfy them, they are unlikely to vote for unionization.

While wages, benefits, working conditions, and job security are the main issues contributing to the decision to join a union, other factors include employees' desires for

1. Better communication with management.
2. Higher quality of management and supervision.
3. Increased democracy in the workplace.
4. Opportunity to belong to a group where they can share experiences and comradeship.

The Opposition View

Understanding why employees oppose unionization is as important as knowing why they favor it. The major reasons for not joining a union are satisfactory wages, benefits, working conditions, and job security. Some employees also have a negative image of labor unions, believing unions have too much political influence, require members to go along with decisions made by the union, and have leaders who promote their own self-interests. Other reasons include the belief that unions abuse their power by calling strikes, causing high prices, and misusing union dues and pension funds.

Some employees identify with management and view unions as adversaries. However, dissatisfaction with wages, benefits, and working conditions can quickly break down this negative attitude toward unions.

Many organizations have avoided unionization. In most cases, the managements of those organizations have provided satisfactory wages, benefits, working conditions, and job security for their employees. Other management practices that decrease the likelihood of unionization include creating a procedure for handling employee complaints, eliminating arbitrary and heavy-handed management and supervisory practices, establishing a meaningful system of two-way communication between management and employees, eliminating threats to employees' job security, and making employees feel that they are part of the organization.

UNION ORGANIZING CAMPAIGN

Web site: United States National Labor Relations Board
www.nlrb.gov

Most often, union organizing campaigns begin when one or more employees request that the union begin an organizing campaign. In some instances, national and international unions contact employees in organizations that have been targeted for organizing campaigns. Generally, however, unions will not attempt to organize a facility unless there is a strong body of support among the employees. Typically, the union begins a campaign to interest employees in joining it. After the union generates sufficient interest, employees sign authorization cards indicating they would like to have an election to vote for or against representation by a union. If 30 percent of the employees sign these authorization cards, the National Labor Relations Board (NLRB) may be requested to come in and supervise an election. In practice, it is unlikely the NLRB will be petitioned unless over 50 percent sign authorization cards.

Several restrictions have been placed on where and when support for the unions can be solicited. Generally, employees in favor of the union can orally solicit support from other employees in work and nonwork areas, but only on nonwork time. In addition, if management allows employees to engage in casual conversation while they are working, the employees can discuss union matters if production is not hindered. Union literature can be distributed only on nonworking time, and management can limit the distribution of literature to nonwork areas.

The NLRB rarely approves exceptions to the general rules for oral solicitation and distribution of union literature. However, some exceptions have been granted. For example, department stores can establish rules prohibiting oral solicitation on the sales floor, provided employees are generally prohibited from casual conversations on the sales floor because customers are waiting for service.

The rights to orally solicit union support and distribute union literature on company property apply only to employees. Generally management can prohibit union organizers from entering company property for these purposes. One exception in this area is that if management allows other solicitors to enter company property, they cannot exclude union organizers.

captive-audience doctrine
Management's right to speak against a union to employees on company time and to require employees to attend the meeting.

Under the so-called **captive-audience doctrine,** management has the right to speak against the union on company time to employees and require employees to attend the meeting. On the other hand, the union does not have the right to reply on company time. The primary exception to the captive-audience doctrine is that management is prohibited from giving a speech on company time to a mass employee audience in the 24 hours immediately before an election. However, the 24-hour rule applies only to a speech before a large group. Managers are permitted to talk against the union to employees individually or in small groups during the last 24 hours.

Determining the Bargaining Unit

When the union obtains signed authorization cards from at least 30 percent of the employees, either the union or the employer can petition the National Labor Relations Board to conduct a representation election. In the event the union has signed authorization cards from more than 50 percent of the employees, the union can make a direct request to the employer to become the bargaining agent of the employees. When this happens, the employer normally refuses, and the union then petitions the NLRB for an election.

bargaining unit
Group of employees in a plant, firm, or industry that is recognized by the employer, agreed on by the parties to a case, or designated by the NLRB as appropriate for the purposes of collective bargaining.

consent elections
Union elections in which the parties have agreed on the appropriate bargaining unit.

community of interest
Concept by which the NLRB makes a bargaining unit decision based on areas of employee commonality.

After a petition is filed, a representative of the NLRB (called an *examiner*) verifies that the authorization requirement has been fulfilled and then makes a determination as to the appropriate bargaining unit. A **bargaining unit** (or *election unit*) is defined as a group of employees in a plant, firm, or industry that is recognized by the employer, agreed on by the involved parties, or designated by the NLRB or its regional director as appropriate for the purposes of collective bargaining.

Although the NLRB is ultimately responsible for establishing an appropriate bargaining unit, the parties usually have a great deal of influence on this decision. Most elections are known as **consent elections,** in which the parties have agreed on the appropriate bargaining unit. When this is not the case, the NLRB must make the bargaining unit decision guided by a concept called **community of interest.** Community-of-interest factors include elements such as similar wages, hours, and working conditions; the employees' physical proximity to one another; common supervision; the amount of interchange of personnel within the proposed unit; and the degree of integration of the employer's production process of operation.

Election Campaigns

During the election campaign, certain activities, called *unfair labor practices,* are illegal. These include (1) physical interference, threats, or violent behavior by the employer toward union organizers; (2) employer interference with employees involved in the organizing drive; (3) discipline or discharge of employees for prounion activities; and (4) threatening or coercing of

informational picketing
Patrolling at or near an employer's facility by individuals carrying signs to publicize the fact that the union is requesting an election to become the bargaining agent for the employees of the organization.

employees by union organizers. After filing for an election with the NLRB, a union can picket an employer only if the employer is not presently unionized, the petition has been filed with the NLRB within the past 30 days, and a representation election has not been conducted during the preceding 12 months. Picketing of this type is called **informational picketing.** Individuals patrol at or near the place of employment carrying signs to publicize the fact that the union is requesting an election to become the bargaining agent for the employees.

During the election campaign, management usually initiates a campaign against a union, emphasizing the costs of unionization and the loss of individual freedom that can result from collective representation. Management can legally state its opinion about the possible ramifications of unionization if its statements are based on fact and are not threatening. Management can also explain to employees the positive aspects of their current situation. However, promises to provide or withhold benefits in the future in the event of unionization or nonunionization are prohibited. An employer can conduct polls to verify union strength prior to an election, but in general it may not question employees individually about their preferences or otherwise threaten or intimidate them.

During the election campaign, unions emphasize their ability to help employees satisfy their needs and improve their working conditions. The ability of the union to sell these concepts to employees is a critical factor in the union's success in an election campaign. Employees must believe the union cares about their problems, can help resolve them, and can assist in improving their wages, benefits, and working conditions. Unions are legally prohibited from coercing or threatening individual employees if they do not join the union.[1]

The actual impact of an election campaign is unclear. However, the campaign tactics of both management and the union are monitored by the NLRB. If the practices of either party are found to be unfair, the election results may be invalidated and a new election conducted. Furthermore, charges of unfair labor practices against management, if serious enough, can result in the NLRB ordering management to bargain with the union. Such situations are called **Gissel bargaining orders.** Gissel bargaining orders are named after a landmark Supreme Court decision, *NLRB* v. *Gissel Packing Company,* which held that bargaining orders by the NLRB are an appropriate remedy for certain types of employer misconduct. Gissel bargaining orders are rarely issued by the NLRB.

Gissel bargaining orders
Situations in which the NLRB orders management to bargain with the union; named after a landmark Supreme Court decision, *NLRB* v. *Gissel Packing Company.*

Election, Certification, and Decertification

If management and the union agree to conduct the election as a consent election, balloting often occurs within a short period of time. However, if management does not agree to a consent election, a long delay may occur. Delays in balloting often increase the likelihood that management will win the election. As a result, management frequently refuses to agree to a consent election.

12-month rule
Provides that no election can be held in any bargaining unit within which a valid election has been held within the preceding 12-month period.

In union elections, the time when an election can be held is an important issue. The so-called **12-month rule** provides that no election can be held in any bargaining unit within which a valid election has been held within the preceding 12-month period. Also, the NLRB will not permit another election in the bargaining unit within 12 months of a union's certification. This is called a **certification bar.** The NLRB also prohibits an election for up to 12 months after an employer voluntarily recognizes a union. This is called a **recognition bar.** Finally, after a contract is agreed on by both parties, the NLRB does not normally permit an election in the bargaining unit covered by a contract until the contract expires, up to a maximum of three years. This is known as the **contract bar doctrine.**

certification bar
Condition occurring when the NLRB will not permit another election in the bargaining unit within 12 months of a union's certification.

When the exact date for the election is finally established, the NLRB conducts a secret-ballot election. If the union receives a majority of the ballots cast, it becomes certified as the exclusive bargaining representative of all employees in the unit. *Exclusive bargaining representative* means the union represents all employees (both union members and nonmembers) in the bargaining unit in negotiating their wages, hours, and terms and conditions of employment. It is important to note that the union does not have to receive a positive vote from a majority of employees in the bargaining unit. It has to receive only a majority of the votes cast.

recognition bar
Condition occurring when the NLRB prohibits an election for up to 12 months after an employer voluntarily recognizes a union.

After a union has been certified, it remains by law the exclusive bargaining representative for all employees until the employees within the unit desire otherwise. In the event the employees want to oust the union, they can file a petition with the NLRB for a decertification election. If 30 percent of the employees support the petition to decertify and a valid election

contract bar doctrine
Doctrine under which the NLRB will not permit an election in the bargaining unit covered by a contract until the contract expires, up to a maximum of three years.

FIGURE 19.1
Steps Involved in a Union Organizing Campaign

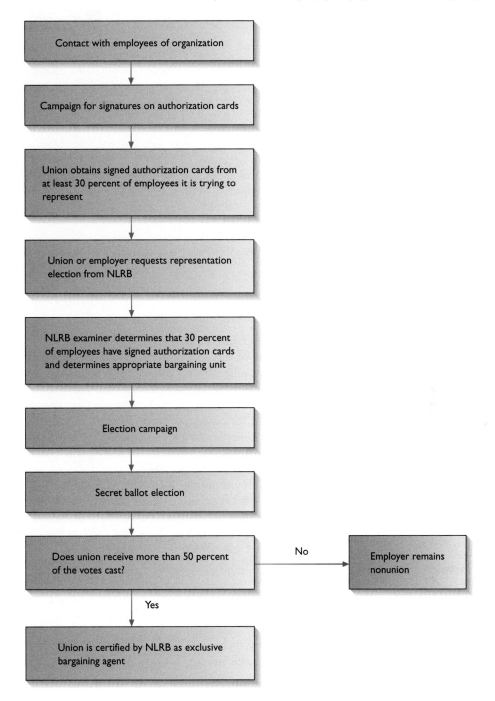

to oust the union has not been held within the preceding year, a decertification election is conducted. If a majority of the voting employees vote to decertify the union, it no longer legally represents them. Figure 19.1 summarizes the steps involved in an organizing campaign. HRM in Action 19.1 describes a decertification campaign.

GOOD-FAITH BARGAINING

good-faith bargaining
Sincere intention of both parties to negotiate differences and reach a mutually acceptable agreement.

After a union is certified, the employer is required by law to bargain in good faith with the union. Of course, bargaining between an employer and the union also takes place before the expiration of an existing contract. The National Labor Relations Act stipulates the legal requirement of **good-faith bargaining** for private enterprise organizations, whereas the Civil Service Reform Act of 1978 make the same requirement of federal agencies. Unfortunately,

DECERTIFICATION OF A UNION

Nearly 1,000 Comcast employees in the Pittsburgh area are scheduled to vote on whether to decertify the Communication Workers of America (CWA) as their bargaining agent. Comcast inherited the CWA-represented employees when it combined with AT&T Broadband. The CWA has charged that the company is encouraging employees to vote for decertification. Comcast says it simply wants employees to be properly informed before they exercise their legal rights regarding union representation. The CWA says that Comcast has encouraged employees to vote against the union through captive audience meetings, picnics, and Monday night football parties. The CWA has been running radio advertisements and posting yard signs criticizing Comcast's use of outside contractors to perform customer service work.

The union was never able to negotiate a first contract in the Pittsburgh area with either AT&T or Comcast. The union was close to tentative agreement on several occasions and claims that each time the company would change lawyers and start bargaining anew. The first contract is essential to union success because if a new bargaining unit goes for a year without obtaining a first contract, employees can petition the National Labor Relations Board (NLRB) for a decertification election to vote the union out.

However, in 2005, after years of fighting, the CWA won contracts at Comcast.

Source: Adapted from Jim McKay, "Pittsburgh-Area Comcast Workers to Vote on Whether to Keep Union," *Knight Ridder Tribune Business News,* November 11, 2003, p. 1.

Web site: Federal Labor Relations Authority
www.flra.gov

boulwarism
Named after a General Electric vice president; occurs when management makes its best offer at the outset of bargaining and firmly adheres to the offer throughout the bargaining sessions. The NLRB has ruled that this is not good-faith bargaining and is therefore illegal.

good faith—or the lack of it—is not explicitly defined in either of these laws. Over the years, however, decisions of the NLRB, the Federal Labor Relations Authority (FLRA), and the courts have interpreted good-faith bargaining to be the sincere intention of both parties to negotiate differences and to reach an agreement acceptable to both. Good-faith bargaining does not require the parties to agree; it merely obligates them to make a good-faith attempt to reach an agreement. Thus, the existence of good faith is generally determined by examining the total atmosphere in the collective bargaining process. The essential requirement is that a bona fide attempt be made to reach an agreement. HRM in Action 19.2 describes a charge that the union charged a lack of good faith bargaining.

Several bargaining situations have been taken to the NLRB to determine the presence or lack of good-faith bargaining. A key case involved General Electric Company's use of **boulwarism,** which was named after a General Electric vice president, Lemuel Boulware, and means that management makes its best offer at the outset of bargaining and firmly adheres to the offer throughout the bargaining sessions. The NLRB has ruled that boulwarism is not good-faith bargaining. In its decision, the NLRB held that boulwarism was illegal because the company not only adhered to a rigid position at the bargaining table but, in this case, had also mounted a publicity campaign to convince its employees that the company's offer was best. The company belittled the union in its literature. Since the employer simply ignored the union and went directly to the employees with its proposal, it violated its duty to bargain in good faith with the employees' exclusive bargaining representative (i.e., the union).[2]

PARTICIPANTS IN NEGOTIATIONS

A number of parties may be either directly or indirectly involved in the collective bargaining process. The primary participants are, of course, the employer and union representatives. However, several third parties can play a significant role.

Employer's Role

The employer's participation in collective bargaining may take one of several forms. The single-company agreement is most common. Under this approach, representatives of a single company meet with representatives of the union and negotiate a contract. Of course, it is possible for one company to have several unions representing different groups of employees. In this situation, representatives of the company would negotiate a different contract with each union. Furthermore, it is possible for one company and one union to negotiate different contracts for each of the company's facilities or plant locations.

REFUSING TO BARGAIN IN GOOD FAITH

The United Public Workers claimed that Gov. Linda Lingle and her labor negotiator are not bargaining in good faith. The UPW claims Lingle has been cancelling and walking out of negotiation sessions. The union filed a prohibited practices complaint with the Hawaii Labor Relations Board.

Lingle, however, believes the claims of the UPW are inaccurate. Through Lingle's team, they claim there was no meeting set for the date the UPW claims and that a second meeting was never confirmed.

Lingle had ordered state employees to take three furlough days a month to help close a huge budget deficit.

Source: Adapted from Derrick DePledge, "UPW Files Labor Complaint: Lingle, Chief Negotiator Refusing to Bargain in Good Faith, Union Says," *McClatchy-Tribune Business News,* July 8, 2009.

In some industries, multiemployer agreements are common. Generally, individual employers in these industries are small and are in a weak position relative to the union. Employers then often pool together in an employer association, which negotiates a single agreement for all involved employers. Multiemployer agreements may be on a local level (e.g., the construction industry within a city), a regional level (e.g., coal and mining), or at the national level (railroad industry). When multiemployer bargaining occurs on a regional or national basis, it is often referred to as *industrywide bargaining.*

Web site: United Auto Workers
www.uaw.org

In large organizations such as General Motors, master agreements on wage and benefit issue are negotiated between corporate officials and officials of the national or international union. However, in addition to the master agreement, local supplements are negotiated at the plant level. Local supplements deal with issues that are unique to each plant.

Union's Role

Union participation in negotiations can take several forms. In single-company agreements, the size of the company determines the nature of the union participation. For smaller companies, the local union normally works closely with a field representative of the international or national union in negotiations. In these instances, the international representative gives advice and counsel to the local union and frequently serves as the principal negotiator for the union.

In large companies with multiple plants, the top officials of the national or international union conduct negotiations. For example, the president of the United Automobile Workers (UAW) is normally a chief negotiator in negotiations with Ford, General Motors, and Chrysler. Local union officials and a field representative of the national or international union negotiate local supplements to the master agreement for large companies.

coordinated bargaining
A form of bargaining in which several unions bargain jointly with a single employer.

In those industries with multiemployer agreements, union participation is usually directed by the president of the national or international union. However, in these types of negotiations, representatives of the local unions to be covered by the multiemployer agreement normally serve on the union's negotiating committee. It is also possible for several unions to bargain jointly with a single employer. This type of negotiation is called **coordinated bargaining.**

Role of Third Parties

Several third parties can and frequently do become involved in the collective bargaining process. Typically the services of third parties are not required unless one or both parties feels the other party is not bargaining in good faith or the parties reach an impasse in negotiations.

National Labor Relations Act

The National Labor Relations Act (discussed in Chapter 18) requires both unions and management to bargain in good faith. Refusal to bargain by either party can be overridden by an order of the National Labor Relations Board (NLRB). Furthermore, if the board's order has been properly issued, the U.S. Court of Appeals is required to order enforcement under the threat of contempt-of-court penalties.

Besides refusing to bargain, other kinds of behavior can be held to be unfair labor practices. Some of these were described earlier in this chapter. The NLRB has the authority to determine whether a particular behavior is unfair. If either party believes an unfair labor practice has occurred during negotiations, a charge can be filed with the NLRB. An NLRB representative then investigates the charge and determines whether it is warranted. If so, the parties are given the opportunity to reach an informal settlement before the NLRB takes further action. If an informal settlement cannot be reached, the NLRB issues a formal complaint against the accused party, and an NLRB trial examiner then conducts a formal hearing. Upon completion of the hearing, the examiner makes recommendations to the NLRB. Either party may appeal the recommendations of the examiner to the board. If the board decides the party named in the complaint has engaged or is engaging in an unfair labor practice, it can order the party to cease such practice and can take appropriate corrective action. Either party can appeal decisions of the NLRB to the U.S. Circuit Court of Appeals and even the U.S. Supreme Court.

Federal Labor Relations Authority (FLRA)

The Federal Labor Relations Authority (FLRA) was given its authority by the Civil Service Reform Act of 1978 and serves as the counterpart to the NLRB for federal sector employees, unions, and agencies. Under procedures similar to those of the NLRB, the FLRA investigates unfair labor practice charges, conducts hearings on unfair labor practices, and can issue orders to cease from any such practices.

Federal Services Impasses Panel (FSIP)

If the parties in the federal sector reach an impasse in negotiations, either party may request the Federal Services Impasses Panel (FSIP) to consider the matter. The FSIP, an entity within the FLRA, has the authority to recommend solutions to resolve an impasse and take whatever action is necessary to resolve the dispute, as long as the actions are not inconsistent with the Civil Service Reform Act of 1978. In addition, the parties may agree to adopt a procedure for binding arbitration of a negotiation impasse, but only if the procedure is approved by the FSIP. The FSIP is considered to be the legal alternative to a strike in the federal sector.

Federal Mediation and Conciliation Service (FMCS)

Created by the National Labor Relations Act, the **Federal Mediation and Conciliation Service (FMCS)** is an independent agency within the executive branch of the federal government. The jurisdiction of the FMCS encompasses employees of private enterprise organizations engaged in interstate commerce, federal government employees, and employees in private, nonprofit hospitals and other allied medical facilities.

One of the responsibilities of the FMCS is to provide mediators to assist in resolving negotiation impasses. **Mediation** (or *conciliation,* as it is often called) is a process whereby both parties invite a neutral third party (called a *mediator*) to help resolve contract impasses. Mediators help the parties find common ground for continuing negotiations, develop factual data on issues over which the parties disagree, and set up joint study committees involving members of both parties to examine more difficult issues. In negotiations where the parties have become angry and/or antagonistic toward each other, the mediator often separates them and serves as a buffer, carrying proposals and counterproposals between the parties. Mediators cannot impose decisions on the parties. Various state agencies and private individuals, such as lawyers, professors, and arbitrators, also provide mediation services.

Arbitrators

Although **arbitration** is most frequently used in the resolution of grievances during a contract period, it can be used to resolve impasses during collective bargaining. Arbitration of contract terms is called *interest arbitration* or *contract arbitration.* Interest arbitration is rarely used in the private sector but is common in the public sector. Such arbitration can take one of two forms: conventional and final-offer. Under **conventional interest arbitration,** the arbitrator listens to arguments from both parties and makes a binding decision, which

---

Web site: Federal Labor Relations Authority
www.flra.gov/fsip/panel.html

Occasionally mediators are invited as a third party to find common ground among parties. Eric Audras/Photoalto/PictureQuest

Federal Mediation and Conciliation Service (FMCS)
Independent agency within the federal government that provides mediators to assist in resolving contract negotiation impasses.

mediation
Process whereby both parties invite a neutral third party (called a mediator) to help resolve contract impasses. The mediator, unlike an arbitrator, has no authority to impose a solution on the parties.

Web site: Federal Mediation and Conciliation Service
www.fmcs.gov

arbitration
Process whereby the parties agree to settle a dispute through the use of an independent third party (called an arbitrator). Arbitration is binding on both parties.

conventional interest arbitration
Form of arbitration in which the arbitrator listens to arguments from both parties and makes a binding decision, which can be identical to the position of either party or different from the positions of both parties.

final-offer interest arbitration

Form of arbitration in which the arbitrator is restricted to selecting the final offer of one of the parties.

can be identical to the position of either party or different from the positions of both parties. In **final-offer interest arbitration,** the arbitrator is restricted to selecting the final offer of one of the parties. Furthermore, interest arbitration can be either voluntary or mandatory. Both the Federal Mediation and Conciliation Service and the American Arbitration Association (AAA) provide lists of certified arbitrators. HRM in Action 19.3 describes a ruling by the Supreme Court on mandatory arbitration clauses.

COLLECTIVE BARGAINING AGREEMENTS

The collective bargaining agreement (or union contract) results from the bargaining process and governs the relations between employer and employees for a specific period of time. The contract specifies in writing the mutual agreements reached by the parties during the negotiations. Under the Taft–Hartley Act, collective bargaining agreements are legally enforceable contracts. Suits charging violation of contract between an employer and a union may be brought in any district court of the United States having jurisdiction over the parties.[3]

As discussed earlier in this chapter, the National Labor Relations Act obligates employers and unions to bargain in good faith on wages, hours, and other terms and conditions of employment. These are called mandatory subjects of negotiation. However, as would be expected, controversy has developed over the subjects covered by the phrase "other terms and conditions of employment." Unions attempt to expand the mandatory area by giving a broad interpretation to the phrase. Employers, on the other hand, naturally resist this expansion. Numerous NLRB and court decisions have been rendered concerning this issue. For example, the Supreme Court ruled in one decision that all management decisions representing a departure from prior practice that significantly impair (1) job tenure, (2) employment security, and (3) reasonably anticipated work opportunities must be negotiated as mandatory subjects. The number of mandatory bargaining items has definitely expanded over the years.

An issue on which the parties are not required to bargain is called a *nonmandatory,* or *permissive, issue.* During contract negotiations, the parties (if both agree) may bargain about permissive issues, but neither party is legally required to do so. Furthermore, it is an illegal labor practice for one party to insist on bargaining about a permissive issue.

The difficulties of establishing a group of mandatory and permissive issues for all organizations are great. Subjects in one industry or organization that are appropriately handled through collective bargaining may be inappropriate in another industry or organization. Ultimately, however, the courts and the NLRB decide whether an issue is mandatory or permissive.

In addition to mandatory and permissive issues, there is a small group of prohibited issues that cannot be included in a collective bargaining agreement. The leading examples are the closed shop and a hot-cargo clause. A *closed shop* requires employers to hire only people who are union members. A *hot-cargo clause* results when an employer agrees with a union not to handle or use the goods or services of another employer.

TABLE 19.1
Prohibited and Permitted Collective Bargaining Issues in the Federal Sector

Prohibited Issues

Negotiation of wage rates

Mission, budget, or organization of the agency

Number of employees

Internal security practices of the agency

Hiring, assigning, directing, laying off, and retaining employees in the agency; suspending, removing, reducing grade or pay; or taking other disciplinary action against employees

Assigning work, making determinations with respect to contracting work, and determining the personnel by which agency operations shall be conducted

Filling vacant positions from properly ranked and certified candidates

Taking whatever actions may be necessary to carry out the agency mission during emergencies

Permitted Issues

Numbers, types, and grades of employees or positions assigned to any organizational subdivision, work project, or tour of duty

Technology, means, and methods of performing work

Procedures used by the agency management to exercise its authority in carrying out duties that cannot be negotiated

Arrangements for employees adversely affected by the exercise of management's authority in carrying out duties that cannot be negotiated

For the federal sector, the Civil Service Reform Act of 1978 makes it mandatory to bargain over "conditions of employment." The act defines conditions of employment as personnel policies, practices, and matters affecting working conditions. Table 19.1 summarizes the prohibited and permitted issues for federal government employees.

SPECIFIC ISSUES IN COLLECTIVE BARGAINING AGREEMENTS

While each contract is different, most contracts include five issues: (1) management rights, (2) union security, (3) wages and benefits, (4) individual security (seniority) rights, and (5) dispute resolution.

Management Rights

The question of how many of their prerogatives can be retained in the union–employer relationship is of great concern to most employers. The primary purpose of the management rights clause is to retain for management the right to direct all business activities. Items that are normally regarded as an integral part of management rights include the rights to direct the workforce, determine the size of the workforce (including the number and class of employees to be hired or laid off), set working hours, and assign work. Generally, in the management rights clause, the union insists on a sentence specifying that management will not discriminate against the union.

Union Security

Union security clauses deal with the status of employee membership in the union and attempt to ensure that the union has continuous strength. Nearly all contracts provide some type of union security clause. Union security is provided in several forms. A **union shop** requires that all employees in the bargaining unit join the union and retain membership as a condition of employment. A modified union shop requires all employees hired after the effective date of the agreement to acquire and retain union membership as a condition of employment. The inclusion of a "grandfather" clause enables employees who are not members of the union as of the effective date of the contract to remain nonmembers. Under an **agency shop** provision, employees are not required to actually join the union, but they are required to pay a representation fee as a condition of employment. A provision for **maintenance of membership** does not require that an employee join the union, but employees who do join are required to remain members for a stipulated period of time as a condition of employment.

union shop
Provision in a contract that requires all employees in a bargaining unit to join the union and retain membership as a condition of employment; most right-to-work laws outlaw the union shop.

agency shop
Contract provision that does not require employees to join the union but requires them to pay the equivalent of union dues as a condition of employment.

maintenance of membership
Contract provision that does not require an employee to join the union but does require employees who do join to remain members for a stipulated time period.

As discussed in the previous chapter, the Taft–Hartley Act permits states to pass legislation that guarantees the right to work regardless of union membership. States that have passed this legislation are known as right-to-work states. The Taft–Hartley Act also prohibits two additional forms of union security: the closed shop and the preferential shop. In a closed shop, only union members can be hired, whereas the preferential shop requires that union members be given preference in filling job vacancies. However, in certain industries, such as construction, exceptions to the act's provisions are permitted.

In addition to providing a means for maintaining union membership, union security provisions often include checkoff procedures. A **checkoff** is an arrangement made with the company under which it agrees to withhold union dues, initiation fees, and assessments from the employees' paychecks and submit this money to the union. Individual union members must sign cards authorizing the withholding before such arrangements can be made.

Wages and Employee Benefits

Traditionally, increased wages have been the primary economic goal of unions. Most contracts contain a provision for general wage increases during the life of the contract. **Cost-of-living adjustments (COLA)** are common in many industries. COLA clauses tie wage increases to rises in the Bureau of Labor Statistics consumer price index (CPI). Most COLA clauses call for hourly increases in wages for each specified rise in the CPI. Adjustments can be made on a quarterly, semiannual, or annual basis. A recent trend has been an attempt by the management of many organizations to eliminate or restrict the use of COLA clauses.

Other wage issues specified in contracts include overtime pay and rates of pay for work on Saturdays, Sundays, holidays, and the sixth or seventh consecutive day of work. Other employee compensation items normally contained in contracts include supplementary pay for shift differentials, reporting and call-in or call-back pay, temporary-transfer pay, hazardous-duty pay, and job-related expenses. Each of these terms is defined in Table 19.2.

The benefits normally covered in union contracts include holidays, vacations, insurance, and pensions. Pay is usually required in union contracts for all recognized holidays. Eligibility for holiday pay is of one or two types: a length-of-service requirement or a work requirement. Normally, an employee must have worked a minimum of four weeks with the employer before being eligible for holiday pay. Furthermore, an employee generally must work the day before and the day after a holiday to receive holiday pay.

Most union contracts provide vacation provisions. Vacation entitlement is usually tied directly to the employee's length of service. One trend in contracts has been an increase in the amount of vacation time per year and a reduction in the amount of service required for receiving increased vacations.

Most union contracts contain clauses providing health, accident, and life insurance benefits. Many union contracts also contain major medical insurance, accidental death and dismemberment benefits, dental insurance, and coverage for miscellaneous medical expenses such as prescription drugs.

---

checkoff
Arrangement between an employer and a union under which the employer agrees to withhold union dues, initiation fees, and assessments from the employees' paychecks and submit this money to the union.

cost-of-living adjustments (COLA)
Contract provision that ties wage increases to rises in the Bureau of Labor Statistics consumer price index.

TABLE 19.2
Definitions of Typical Supplementary Pay Items

Item	Definition
Shift differential pay	Bonus paid for working less desirable hours of work
Reporting pay	Pay given to employees who report for work as scheduled but find on arrival that no work is available
Call-in or call-back pay	Pay earned when employees are called in or back to work at some time other than their regularly scheduled hours
Temporary-transfer pay	Pay given when employees are temporarily transferred to another job (if the transfer is to a lower-paying job, normally the employee continues to receive the old rate of pay; if to a higher-paying job, the employee is usually paid the higher rate)
Hazardous-duty pay	Pay given for performing jobs that, from a safety or health point of view, are considered to be riskier than usual
Job-related expenses	Remuneration for travel expenses, work clothes, or tools required for the job

Individual Security (Seniority) Rights

Seniority refers to an employee's relative length of service with an employer. Seniority may be measured on the basis of the employee's length of service in a job classification or a department or on the individual's length of service with one plant or with the company as a whole.

Job security for employees is a basic concern for unions. The seniority system is the method most commonly used to achieve job security. In general, union contract provisions specify that seniority is to be used within the bargaining unit for transfers to higher-level jobs, layoffs, recalls from layoffs, and choice of work shifts and vacation periods.

Seniority systems are designed to benefit employees with greater length of service. Thus, women and minorities, generally the most recently hired employees, can be adversely affected by a seniority system. Section 703(a) of the 1964 Civil Rights Act prohibits discrimination on the basis of race, color, religion, sex, or national origin. However, Section 703(h) exempts bona fide seniority systems from the mandate of Section 703(a). Section 703(h) suggests that bona fide seniority may have a disproportionate impact on a certain class of people and still be deemed valid. However, such a system may not be the result of intent to discriminate against a class of individuals. In the Stotts case, discussed in Chapter 2, the Supreme Court ruled that a judge could not impose an affirmative action plan that required white employees to be laid off when the otherwise applicable system would have required the layoff of African American employees with less seniority. It is important to note that this decision did not ban affirmative action programs. It did indicate, however, that seniority systems may limit the application of certain affirmative action measures.

Dispute Resolution

Inevitably, disputes arise during the life of a contract. Most contracts contain specific clauses describing how disputes are to be resolved.

A "no-strike" clause pledges the union to cooperate in preventing work stoppages. No-strike pledges can be either unconditional or conditional. Unconditional pledges ban any interference with production during the life of the contract. Conditional pledges permit strikes under certain circumstances. The no-strike ban most commonly is lifted after exhaustion of the grievance procedure or after an arbitration award has been violated. In return for a no-strike pledge, the union normally asks for a promise on the part of the company not to engage in lockouts during the term of the contract. A **lockout** is a refusal of the employer to let employees work.

The grievance procedure provision is the most common method for resolving disputes arising during the term of the contract. The final step in the dispute resolution procedure is usually arbitration. Both grievance procedures and arbitration were discussed in Chapter 17.

IMPASSES IN COLLECTIVE BARGAINING

At the end of the contract period, if a new agreement has not been reached, employees can continue working under the terms of the old contract until a new agreement is reached or a strike is called. Union officials will not recommend that the employees continue working unless significant progress is being made in contract negotiations.

If no progress is being made and the contract expires, a strike is frequently called. A **strike** occurs when employees collectively refuse to work. Strikes are not permitted for most public employees. To strike, the union must first hold a vote among its members. Unless the vote is heavily in favor of a strike, one will not be called. When a strike does occur, union members picket the employer. In picketing, individual members patrol at or near the place of employment to publicize the existence of a strike, discourage employees from working, and discourage the public from dealing with the employer. Frequently, members of other unions will refuse to cross the picket line of a striking union. For example, unionized truck drivers often refuse to deliver goods to an employer involved in a strike. HRM in Action 19.4 describes a potential strike at a correctional institution.

The purpose of a strike is to bring economic hardship to the employer, forcing the employer to agree to union demands. The success of a strike is determined by how severely the union is

CORRECTION SUPERVISOR FIRED

Steven Kennaway, president of the Massachusetts Correction Officers Federated Union, says that a supervisor was fired and five other supervisors were demoted and transferred to other correctional institutions as a result of an incident that occurred on January 28, 2004. The union represents nearly 5,000 correction officers in Massachusetts. The union said that the incident that precipitated this action by management was a situation in which an inmate being escorted to the prison's health services unit kicked an officer in the groin. The inmate was then subdued by six guards who held him down on a gurney as he thrashed his legs. The union alleged that the inmate received a black eye and two small lacerations near his eye. The officer who was kicked in the groin was fired because the investigation by management determined that he gave the inmate his injury. The union was told that two lieutenants and three sergeants were stripped of their ranks and demoted after an investigation by management found that they engaged in misconduct and were unable to account for how the inmate received his injury.

This is the same correctional facility in which the defrocked priest John Geoghan was killed during the summer of 2003. Geoghan was beaten and strangled to death by another inmate. An investigation found that a handful of guards wrote trumped-up disciplinary reports that prompted Geoghan's transfer to the dangerous inmate unit where he was killed.

Union officials stated they were considering calling for a strike vote to protest the guards' treatment after the incident of January 28.

Source: Adapted from Denise Lavoie, "Strike Threatened over Discipline; Correction Supervisor Fired," *Telegram & Gazette,* April 15, 2004, p. A.2.

able to interrupt the organization's operations. Employers often attempt to continue operations by using supervisory and management personnel, people not in a striking bargaining unit, people within the bargaining unit who refuse to go on strike, or people hired to replace striking employees. Attempts to continue operations through these methods can increase the difficulty of reaching an agreement and often result in violence.

When the president of the United Sates believes a strike may jeopardize the national health and safety, the emergency dispute provisions of the Taft–Hartley Act can be used. Under these provisions, the president is authorized to appoint a special board of inquiry, which makes a preliminary investigation of the impasse prior to issuing an injunction to halt the strike. If the impasse is not resolved during this preliminary investigation, the president can issue an injunction prohibiting the strike action for 80 days. This is called a *cooling-off period.* The parties then have 60 days to resolve the impasse, after which the NLRB is required to poll the employees to see whether they will accept the employer's last offer. If the employees do not agree to accept the employer's last offer, the injunction is dissolved and the president can refer the impasse to Congress and recommend a course of action.

TRENDS IN COLLECTIVE BARGAINING

Technological change and increased use of automation, changing government regulations, rising foreign competition, the decline in the percentage of blue-collar employees, and high rates of unemployment are just some of the variables that influence the collective bargaining process.[4] These and other variables can change rapidly, making virtually useless a contract provision negotiated two years earlier.

One form of collective bargaining that has evolved to cope with these rapidly changing variables involves the establishment of joint labor–management committees that meet regularly over the contract period to explore issues of common concern. The essential characteristics of this new form of collective bargaining are as follows:

1. Meetings are held frequently during the life of the contract and are independent of its expiration.
2. Discussions examine external events and potential problem areas rather than internal complaints about current practices.
3. Outside experts such as legal, economic, actuarial, medical, and industry specialists play a major role in making the final decision on some issues.
4. Participants in the meetings are encouraged to take a problem-solving, rather than an adversarial, approach.

Another likely trend in collective bargaining within U.S. companies is productivity bargaining. Under productivity bargaining, unions and management develop a contract whereby the union agrees to exchange old work procedures and methods for new and more effective ones in return for gains in pay and working conditions. Productivity bargaining involves not only reaching an agreement but also creating an atmosphere of ongoing cooperation in which the changes called for in the agreement can be implemented.

A final trend involves what has been called "take-back-bargaining." This form of bargaining involves asking unions to make concessions on wages and benefits. It has occurred in industries especially hard hit by foreign competition.

Summary of Learning Objectives

1. **Define *collective bargaining*.**

   Collective bargaining involves the negotiation, drafting, administration, and interpretation of a written agreement between an employer and a union for a specific period of time.

2. **Explain the captive-audience doctrine.**

   Under this doctrine, management has the right to speak to employees against the union on company time and require employees to attend the meeting. The union does not have the right to reply on company time. However, management is prohibited from giving a speech on company time to a mass-employee audience in the 24 hours immediately before a union election.

3. **Define *bargaining unit*.**

   A bargaining unit is a group of employees in a plant, firm, or industry that is recognized by the employer, agreed on by the parties to a case, or designated by the NLRB or its regional director as appropriate for the purposes of collective bargaining.

4. **Explain certification, recognition, and contract bars.**

   Under a certification bar, the NLRB will not permit another election within 12 months of a union's certification. Under a recognition bar, the NLRB will not permit an election for up to 12 months after an employer voluntarily recognizes a union. Under a contract bar, the NLRB does not normally permit an election on the bargaining unit covered by a contract until the contract expires, up to a maximum of three years.

5. **Describe good-faith bargaining.**

   Good-faith bargaining is the sincere intention of both parties to negotiate differences and reach an agreement acceptable to both.

6. **Discuss boulwarism.**

   Boulwarism is a form of collective bargaining under which management makes its best offer at the outset of bargaining and adheres to its position throughout the bargaining sessions. Boulwarism is in violation of an employer's obligation to negotiate in good faith and is illegal.

7. **Explain mediation.**

   Mediation is a process whereby both parties invite a neutral third party to help resolve contract impasses.

8. **Define *checkoff*.**

   Checkoff is an arrangement a union makes with a company under which the company agrees to withhold union dues, initiation fees, and assessments from the employees' paychecks and submits this money to the union.

9. **Explain seniority.**

   Seniority refers to an employee's relative length of service with an employer.

10. **Define *lockout* and *strike*.**

    A lockout is a refusal of the employer to let employees work. A strike occurs when employees collectively refuse to work.

Key Terms

12-month rule, *376*
agency shop, *382*
arbitration, *380*
bargaining unit, *375*
boulwarism, *378*
captive-audience doctrine, *375*
certification bar, *376*
checkoff, *383*
collective bargaining, *373*
community of interest, *375*
consent elections, *375*

contract bar doctrine, *376*
conventional interest arbitration, *380*
coordinated bargaining, *379*
cost-of-living adjustments (COLA), *383*
Federal Mediation and Conciliation Service (FMCS), *380*
final-offer interest arbitration, *381*

Gissel bargaining orders, *376*
good-faith bargaining, *377*
informational picketing, *376*
lockout, *384*
maintenance of membership, *382*
mediation, *380*
recognition bar, *376*
seniority, *384*
strike, *384*
union shop, *382*

Review Questions

1. What is collective bargaining?
2. Describe some of the reasons employees join unions.
3. What is a bargaining unit?
4. Define some unfair labor practices that can occur during a union election campaign.
5. Define *good-faith bargaining.*
6. What is a multiemployer agreement?
7. Describe the roles of the following third parties in the collective bargaining process:
   a. NLRB
   b. FLRA
   c. FSIP
   d. FMCS
   e. Mediators
   f. Arbitrators
8. Define the following union security clauses:
   a. Union shop
   b. Agency shop
   c. Maintenance of membership
   d. Closed shop
   e. Preferential shop
9. What is the purpose of COLA clauses in a union contract?
10. Define *seniority.*
11. What is a strike?

Discussion Questions

1. "Seniority provisions in a contract discriminate against women and minorities." What is your opinion of this statement?
2. "Right-to-work laws should be rescinded." Discuss.
3. Identify several management rights that you believe should not be subject to collective bargaining.
4. Why do you think collective bargaining is increasing among white-collar employees?

Incident 19.1

Florida National Guard and NAGE

The Florida National Guard employs full-time civilian technicians to assist in training the guard and to help repair and maintain the guard's equipment and supplies. As a condition of their employment, these technicians are required to maintain membership in the guard. The technicians are represented by the National Association of Government Employees (NAGE).

During negotiations between NAGE and the Florida National Guard, the technicians submitted through their unions a proposal whereby the technicians could opt to wear either their military uniform or agreed-on civilian attire while performing their technician duties. The parties were unable to reach an agreement on this issue. Consequently, NAGE asked the Federal Services Impasses Panel (FSIP) to resolve the matter. FSIP directed the parties to adopt the proposal as part of their collective bargaining agreement. The guard refused.

NAGE then filed an unfair labor practice charge with the Federal Labor Relations Authority (FLRA). The FLRA concluded that wearing the uniform was not within the guard's duty to bargain and dismissed the charge.

Questions

1. Do you feel that the National Guard should bargain over this issue?

2. If you had been advising the National Guard, would you have recommended that it bargain over this issue? Why or why not?

Incident 19.2

Retiree Benefits

Federal courts have ruled that two companies cannot require retirees and their dependents covered by collective bargaining agreements to pay part of their health care costs. One company is trying to make its retirees pay monthly premiums and deductibles, while the second company is trying to impose copayments and deductibles on its retirees. In the case of the first company, a federal judge reinstated the benefits to retirees since the benefits were intended to outlast the life of the labor contract. In the case of the second company, a U.S. district court ordered the company to reinstate the benefits of the retirees pending the outcome of a jury trial.

Questions

1. Should a company be allowed to make changes to the health benefits of retired employees who are covered by a collective bargaining agreement? Why or why not?

2. Why do you think the court system was involved in the resolution of this disagreement?

EXERCISE 19.1
Contract Negotiations*

*Adapted from James A. Vaughan and Samuel D. Deep, "Exercise Negotiations," *Program of Exercises for Management and Organizational Behavior* (Beverly Hills, Calif.: Glencoe Press, 1975), pp. 137–52.

You will be put on a team of three to four students. Each team will be required to negotiate a contract for a company or a union.

The company's wage scale, $14.00 per hour, compares favorably with most firms in its area but is about 8 percent below those firms that employ workers of equivalent skill. Wages have not increased in proportion to cost-of-living increases over the past three years.

At the last bargaining session, the company and union took the following positions:

1. *Hospital and medical plan*

   Past contract: Company paid one-fourth of cost, employee paid remaining three-fourths.

   Union: Demanded that company pay full cost.

   Company: Refused to pay more than one-fourth.

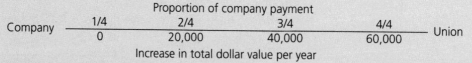

Proportion of company payment

Company	1/4	2/4	3/4	4/4	Union
	0	20,000	40,000	60,000	

Increase in total dollar value per year

2. *Wages*

   Past contract: $14.00 per hour.

   Union: Demanded an increase of 60 cents per hour.

   Company: Refused outright.

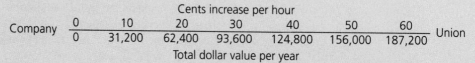

Cents increase per hour

Company	0	10	20	30	40	50	60	Union
	0	31,200	62,400	93,600	124,800	156,000	187,200	

Total dollar value per year

3. *Sliding pay scale to conform to cost of living*

Past contract: Pay scale is fixed through the term of the contract.

Union: Demanded pay increases in proportion to increases to the cost of living.

Company: Rejected outright.

Company	No	Yes	Union
	0	120,000	

Total dollar value per year

4. *Vacation pay*

Past contract: Two weeks' paid vacation for all employees with one year of service.

Union: Wants three weeks' paid vacation for employees with 10 years of service.

Company: Rejected.

Company	2 weeks/ 1 year	3 weeks/ 20 years	3 weeks/ 15 years	3 weeks/ 10 years	Union
	0	10,000	20,000	30,000	

Total dollar value per year

Each week on strike (10 minutes of negotiations in the exercise) costs the company $40,000 in lost profits and the employees $40,000 in lost wages.

1. Negotiate the above contract issues with another team (as assigned by your instructor).

2. At the end of negotiations, your instructor will summarize the beginning, ending, and costs for each negotiation.

Notes and Additional Readings

1. For discussion of organizing tactics by unions, see Gillian Flynn, "When the Unions Come Calling," *Workforce,* November 2000, pp. 82–86.

2. See Terence K. Huwe and Janice Kimball, "Collective Bargaining in the Private Sector," *Industrial Relations,* October 2003, p. 779.

3. See Marc Boulanger and Brian H. Kleiner, "Preparing and Interpreting Collective Bargaining Agreements Effectively," *Management Research News* 26 (2003), pp. 193–200.

4. Stuart R. Korshak, "Good Union Relationships Are Best," *Workforce,* January 26, 2001.

Glossary

A

absorption   Union merger that involves the merging of one union into a considerably larger one.

acquired immunodeficiency syndrome (AIDS)   A life-threatening disease that, although not communicable in most work settings, is causing many work-related debates that have yet to be legally resolved.

adventure learning   Programs that use many kinds of challenging outdoor activities to help participants achieve their goals.

adverse impact   Condition that occurs when the selection rate for minorities or women is less than 80 percent of the selection rate for the majority group in hiring, promotions, transfers, demotions, or any selection decision.

affirmative action plan   Written document outlining specific goals and timetables for remedying past discriminatory actions.

Age Discrimination in Employment Act (ADEA)   Prohibits discrimination against employees over 40 years of age by all companies employing 20 or more people in the private sector.

agency shop   Contract provision that does not require employees to join the union but requires them to pay the equivalent of union dues as a condition of employment.

Alexander v. Gardner-Denver   Supreme Court decision in 1974 that ruled that using the final and binding grievance procedure in an organization does not preclude an aggrieved employee from seeking redress through court action.

amalgamation   Union merger that involves two or more unions, usually of approximately the same size, forming a new union.

Amended Age Discrimination in Employment Act (ADEA)   Forbids mandatory retirement at any age for all companies employing 20 or more people in the private sector and in the federal government.

American Federation of Labor–Congress of Industrial Organizations (AFL–CIO)   Combination of national, international, and local unions joined together to promote the interests of unions and workers. The AFL–CIO was formed in 1955 by the amalgamation of the American Federation of Labor (AFL) and the Congress of Industrial Organizations (CIO).

Americans with Disabilities Act (ADA) (1990)   Gives disabled persons sharply increased access to services and jobs.

applicant flow record   Form completed voluntarily by a job applicant and used by an employer to obtain information that might be viewed as discriminatory.

apprenticeship training   Giving instruction, both on and off the job, in the practical and theoretical aspects of the work required in a skilled occupation or trade.

aptitude tests   Means of measuring a person's capacity or latent ability to learn and perform a job.

arbitration   Process whereby the parties agree to settle a dispute through the use of an independent third party (called an arbitrator). Arbitration is binding on both parties.

assessment center   Formal method used in training and/or selection and aimed at evaluating an individual's potential as a manager by exposing the individual to simulated problems that would be faced in a real-life managerial situation.

B

bargaining unit   Group of employees in a plant, firm, or industry that is recognized by the employer, agreed on by the parties to a case, or designated by the NLRB as appropriate for the purposes of collective bargaining.

base wage or salary   Hourly, weekly, or monthly pay that employees receive for their work.

behaviorally anchored rating scale (BARS)   Method of performance appraisal that determines an employee's level of performance based on whether or not certain specifically described job behaviors are present.

behavior modeling (interaction management)   Method of training in which interaction problems faced by managers are identified, practiced, and transferred to specific job situations.

benchmarking   Thoroughly examining internal practices and procedures and measuring them against the ways other successful organizations operate.

benefits   Rewards employees receive as a result of their employment and position with the organization.

board or panel interview   Interview method in which two or more people conduct a single interview with one applicant.

bona fide occupational qualification (BFOQ)   Permits employer to use religion, age, sex, or national origin as a factor in its employment practices when reasonably necessary to the normal operation of that particular business.

bonus   Reward that is offered on a one-time basis for high performance.

bottom line concept   When the overall selection process does not have an adverse impact, the government will usually not examine the individual components of that process for adverse impact or evidence of validity.

boulwarism   Named after a General Electric vice president; occurs when management makes its best offer at the outset of bargaining and firmly adheres to the offer throughout the bargaining sessions. The NLRB has ruled that this is not good-faith bargaining and is therefore illegal.

***Bowen v. United States Postal Service* (1983)**   Supreme Court decision that established that an employee may be entitled to recover damages from both the union and the employer in cases where the employer has violated the labor agreement and the union has breached its duty of fair representation.

broadbanding   A base-pay technique that reduces many different salary categories to several broad salary bands; broadbanding collapses job clusters or tiers of positions into a few wide bands to manage career growth and deliver pay.

burnout   Occurs when work is no longer meaningful to a person; can result from stress or a variety of other work-related or personal factors.

business necessity   Condition that comes into play when an employer has a job criterion that is neutral but excludes members of one sex at a higher rate than members of the opposite sex. The focus in business necessity is on the validity of stated job qualifications and their relationship to the work performed.

business simulation   Method of classroom training that simulates an organization and its environment and requires participants to make operating decisions based on the situation.

C

cafeteria plans of benefits   Plans that give employees the opportunity to choose, from among a wide range of alternatives, how their benefits will be distributed.

campus recruiting   Recruitment activities of employers on college and university campuses.

captive-audience doctrine   Management's right to speak against a union to employees on company time and to require employees to attend the meeting.

career development   An ongoing formalized effort by an organization that focuses on developing and enriching the organization's human resources in light of both the employees' and the organization's needs.

career pathing   A technique that addresses the specifics of progressing from one job to another in an organization; sequence of developmental activities involving informal and formal education, training, and job experiences that help make an individual capable of holding a more advanced job in the future.

career planning   Process by which an individual formulates career goals and develops a plan for reaching those goals.

career plateau   Point in an individual's career where the likelihood of an additional promotion is very low.

career self-management   The ability to keep up with the changes that occur within the organization and industry and to prepare for the future.

cascade approach   Objective-setting process designed to involve all levels of management in the organizational planning process.

case study   Method of classroom training in which the trainee analyzes real or hypothetical situations and suggests not only what to do but also how to do it.

central tendency   Tendency of a manager to rate most employees near the middle of the performance scale.

certification bar   Condition occurring when the NLRB will not permit another election in the bargaining unit within 12 months of a union's certification.

checklist   Method of performance appraisal in which the rater answers, with a yes or no, a series of questions about the behavior of the employee being rated.

checkoff   Arrangement between an employer and a union under which the employer agrees to withhold union dues, initiation fees, and assessments from the employees' paychecks and submit this money to the union.

Civil Rights Act (1991)   Permits women, persons with disabilities, and persons who are religious minorities to have a jury trial and sue for punitive damages if they can prove intentional hiring and workplace discrimination. Also requires companies to provide evidence that the business practice that led to the discrimination was not discriminatory but was job-related for the position in question and consistent with business necessity.

Civil Service Reform Act   Legislation enacted in 1978 regulating labor–management relations for federal government employees.

classroom training   Most familiar training method; useful for quickly imparting information to large groups with little or no knowledge of the subject.

coaching   Method of management development conducted on the job, which involves experienced managers advising and guiding trainees in solving managerial problems.

collective bargaining   Process that involves the negotiation, drafting, administration, and interpretation of a written agreement between an employer and a union for a specific period of time.

commission plan   Incentive plan that rewards employees, at least in part, based on their sales volume.

commitment manpower planning (CMP)   Systematic approach to human resource planning designed to get managers and their subordinates thinking about and involved in human resource planning.

Commonwealth v. Hunt   Landmark court decision in 1842 that declared unions were not illegal per se.

communication   Transfer of information that is meaningful to those involved.

community of interest   Concept by which the NLRB makes a bargaining unit decision based on areas of worker commonality.

comparable worth theory   Idea that every job has a worth to the employer and society that can be measured and assigned a value.

compensable factors   Characteristics of jobs that the organization deems important to the extent that it is willing to pay for them.

compensation   All the extrinsic rewards that employees receive in exchange for their work; composed of the base wage or salary, any incentives or bonuses, and any benefits.

competency-based pay system   Rewarding employees based on knowledge, skills, and behaviors that result in performance.

concentration   Practice of having more minorities or women in a job category than would reasonably be expected when compared to their presence in the relevant labor market.

concurrent validity   Validity established by identifying a criterion predictor, administering it to current employees, and correlating the test data with the current employees' performance.

consent elections   Union elections in which the parties have agreed on the appropriate bargaining unit.

conspiracy doctrine   Notion that courts can punish a union if they deem that the means used or the ends sought by the union are illegal.

construct validity   Extent to which a selection criterion measures the degree to which job candidates have identifiable characteristics determined to be relevant to successful job performance.

content validity   Extent to which the content of a selection procedure or instrument is representative of important aspects of job performance.

contingent workers   Employees who are independent contractors and on-call workers or temporary short-term workers.

contract bar doctrine   Doctrine under which the NLRB will not permit an election in the bargaining unit covered by a contract until the contract expires, up to a maximum of three years.

conventional interest arbitration   Form of arbitration in which the arbitrator listens to arguments from both parties and makes a binding decision, which can be identical to the position of either party or different from the positions of both parties.

coordinated bargaining   Form of bargaining in which several unions bargain jointly with a single employer.

corrective (progressive) discipline   Normal sequence of actions taken by management in disciplining an employee: oral warning, written warning, suspension, and finally discharge.

cost-of-living adjustments (COLA)   Contract provision that ties wage increases to rises in the Bureau of Labor Statistics consumer price index.

craft unions   Unions having only skilled workers as members. Most craft unions have members from several related trades (e.g., Bricklayers, Masons, and Plasterers International Union).

criteria of job success   Ways of specifying how successful performance of the job is to be measured.

criterion predictors   Factors such as education, previous work experience, and scores on company-administered tests that are used to predict successful performance of a job.

critical-incident appraisal   Method of performance appraisal in which the rater keeps a written record of incidents that illustrate both positive and negative employee behaviors. The rater then uses these incidents as a basis for evaluating the employee's performance.

cross training   *See* Job rotation.

D

Danbury Hatters case   Landmark case of 1908 in which the Supreme Court decided that the Sherman Anti-Trust Act applied to all unions.

data   Raw material from which information is developed: composed of facts that describe people, places, things, or events and that have not been interpreted.

deadwood   Individuals in an organization whose present performance has fallen to an unsatisfactory level and who have little potential for advancement.

defined-benefit plan   Pension plan under which an employer pledges to provide a benefit determined by a definite formula at the employee's retirement date.

defined-contribution plan   Pension plan that calls for a fixed or known annual contribution instead of a known benefit.

degree statements   Written statements used as a part of the point method of job evaluation to further break down job subfactors.

Delphi technique   Judgmental method of forecasting that uses a panel of experts to make initially independent estimates of future demand. An intermediary then presents each expert's forecast and assumptions to the other members of the panel. Each expert is then allowed to revise his or her forecast as desired. This process continues until some consensus or composite emerges.

departmental and job orientation   Specific orientation that describes topics unique to the new employee's specific department and job.

differential piece rate plan   Piece rate plan devised by Frederick W. Taylor that pays one rate for all acceptable units produced up to some standard and then a higher rate for all pieces produced if the output exceeds the standard.

direct feedback   Process in which the change agent communicates the information gathered through diagnosis directly to the affected people.

disability insurance   Designed to protect employees who experience a long-term or permanent disability.

disabling injuries   Work-related injuries that cause an employee to miss one or more days of work.

discipline   Action taken against an employee who has violated an organizational rule or whose performance has deteriorated to the point where corrective action is needed.

disparate impact   Unintentional discrimination involving employment practices that appear to be neutral but adversely affect a protected class of people.

disparate impact doctrine   States that when the plaintiff shows that an employment practice disproportionately excludes groups protected by Title VII, the burden of proof shifts to the defendant to prove that the standard reasonably relates to job performance.

disparate treatment   Intentional discrimination; treatment of one class of employees differently from other employees.

downsizing   Laying off large numbers of managerial and other employees.

due process   Right of an employee to be dealt with fairly and justly during the investigation of an alleged offense and the administration of any subsequent disciplinary action.

Duplex Printing Co. v. Deering   Case in which the Supreme Court ruled that unions were not exempt from the control of the Sherman Anti-Trust Act.

duties   One or more tasks performed in carrying out a job responsibility.

duty of fair representation   Under the National Labor Relations Act of 1935, the statutory duty of a union to fairly represent all employees in the bargaining unit, whether or not they are union members.

E

element   Aggregation of two or more micromotions; usually thought of as a complete entity, such as picking up or transporting an object.

employee assistance programs (EAPs)   Company-sponsored programs designed to help employees with personal problems such as alcohol and drug abuse, depression, anxiety, domestic trauma, financial problems, and other psychiatric/medical problems.

employee benefits (fringe benefits)   Rewards that an organization provides to employees for being members of the organization and for their positions in the organization; usually not related to employee performance.

employee leasing companies   Provide permanent staffs at customer companies.

Employee Retirement Income Security Act (ERISA)   Federal law passed in 1974 designed to give employees increased security for their retirement and pension plans and to ensure the fair treatment of employees under pension plans.

employee stock ownership plan (ESOP)   Form of stock option plan in which an organization provides employee purchase of its stock at a set price for a set time period based on the employee's length of service and salary and the profits of the organization.

Employer Information Report (Standard Form 100)   Form that all employers with 100 or more employees are required to file with the EEOC; requires a breakdown of the employer's workforce in specified job categories by race, sex, and national origin.

employment arbitration program   A dispute resolution program for employees in nonunionized organizations that requires a signed arbitration agreement as a condition of employment.

employment at will   Allows either the employer or employee to terminate his or her employment relationship at any time for virtually any reason for no reason at all.

employment parity   Situation in which the proportion of minorities and women employed by an organization equals the proportion in the organization's relevant labor market.

empowerment   Form of decentralization that involves giving subordinates substantial authority to make decisions.

Enterprise Wheel   Supreme Court ruling in 1960 holding that as long as an arbitrator's decision involves the interpretation of a contract, the courts should not overrule the arbitrator merely because their interpretation of the contract was different from that of the arbitrator.

equal employment opportunity   The right of all people to work and to advance on the basis of merit, ability, and potential.

Equal Employment Opportunity Commission (EEOC)   Federal agency created under the Civil Rights Act of 1964 to administer Title VII of the act and to ensure equal employment opportunity; its powers were expanded in 1979.

Equal Pay Act   Prohibits sex-based discrimination in rates of pay for men and women working on the same or similar jobs.

ERISA   *See* Employment Retirement Income Security Act.

ESOP   *See* Employee stock ownership plan.

essay appraisal   Method of performance appraisal in which the rater prepares a written statement describing an employee's strengths, weaknesses, and past performance.

executive orders   Orders issued by the president of the United States for managing and operating federal government agencies.

external equity   Addresses what employees in an organization are being paid compared to employees in other organizations performing similar jobs.

extrinsic rewards   Rewards that are controlled and distributed directly by the organization and are of a tangible nature.

F

factor comparison method   Job evaluation technique that uses a monetary scale for evaluating jobs on a factor-by-factor basis.

Family and Medical Leave Act (FMLA)   Enables qualified employees to take prolonged unpaid leave for family- and health-related reasons without fear of losing their jobs.

Federal Labor Relations Authority (FLRA)   Three-member panel created by the Civil Service Reform Act whose purpose is to administer the act.

Federal Mediation and Conciliation Service (FMCS)   Independent agency within the federal government that, as one of its responsibilities, provides mediators to assist in resolving contract negotiation impasses.

Federal Register   Periodical found in many public and college libraries that regularly publishes all OSHA standards and amendments. The official daily publication for rules, proposed rules, and notices of federal agencies and organizations. http://www.gpoaccess.gov/fr/

Federal Services Impasses Panel (FSIP)   Entity within the FLRA whose function is to provide assistance in resolving negotiation impasses within the federal sector.

final-offer interest arbitration   Form of arbitration in which the arbitrator is restricted to selecting the final offer of one of the parties.

flexible-benefit plan   Benefit plan that allows employees to select from a wide range of options how their direct compensation and benefits will be distributed. *See also* cafeteria plan of benefits.

floating holiday   Holiday that may be observed at the discretion of the employee or the employer.

forced-choice rating   Method of performance appraisal that requires the rater to rank a set of statements describing how an employee carries out the duties and responsibilities of the job.

4/5ths or 80 percent rule   Limit used to determine whether or not there are serious discrepancies in hiring decisions and other employment practices affecting women or minorities.

401(k) plan   Most popular type of defined contribution plan, named after section 401(k) of the Internal Revenue Code. Allows employees to defer a portion of their pay into the plan, thus making contributions tax deductible (up to a limit).

frequency rate   Ratio that indicates the frequency with which disabling injuries occur.

G

gain sharing   Programs also known as *profit sharing, performance sharing,* or *productivity incentives;* generally refers to incentive plans that involve employees in a common effort to achieve the company's productivity objectives. Based on the concept that the resulting incremental economic gains are shared among employees and the company.

garnishment   Legal procedure by which an employer is empowered to withhold wages for payment of an employee's debt to a creditor.

general-duty clause   Clause in the Occupational Safety and Health Act covering those situations not addressed by specific standards; in essence, it requires employers to comply with the intent of the act.

Gissel bargaining orders Situations in which the NLRB orders management to bargain with the union; named after a landmark Supreme Court decision, *NLRB* v. *Gissel Packing Company.*

good-faith bargaining Sincere intention of both parties to negotiate differences and reach a mutually acceptable agreement.

graphic rating scale Method of performance appraisal that requires the rater to indicate on a scale where the employee rates on factors such as quantity of work, dependability, job knowledge, and cooperativeness.

graphology (handwriting analysis) Use of a trained analyst to examine a person's handwriting to assess the person's personality, emotional problems, and honesty.

grievance arbitration Arbitration that attempts to settle unresolved disputes arising during the term of the collective bargaining agreement that involve questions of its interpretation or application.

grievance procedures Outline of the steps to be taken by employees appealing any management action they believe violates the union contract or corporate procedures agreed to in negotiations.

group incentives Incentives based on group rather than individual performance.

group interview Interview method in which several applicants are questioned together.

H

halo effect Occurs when managers allow a single prominent characteristic of an employee to influence their judgment on separate items of a performance appraisal.

handicapped individual Person who has a physical or mental impairment that substantially limits one or more major life activities, has a record of such impairment, or is regarded as having such impairment.

Hazard Communication Standard Standard issued by OSHA in the early 1980s that established uniform requirements to ensure that the hazards of all chemicals produced or used in, or imported into, the workplace are evaluated and that the results of these evaluations are transmitted to affected employers and exposed employees.

headhunter A type of private employment agency that seeks candidates for high-level, or executive, positions.

health maintenance organization (HMO) Health service organization that contracts with companies to provide certain basic medical services around the clock, seven days a week, for a fixed cost.

Hitchman Coal & Coke Co.* v. *Mitchell Supreme Court case of 1917 that upheld the legality of yellow-dog contracts.

hot-stove rule Set of guidelines used in administering discipline that calls for quick, consistent, and impersonal action preceded by a warning.

HR Scorecard A measurement and control system that uses a mix of quantitative and qualitative measures to evaluate performance.

human resource functions Tasks and duties human resource managers perform (e.g., determining the organization's human resource needs; recruiting, selecting, developing, counseling, and rewarding employees; acting as liaison with unions and government organizations; and handling other matters of employee well-being).

human resource generalist Person who devotes a majority of working time to human resources issues, but does not specialize in any specific area.

human resource information system (HRIS) A database system that contains all relevant human resource information and provides facilities for maintaining and accessing these data.

human resource management (HRM) Activities designed to provide for and coordinate the human resources of an organization.

human resource planning (HRP) Process of determining the human resource needs of an organization and ensuring that the organization has the right number of qualified people in the right jobs at the right time.

human resource specialist Person specially trained in one or more areas of human resource management (e.g., labor relations specialist, wage and salary specialist).

I

Immigration Reform and Control Act 1986 act making it illegal to hire, recruit, or refer for U.S. employment anyone known to be an unauthorized alien.

in-basket technique Method of classroom training in which the trainee is required to simulate the handling of a specific manager's mail and telephone calls and to react accordingly.

incentive or variable pay plans Pay plans designed to relate pay directly to performance or productivity; often used in conjunction with a base wage/salary system.

incentive stock option (ISO) Form of qualified stock option plan in which the manager does not have to pay any tax until the stock is sold.

incentives Rewards offered in addition to the base wage or salary and usually directly related to performance.

incident method Form of case study in which students are initially given the general outline of a situation and receive additional information from the instructor only as they request it.

individual equity Addresses the rewarding of individual contributions; is very closely related to the pay-for-performance question.

individual retirement account (IRA) Individual pension plan for employees not covered by private pension plans.

industrial unions Unions having as members both skilled and unskilled workers in a particular industry or group of industries.

information Data that have been interpreted and that meet a need of one or more managers.

informational picketing Patrolling at or near an employer's facility by individuals carrying signs to publicize the fact that the union is requesting an election to become the bargaining agent for the employees of the organization.

initial impressions Interviewer draws conclusions about job applicant within the first ten minutes of the interview.

injunction Court order to stop an action that could result in irreparable damage to property when the situation is such that no other adequate remedy is available to protect the interests of the injunction-seeking party.

interaction management *See* Behavior modeling.

interest tests Tests designed to determine how a person's interests compare with the interests of successful people in a specific job.

internal equity Addresses what an employee is being paid for doing a job compared to what other employees in the same organization are being paid to do their jobs.

intrinsic rewards Rewards internal to the individual and normally derived from involvement in certain activities or tasks.

J

job Group of positions that are identical with respect to their major or significant tasks and responsibilities and sufficiently alike to justify their being covered by a single analysis. One or many persons may be employed in the same job.

job advertising Placement of help-wanted advertisements in daily newspapers, in trade and professional publications, or on radio and television.

job analysis Process of determining and reporting pertinent information relating to the nature of a specific job.

job classification method Job evaluation method that determines the relative worth of a job by comparing it to a predetermined scale of classes or grades of jobs.

job depth Freedom of jobholders to plan and organize their own work, work at their own pace, and move around and communicate.

job description Written synopsis of the nature and requirements of a job.

job design Process of structuring work and designating the specific work activities of an individual or group of individuals to achieve certain organizational objectives.

job evaluation Systematic determination of the value of each job in relation to other jobs in the organization.

job knowledge tests Tests used to measure the job-related knowledge of an applicant.

job posting and bidding Method of making employees aware of job vacancies by posting a notice in central locations throughout an organization and giving a specified period to apply for the job.

job ranking method Job evaluation method that ranks jobs in order of their difficulty from simplest to most complex.

job rotation (cross training) Training that requires an individual to learn several different jobs in a work unit or department and perform each for a specified time period.

job satisfaction An employee's general attitude toward the job.

job scope Number and variety of tasks performed by the jobholder.

job specification Description of the competency, educational, and experience qualifications the incumbent must possess to perform the job.

job subfactor Detailed breakdown of a single compensable factor of a job.

just cause Requires that management initially bear the burden of proof of wrongdoing in discipline cases and that the severity of the punishment must coincide with the seriousness of the offense.

K

Keogh plan Retirement plan allowing self-employed persons to have their own 401(k) plan following the same rules as other 401(k) plans.

L

Labor–Management Relations Act (Taft–Hartley Act) Legislation enacted in 1947 that placed the federal government in a watchdog position to ensure that union–management relations are conducted fairly by both parties.

Labor–Management Reporting and Disclosure Act (LMRDA) (Landrum–Griffin Act) Legislation enacted in 1959 regulating labor unions and requiring disclosure of certain union financial information to the government.

Landrum–Griffin Act of 1959 Labor–Management Reporting and Disclosure Act, regulating labor unions and requiring disclosure of certain union financial information to the government.

learners Individuals in an organization who have a high potential for advancement but who are currently performing below standard.

leniency Occurs in performance appraisals when a manager's ratings are grouped at the positive end instead of being spread throughout the performance scale.

lockout Refusal of an employer to let its employee work.

M

maintenance of membership Contract provision that does not require an employee to join the union but does require employees who do join to remain members for a stipulated time period.

management by objectives (MBO) Consists of establishing clear and precisely defined statements of objectives for the work to be done by an employee, establishing an action plan indicating how these objectives are to be achieved, allowing the employee to implement the action plan, measuring objective achievement, taking corrective action when necessary, and establishing new objectives for the future.

management development Process concerned with developing the experience, attitudes, and skills necessary to become or remain an effective manager.

management inventory Specialized, expanded form of skills inventory for an organization's current management team; in addition to basic types of information, it usually includes a brief assessment of past performance and potential for advancement.

management succession plan Chart or schedule that shows potential successors for each management position within an organization.

managerial estimates Judgmental method of forecasting that calls on managers to make estimates of future staffing needs.

market-based pay systems Systems that focus on external rather than internal equity and operate without traditional pay ranges.

Marshall* v. *Barlow's, Inc. 1978 Supreme Court decision that ruled that employers are not required to admit OSHA inspectors onto their premises without a search warrant; also ruled that probable cause needed to obtain the search warrant is much less than that required in a criminal matter.

mediation Process whereby both parties invite a neutral third party (called a mediator) to help resolve contract impasses. The mediator, unlike an arbitrator, has no authority to impose a solution on the parties.

merit pay increase   Reward based on performance but also perpetuated year after year.

metrics   Any set of quantitative measures used to assess workforce performance.

microcomputer   Very small computer, ranging in size from a "computer on a chip" to a typewriter-size unit.

micromotion   Simplest unit of work; involves very elementary movements such as reaching, grasping, positioning, or releasing an object.

motion study   Job analysis method that involves determining the motions and movements necessary for performing a task or job and then designing the most efficient methods for putting those motions and movements together.

N

National Labor Relations Act (Wagner Act)   Prolabor act of 1935 that gave workers the right to organize, obligated the management of organizations to bargain in good faith with unions, defined illegal management practices relating to unions, and created the National Labor Relations Board (NLRB) to administer the act.

National Labor Relations Board (NLRB)   Five-member panel created by the National Labor Relations Act and appointed by the president of the United States with the advice and consent of the Senate and with the authority to administer the Wagner Act.

needs assessment   Systematic analysis of the specific training management development activities required by an organization to achieve its objectives.

NLRB v. Weingarten   Supreme Court decision in 1975 holding that an employee has the right to refuse to submit to a disciplinary interview without union representation.

nonqualified stock options   Similar to qualified options, except that they are subject to less favorable tax rate and are not subject to the same restrictions.

Norris–La Guardia Act of 1932   Prolabor act that eliminated the use of yellow-dog contracts and severely restricted the use of injunctions.

O

occupation   Grouping of jobs or job classes that involve similar skill, effort, and responsibility within a number of different organizations.

Occupational Informational Network (O*NET)   The United States' primary source of occupational information. The O*NET database is a comprehensive online database of employee attributes and job characteristics. www.onet.center.org

occupational parity   Situation in which the proportion of minorities and women employed in various occupations within an organization is equal to their proportion in the organization's relevant labor market.

Occupational Safety and Health Act   Federal law enacted in 1971 to ensure safe and healthful working conditions for every working person.

Office of Federal Contract Compliance Programs (OFCCP)   Office within the U.S. Department of Labor that is responsible for ensuring equal employment opportunity by federal contractors and subcontractors.

Office of the General Counsel   Separate and independent office created by the Taft–Hartley Act to investigate unfair labor practice charges and present those charges with merit to the NLRB.

Older Workers Benefit Protection Act of 1990   Provides protection for employees over 40 years of age in regard to fringe benefits and gives employees time to consider an early retirement offer.

on-the-job training (OJT)   Training showing the employee how to perform the job and allowing him or her to do it under the trainer's supervision.

operating manager   Person who manages people directly involved with the production of an organization's products or services (e.g., production manager in a manufacturing plant, loan manager in a bank).

organizational development (OD)   Organizationwide, planned effort managed from the top, with the goal of increasing organizational performance through planned interventions and training experiences.

organizational equity   Addresses how profits are divided up within the organization.

organizational inducements   Positive features and benefits offered by an organization to attract job applicants.

organizational morale   An employee's feeling of being accepted by and belonging to a group of employees through common goals, confidence in the desirability of those goals, and the desire to progress toward the goals.

organizational objectives   Statements of expected results that are designed to give the organization and its members direction and purpose.

organizational orientation   General orientation that presents topics of relevance and interest to all employees.

organizational replacement chart   Chart that shows both incumbents and potential replacements for given positions within an organization.

organizational rewards   Rewards that result from employment with the organization; includes all types of rewards, both intrinsic and extrinsic.

organizational reward system   Organizational system concerned with the selection of the types of rewards to be used by the organization.

organizational vitality index (OVI)   Index that results from ratio analysis; reflects the organization's human resource vitality as measured by the presence of promotable personnel and existing backups.

organizationwide incentives   Incentives that reward all members of the organization, based on the performance of the entire organization.

orientation   Introduction of new employees to the organization, work unit, and job.

orientation kit   Packet of written information given to a new employee to supplement the verbal orientation program.

OSHA Forms 300 and 300A   Forms for recording all occupational injuries and illnesses. Each occurrence must be recorded within six working days from the time the employer learns of the accident or illness.

OSHA Form 301 Form that requires much more detail about each injury or illness. Form 301 must be completed within six working days from the time the employer learns of an occupational injury or illness.

outplacement Benefit provided by an employer to help an employee leave the organization and get a job someplace else.

outsourcing Subcontracting work to an outside company that specializes in that particular type of work.

P

panel interview *See* Board interview.

parallel forms Method of showing a test's reliability; involves giving two separate but similar forms of the test at the same time.

pay Refers only to the actual dollars employees receive in exchange for their work.

pay grades Classes or grades of jobs that for pay purposes are grouped on the basis of their worth to an organization.

pay range Range of permissible pay, with a minimum and a maximum, that is assigned to a given pay grade.

performance Degree of accomplishment of the tasks that make up an employee's job.

performance appraisal Process of evaluating and communicating to an employee how he or she is performing the job and establishing a plan for improvement.

performance share plan (unit plan) Incentive plan that awards top executives a set number of performance units at the beginning of the performance period; actual value of the units is then determined by the company's performance over the performance period.

performance-vesting options Stock options priced at market price but only exercisable if stock price reaches or exceeds price goal within defined period.

personality tests Tests that attempt to measure personality traits.

personnel requisition form Describes the reason for the need to hire a new person and the requirements of the job.

phantom stock plan Special type of stock option plan that protects the holder if the value of the stock being held decreases; does not require the option holder to put up any money.

Philadelphia Cordwainers (shoemakers) case of 1806 Case in which the jury ruled that groups of employees banded together to raise their wages constituted a conspiracy in restraint of trade.

point method Job evaluation method in which a quantitative point scale is used to evaluate jobs on a factor-by-factor basis.

polygraph Machine that records fluctuations in a person's blood pressure, respiration, and perspiration on a moving roll of graph paper in response to questions asked of the person; commonly known as a *lie detector*.

position Collection of tasks and responsibilities constituting the total work assignment of a single employee.

predictive validity Validity that is established by identifying a criterion predictor such as a test, administering the test to all job applicants, hiring people without regard to their test scores, and at a later date correlating the test scores with the performance of these people on the job.

preferred provider organization (PPO) Formed by contracting with a group of doctors and hospitals to provide services at a discount or otherwise attractive price. Such providers are designated as "preferred" providers of care.

Pregnancy Discrimination Act (PDA) Requires employers to treat pregnancy just like any other medical condition with regard to fringe benefits and leave policies.

premium-priced options Stock options with an exercise price significantly above stock's current market price.

private plans Employee benefit that provides a source of income to people who have retired; funded either entirely by the organization or jointly by the organization and employee during employment.

proficiency tests Tests that measure how well a job applicant can do a sample of the work that is to be performed.

psychomotor tests Tests that measure a person's strength, dexterity, and coordination.

Q

qualified stock options Stock options approved by the Internal Revenue Service for favorable tax treatment.

R

Railway Labor Act An act enacted in 1926 that set up the administrative machinery for handling labor relations within the railroad industry; the first important piece of prolabor legislation.

ranking methods Methods of performance appraisal in which the performance of an employee is ranked relative to the performance of others.

ratio analysis Tool used in human resource planning to measure the organization's human resource vitality as indicated by the presence of promotable personnel and existing backups.

realistic job previews (RJP) Method of providing complete job information, both positive and negative, to the job applicant.

recency Tendency of a manager to evaluate employees on work performed most recently—one or two months prior to evaluation.

recognition bar Condition occurring when the NLRB prohibits an election for up to 12 months after an employer voluntarily recognizes a union.

recruitment Process of seeking and attracting a pool of people from which qualified candidates for job vacancies can be chosen.

reengineering Fundamental rethinking and radical redesign of business processes to achieve dramatic improvements in cost, quality, service, and speed.

Rehabilitation Act of 1973 Prohibits discrimination against handicapped individuals.

relevant labor market The geographical area in which a company recruits its employees.

reliability Refers to the extent to which a criterion predictor produces consistant results if repeated measurements are made.

responsibilities Obligations to perform certain tasks and assume certain duties.

restricted stock plan Plan under which a company gives shares of stock to participating managers, subject to certain restrictions; major restriction of most plans is that shares are subject to forfeiture until "earned out" over a stipulated period of continued employment.

Retirement Equity Act Act passed in 1984 that liberalized eligibility requirements, vesting provisions, maternity/paternity leaves, and spouse survivor benefits of retirement plans.

reverse discrimination Condition under which there is alleged preferential treatment of one group (minority or women) over another group rather than equal opportunity.

rightsizing Continuous and proactive assessment of mission-critical work and its staffing requirements.

right-to-sue-letter Statutory notice by the EEOC to the charging party if the EEOC does not decide to file a lawsuit on behalf of the charging party.

right-to-work laws Legislation enacted by individual states under the authority of Section 14(b) of the Taft–Hartley Act that can forbid various types of union security arrangements, including compulsory union membership.

Roth IRA Retirement plan that allows individuals to make nondeductible contributions and tax-free withdrawals with certain restrictions.

S

Scanlon plan Organizationwide incentive plan that provides employees with a bonus based on tangible savings in labor costs.

scenario analysis Using workforce environmental scanning data to develop alternative workforce scenarios.

secondary boycott Issue involving other employers (secondary employers) in the relationship between a union and an employer (the primary employer).

selection Process of choosing from those available the individuals who are most likely to perform successfully in a job.

self-managed work teams Groups of peers are responsible for a particular area or task.

seniority An employee's relative length of service with an employer.

sensitivity training Method used in OD to make one more aware of oneself and one's impact on others.

SEP-IRA Retirement plan that allows small businesses and sole proprietors to make deductible contributions.

severity rate Ratio that indicates the length of time injured employees are out of work.

sexual harassment Unwelcome sexual conduct that has the purpose or effect of unreasonably interfering with an individual's work performance or creating an intimidating, hostile, or offensive work environment.

skill-based pay systems Systems that compensate employees for the skills they bring to the job.

skills inventory Consolidated list of biographical and other information on all employees in the organization.

social security Federally administered insurance system designed to provide funds upon retirement or disability or both and to provide hospital and medical reimbursement to people who have reached retirement age.

software as a service (SaaS) Standard business applications that are delivered over the Internet on a pay-as-you-go basis.

solid citizens Individuals in an organization whose present performance is satisfactory but whose chance for future advancement is small.

split halves Method of showing a test's reliability; involves dividing the test into halves.

stars Individuals in an organization who are presently doing outstanding work and have a high potential for continued advancement.

stock appreciation rights (SARs) Type of nonqualified stock option in which an executive has the right to relinquish a stock option and receive from the company an amount equal to the appreciation in the stock price from the date the option was granted. Under an SAR, the option holder does not have to put up any money, as would be required in a normal stock option plan.

stock-for-stock swap Allows options to be exercised with shares of previously purchased company stock in lieu of cash; postpones the taxation of any gain on stock already owned.

stress Mental and physical condition that results from a perceived threat of danger (physical or emotional) and the pressure to remove it.

stress interview Interview method that puts the applicant under pressure to determine whether he or she is highly emotional.

strike Collective refusal of employees to work.

structured interview Interview conducted using a predetermined outline.

subfactor Detailed breakdown of a single compensable factor of a job.

succession planning Technique that identifies specific people to fill future openings in key positions throughout the organization.

suggestion systems Systems that usually offer cash incentives for employee suggestions that result in either increased profits or reduced costs.

systemic discrimination Large differences in either occupational or employment parity.

T

Taft–Hartley Act of 1947 Labor–Management Relations Act, which placed the federal government in a watchdog position to ensure that union–management relations are conducted fairly by both parties.

talent management The broad spectrum of HR activities involved in obtaining and managing the organization's human resources.

task Consisting of one or more elements, one of the distinct activities that constitute logical and necessary steps in the performance of work by an employee. A task is performed whenever human effort, physical or mental, is exerted for a specific purpose.

team building Process by which a work group develops awareness of conditions that keep it from functioning effectively and takes action to eliminate these conditions.

telecommuting Working at home by using an electronic linkup with a central office.

temporary help People working for employment agencies who are subcontracted out to businesses at an hourly rate for a period of time specified by the businesses.

test-retest One method of showing a test's reliability; involves testing a group and giving the same group the same test at a later time.

time study Job analysis method that determines the elements of work required to perform the job, the order in which these elements occur, and the times required to perform them effectively.

Title VII of the Civil Rights Act of 1964 Keystone federal legislation that covers disparate treatment and disparate impact discrimination; created the Equal Employment Opportunity Commission.

Toxic Substance Control Act Federal law passed in 1976 requiring the pretesting of new chemicals marketed for safety.

training Learning process that involves the acquisition of skills, concepts, rules, or attitudes to increase employee performance.

12-month rule Provides that no election can be held in any bargaining unit within which a valid election has been held within the preceding 12-month period.

U

understudy assignments Method of on-the-job training in which one individual, designated as the heir to a job, learns the job from the present jobholder.

underutilization Practice of having fewer minorities or women in a particular job category than their corresponding numbers in the relevant labor market.

unemployment compensation Form of insurance designed to provide funds to employees who have lost their jobs and are seeking other jobs.

union shop Provision in a contract that requires all employees in a bargaining unit to join the union and retain membership as a condition of employment; most right-to-work laws outlaw the union shop.

unstructured interview Interview conducted without a predetermined checklist of questions.

utilization evaluation Part of the affirmative action plan that analyzes minority group representation in all job categories, past and present hiring practices, and upgrades, promotions, and transfers.

V

Vaca v. *Sipes* Supreme Court decision that held that a union is not obligated to take all grievances to arbitration but has the authority to decide whether or not the grievance has merit. If such a decision is made fairly and nonarbitrarily, the union has not breached its duty of fair representation.

validity Refers to how accurately a predictor actually predicts the criteria of job success.

vesting Right of employees to receive the money paid into a pension or retirement fund on their behalf by their employer if they leave the organization prior to retirement.

Vietnam-Era Veterans Readjustment Assistance Act of 1974 Prohibits federal government contractors, and subcontractors with federal government contracts of $10,000 or more from discriminating in hiring and promoting Vietnam and disabled veterans.

vision statement A concise statement of career goals in measurable terms.

Vocational Rehabilitation Act Legislation enacted in 1973 that prohibits discrimination against otherwise qualified handicapped individuals solely on the basis of their disability; applies only in certain situations involving federal contracts, recipients of federal assistance, or federal agencies.

W

wage and salary curves Graphical depiction of the relationship between the relative worth of jobs and their wage rates.

wage and salary survey Survey of selected organizations within a geographical area or industry designed to provide a comparison of reliable information on policies, practices, and methods of payment.

Wagner Act of 1935 National Labor Relations Act; prolabor act that gave workers the right to organize, obligated the management of organizations to bargain in good faith with unions, defined illegal management practices relating to unions, and created the National Labor Relations Board (NLRB) to administer the act.

Web-based training Method of training in which material is presented on computer video screens via either the Internet or company intranet; participants are required to answer questions correctly before being allowed to proceed.

weighted application form Assigns different weights or values to different questions on an application form.

wellness programs Company-implemented programs designed to prevent illness and enhance employee wellness.

work sampling Job analysis method based on taking statistical samples of job actions throughout the workday and then drawing inferences about the requirements and demands of the job.

work standards approach Method of performance appraisal that involves setting a standard or expected level of output and then comparing each employee's level to the standard.

workers' compensation Form of insurance that protects employees from loss of income and extra expenses associated with job-related injuries or illness.

Y

yellow-dog contract Term coined by unions to describe an agreement between an employee and employer stipulating that, as a condition of employment, the worker would not join a labor union. Yellow-dog contracts were made illegal by the Norris–La Guardia Act of 1932.

Name Index

A

Adams, Graham, Jr., 358
Adkins, John I., Jr., 340
Al-Hawamdeh, Suliman, 185
Alvarez, Ralph, 101
Andler, Edward C., 144
Applebaum, Steven H., 210, 340
Aquilano, Nicholas J., 83
Arnold, Edwin W., 230, 272
Atchison, Thomas J., 253
Auster, Ellen R., 250

B

Bach, Pete, 84
Baker, Carolyn A., 316
Bakke, Allan, 35
Balderrama, Jose, 271
Bambacas, Mary, 209
Banik, Joseph A., 21
Bankston, Karen, 271
Banning, Kevin C., 185
Barcellos, David, 271, 272
Bardwick, Judith M., 210
Barlow, Wayne E., 73, 83,
    250, 337
Barrier, Michael, 341
Beard, L. Michelle, 210
Beatty, R. W., 219
Beck, Evelyn, 340
Beckham, Renee, 290
Belcher, David W., 253
Bell, Bradford S., 21
Benge, Eugene, 257
Benjamin, Ellen R., 272
Benko, Cathleen, 210
Bergel, Gary L., 272
Berry, Mike, 316
Biggs, W. D., 316
Blanton, Kimberly, 294
Blasi, Joseph R., 290
Bonache, Jaime, 290
Bonney, Joseph, 371
Bordia, Prashant, 209
Boulanger, Marc, 389
Boulware, Lemuel, 378
Boyle, Matthew, 209
Bradner, Tim, 334
Brady, Teresa, 243
Brandau, Mark, 101
Breaugh, James A., 124
Brennan, C. W., 290
Brown, Trevor C., 166
Buhler, Patricia M., 108
Burack, E. H., 195, 209
Burne, James A., Jr., 60
Burns, LaShonda, 46

Burr, Barry B., 289
Burrows, Donald M., 21
Byars, Lloyd L., 352

C

Caldwell, Cam, 185
Camardella, Matthew J., 229
Camden, T. M., 210
Cantalupo, Jim, 101
Capozzoli, Thomas, 290
Captain, Lori, 301
Carberry, Ed, 290
Carey, John, 339
Cargemi, J. P., 310
Carlson, D. G., 302
Carroll, Kathleen, 271
Carter, Nancy, 210
Case, John, 250
Case, Stanley R., 108
Catalanello, Ralph E., 108
Caudron, Shari, 21, 83, 249, 271, 272
Cavanagh, Michael E., 339
Champy, J., 21
Chase, Richard B., 83
Chavez, Linda, 250
Cherniphenko, Oleksandr S., 316
Chicci, D. L., 109
Cira, Darrell J., 272
Claypool, J. C., 310
Cohen, Alan, 21
Colella, Adrienne, 250
Conger, Jay A., 229
Conlin, Michelle, 339
Conway, Michael A., 271
Cooke, Rhoda, 340
Cornelius, Nelarine E., 109
Cornell, Christopher, 315
Crawford, Neil, 9
Crawford, Vicky, 55
Crispell, Diane, 243
Csiernik, Rick, 340
Cummings, Larry I., 249
Cutler, W. Gale, 208

D

Dahl, Darren, 109
Daughtery, Chad, 316
David, Fred R., 185
Davidson, Duncan, 21
Davidson, Linda, 108
Davis, Jeff, 334
Davis, Louis E., 83
Davis, Paula, 289
Deep, Samuel, D., 388
Delaney, John, 272

Demby, Elayne Robertson, 340
DePledge, Derrick, 379
Dickmeyer, William, 271
Dickson, Duane, 21
Dobson, Sarah, 195
Dominguez, Cari M., 210
Donovan, Tristan, 78
Drozdowski, Lisa, 26
Dugal, Sanjiv S., 290
Dysart, Ted, 100

E

Eargle, Fred L., 271
Eimicke, Victor W., 114
Eisenberg, Daniel, 236
Elswick, Jill, 271
Emens, Paul, 42
Epstein, Gene, 210

F

Fandray, Dayton, 229
Faria, A. J., 185
Farish, Phil, 21
Farr, Stephanie, 26
Farrell, Christopher, 290
Farzad, Roben, 280
Fasoldt, Gene F., 303
Feldman, B. H., 194
Ference, T. P., 199, 209, 210
Feyerherm, Ann E., 185
Finnie, Bruce, 76
Firestone, David, 209
Firestone, Dvorah, 210
Fisher, Anne, 209
Fisher, Cynthia D., 249
Fisscher, Olaf A. M., 230
Fleming, Sue, 300
Flynn, Gillian, 144, 389
Foust, Dean, 280
Frauenheim, Ed, 191

G

Gale, Sarah Fister, 83, 210
Garlough, Cory, 9
Garvey, Thomas W., 21
Geisel, Jerry, 300
Gerhart, Barry, 265
Giancola, Frank L., 272
Gibbons, John, 237
Gibson, Linda, 76
Gilbert, Jacqueline A., 20
Gill, Brian, 83
Gill, Jennifer, 236

Subject Index